**DO NOT REMOVE
CARDS FROM POCKET**

MONTHLY
TERRORS

MONTHLY TERRORS

AN INDEX TO THE WEIRD FANTASY MAGAZINES PUBLISHED IN THE UNITED STATES AND GREAT BRITAIN

COMPILED BY FRANK H. PARNELL
WITH THE ASSISTANCE OF MIKE ASHLEY

Foreword by Peter Haining

Bibliographies and Indexes in World Literature, Number 4

GREENWOOD PRESS
WESTPORT, CONNECTICUT • LONDON, ENGLAND

Library of Congress Cataloging in Publication Data

Parnell, Frank H.
   Monthly terrors.

   (Bibliographies and indexes in world literature,
ISSN 0742-6801 ; no. 4)
   Bibliography: p.
   1. Fantastic fiction, American—Periodicals—Indexes.
2. Fantastic fiction, English—Periodicals—Indexes.
I. Ashley, Michael. II. Title. III. Series.
PS374.F27P37 1985   016.823'0876   84-19225
ISBN 0-313-23989-4 (lib. bdg.)

Library of Congress Catalog Card Number: 84-19225
ISBN: 0-313-23989-4
ISSN: 0742-6801

First published in 1985

Greenwood Press
A division of Congressional Information Service, Inc.
88 Post Road West, Westport, Connecticut 06881

Printed in the United States of America

10 9 8 7 6 5 4 3 2 1

To my Wife, Evelyn

HAUNTED HERITAGE

Primeval campfire bards intone their tale
   Of fairyland, where human beings dare not stray -
   A nether-realm of water-sprite and fay,
Evoked by incantations and the banshee's wail.
From out of ancient balladry, Man's myths prevail,
   As legends from a far-gone pagan day
   Evolve, and make their immemorial way
Down centuries. Old ghosts, old magic, cannot fail.

They live as fiction on the printed page,
   To thrill a reader on a winter's night
     In some Victorian book, shelved by the bed.
Such phantoms mock our glib, computor age,
   Where even science cannot point the light
    To drive the cosmic specters from our head.

                    -- Steve Eng

Contents

▃Acknowledgements▃▃▃▃▃

Although most of the entries herein stem from my own collection and that of Mike Ashley's, I must acknowledge the debt I owe to many people in Britain and America who helped me where our collections failed.

First and foremost I must tender special thanks to Mike Ashley, without whose assistance this Index may never have been published.

It is dangerous to isolate too many names at the peril of upsetting others, but I cannot let the moment pass without extending my thanks to Steve Miller who seldom failed to find some obscure item in his bottomless collection; R. Alain Everts and Sam Moskowitz who provided Mike with much useful data on magazines and authors from their years of research; Randall Larson, Jessica Salmonson and Paul C. Allen who provided many details on small press magazines; Chester D. Cuthbert who at the last minute came up trumps with full details of the Canadian *Weird Tales*, and those editors like Gordon Linzner, David Warren and Chet Clingan who generously supplied complete or near-complete runs of their magazines. There were many editors and writers who responded to Mike's enquiries for details about themselves and their magazines, and to them, all our thanks.

To all those not already mentioned I hope inclusion in the following complete list of aiders and abettors goes at least some way to thanking you. And to those, possibly forgotten over the years, I tender my thanks and sincere apologies.

The roll of honor ...

Paul C. Allen
Michael E. Ambrose
James Anderson
Ted Ball
Edward Paul Berglund
Eddy C. Bertin
Bill Blackbeard
Leigh D. Blackmore
Gerald J. Brown
Joseph Payne Brennan
A. Vincent Clarke
C. C. Clingan
John Robert Colombo
Michael L. Cook
Ian Covell
Chester D. Cuthbert
Richard Dalby
Charles de Lint
Howard DeVore
Alistair Durie
John Eggeling
Stephen Eng
R. Alain Everts
Leslie Flood
Janet Fox
Brian J. Frost
W. Paul Ganley
Alan J. Gobel
Richard Lancelyn Green
Peter Haining
John Hale
Jon Harvey
Ewen Hedger
Steve Holland
Ben P. Indick
Terry Jeeves
Kenneth R. Johnson

Stephen Jones
Ken Krueger
Randall D. Larson
Joe Lewandowski
Dennis Lien
Gordon Linzner
George W. Locke
W. O. G. Lofts
David Longhurst
Glenn Lord
Robert A. Madle
Albert J. Manachino
Steve Miller
Richard Minter
Nancy Mortensen
Sam Moskowitz
Will Murray
Mark Owings
Rosemary Pardoe
Gerry de la Ree
Dave Reeder
Andy Richards
Jessica Amanda Salmonson
Robert Sampson
Darrell Schweitzer
A. Langley Searles
David A. Sutton
Grant Thiessen
Donald H. Tuck
Richard Wald
David R. Warren
Robert Weinberg
Walt Willis
Billy Wolfenbarger
Donald A. Wollheim

FOREWORD
BY PETER HAINING

There is only one thing I can think of that would be better than having a copy of this book on your shelf - and that is constant access to its compiler, Frank Parnell. For Frank, you see, is quite simply a walking encyclopedia of knowledge on weird and fantasy magazines. Not only does he possess a most wide-ranging and enviable collection of these magazines covering over half a century (including an almost complete run of *Weird Tales* that makes the mouth water just to think about it!); but as a result of his years of dedicated research into this particular area of publishing, he has become literally *vade mecum* (walking dictionary, if you prefer) of who wrote what and where in the world's fantasy magazines, big and small, new and old, long-lived and (in some cases perhaps most suitably) almost still-born.

I have known Frank for the best part of a decade now and I owe him and his knowledge of the weird and fantasy field a great deal. Perceptive readers of the Acknowledgements in many of my anthologies (if such dedicated souls actually exist!) will no doubt have seen his name listed with persistent regularity. Indeed, there is hardly a book I have compiled or written over this period that I have not discussed at some time with Frank; and both I - and more particularly the book - have benefited from his fund of knowledge about material related to the subject or theme, and also his

suggestions of items in a variety of magazines that I might like to consider. And when locating any of the publications concerned has proved impossible from my own re-sources, there has been Frank to loan what is invariably a rare and much-treasured item. Would that all collectors were as generous to re-searchers and anthologists as Frank!

The idea for this Index has been with Frank for many years - though perhaps not as far back as those days before World War II when he first began to pick up copies of the American pulp magazines that today form the core of his collection (and this book). They cost a few pennies then, and were mostly found in Wool-worth's where they had been dumped after an unceremonious journey across the Atlantic as ballast in returning cargo ships. It's a re-markable fact that what were then no more than remainder copies of 'Yank' magazines sold off by the publish-ers to keep their (financial) heads above water, are now some of the most sought-after and valuable items for collectors of weird and fantasy fiction. (Frank, incidentally, will tell you ruefully of the many maga-zines he bought in those far-off days which later, because of the ex-igencies of a small house and a growing family, he had to part with for a few shillings. He admits he pines after some of those departed souls today just like any other collector!)

To assemble this most comprehensive and fascinating listing - the first of its kind - has been a painstaking and at times frustrating labor of love. Yet Frank has clearly toiled long and hard in the dusty vineyards of fantasy fiction to produce a bibliography which I have found full of surprises - as I am sure you will too. Although I was familiar with such legendary American pulps as *Weird Tales*, *Strange Tales* and *Unknown Worlds*, my eye lighted with delight on titles both amateur and professional that I had never heard of, let alone seen: magazines with such fantastic titles as the Canadian *Copper Toadstool*, the unlikely sounding (in the context of this particular index) *Etchings & Odysseys* from America, and the short-lived British publication *Yankee Weird Shorts* (which immediately gave me visions of those abominations so popular a few years ago - Bermuda shorts). I was intrigued too by *Moonbroth*, *Midnight Sun* and *Dragonbane*, the almost unpronounceable *Airgedlamh* and such titilating and very typical 'spicy' titles as *Horror Sex Tales*, *Legendary Sex Tales* and even *Weird Sex Tales*! (Where would you keep them, Frank, under the bed?)

As I was aware that many now-famous writers had begun their careers in magazines such as those listed here - indeed, I have rescued many tales from their pages for my collections - I was also most interested in the listing of authors. And, just as with the titles, I found names that were both unexpected and surprising - as well as in the most unlikely pages! Just who they were - and where I found them - I'll leave you to discover for yourselves.

So, as I said earlier, Frank himself is still the best possible source on information on weird and fantasy fiction. But there is more than a little of him in this remarkable book, and even though I know him well, and hope to continue to do so for many more years, I nevertheless plan to have a copy of it close to my desk at all times. And I would urge you to do the same.

Peter Haining

***

_INTRODUCTION_____

The aim of this book is to provide an index to all weird fantasy
magazines published in the English
language.

But what is weird fantasy, you
may ask. I am afraid that there is
no easy answer, and to attempt a
definition will be to encourage a
response into the realms of seman-
tics that would prove fruitless.
Let us simply say that it is fiction that deals with non-everyday
happenings - the bizarre, the outre,
the macabre - all tinged with an
infusion of the supernatural. These
tales may be set in the here and
now, the past, the future, or some
other world entirely.

Because weird fantasy is best
not defined, like all good stories,
it has areas of _terra incognita_, where
it overlaps with other worlds. Thus,
inevitably, this index contains
stories that are straight science
fiction, mystery and horror with
none of the supernatural. These
stories are in the minimum, and I
don't think any index could be pre-
pared without such overlaps.

This index is not comprehensive.
It is doubtful if such is possible.
It is those borderline cases that
will cause controversy amongst the
weird fantasy fans, but they have
been included on the well tried
principle of: if in doubt, put it
in. The original guideline for the
index was that the magazine had to
contain more than 50% weird fantasy
fiction - not necessarily in each
issue, but over the full run. This
means that some magazines are included which, for certain periods,

were devoted more to science fiction
- _Fantastic_ and _Science Fantasy_ being the
most obvious examples. By the same
token _The Magazine of Fantasy and Science
Fiction_ - which currently is a major
market for fantasy and which may well
be expected to be included in this
index - is excluded because when its
entire run is considered it is predominantly science fiction.

Nevertheless rules are made to be
broken, and though that yardstick
has been adhered to throughout it
has not been at the cost of omitting
magazines that would be of major
value to the researcher. Thus a few
exceptions were made to include
magazines which are predominantly
non-fiction, such as _Gothic_ and _Nycta-
lops_, where the value of their contents was indisputable.

On the whole sado-sexual mystery
and horror magazines - the weird
menace pulps - have been omitted,
mostly because the stories have
natural (or perhaps I should say
unnatural) rather then supernatural
solutions. There are, needless to
say, a few exceptions, when such
magazines did print a high quota of
fantasy. Thus you will find in this
index entries for _Uncanny Tales, Eerie
Mysteries, Ace Mystery_ and a few others,
but you won't find _Terror Tales, Horror
Stories_ or _Thrilling Mystery_ despite what
their titles might imply.

Also omitted are the 'true' magazines in this field such as _True
Strange Stories_ or _The Hidden World_, regardless of the veracity - or perhaps lack of it - of the contents.
There are, though, magazines which
are included which did regularly

feature 'true stories' as part of their content, such as *Ghost Stories* and *Mystic*. Even *Weird Tales* did on a few occasions!

In the past, most indices have concentrated on professional magazines and little attention has been paid to the vast depth of small press and amateur publications that have appeared during this century. This index attempts to redress that balance. Over a third of the entries relate to small press magazines, most of them in the vague and ill-defined 'semi-professional' category. Only those magazines which made a serious attempt to publish weird fantasy have been included, even if these means including very rare, hectographed magazines from the thirties and forties. Few collectors have the privilege of owning sets of these titles, but that does not mean that others should be denied knowledge of what those issues contained. Thus, this index will preserve information that otherwise might have become irretrievably lost.

Few of the magazines listed here had a long life. Exceptions are *Weird Tales*, *Ghost Stories*, *Unknown Worlds* and *Fantastic* in America, and in Britain *Science Fantasy*, *Supernatural Stories* and, to a lesser degree, the British edition of *Unknown Worlds*. To aid in establishing the significance and importance of these magazines, a brief historical survey is provided starting on page xv.

This index is divided into two main parts and several smaller (though not lesser) parts. There is a listing by issue - and for the statistically minded this covers 168 different magazines running to 1733 issues. This lists the contents of each issue and provides some basic publishing data on each title.

This is followed by the Author Index (this time the statistically minded can work totals out for themselves!) which not only lists all authors' contributions to the magazines but also provides some basic biographical data on many of the entries.

A third index covers all artists. It was not practical to list all artwork, but here note is made of all cover art, portfolios, graphic features, comic strips and all major free-standing art.

Other indices are provided to Editors and Publishers, and to Series and Connected Stories. There is also a chronological and geographical listing, plus a nod to those titles that nearly made the index, but didn't quite, in the "Honorable Mentions".

Great care has been taken in the compilation of this index to ensure accuracy, but due to the sheer size errors must have crept in. For these we apologise, and all corrections are welcome.

I hope this index will help those who have wondered about the contents of the weird and wonderful magazines. I also hope it may play a part in generating a revival of interest in weird fantasy magazines which are currently on hard times.

Good hunting.

Frank Parnell
Ipswich
1984

THE WEIRD FANTASY MAGAZINES
A HISTORICAL SURVEY
1919–1983

I – UNITED STATES

There has been weird fantasy in the popular magazines for well over a century, but the first magazine to contain a sufficient quota of weird fiction to justify the honor of that epithet – and its inclusion in this index – was *The Thrill Book*, published during 1919. Toward the end of its short-life it deteriorated into a basic adventure magazine.

The first magazine to be devoted entirely to weird fantasy, the granddaddy of them all, was *Weird Tales*, which ran from 1923 to 1954 and has justifiably acquired legendary status, regardless of the real quality of many of its issues. The magazine has had two short-lived revivals and is currently in the throes of a third, but to most collector's the magazine had one and only one incarnation. Its heyday was under the editorship of Farnsworth Wright from 1924-1939. During these years it could boast publication of the best work of H.P.Lovecraft, Robert E. Howard, Clark Ashton Smith, Edmond Hamilton, Seabury Quinn, August Derleth, E. Hoffmann Price and a young Robert Bloch. It also printed some early or one-off items by a surprising cast of notables such as Tennessee Williams, Robert Spencer Carr, L.M.Montgomery, Edward Lucas White and Vincent Starrett. It also displayed such wonderful covers and interior art by Virgil Finlay, J.

Allen St. John and the irreplaceable Margaret Brundage.

In the 1940s, under editor Dorothy McIlwraith, the magazine lost some of that uniqueness that gave it its sub-title, 'The Unique Magazine', although it could still claim some of the more original fiction by Ray Bradbury, Robert Bloch, Manly Wade Wellman and even writers like Frank Gruber, Carroll John Daly and Michael Avallone.

Its lifetime spanned an era – from the start of the specialised pulps to the death of the pulps. When it went it left a void which, to its devotees, has never been filled.

During its lifetime *Weird Tales* had few rivals. *Ghost Stories* certainly constituted no threat, with its total emphasis on formula ghost tales in a confessions mold. Perhaps the most remarkable fact about that magazine was that it lasted as long as it did, from 1926 to 1931. *Tales of Magic and Mystery* was another non-rival, concentrating more on stage magic than weird fantasy. Because of its publication of one story by H.P.Lovecraft it has taken on a greater legendary aura than it deserves.

One magazine that has virtually been forgotten, and has certainly never been indexed before is *Mind Magic*, retitled *My Self* for its last two issues. Unfortunately it published nothing of note, but is a another rare collector's item.

Strange Tales was the closest *Weird Tales* had to a serious rival, and there is some justification to claiming *Strange Tales* the better magazine. Unfortunately it never survived long enough to establish itself - only seven issues, before its publisher fell victim to the Depression. Ironically, although the title was acquired by another publisher - Street & Smith - the magazine was never revived, although six years later, as we shall see, Street & Smith launched another magazine that became equal in legend to *Weird Tales*.

The 1930s were not the best years for new magazines. It was the hey-day of the weird menace and super-hero pulps, with *Horror Stories* typi-fying the first category and *Doc Savage* the second. Neither of these magazines are included in this index but in the first vein you will find *Ace Mystery, Eerie Stories, Eerie Myster-ies* and *Uncanny Tales*. In the second vein only the super-villain pulp *Dr.Death* qualifies.

The 1930s saw cross-fertilization between the pulps and radio, mostly in the character pulps like *The Shadow* and *Doc Savage*. The weird fantasy field saw only the short-lived *The Witch's Tales* in 1936. The practice returned in the 1950s, though, with such titles as *The Mysterious Traveler Magazine, Suspense* and *Tales of the Fright-ened*. One could say the practice is still alive today, with the greater in-fluence coming from television, esp-ecially the in light of one of the latest magazines in this index, *Rod Serling's 'The Twilight Zone' Magazine*.

Perhaps of greater significance in the thirties was the appearance of the amateur small press magazines. Most of these related to the science fiction field, and concentrated more on news and articles than fiction. The man who made the greatest effort to bridge the gap between the ama-teur and professional magazines was the late William L. Crawford who heroically struggled to publish two such magazines *Unusual Stories* and *Marvel Tales*, thereby starting a move-ment which today is almost the sole haven and protector of the weird fantasy short story. These magazines are rare, especially the incomplete advance issue of *Unusual Stories* and full sets are a collector's dream. A third small press item from this period included in this index is Donald Wollheim's *Fanciful Tales*, and of special interest is Robert Bar-low's rare and legendary *Leaves*.

The thirties ended with the birth of two new magazines. The first, *Strange Stories* was an unsuccessful attempt to copy *Weird Tales*, and though it used fiction by many of that magazine's leading writers - especially August Derleth, Henry Kuttner and Robert Bloch - it failed to capture the spirit and character of the elder pulp.

The other magazine was another story. Edited by John W. Campbell, the father of modern science fiction, *Unknown* (later *Unknown Worlds*), established a new dimension in weird fiction. Despite the success (intangible though that was) of *Weird Tales* few will deny that *Unknown* was a more mature and literary magazine and a far higher percentage if its stories stay readable today than those in *Weird Tales*. *Unknown* was certainly the aristocrat of weird fantasy magazines. Macabre humor by leading authors was a strong feature and a large number of the stories have been reprinted, many as hardcover novels. Full files of this magazine are highly prized.

Few other magazines survived in the shadow of these two pulps, and even fewer in the shadow of World War II. After the war there came a resurgence of interest, although this was directed mainly at science fiction. A few fantasy magazines were whisked along in this wake, most of which captured the public's yearning for the less complicated past - hence the existence of *The Avon Fantasy Reader, The Arkham Sampler* and *A.Merritt's Fantasy Magazine*. It was also a time when fans, once out of the Army, invested their funds in small press magazines, including *The Vortex, The Gorgon* and *The Nekromantikon*. It was all rather short-lived however. Fantasy was becoming a publishing liability, and few titles survived beyond their first or second issue.

It was a bold gamble in 1952 when, with much financial backing, Ziff-Davis launched *Fantastic* as a mature, up-market fantasy maga-zine. For a few issues it was, without a doubt, amongst the best of all magazines, but the publisher soon lost interest, and *Fantastic* rapidly deteriorated in quality. To the publisher's credit it was not dropped, but the emphasis switched to the more saleable comm-odity of science fiction. A less kindly fate befell *Fantasy Magazine* and *Beyond*, two equally superior magazines which were unable to reach a viable market and ceased publication.

For a brief period *Fantastic* had a companion fantasy magazine in the form of *Dream World* born out of the success of a special wish-fulfilment issue of *Fantastic*. But the success was not to be repeated. A few other short-lived magazines appeared; some, like *Fear!* and *Shock* had promise, whilst others, like *Thriller* were best forgotten.

It was left to *Fantastic* under new editor Cele Goldsmith, to start a revival in fantasy. Beginning in 1958 and reaching a peak in the period 1962-64 *Fantastic* became the major market for fantasy publishing a wide variety of original and experimental stories. It was a shame that Ziff-Davis sold *Fantastic* in 1965, just at the time that the paperback publication of J.R.R. Tolkien's *Lord of the Rings* and the start of the complete Conan stories of Robert E. Howard brought about a resurgence of interest in fantasy. *Fantastic* became predominantly a reprint magazine for the rest of the sixties and thus played no part in the development of a genre that it had helped survive through the lean fifties.

Few other regular professional markets existed for fantasy and horror during the 1960s. A number of reprint magazines appeared, most under the discerning editorship of Robert A.W. Lowndes. Starting with *Magazine of Horror* and subsequently *Startling Mystery Stories*, *Bizarre Fantasy Tales* and *Weird Terror Tales*, Lowndes created a family of magazines that generated a warm and nostalgic atmosphere and were sadly missed when a change in publisher saw their demise. The contents were drawn from a number of sources, mostly *Weird Tales* and *Strange Tales*, but they carried some new stories and if the magazines were remembered for nothing else, they can at least claim that in their pages the work of Stephen King first saw print.

Few of the other professional magazines of the sixties held much promise. Only *Gamma*, which staggered through five issues in three years, and *Worlds of Fantasy* which saw only four issues in as many years, had any potential and originality. For a brief period *Fantastic* fostered a number of companion reprint titles with contects selected from its own past or that of its predecessor *Fantastic Adventures* or its stable mate *Amazing Stories*. These magazines - *Weird Mystery*, *Strange Fantasy*, *The Strangest Stories Ever Told* and much later the *Sword and Sorcery Annual* - contained

mostly minor works, but their very existence allowed *Fantastic* to drop its reprint policy and once again become a market - albeit an irregular one - for new fiction.

One other reprint magazine made a brief but welcome appearance at the start of the seventies - *Forgotten Fantasy* - a most attractive and readable magazine which demonstrated what could be achieved with caring and diligent publishers and editors. Unfortunately the distributor was not so altruistic and the magazine ended abruptly after five issues.

Another casualty was *Coven 13* a very promising market for new fiction. This magazine was saved, however, when its mailing list was taken over by William Crawford - the same man who had bravely tried to issue *Marvel Tales* and *Unusual Stories* a quarter of a century before. Crawford never had much success with his magazines, however, and though the newly retitled *Witchcraft & Sorcery* contained much of interest, it again failed to capture a market and eventually dwindled away.

Its demise, and the rapid appearance and disappearance of the potentially significant *The Haunt of Horror* left *Fantastic* as the only professional market for fantasy, and as that magazine seldom sustained its bi-monthly schedule, the prospect for readers and writers would appear bleak. There was one other regular market - *The Magazine of Fantasy and Science Fiction* - a publication not covered in this Index because over its 35 years (it appeared in 1949) its contents have been predominantly science fiction. Nevertheless during the 1970s it did increase its quota of fantasy and weird fiction, but was still only a limited market.

The real salvation came in the small press field. Most of the amateur magazines that appeared during the 1950s and treated their subject with any degree of seriousness concentrated on science fiction as the interest in weird fantasy had all but vanished. One man, however, determined to fill that gap, especially with the passing of *Weird Tales*, and in 1957 writer Joseph Payne Brennan launched *Macabre*. Its contents were mostly poetry, and Brennan could afford to produce it only twice a year at best, but it was a start. For nearly ten years *Macabre* weathered it alone until the late sixties saw the start of a resurgence in the amateur fantasy field.

One of the first was *Anubis* which set out to establish itself as a major market for weird fantasy but which unfortunately foundered after four issues. Of greater significance was *The Arkham Collector* launched by author/editor/publisher August Derleth to replace his regular catalog, and which soon took on an identity of its own. It is almost certain that this little magazine created a form that other fans realized they could imitate, and when *The Arkham Collector* folded with Derleth's death in 1971, the vacuum was soon filled. By far the most important successor was *Whispers* which deliberately set out to follow *The Arkham Collector* (the title was originally going to be *Whispers From Arkham*). From an auspicious start *Whispers* rapidly established itself as the major small-press market for weird fantasy and is, for that matter, superior to almost all professional markets.

Another of the early markets in the late sixties was *Weirdbook* which whilst never having the meteoric rise achieved by *Whispers* has slowly and methodically risen in both quality and presentation to become another of the major small press markets of the 1980s.

Probably overlooked at the time of its birth, the other sixties market has since become something of a small press phenomenon. *Space and Time*, which originally placed its emphasis on science fiction, has appeared with unfailing regularity since 1966, and with sixty-five issues published at this time of writing, is the longest-running fantasy fiction small press magazine. *Space and Time* soon generated its own imitators, so that during the 1970s there was a wealth of semi-professional publications of variable quality and content such as *The Argonaut, The Diversifier, Wyrd, Fantasy & Terror, Astral Dimensions, Jeet* and *Evermist*.

Two of the biggest influences on fantasy fiction were the works of H.P.Lovecraft and Robert E. Howard, and during the 1970s a host of magazines appeared devoted to discussing, dissecting, imitating and emulating them. On the Lovecraft side were *Nyctalops, From Beyond the Dark Gateway, Spoor Anthology* and *The Dark Messenger Reader* (now *Eldritch Tales*); whilst batting for Howard were *Fantasy Crossroads* and several not included in this index such as *Cross Plains, The Howard Reader* and the impressive *REH: Lone Star Fictioneer*. This last title was produced by Arnie Fenner and Byron Roarke and these two also produced *Chacal* which, in order to shake off the Howardian shadow, soon evolved into *Shayol* one of the most attractive of all small press magazines. When it comes to superiority of presentation, however, the title must go to *Ariel* which, after its first issue, was a stunningly designed and decorated phantasmagoria.

The small press field has dominated the weird fantasy genre since the early seventies, and there are as many, if not more, amateur magazines omitted from this index as are included. At present in the professional field only one regular magazine exists - *Rod Serling's 'The Twilight Zone' Magazine* - *Fantastic* having merged with *Amazing Stories* in 1980. *The Magazine of Fantasy & Science Fiction* continues to serve as a divided market, but today the leading markets for weird and fantasy fiction are all semi-professional magazines: *Whispers, Weirdbook,* the new *Fantasy Book* and, to a lesser degree *Space & Time*. That these magazines survive is due to the dedication of their editors and publishers. One can only dream at what might have been achieved had professional distributors attached even a fraction of that dedication in reaching the full market potential for all those other magazines that have passed away.

II - CANADA

Weird fantasy in Canada has been almost totally eclipsed by its southern neighbor. Its earliest independent magazine, *Uncanny Tales*, contained a mixture of fantasy and science fiction most of it reprinted from American sources. Nevertheless it survived for three years (1940-1943) and allowed a number of Canadian authors to experiment with a home market. It even had a short-lived companion title in *Eerie Tales*.

Excluding a couple of one-shot reprint magazines, and the longer-running Canadian edition of *Weird Tales* (which has sufficient variances from its progenitor to be of special interest to collectors) no other professional weird fantasy magazines have appeared in Canada. It was not until the 1970s when the small-press fever in the States spread north, that the Canadian fantasy potential was at last tapped.

Three small press magazines appeared all of which were of a good, even high quality - *Dark Fantasy, The Copper Toadstool* and *Dragonfields*. This last first appeared as two separate magazines - *Dragonbane* and *Beyond the*

Fields We Know before merging to become what is currently Canada's only significant market for weird fantasy.

III - UNITED KINGDOM

Unlike the United States, Britain did not pursue the publication of a variety of specialized fiction pulps until quite late. What weird fiction there was appeared in the general periodicals like *The Red Magazine* and *Hutchinson's Mystery Magazine*, and it was not until an experiment by the South London firm of World's Work that a whole series of specialized pulps appeared in the shape of the Master Thriller series. These presented both new and reprint stories by a variety of popular and unknown writers, and covered all fields of adventure, mystery and horror. The first, *Tales of Mystery and Detection* was a mixture of crime and fantasy fiction, but it was soon followed by *Tales of the Uncanny* and *Tales of Terror* which presented all weird fiction. The year was 1934, the same year that saw Britain's first science fiction magazine *Scoops*, so 1984 was something of a double anniversary.

Later titles in the series included *Fireside Ghost Stories, Ghosts & Goblins, Tales of Crime and Punishment* and *Tales of Ghosts and Haunted Houses*, the series ending with the advent of World War II, which also curtailed the companion series *Mystery Stories*.

With the War restricting the import of American magazines, the firm of Atlas, which had originally distributed US titles, now began to publish British editions. Thus a home grown *Unknown* appeared which, whilst drawing its contents wholly from its mother title, outlived the parent, and survived until 1949.

The only other company to provide fantasy matter during the War was that of the enterprising publisher Gerald G. Swan. Having stockpiled paper before the War, Swan had more than enough when paper was rationed and he was able to produce a regular supply of books and magazines right through the war years. The quality was minimal, however, but to a nation starved of reading matter, no questions were asked. Swan's fantasy titles included *Weird Story Magazine, Yankee Weird Shorts, Weird Pocket Library, Weird Shorts* and *Occult Shorts*. By the end of the War, Swan had accumulated so many manuscripts in his warehouse that he still published magazines for another fifteen years drawing on that stock. 1960 saw the last of them in the form of *Weird and Occult Library*.

After the War there was a sudden boom in book and magazine publishing in Britain, much of it inferior. The more dedicated of British fans, Walter Gillings and Leslie Johnson, produced the reprint *Strange Tales* and the new *Outlands* respectively, but it was not until the formation of the fan-financed Nova Publications that a major magazine could be launched. With Gillings as editor, *Science-Fantasy* appeared in 1950 as companion to the sf magazine *New Worlds*. Gillings was soon replaced as editor by John Carnell, and as the 1950s progressed Carnell gradually converted *Science-Fantasy* from a predominantly science fiction publication to the only regular fantasy market Britain has ever had. During the 1950s it presented highly original fantasies by John Brunner, Kenneth Bulmer and others, and by the early 1960s was publishing the Elric stories by Michael Moorcock and the exquisite historical fantasies of Thomas Burnett Swann.

The only other regular fantasy publication at this time was *Supernatural Stories* but it was no market for aspiring authors as the contents were almost entirely the work of just two men, R. Lionel Fanthorpe and John S. Glasby. Producing fiction in such quantity it is no surprise that the quality suffered.

Science Fantasy folded in 1964 but the title was taken over by a new publisher and a new editor and continued through to 1966. Editor Kyril Bonfiglioli changed the emphasis of the magazine so that less weird fantasy appeared. In the end he even changed the title to *Impulse* and whilst it published much of interest, especially the work of Keith Roberts, it had lost the excitement of the Carnell issues.

The only other professional magazines to appear in Britain in the 1950s were *Weird World* and its longer lived foster child *Phantom*. *Phantom*'s editor, Cliff Lawton, made contact with US agent Forrest Ackerman who supplied a number of new and reprint items for later issues. Lawton and Ackerman again teamed up for an all-reprint *A Book of Weird Tales* in 1960, but the intended series never eventuated.

With the demise of *Impulse* in 1967 Britain was left without a market for weird fantasy. Once again, as in America, it was the small press field that saved it. The pioneer in this respect was David A. Sutton who published the scholarly magazine

Shadow. In 1970/1 Sutton produced two issues of a companion fiction magazine *Weird Window.* He was also one of the fans instrumental in founding the British Fantasy Society which issued its own magazine *Dark Horizons* which Sutton currently edits. The founding editor of *Dark Horizons* was Rosemary Pardoe, who subsequently launched her own publication *Ghosts & Scholars* in honor of the master British fantasist M.R.James.

Another editor of *Dark Horizons*, Steve Jones, joined forces with David Sutton in 1977 to publish *Fantasy Tales*, Britain's leading small press magazine, and the only regular market for fantasy in Britain. Sutton and Jones also produced a memorial issue of *Airgedlamh* in tribute to its editor Dave McFerran who died before completing the issue.

The work of David Sutton and Steve Jones and other dedicated fans like Rosemary Pardoe, Jon Harvey and Charles Partington, has kept fantasy markets alive in Britain at a time when the professional publishers abandoned the field. Indeed Sutton and Jones also assisted the Italian fan Francesco Cova in producing his Anglo-Italian magazine *Kadath* and there is no denying the the fantasy field would be so much the poorer had it not been for this handful of devotees.

Mike Ashley &
Frank Parnell
1984

* * *

_User's Guide

The index is divided into four main sections:

(1) Issue Index

Every entry opens with a brief descriptive passage detailing the magazine's status (e.g. small press, horror/mystery etc.), country of origin, publishing schedule (monthly, bi-monthly, irregular), publisher, place of publication and editor. It will also make reference to the magazine's format, and for this volume the following designations have been used regarding a magazine's size and appearance:

Digest	$7\frac{1}{2}$ x $5\frac{1}{2}$ inches approx. Usually printed on pulp paper. The size can vary to Large Digest, i.e. $8\frac{1}{4}$ x $5\frac{1}{2}$.
Pulp	10 x 7 inches, printed on low quality pulp paper. A larger format exists, sometimes erroneously called 'bedsheet' size, which is $11\frac{1}{2}$ x $8\frac{1}{2}$.
Neo-pulp	$10\frac{1}{2}$ x $8\frac{1}{4}$ inches, printed on pulp paper but with high quality gloss covers.
Slick	11 x 8 inches, printed on high quality glossy stock throughout. Some magazines may use glossy stock for part of the issue and standard grade for the rest, and these I have refered to as quasi-slick.
Chapbook	7 x 5 inches. Small booklet format, usually without standard covers, though often on good quality paper.
Quarto	11 x $8\frac{1}{2}$ in US: 10 x 8 in UK. Standard imperial size for most duplicated amateur magazines on low quality stock. The metric equivalent is A4.size $29\frac{1}{2}$ x 21mm.
Octavo	$8\frac{1}{2}$ x $5\frac{1}{2}$ in US; 8 x 5 in UK. Also used on most printed or duplicated amateur magazines, usually on paper of a reasonable quality stock. Metric requivalent is A5 21 x $14\frac{1}{2}$mm.

Every issue entry follows the same format. The top line begins with the cover date. Where no date is given the publication date is given in brackets, e.g. [June] 1974, [Summer] 1980. This is followed by the volume and issue number, thus: 1/1 equals Volume 1, Number 1. Where no volume sequence is retained the issue number only is cited, e.g. No.1. Where the volume numbering exceeds the first, a further figure in brackets gives the total issue numbering to date. The final entry on the top line

names the cover artist if known. Thus a full entry, as taken here from
Weird Tales reads:

<u>November 1941</u>   36/2 (202)   Hannes Bok

Means the November 1941 issue was Volume 36, Number 2, Whole Number
202, and featured a cover painted by Hannes Bok.

The contents are then listed with the title on the left and the author
on the right. If a story is a reprint it is preceded by an asterisk: *.
Between the title and the author will be given some kind of content identification. All contents are presumed to be short stories (under 10,000
words) unless otherwise designated. Otherwise fiction is noted thus:

nt   novelette   [10,000 - 20,000 words]
na   novella   [20,000 - 30,000 words]
sn   short novel [30,000 - 40,000 words]
n   novel   [above 40,000 words]
abr.n abridged novel
s   short story [used rarely]

If a story is serialized the episode is noted following the story
designation, thus:

n1/4 a four-part serialized novel of which part one is
      in this issue.
s2/2 a two-part serialized short story of which the
      second and final instalment is in this issue.

A full list of these abbreviations will be found at the end of this
User's Guide. Suffice it here to say the code will identify whether
the item is fiction, non-fiction, poetry, a particular editorial or
pictorial feature, a comic strip, interview or even a play.

Thus a full entry taken from the September 1931 *Weird Tales* reads:

*The Wolf-Leader [n2/8]   Alexandre Dumas

Means the issue contains part two of an eight-part serialization of
the novel "The Wolf-Leader" by Alexandre Dumas, which is a reprint.
[For original publication data on reprints see the Author Index.]

(2) Author Index

The first line of entry gives the author's full name and birth/death
details. If the by-line varies the variable part is printed in capitals
within brackets. That part of the author's name which never appears in
print is included in further brackets in lower case. A variant name
such as MIKE/MICHAEL or RAY/RAUL is indicated as shown.

Names are listed in alphabetical order. Mc is treated as spelled Mac,
and d' as if spelled de. Thus D'ORSAY appears alphabetically as if
DE ORSAY. DE is treated as a separate word, thus all DE surnames will
appear together, before surnames starting DEAN, DEATON etc.

Following the name and birth/death data, the second line will give,
if known, a brief author identification in italics, usually designating
nationality and occupation. A full example reads:

<u>WEST, WALLACE</u> [G(eorge)] [1900-80]
<u>US pollution control expert</u>

Means that although West's full name is Wallace George West it
usually appears as Wallace West and sometimes as Wallace G. West.
He lived from 1900-1980 and was American and a pollution control
expert.

The entries themselves are in alphabetical order of contribution.
However, any items about the author, e.g. interviews, profiles or bibliographies are always listed first in italics.

The same notations apply as used in the Issue Index. A title preceded
by an asterisk (*) denotes a reprint. In these cases the original source
of publication is listed immediately below that entry. Wherever possible
the first known publication has been listed (usually in magazine form);
failing that the first known book publication is cited; in rare cases
where neither is known the source used for the reprint is cited. Alternate

titles or title changes are also indicated.

Following the title is an indication of the type of content, as in the issue index (see List of Abbreviations). If the story forms part of a series or is connected to another story this is indicated in italics in brackets. If short enough the full name of the series is used; otherwise it is abbreviated to some still recognizable form and an explanation is given at the end of each author entry. There is a full index to the series in Appendix I.

Finally, the right-hand column lists the magazine issue in which the story appeared. The magazine title is abbreviated and full details will be found in the List of Abbreviations. The issue date is abbreviated to the first three characters of the month or season, and the last two of the year. [Note: this format is used throughout to any reference of a month and year. If there is any doubt as to whether the year may be a monthly date (in the case of weekly publications) the year is given in full. Similarly all years prior to this century are given in full.] If the magazine carries no issue date, reference is made by issue number with the year of publication only given. Where a magazine is known better by its issue number than the cover date (even when it has one) then both details are given - this is common for small press magazines. Thus the three variants are:

              WT Sum 73   =   Weird Tales Summer 1973
           AFR 14,1950   =   Avon Fantasy Reader No.14 in 1950
          Div 21,Jul 77   =   The Diverisifer No.21, July 1977

A full example selected from the entry for Ray Bradbury is as follows:

          The Wind   WT Mar 43
         *The Wind   MysT Nov 51
         *The Wind   Div 21,Jul 77
         *Ylla   [MC]   AFR 14,1950
          [*orig."I'll Not Look For Wine"
          Maclean's Magazine Jan 1,1950]

> Means "The Wind" will be found in its original publication in the March 1943 *Weird Tales* and will subsequently be found reprinted in the November 1951 *The Mysterious Traveler Magazine* and issue number 21 (dated July 1977) of *The Diversifier*. "Ylla", which forms part of the Martian Chronicles series, will be found reprinted in issue number 14 of *The Avon Fantasy Reader* published in 1950 but was originally published under the title "I'll Not Look For Wine" in the January 1st 1950 issue of *Maclean's Magazine*. As there is no other indication, both stories are short stories (i.e. under 10,000 words).

Under each author entry the first grouping lists all those stories written by that author alone and published under the name cited above. In most cases this is the author's real name. In rare instances, where an author's pseudonym has totally supplanted his real name, entries will be found under the pen name. Following that entry are stories written by that author under pseudonyms; and following those are any stories written in collaboration. Thus, under Robert Silverberg, first are listed those stories published as by Silverberg, then those published under the pseudonyms Ralph Burke, Ivar Jorgensen, Calvin M. Knox, Dan Malcolm, Alex Merriman, Hall Thornton and Richard F. Watson, and then are listed his collaborations with Randall Garrett, first as Clyde Mitchell and then as Robert Randall.

(3) Artist Index

As with the Author Index each entry opens with the Artist's Name, birth/death details and a brief artist identification. The entries are then sub-divided into the three areas indexed:

          (1) Front Covers   (2) Back Covers   (3) Interiors

Front and back covers are, I hope, self-explanatory. Interior art does not cover all illustrations. Those incidental to the contents have been excluded. What are covered are all art portfolios, free-standing major illustrations (not fillers), frontispieces and endpapers, graphic features, pictorials (meaning an illustration with some brief textual comment) comic strips and graphic stories. Where these items have titles these are also listed.

   Each section takes the same format. The magazine title (in its abbreviated form) is listed first followed by the year and issue date. Where
issues are known by their serial number this is given in brackets after
the date. Reprinted artwork, where known, is again indicated by an asterisk and the source given in brackets immediately following. Thus, an example selected from within the entry for Virgil Finlay reads:

   covers
   BFT 1970*Fal(1) [*SS Jan 52]
   MoH 1968*May(21) [*WT May 38]

   backcovers
   Ftc 1961 Sep; 1962 Jan,Mar
       1963 Feb,Jul,Nov; 1964 Jan

   interiors
   Ftc 1966*Jul [ap:*AS Feb 43,*FA Feb 48,*FA Jul 48]
   WT 1937 Dec The Vampire [pic]
       1938 Jan "Her Demon Lover" [pic]

Means Finlay's artwork appears on the cover of the Fall 1970 *Bizarre
Fantasy Tales* (Issue No.1) reprinted from the January 1952 *Startling
Stories*; and on the May 1968 *Magazine of Horror* (Issue No.21), reprinted from the May 1938 *Weird Tales*.
   Finlay provided back cover art for the September 1961, January
1962 and so on through to the January 1964 issue of *Fantastic*.
   The July 1966 *Fantastic* contains a portfolio of Finlay artwork
reprinted from the February 1943 *Amazing Stories* and the February
and July 1948 issues of *Fantastic Adventures*. The December 1937 issue
of *Weird Tales* contains a Finlay pictorial feature entitled "The
Vampire", and the January 1938 issue contains another pictorial feature entitled "'Her Demon Lover'".

(4) Editor Index

   Following the Editor's name and birth/death details (if known),
the entries cite the editorial or publishing post held and the magazine
and issues for which he/she was responsible. The issues cited are as
per the cover date and not necessarily related directly to the dates of
the editor's employment. The posts listed cover all those which will
relate directly to the selection of manuscripts, compilation of the
issues and publication of the magazine together with policy directives.
Thus posts include Publisher, Editor-in-Chief, Editor, Executive Editor,
Managing Editor, Assistant Editor, Associate Editor and Editorial
Assistants. As a rule consulting editors are excluded.

   The magazines are detailed in the same abbreviated form as used in
the Artist's Index. The list of all abbreviations will be found on the
following page.

ABBREVIATIONS USED

DESCRIPTIVE OR EXPLANATORY

a	article (non-fiction)
abr	abridged from a longer work
aka	also known as
ap	art portfolio
bib	bibliography
col	column or feature
cs	comic strip (see also gs)
ed	edited by/editorial
ex	excerpt or extract from a longer work
ged	guest editorial
gf	graphic feature
gs	graphic story (see also cs)
gv	graphic verse
ill	illustration (refers to a full-page free-standing illustration with no accompanying text; see also pic)
in	interview
intro	introduction
ltr	letter
n	novel (fiction above 40,000 words. If serialized will be followed by the number of instalments, e.g. n3 means a three-part serialized novel)
na	novella (20-30,000 words)
nt	novelette (10-20,000 words)
obit	obituary/memoriam
orig	originally
pic	pictorial feature (an illustration with text; see ill)
pseud	pseudonym
pub'd	published
ret	retitled
rev	revision of/revised
rr	round-robin (story written in sequence by more than one writer)
rv	review
s	short story (under 10,000 words)
sc	script
sf	science fiction
sn	short novel (30-40,000 words)
spf	spoof
sr	serial
ss	short-short story (under 500 words)
sym	symposium
tp	teleplay
trans	translator/translation
ts	'true' story/experience
v	verse (may include prose poems, though these usually indicated by ss for very short story)

MAGAZINE TITLES

Ace	Ace Mystery
AD	Astral Dimensions
AdH	Adventures in Horror (includes Horror Stories)
AFR	Avon Fantasy Reader
Agd	Airgedlamh
AMF	A. Merritt's Fantasy Magazine
Anu	Anubis
Arg	The Argonaut (orig. Macabre)
Ariel	Ariel, the Book of Fantasy
ArkC	Arkham Collector
ArkS	The Arkham Sampler
AS	Amazing Stories
ASFFR	Avon Science Fiction & Fantasy Reader
ASFR	Avon Science Fiction Reader
BC	The Black Cat
BFF	Beyond Fantasy Fiction
BFT	Bizarre Fantasy Tales
BFWK	Beyond the Fields We Know
BI	Beyond Infinity
Biz	Bizarre
BL	Black Lite
BMM	Bizarre! Mystery Magazine
BoT	The Book of Terror
BrFT	Brief Fantastic Tales
BWT	A Book of Weird Tales
Chac	Chacal
Chl	Chillers
Cov	Coven 13
CT	The Copper Toadstool
Cth	Cthulhu
Db	Dragonbane
DDH	Dreams of a Dark Hue
DFd	Dragonfields
DFy	Dark Fantasy
DH	Dark Horizons
Div	The Diverisifer
DMR	The Dark Messenger Reader
DrD	Doctor Death
DW	Dream World
E&O	Etchings and Odysseys
EC	Eerie Country
Eld	Eldritch Tales
EM	Eerie Mysteries
ES	Eerie Stories
Esc	Escape
ET	Eerie Tales
EvM	Evermist
FA	Fantastic Adventures
F&T	[The Literary Magazine of] Fantasy & Terror
FB	Fantasy Book
FBDG	From Beyond the Dark Gateway
FC	Fantasy Classics
FCr	Fantasy Crossroads
FCw	Fantasy Crosswinds
Fear	Fear!
FF	Fantasy Fiction/Fantasy Stories
FFy	Forgotten Fantasy
FGS	Fireside Ghost Stories
FM	Fantasy Magazine
FT	Fanciful Tales
Ftc	Fantastic
FUW	From Unknown Worlds
FUWB	From Unknown Worlds - British
FyM	Fantasy Macabre
FyT	Fantasy Tales
Gam	Gamma
G&G	Ghosts and Goblins
G&S	Ghosts and Scholars
Ggn	The Gorgon
Goth	Gothic

GS	Ghost Stories		TB	The Thrill Book
GSTZ	Great Stories From Rod Serling's 'The Twilight Zone' Magazine		TCP	Tales of Crime and Punishment
HoH	The Haunt of Horror		TF	Tales of the Frightened
Hor	Hor-Tasy		TGHH	Tales of Ghosts and Haunted Houses
HPL	H.P.L.		Thrl	Thriller
HST	Horror Sex Tales		TMD	Tales of Mystery and Detection
Imp	Impulse [later sf Impulse]		TMM	Tales of Magic and Mystery
Jeet	Jeet		ToF	Threshold of Fantasy
Kad	Kadath [Italian]		ToT	Tales of Terror
Kdth	Kadath [US]		TTFB	Tales of Terror From the Beyond
LST	Legendary Sex Tales		TTT	True Twilight Tales
Lvs	Leaves		TU	Tales of the Uncanny
Mac	Macabre		TW	Toadstool Wine
M&T	Monsters and Things		TZ	Rod Serling's 'The Twilight Zone' Magazine
Mb	Moonbroth			
MM	Mind Magic/My Self Magazine		Unk	Unknown [see UW]
MoH	Magazine of Horror		UnkB	Unknown [British edition]
MP	Monster Parade		Unq	Unique
MS	Midnight Sun		UnS	Unusual Stories
MST	Monster Sex Tales		UnT	Unique Tales
MT	Marvel Tales		US	Uncanny Stories
MyS	Mystery Stories		UT	Uncanny Tales [US]
MysT	The Mysterious Traveler Magazine		UTC	Uncanny Tales [Canadian]
Mystic	Mystic Magazine		UW	Unknown Worlds [see Unk]
Nek	The Nekromantikon		UWB	Unknown Worlds [British edition]
NF	Night Flights		Vor	The Vortex
NFJ	The New Fantasy Journal		WA	Weird Adventures
Nov	November Magazine		W&S	Witchcraft & Sorcery
NV	Night Voyages		WB	Worlds Beyond
Nyc	Nyctalops		Wbk	Weirdbook
OS	Occult/Occult Shorts		WD	The Wax Dragon
OTW	Out of This World		Whsp	Whispers
Out	Outlands		WM	Weird Mystery
PD	Phantasy Digest		WoF	Worlds of Fantasy
Pgn	Paragon		WOL	Weird and Occult Library
PGS	Prize Ghost Stories		WOM	Weird and Occult Miscellany
Phtm	Phantom		WPL	Weird Pocket Library
PtF	Prelude to Fantasy		WS	Weird Shorts
S&S	Sword and Sorcery Annual		WSM	Weird Story Magazine
S&T	Space and Time		WST	Weird Sex Tales
SCMS	Screen Chills and Macabre Stories		WT	Weird Tales [WT(Can) refers to the Canadian edition]
SE	Something Else			
SFF	Stirring Fantasy Fiction		Wtch	The Witch's Tales
SFy	Science Fantasy		WTT	Weird Terror Tales
Shk	Shock		WW	Weird Window
Shyl	Shayol		WWd	Weird World
SMS	Startling Mystery Stories		Wyrd	Wyrd
SN	Supernatural Stories		YWS	Yankee Weird Shorts
Spoor	Spoor Anthology			
SPWAO	SPWAO Showcase [SPWAO = Small Press Writers and Artists Organization]			
SSET	The Strangest Stories Ever Told			
ST	Strange Tales [US]			
STB	Strange Tales [British]			
StF	Strange Fantasy			
StS	Strange Stories			
Sus	Suspense			

****

Issue Index:
A Chronological
Listing
of Contents of
Magazines

A

ACE MYSTERY

A weird menace pulp published bi-monthly by Periodical House, 67 West 44th Street, New York. Editor: Harry Widmer.

May 1936	1/1	Sherman
The Singing Scourge [nt]		Frederick C. Davis
Death's Heiress		Laurence Hammond
Cat-Man		Ben George
Priestess of Pain [nt]		Maitland Scott
Satan's Faceless Henchmen		Steve Fisher
Wolf Vengeance		Rex Grahame
The Corpse Queen's Lovers		John H. Knox
Nightmare House		Paul Ernst
The Horde of Silent Men [nt]		Hugh B. Cave

July 1936	1/2	Sherman
The Destroying Angel [nt]		Frederick C. Davis
Satan's Armchair		Maitland Scott
Mistress of the Snarling Death		Paul Chadwick
The Beast Mark [nt]		Laurence Hammond
Coyote Woman		Charles Marquis Warren
The Devil's Nightmare		Robert C. Blackmon
Witch Girl		Ralph Powers
Blade of the Doomed		N. L. Clarke
Death Lovers [nt]		George A. Starbird

September 1936	1/3	R. M. de Soto
Princess of Death's Desire [nt]		Frederick C. Davis
Satan's Forge		G. T. Fleming-Roberts
Doomsday Fate		Jeffery Strictland
Milady's Black Bondage		Henry Treat Sperry
Bride For the Half-Dead [nt]		Charles Marquis Warren
The Massacre Curse		Maitland Scott
Shackled Doom		Frank Gruber
Terror's Temptors		MacAllister Street

***

ADVENTURES IN HORROR

A low quality weird menace neo-pulp published bi-monthly by Stanley Publications, 261 Fifth Ave., New York. Editor: Theodore S. Hecht. Was retitled Horror Stories from the third issue. Illustrated in part with stills from low grade horror movies, which were also used for the covers.

October 1970   1/1
Love is the Color of Blood
                   J. Philip Tarleton
Howl, Wolf, Howl   William Cornish
Gory Terror in the Night   Dave Kingston
The Naked Slaves of the
   Master of Hell   William Dunlappe
The Spell of the Witch   Thomas Arnes
The Unholy Six   Bill Prescott
The Devil of Denham Swamp Howard Cherna
Adventures in the Occult [col]
                 Whittier Fowles

December 1970   1/2
Bony Fingers From the Grave
                 Robert Lawrence
Trapped in the Vampire's Web
   of Icy Death   Harlan Williams
One More Victim for the Coffin's
   Curse of Horror Michael Pretorius
The Blood-Drenched Corpse of the
   Priestess of Satan William Dunlappe
The Doll-Maker's Revenge   Thomas Arnes
It Takes Two For Terror   Obadiah Kemph
Evil Stranger in the House
   of Doom   Norman Nickerson
Adventures in the Occult [col]
                 Whittier Fowles

retitled HORROR STORIES

February 1971   1/3
Screaming Terror on the Night
   the Zombies Walked   George Bruno
The Ghost is Coming to Take
   Me to Hell   Charles Dobey
The Devil Needs Your Soul Edward Hampton
The Vampire's Fangs Were Red
   With My Woman's Blood Andre Palmer
Trapped in a Room of Horror
   With the Slave of Satan T. W. Mannering

One Last Death Prowl For the Man
   Who Howled Like a Wolf Michael Pretorius
The Mad Monster Strikes Again Alden Franz
Adventures in Witchcraft [col]
                 Whittier Fowles

April 1971   1/4
The Ghost Wanted My Heart Thomas Campion
Revenge From Hell   Obadiah Kemph
The Curse of the Burning Witch
                 Michael Pretorius
The Night the Zombies Walked
                 Geoffrey Jack
Feast of Blood For the Girl
   Who Couldn't Die   Martha Scott
Screaming Horror of the Devil's
   Spawn   James Forrester
We Faced the Silent Spirit From
   the Grave   Gabriel Varney
Adventures in Witchcraft [col]
                 Whittier Fowles

June 1971   1/5
The Howling Ghost of the
   Spiral Staircase   Gabriel Varney
Long Night in the Hellfire
   Mansion   Obadiah Kemph
She Tried to Sell My Soul
   to Satan   George Venner
Feast of Blood in the House
   of the Vampire   Henry Lawes
Lamp of the Laughing Witch
                 Michael Pretorius
The Death Dance of the
   Fisherman's Devil Joseph Glanyil
The Shrieking Curse of the
   Voodoo God   Nicholas Flamel
Adventures in Witchcraft [col]
                 Whittier Fowles

August 1971   1/6
The Slave of Satan Who Stalked
    By Night   William Arnes
Seven Victims For a Blood-Mad
    Ghost   Charles Thompson
Revenge of the Witch   Avery West
The Phantom of Kensington Theatre
                         Gabriel Varney
Trapped Without Hope on the
    Ship of the Dead   Franklin Chase
Fangs of a Fiend for the Girl
    Who Died Twice   Obadiah Kemph
"Tomorrow We'll Dance in the
    White Man's Blood"   Roy Marvin
Adventures in Witchcraft   [col]
                         Whittier Fowles

October 1971   1/7
Shrieking Victim of the
    Vampire's Curse   William Arnes
The Army of Marching Corpses John D. Craig
"Giant Spiders Are Attacking
    Our Town"   Avery West
Sweet Violets of Death   Gabriel Varney
"I Was Raised From the Grave" Earl Martin
The Howling Demon Who
    Hungered for Blood   Michael Pretorius
Terror From the Mummy's Eyes
                         Charles Thompson
Adventures in Witchcraft   [col]
                         Whittier Fowles

***

AIRGEDLAMH

An Irish small press fantasy magazine published by Stephen Jones & David A. Sutton, in London, England on behalf of the editor, Dave McFerran. The magazine was the brainchild of McFerran and the issue was published as a tribute and memorial to McFerran following his death in February 1980, with all profits going to the Cancer Research Campaign.

<table>
<tr><td>Autumn 1980</td><td>[1]</td><td>Jim Pitts</td></tr>
<tr><td>Manslayer!</td><td></td><td>Simon R. Green</td></tr>
<tr><td>The Famulus in the Talisman</td><td>[v]</td><td></td></tr>
<tr><td></td><td></td><td>John Hurley</td></tr>
<tr><td>Two Sorrows and a Joy</td><td></td><td>Gordon Larkin</td></tr>
<tr><td>Jim Fitzpatrick: The Early</td><td></td><td></td></tr>
<tr><td> Years [in]</td><td></td><td>Dave McFerran</td></tr>
<tr><td>Nuada Airgedlamh [ill]</td><td></td><td>Jim FitzPatrick</td></tr>
<tr><td>The Universe of Islands [nt]</td><td></td><td>Adrian Cole</td></tr>
<tr><td>The Prophecy, or The Witchwoman</td><td></td><td></td></tr>
<tr><td> [v]</td><td></td><td>Marion Pitman</td></tr>
<tr><td>In Memoriam: Dave McFerran</td><td></td><td></td></tr>
<tr><td> [obit]</td><td></td><td>Peter Tremayne,
Karl Edward Wagner</td></tr>
</table>

***

A. MERRITT'S FANTASY MAGAZINE

A fantasy pulp published bi-monthly by Recreational Reading Inc., an affiliate of Popular Publications, 205 East 42nd St., New York. Editor: assumed to be Mary Gnaedinger who edited the companion magazines Famous Fantastic Mysteries *and* Fantastic Novels *(see Appendix II). Canadian issues were identical in fictional content to the US. Contents were reprinted from the Munsey magazines, in particular* Argosy/All-Story Weekly.

December 1949   1/1 (1)   [L. Stevens]
*Creep, Shadow! [n]   A. Merritt
*Footsteps Invisible   Robert Arthur

February 1950   1/2 (2)   [N. Saunders]
*The Smoking Land [n]   George Challis
*Three Lines of Old French   A. Merritt
*The Science of Time Travel [a]
                              Ray Cummings
*The Seal Maiden   Victor Rousseau

April 1950   1/3 (3)   N. Saunders
*The Ninth Life [n]   Jack Mann
*The Little Doll Died   Theodore Roscoe

July 1950   1/4 (4)   N. Saunders
*The Face in the Abyss [na]   A. Merritt
*The Green Flame [na]   Eric North

October 1950   2/1 (5)   N. Saunders
*The Elixir of Hate [n]
                          George Allan England
A Glimpse of A. Merritt [a]   [The Editor]
*The Devil-Fish   Elinore Cowan Stone
*Racketeers in the Sky   Jack Williamson

                    ***

ANUBIS

A weird fantasy amateur magazine printed (offset) and published quarterly by Ronald J. Willis under the imprint Golden Goblin Press, Arlington, Virginia. Editor: Paul J. Willis. It strove to follow in the tradition of Weird Tales.

Autumn 1966   1/1   P. Willis
The Hidden Ones [v]   George Keneboros
Realism [v]   Norman G. Markham
H. P. Lovecraft and the
    Voynich Manuscript [a] Paul J. Willis
Leaves From the *Necronomicon*   P. J. Willis
    [graphics by M. Philippe Druillet]
The Amulet   Ronald J. Willis &
                           Paul J. Willis
The Horrible Effigy   Norman G. Markham
The Parable of Keys: An
    Allegory   John W. Andrews
The Beast From Baalazz   Lyle Gaulding
Pan's Pipes   Henry Vandervort
Le Tombeau de Howard Phillips
    Lovecraft [v]   Ronald J. Willis
Prolegomenon on Little Green
    Men [a]   Ronald J. Willis
Last Words [v]   Norman G. Markham

Spring 1967   1/2   R. E. Jennings
Take a Giant Step   Paul J. Willis
The Black Bishop   Ronald J. Willis
More Leaves From the
    Necronomicon [a]   [Paul J. Willis]
Irem [v]   Philip Canning
A Knight of Uthar-Pent   Philip Canning
My Lords, a Fretful Spirit
    Speaks ... [v]   Philip Canning
Arizona's Lost Death Trap [a]
                           Vincent H. Gaddis
Tit For Tat   Norman G. Markham
The Bookseller's Tale   Walter J. Wentz
Illumination [v]   Philip Canning
Fullfillment   R. Edwards Jennings
*Charles Fort and a Man Named
    Thayer [a]   Robert Barbour Johnson
Dust [v]   Ronald J. Willis
The Inheritor   Henry Vandervort

[Spring] 1968   1/3   ·   T. Kirk
Corrida   Roger Zelazny
The Gate of Diminishingness
                           Andrew E. Rothovius
*Caves [v]   Evelyn Thorne
*The Book of the Dead:
    Farnsworth Wright [a] E. Hoffman Price
Snatchment   Norman G. Markham
Daedalus Speaks [v]   Bennett Weinberg
Hallucination   Gerald W. Page
The Diary of Prof. Leman   Ronald J. Willis
The Altar of Flame   Lyle Gaulding
Vanished Hunters [v]   Philip Canning
Commentary on the *Necronomicon*
                           Dr. Franklin E. Tillinghast

Autumn 1968   1/4   D. B. Berry
The History of Greeley   Mose Mollette
Colloquy on a Field of Skulls
    [ss]   Philip Canning
The Huddlestone Horror   Robert M. Slater
Chimera [v]   Bennett Weinberg
When Gknorf, the Kingly
    Jester, Sat ... [v]   Bennett Weinberg
The Treason of Morn Connacht
                           Carleton Grindle
Eine Kleine Nachtmusik [ss]
                           Philip Canning
The Murals   Norman G. Markham
The Madman [v]   Roger Wilson Cook
Dead Sea [v]   Emilie Glen
Possible Sources for Lovecraftian
    Themes [a]   Ronald J. Willis
From the Diary of a Corpse [v]
                           Philip Canning
Dead Bone [gs]   Vaughn Bode
Overhill Mountain   Gerald W. Page
The Perfumed Room   Philip Canning
What Rattles Now ... [v]Mercer M. McDowell
Three Night Hours [v]   Douglas Kames
The Egg   L. E. Preston

* * *

THE ARGONAUT

A small press digest fantasy/sf magazine published irregularly by Michael Ambrose, Austin, Texas. The first three issues were entitled Macabre, thus causing confusion with Joseph Payne Brennan's magazine, also included in this Index. The first two issues were produced at high school by carbon copy with a circulation of less than a dozen and are included here for completeness. The magazine then suspended circulation until 1976.

entitled MACABRE

May 1972   1/1 (1)   –
Unknown Lust   Randy Philips
Wei-Thogga   Mike Ambrose
Tormented   Randy Philips

July 1972   1/2 (2)   –
Mr. Smith   Randy Philips
A Short Untitled Piece [ss]   Mike Malia
Curse of the Harz Mountains   Mike Ambrose
Valaric   Ronnie Thrasher
Rebirth of Essential Thought
                                William Ambrose

Summer 1976   2/1 (3)   [M. E. Ambrose]
Origin Point   Joel Harbin
Fragments from 'The Old
   Path' [v]   C. T. Thackeray
A Fable   Reginald Brane

retitled THE ARGONAUT

Spr/Sum 1977   No.4   M. E. Ambrose
Goodbye Mother Dear   Albert J. Manachino
Conquest   Joel Harbin & Duncan Moss
Fragments from 'The Old Path'
   [v]   C. T. Thackeray
*Silence – A Fable   Edgar Allan Poe

Win/Spr 1979   No.5   David Vosburgh
St. George and the Mushroom
                            Albert J. Manachino
Xeethra [v]   Michael Danagher
3...2...1   Phillip C. Heath
Genesis [v]   William A. Conder
Zithiquenne [v]   Michael Danagher
Shadows   Dewi McS
H.P. Lovecraft: A European
   Tribute [a]   Dirk W. Mosig

The Images of a Pale Dragon
   [v]   Michael Danagher
Death-Blow [v]   Joey Froehlich
The Children [v]   D. D. Marlan
Horror in the Rain [v]   Joey Froehlich
The Imaginary Emperor   Irvin L. Wagner
I've Got a Feeling [v]   Dale Hammell
Master of the Hunt of Time
                            An Clovis & Eric Hope
Poems, to the Poet [v]   Phillip C. Heath
Tryst [v]   William A. Conder
Chu-Tang at the Willow
   Bridge Inn   Gene Phillips
The Chant of Hearses
   Moving [v]   Joey Froehlich
To Mankind [v]   Carl Scott Harker
The Crossing   Brenda F. Watkinson
Reasons [v]   Carl Scott Harker

Sum/Fall 1979   No.6   Gary Kato
The Shadow   Albert J. Manachino
And the Winner Is... [v]   Dewi McS
Black Things   Brenda F. Watkinson
Justice [v]   Steve Eng
The Thing That Counts   Randall D. Larson
A Good Sense of Humor   Lawson W. Hill
Last Kiss [v]   Mark McLaughlin
Alanna   Gordon Linzner
A Wee Visitor [v]   Mark McLaughlin
The Babysitter [v]   William A. Conder
The Fall of Commorrium [v]
                            Michael Danagher
Transformation [v]   Joey Froehlich
Valley of the Lost Soul   M. E. Tyrell
Witness the Conestoga Wagon
   [v]   Venkatesh Srinivas Kulkarni
Forbidden Corner   Dewi McS
The Seeker From the Stars
   [v]   K. Allen Daniels

* * *

ARIEL

An ultra-slick fantasy magazine published quarterly by The Morning Star Press, Leawood, Kansas (from Vol.3 changed to Ariel Books, Kansas City, Missouri), under publisher Armand Eisen. Editor: Thomas Durwood. In large format (12" x 9"), Ariel was sub-titled 'The Book of Fantasy' from the second issue and was distributed by Ballantine Books as one of their art series. The emphasis was on fantasy art and graphics.

* * *

11

THE ARKHAM COLLECTOR

A chapbook-style magazine published twice-yearly by Arkham House, Sauk City, Wisconsin. Editor and Publisher: August Derleth. Originally issued to replace the company's annual publishing bulletin it initially consisted of mostly news and announcements but later gave greater emphasis to verse and fiction. Only these latter items are listed here, plus the more extensive non-fiction entries.

Summer 1967   No.1
Graveyard in April [v]
                    Joseph Payne Brennan
H.P. Lovecraft & Science Fiction
   [a]   [August Derleth]
The Mrs Ann Radcliffe Literature
   Award [speech]   Robert Bloch
*Someone at the Pasture Gate
   [v]   August Derleth
Nightmare [v]   Walter Shedlofsky
The Key [v]   Duane Rimel
Nocturne [v]   Herman Stowell King
Necrology [obit]   [August Derleth]
Colin Wilson [a]   [August Derleth]
Tintagel [v]   L. Sprague de Camp

Winter 1968   No.2
*Notes on the Writing of
   Weird Fiction [a]   H.P. Lovecraft
Lorenzo's Visit [v]   Raymond Roseliep
Alas [v]   Arthur M. Sampley
Down Endless Years [v]
                    Joseph Payne Brennan
The First PSI Annual Dinner
   [speech]   Robert Bloch
No Limit on Hippogrifs [v]   David Drake
H.P. Lovecraft [v]   William Fagan
More Than Twice Told Tales:
   1. The Valley [v]   Edna Meudt
   2. Leaves From Family Trees [v] Edna Meudt
   3. Once on a Country Road [v] Edna Meudt
   4. Frances: Fears That Pinch
      the Breastbone [v]   Edna Meudt
Hugo Gernsback [obit] [August Derleth]
The Visitant [v]   Wade Wellman
Connaissance Fatale [v]   Donald S. Fryer

Summer 1968   No.3
*Poe [v]   Thomas Bailey Aldrich
The Lemurienne [v]   Clark Ashton Smith
The Cyprus Shell   Brian Lumley
*Edith Miniter [v]   H.P. Lovecraft
Atlas in a Fourth Avenue Bar
   [v]   Arthur M. Sampley
Revelation [v]   Jack Hajdu
Cthulhu in Celluloid [a]
                    J. Ramsey Campbell
*Mary's Ghost [v]   Thomas Hood
Night [v]   L. Sprague de Camp
Clifford M. Eddy/Anthony
   Boucher [obit]   [August Derleth]
The Chain [v]   Frances May
The Vampire's Tryst [v]   Wade Wellman

Winter 1969   No.4
*"Till All the Seas"   Robert H. Barlow &
                       H.P. Lovecraft
Bleak November Days [v]
                    Joseph Payne Brennan
Lovecraft's Last Letter [ex]
                       H.P. Lovecraft
The Purple Door [v]   Walter Shedlofsky
*The Thing in the Moonlight:I
                       H.P. Lovecraft
The Thing in the Moonlight:II Brian Lumley
*To An Infant [v]   H.P. Lovecraft
Memories of Lovecraft:I [ex]
            Sonia Haft Lovecraft Davis
Memories of Lovecraft:II [a] Helen Sully
In Memoriam: H.P. Lovecraft [v] James Wade

Summer 1969   No.5
A Twist of Frame [v]   William D. Barney
Under the Eaves   Lin Carter
Nightmare Three [v]   Joseph Payne Brennan
Shadow on the Wall [v]   Duane Rimel

12

*Of William Hope Hodgson
  [ex]   A. St. John Adcock
*Lost [v]   William Hope Hodgson
*Shoon of the Dead [v]
                     William Hope Hodgson
The Crack in the Wall   Walter Jarvis
Ghosts [v]   L. Sprague de Camp
A Fragment From the Atlantean
  [v]   Donald S. Fryer
The Onlooker [v]   Wade Wellman
A Darker Shadow Over Innsmouth James Wade
Carcosa [v]   Richard L. Tierney
What It Is [v]   Roger Mitchell

Winter 1970   No.6   photo
Poe's Lake [v]   Joseph Payne Brennan
To Clark Ashton Smith [v]   Lin Carter
A Night For a Shearing Wind [v]
                     William D. Barney
*Nyarlathotep   H. P. Lovecraft
The Gate in the Mews [v]
                     Meade Frierson III
Star Winds [v]   Walter Shedlofsky
The Edomite Kings [v] Frank D. Thayer, Jr
Billy's Oak   Brian Lumley
The Wendigo [v]   Richard L. Tierney
The Hour of the Wolf [v] Viktor R. Kemper
Necrology: Greye La Spina/
  Margery Lawrence [obit]
                     [August Derleth]

Summer 1970   No.7
Marsh Moment [v]   Joseph Payne Brennan
The House of the Worm   Gary Myers
Judgement Day [v]   Joseph Payne Brennan
Bertrand Russell in Hell [v]
                     William D. Barney
Moonlight [v]   Clark Ashton Smith
The Sorcerer [v]   Wade Wellman
Miss McWhortle's Weird Donald A. Wollheim
Map of Arkham, c 1930 [map]   Gahan Wilson
All Hallows' Eve [v]   Lin Carter
An Item of Supporting Evidence
                     Brian Lumley
Vapor Fetch [v]   Walter Shedlofsky
Not to Hold [v]   Joyce Odam
Necrology: Seabury Quinn
  [obit]   [August Derleth]
The Lost Moon [v]   Donald Wandrei
An Epitaph on Jupiter [v] Donald Wandrei

Winter 1971   No.8   D. Tiani
To His Mistress, Dead and
  Darkly Returned [v]   Roger Johnson
The Cocomacaque   Carl Jacobi
*To Howard Phillips Lovecraft
  [v]   Clark Ashton Smith
Black Thirst [v]   Lin Carter
Enough [v]   Brian Lumley
Yohk the Necromancer   Gary Myers
K'n-Yan [v]   Walter C. DeBill, Jr
Summer Night [v]   Joseph Payne Brennan
Lovecraft on Love [ex]   H. P. Lovecraft
The Jersey Devil [v]   Barbara A. Holland
Strange Flowers Bloom [v]   Duane Rimel
The Shade in the Old Apple
  Tree [v]   Walter H. Kerr
A Presentation to George   Miki Myrick
Necrology: R. L. D. Taylor
  [obit]   [August Derleth]

Spring 1971   No.9
To Great Cthulhu [v]   Richard L. Tierney
Passing of a Dreamer   Gary Myers
May-Eve [v]   Steve Eng
The Aphids [v]   William D. Barney
*The Waiting Room   Robert Aickman
Ghost Stories, Fairy Tales
  and Riddles [v]   Joyce Odam
Dream For a Windy Night   Caryl Porter
When the Moon is Pale [v]   Wade Wellman
The Relic [v]   Roger Johnson
After You, Montagu   Howard Wandrei
In Pressure-Pounded Chasms [v] Brian Lumley
Necrology: Virgil Finlay
  [obit]   [August Derleth]
Panels For a Nativity [v]   James Wade
Atlantic City: 5.30 PM [v]   W. P. Ganley

Summer 1971   No.10
III Samuel [v]   William D. Barney
The Mass Media Horror [a]   James Wade
The Crest of Satan   Sara Lindsay Rath
Where They Rule [v]   Meade Frierson III
The Doom of Yakthoob   Lin Carter
In Intricate Magicks [v]   Walter H. Kerr
To My Masters [v]   Roger Johnson
Notes Concerning a Green Box
                     Alan Dean Foster
Night Sounds [v]   Walter C. DeBill
Shadow Game   George Wetzel

* * *

THE ARKHAM SAMPLER

Weird/sf magazine in larger-than-digest format published quarterly by Arkham House, Sauk City, Wisconsin. Editor and Publisher: August W. Derleth. Used as a vehicle to show the type of fiction published by Arkham House, but also served as a literary quarterly with extensive reviews and comment. In this respect it was one of the earliest academic journals. There was no cover artwork.

Winter 1948   1/1 (1)
Messrs Turkes and Talbot
                        H. Russell Wakefield
*History and Chronology of
   the Necronomicon [a]   H. P. Lovecraft
Three Poems [3v]   Clark Ashton Smith
Introduction: Strange Ports
   of Call [a]   August Derleth
Mara   Stephen Grendon
A Hornbook For Witches [v]
                        Leah Bodine Drake
The Carvings of Clark Ashton
   Smith [bib]   [no credit]
*The Dream-Quest of Unknown
   Kadath [sn1/4]   H. P. Lovecraft

Spring 1948   1/2 (2)
A Damsel With a Dulcimer Malcolm Ferguson
Hellenic Sequel [a]   Clark Ashton Smith
A Group of Letters [a]   H. P. Lovecraft
The Blindness of Orion [v]
                        Clark Ashton Smith
The Wind in the Lilacs   Stephen Grendon
Unhappy Endings [v]   Leah Bodine Drake
Fantasy on the March   Fritz Leiber, Jr
Random Notes:
   On the Cthulhu Mythos [a]
                        George T. Wetzel
   On "The Lurker at the
      Threshold" [a]   August Derleth
   From a Letter [a]   Clark Ashton Smith
*A Memoir of Lovecraft [a]
                        Rheinhart Kleiner
*The Dream-Quest of Unknown
   Kadath [sn2/4]   H. P. Lovecraft
W. Paul Cook [obit]   August Derleth

Summer 1948   1/3 (3)
A Kink in Space-Time H. Russell Wakefield
Night in the City [v]   Geraldine Wolf

The Novels of M. P. Shiel [a]
                        A. Reynolds Morse
No Stranger Dream [v] Clark Ashton Smith
*The Loved Dead   C. M. Eddy, Jr
On the Mount of Stone [v]
                        Clark Ashton Smith
*Howard Phillips Lovecraft [a]
                        Samuel Loveman
A Letter to E. Hoffman Price
   [ltr]   H. P. Lovecraft
Old Wives' Tales [v]   Leah Bodine Drake
Strangers From Hesperus [a] Norman Markham
*The Dream-Quest of Unknown
   Kadath [sn3/4]   H. P. Lovecraft

Autumn 1948   1/4 (4)
*The Sign   Lord Dunsany
Providence: Two Gentlemen Meet
   at Midnight [v]   August Derleth
A Note on Aubrey Beardsley [a]
                        Malcolm Ferguson
Only to One Returned [v]
                        Clark Ashton Smith
A Spell Useful Near Water [v]
                        Peter Viereck
*Nut Bush Farm [nt]   Mrs J. H. Riddell
The Unknown Land [v]   Leah Bodine Drake
*The Dream-Quest of Unknown
   Kadath [sn4/4]   H. P. Lovecraft
Change of Heart   Robert Bloch
*Anterior Life [v]   Charles Baudelaire

Winter 1949   2/1 (5)
A Basic Science Fiction Library
   [sym]   F. J. Ackerman, E. Bleiler
   D. H. Keller, S. Merwin, Jr, P. S. Miller,
      S. Moskowitz, L. Padgett, P. L. Payne,
   A. L. Searles, T. Sturgeon, A. E. van Vogt,
                        D. Wandrei
Avowal [v]   Clark Ashton Smith

SECOND SERIES

In 1983, during the preparation of this Index, The Arkham Sampler was revived, not as an individual magazine, but as a supplement to Etchings & Odysseys (q.v.). Published by The Strange Company, Madison, Wisconsin and edited by R. Alain Everts it appears in chapbook format (5x7 inches) and is included here for completeness. Like The Arkham Collector, the revived Arkham Sampler serves a dual purpose as magazine supplement and publisher's catalogue.

***

ASTRAL DIMENSIONS

A small press litho'd magazine in octavo format, co-published and co-edited by Chris Marler and Mark Jacobs from Staatsburg, New York. Although sub-titled 'The Magazine of Illustrated Fantasy & Science Fiction' the quantity of sf was minimal. Issue 6 was an 'All Weird Tales issue'.

Winter 1975	No.1	Alvin Bahret
Bron Haldrathe [s1/2]		Chris Marler
A Case of Genocide		Chris Marler
The Brain Death		Mark Jacobs
The Drug		Mark Jacobs
The Death Toller		Mark Jacobs

Winter 1975/6	No.2	Alvin Bahret
No Place Like Home		Mark Jacobs
Bron Haldrathe [s2/2]		Chris Marler
Spiders Are Harmless		Mark Jacobs
Not the Nova said Seven		Mark Jacobs
The Monk and the Minstrel		Chris Marler

Spring 1976	No.3	Alvin Bahret
Return to Quandar [s1/3]		C.C. Clingan
A Castle		Chris Marler
To View an Eagle		Mark Jacobs
The Pleasure Stones of Karina		Mark Jacobs
Of Ants and Men		Chris Marler
A Shadow Review [a]		Mark Jacobs

Fall 1976	1/4 (4)	Gene Day
Advice of a Friend		Michael Bell
The Waiting Game [v]		Steve Sneyd
The Temple in the Pines		Jim Coplin & Chris Marler
Malvoisie for Icarus [v]		Niel Kvern
The Hunt		David Madison
The Value of Pulp Fiction [a]		William H. Pugmire
Sky Castle of Quandar [s2&3/3]		C.C. Clingan
Teacher		Mark Jacobs
Last Killing		Frank Watson

Winter 1977	2/1 (5)	Ken Raney
The Cats in the Cellar		Charles R. Saunders
Tactics of Survival		C.C. Clingan & Ron Fortier
The Virtue of War		Wayne Hooks
The Devil, You Say?		Stephanie Stearns
A Doll for Susan		Phillip C. Heath
A Portfolio of Pulp Characters [ap]		Gene Day
Lord Tremaine and Squig the River Rat		Ken Hahn
Garden of Time [v]		Joseph Payne Brennan
*A Cry at Night [v]		Brian Lumley

Fall 1977	2/2 (6)	Clifford Bird
The Martin Gorsham Case		A.K. Molnar
The Lost Mind of Kerr Gulch		Glenn Rahman
Nightmare Circus		Jessica Amanda Salmonson
The Red Leather Book		David Madison
On H.P. Lovecraft's Views of Weird Fiction [a]		Robert A.W. Lowndes
Why Does One Write? [a]		H. Warner Munn
[with an intro. by E. Hoffman Price]		
The Terror of Time [a]		Joseph Payne Brennan
The Dead Lovers [v]		Michael Fantina
Evil Unseen		Gary Robert Muschla
H.P. Lovecraft: A Portfolio		
The Dunwich Horror [ill]		Gene Day
The Silver Key [ill]		Stephen Riley
Dagon [ill]		Allen Koszowski
The Cats of Ulthar [ill]		Todd Klein
Dream-Quest of Unknown Kadath [ill]		Clifford Bird
The Children's Hour		Frances Watson
Crimson and Clown White		William H. Pugmire
Tale Told by Moonlight [v]		Stephanie Stearns
Author! Author! [v]		Brian Lumley

* * *

AVON FANTASY READER

A fantasy/sf paperback anthology series published by Avon Book Co., 119 West 57th St., New York (later Avon Novels Inc., 575 Madison Ave., New York). Editor: Donald A. Wollheim. Due to its digest format and regular publication (initially bi-monthly, but became irregular) it was regarded by the sf community as a magazine (at a time when sf paperbacks were a rarity) and it has been regarded as such ever since. The covers were always colorful and attractive but, apart from issue 17, the artists have not been identified.

February 1947   No.1   ?
*The Power Planet [nt]   Murray Leinster
*The Shuttered House   August Derleth
*Justice [ss]   The Gibsons
*The Voice in the Night
                    William Hope Hodgson
*The Woman of the Wood [nt]   A. Merritt
*The Truth About Pyecraft   H. G. Wells
*The Vaults of Yoh-Vombis
                         Clark Ashton Smith
*Nostalgia [v]   H. P. Lovecraft
*The Central Figure   H. Russell Wakefield
*Three Infernal Jokes   Lord Dunsany
*Climax For a Ghost Story [ss]
                             I. A. Ireland

[April] 1947   No.2   ?
*Stenographer's Hands   David H. Keller
*The Strange Case of Lemuel
  Jenkins [nt]   Philip M. Fisher, Jr
*The Day of the Dragon   Guy Endore
*The Mirrors of Tuzun Thune
                         Robert E. Howard
*The Yellow Sign   Robert W. Chambers
*Automata   S. Fowler Wright
*The City of the   Laurence Manning &
  Living Dead   Fletcher Pratt

[June] 1947   No.3   ?
*Rhythm of the Spheres   A. Merritt
*The Phantom Wooer [v]
                     Thomas Lovell Beddoes
*The Silent Trees   Frank Owen
*The Queer Story of Brownlow's
  Newspaper   H. G. Wells
*Ozymandias of Egypt Percy Bysshe Shelley

*The Silver Key   H. P. Lovecraft
*The Grocer's Knock   Andrew Lang
*Black Thirst [nt]   C. L. Moore
*Mimic   Donald A. Wollheim
The Bishop's Gambit   Stephen Grendon
*"Let's Talk of Graves..." [v]
                       William Shakespeare
*Evening Primrose   John Collier
*Homecoming   Ray Bradbury

[Fall] 1947   No.4   ?
*The Arrhenius Horror [nt]
                        P. Schuyler Miller
*The Hollow Man   Thomas Burke
*Conqueror's Isle   Nelson S. Bond
*The Hoard of the Gibbelins   Lord Dunsany
*The Derelict [nt] William Hope Hodgson
*The Man Upstairs   Ray Bradbury
*The Planet of the Dead Clark Ashton Smith
*A Warning to the Curious   M. R. James
Defense   A. E. van Vogt

[Spring] 1948   No.5   ?
*Scarlet Dream   C. L. Moore
*Sambo   William Fryer Harvey
*Fane of the Black Pharaoh   Robert Bloch
The Random Quantity   Carl Jacobi
*The Gold Dress   Stephen Vincent Benet
*The Miracle of the Lily
                       Clare Winger Harris
*In the Court of the Dragon
                       Robert W. Chambers
*A Study in Amber   Frank Owen
*The Words of Guru   C. M. Kornbluth

17

* * *

AVON SCIENCE FICTION AND FANTASY READER

A digest magazine published by Avon Novels Inc., 575 Madison Ave., New York. Editor: Sol Cohen. In theory the merger of Avon Fantasy Reader and Avon Science Fiction Reader but with new stories instead of reprints. The contents were still 60% fantasy.

January 1953	1/1	
		Leo Manso
For Humans Only		Alfred Coppel
Like Gods They Came		Irving Cox, Jr
The Forgotten Enemy		Arthur C. Clarke
The Agents		Bryce Walton
Mr Kowtshook		John Christopher
The Shed		E. Everett Evans
Come Blow Your Horn		Milton Lesser
The Call of the Black Lagoon		
		Charles L. Harness
Agratha		Glen Malin
Checkmate Morning		John Jakes
*One-Man God		Frank Owen
The Short Count		Theodore R. Cogswell

April 1953	1/2	
		Leo Manso
DP!		Jack Vance
The Rather Improbable History		
of Hillary Kiffer		William Vine
Survivor		Irving E. Cox, Jr
*Breaking Point		John Christopher
As Holy and Enchanted		Henderson Starke
Hunt the Red Roe		Alan Payne
Crack of Doom		Milton Lesser
The Agent		Stephen Marlowe
Forever is so Long		John Jakes
A Night on Mars Hill [a]		
		Dr R.S. Richardson
The Parasite		Arthur C. Clarke

* * *

AVON SCIENCE FICTION READER

A paperback anthology in digest format published by Avon Novels Inc., 575 Madison Ave., New York; companion to Avon Fantasy Reader. *Editor: Donald A. Wollheim. Despite the title it was still over 50% fantasy.*

[Spring] 1951   No.1   ?
*The War of the Sexes [nt] Edmond Hamilton
*Green Glory   Frank Belknap Long
*The Immeasurable Horror
                     Clark Ashton Smith
*The Morrison Monument [nt]
                      Murray Leinster
*The Incubator Man   Wallace West
*The Dark Side of Antri [nt]
                 Sewell Peaslee Wright
*Blind Flight   Donald A. Wollheim
*Rhythm of the Spheres   A. Merritt
*Madness of the Dust   R. F. Starzl
*The Cosmic Express   Jack Williamson

[Summer] 1951   No.2   ?
*Priestess of the Flame [nt]
                 Sewell Peaslee Wright
*The Whisperers   Donald Wandrei
*When Half-Worlds Meet   John Michel
*The Superperfect Bride   Bob Olsen
*Vulthoom   Clark Ashton Smith
*The Man Who Discovered Nothing
                     Ray Cummings
*Highway   Robert W. Lowndes
*When the Flame Flowers Blossomed
                   Leslie F. Stone
*The Book of Worlds   Miles J. Breuer
*The Rebuff   Lord Dunsany

[Winter] 1952   No.3   Earle K. Bergey
*The Robot Empire   Frank Belknap Long
*P. N. 40   S. Fowler Wright
*The Master Ants   Francis Flagg
*In the Walls of Eryx Kenneth Sterling &
                    H. P. Lovecraft
*The Black Stone Statue
          Mary Elizabeth Counselman
*The Planet of Dread   R. F. Starzl
*The Alien Vibration   Hannes Bok
*The Ultimate Paradox Thorp McClusky

                ***

B

BEYOND FANTASY FICTION

*A digest fantasy magazine published bi-monthly by Galaxy Publishing Corp.,
421 Hudson St., New York. Editor: Horace L. Gold. A prestigeous magazine,
it failed to sustain the quality of the early issues. The word 'Fantasy'
was omitted from the cover and spine (but not the masthead) of the last two
issues. A British edition of the first four issues was published bi-monthly
by Strato Publications, East Street, Oadby, Leicester. It omitted those stories
marked with a ↑ below.*

July 1953   1/1 (1) Richard Powers
[UK issue released undated November 1953]
...And My Fear is Great [na]
                    Theodore Sturgeon
All of You   James McConnell
The Day the World Ended Frank M. Robinson
The Springbird   Roger Dee
Babel II [nt]   Damon Knight
Share Alike   Jerome Bixby & Joe E. Dean
The Wedding   Richard Matheson
↑Eye For Iniquity   T. L. Sherred

September 1953   1/2 (2) Richard Powers
[UK issue released undated January 1954]
The Wall Around the World [nt]
                    Theodore R. Cogswell
Wire-Haired Radical   Joseph Shallit
↑Can Such Beauty Be?   Jerome Bixby
↑Talent   Theodore Sturgeon
The Dream Makers [nt]   Robert Bloch
A Little Pile   M. C. Pease
How Do I Do?   John Wyndham
And Not Quite Human   Joe L. Hensley
Kid Stuff   Isaac Asimov
The Goddess on the Street
   Corner   Margaret St. Clair
The King of the Elves   Philip K. Dick

November 1953   1/3 (3)   Rene Vidmar
[UK issue released undated March 1954]
The Real People [na]   Algis Budrys
The Helpful Haunt   Richard Deming
↑Hush!   Zenna Henderson
House ... Wife [nt]   Boyd Ellanby
Just Imagine   Ted Reynolds
↑The Big Breeze   Franklin Gregory
↑Sorry, Right Number   Richard Matheson
My Darling Hecate   Wyman Guin

January 1954   1/4 (4)   Rupert Conrad
[UK issue released undated May 1954]
Call Me Wizard [na]   Evelyn E. Smith
↑Tag   Robert Abernathy
The Ghost Maker   Frederik Pohl
Perforce to Dream   John Wyndham
G'rilla   William Morrison
↑The Man Who Got Around   Joseph Satin
↑Wolfie   Theodore Cogswell
Halfway to Hell   Jerome Bixby

March 1954   1/5 (5)   Scott Templar
The God Business [na] Philip Jose Farmer
Lover Boy   Theodore R. Cogswell
The Green-Eyed Corner   Jay Clarke
Henry Martindale, Great Dane
                   Miriam Allen deFord
Hell to Pay [nt]   Randall Garrett
Then — Nothing   D. V. Gilder
The Watchful Poker Chip   Ray Bradbury
Gone Witch   Roy Hutchins

May 1954   1/6 (6)   Arthur Krusz
Sine of the Magus [na]   James E. Gunn
The Afterlife of Reilly   Richard Deming
Heads You Lose   William Morrison
High Man, Low Man   R. Bretnor
Illogistics   Stewart Kaser
I'd Give a Dollar   Winston Marks
Bottled in Russia   A. J. Greenwald

July 1954   2/1 (7)   Rene Vidmer
No More Stars [nt]   Charles Satterfield
Disassembly Line   Theodore R. Cogswell
A Brush With the Enemy H. Chandler Elliott
The Agony of the Leaves [nt]
                    Evelyn E. Smith
Yours For the Asking   Winston Marks

22

It's a Gift   George Hayman
Miss Tarmitty's Profession   Roy Hutchins

September 1954   2/2 (8)   Arthur Krusz
The Beautiful Brew   James E. Gunn
Earth Shaker   Franklin Gregory
Room Without Windows   Manly Banister
It's Not the Heat   Sam Merwin, Jr
Double Whammy: [2ss]
    Naturally / Voodoo   Fredric Brown
See Me in Black   Robert Beine
Kash and the Lemurs   ·Ralph Spencer
The Root and the Ring   Wyman Guin

[November] 1954   (2/3) 9   Rene Vidmer
The Green Magician [na]
        L. Sprague de Camp & Fletcher Pratt
The Upholstered Chaperone   Jeanne Williams

Upon the Dull Earth   Philip K. Dick
Reluctant Adam   Robert Richard
Queen's Mate   Jean M. Janis

[January] 1955   (2/4) 10   Rupert Conrad
Dragon Lady   Evelyn E. Smith
Stream of Consciousness [na] Roy Hutchins
The Paynim's Flute   Ralph Spencer
Sizzlestick   Sam Merwin, Jr
It's Colder Inside   E. B. Battles
Age Cannot Wither   [nt]   Cleve Cartmill
They   D. V. Gilder

***

BEYOND INFINITY

Planned as a bi-monthly digest magazine, published by I. D. Publications, Inc., 8383 Sunset Blvd., Hollywood, California. Editor: Doug Stapleton. Subtitled 'Strange Tales From Other Dimensions' it was a 50/50 blend of sf and horror. Poorly produced and poorly distributed it did not survive its first issue.

Nov/Dec 1967	1/1	[Lynn Goller]
Of Human Heritage		Wade Hampton
Communication Problem		John Christopher
Whirligig!		John Brunner
Talk to Me, Sweetheart		Ben Bova
5 - 4 - 3 - 2 -		James McKimmey
Deadly Image		McHugh Ferris
Revenge at the TV Corral!		
		J. de Jarnette Wilkes
The Thirteenth Chair		
		Michael Quentin Lanz
Upon Reflection		Gilmore Barrington
Mommy, Mommy, You're a Robot!		
		Dexter Carnes
Greetings, Friend!		
		Douglas & Dorothy Stapleton
The New Way		Christopher Anvil

***

BIZARRE

*A semi-professional sf/fantasy magazine published (with an intended bi-monthly
schedule) by Bizarre, 5000 Train Ave., Cleveland, Ohio. Published and Edited by
Jack Chapman Miske and Walter E. Marconnette. Printed by W. Lawrence Hamling.
Formerly a fanzine entitled* Scienti-Snaps *which had seen 13 issues since January 1938, in its new incarnation it lasted just the one issue.*

<u>January 1941</u>   4/1   Hannes Bok
The Thing in the Moonlight
  [fragment]   H. P. Lovecraft
To Write - Be Wrong! [a]
               John W. Campbell, Jr
Fantasy Footnotes [col] Harry Warner, Jr
The Dwellers in the Mirage A. Merritt
A Brief Autobiography [a]   Hannes Bok
The Open Mind [a]   E. E. Smith, Ph. D.
On H. P. Lovecraft's "The
  Festival" [v]   Earl Singleton

* * *

25

BIZARRE ʀANTASY TALES

A quarterly digest weird fantasy magazine published by Health Knowledge Inc., 140 Fifth Ave., New York, and companion to Magazine of Horror. Editor: Robert A.W. Lowndes.

Fall 1970   1/1   *Virgil Finlay
*The Great Circle [na]
                        Henry S. Whitehead
*The Doom That Came to Sarnath
                        H. P. Lovecraft
*Never Bet the Devil Your Head
                        Edgar Allan Poe
A Taste of Rain and Darkness
                        Eddy C. Bertin
*The 'V' Force   Fred C. Smale

March 1971   1/2   [uncredited]
*The Nemesis of Fire [na]
                        Algernon Blackwood
*My Favorite Murder   Ambrose Bierce
*The Holiness of Azederac
                        Clark Ashton Smith
The Ashley Premiere   Eddy C. Bertin
Cacillia   Reinsmith
*The Woman in Gray   Walker G. Everett

* * *

26

BIZARRE! MYSTERY MAGAZINE

A mystery/horror digest published monthly (bi-monthly from issue 3) by Pamar Enterprises, 122 East 42nd St., New York. Editor: John Poe. Covers are not credited but may have been by Art Director Hillary Wilson.

October 1965   1/1   ?
*One Drop of Blood   Cornell Woolrich
The Rats of Dr Picard   Henry Slesar
*The Living Statue   Romain Gary
Coup de Grace   Robert Edmond Alter
A Civilized Community   Arthur Porges
The Renter   Edward Preston
That Warm, Dead Brain   Donald Honig
A Loveable, Old Ritual   Warner Barth
Jack Be Nimble - Jack Be Quick,
   Jack Jump Over the Candlestick
                    Avram Davidson
Leader of the Revolution   Thomas M. Disch
"Let's Change Bodies!"   Arthur Kaplan
*The Horror at Redhook   H. P. Lovecraft
106   Andy Sugar

November 1965   1/2   ?
The Creep Brigade   Arthur Porges
Fear   Hal Ellson
*Enoch   Robert Bloch
The Last Command   Arthur C. Clarke
The Pledge   Lawrence Carney
Only For You   Jules Black
Comrade Vukashin's Clock
                    Robert Edmond Alter
Man and Wife   Andrew Prince
The Many Dooms of Harold Hall
                    Charlotte Corday-Marat
The 60-Minute Egg   Derek Page
The Marinus Ghost   Robert Retla
The Emperor's Dogs   Abel Jacobi
*Planet of the Apes [abr/nt] Pierre Boulle

January 1966   1/3   ?
Walpurgisnacht   August Derleth
Love is a Punch in the Nose   John Jakes
*The Lady Says Die   Mickey Spillane
The Way to a Man's Heart   Tom Disch &
                    John Sladek
Too Nice a Day to Die   Cornell Woolrich
Faddist   James H. Schmitz
A Therapeutic Success   Michael J. Kelley
Bad Tommy   Eric Corder
A Living Doll   Helen Santori
The Bet   Talmage Powell
A Matter of the Mind   Rita Ritchie
Pride Goeth   Peter Bassey
The Rabbit Box   J. O. Council
Frog Man   Harry Emerson Machen
The Death Wish   Richard O. Lewis
Die, Damn You   Jim McCormick
The Last Moments of Cornell Allen
                    Fletcher Flora

                    ***

27

THE BLACK CAT

*A Canadian small press weird fantasy magazine published by Memory Lane Public-
ations, 594 Markham Street, Toronto, Ontario. Publisher/Editor: George Henderson.*

Winter 1970/71   No.1 [*Virgil Finlay?]
*A Dose of Hasheesh [ex] Fitzhugh Ludlow
*The Man With the Brain of
   Gold   Alphonse Daudet
*The Bell of Kuang Sai   Edward W. Gilbert
*In the Hands of Fear   Harris Symmes
*The Cask of Amontillado   Edgar Allan Poe
*How It Feels to Die [ex]
                        Count Leo Tolstoy
*The Attribute of Fools
                   Mary Wilhelmina Hastings
*Frankenstein's Monster [ex] Mrs. Shelley
*The Love-Affair of a Freak
                   Mary Roberts Rinehart
*The Silent Prison [ex]   Charles Dickens
*The Iron Shroud   William Mudford
*The Murders in the Rue
   Morgue   Edgar Allan Poe
[*Introduction by Frederic Taber Cooper,Ph.D]
*Ariel's Song [pic]   Virgil Finlay

***

BLACK LITE

A small press (quarto,litho) sf/fantasy magazine published and edited by John DiPrete, 45 Vale Avenue, Cranston, Rhode Island.

August 1976   No.1   Gene Day
When the Universe Imploded [v]
                            John DiPrete
To Sleep, Perchance To ... Eric Vinicoff &
                            Marcia Martin
The One True God   Darrell Schweitzer
Limelost [v]   Jon Inouye
Grand Central Savior   A.K. Molnar
*Work Break   John DiPrete
Starllorn, the Philosopher [cs1/3]
  [art: Gene Day]   John DiPrete

October 1976   No.2   Mark Gelotte
Death-Cattle of Djenne Charles R. Saunders
Falling Doom   Gordon Linzner
Starllorn, the Philosopher [cs2/3]
  [art: Gene Day]   John DiPrete

March 1977   No.3   Gene Day
The Vision of Tseng Yuan-Li
                            Darrell Schweitzer
For Their People   Ken Hahn
Starllorn, the Philosopher [cs3/3]
  [art: Gene Day]   John DiPrete

January 1978   Nos.4/5   Gene Day
Angel's Gambit   D. Skov
Last Redwood   Davida McLean
Lobsters [v]   Neil Kvern
British and American SF: 'Waves'
  Apart? [a]   Cy Chauvin
Black Market Tape   Ken Hahn
Ghost Food   A.K. Molnar
Cold Sea   Kenneth Huff

* * *

THE BOOK OF TERROR

A Canadian pulp magazine published by the Metropolitan Publishing Co., Toronto.
Editor: 'The Black Prince'. Relied on reprints of occult and weird menace
material from the US pulps.

December 1949	?
*Rivers of Doom	Kenneth Miller
*Dark Depths of Human Madness	
	E. Hoffmann Price
*From An Old Egyptian Tomb	[no credit]
*From the Depths of the Unknown	
Came a Strange Desire	
	Gladys E. Dansfield
*The Witch Hunter's Bible [a]	[no credit]
*A Nightmare of Devil-Spawned	
Mysticism	Carl Moore
*Nameless Dread of the Savage	
Sirens	Robert Leslie Bellem

***

A BOOK OF WEIRD TALES

A British weird fantasy digest published by Veevers & Hensman Ltd., Burnley, Lancashire. Editor: Cliff Lawton, though issue assembled entirely from material submitted by US agent Forrest J. Ackerman, who is credited as Associate Editor. See also associational magazines Phantom *and* Screen Chills & Macabre Stories.

[Autumn] 1960   1/1   [Cliff Lawton]
*The Curse of Amen-Ra [na]
                          Victor Rousseau
*The Terror From Transylvania
   [a]   Dr. Acula
*The Dead Walk Softly [nt]
                Sewell Peaslee Wright
*Second Chance   L. Major Reynolds
*The Hunters From Beyond
                 Clark Ashton Smith
*The Wild One   Marion Zimmer Bradley
*Chained to a Bed of Roses   Jack Bechdolt

***

BRIEF FANTASTIC TALES

A scarce and little known Canadian fantasy magazine published in vest-pocket-size format by Studio Publications, 2842 Bloor Street West, Toronto, Ontario. No editor credited. Contains reprints from the Canadian Uncanny Tales.

[c1950]   [1]   -
*Strong Fingers of Death   D. H. Fairley
*The Man Who Remembered   Thomas S. Gardner
*The Thing Creeps   Geoffrey Myers
*Nightmare Murder   Lyle Cranston

***

C

CHACAL

A fantasy/sf small press magazine published quarterly by Nemedian Chronicles (Daemon Graphics for the second issue), Shawnee Mission, Kansas. Publisher: Arnie Fenner. Editor: Byron Roark (first issue), Arnie Fenner (second issue) assisted by Pat Cadigan. One of the most attractive small press publications in neatly printed and illustrated slick format, Chacal *(which is the French for 'jackal') was the successor to* REH: Lone Star Fictioneer, *a magazine which was dedicated to the writer Robert E. Howard and which the editors began to feel was too limiting.* Chacal *was in turn succeeded by* Shayol.

Winter 1976	1/1	Jeff Easley
The Road of Azrael [nt]		Robert E. Howard
Kirk's Corner [ill]		Tim Kirk
Der Untergang des Abendlandesmenschen		
		Howard Waldrop
Reflections on the Winter of My Soul		
[ap]		Jeff Easley
C. L. Moore Talks to Chacal [in]		
		Byron Roark
The Ballad of Singapore Nell [v]		
		Robert E. Howard
Mistress of Windraven		Tom Reamy
The End of Days [na1/2]		David C. Smith
Hannes Bok: Artist and Man [a]		
		Ben Indick
Sing a Last Song of Valdese		
		Karl Edward Wagner

Spring 1977	1/2	Jeff Easley
The Adventure of the Grinder's		
Whistle		Howard Waldrop
Raven's Eyrie [na]		Karl Edward Wagner
Daughter of Evil [v]		Robert E. Howard
Kirk's Corner [ill]		Tim Kirk
Celtia [ap]		Jim Fitzpatrick
Last Chance For Angina Pectoris		
at Miss Sadie's Saloon, Dry		
Gulch		Pat Cadigan
Palace of Bast [v]		Robert E. Howard
Interview: Manly Wade Wellman		
[in]		Karl Edward Wagner
The Next to the Last Voyage of		
the Cuttle Sark		Bill Wallace &
		Joe Pumilia
The End of Days [na2/2]		David C. Smith
A Fevered Glimpse of Chaos		
[a]		Dave McFerran
To 1966		Steven Utley

***

CHILLERS

A neo-pulp dedicated to horror films but containing a high percentage of fiction. Published bi-monthly by Charlton Publications, Charlton Building, Derby, Connecticut. Editor: Roger Elwood. All covers were film stills. The following list excludes the film previews.

July 1981   1/1
*Black Magic   Jessie Adelaide Middleton
Requiem   Gail Kimberly
Tarantula   Ward Smith
Night Prowler   William Colbert
Fire of Spring   George Zebrowski
Homecoming   Howard Goldsmith
The Final Conflict: Richard
   Donner [in]   [no credit]
Is the Dreadful 'Beast' of the
   Apocalypse About to Emerge?
   [a]   Dr W. S. McBirnie
Harvey Bernhard [in]   [no credit]

September 1981   1/2
Spare Change   Bill Clayton
An Interview With John
   Newland [in]   [no credit]
*The Witch of the Marsh
                     Ethel Marriott-Watson
Earth Around His Bones   George Zebrowski
Shadow, Shadow   Anton Shayne
The Undead   Thomas Paul

November 1981   1/3
Cancellation of the Candidate Steve Vance
Stephen King: King of the
   Beasties [a]   Bill & Debra Clayton
Feast   Philip Coolidge
The Alternate   George Zebrowski
Irwin Allen - Master of
   Disaster [a]   Tony Habeeb
*The Demon Cat   Lady Wilde
An Interview With Peter Hyams
   [in]   [no credit]
*The Vampire of Croglin Grange
                            Augustus Hare

                    ***

THE COPPER TOADSTOOL

A Canadian small press fantasy magazine published by Soda Publications, 750 Bridge Street, Richmond, British Columbia (final issue from 1235 Nelson St., Vancouver, B.C.). Publisher/Editor: Dale Hammell. Published in octavo digest format, the final issue appeared as a trade paperback under the title The Storyteller.

December 1976	1/1	Dale Hammell
By Power of Scalpel		Gene Day
The Black Swans of Loch		
Lothlomond		Dale Hammell
Siren [ill]		Tim Hammell
Schizoid [v]		D. D. Marlan
Saruman [ill]		Dale Hammell
The End [v]		Dale Hammell
July 1977	1/2	Tim Hammell
Tower of Babel		Al Manachino
Looking to the Sun		Gale Jack
Armagma Polareddon		Dale Hammell
Proxy	Gene Day & Gale Jack	
Roundstones and Sunchild		Gale Jack
Dollars		Gord Smith
The Great Matriarch Snatch		Steve Clement
Zap!	Alan & R. Limacher	
Fever Time		Gene Day
Ipswich		[no credit]
Alive and Living In		Gale Jack
January 1978	1/3	Tim Hammell
Far-Flung From an Ill-Spawned		
Galaxy		Randall Larson
The Cure [v]		Gary Philips
Setting Traps		Donald Legault
The Sea-Cave		Michael Ambrose
A Shade's Lament [v]		Galad Elflandson
The Old Stones [v]		Dale Hammell
The Piper of Dray		Galad Elflandson
The Wailers [v]		D. D. Marlan
St. George and the Mushroom		
		Albert Manachino
Social Comment [a]		Joe Pearson
In the Slums of Slumberland		Greg Gabbard
Boneless or Whole [v]		D. D. Marlan
R'lyeh Redux [a]		Charles Saunders
Grog [ap]		John Dods

May 1978	1/4	Tim Hammell
The Dark Dream of Ross Henderson		
		Phillip Heath
Sundown / Sewer [2v]		LeRoy Gorman
Slave to Tradition		An-Clovis
The Pythagorean Connection [a]		
		Lawrence Russell
The Great Garbage Strike		Donald Legault
The Virgins of Po		Galad Elflandson
Growth [v]		LeRoy Gorman
Raphael de Soto [a/ap]	Albert Manachino &	
		Dale Hammell
Of Bejewelled Hides [a]		Dale Hammell
The Day Frank Schoonover Died		John Bell
Gift From the Universe		Dewi McS
One Left Turn Too Many		Steve Clement
Splashdown [v]		LeRoy Gorman
Release [v]		Galad Elflandson
The Universe Makers		Paul Payack
Untitled Verse [v]		Dan Brady
January 1979	No.5	Larry Dickison
The Three That Came		Charles de Lint
Full Circle		Richard Marsh
Beloved Nephew, Loving Not		D. M. Vosk
The Great Sardine of Sardis		G. N. Gabbard
The Basilisk [nt]		Galad Elflandson
Fire on Yellow Mountain		Peter Werner
The Mad Maestro of Gananoque		
[in]		Larry Dickison
Bride of the Vodyanyk		Gordon Derevanchuk
The Lure [v]		Steve Sneyd
Nocturne [v]		G. N. Gabbard
Quo Arbitrium [v]		R. A. Heath
Autumn [v]		Wendelessen
Green Bride [v]		Steve Eng
Butterfly [v]		Sharon Sinner
Cremation Trot [v]		LeRoy Gorman
Fairy [v]		Sharon Sinner

```
Grimoire  [v]                    Steve Eng
Lily of Egypt  [v]              Steve Sneyd
Crimson Witch  [v]               Steve Eng
Unicorn  [v]                  Sharon Sinner
```

[THE STORYTELLER]

July 1979   No.6/7   Tim Hammell
Myth and Mystery: Some Thoughts
   on Fantasy [a]   Mike Ambrose
Day of the Skeleton, Night of
   the Pumpkin   Ralph Stephen Harding
My Ainsel'   Charles de Lint
The End of the Dream   An Clovis
Space Modesty   Christopher Merry
Night Drive   Caroline Kimble
A Great King Called Ile Phant Peter Werner
A Stitch in Time   Glenn Lisle
Snowbound in Glimmerwhite
   Hall [nt]   Galad Elflandsson
Inn of the Dutchman   Steve Eng
A Little Walk in Corduene   Steve Sneyd
St.George and the Bed Albert J. Manachino

                 ***

COVEN 13

A weird fantasy digest magazine published bi-monthly by Camelot Publishing Co., 2412 West 7th St., Los Angeles, California. Editor: Arthur H. Landis. From the fifth issue the magazine was purchased by William Crawford and was retitled Witchcraft & Sorcery. *Although it continued the issue numeration, the format and content are sufficiently varied for it to be regarded as a different magazine, and it is thus accorded a separate entry in this Index.*

September 1969	1/1	William Stout
Odile [na]		Alan Caillou
Potlatch		Joseph Harris
In Markham Town!		Jack G. Levine
The Postman Always ...		Richard P. Flanagan
Of Brides and Brimstone		Lenore Betker
I'll Come to You by Moonlight!		
		Jean W. Cirrito
The Visitor [v]		Walden Muns
A Spell of Desperation		G. Kissinger
Let There Be Magick [n1/4]		
		James R. Keaveny

November 1969	1/2	William Stout
Once Upon a Werewolf		Robert L. Davis
A Message For Brother		John Lipford
Double Hex		Samuel M. Clawson
About Witches and Such [a]		Jean Cirrito
The Transmogrification of		
Ridgely P. Winters		Joseph Harris
The Shadow Trader		Wylly Folk St. John
Moorfire Foxfire [v]		Walden Muns
Rock God		Harlan Ellison
Let There Be Magick! [n2/4]		
		James R. Keaveny
Pia		Dale C. Donaldson

January 1970	1/3	William Stout
Leona! [nt]		Alan Caillou
Song of the Undead [v]		Wade Wellman
Nightmare [v]		Wade Wellman
Bell, Book and Tarot: The		
Evil Eye [a]		Jean Cirrito
The Strawhouse Pavillion		Ron Goulart
The Little People		Robert E. Howard
The Turn of the Screw [a]		Arthur Jean Cox
Witch Fish		Dennis Quinn
Last Rites		Pauline Smith
Don't Open 'til X-Mas		James Benton Carr
Let There Be Magick! [n3/4]		
		James R. Keaveny

March 1970	1/4	William Stout
The Bidderfrost Dragon		Buddy Saunders
I, Vampire! '		Bill Pronzini &
		Jeffrey Wallman
Bell, Book and Tarot: About		
Poltergeists [a]		Jean Cirrito
The Convert		S. M. Clawson
Feach Air Muir Lionadhi Gealach		
Buidhe Mar Or [v]		Robert E. Howard
The Thing on the Stairs		Lee Chater
Eats		Sidney Harriet
Let There Be Magick! [n4/4]		
		James R. Keaveny

Continued as *Witchcraft & Sorcery*

***

CTHULHU

Tales of the Cthulhu Mythos

*A small press weird fiction magazine published by Spectre Press, 18 Cefn Road,
Mynachdy, Cardiff. Publisher/Editor: Jon M. Harvey. Although published in chapbook format* Cthulhu *was arguably an anthology series (it bore an ISBN reference,
0 905416 00 7 for the first issue, instead of an ISSN code) but as a hybrid
publication is included for completeness. See also* Dreams of a Dark Hue.

[1976]	No.1	Jim Pitts
Harold's Blues		Glen Singer
Baptism of Fire		Andrew Darlington
1977	No.2	Jim Pitts
The Guardians of the Gates [nt]		
		Brian Mooney
1978	No.3	Jim Pitts
*Demoniacal		David Sutton
The Kiss of Bugg-Shash		Brian Lumley

***

D

DARK FANTASY

A Canadian small press weird fantasy magazine published in octavo format by Shadow Press, Gananoque, Ontario. Publisher/Editor: Howard E. Day. Regarded by many as the leading Canadian 'fanzine', Dark Fantasy was responsible for introducing the work of many writers later to establish themselves such as Charles R. Saunders and Galad Elflandsson. The original issues 12 and 13 were lost by the printer. A revised issue 12 appeared two years later (hence the jump in sequence) but issue 13 was never published.

Summer 1973 1/1 (1) Gene Day	
One Million Einsteins Howard E. Day	
Payment [v] Gale A. Jack	
The Island [ss] A. A. Crawford	
White Room Augustine Funnell	
Beyond the Gates of Amber [v] Gale A. Jack	
The Immortal Howard E. Day	
Tomorrow is Such a Long Time Gale A. Jack	
Sundown Augustine Funnell	
"How Much Do You Love Me,	
John Barthalamew?" Howard E. Day	
A Poem of Terror [v] Howard E. Day	
Fall 1973 1/2 (2) Gene Day	
A Cut Above Augustine Funnell	
The Cripples of the Earth [v]	
Howard E. Day	
Shooting Star Richard H. DeWolfe	
An Angel [v] Gale A. Jack	
Andrea Augustine Funnell	
The Hall of Rune Howard E. Day	
United [v] Gale A. Jack	
March 1974 1/3 (3) Gene Day	
The Gamble James W. Smith	
Oh My God! They Come Again [v]	
W. B. McMaster	
Riders in the Storm Howard E. Day	
Presence of Mind [v] David T. Krippner	
July 1974 1/4 (4) Gene Day	
There Used to be a Time [v] Gale A. Jack	
M'Ji Ya Wazimu (City of	
Madness) [nt1/2] Charles R. Saunders	
Marangue Tribunal [v] M. David Rich	
The Painter Richard DeWolfe	
An Obstacle Grotesque [v] Gale A. Jack	

October 1974 2/5 (5) Gene Day	
Godseye [v] Howard E. Day	
M'Ji Ya Wazimu (City of	
Madness) [nt2/2] Charles R. Saunders	
Glories Lost and Won Joseph P. D. Sullivan	
Blackwood [v] Gale A. Jack	
January 1975 2/6 (6) Gene Day	
Zothique [v] Walter Shedlofsky	
Two-Edged Fate Wayne Hooks	
Last of the Caravans [v] Gale A. Jack	
Corsairs James W. Smith	
The Black Gauntlet George Duck	
Words, Dreams and a Blade	
Joseph P. D. Sullivan	
September 1975 2/7 (7) Gene Day	
The Dream [v] Gale A. Jack	
The Princess' Prime Possession	
Al D. Cockrell	
The Waters of Meron James Lankashire	
Kibanda Ya Kufa (The Hut of	
Death) Charles R. Saunders	
The Flames of Hell [v] W. B. McMaster	
May 1976 2/8 (8) Tim Hammell	
Synthetic Realm [v] Gale A. Jack	
An Evening in the Wood William Bitner	
Grass David Madison	
The Ghost Sword [v] Walter Shedlofsky	
Scriptures Neal Wilgus	
Bwala Li Mwesu (The Moon	
Pool) Charles R. Saunders	
September 1976 3/9 (9) Steve Fabian	
A Pillow of Wind [v] Gale A. Jack	
Shadows Wayne Hooks	

[Editor Howard (Gene) Day died in October 1982 of a heart attack, at the age of 31]

***

DARK HORIZONS

A small press fantasy magazine, official journal of the British Fantasy Society (Current Secretary, David A. Sutton, 194 Station Rd., Kings Heath, Birmingham). Editors: Rosemary Pardoe, Nos. 1-4; Trevor Hughes, No.5; Adrian Cole, No.6; Adrian Cole & David A. Sutton, No.7; Darroll Pardoe, No.8; Steve Jones, Nos.9-15; Geoffrey N. Smith, Nos.16 & 17; John Heron, No.18; Mike Chinn & John Merritt, Nos. 19-22; David A. Sutton, Nos. 23-current.

[Autumn] 1971   1/1
Treasure Hunting [a]   Brian Talbot
The Unicorn of Fame [v]   Brian Mooney
     David Weldrake
The Golden Age of the
   British Horror Fanzines
   [a1/2]   David A. Sutton
What is Fantasy? [a]   Keith Walker
Conan, Champion of Champions
   [a]   A. R. Fallone
Don't Knock Alan Garner [a]
     Rosemary Pardoe

[Spring] 1972   1/2   David A. Riley
The Lovecraftian Works of
   Colin Wilson [a]   Eddy C. Bertin
The Golden Age of the British
   Horror Fanzines [a2/2]   David A. Sutton
Rain [v]   David A. Riley
Not Your Philosophy, Horatio!
   [nt1/4]   Roberta Gray

[Summer] 1972   1/3   David A. Riley
Kenneth Grant: A New Viewpoint
   of H. P. Lovecraft [a]   Brian Mooney
For Whom the Ghouls Troll   Brian Mooney
On C. S. Lewis [a]   Alan Parkes
Not Your Philosophy, Horatio!
   [nt2/4]   Roberta Gray
Wanderings in the Weird [col] John Godrich
Olympiad of Ghosts [v]   David A. Riley

[Autumn] 1972   1/4   Mike Higgs
Fantasy and a Place for
   Contemporary Music [a]   Adrian Cole
The Magical Fire [v]   Allan W. Parkes
Wanderings in the Weird [col] John Godrich
A Checklist of the Works of
   'Monk' Lewis [bib]   Rosemary Pardoe

Not Your Philosophy, Horatio!
   [nt3/4]   Roberta Gray
Something in Wood [a]   Brian Mooney

[Spring] 1973   2/5   A. R. Fallone
As Silver Dusk Suffuses Red
   [v]   David A. Riley
Waiting in the Dark [v]   Eddy C. Bertin
The Crime of the Ancient
   Mariner [v]   Allan W. Parkes
Then and Now [a]   Allan W. Parkes
Thoughts in a Solitary
   Churchyard [v]   David A. Riley
The Powers of Darkness [v] Allan W. Parkes
Not Your Philosophy, Horatio!
   [nt4/4]   Roberta Gray
That Greater Death [v]   David A. Riley

[Summer] 1973   3/6   Adrian Cole
The Missile   John Hurley
L'Inferno   Allan W. Parkes
In Fantasy [v]   R. D. Ford
Antarctica [v]   Thelma Collins
Worship Me [v]   John Hurley
Wired Tales [spf]   Adrian Cole
The Lay of the Last Zydrin   Gordon Larkin
In Piece [v]   David A. Riley

December 1973   No.7   Jim Pitts
Derleth As I Knew Him [a1/2]
     Ramsey Campbell
The Spell of Lankya   Glen Symonds
Do Not Disturb   David Lloyd

April 1974   No.8   *Dietterlin
Derleth as I Knew Him [a2/2] Ramsey Campbell
The Cosmic in Fiction [a]   Dave Sutton
Belendon's Chair   Gordon Larkin

***

THE DIVERSIFIER

(including PARAGON)

A fantasy/sf small press magazine published and edited monthly (bi-monthly from issue 6) by the brothers A.B. and C.C. Clingan, Leah Court, Oroville, California (under the imprint Castle Press from issue 4). The first five issues were mimeographed, changing to offset-litho from issue 6. The first seven issues were in quarto format, the remainder octavo. C.C. Clingan continued as sole editor from issue 23, but from issue 25 he was joined by Ralph Stephen Harding, Joey Froehlich, Jon Inouye and Robert Medcalf. Thereafter Harding and Froehlich remained as editors with Clingan departing after issue 26/27. After issue 28/29 the magazine was revived under the name Paragon *with C.C. Clingan as sole editor.*

[June] 1974   1/1 (1)   Verna Dixon
The Monument   V.L. Dixon
Past Times [a]   Charles E. Miller
The White Stone   Marge V. Garrett
An Incredibly Stupid Poem
    [v]   Amos Salmonson
Sky Castle of Quandar [s1/3] C.C. Clingan
Eternal Time [v]   A.B. Clingan
Resting Place [v]   A.B. Clingan
Unanswered [v]   A.B. Clingan
In The Beginning [v]   A.B. Clingan

July 1974   1/2 (2) Sheryl Birkhead
Someday We May Look Back on
    This and Shudder   Irvin L. Wagner
First 4th [v]   A.B. Clingan
All That Glitters in California
    is not Gold [a]   C.C. Clingan
Sky Castle of Quandar [s2/3] C.C. Clingan
Images [v]   Karen Burgett
Slumber's Lost Ship [v] George Diezel II
Slowly, Slowly, Wheels the
    Midnight Star [v]   Verna Lee Dixon
Frankenstein: The True Story
    [a]   Roger D. Sween
The Watcher   Gerard Houarner

August 1974   1/3 (3)   Kurt Erichsen
Lost [v]   George Diezel II
It Was a Hell of a Spell, HPL
    [a]   Stanislaus Clutchpin
Sky Castle of Quandar [s3/3] C.C. Clingan
Captive [v]   Chet Hendrix

Profound/Profundity [col] Amos Salmonson
Solitude [v]   Dan Cohenour
The Decision   Karen Burgett
The Sadhu   Joseph A. West

September 1974   1/4 (4)   Gary Winnick
The Lord's Flower Box   Chet Hendrix
Wandering [v]   Debra Susan Elder
Curse of the Black One   Lew M. Cabos
Whiffling Turgidly [spf]
                          Stanislaus Clutchpin
Death Without a Funeral [v] Bill Breiding
The Vault of the Spider   Ed Newby
Cyclic Entropy [v]   Dan Cohenour
Profuse Redundancy [col] Amos Salmonson
Farewell [v]   Sutton Breiding

October 1974   1/5 (5)   Don Herron
Barbarian King [v]   Tim C. Marion
Lawbooks of Necrophilia [a]
                              Sutton Breiding
Nothing Gained But Friendship
                             Michael J. Bell
Dark Pursuer [v]   George Dietzel II
Closet Friend   Wayne C. Hooks
Re-Enter the Dragon [a]   Don Herron
The Dreadful City [v] Richard L. Tierney
Profuse Redundancy [col] Amos Salmonson

December 1974   1/6 (6)   Joseph A. West
We Have Lift Off   Steve Sneyd
Fat Chance [a]   Donn Brazier
Gems For the Hunter   Deems Ortega

44

*Sorry, Wrong Dimension
  [play]   Ross Rocklynne
*Bitter Sweet   E. C. Tubb
Shapechangers and Fearmongers
  [a]   James Gunn
The Family D'Alembert [a]   Ron Fortier

May/July 1978   (4/5-6) 26-27 Cliff Bird
Recipe For Survival [v]   Ruth Lechlitner
Landscape With Ghouls   Jeffrey Goddin
A Druid Prayer Translated [v]
                             Denise Dumars
Savages and Scriveners [a]
                       L. Sprague de Camp
Leaving Earth [v]   Mike Manis
Small is Beautiful   Jim Morgan
Willie [v]   Stephanie Stearns
Robert Bloch [in]   Jeffrey Elliot
Lovesong to a Woodnymph [v]
                           Sutton Breiding
Won'ter   Keith Figley
Wendayne Ackerman [in] Frederick J. Mayer
Dark Host   Ken Huff
A Frog In Search of a Princess
                         G. Arthur Rahman
Lion Wizardry [v]   Joey Froehlich
The Other Gothic [a]   M. E. Tyrrell
St. Louis Tickle   Grant Carrington
Poxy   Robert Bolin
The Saga of Special Effects [a]
                           Craig Anderson
Magic [v]   Don Herron
Tiger By the Tail   Irene Eugenia
My Favorite Things   B. F. Watkinson
Academy's Film Seerer [a]
                        Frederick J. Mayer
Devil Cat [v]   Frederick J. Mayer
Shadow Shapes   Paul McQuire III
Conflict [s2/2]   Gary Muschla
And the Dead [v]   Denise Dumars

Feb/March 1979   (5/1-2) 28-29   Al Sirois
The Hungry Apples   Richard Lyon &
                            Andrew Offutt
C. L. Moore: Poet of Far Distant
  Futures [in]   Jeffrey Elliot
The Vampires [v]   Mark McLaughlin
The Solution   Sydney J. Bounds
Invitation to a Shy Satyr [v]
                         Sutton Breiding
The Different Man: Dickson's
  Donal Graeme [a]   Clifford McMurray
The Song the Brahmin Sings   Janet Fox
Grotesque [v]   Mark McLaughlin
Amateur Night   Gordon Linzner
A New Age   Paul Collins
The October Pumpkins   Michael Capobianco

+ magazine suspended +

relaunched as

PARAGON

May 1980   1/1   Craig Anderson
The Red Shift   William Scott Home
Poet of the Unconscious [a]   Dirk Mosig
Interlude at the Bridge Franklyn Searight
Hyborian Africa [a]   Charles Saunders
An Interview With John Varley
  [in]   Darrell Schweitzer
The Clark Ashton Smith Boom?
  [a]   Robert Weinberg

*   *   *

DOCTOR DEATH

A weird menace character pulp published monthly by Dell Publications, New York.
Editor: Carson W. Mowre.

February 1935	1/1	?
Twelve Must Die [n]		Zorro
The Beast That Talked		Damascus Blount
The Black Orchids		A. J. Burks
The Skeleton Scream		O'Casey Holt

March 1935	1/2	?
The Gray Creatures [n]		Zorro
The Man Who Didn't Exist		A. J. Burks
"I Am Dead!"		Harold Ward

April 1935	1/3	Rudolph Zirn
The Shriveling Murders [n]		Zorro
Web of Terror		Michael Crowley
Vampire Meat		Fred C. Painton
Five Minutes of Life		John Carpenter

***

48

DRAGONFIELDS

A small press magazine published irregularly in large digest format by Charles de Lint's Triskell Press, Ottawa, Ontario, Canada. Editors: Charles de Lint & Charles R. Saunders. It was originally two separate magazines: Dragonbane, *edited by Saunders, and* Beyond the Fields We Know, *edited by de Lint each of which saw a single issue before they were merged as issue No.3.* Dragonbane *had been published in Demy-Quarto size.*

DRAGONBANE

Spring 1978	No.1	John Charette
Sleeping Tiger		Tanith Lee
Arthur Machen [v]		Michael Danagher
From Under the Hills		David Madison
Wings Over Antar		Charles de Lint
Lord Dragon's Bane [v]		Wendelessen
How Darkness Came to Carcosa		
		Galad Elflandsson
The Moons of Glass [v]		Gene Phillips
Continuing the Characters of		
Robert E. Howard [col]		David C. Smith
The Poetry of Clark Ashton		
Smith [a]		Michael E. Ambrose
Clark Ashton Smith [v]		Michael Danagher
Turkhana Knives		Charles R. Saunders

BEYOND THE FIELDS WE KNOW

Autumn 1978	No.1	Danielle Dupont
"Far From the Rush..." [v]		Wendelessen
A Tapestry of Dreams		Galad Elflandsson
Po Bos yn Weir [v]		Jan Penalurick
*Riddle [v]		Robin Williamson
The Last Elf		Angus C. Wilson
Night Song [v]		Billy Wolfenbarger
A Problem of Adjustment		
		Thomas Burnett Swann
Honey-Pale [v]		Henri Cuiscard
Amma		Charles R. Saunders
The Bear [v]		Diana L. Paxson
"Spring, the Young Warrior" [v]		Joy Chant
Visionary Poet of the Past:		
William Morris [a]		Michael E. Ambrose
The Grail [v]		Thomas M. Egan
Mad Michael		Ron Nance
Glamour-Guiled [v]		Wendelessen
Spinning Song [v]		Marion Zimmer Bradley

An Interview with Terry

Brooks [in]		Charles de Lint
Winter Night [v]		Joseph Payne Brennan
The Black Crusader [v]		
		Jessica Amanda Salmonson
Curuthann's Barr		J. E. Coplin
Beyond the Wall of Clouds		
[v]		Galad Elflandsson
Twilight Tracings [v]		Wendelessen
The Veiled Pool of Mistorak		
		Darrell Schweitzer
The Kraken [v]		Diana L. Paxson
Dunsany: The Man and the		
Influence [a]		Loay H. Hall
Lord Dunsany [v]		Michael Danagher
A Kingly Thing		Charles de Lint
"Old the Hills of Kernow"		
[v]		Jan Penalurick

DRAGONFIELDS

Summer 1980	No.3	Donna Gordon
In Remembrance of David		
Madison [obit]		Charles R. Saunders
The City of Silence		David Madison
*Invocation [v]		Robin Williamson
Cyrion in Wax		Tanith Lee
The Desolation of Yr		
(Marcus's Song) [v]		David Madison
Keeper of the Wood		Caradoc A. Cador
Troll Woman [ss]		Georgie Schnobrich
The Fisher King [a]		Thomas M. Egan
Puck's Invitation [v]		Sharrie n'ha Verana
White are the Horns of		
the Horses [v]		Joy Chant
Reflections of Terrance		
Whitley		Adrian Chadwick
The Sands of the Desert [v]		
		Robert E. Howard

The Heroes in Heroic Fantasy
  [a]   Michael Moorcock
Sandy Denny [v]   Gregg Jones Muller
Devil on my Stomache   Richard K. Lyon &
                         Andrew J. Offutt
Scarlet Night [v]   Dwight E. Humphries
Enemy, Enemy [v]   Stephanie Stearns
The Game of Burke and
  Hare   Albert J. Manachino
William Hope Hodgson [v] Michael Danagher
Ship of the Hundred Flames
  [v]   Joey Froehlich
Withered Trickster [v]   Wendelessen
The Way of Wizards   Galad Elflandsson
Desiring Dragons [v]   Diana L. Paxson
Continuing the Characters of
  Robert E. Howard [col]
  - Bran Man Morn   Don Herron
  - Wasn't Bran Mak Morn a
    Cereal?   Karl Edward Wagner
King Kull in Valusia [v] Thomas M. Egan
Along the Borders [v]   Wendelessen
The Windspell   Diana L. Paxson

Winter 1983   No.4   Donna Gordon
Meet on the Road   Georgie Schnobrich
A Celebration of Tanith Lee:
The Wooing of the Blue Rose   J. E. Coplin
An Empress of Dreams [a]
                         Galad Elflandsson
The Interview [in]   Charles de Lint
The Fiction of Tanith Lee:
  1971-1983 [bib]   Charles R. Saunders
Memorial Stone: 1945 [v]   Tanith Lee
Blue Vase of Ghosts   Tanith Lee
Duel [v]   John Bell
Masquerade   Albert J. Manachino
The Five Horns of Artaius [v]
                              Linda Kellar
Ichiyusai's Curse   Gordon Linzner
*Illuminations [v]   John Bell
Darkdreamer [v]   Helen Stegall
Incarnation [v]   Steve Eng
Merlin's Song [v]   Karen Willson
Refuge [v]   Billy Wolfenbarger
*Coils [v]   John Bell
Nemesis [v]   Cathy Young Czapla
Cymru, Ambyth [v]   Gregg Jones Muller
Shadows of Doom [v]   Joey Froehlich
Haiku [v]   Tanuki Aki
We Walked These Hills But
  Never Knew [v]   Carol Ann Cupitt
Stolen Laughter   Sharon Lee
Changeling [v]   David F. Nalle
Grittel   Ardath Mayhar
The Rolling of the Stones [v]
                             Wendelessen
Stonehill   Georgie Schnobrich
At the Edge of the Wood [ss]
                           Jeffrey Goddin

* * *

DREAM WORLD

A 'dream-fantasy' digest published quarterly by Ziff-Davis Publishing Co., 366 Madison Ave., New York. Editor: Paul W. Fairman.

February 1957   1/1   Edward Valigursky
Legs on Olympus   Adam Chase
*Ways To Get a Gal   P. G. Wodehouse
The Devil Never Waits   Randall Garrett
*Sex, Love and Mr Owen   Thorne Smith
Time Out   Darius John Granger
The Man With X-Ray Eyes [nt]
                          Leonard G. Spencer
A Bucketful of Diamonds   Harlan Ellison
Oswald's Willing Women   Bill Majeski
Windfalls [col]   Paul Steiner
A Strange Lady Called Luck [a]
                          Villiers Gerson

May 1957   1/2   John Parker
The Man Who Made His Dreams
   Come True [nt]   C. H. Thames
You Too Can Win a Harem   Randall Garrett
So You Want to be President   Adam Chase

I'm Listening to Your Thoughts
                             Walt Sheldon
He Fired His Boss   Darius John Granger
To Walk Through Walls   James Cooper
Success Story - Complete With
   Genie   Ivar Jorgensen
Boy Meets Dream Girl [col]   Paul Steiner

August 1957   1/3   Edward Valigursky
His Touch Turned Stone to Flesh
   [nt]   Adam Chase
Mr Milford's Magic Camera   Forrest Norton
The Big Trance   Harlan Ellison
The Man Who Couldn't Lose
   [nt]   G. L. Vandenburg
Anything His Heart Desires
                          Robert Silverberg

***

DREAMS OF A DARK HUE

A British small press magazine published in chapbook format by Spectre Press, 18 Cefn Road, Mynachdy, Cardiff, Wales. Publisher/Editor: Jon M. Harvey.

December 1978	[1]	David Lloyd
A Halloween Story		Gregory FitzGerald
Toppling [v]		Ronnie M. Lane
Gertrude [nt]		Alex Kernaghan
Dreamt ... [v]		Leon Spiro
Pursuit		David Lloyd
The Sea is My Bed		Eddy C. Bertin
Things That Go Bump in the Night [v]		Ronnie M. Lane
All in the Appearance [v]		Gregory FitzGerald
The Bad Dreamer [ss]		Antonin Artaud

***

E

EERIE COUNTRY

A weird fantasy small press magazine published irregularly by Weirdbook Press, Amherst Branch, Buffalo, New York. Editor: W. Paul Ganley. Companion to Weirdbook. Offset printed in quarto format. A current publication.

July 1976 No.1 Daniel Loge
The Preacher Richard Addison Stewart
Ye Gods and Little Fishes Walter Quednau
Embroidered Curse Eleanor Roth
Future, Inc. J. Yeskovich
Sheena O'Meara W. Fraser Sandercombe
The Smell of Witchcraft Joshua Mostow
The Lark William S. Doxey
Roots Valerie Wood
The Gathering Jerry C. Brigham
The Pictures Barbara Denbrook
A Piece of the Action P. Scott Hollander
Only Toys Janet Fox
Reflections [v] Darrell Schweitzer
Century's End [v] Joseph Payne Brennan
Prophecy [v] A. Arthur Griffin
Untitled Verse [v] A. E. Darmstadt
He Is Satisfied [v] W. Fraser Sandercombe
Haunted Glen [v] William Scott Home
Nightly [v] Alixandra Lee
Prayer of Kadru-Sekoth [v] Gene Phillips
The Scorched Streets [v] Kristi Kamerer
The Practical Joker [v] Betty M. Lee
A Prophecy [v] David Reissig
Whistler [v] Brian Lumley
Walking in New Haven [v]
  Joseph Payne Brennan

[January] 1979 No.2 Todd Klein
Plike Ruth M. Walsh
Revenge [v] Andrew Duane
Weird of the Bald Branley Allan Branson
Breath of Ages Ray Jones
The Light at Curry's Point Ernest Johnson
Mammoths [v] Paul Garson
Mother Love E. S. Burroughs
Invocation [v] Bernadette Lynn Bosky
A Fork in the Road Raymond Kaminski
We Remember, Vincent [v]
  Joseph Payne Brennan
Return [v] Steve Eng

House of the Nightquesters [v]
  Steve Troyanovich
Cold Touch [v] William Scott Home
At The Sea [v] Joey Froehlich

[July] 1980 No.3 Frank Hamilton
The Cross and the Grave
  W. Fraser Sandercombe
Edward Phillip C. Heath
The Path of Gods [v] A. Arthur Griffin
The Cross-Town Void Maker Robert Ritter
From the Crypts By Our Side [v]
  Patrick Alther
The Winged Llama of the Mesa
 [ss] Jessica Amanda Salmonson
Urlea [v] Steve Troyanovich
The Quilt John Taylor
Night of Owls [v] Joseph Payne Brennan
Nameless Things [v] Joseph Payne Brennan
Everyman's Epitaph [v]
  Joseph Payne Brennan
Nemesis Gerald Barnes
The Walls Ray Jones
Ghosts / Garden Guests [2v] Steve Eng
Thou Shalt Not Suffer John Wysocki
The Visitor From Beyond Dave Reissig

[December] 1980 No.4 Thomas F. Kuras
The Phantasist [v] Michael R. Little
Deep Calls to Deep John Taylor
Custodian of the Latter
 Warlocks' Tears [v] William Scott Home
Better Oblivion's Leaf [v]
  Joseph Payne Brennan
The Soft [v] Jean Marie Ward
Strange Morning [v] B. R. Strahan
Candles in Kaldesh Gene Phillips
The Cohorts of the Damned John Wysocki
When Wakes a God Clifford Blair
Invocation [v] William A. Conder
Elise Beckoning Patrice Schroeder

***

EERIE MYSTERIES

*A weird menace pulp published bi-monthly by Ace Magazines, 67 West 44th St.,
New York. Editor: Harry Widmer. Some of the stories were reprints from other
Ace Magazines, retitled and with new pseudonymous by-lines. These stories have
not been identified.*

August 1938   1/1   Norman Saunders
City of Stone Corpses   Ralph Powers
Tomb Treachery   Ronald Flagg
Brotherhood of the Damned   Harris Clivesey
Immortal Murder   Cliff Howe
Scourge of the Death Master
                         Charles Q. Evans
Satan's Trio   Robert A. Gustin
The Garden of Fate   Eric Lennox
Curse of a Thousand Cats   Leon Dupont
Thirsty Steel   Rexton Archer
Midnight's Sinister Snare   Dennis Storm

November 1938   1/2   Norman Saunders
When It Rained Corpses   Ralph Powers
Satan's Ante-Chamber   Vance Leighton
The Carnivorous Bubble   Lorne Balsley
Executioner's Playday   Clint Douglas
The Three From Nowhere   Rexton Archer
Song of the Spectre   Ronald Flagg
Homicide House   Cliff Howe
The Robot's Revenge   Dennis Storm
Modelled in Death   Norman Daniels
Skull and Double-Cross Bones   Eric Lennox

February 1939   1/3   Norman Saunders
Horror's Handshake   Ralph Powers
Mr Justice Sits In   Arden Anthony
Abyss of the Wailing Dead Stephen McBarron
Time Takes a Holiday   Frank Airth
Street of Ghouls   John Clemmons
Unwilling Corpse   Edgar Allan Martin
The Hounds of Purgatory   Eric Thane
The Cobra Strikes   Cliff Howe
Realm of Liquid Death   Chester Brand
Fangs of the Soul   Robert C. Blackmon

April/May 1939   1/4   Norman Saunders
The Corpse Symphony   Lorne Balsley
Tomb of Torment   Arden Anthony
Spider's Realm   Stephen McBarron
Havoc For Sale   Frank Airth
Call of the Claw   Laurence D. Smith
The Fear Fetish   Eric Lennox
Time For Death   Ralph Powers
Song of the Damned   John Clemmons
Wedding Hells   David Bernard
Invitation to Murder   Cliff Howe

***

EERIE STORIES

A weird menace pulp, planned as a bi-monthly, published by Ace Magazines, 67 West 44th St., New York. Editor: Harry Widmer. Companion to Ace Mystery and Eerie Mysteries.

<u>August 1937</u>   1/1   Norman Saunders

Virgins of the Stone Death	
	Gates Alexander
The Soul-Scorcher's Lair	Ronald Flagg
The Corpse-Girl's Return	Eric Lennox
Devil's Brew	Branton Black
Her Island of Horror	Cliff Howe
The Pain Master's Bride	Rexton Archer
Sinister Skein	Horace Stoner
Rehearsal With Doom	Terrance Flint
Lust For Blood	Clifford Gray
*Mate of the Beast	Leon Dupont
Terror's Tomb	John Gregory
Step-Daughter to Greed	Peter Reginald

***

EERIE TALES

A Canadian weird fantasy pulp published by CK Publishing, 84 Adelaide Street West, Toronto, Ontario. No editor credited but possibly Melvin Colby.

July 1941	1/1	John K. Hilkert
The Hound		Thomas P. Kelley
A Dictator Dies		Leslie A. Croutch
Tales of the Long Ago [a]		
		Ethel G. Preszcator
The Phantom Trooper		Scott Malcolm
Horror in the Dungeon		George Grant
The Man Who Killed Mussolini		
		Valentine Worth
The Weird Queen [n1/?]		Thomas P. Kelley

***

ELDRITCH TALES

A small press weird fantasy digest published by Yith Press, 1051 Wellington Rd., Lawrence, Kansas. Editor/Publisher: Crispin Burnham. Originally entitled The Dark Messenger Reader *(published by The Strange Company, Madison, Wisconsin and co-edited with E. P. Berglund) it was an extension of Burnham's earlier fanzine* The Dark Messenger. *Issue 2 was lost by the printer and was only eventually published four years later (hence the loss of sequence below). Bannered as 'A Magazine in the Weird Tales tradition'* Eldritch Tales *is heavily influenced by the works of H. P. Lovecraft.*

entitled THE DARK MESSENGER READER

[Winter] 1975   No.1   -

Images in Stone	Crispin Burnham
Sonnet to a Boxelder Bug	
[v]	Richard L. Tierney
Beneath the Sleeping City	
	Llewellyn M. Cabos
Second Time in Twenty Years	Ross Marchmont
Descent Into Madness	J. J. Koblas
Mad Eyes in Darkness	C. H. Mallory
The Innsmouth Head	Franklyn Searight
Wings in the Night	Edward P. Berglund
Aphrodite's Gift	Tad Crawford
Demon Day	Ted Pons
The Still Ones	F. C. Adams
Promise of the Black Goat	Edward M. Kane

retitled ELDRITCH TALES

[Winter 1976]   [No.2]

unpublished, but see after issue 7.

March 1978   1/3 (3)   Michael Martin

Sword of the Seven Suns	E. P. Berglund
Dreams of the Dreamer [n1/4]	
	Joeseph Hammond
The Creatures	Richard L. Tierney
Dreams of Darkness [v]	Jim Pianfetti
Where the Old Ones Dwell [v]	Randy Medoff
...And the Sleepers Woke	A. Aspromatis
The Sun Doth Set [v]	Ken Schrauzer
And the Earth Brought Forth	
	William Scott Home
The City of Hastur [v]	Tom Egan
Love Unveiled [v]	William A. Conder

*The Minneiska Incident

                    Philip & G. Arthur Rahman

October 1978   1/4 (4)   John Tibbetts

The Black Chaos	Kenneth Huff
Dreams of the Dreamer [n2/4]	
	Joeseph Hammond
The Awakening	Edward M. Kane
Ghoul-Rider [v]	Steve Eng
Beneath College Hill	
	Gerard E. Giannattasio
The Sorcerer's Pipe	Franklyn Searight
Incident in Newark	Phyllis Rose
The Shadow Vampire	Leon Gammell
The Color From Beyond	Llewellyn M. Cabos
A Few Words With a Friend	
[v]	Jim Pianfetti
*The Dead Are Not Grateful	Randall Larson
Father of Darkness	Bill R. Wolfenbarger
Haven	Ted Pons

April 1979   1/5 (5)   John Tibbetts

Be Prepared!	Fred Croft
Gunfight Against Nyarlathotep	
· [nt1/2]	Randall Larson
Joie de Morte [v]	Frederick J. Mayer
Recurrent Dream [v]	Steve Eng
The Well at the Half-Cat	John Tibbetts
Quest [v]	Jim Pianfetti
Dreams of the Dreamer [n3/4]	
	Joeseph Hammond
Midnight Dance [v]	Don R. Broyles
The Thing in the Abyss	Llewellyn M. Cabos
A Novice Conductor	Douglas Roome
Arkham By Moonlight [v]	Janet Fox
Creatures in the Fog [v]	Joey Froehlich

***

ESCAPE!

A small press fantasy magazine, printed in quarto format, and published by Crystal Visions Press, 809 Cleermont Drive, Huntsville, Alabama. Publisher and Editor: Charles W. Melvin.

Fall 1977   No.1   Clyde Caldwell
Escape! [v]   Brian Lumley
Cryptically Yours...   Brian Lumley
The Labyrinth of Braneth-
   Dulzuum   Michael Fantina
The Vampire [v]   Edith Ogutsch
The Rambunctious Bok [a] Edith Ogutsch
Psychodyssey [v]   Hannes Bok
The Other One   Karl Edward Wagner
The Corrie of the Howlings [v]
                          J. E. Coplin
My Lady of the Darkwood
                     Darrell Schweitzer
Within [v]   Joseph Payne Brennan
Heat [v]   Joseph Payne Brennan
To the Philaticus Eroticus Upon
   Being Eaten By the Baddosaurus
   [v]   Hannes Bok
The Frightened Waltz   Walter Shedlofsky
The Maiden of Ice and Steel   J. E. Coplin
The Blacksmith and the Bambuti
                      Charles Saunders
The Landlords [v]   Marc Laidlaw
Darius   L. Sprague de Camp
Lethal Lure [v]   Edith Ogutsch
Crystal Visions [a]   John Reiber
Something Like the Hobo Bird
                     Darrell Schweitzer
Thoth-Amon [v]   John Reiber
Another Time, Another Place [v]
                       Stephanie Stearns

***

61

ETCHINGS AND ODYSSEYS

A small press spiral-bound magazine, subtitled 'A Tribute to the Weird' and published by MinnCon Publications, Duluth, Minnesota. Editors: Eric Carlson and John Koblas. Finances precluded further issues until ten years later when assisted by R. Alain Everts who served as publisher and co-editor the magazine was revived on a quarterly basis, published by The Strange Company, Madison, Wisconsin in a more conventional quasi-slick format. Issue 1 was limited to an edition of 250 copies, issues 2 and 3 of 500 copies.

[Spring] 1973   No.1   Herb Arnold
First Love   Joseph Payne Brennan
White Witch [v]   John Bredon
Hate [v]   Richard L. Tierney
The Mound of Yig? [a]   W. E. Baardson
Kiss an Angel Good Morning   Robert Borski
Where Are Yesterday's Castles?
     [v]   Eddy C. Bertin
A Song For the Living, A Song
     For the Dead [v]   Eddy C. Bertin
The Left Behind   John Jacob
Letters of Reminiscence
     [ltrs]   E. Hoffmann Price
Ice Dwarf [v]   John Bredon
Places to Avoid! [col]   [The Editors]
What Lurks Among the Dunes
                           Walter C. DeBill, Jr
*Rune [v]   Robert E. Howard
Guess Whut's Coming to Dinner
     [spf play]   J. J. Koblas
Lunar Liturgy [v]   Alan Gullette
Carl Jacobi [in]   Eric Carlson,
               John Koblas & Joseph A. West
Death [v]   Joseph Payne Brennan
*Homecoming   E. P. Berglund
When the Stars are Right [a]
                           Richard L. Tierney
For Fear [v]   Alan D. Gullette
Brandon's Pipe   Joseph A. West
Filming "The Outsider" [a]
                           Darrell Schweitzer
The Lost Man [v]   Kenneth W. Faig, Jr
The Last Song   John Bredon
*Voices of the Night [2v] Robert E. Howard
  [The Voices Waken Memory; Babel]
And the Darkness Never
     Answers [v]   Eddy C. Bertin
A Man of Discretion   Richard L. Tierney

Dumb-Show [v]   John Bredon
Robert E. Howard: The Other
     Heroes [a]   Ted Pons
*Badland Ballad [v]   John Bredon
The Scrolls [v]   Richard L. Tierney
Casonetto's Last Song   Robert E. Howard
*Reborn [v]   John Bredon
Catherine Duval: Modern Master
     of Gothic Horror [a]   Eddy C. Bertin
Poem to Polymnia [v]   Alan Gullette
Jack the Ripper [v]   Richard L. Tierney
Moubata [v]   Richard L. Tierney
*Extermination   Joseph Payne Brennan
Canons I / Canons II [2v]   John Jacob

[May] 1983   No.2 *Margaret Brundage
The Syndicate of the Snake   Carl Jacobi
The Gilded Mask [v]   Fred Croft
In Loving Tribute: I Remember
     Seabury [a] Mary Elizabeth Counselman
Eve Two [ill]   Jim Garrison
The Room of Fear   William Hope Hodgson
Astarte [v]   Fred Croft
He Hunts [v]   Scott Wyatt
*The Light-House   Edgar Allan Poe &
                           Richard L. Tierney
Wolf-Moon [v]   Fred Croft
To Poe, the Master [v]   William A. Conder
To Lovecraft, the Second
     Master [v]   William A. Conder
The Dream [v]   William A. Conder
Nocturnal Goddess [v]   William A. Conder
*Love Unveiled [v]   William A. Conder
Cthulhu Speaks [v]   William A. Conder
Lycanthrope [v]   William A. Conder
Al Azif [v]   William A. Conder
Places to Avoid! [col]   [The Editors]
The Thing in the Museum   William H. Stout

Cursed [v]   John Bredon
*Madman's Song [v]
                   Mary Elizabeth Counselman
In the Toad God's Land [cs]   Tim Draus
Soon To Be Retired   J. Vernon Shea
Eldoor [v]   Bill Guy
The Hour of Demons   Llewellyn M. Cabos
Margaret Brundage [a]   R. Alain Everts
Margaret Brundage [in]   R. Alain Everts
The Harlequin   Walter C. DeBill
Ringstones [v]   Bill Guy
The Shadow [v]   William A. Conder
The Jewel of the Sorcerer's
    Daughter   David C. Smith
Discovery [ill]   Jim Garrison
The Cosmic Spectre [v]
                      George C. Diezell II
Red Men Know [v]   George C. Diezell II
Love At First Sight   William A. Conder
Shub-Niggurath [ill]   D. A. Riley
Some Correspondence [a]   Carl Jacobi
Nightmare's Promise   Robert Borski
The Cyclops [v]   Steven Sinatra
Lovecraft, My Childhood Friend
    [a]   Harold W. Munro

[October] 1983   No.3   Jon D. Arfstrom
Pyramid   Mary Elizabeth Counselman
Some Antecedents of the Shining
    Trapezohedron [a]   Steve Mariconda
*The Dark Tower   Robert M. Eber
Those of the Bluestone [v]
             Reinhold Johannes Kaebitzsch
Demon Wind [v]   Michael Fantina
Vivisection [v]   David E. Schultz
169 Clinton Street [pic]   -
Mortal Combat [v]   Steve Eng
Haven in the Head [v]   Steve Eng
Humanchange [v]   Janet Fox
The Ancestral Memory and Rein-
   carnation in Robert E. Howard's
   Fiction [a]   Llewellyn M. Cabos
The Original Cover for "The
    Purcell Papers" [a]   R. Alain Everts
Jon D. Arfstrom [in]   R. Alain Everts
Nightmare [v]   Lew Cthew
An Appreciation of 'He Hunts' [v]
                              Lew Cthew
*Farnsworth Wright [a]   E. Hoffmann Price
*Self-Portrait [v]   Farnsworth Wright
The Cenote   Joan Garrison
The Yowlings of Yog-Sothoth [ap]
                           Michael Cline
*The Traveller   W. F. Harvey
The Lovecraft Illustrator
    [ill]   Harry O. Morris
The Strange Boy   William A. Conder
Echoes and Mirrors   Robert Borski
Innsmouth Update [v]   Janet Fox
Lost in the Corridors of Time
                          J. Vernon Shea
*The Riven Night   William Hope Hodgson
Lillith [v]   Janet Fox

                 ***

EVERMIST

*A small press fantasy magazine published quarterly by Evermist Publications,
LaBelle, Florida. Publisher and Editor: David R. Warren. Printed offset, in
octavo format, it began as an amateur enterprise and turned semi-professional
with its tenth issue in Spring 1977.*

December 1974   1/1 (1)   John A. Little
Thing of Your Dreams [v]   David R. Warren
The Vision of Asthomos   John A. Little
Moonmist [v]   David R. Warren
A Song is Born [v]   John A. Little
The Battle of Evermist [nt1/9]
                        David & Marjorie Warren

Spring 1975   1/2 (2)   John A. Little
The Battle of the Wizards [v]
                              David R. Warren
Generation Gap   J. Schaefer
Knabos [v]   John A. Little
Helios [v]   David R. Warren
I Shun the Night   John A. Little
A Short History of the History
    of the World   David Weisberg
The Battle of Evermist [nt2/9]
                        David & Marjorie Warren
Starlight Battle [v]   John A. Little

Summer 1975   1/3 (3)   John A. Little
Return of the Twilight
    Wanderer [v]   John A. Little
The Star   David R. Warren
Fantasy is ... [v]   Marjorie Warren
The Guardian of the Gate   John A. Little
Menace Beneath the Marsh   Eric Storm
The Wizard's Castle [v]   David R. Warren
The Battle of Evermist [nt3/9]
                        David & Marjorie Warren

Fall 1975   1/4 (4)   John A. Little
The Way to Faery [v]   John A. Little
Unicorn [v]   John A. Little
Debut From Olympus   David R. Warren
To Become a Wizard   Eric Storm
The City in the Sky [v]   David R. Warren
Twelve Inches High   Marjorie Warren
The Battle of Evermist [nt4/9]
                        David & Marjorie Warren

Winter 1975   2/1 (5)   John A. Little
    [Special H. P. Lovecraft issue]
Bird of Hell [v]   John A. Little
Howard Phillips Lovecraft [a]
                        Dirk W. Mosig, Ph.D.
The Fearful Fane [v]   Daniel Bailey
The Shadow That Lurked in
    Twilight   John A. Little
The Battle of Evermist [nt5/9]
                        David & Marjorie Warren

Spring 1976   2/2 (6)   John A. Little
Remembering [v]   David R. Warren
The Phoenix Time   Eric Storm
Death Entertains   John A. Little
The Sword   John R. Woodward
The Ruin   David R. Warren
Songs of a Spring in Spring
    [v]   John A. Little
The Battle of Evermist [nt6/9]
                        David & Marjorie Warren

Summer 1976   2/3 (7)   John A. Little
The Vision Pool [v]   David R. Warren
A Western Tale   John A. Little
The Sorcerer [v]   Steve Houser
The Beauty and the Beast   Peggy Gemignani
Ship of Death [v]   John R. Woodward
Deliverance [v]   Doug Baker
The Battle of Evermist [nt7/9]
                        David & Marjorie Warren

Fall 1976   2/4 (8)   Jeff Adams
My Torment [v]   John A. Little
The Finding of the Sword   Eric Storm
An Artist's Vengeance   Marjorie Warren
The Flight of the Toad [v]   David R. Warren
The Day King Hiram Pomp Made
    War on the Dwarves   John A. Little
Stalemate   Ken Hahn
Holocaust [ss]   John R. Woodward

64

The Battle of Evermist [nt8/9]
                    David & Marjorie Warren

Winter 1976/77   3/1 (9)   John A. Little
  [Special Tolkien issue]
Seagulls   David R. Warren
The Hocket [spf]   Eric Storm
Black Riders   Marjorie Warren
Leaf By Niggle [a]   Rebecca J. Hoffman
The Battle of Evermist [nt9/9]
                    David & Marjorie Warren

Spring 1977   3/2 (10) Sabrina Jarema
Evermisty Morning [v]   John A. Little
The Book of Sukla-Tet Gary Robert Muschla
Time Enough [v]   Neal R. Blaikie
Charlie of Shrall   Ken Hahn
Miriam [v]   John Thiel
The Pass of Thor   Marjorie Warren

Summer 1977   3/3 (11) Rick Harrison
Winter Vision [v]   John A. Little
An Afternoon Off   Ken Hahn
The Tragedy [v]   William R. Barrow
Billy's Chameleon   J. T. McDaniel
Mourning Has Broken [v] Neal R. Blaikie
An Evil Out of Krak [ex] William Monaghan
The Grey Steppes   David R. Warren

Fall 1977   3/4 (12) David Vosburgh
Daybreak on the Last Moor
  [ss]   John A. Little
Promises Are Forever   A. B. Clingan

Atlantis Founders [play] John R. Woodward
The Dwarven Way   Bret Ryan Rudnick
The Watcher [v]   David R. Warren
A Dead Frog   Keith Figley

Winter 1977/78   4/1 (13) Sabrina Jarema
I Am the Corpse [v] Ralph Stephen Harding
The Courage   John Kelly
The Scoffers [v]   John A. Little
The Night Keeper   Ken Hahn
The Gift   Marjorie Warren
The Dancer in the Storm   G. Arthur Rahman

Spring 1978   4/2 (14)   M. Littlejohn
A Song For Howard Phillips
  Lovecraft [v]   Joey Froehlich
Perfect Angels   Albert J. Manachino
The Golden Glow   David R. Warren
The Perfect Haunted House J. T. McDaniel
The Winds of Weir [v]   Wendelessen
Survival of the Fittest [s1/2] Ken Parker

Summer 1978   4/3 (15)   Morno
The White Shirts   William R. Barrow
The Death Tree   Gary Robert Muschla
Lara [v]   John A. Little
Survival of the Fittest [s2/2]
                              Ken Parker
The Wild and Ancient Sea [v]
                          Joey Froehlich

***

F

FANCIFUL TALES

OF TIME AND SPACE

A small press fantasy/sf magazine in octavo format published by Wilson Shepherd and Donald A. Wollheim. Printed by Shepherd from Oakman, Alabama. Editor: Donald A. Wollheim.

Fall 1936	1/1 Clay Ferguson, Jr
The Nameless City	H. P. Lovecraft
Umbriel	Donald A. Wollheim
The Forbidden Room	Duane W. Rimel
Solomon Kane's Homecoming [v]	Robert E. Howard
The Typewriter	David H. Keller, MD
The Man From Dark Valley	August W. Derleth
The Globe	William S. Sykora
The Electric World	Kenneth B. Pritchard

***

FANTASTIC

A fantasy/sf digest, the second longest running magazine included in this Index.
Published by Ziff-Davis Publishing (366 Madison Ave., New York until 1958, then
1 Park Ave., New York) until June 1965; then Ultimate Publishing Co., (Oakland Gdns.,
Flushing, New York until January 1979, then Scottsdale, Arizona) until October
1980. Editors: Howard Browne Summer 1952 - August 1956; Paul W. Fairman October
1956 - November 1958; Cele Goldsmith [Lalli] December 1958 - June 1965; Joseph Ross
September 1965 - November 1967; Harry Harrison January - October 1968; Barry Malzberg
December 1968 - April 1969; Ted White June 1969 - January 1979; Elinor Mavor April
1979 - October 1980. Quarterly for the first two issues, it became bi-monthly and
then monthly from February 1957 - June 1965, thereafter reverting to bi-monthly
with occasional periods as a quarterly. After October 1980 was merged with Amazing
Stories *though it may be revived as a separate magazine under its new publisher.*
Although always a fantasy magazine it did feature a high percentage of sf under
Paul Fairman, and its name was even changed to Fantastic Science Fiction *from*
April 1955 - September 1960, when it reverted to Fantastic *and was given the sub-*
title 'Stories of Imagination'. From September 1965 the spine bore the title
Fantastic Stories, *though this was never officially the title.*
   A British reprint edition was published bi-monthly by Strato Publications,
Oadby, Leicester between December 1953 and February 1955. Variations in content
are noted below. Stories omitted from the British edition are marked †.

Summer 1952	1/1 (1)	B. Phillips &
		L. R. Summers
Six and Ten are Johnny [nt]		
		Walter M. Miller, Jr
For Heaven's Sake		Sam Martinez
"Someday They'll Give Us Guns"		
		Paul W. Fairman
Full Circle		H. B. Hickey
The Runaway		Louise Lee Outlaw
The Opal Necklace		Kris Neville
The Smile		Ray Bradbury
And Three To Get Ready		H. L. Gold
What If		Isaac Asimov
*Professor Bingo's Snuff [nt]		
		Raymond Chandler

Fall 1952	1/2 (2)	L. R. Summers
Angels in the Jets		Jerome Bixby
I'm Looking For Jeff		Fritz Leiber
The Sin of Hyacinth Peuch		
		Eric Frank Russell
The Star Dummy		Anthony Boucher
*Famous Fantasy Masterpieces		Heinrich Kley
The Sex Opposite [nt]		Theodore Sturgeon

Beatrice	Dean Evans
Man in the Dark [nt]	Roy Huggins
*Miriam	Truman Capote
*The Tell-Tale Heart	Edgar Allan Poe

Nov/Dec 1952	1/3 (3)	B. W. Phillips
The Veiled Woman [nt]		Mickey Spillane
To Fit the Crime		Richard Matheson
Final Exam		Chad Oliver
Candlesticks		Dean Evans
The Moon of Montezuma [nt]		
		Cornell Woolrich
The Missing Symbol		Ivar Jorgensen
Rabbit Punch		Ralph Robin
*The Celestial Omnibus		E. M. Forster
*The Cask of Amontillado		Edgar Allan Poe
The Opener of the Crypt		John Jakes

Jan/Feb 1953	2/1 (4)	R. Frankenberg
Wonder Child [nt]		Joseph Shallit
Love is a Barometer		Del Molarsky
Mad House [nt]		Richard Matheson
Isle of Blight		Samuel Hopkins Adams
The Man With the Fine Mind		Kris Neville

The Yellow Needle [nt]   Gerald Vance
[Something For the Woman (UK)
                        Ivar Jorgensen]
[Stellar Pincushion [a] (UK) Conrad Kyle]
[Heli-Cab Hack [a] (UK)   John Weston]
[Pituitary Mystery [a] (UK)   A. Morris]

December 1954   3/6 (15) Ralph Castenir
[UK issue 1/8 released undated Feb 1955]
[Hydrogen is All [a] (UK)   Carl Webb]
[Energy Sink [a] (UK)   Bernard Lytle]
Water Cure [na]   John Toland
The Spidery Pied Pipers
                    Robert Moore Williams
The Courtship of 53 Shotl 9G   Niall Wilde
The Vicar of Skeleton Cove [nt]
                      Lawrence Chandler
 (author given as Ivar Jorgensen on story)
The Appointment   Raymond Stark
*[*Operation Decoy (UK)   Walt Sheldon]*

February 1955   4/1 (16)   Henry Sharp
The Patty-Cake Mutiny [nt] Winston Marks
The Gun   John Bernard Daley
The Day After Eternity [nt]
                      Lawrence Chandler
Ourselves of Yesterday   T. D. Hamm
While My Love Waits   Henry Still
Cross Index   Randall T. Ross
End of the Line   Thomas N. Scortia
Love That Potion   William P. McGivern

April 1955   4/2 (17) E. Valigursky
The Eye and I [nt]   C. H. Thames
Gold is Anywhere   Henry Still
Death Has Strong Hands Lawrence Chandler
Silent Night   Lysander Kemp
The Still Waters   Joy Hall
Killer in the Crib   Richard Wilson
The Big Bluff   Milton Lesser

June 1955   4/3 (18) E. Valigursky
Beyond the Black Horizon [nt]
                        Paul W. Fairman
The Typewriter   J. J. Allerton
Too Tough to Bury   Ron Butler
For the Greater Good   P. F. Costello
The Killer Within   C. H. Thames

August 1955   4/4 (19) E. Valigursky
The Girl in Tube 14 [nt]   Dick Purcell
Come Tuesday   Winston Marks
Occupation Force   Frank Herbert
The Smashers [nt]   Paul W. Fairman
He Ran All the Way   Milton Lesser

October 1955   4/5 (20) [E. Valigrsuky]
Scavengers of Space [nt]   Clee Garson
Signal Thirty-Three [nt]   Lee Grant
What Number Are You Calling? Ron Butler
Recruiting Officer   Alice Eleanor Jones
This is My Son   Paul W. Fairman

December 1955   4/6 (21) E. Valigursky
All Walls Were Mist [nt] Paul W. Fairman
"Madam, I Have Here - "   Ivar Jorgensen
The Man Who Read Minds   John Toland
He Took What He Wanted   C. H. Thames
Between Two Worlds   Milton Lesser

February 1956   5/1 (22) E. Valigursky
Black Blockade [nt]   Paul W. Fairman
Quick Cure   Randall Garrett
The Sore Spot   Ivar Jorgensen
Mind Bet   George Julius
Leave it to Umpax   Eric Dean

April 1956   5/2 (23) E. Valigursky
The Monarch of Mars [nt]   John Pollard
The Hero   Milton Lesser
The Rough Rock Road [nt]   E. K. Jarvis
House of Toys   Karl Stanley

June 1956   5/3 (24) E. Valigursky
Conception, Zero [nt]   Gerald Vance
Dream Girl   Robert Silverberg
All Good Men   Milton Lesser
Everybody's Watching You [nt] C. H. Thames
Round Trip   Karl Stanley

August 1956   5/4 (25) E. Valigursky
Guardian of the Crystal Gate
     [nt]   Robert Silverberg
The Long Forgotten   Henry Still
O' Captain, My Captain   Ivar Jorgensen
Growing Pains   Robert Arnette
The Slow and the Dead [nt] Robert Randall
Revolt of the Synthetics   Ralph Burke

October 1956   5/5 (26) E. Valigursky
The Passionate Pitchman [nt]
                       Stephen Wilder
The Man Who Knew Everything
                      Randall Garrett
An Eye For the Ladies Darius John Granger
Peter Merton's Private Mint   Lee Archer
The Girl From Bodies, Inc [nt]
                     Leonard G. Spencer
The Pint-Size Genie   Kate Wilhelm

December 1956   5/6 (27) E. Valigursky
The Mummy Takes a Wife [nt]
                       Clyde Mitchell
Death Rattle   O. H. Leslie
The Fifth Stone   Alfred Coppel
Coward's Death   Ivar Jorgensen
Choke Chain   Robert Silverberg
The Chimp   Henry Slesar
Man of Many Bodies   Ralph Burke

February 1957   6/1 (28) E. Valigursky
Biddy and the Silver Man [nt] E. K. Jarvis
World of Women [nt]   Harlan Ellison
The Mystery of Deneb IV Robert Silverberg
Beauty Contest?   Henry Slesar
My Robot   O. H. Leslie
An Enemy of Peace   Ralph Burke
A Kiss For the Conqueror   Clyde Mitchell

March 1957   6/2 (29) E. Valigursky
The Goddess of World 21 [nt] Henry Slesar
Forgotten World   Robert Silverberg
Citadel of Darkness   Ralph Burke
The Dead Companions   Stanley Mullen
Swords Against the Cutworlders
                         Calvin Knox
Freak Show   Hall Thornton
It Sounds Fantastic, But ...
     [col]   Paul Steiner

July 1958   7/7 (45)   Leo Summers
The Dream Makers [sn]   Richard S. Shaver
The Facts Behind the Mystery
    [a]   Raymond A. Palmer
The Shaver Mystery - A Defense
    [a]   Richard S. Shaver
The Shaver Mystery - Dangerous
    Nonsense [a]   A. J. Steichert
*The Key to Mantong, the Ancient
    Language [a]   Richard S. Shaver &
                              Joel Kos

August 1958   7/8 (46)   Leo Summers
The Girl Who Played Wolf   G. Dickson
Magic Window   Robert F. Young
Patented Paradise [nt]   Bryce Walton
Somebody Up There Typed Me   Gerald Vance
Operation Scrumblies   Henry Still
The Hunter and the Cross   Jeanne Williams
Cat Island Hoax [a]   G. L. Vandenburg
Satan's Footprints [a] Eric Frank Russell

September 1958   7/9 (47)   E. Valigursky
Call Me Monster [nt]   G. L. Vandenburg
Time Squeeze   Paul Dallas
A Slight Case of Genius   E. K. Jarvis
In This Dark Mind   Inez McGowan
Psychoanalysis by Telepathy
    [a]   Ellery Lanier
Jason's Secret   Rog Phillips
The Thousand Dollar Wish   Jack Milton

October 1958   7/10 (48)   Gabe Keith
Suicide World [nt]   Harlan Ellison
Who Steals My Mind ...   Lloyd Biggle, Jr
Dark Menace   J. Anthony Ferlaine
Figurex   Paul Dallas
Report on a Backward Planet
                    Russ Winterbotham
A Lesson For the Teacher   Robert Bloch
Voodoo Queen of New Orleans [a]
                        Bryce Walton
Hello, Young Lover   Lawrence Chandler
Shadows Over the White House [a]
                        Vincent Gaddis

November 1958   7/11 (49)   Gabe Keith
The Troons of Space:
    The Space Station, AD 1994 [nt]
                        John Wyndham
F. O. B. Venus   Robert Bloch
The Picture   John Boland
Mr and Mrs Saturday Night Robert F. Young
Intermission   E. K. Jarvis
The Savage Machine [nt]   Randall Garrett
Spontaneous Generation [a] Ellery Lanier

December 1958   7/12 (50)   Gabe Keith
Jungle in Manhattan [nt] G. L. Vandenburg
The Eleventh Plague [nt]   Henry Slesar
The Troons of Space: The
    Moon, AD 2044 [nt]   John Wyndham
Enough Rope   Louis Fisher

January 1959   8/1 (51)   Phil Berry
The Screaming People [nt]   Robert Bloch
The Troons of Space: Mars
    A D 2094 [nt]   John Wyndham
Replace the Horse   Larry M. Harris
Passage to Gomorrah   Robert F. Young

Last Laughter   Robert Chase
Fish Talk   Winston K. Marks
Nothing But Terror   J. F. Bone

February 1959   8/2 (52)   Gabe Keith
The Body Hunters [nt]   Paul W. Fairman
Like Father - Like Son   Henry Slesar
The Creeper in the Dream [nt] Rog Phillips
The Garden of Fast   Dick Ashby
The Troons of Space: Venus
    A D 2144 [nt]   John Wyndham

March 1959   8/3 (53)   E. Valigursky
The Trouble With Magic [nt]
                        Randall Garrett
The Captain of His Soul   Jack Sharkey
The Obvious Solution   Jack Sharkey
The Last Hero   Robert F. Young
The Girl of Many Bodies [nt] Wilson Kane
East is East   Richard DeMille
The Little One?   Barbara J. Griffith
What Crouches in the Deep   Arthur Porges

April 1959   8/4 (54)   E. Valigursky
The Abnormals   Harlan Ellison
After the Funeral   Gordon Dickson
Second Man to the Moon   Jack Williamson
Hear a Pin Drop   Edward Wellen
Keepers in Space   Rog Phillips
A Dozen of Everything
                    Marion Zimmer Bradley
The Ecstasy of It [nt]   Kate Wilhelm
The Arm of Enmord   Jack Sharkey
A Touch of Sun   Arthur & Irwin Porges

May 1959   8/5 (55)   Jed Thayer
Guest Editorial [ged]   Arthur Porges
The Hungry Eye   Robert Bloch
Queen of the Green Sun   Jack Sharkey
Guardian Devil [nt]   Robert Silverberg
The Convention   Ede Witt
More Like Home   Raymond E. Banks
The Middle-Aged Rookie Charles D. Hammer
The Only One That Lived   Rog Phillips

June 1959   8/6 (56)   E. Valigursky
Give Me My Body! [nt]   Paul W. Fairman
Blurble   M. G. Zimmerman
The Lurker   Rog Phillips
What Other Color is There? Jeanne Williams
A Desert Incident   Will Worthington
The Fife of Bodidharma   Cordwainer Smith
Cedric   Winston Marks
The Worth of a Man   Henry Slesar
The Warren   Richard Brian
Bedside Monster   Jack Sharkey

July 1959   8/7 (57)   Leo Summers
The Last Plea [nt]   Robert Bloch
The Gift   Ray Bradbury
The Forerunner   Arthur Porges
The Kink-Remover   Jack Sharkey
The Key [nt]   A. Bertram Chandler
Bottle It Up   Ron Goulart
40 - 26 - 38   Robert F. Young
*The Four-Sided Triangle William F. Temple

August 1959   8/8 (58)   E. Valigursky
Damnation Morning   Fritz Leiber
Let X = Alligator   Jack Sharkey

November 1960   9/11 (73) Alex Schomburg
Deadly Moon [nt]   Fritz Leiber
Mariwite   Charles L. Fontenay
Donor [nt]   James E. Gunn
A Diversion for the Baron   Arthur Porges
A World to Choose   Poul Anderson
Long Shot   Henry Slesar

December 1960   9/12 (74)   Leo Summers
A Plague of Masters [sn1/2] Poul Anderson
The Melanas   Arthur Porges
Summons of the Void   Daniel F. Galouye
The Eye of Aesculapius   Stanley R. Lee
Remember Me, Peter Shepley [nt]
                        Charles W. Runyon
The Radio   Peter Arthur

January 1961   10/1 (75) Alex Schomburg
The Reality Paradox   Daniel F. Galouye
Dreaming Eyes   Miriam Allen deFord
According to Plan   Jack Sharkey
Degree Candidate   Peter Arthur
Dr Blackadder's Clients   Arthur Porges
A Plague of Masters [sn2/2] Poul Anderson

February 1961   10/2 (76)   Leo Summers
Worlds of the Imperium [n1/3]
                            Keith Laumer
The Other Side   Arthur Porges
Visiting Professor   Rosel George Brown
A Thread in Time   Jack Sharkey
Project   Steven Terry
Catalyst   Henry Still
We Regret ...   David R. Bunch

March 1961   10/3 (77) Alex Schomburg
The Big Blow-Up   Daniel F. Galouye
Night Caller   Jack Sharkey
Random Choice   Randall Garrett
Temptation   Ida Helmer
Worlds of the Imperium [n2/3]
                            Keith Laumer
Last Zero   David R. Bunch

April 1961   10/4 (78)   Ed Emshwiller
Descent Into the Maelstrom [nt]
                        Daniel F. Galouye
The Violin String   Henry Hasse
Mulberry Moon   Arthur Porges
Discoverers   Henry Slesar
Worlds of the Imperium [n3/3] Keith Laumer

May 1961   10/5 (79) Vernon Kramer
Scylla's Daughter [na]   Fritz Leiber
*The Garden of Fear   Robert E. Howard
    [introduction by Sam Moskowitz]
The Problem was Lubrication David R. Bunch
Are You Now or Have You Ever
    Been? [nt]   Jack Sharkey
The Arrogant Vampire   Arthur Porges

June 1961   10/6 (80) Alex Schomburg
Second Ending [sn1/2]   James White
A Small Miracle of Fishhooks
    and Straight Pins   David R. Bunch
The Face in the Mask   Estelle Frye
I.Q.   Mack Reynolds
*The Cosmic Relic [nt] Eric Frank Russell
    [introduction by Sam Moskowitz]
One Bad Habit   Arthur Porges

July 1961   10/7 (81)   Vernon Kramer
*The Creator   Clifford D. Simak
    [introduction by Sam Moskowitz]
The Forest of Unreason   Robert F. Young
No Harm Done   Jack Sharkey
Second Ending [sn2/2]   James White
The Goggles of Dr Dragonet   Fritz Leiber
Solomon's Demon   Arthur Porges

August 1961   10/8 (82)   Leo Summers
Goodbye, Atlantis   Poul Anderson
*The Root of Ampoi   Clark Ashton Smith
    [introduction by Sam Moskowitz]
One Small Drawback   Jack Sharkey
Stranger in Paradox   Keith Laumer
Report on the Magic Shop   Arthur Porges
Passage to Malish   Theodore L. Thomas
Policeman's Lot   Henry Slesar

September 1961   10/9 (83) Alex Schomburg
*Ship of Darkness   A. E. van Vogt
    [introduction by Sam Moskowitz]
Magnanthropus [sn1/2]   Manly Banister
The Trekkers   Daniel F. Galouye
Specimen   C. C. MacApp
The Genie   A. Bertram Chandler

October 1961   10/10 (84) Alex Schomburg
Deluge II [nt]   Robert F. Young
*The Mother   David H. Keller, M.D.
    [introduction by Sam Moskowitz]
Magnanthropus [sn2/2]   Manly Banister
A Cabbage Named Sam   John Jakes
The Last Druid   Joseph E. Kelleam
Court of Judgement   David Ely

November 1961   10/11 (85) L. Birmingham
Hatchery of Dreams   Fritz Leiber
Special Effect [na]   J. F. Bone
*To Heaven Standing Up   Paul Ernst
    [introduction by Sam Moskowitz]
The Living End   Henry Slesar
...But Who Knows Huer, or Huen?
                            Rog Phillips

December 1961   10/12 (86) L. Birmingham
Spawn of Doom [nt]   Daniel F. Galouye
The Last Friday in August   David Ely
Point [na]   John T. Phillifent
The Voice Box   Allan W. Eckert
*The Dead Remember   Robert E. Howard
    [introduction by Sam Moskowitz]

January 1962   11/1 (87) L. Birmingham
Hepcats of Venus   Randall Garrett
*The Human Zero [nt] Erle Stanley Gardner
    [introduction by Sam Moskowitz]
Rat Race   Paul Dellinger
This is Your Death [nt]   Albert Teichner
Atonement   Jesse Roarke
The Empathic Man   Gordon Browne

February 1962   11/2 (88)   Leo Summers
A Bit of the Dark World [nt] Fritz Leiber
A Silence of Wings [nt] Daniel F. Galouye
The Red Flowers of Tulp Joseph E. Kelleam
*The Shadow Out of Space
    H. P. Lovecraft & August W. Derleth
    [introduction by Sam Moskowitz]
What If?   William W. Stuart

June 1963   12/6 (104) Lee Brown Coye
The Mirror of Cagliostro [nt]
                              Robert Arthur
Plumrose   Ron Goulart
On the Mountain   Dave Mayo
The Penalty   John J. Wooster
A Hoax in Time [n1/3]   Keith Laumer
The Hall of C D   David R. Bunch
A Museum Piece   Roger Zelazny

July 1963   12/7 (105)   J. Blair
The Trouble With Tweenity   Jack Sharkey
*He That Hath Wings [nt] Edmond Hamilton
   [introduction by Sam Moskowitz]
A Hoax in Time [n2/3]   Keith Laumer
The Recurrent Suitor   Ron Goulart
A Contract in Karasthan Phyllis MacLennan
Final Audit   Thomas M. Disch

August 1963   12/8 (106) Vernon Kramer
Bazaar of the Bizarre [nt]   Fritz Leiber
The Red Tape Yonder   Vance Simonds
The Grass, More Green   W. Lee Tomerlin
A Hoax in Time [n3/3]   Keith Laumer
Two More Tales For the Horrid
   at Heart: Sacrifice Play
         One Too Many   Brad Steiger
*The Devil in Hollywood   Dale Clarke
   [introduction by Sam Moskowitz]
Sometimes I Get So Happy   David R. Bunch
Fables of the Past & Future:
   The Return of the Medusae
   Master Said-and-Done
   The Enchanted Prince, 1963
                              Thomas M. Disch
Cornie on the Walls   Sidney Van Scyoc

September 1963   12/9 (107) Paula McLane
The House That Time Forgot [nt]
                              Robert F. Young
The Sudden Afternoon   J. G. Ballard
*The Singing Sands of Prester John
                              H. Bedford-Jones
   [introduction by Sam Moskowitz]
Vanity, Thy Name Is   Ron Goulart
The Demon of the North [nt]   C. C. MacApp
Adjustment   Wilton G. Beggs

October 1963   12/10 (108)   Emsh
The Screen Game [nt]   J. G. Ballard
*The Wolf Woman   H. Bedford-Jones
   [introduction by Sam Moskowitz]
King Solomon's Ring   Roger Zelazny
Let There Be Night [nt]   Robert F. Young
The Mating Season   Wilton G. Beggs
A Night With Hecate   Edward W. Ludwig

November 1963   12/11 (109) A. Schomburg
The Aftertime [nt]   Jack Sharkey
"I Was a Spider for the SBI"
   [nt]   Neal Barrett, Jr
Witch of the Four Winds [n1/2] John Jakes
Darkness Box   Ursula K. LeGuin
And on the Third Day   John J. Wooster

December 1963   12/12 (110) Paul Wenzel
After a Judgement Day   Edmond Hamilton
Lilliput Revisited [nt] Adam Bradford, M.D.
The Soul Buyer [nt]   Keith Laumer
Witch of the Four Winds [n2/2] John Jakes

January 1964   13/1 (111)   Emsh
The Lords of Quarmall [sn1/2]
                    Fritz Leiber & Harry Fischer
Minnesota Gothic   Dobbin Thorpe
The Word of Unbinding   Ursula K. LeGuin
Last Order [nt]   Gordon Walters
A Thesis on Social Forms &
   Social Controls in the
   U.S.A. [spf]   Thomas M. Disch

February 1964   13/2 (112)   Emsh
Novelty Act [nt]   Philip K. Dick
The Soft Woman   Theodore L. Thomas
The Orginorg Way   Jack Sharkey
The Lords of Quarmall [sn2/2]
                    Fritz Leiber & Harry Fischer
They Never Come Back From
   Whoosh!   David R. Bunch
Return to Brobdingnag Adam Bradford, M.D.
Death Before Dishonor   Dobbin Thorpe

March 1964   13/3 (113) Paula McLane
Iron   Robert H. Rohrer, Jr
The Graveyard Heart [na]   Roger Zelazny
*The Coming of the Little People
   [nt]   Robert Spencer Carr
   [introduction by Sam Moskowitz]
Training Talk   David R. Bunch
Identity Mistaken   Rick Raphael

April 1964   13/4 (114)   Frank Bruno
Centipedes of Space [nt] Daniel F. Galouye
The Dunstable Horror   Arthur Pendragon
A Ritual For Souls   Albert Teichner
The Rule of Names   Ursula K. LeGuin
*The Devil Came to Our Valley
   [nt]   Fulton T. Grant
   [introduction by Sam Moskowitz]

May 1964   13/5 (115)   Emsh
*Adept's Gambit [na]   Fritz Leiber
To The Victor   Leo P. Kelley
Master of Chaos   Michael Moorcock
All For Nothing   David R. Bunch
Gulliver's Magic Islands [nt]
                       Adam Bradford, M.D.

June 1964   13/6 (116) Robert Adragna
Paingod   Harlan Ellison
Testing [nt]   John J. McGuire
Body of Thought [nt]   Albert Teichner
Illusion   Jack Sharkey
Genetic Coda   Thomas M. Disch
*From the Beginning [nt]   Eando Binder
   [introduction by Sam Moskowitz]

July 1964   13/7 (117)   Emsh
The Kragen [na]   Jack Vance
Descending   Thomas M. Disch
The College of Acceptable Death
                              David R. Bunch
The Boundary Beyond Florence Engel Randall
The Venus Charm   Jack Sharkey
The Thousand Injuries of Mr
   Courtney   Robert F. Young

August 1964   13/8 (118)   Emsh
When the Idols Walked [n1/2]   John Jakes
The Scent of Love   Larry Eisenberg
The Failure   David R. Bunch

Science Fiction and Drugs [a]
                          Donald K. Arbogast

August 1970   19/6 (158)   Jeff Jones
The Good Trip   Ursula K. LeGuin
Music in the Air   Ova Hamlet
A Gift From the Gozniks   Gordon Eklund
Say Goodbye to the Wind   J. G. Ballard
Always the Black Knight [n2/2] Lee Hoffman
Directions Into the Darkness
                          Robert E. Toomey, Jr
*The Elixir of Invisibility [nt]
                          Henry Kuttner
Treaty   Lincoln Albert
The Nature of Science Fiction
   [a]   Alexei Panshin
Fantasy Fandom [a]   John J. Pierce

October 1970   20/1 (159)   Gray Morrow
The Crimson Witch [n]   Dean R. Koontz
The Movement   Greg Benford
A Glance at the Past   David R. Bunch
As Between Generations   Barry N. Malzberg
Unbinding Science Fiction [a]
                          Alexei Panshin
*Spook For Yourself [nt]
                          David Wright O'Brien
Fantasy Fandom [a]   Michael Juergens
2000 A.D. Man [cs]   Jay Kinney

December 1970   20/2 (160)   M. W. Kaluta
The Shape Changer [n1/2] Keith Laumer
Cardiac Arrest [nt]   Brian Aldiss
Walk of the Midnight Demon
                          Gerard F. Conway
Been a Long, Long Time   R. A. Lafferty
The New Rappacini   Barry Malzberg
Battered Like a Brass Bippy Ova Hamlet
*The Bottle Imp [nt]   Dwight V. Swain
Science Fiction and Creative
   Fantasy [a]   Alexei Panshin

February 1971   20/3 (161)   Steve Harper
Bowerbird   Verge Foray
A Soul Song to the Sad Silly
   Soaring Sixties   Barry N. Malzberg
Nancy   David Redd
How Eliot Met Jeanie   Laurence Littenberg
The Shape Changer [n2/2] Keith Laumer
*The Magic Flute   David V. Reed
The Nature of Creative Fantasy
   [a]   Alexei Panshin

April 1971   20/4 (162)   Gray Morrow
Wolf Quest [na]   Ted White
Dread Empire [nt]   John Brunner
The Eight Thirty to Nine Slot
                          Geo. Alec Effinger
How Georges Duchamps Discovered a
   Plot to Take Over the World [ss]
                          Alexei Panshin
The Iconoclasts   Dennis O'Neil
*The Garden of Hell [nt] Leroy Yerxa
The Short History of Science
   Fiction [a]   Alexei Panshin

June 1971   20/5 (163)   Dan Adkins
The Byworlder [n1/2]   Poul Anderson
War of the Doom Zombies   Ova Hamlet
No Exit   Larry Niven & Hank Stine
The Man Who Faded Away   Richard E. Peck

The Lurker in the Locked Bedroom
                          Ed Bryant
*War of the Human Cats [nt]
                          Festus Pragnell
Skald in Post Oaks [a] L. Sprague de Camp
New Perspective [a]   Alexei Panshin

August 1971   20/6 (164)   Paula McLane
The Joke   David R. Bunch
Extra Ecclesiam Nulla Salus Eugene Stover
Sentence in Binary Code Christopher Priest
Pulse   James Benford
The Byworlder [n2/2]   Poul Anderson
*The Electric Butterflies   Ross Rocklynne
Eldritch Yankee Gentleman
   [a1/2]   L. Sprague de Camp
A New Paradigm: I   Alexei Panshin

October 1971   21/1 (165)   Todd & Bode
The Dramaturges of Yan [n1/2] John Brunner
Shadow-Led   Wilmar H. Shiras
Doll For the End of the Day David R. Bunch
How Eliot and Jeanie Became
   Parents   Laurence Littenberg
*The Meteor Monsters [nt] Arthur R. Tofte
Eldritch Yankee Gentleman
   [a2/2]   L. Sprague de Camp
A New Paradigm: II   Alexei Panshin

December 1971   21/2 (166)   Doug Chaffee
[Special Guilford Conference Writers' issue]
The Awesome Menace of the
   Polarizer   Geo. Alec Effinger
Things Are Tough All Over   Ted White
Cartoon   Jack M. Dann
Garden of Eden   Jack C. Haldeman II
Wires   Gardner Dozois
The Dramaturges of Yan [n2/2] John Brunner
*Madamoiselle Butterfly [nt] Don Wilcox
SF and Academia [a]   Alexei Panshin

February 1972   21/3 (167)   Mike Kaluta
The Sleeping Sorceress [nt]
                          Michael Moorcock
Djinn Bottle Blues   John Brunner
The Exit to San Breta George R. R. Martin
Death Card   Ken McCullough
After the Last Mass   Roger Ebert
Timmy Was Eight   Susan Doenim
The Horror South of Red Hook Ova Hamlet
Reality   Wilmar H. Shiras
Two Men in One [a] L. Sprague de Camp
Metaphor, Analogy, Symbol and Myth
   [a]   Alexei Panshin
*Master of the Fantastic
   [ap]   Julian S. Krupa

April 1972   21/4 (168)   Mike Hinge
Beyond the Resurrection [n1/2]
                          Gordon Eklund
A Dome of Many-Colored Glass Bob Shaw
Thus I Refute   Terry Carr
Up to the Edge of Heaven David R. Bunch
The Puiss of Krrlik   F. M. Busby
The Pill   Maggie Nadler
Nice Trees Don't   B. Mebane
The Resurrection of SF - 1 [a]
                          Alexei & Cory Panshin
*Slaves of the Fish Men [ap]
                          J. Allen St. John

July 1979   27/6 (203)   Elinor Mavor
Hessie and the Spaced-Out
 Demon   William E. Fark
*The Worm   David H. Keller, M.D.
Daemon [gs1/5]   Stephen & Chip Fabian
*The Success Machine   Henry Slesar
*The Bald-Headed Mirage   Robert Bloch
*A Museum Piece   Roger Zelazny
Between the Lines [col] Robert H. Wilcox
Sex Queens of Outer Space [gf] Jon Gerung
The Non-Existent Man   Wynne Whiteford
*Now is Forever   Dobbin Thorpe
*The Big Blow-Up   Daniel F. Galouye
Early Winter   John E. Stith

October 1979   27/7 (204)   Elinor Mavor
A Logical Resolution   Robert Stearns
The Ones That Got Away   Gus Dallas
Daemon [gs2/5]   Stephen & Chip Fabian
The Weird of Yothlant Hollow
                        Romuald M. Tallip
*Tumithak of the Corridors
 [na]   Charles R. Tanner
Between the Lines [col] Robert H. Wilcox
Into the Valley of Doom [v]
                        Kurt von Stuckrad

January 1980   27/8 (205)   Elinor Mavor
The Martian Chronicles [a]   Steven Dimeo
Murvyn the Magnificent   William E. Fark
The Cliffhanger Sound   Paul Dellinger
Daemon [gs3/5]   Stephen & Chip Fabian
*Never Argue With Antique
 Dealers   Darrell Schweitzer
Alternative Worlds Ghazal [v] Steve Rasnic
Alpha Centauri A Nine   L. A. P. Moore
Person to Person   Robert H. Brown
Frozen Star   Allan D. Maurer
Pawn Shop Camera   Leland G. Griffin
*The Runaway Skyscraper [nt]
                        Murray Leinster
Between the Lines [col] Robert H. Wilcox
Inner Space   Vincent Argondezzi

April 1980   27/9 (206) *Hildebrandts
The White Isle [sn1/2] Darrell Schweitzer
Encounter With the Universe   Thea Carvel
Daemon [gs4/5]   Stephen & Chip Fabian
A Message From the Medium Israel O'Rourke
Lay of the Line-boat Lovers
 [v]   Frank C. Gunderloy, Jr
Blood Money   Edward Uchno
*Damned Funny   Marvin Kaye
Weather Report: Chicago 2000
                        Thomas A. Easton
Creator of Tomorrow   Dave Stover

July 1980   27/10 (207)   *W. Barlowe
Prophet of Doom and Gloom [in]
                        Brian M. Fraser
Adapting Ursula LeGuin's "The
 Lathe of Heaven" [a]   Steven Dimeo
A Funny Thing Happened [a] Robert Wilcox
The White Isle [sn2/2] Darrell Schweitzer
The Imprecise Delights of
 Love   Wayne Wightman
Rope the Hornet   Lawrence C. Connolly
A Visit With Lenny   K. L. Jones
Daemon [gs5/5]   Stephen & Chip Fabian
The Compromise
           Eric Vinicoff & Marcia Martin
New Member   David R. Bunch
The Competitor   Brad Linaweaver
Parable of Barter   Jose Juan Arreola

October 1980   27/11 (208)   *R. Petillo
Putting the Past into the
 Future [in]   Brian M. Fraser
Alternate Worlds [a]   Thomas Easton
Off the Rack Space Suits [a]
           Walter B. Hendrickson, Jr
The Amorous Umbrella [nt]   Marvin Kaye
Evening Promenade   Wayne Wightman
The Small One   M. Lindholm
The Headless Horseman Darrell Schweitzer
Girl of My Dreams   Paul Dellinger
Main Street Stars [a]   Britton Bloom
Great 10^{24} Grandfathers [a] Britton Bloom
What's in a Wave? [a]   Britton Bloom
Seeds of the Future [a]   Tom Easton
The Songs Are of Earth   R. G. Steinhauer
Wonders of the Gods?   J. J. Miller

                    ***

Hereafter combined with AMAZING STORIES

FANTASY AND TERROR

A small press quarto magazine published by the Fellowship of Odysseans, Zenith, Washington. Publisher and Editor: Jessica Amanda Salmonson [formerly Amos Salmonson]. Full title: The Literary Magazine of Fantasy and Terror. The last issue was a triple volume. Although further issues were announced F&T folded and most of the material was used in Salmonson's Windhaven. A second series of F&T has appeared as from 1984, and thus beyond the cut-off date for this Index. [Note: see also the sampler magazine Toadstool Wine.]

[Spring] 1973   1/1 (1)   A. Salmonson
Ray   Mel Horman
Youngin   Josiah Kerr
Legendary Korm [v]   [Amos Salmonson]
If I Were God [v]   [Amos Salmonson]
A Great Experience   Patrick Lean
Quest For Life   Amos Salmonson

[Summer] 1973   1/2 (2)   A. Salmonson
The Winged Demon   Gordon Linzner
Never Kill a Fly!   F. C. Adams
The Mountain Witch's Dying
   Curse [v]   Josiah Kerr
The Continuing Story of Joe
   and Mac [cs]   Cam Broze
Ladamir's Gem of Life   Amos Salmonson

[Fall] 1973   1/3 (3)   *Gustav Dore
Elimdorath   Darrell Schweitzer
The Cube-Root of Richard Dunn   Peter Glass
Cemetery Hill   R. Neil Horman
*The Gustav Dore Sampler [ap] Gustav Dore
City of the Enlightened   Amos Salmonson

[Winter] 1973   1/4 (4)   Jenny Hunt
Orb of the Wizard King   Ron Nance
The Follower [v]   Joseph Payne Brennan
Halloween Snow [v]   Joseph Payne Brennan
The Older Gods [v]   Joseph Payne Brennan
Refrain [v]   Joseph Payne Brennan
Cosmic Jesters   C. C. Clingan
A Matter of Competition   Eddy C. Bertin
Archives of Fear   Rhondi Greening
Demonology of the Pacific North-
   West American Indian [pic] Ian Walker,
            Joy Long & Margaret Smith
The Alchemists of Ivis   Amos Salmonson

[Spring] 1974   1/5 (5) James Garrison
The Devil's Tooth [nt]   Glen Cook
Two Bards Recite:
   Happiness [v]   L. Sprague de Camp
   The Haunting Beauty [v]   Tawnya Ison
Where Walked a Tree [ap]   Jenny Hunt
Once Upon a Pentacle   Mel Horman
Green Temple   F. C. Adams
Pril and the Wizard's Spirit
                            Amos Salmonson
Mythconception [v]   Dale C. Donaldson

[Summer] 1974   1/6 (6)   Al B. Cox
Toyman's Trade   Phyllis Anne Karr
Returning [v]   Josiah Kerr
The Last Words of Imatus Istum
                            David C. Smith
The Singing Sword Trilogy:
   The Sword That Sings [v]
   Sword Song [v]
   Song of the Minstrel [v]
                          Stephanie Stearns
Gods of Aduil   Darrell Schweitzer
Nightmares! [sym]   Amos Salmonson,
            William R. Barrow, Isaac Asimov,
                         & Phyllis Anne Karr
Treasure Quest [v]   Susan L. Tannahill
The Dream Child [v]   Walter Shedlofsky
Satanesque   Allan Weiss
Mihera - Mahura   Amos Salmonson
*That Is Our Eden's Spring,
   Once Promised [v]   Ray Bradbury

[Summer] 1975   2A/1 (7)   Mark Gelotte
Wake Unto Me   Jean Thompson
The Shadow of Monya Khan
                        Ed & George S. Howard

84

The Trophy [gs]   James Garrison
Return of the Jaward [nt] Gordon Linzner
Of Sorcerers and Salamanders
                             Rhondi Greening
More Sword Poems:
    Song For a Queen [v]
    Song For a Kingdom [v]
    Song For a Son [v]   Stephanie Stearns
The Night of the Hanged Men George Kelley
Lays Without Tunes and Bardic Runes
*[Special verse supplement serving as first
 issue of the magazine BARDIC RUNES]*
    The Demon Lover [v]   Jefferson Davis
    Feigned Death [v] Jessica A. Salmonson
    Verse of Necromancy [v]
                             Walter Shedlofsky
    To Robin Hood [v] Jane Gabrielle Beckman
    The Lovers: Three Nights Beneath
      a Balcony [v]   Darrell Schweitzer
    Unquiet Death [v] Jane Gabrielle Beckman
    Gods [v]   Richard L. Tierney
    Tahuantin-Suyu [v]   Richard L. Tierney
    The Prophet [v]   Frank Belknap Long
What Do the Flowers Tell?   Helen Knight
One Man's View of the Death
    of the Pulp Era [a]   E. Hoffman Price
Love Tryst   Wayne Hooks
The Walking Cane   David Jackson
Sunset on Paradise   Gary Muschla
Artist of the Impossible [a]   John Hartl
A Tribute to Ray Harryhausen [pic]   -
Death and Sir Penelain Darrell Schweitzer
Parable of Three Nations [nt]
        Jessica Amanda Salmonson & Ron Nance

                    ***

FANTASY BOOK

A small press fantasy magazine published quarterly (originally bi-monthly) in quasi-slick format by Fantasy Book Enterprises, 1441 N. Altadena Drive, Pasadena, California. Editor: Nick Smith. Not to be confused with an earlier sf/fantasy magazine of the same name (see Appendix II).

October 1981   1/1 (1)   Cathy Hill
The Assiz Dragon   Sherwood Springer
*A Symphony for Sarah Ann
                        Sheila Finch-Rayner
The Ballad of Lookhma [spf]   Jon L. Breen
We Take Care of Our Own   Terri Pinckard
Another Creator   Kris Neville
The Room at Inglenook   Walt Liebscher
*The Marriage of Heaven and
  Hell [v]   William Blake
Wasps   Walter Beckers
The Hour of the Anvil [v]   Jim Neal
The Were-Human   L. Ron Hubbard
The Devil Behind the Leaves
            Kathleen Sky & Stephen Goldin
The Musician   J. Neil Schulman
[contains textual errors; see next issue]
Bourbon, Water, and Djinn   Boyd Correll
*Warm, Dark Places   H. L. Gold

December 1981   1/2 (2)   Charles Vess
Won't You Have a Cup of Tea,
  Dearie?   Terri Pinckard
Among the Wilder Talents Sherwood Springer
Great Gog's Grave   Forrest J Ackerman &
                      Donald A. Wollheim
Camber the Heretic [ex]   Katherine Kurtz
*Death Talk   A. E. van Vogt
Herbie Feamster, Lord of
  Dimensions!   K. L. Jones
Deal With the D.E.V.I.L.
                      Theodore R. Cogswell
The Dark Country   Dennis Etchison
Necromantic [v]   Leilah Wendell
It Ain't Missed Yet   Michael Bernard
Transylvanian Roots   Thomas R. McDonough
M-M-Magic   Rory Harper
Of Mice and Monsters   Al Hernhuter
In All Things Moderation Steve Rasnic Tem
Challenge [v]   Jim Neal

The Musician   J. Neil Schulman
  [corrected version; see last issue]

February 1982   1/3 (3)   Lela Dowling
The Return of Mad Santa   Al Sarrantonio
A Shade of Jealousy   C. Bruce Hunter
The Pegasus Suit   Frank Ward
Dance of the Dwarfs [nt]   John F. Carr
These Shrunken Men [v]   Joel Hagen
The Christmas Demon   James B. Hemesath
The Summer's Garden   Eric G. Iverson
Mr. Hancock's Last Game   David Kaufman
The Carrot of Doom   Edward DeGeorge
Second Chance   Mike Hodel
Milk Into Brandy   Lil & Kris Neville
Friend in Need [ss]   Paul Collins
The Spotted Horse [v]   Nancy Springer
Look Behind Me   Ray Capella
*Borderland   Arthur J. Burks

May 1982   1/4 (4)   Corey Wolfe
Profit and the Grey Assassin
                        Raymond E. Feist
Meadow Silence   Jessica Amanda Salmonson
Minutes of the Last Meeting of
  the Heroes Club [v]   Jim Neal
Earth Mother, Sky Father
                      Bill & Lois Thomas
The Handsome Prince   Sharon Lee
The Elementals [v]   Chris Weber
Chrysalis   Jean Darling
The Loneliest Unicorn [nt]   R. Bretnor
The Woodcutter's Dream [ss]Andrea Schlecht
Cellini's Pitchfork
                  Mary Elizabeth Counselman
Triage   M. D. Copely
The Lynxidopteron [pic]   Lynn Glasenapp
Telepathetique   Jack Wodhams
*Love in the Year 93 E.E. S. Fowler Wright

86

***

FANTASY CLASSICS

A weird fantasy large-size slick magazine published monthly by Fantasy House, 6045 Vineland Ave., North Hollywood, California. Editor: Ken Krueger. Despite its format, its reliance on reprints has caused some to regard it as an anthology series, but the editor always regarded it as a magazine. Issues were undated, other than by copyright, which was 1973 for the full run. After five issues the series was aborted in favor of printing paperback books, but a spiritual descendant of the magazine later appeared as Unique *[see entry].*

1973   No.1   John Pound
*The Terror [sn]   Arthur Machen
*The Elixir of Life   Richard Garnett
*An Odd Sort of People [ex]
                          Sir John Mandeville

1973   No.2   [John Pound?]
*Werewolf [nt]   Clemence Housman
*The Plant Thing   R. G. Macready
*The Diamond Lens [nt] Fitz-James O'Brien
*The Third Thumb Print   Mortimer Levitan
*The Tortoise-Shell Cat   Greye La Spina

1973   No.3   Gerry Mooney
*The Obsidian Ape [sn] Robert Neal Leath
*True History of the Hare and
  the Tortoise   Lord Dunsany
*Lives of Highwaymen, Pirates
  and Robbers [ex]   Sawney Beane

1973   No.4   John Pound
*Ancient Sorceries [nt]
                          Algernon Blackwood
*The Vanguard of Venus [nt]
                          Landall Bartlett
*A Hand From the Deep   Romeo Poole
*Dialogue of the Dead   Lucian

1973   No.5   John Pound
*The Jewel of the Seven Stars
  [abr.n]   Bram Stoker
*The Case of the Russian
  Stevedore   Henry W. Whitehill
*Lips of the Dead   W. J. Stamper

                    ***

FANTASY CROSSROADS

A small press quarto magazine published quarterly by Stygian Isle Press. Publisher/ Editor: Jonathan Bacon, Lamoni, Iowa until issue 11; Clifford Bird, Huston, Texas, for issue 12; then Jonathan Bacon, now at Shawnee Mission, Kansas. Dedicated to all aspects of fantasy but with special emphasis on the life and work of Robert E. Howard.

November 1974	1/1	Mike Ball

Jack Kirby: Myth Maker [in] Jonathan Bacon
Eisner and The Spirit [in] Jonathan Bacon
Nostalgia [pic]   [old film stills]
Fan Art Portfolio [ap]   [various]
*Recompense [v]   Robert E. Howard
*The Singer in the Mist [v]
                        Robert E. Howard
Conan the Barbarian checklist
    [bib]   Jonathan Bacon
Synopsis [fragment]   Robert E. Howard
*The Song of a Mad Minstrel [v]
                        Robert E. Howard
*Delenda Est   Robert E. Howard

February 1975	1/2	Bob Hanley

*Two Letters to Harold Preece
    [ltrs]   Robert E. Howard
*The Curse of the Golden Skull
                        Robert E. Howard
*The Last Celt [a]   Harold Preece
*Heritage [v]   Robert E. Howard
The Last Celt - an Epilogue [a]
                        Harold Preece
Heritage [v]   Robert E. Howard
*Always Comes Evening [v] Robert E. Howard
*The Poets [v]   Robert E. Howard
Kull the Conqueror checklist
    [bib]   Jonathan Bacon
Kung Who? [cs]   Gary Sassaman
                [art: Mike Hodge]
Mars Reporter [cs]   David Heath, Jr
Trader [cs]   Frank Cirocco
Volsunga Saga [cs1/2]   Coreen Casey
                [art: Ronn Foss]
The Sons of Liberty [cs]   Richard Lynn
Fan Art Portfolio [ap]   [various]
A Conversation with A.J.
    Hanley [in] Mike Hodge & Jonathan Bacon

*Drums of the Sunset   Robert E. Howard

May 1975	1/3	Sam de la Rosa

*Blank   Harlan Ellison
Howard's Women [ap]   [various]
Women and Robert E. Howard [a]
                        Harold Preece
*The Good Knight   Robert E. Howard
*A Letter to Harold Preece
    [ltr]   Robert E. Howard
The Treasures of Ali Akbar Khan
    [a] George T. Hamilton & Wayne Warfield
*The Ghost Kings [v]   Robert E. Howard
Flint's Passing [v]   Robert E. Howard
Richard Lynn [in]   T. L. Trisler
Our World [cs]   David Heath, Jr
Lev's [cs]   David Heath, Jr
The Sons of Liberty [cs]   Richard Lynn
Benji the Barbarian [cs1/2] Brent Anderson

August 1975	1/4-5	Broc Sears

Lovecraft: A Review and a Dirk W. Mosig &
    Response [a1/2]   L. Sprague de Camp
The Hobbit Portfolio [ap]   C. C. Beck
Tolkien and the Elves [a] Ruth Ann Moore
Middle Earth and the Bible
    [a]   David J. Grant
Ten Tuesdays Down a Rabbit
    Hole [a]   Leslie Kay Swigart
*Reaping the Whirlwind [a] Harlan Ellison
*Knox   Harlan Ellison
*Man With the Mystery Mitts
                        Robert E. Howard
War to the Blind [v]   Robert E. Howard
The Abbey [fragment]   Robert E. Howard
The Sending of the Singing
    Bones [long v]   James Coplin
Conan and Other Fantasy
    Swordsmen [ap]   [various]

November 1977   3/12   Clifford W. Bird
Who Make Their Bed in Deep
   Waters [v]   William Hope Hodgson
Genseric's Fifth-Born Son [rr]
   4. The Ice Woman's Prophecy
                          Richard L. Tierney
   5. The Nemedians   Michael Moorcock
   6. Betrayal in Belverus
                        Charles R. Saunders
Of Swords and Sorcery [col] Paul C. Allen
Broken Hills and Diamond
   Valleys [a]   Charles R. Saunders
On an Ancient Shore [v]
                      Tevis Clyde Smith, Jr
The Silver Ape   Clifford W. Bird
The Victor [v]   Clifford W. Bird
The Toad [v]   Clifford W. Bird

June 1978   3/13   [photo]
Leopard Night [v]   Winona Morris Nation
Prayer to Zathog [v]   Richard L. Tierney
What Robert Howard said on
   Wednesday Night [v] Tevis Clyde Smith
Limericks [v]   James Wade
*The Invaders   Henry Kuttner
To a Meteor in a Planetarium
   [v]   Edith Ogutsh
Hexagondra: A Myth in Poetry
   [v]   Ruth M. Eddy
Lunar Fantasy [v]   Lucile Coleman
Ghor, Kin-Slayer [rr, retitle of
   Genseric's Fifth-Born Son]
   7. Lord General of Nemedia
                        Andrew J. Offutt
   8. The Oath of Agha Junghaz
                      Manly Wade Wellman
[Untitled Centerpiece] [v]   James Garver
The Feud [v]   Robert E. Howard
The Ballad of Robbie Adam [v]   Jay Sher
Paganini [v]   Tevis Clyde Smith
The Ghost-Child [v]   Walter Shedlofsky
The Last Passover [v]   Neal Wilgus
Gate of Doom [v]   Bruce D. Griffiths
Of Swords and Sorcery [col] Paul C. Allen

September 1978   3/14   Bok & Fabian
The Curse of Bana-gui [nt]
                     Charles R. Saunders
Miracle in a Bottle [v]   W. Paul Ganley
The Creator Meditates [v] H. Warner Munn
Ghor, Kin-Slayer [rr]
   9. The Mouth of the Earth
                        Darrell Schweitzer
   10. The Gods Defied   A. E. van Vogt
Kenneth Smith: An Appreciation
   [a]   Stephen T. Riley
Portfolio [ap]   Kenneth Smith
Gizzlestines and Goblin Roses
   Previsited [a]   Hannes Bok
Death Lurks in the Seaweed [v] Hannes Bok
Escape [v]   Hannes Bok
Vision [v]   Hannes Bok
Dream [v]   Hannes Bok
The Road 'Cross the Rushes [v]
                        James E. Coplin
The Garden of Old Night
                      Stephen G. Mitchell
*Oh Babylon, Lost Babylon [v]
                      Robert E. Howard
Nightwalkers [v]   C. C. Norton

January 1979   3/15   Stephen E. Fabian
Minas Morgul [v]   Richard L. Tierney
Ghost [v]   Gordon Larkin
Stephen R. Donaldson [in]   Jonathan Bacon
The Ocean of Souls   Adrian Cole
Of Swords and Sorcery [col] Paul C. Allen
Ghor, Kin-Slayer [rr]
   11. Swordsmith and Sorcerer   Brian Lumley
   12. The Gift of Lycanthropy
                      Frank Belknap Long

* * *

FANTASY CROSSWINDS

A small press fantasy magazine publishing by Stygian Island Press, Lamoni, Iowa. Publisher/Editor: Jonathan Bacon. Companion to Fantasy Crossroads, though with a stronger emphasis on verse.

January 1977   No.1   Stephen T. Riley
The Story of the Brown Man
                              Darrell Schweitzer
Flying Fish [v]   L. Sprague de Camp
The Antique Hunters   James A. McKracken
Goodbye Iprezgala [v]   John Hurley
The Outcast [v]   Robert E. Howard
An Arbiter of Destiny Clifford M. Eddy, Jr
The Dead's Doom [v]   John Bredon
Enough Rope?   John Bredon
Wulfdene [v]   Tevis Clyde Smith
Wolf-Meal [v]   John Bredon
Norumbega [v]   Michael Fantina
Limerick [v]   Mark Anspach
The Elephant Tree   Arthur Metzger
Epitaph   James Wade
The Curse of Greed   Robert E. Howard
The Kiowa's Tale [v]   Robert E. Howard
The Beginning [v]   Deborah K. Raney
Ulysses [v]   William A. Conder
Hell's Artist [v]   William A. Conder
Hymn to Apollo [v]   William A. Conder
A Wraith [v]   Michael Fantina
Loch Ness [v]   Thomas M. Egan
Crimson Witch [v]   John Bredon
Lament [v]   Don R. Broyles
The Ballad of Lonny McBride
    [v]   Bruce D. Griffiths
Macabre [v]   William A. Conder
Portfolio [ap]   Gene Day

February 1977   No.2   Jeff Easley
The Book of Belialon   G. Arthur Rahman
The Red Rain [v]   Winona Morris Nation
John Bourbon [v]   Tevis Clyde Smith
*Jennifer's Song [v]   Poul Anderson
He Who Laughs   Joseph W. Hinton
The Witch of Atahualpa [v]
                              Steve Troyanovich
The Veiled Pool of Mistorak
                              Darrell Schweitzer

A-Waiting Till the Air Runs Out
                              Frances Watson
Turlogh's Hymn [v]   Steve Troyanovich
Turlough in New York [v] Steve Troyanovich
Yule [v]   Steve Troyanovich
Seeker of Power, Finder of
    Doom [v]   Don Fioto
Death of a Ghost [v]   Deborah Raney
Door to the Garden   Robert E. Howard
*Monody on the Late King
    Alcohol [v]   H. P. Lovecraft
*Hylas [v]   August Derleth
Some Poetry [v]   Bill Orlikow
Me [v]   Edith Ogutsch
A Tolkien Portfolio [ap]   Tim Foster
Reflected Bale [v]   Michael Fantina
*Hellas [v]   H. P. Lovecraft
The Parade [v]   Edith Ogutsch
Atonement [v]   John Bredon

February 1977   No.3   Jeff Easley
The Horror Out of Time   Leon L. Gammell
Trouble With Tezcatlipoca
    [v]   Tevis Clyde Smith
King Clair's Defeat [v] Deborah K. Raney
Worms of Death [v]   Don R. Broyles
Blue Shadows of the Sahara James E. Coplin
The Dark Road   Muriel Eddy
The Last Horror Out of
    Arkham   Darrell Schweitzer
Roar, Silver Trumpets [v] Robert E. Howard

***

92

FANTASY FICTION

A digest fantasy magazine styled after the confession pulps, published quarterly by Magabook Inc., 420 Lexington Ave., New York. Editor and Publisher: Curtis Mitchell. With second issue changed title to Fantasy Stories.

May 1950   1/1 (1)   Bill Stone
The Voice in the Foxhole
  [ts]   Corp. Waldo McQueen
*She Said "Take Me ... If
  You Dare" [nt]   Theodore Roscoe
*The Strange Loves of Beatrice
  Jervan   Max Brand
*The Flying Eye   Robert Arthur
The President's Daughter   Anton Kermac
*The Benevolent Ghost and
  Captain Lowrie   Richard Sale
The Moose That Talked [ts]   C. A. Dixon
*Speak to Me of Death [nt]
                Cornell Woolrich
Treasure Accursed!   Otis Adelbert Kline

November 1950   1/2 (2)   Bill Stone
Secrets of the Flying Saucers
  Told at Last [a]   Maj. Vernon Piper
*Blood-Brother of the Swamp
  Cats   Irvin S. Cobb
*Her Love Was Jungle Gold Theodore Roscoe
Reach For the Stars   V. E. Thiessen
College of Scientifictional
  Knowledge [quiz] Forrest J. Ackerman
You Must Flee Again   Paul Spencer
*The Vengeful Pearls of Madame
  Podaire   Robert Arthur
*Both Feet in Eternity   Robert W. Sneddon
*Cut Out This Aztec Heart   Brice Purcell

***

FANTASY MACABRE

Although a British small press weird fantasy magazine it is published, in octavo format, in the United States, by Richard Fawcett, 61 Teecomwas Drive, Uncasville, Connecticut. Editor: Dave Reeder.

September 1980   No.1   Dave Carson
Leopard Eyes [v]   Dave Reeder
Goldenhair   Tanith Lee
Corruption   David Sutton
The Mythos Writers: Colin
    Wilson [in]   [Dave Reeder]
A Gent.of Providence   Dave Reeder
The Horror in the Cave   Jeffrey Goddin

April 1981   No.2   Dave Carson
The Mythos Writers: Ramsey
    Campbell [in]   [Dave Reeder]
Allan & Adelaide - an Arabesque
                                    Thomas Ligotti
A Greater Darkness   Richard Fawcett
The David H.Keller Bibliography
    [bib1/2]   Mike Ashley
Portfolio [ap]   Allen Koszowski
Testing the Spirits   Stephen Gresham
Cae Coch   Dave Reeder

June 1982   No.3   Dave Carson
The Ploughing of Pras-a-Ufereth
                                   Peter Tremayne
To Innsmouth / To R'lyeh [2v]
                          David Cowperthwaite
The House Next Door to the House
    on the Borderland [v]   Allen A. Lucas
*Granny's Last Meal   David H. Keller
In the Bayou   Ed Lesko
At the Foot of the Bed [v] Denise Dumars
The David H.Keller Bibliography
    [bib2/2]   Mike Ashley & Paul Spencer
Wishful Thinking   C. Bruce Hunter
Soulhunter   Simon R. Green
Apocalypse [v]   Richard L. Tierney
Red is the Colour of Blood
    and Roses   Joe R. Lansdale
The Festering [v]   Billy Wolfenbarger
Inquest   Michael D. Toman

In the Valley of the Old Gods
    [ss]   Thomas Wiloch
Marianntha [v]   Morgan Griffith
If Only in the Mind   George W. Smyth
Away ... Away [v]   Dave Reeder
If Only   James Piatt

July 1983   No.4   'Emmanuel'
Problem Child   Frank Belknap Long
Death [v]   Janet Fox
Jungle Breath, Jungle Death
                   Robin Ansell & Karen Young
Portfolio [ap]   'Emmanuel'
Come the Eaters Jessica Amanda Salmonson
The Tanith Lee Bibliography
    [bib]   Mike Ashley
The Enchanted Maze [ss]   Thomas Wiloch
Incident in a Graveyard [v]
                        David Cowperthwaite
Water Above Electricity   Herbert Swartz
Cobweb and Clay [v]   Joel Lane
The Kelpie's Mask   Peter Tremayne

***

FANTASY MAGAZINE

A fantasy digest published bi-monthly by Future Publications, 80 Fifth Ave., New York. Editor: Lester del Rey [on all issues, although last pseudonymous credited to 'Cameron Hall']. From the second issue was re-titled Fantasy Fiction Magazine.

Feb/Mar 1953   1/1 (1)   Hannes Bok
The Black Stranger [na] Robert E. Howard &
                                L. Sprague de Camp
Too Gloomy For Private Pushkin
                                Richard Deming
The Demons   Robert Sheckley
Ashtaru the Terrible   Poul Anderson
Feeding Time   Finn O'Donnevan
The Night Shift   Frank Robinson
Dragon Fires [nt]   Steve Frazee

June 1953   1/2 (2)   Hannes Bok
The Wall of Serpents [na]
        L. Sprague de Camp & Fletcher Pratt
The Weeblies   Algis Budrys
Emissary   Charles E. Fritch
Samsi   Peter Coccagna
Rachaela   Poul Anderson
The Cookie Lady   Philip K. Dick
Sylvia   Peter Phillips
More Spinned Against   John Wyndham

August 1953   1/3 (3)   Hannes Bok
"So Sweet as Magic..." [na] Bruce Elliott
Out in the Garden   Philip K. Dick
Much Ado About Plenty   Charles E. Fritch
The Frost Giant's Daughter
        Robert E. Howard & L. Sprague de Camp
A Stray From Cathay   John Wyndham
Koenigshaufen's Curve   H. B. Fyfe
Foxy's Hollow   Leah Bodine Drake
Mr Mottle Goes Pouf   Laurence Manning
The Other Ones   David Alexander
Nom d'un Nom   Randall Garrett

November 1953   1/4 (4)   Hannes Bok
Web of the Worlds [na]
        Katherine MacLean & Harry Harrison
Nothing To It   William S. Corwin
Schizoid Creator   Clark Ashton Smith
Medicine Dancer   Bill Brown
Capital Expenditure [nt]   Fletcher Pratt
De Demon- Natur-   Wesley Barefoot
The Stronger Spell   L. Sprague de Camp
The Apprentice Sorcerer   Stephen Arr

***

FANTASY TALES

British small press fantasy magazine published in digest format by the Editor, Stephen Jones, 130 Park View, Wembley, Middlesex.

Summer 1977   1/1 (1)   Jim Pitts
Naked as a Sword   Kenneth Bulmer
Fog Upon Ynth [v]   Gordon Larkin
*A Madness From the Vaults Ramsey Campbell
Morvenna [v]   John Grandfield
*The Price to Pay   Eddy C. Bertin
Mylakhrion the Immortal   Brian Lumley
*The Stone Thing [spf]   Michael Moorcock
The Dream Shop   Brian Mooney
Milk of Kindness   Steve Sneyd

Winter 1977   1/2 (2)   Jim Pitts
Scars   Adrian Cole
The Hypnocosm   William Thomas Webb
Accident Zone   Ramsey Campbell
*The Last Wolf   Karl Edward Wagner
City Out of Time [gv]   Brian Lumley
                         [art: Graham Manley]
Borden Wood   Sydney J. Bounds
Undead [v]   Brian Mooney
The Feast of Argatha   F. C. Adams

Summer 1978   2/3 (3)   S. E. Fabian
At the End of the Road   Patrick Connolly
A Sonnet for Insanity [v]   Marion Pitman
The Lean Wolves Wait   John Wysocki
Beruthiel [v]   Pat McIntosh
The Last Sleeping God of Mars
                              Andrew Darlington
Fantasy Tales [v]   Brian Lumley
*The Inheritance   Denys Val Baker
The Exhumation   Peter Coleborn

Spring 1979   2/4 (4)   Jim Pitts
First Make them Mad   Adrian Cole
Love Philtre [v]   H. Warner Munn
The Chinese Box   Ken Dickson
Mourning of the Following Day
    [v]   Karl Edward Wagner
Bloodgold   Joe R. Schifino
At Last the Arcana Revealed A. J. Silvonius
Mausoleum [v]   Gordon Larkin

Tomb-Time [v]   Steve Eng

Winter 1979   3/5 (5)   David Lloyd
Extension 201   Cyril Simsa
*The Thing in the Moonlight
            H. P. Lovecraft & Brian Lumley
An Agonising Choice [v]   Gordon Larkin
For the Life Everlasting   Brian Mooney
*Don't Open That Door   Frances Garfield
The Exiles [v]   H. Warner Munn
Just Another Vampire Story Randall Garrett
The Seafarers [v]   Simon Ounsley
Morsel [v]   Steve Eng

Summer 1980   3/6 (6) *Jim FitzPatrick
*Ever the Faith Endures Manly Wade Wellman
The Wind-Walker [v]   Brian Lumley
Lair of the White Wolf   J. R. Schifino
The Blades of Hell [v]   Don Herron
*Dreams May Come   H. Warner Munn
The Elementals   Frances Garfield
The Last Trick   Dave Reeder
*The Story of the Brown Man
                          Darrell Schweitzer
Bone-Yowl [v]   Steve Eng

Spring 1981   4/7 (7)   Jim Pitts
*The Other One   Karl Edward Wagner
The Wedding Guest [v]
                      Steven Edward McDonald
Reflections on a Dark Eye   Peter Tremayne
*Payment in Kind   C. A. Cador
A Death-Song for Gondath [v] Marion Pitman
Wrapped Up   Ramsey Campbell
The Woodcarver's Son   Robert A. Cook
Limbo [v]   H. Warner Munn
*The Last Horror Out of
   Arkham   Darrell Schweitzer
Bleak December   Dave Ward

96

Summer 1981   4/8 (8)   Dave Carson
The Dark Country   Dennis Etchison
A Place of No Return   Hugh B. Cave
The Elevation of Theosophus
    Goatgrime   Brian Mooney
The Legacy   James Glenn
Sic Transit...   Mike Chinn
Shadows From the Past   Mary Clarke
Swamp Call [v]   Brian Lumley
Weirwood   Michael D. Toman

Spring 1982   5/9 (9)   Jim Pitts
Dead Bird Singing in the
    Black of Night   Adam Nichols
The Changeling [v]   H. Warner Munn
The Grey Horde   David Malpass
The Frolic   Thomas Ligotti
In Lieu of Applause   [v]   Steve Eng
The Laughter of Han   Lin Carter
Initiation [v]   George A. McIntyre
The Strange Years   Brian Lumley
October Treat   Phillip C. Heath
Lee Brown Coye   [obit] Karl Edward Wagner

Summer 1982   5/10 (10)   David Lloyd
The Voice of the Beach   Ramsey Campbell
*A Witch For All Seasons
                              Manly Wade Wellman
Death Wish [v]   Charlotte Dean
But the Stones Will Stand...   Mike Chinn
Thatcher's Bluff   James Anderson
The Gardens   Peter G. Shilston
The Motel Room   Scott E. Green

Winter 1982   6/11 (11)   Jim Pitts
*A Sprig of Rosemary   H. Warner Munn
The Storm-Devil of Lan-Kern Peter Tremayne
To Welcome One of Their Own
                               C. Bruce Hunter
Seven Kings [v]   Robert E. Howard
Dead to the World   Allen A. Lucas
At the Mouth of Time   Joe R. Lansdale
The Worm   Joel Lane
Legacy of Evil   Peter Bayliss
A Lady's Retribution [v]   Charlotte Dean
The Story of Lallia the
    Slave Girl   Dray Prescot

Winter 1983   6/12 (12)   David Lloyd
*A Question of Identity   Robert Bloch
*You Can Go Now   Dennis Etchison
The Stones Would Weep   Darrell Schweitzer
The Zulu Lord [v]   Robert E. Howard
The Summer House Party   Peter A. Hough
Ballad [v]   Marise Morland
In the Labyrinth   Simon R. Green
The Green Man   Kelvin Jones
A Rock That Loved Jessica Amanda Salmonson
*Pharaoh's Revenge   C. Bruce Hunter

                        ***

FEAR!

*A digest horror magazine published bi-monthly by Great American Publications,
270 Madison Ave., New York. Editor: Joseph L. Marx.*

May 1960	1/1	?
Deus Ex Machina	Martin Weingarten	
Dust to Dust	Alfred Sneider	
Josephus	Arthur Porges	
The Vandal	Evelyn Goldstein	
The Black Sadhu	Theodore Mathieson	
Nightquake	Pat Rogers	
*The Dream Woman [nt]	Wilkie Collins	
The Rainy Night	Hal Ellson	
Of Hairy Snakes	Pat Remlik	
The Girl Who Was God	Newel Bixby	
Haven For the Damned	Robert Cassiday	
Vortex	William Jukes	
If I Die Before I Wake [v]	Peter Gund	
The Strange Paintings of		
Felix A. Orth	John Jakes	

July 1960	1/2	?
Confession	James Harvey	
Account Closed	David Mason	
The Veiled Woman	Larry Bearson	
The Cage	Bryce Walton	
End With the Night	Donald Honig	
Still Life	Mark Richards	
The Persuader	Irving Schiffer	
The Idol	Joe Mackey	
Bourbon on a Champagne Carpet	Albert Bermel	
*How Love Came to Professor		
Guildea [nt]	Robert Hichens	

***

98

FORGOTTEN FANTASY

A digest fantasy magazine published by Nectar Press, 1521 North Vine St., Holly-
wood, California. Editor: Douglas Menville.

October 1970   1/1   Bill Hughes
*The Goddess of Atvatabar
  [n1/4]   William R. Bradshaw
*The Parasite [nt]   Arthur Conan Doyle
*The Phantom-Wooer [v]
                   Thomas Lovell Beddoes
*The Dead Smile   F. Marion Crawford

December 1970   1/2   George Barr
*When the Gods Slept   Lord Dunsany
*The Shadows on the Wall
                   Mary E. Wilkins Freeman
*The Goddess of Atvatabar
  [n2/4]   William R. Bradshaw
*The Fisherman [v] Matthew Gregory Lewis
*Memnon, or Human Wisdom   Voltaire

February 1971   1/3   Bill Hughes
*The Valley of Spiders   H. G. Wells
*The Birthmark   Nathaniel Hawthorne
*Man-Size in Marble   E. Nesbit
*The Goddess of Atvatabar
  [n3/4]   William R. Bradshaw

April 1971   1/4   Tim Kirk
*The Hollow Land [nt]   William Morris
*The Goddess of Atvatabar
  [n4/4]   William R. Bradshaw

June 1971   1/5   Bill Hughes
*Hartmann the Anarchist [n1/2]
                   E. Douglas Fawcett
*Smith: an Episode in a
  Lodging House   Algernon Blackwood
*The Mer-Mother [v] Richard Le Gallienne
*The Pine Lady [v] Richard Le Gallienne
*A Lost Opportunity   Tudor Jenks

                  ***

FROM BEYOND THE DARK GATEWAY

A small press weird fantasy magazine published by Silver Scarab Press, 500 Wellesley S.E., Albuquerque, New Mexico. Editor: Edward P. Berglund. The fiction-based companion to Nyctalops *it concetrates on publishing mostly stories within the Cthulhu Mythos inspired by H. P. Lovecraft.*

April/May 1972   1/1   Steve Riley
The Rynlaerth Megaliths   John Jacob
The Outpost   John J. Koblas
From the Sea   Walter C. DeBill, Jr
*The Trail of *The Necronomicon*
                               Gordon Matthews
The Song of Rhin   Graham Pryor
*The Dark Stairway
             E. P. Berglund & R. E. Weinberg
A Sense of Movement   David Riley

December 1972   1/2   Oscar Crand
Quest of *The Necronomicon*   J. J. Koblas
Our Flesh and Blood is Grown
   so Vile   William Scott Home
The Dream   Richard L. Tierney
The Summons of Hastur   Alan G. Gullette
The Recital   J. J. Koblas
The Lure of Leng   Walter C. DeBill, Jr
The Events at Poroth Farm [na]
                                 T. E. D. Klein

April 1974   1/3   Steve Riley
The Crier in the Vault   Ted Pons
The Bells   Graham Pryor
*Mushroom   John Jacob
Poison Pen   George Wetzel
From Beyond the Dark Gateway
                           Warren Scott Miller
The History of the Great Race   'Drs' Eric
       von Konnenberg & Pierre de Hammais
The Case of Charles Dexter
   Weird [spf]   J. J. Koblas
The New Subscriber   Douglas Roome
A Special Purpose   Darrell Schweitzer
Translations From the Book of Yng:
   I: The Debt of the Summoner
  II: The Punishment of Igharta
 III: The Fleece of Yaggar   F. C. Adams
Magus Imperitus [v]   L. Sprague de Camp

The First Circle [v]   M. K. Sheffield
Perilous Legacy   Walter C. DeBill, Jr
The Disciples of Cthulhu, I
   [a]   Walter C. DeBill, Jr
The Black Bear Bites   Robert E. Howard

October 1977   1/4   A. B. Cox
The Horror in the Blue Glass
   Bottle   Ross F. Bagby
Translations From the Book of Yng:
   The Temple of Bones
   The Son of Nisharga   Fred C. Adams
*The Face in the Desert   Ramsey Campbell
*Reflections on 'The Face
   in the Desert' [a]   Ramsey Campbell
That Dark Gateway [v] George C. Diezel II
The God-Stone   George S. Howard
The Disciples of Cthulhu II
   [a]   Alan D. Gullette
The Apprentice Avenger   Douglas Roome
Candles Burning Blue   Llewellyn M. Cabos
The Temple in the Swamp   Stephen Cross
The Adventure of Gosnell   George Wetzel
The Circular Pathway   Darrell Schweitzer
Colour Poems   John McLoughlin
Hungering After Green Fire
                          William Scott Home
*The Sorcerer's Jewel   Robert Bloch

                        ***

100

G

GAMMA

A fantasy and sf digest published irregularly by Star Press Inc., 10523 Burbank Blvd., North Hollywood, California. Editors: Charles E. Fritch & Jack Matcha, along with William F. Nolan for the first three issues. Bore the sub-title 'New Frontiers in Fiction' and tried to cover all aspects of fantasy and sf without being genre-ised.

[Summer] 1963   1/1 (1)   M. S. Dollens
Mourning Song   Charles Beaumont
Crimes Against Passion [play] Fritz Leiber
*Time in thy Flight   Ray Bradbury
*The Vengeance of Nitocris
          Tennessee Williams
Itself!   A. E.van Vogt
Venus Plus Three   Charles E. Fritch
A Message from Morj   Ray Russell
To Serve the Ship   William F. Nolan
The Gamma Interview:
   Rod Serling [in] [William F. Nolan]
The Freeway   George Clayton Johnson
One Night Stand   Herbert A. Simmons
*As Holy and Enchanted   Kris Neville
Shade of Day   John Tomerlin
*The Girl Who Wasn't There
          Forrest J. Ackerman
*Death in Mexico [v]   Ray Bradbury
Crescendo   Richard Matheson

[Winter] 1963   1/2 (2)   M. S. Dollens
The Granny Woman   Dorothy B. Hughes
The Old College Try   Robert Bloch
Michael   Francesca Marques
Deus Ex Machina   Richard Matheson
*The Kid Learns   William Faulkner
King's Jester   Jack Matcha
Here's Sport Indeed [spf/v]
     William Shakespeare & Ib Melchior
Portfolio [ap]   Burt Shonberg
*The Undiscovered Country
          William F. Temple
The Gamma Interview:
   Robert Sheckley [in] [William F. Nolan]
Castaway   Charles E. Fritch
Something in the Earth Charles Beaumont
I'm Only Lonesome When I'm
   Lonely   William F. Nolan
Sombra y Sol   Ray Bradbury

[Summer] 1964   2/1 (3)   M. S. Dollens
The Girl of Paradise Planet
   [nt]   Robert Turner
The Feather Bed   Shelly Lowenkopf
*Angel Levine   Bernard Malamud
The (In)visible Man   Edward W. Ludwig
Inside Story   Miriam Allen de Ford
The Birth   George Clayton Johnson
Soviet Science Fiction [in]   Ivan Kirov
Buttons   Raymond E. Banks
Society For the Prevention   Ron Goulart
The Snail Watcher   Patricia Highsmith

February 1965   2/2 (4)   John Healey
The Clutches of Ruin [nt]   H. B. Fyfe
The Towers of Kagasi William P. Miller
Food   Ray Nelson
Hans Off in Free Pfall to the
   Moon [spf]   E. A. Poe
Forrest J Ackerman [in] [William F. Nolan]
Open Season   John Tanner
The Woman Astronaut [play] Robert Katz
Happily Ever After   William F. Nolan
Don't Touch Me, I'm Sensitive James Stamers
The Hand of Dr Insidious   Ron Goulart

September 1965   2/5 (5)   John Healey
Nesbit [na]   Ron Goulart
Policy Conference Sylvia Dees & Ted White
Auto Suggestion   Charles Beaumont
Welcome to Procyon IV Chester H. Carlfi
Interest   Richard Matheson
Lullaby and Goodnight
        George Clayton Johnson
*A Careful Man Dies   Ray Bradbury
The Late Mr Adams   Steve Allen
Wet Season   Dennis Etchison

***

GHOST STORIES

A fantasy pulp devoted entirely to ghost stories and styled after the confession magazines. Published monthly by Constructive Publishing, Macfadden Building, Broadway, New York until March 1930; thereafter Good Story Magazine Co., New York. The Editorial responsibility is complicated [moreso since the editors did not write the editorials] but ran approximately Harry A. Keller 1926/27; W. Adolphe Roberts 1928; George Bond 1929; D. E. Wheeler and Arthur B. Howland 1929/30 then, from April 1930 Harold Hersey. Was originally in large format on quality stock until July 1928 then turned pulp, with a brief transition to large pulp between April and December 1929. Two subsequent reprint magazines that relied totally on Ghost Stories *were* Prize Ghost Stories *and* True Twilight Tales *(see entries). For the first two years the covers featured posed photographs.*

July 1926   1/1 (1)
In Touch With the Unknown [ed]
                    George William Wilder
The Phantom of the Fifteenth
   Floor [n1/6]   Fulton Oursler
The Coming of Roger Crane   Al Clifton
In the Shadow of Voodoo   Eugene A. Clancy
He Fell in Love With a
   Ghost   Arnold Fountain
Superman or Clever Trickster
   - Which? [a]   Samri Frikell
The Girl Who Lived With the
   Dead [sn1/4]   Grant Hubbard
*The Transferred Ghost   Frank R. Stockton
Back From Beyond   Hubert V. Coryell
Chained to a Bed of Roses   Jack Bechdolt
The Curse of the House of
   Gables   Edwin A. Goewey
The White Seal of Avalak Walter W. Liggett
Hands in the Dark [ts] Ann Irvine Norment
Convicted By a Silent Witness Emil Raymond

August 1926   1/2 (2)
Are You Haunted By a Shadow?
   [ed]   George William Wilder
The Return of Paul Genstare Gilbert Patten
The Mystery of the Pilotless
   Plane   Eugene A. Clancy
The Ha'nts of Amelia Island
                        T. Howard Kelly
The Phantom of the Fifteenth
   Floor [n2/6]   Fulton Oursler
Hidden in Hollow Men   Emil Raymond

Told by a Talking Table W. Adolphe Roberts
The Man Who Killed a Ghost Edwin A. Goewey
In the Grip of Edgar the Great
                Anita Fitzgerald & Mark Mellen
*The Open Door   Mrs. Margaret Oliphant
Out of a Haunted Camera   Jack Bechdolt
The Girl Who Lived With the
   Dead [sn2/4]   Grant Hubbard
The Voice That Came Through
   the Night   Walter W. Liggett

September 1926   1/3 (3)
Can Science Prove Immortality?
   [ed]   George William Wilder
Into the Valley of Whispering
   Shadows   J. H. Conner
In the Focus of 10,000 Eyes
                        Sylvette De Lamar
The Avenging Haunt From
   Cherokee Lagoon   R. P. Guiler, Jr
Jim Meade's 50,000 Dollar
   Ghost   Eugene A. Clancy
Guided By a Spirit Hand   T. Howard Kelly
But - He Couldn't Kill Her
   Ghost!   Allan Van Hoesen
The Mystery of the Floating
   Head   Johnston Kerkoff
*What Was It?   Fitz-James O'Brien
The Phantom of the Fifteenth
   Floor [n3/6]   Fulton Oursler
The Flaming Specter of Long
   Ridge   Emil Raymond
The Ghost of Flying Nell W. Adolphe Roberts

Under the Spell of the Red
  Circle [sn3/4]   Wilbert Wadleigh
In the Clutches of the
  Black Idol   Vera Darrell
Spirit Tales [col]   Count Cagliostro
Were You Born in January? [col]   'Stella'
How My Baby Came Back From the
  Dead [ts]   Carol Lansing

March 1927   2/3 (9)
What is a 'Soul'? [ed]
                    George William Wilder
The Revelations of an Executioner
  [na1/3]   'John Huberston'
The Mystery of the Clergyman's
  Daughter   James Craig Gordon
The House of Captive Spirits
                    W. Adolphe Roberts
Werewolf   Cassie H. MacLaury
The Voice in the Picture Frame
                    Evelyn Wainwright
My Glimpse into the Unknown [a]
                    Virginia Pearson
John Shard Comes Back   Leonard Hess
Marble Fingers   Kenneth C. Waggoner
The Crystal Gazer   Carol Lansing
Pawn of the Unseen [n6/7]   Lyon Mearson
The Ghost of the Red Cavalier
                    Victor Rousseau
Under the Spell of the Red
  Circle [sn4/4]   Wilbert Wadleigh
"Living or Dead, I'm Your
  Wife"   Mark Mellen
The Phantom Ace [na2/2]   Edwin A. Goewey
"We're Dead, Mates, We're Dead!"
                    Holland Cox
The Woman and the Apparition   Pearl Floyd
Spirit Tales [col]   Count Cagliostro
Were You Born in February? [col]   'Stella'

April 1927   2/4 (10)
What Does Magic Mean to You?
  [ed]   George William Wilder
The Flaming Specter of
  Briarwood [n1/4]   Llewellyn Bronson
The Mystery of the Buried
  Abbey [a]   Samri Frikell
"A Little Child Shall Lead - "
                    Att. Samuel Raines
The Silver Moth   C. H. MacL.
On the Isle of Blue Men   Robert W. Sneddon
*The Red Room   H. G. Wells
He Tried to Forge a Ghost   Philip Ashe
Talking Glass   John Miller Gregory
The Revelations of an Executioner
  [na2/3]   'John Huberston'
The Phantom of the Seven Seas
                    W. Adolphe Roberts
"How Can I Marry a Ghost?"
                    Harold S. Corbin
The Street of Laughing Ghosts   Arthur Lake
Pawn of the Unseen [n7/7]   Lyon Mearson
"He Murdered Me - He Murdered
  Me!"   Frank Hampton Fox
Spirit Tales [col]   Count Cagliostro
Specter of the Night [ts]   L. R. E.
Were You Born in March? [col]   'Stella'

May 1927   2/5 (11)
Can You Take it Seriously? [ed]
                    George William Wilder

The Soul Destroyers [sn1/4]
                    Wilbert Wadleigh
The Phantom Mother   Mark Mellen
On a Haunted Piano   Mary Eugene Pritchard
The Man Who Lived Backwards
                    John H. Shuttleworth
The Mystery of the Vanished
  Bride   Julia Tate Shearon
He Refused to Stay Dead   Nictzin Dyalhis
My Seance with Margery the
  Medium [a]   Col. Norman G. Thwaites
The Flaming Specter of
  Briarwood [n2/4]   Llewellyn Bronson
"Ouija Never Lies"   Anne Irvine Norment
He Told Me He'd Married a
  Ghost!   Victor Rousseau
When the Dumb Speak   Harold Standish Corbin
The Revelations of an Executioner
  [na3/3]   'John Huberston'
"Go Find My Kidnapped Son!"   Carol Lansing
The Haunted Dagger   Blanche Goodman
Spirit Tales [col]   Count Cagliostro
In Flanders Fields [ts]   W. J. McG
Were You Born in April? [col]   'Stella'

June 1927   2/6 (12)
Are You Shackled to a Phantom
  [ed]   George William Wilder
The Specter in Red   Ethel Watts Mumford
Body and Soul [nt1/2]   Lyon Mearson
Who Am I?   Lilith Shell
Whispering Fingers   Clettis Dunn
Paid By a Ghost   Florence E. Hubbard
*The Plattner Story   H. G. Wells
How Can This Man Romano do
  Such Things? [a]   Samri Frikell
The Tale of the Golden Ghost
                    William J. Maddox
Phantom Jazz   W. Adolphe Roberts
The Soul Destroyers [sn2/4]
                    Wilbert Wadleigh
Hands Against the Sky   Tom Ogilvie
Fire - Water - and What?   Victor Rousseau
The Ghost Who Wore Handcuffs
                    Edwin A. Goewey
The Flaming Specter of
  Briarwood [n3/4]   Llewellyn Bronson
The Headless Bride   Rosa Zagnoni
The Haunted Room [ts]   Dr H. Carrington
Were You Born in May? [col]   'Stella'

July 1927   3/1 (13)
Remember the Ghost of Jim Jones!
  [ed]   George William Wilder
The Mind Reader [n1/7] W. Adolphe Roberts
The Ghost Who Reformed   A. R. Browne
"Did I Commit a Murder?"   Harvey S. Cotrell
The Phantom in the Wooden Well
                    Victor Rousseau
The Haunted Necklace
                    Harold Standish Corbin
The Phone Call From the Dead
                    Wayne Drummond
The Soul Destroyers [sn3/4]
                    Wilbert Wadleigh
"Who's Afraid of a Ghost?" Edwin A. Goewey
The Flaming Specter of
  Briarwood [n4/4]   Llewellyn Bronson
The Friendly Ghost   A. M. Church
The Night of a Thousand Eyes
  Charles A. Freeman & George Warburton Lewis

My Adventure in a Haunted Room Dick Quince
Body and Soul [nt2/2]   Lyon Mearson
Spirit Tales [col]   Count Cagliostro
The Phantom Head [ts]
                    Dr Hereward Carrington
Were You Born in June? [col]   'Stella'

August 1927   3/2 (14)
This World - and the Next [ed]
                    George William Wilder
The Curse of the One-Eyed
   Buddha [n1/5]   Lyon Mearson
Port of Dreams   Archie Binns
He Tried to Burn a Ghost   Carol Lansing
Between Two Worlds Harold Standish Corbin
The Riddle of the Floating Arm
                    Dr F. S. O'Hara
The Woman Two Hundred Years Old
                    Gwendolyn White
*The Story of the Late Mr Elvesham
                    H. G. Wells
The Legend of Newbury Castle
                Col.Norman G. Thwaites
The Soul That Lost its Way Victor Rousseau
The Mind Reader [n2/7] W. Adolphe Roberts
Told By a Clergyman [ts]   H. Blose, D.D.
Phantom Drums   Edwin A. Goewey
The Soul Destroyers [sn4/4]
                    Wilbert Wadleigh
The Dead Who Know No Peace
                    A. Hughes Neuport
Spirit Tales [col]   Count Cagliostro
Were You Born in July? [col]   'Stella'

September 1927   3/3 (15)
The Romance of the 'Supernatural'
                    Robert Napier
My Week-End With the Other
   World   Wilbert Wadleigh
Captive Souls [nt1/2] Cassie H. MacLaury
The Ghost Light   C. B. Bigelow
The Haunted Print Shop   Harold S. Corbin
Through the Wall   Arthur T. Jolliffe
The Curse of the One-Eyed
   Buddha [n2/5]   Lyon Mearson
The White Leopard   Julia Tate Shearon
The Phantom of the Big Top
                    Robert W. Spurge
The Mind Reader [n3/7] W. Adolphe Roberts
The House of the Dancing
   Mirrors   Carl Easton Williams
Written in Sand   Edwin A. Goewey
Secrets of a Mysterious Woman
   [a]   Samri Frikell
Dr Blenheim Operates   Paul Hall
Spirit Hands Gilbert Patten & Den O'Brien
My Ghostly Burglar Alarm [ts]
                    Antonie H. Luepke
Spirit Tales [col]   Count Cagliostro
Were You Born in August? [col]   'Stella'

October 1927   3/4 (16)
Spirits, or Mind Reading -
   Which? [ed]   Robert Napier
The Curse That Crossed the World
                    Guy Fowler
The Tiger Woman of the Punjab
   [nt1/2]   Allan Van Hoesen
Spirit Fingers   John Miller Gregory
Arms in the Dark   Emil Raymond

The Specter Cuts the Ace   Edwin A. Goewey
*A Moth - Genus Unknown   H. G. Wells
The Phantom Torturer Harold Standish Corbin
Captive Souls [nt2/2] Cassie H. MacLaury
The Curse of the One-Eyed
   Buddha [n3/5]   Lyon Mearson
"Only By Mortal Hands"
                    Henry W. A. Fairfield
The Mind Reader [n4/7] W. Adolphe Roberts
Conan Doyle's Museum of
   Psychic Wonders [a]   Leonard Crocombe
Out of the Split Wall   Eleanor Carroll
Because Their Bones Were
   Unburied [ts]   Rosalie Evans
The House of Fear   Maybel Sherman
Spirit Tales [col]   Count Cagliostro
Were You Born in September? [col] 'Stella'
On the Frontier of the
   Unseen [ts]   Wilbert Wadleigh

November 1927   3/5 (17)
The Luck of Being Mediumistic
   [ed]   Robert Napier
The Dog With Man's Eyes Lawrence G. Bailey
How I Foretold the Fates of
   Great Men [a1/4]   'Cheiro'
A Spirit Danced For Me Ella Blanche Kelly
The Phantom Pilot   Guy Fowler
The Spirit in the Violin
                    Harold Standish Corbin
The Tiger Woman of the Punjab
   [nt2/2]   Allan Van Hoesen
Yellow Man's Magic   Norton L. James
The Mind Reader [n5/7] W. Adolphe Roberts
My Wreath of Death   Rev. Cowley Cowles
The Curse of the One-Eyed
   Buddha [n4/5]   Lyon Mearson
Sardonic Laughter   Harvey S. Cottrell
Burglars Bewitched   'Ramsey Red'
The Mystery of the Colwell
   House [ts]   Hereward Carrington
The Man Who Died Twice
                    Alice Whitson-Norton
Spirit Tales [col]   Count Cagliostro
Were You Born in October? [col] 'Stella'
The Ghost of the Ball Park
   [ts]   Leroy R. Eisenhower

December 1927   3/6 (18)   Delos Palmer
Now, Let us Discuss Magic
   [ed]   Robert Napier
The House of the Living
   Dead [n1/6]   Victor Rousseau
Invisible Knock-Outs   W. J. Rapp
The Picture That Came to Life
                    Eustache Rops
The Ghost Tiger   Guy Fowler
A Witness From the Bottom of
   the Lake   Edwin A. Goewey
Phantom Perfumes   Ethel Watts Mumford
Vengeance House   Mrs P. G. Wiggins
How I Foretold the Fates of
   Great Men [a2/4]   'Cheiro'
A Haunted Half-Dollar   Paul R. Milton
How I Got Back My Soul
                    Katherine Metcalf Roof
Has Iceland Proved That
   Ghosts Exist? [a]   Samri Frikell
The Mind Reader [n6/7] W. Adolphe Roberts
Signed By a Ghost William Edmund Fillery

The Ghost Car   Ken Batten
When the Red Gods Call [n6/6]
                            Edwin A. Goewey
Were You Born in September? [col]
                                Stella King
Do Animals Come Back? [ed]   Robert Napier
Spirit Tales [col]   Count Cagliostro
Skeletons in the Closets of Famous
    Families VI [a]   Gordon Hillman

November 1928   5/5 (29)   Doris Stanley
The Haunted Harem   Stuart Palmer
Did This Man Have Two Bodies? A. L. Shands
The Ghost of the Sideshow
    [n1/5]   Lyon Mearson
The Strange Wedding at Barlow's
    Dam   Harold Standish Corbin
What Was in the Seaman's Chest?
                            Maria Moravsky
The Sign on the Chinese Rug
    [ts]   Margaret Jackson
Crooked Ghosts   Edwin A. Goewey
The Man in Red   Nell Kay
Pieces of Eight [n6/6] Wilbert Wadleigh
The Copper King Strikes [ts] Allen Schultz
A Medium's Memoirs [a2/6]   Horace Leaf
My Pact With the Beyond   Pauline de Silva
The Prisoner of Life [n4/6]
                            Victor Rousseau
Skeletons in the Closets of
    Famous Families VII [a] Gordon Hillman
Spirits That are Not Ghosts
    [ed]   Robert Napier
Spirit Tales [col]   Count Cagliostro
Were You Born in October? [col] Stella King

December 1928   5/6 (30)   Doris Stanley
My $250,000 Ghost   James Bourgoyne
The Phantom Corporal   Capn. Nevil Gow
The Spider [n1/8]   Grace Oursler
A Strange Experiment With a
    Mad Woman   Doris B. Grigsby
The Flying Fury   Leon N. Hatfield
Haunted River   Alan Schultz
The Prisoner of Life [n5/6]
                            Victor Rousseau
Is the White House Haunted?
    [a]   Uthai Vincent Wilcox
The Ghost of the Sideshow
    [n2/5]   Lyon Mearson
Seven Gray Wolves   Stuart Palmer
The Beloved Specter
            Dr C. Avelasquez de Hindesone
The Thing on the Roof   Margaret Jackson
A Medium's Memoirs [a3/6]   Horace Leaf
The Stolen Crucifix   Eric P. Warndof
She Spent $15,000,000 on
    Ghosts! [ed]   Robert Napier
Skeletons in the Closets of
    Famous Families VIII [a] Gordon Hillman
Spirit Tales [col]   Count Cagliostro
Were You Born in November? [col]
                                Stella King

January 1929   6/1 (31)   ?
The Thing in the Theater   Mark Shadow
The House That Ghosts Built Robert Ainslee
Phantom Lovers [n1/5]   Grant Hubbard
The Leopard Woman   Edith Ross
Conscripted by the Dead [a] Capn. Neil Gow

My Yuletide Phantom   Edwin A. Goewey
The Ghost of the Sideshow
    [n3/5]   Lyon Mearson
At the Threshold of the
    Invisible [a] George Sylvester Viereck
Four Skeptics and the Prowler
                        William Jordan Rapp
How a Woman Saved a Ghost[ed]Robert Napier
The Spider [n2/8]   Grace Oursler
Haunted Gold   Ken Batten
A Medium's Memoirs [a4/6]   Horace Leaf
The Prisoner of Life [n6/6]
                            Victor Rousseau
Skeletons in the Closets of
    Famous Families IX [a] Gordon Hillman
Spirit Tales [col]   Count Cagliostro
Were You Born in December? [col]
                                Stella King

February 1929   6/2 (32)   ?
The Invisible Tenant [ts]
                        Lowell Ames Norris
My Bewitched Lover   Ken Batten
The Specter of the Night Club
                            Edwin A. Goewey
The Red Curse of the Mummy
                        Theodore Orchards
Suicide or - What? [a] Mrs Mary MacGuckin
The Spider [n3/8]   Grace Oursler
Mark Twain's Astounding Vision
    [a]   [no credit]
Burning Eyes   Terrell McKay
The Mystery of the Floating
    Knife   Harold Standish Corbin
The Creature That Rose From
    the Seas   Muriel Hunt
Phantom Lovers [n2/5]   Grant Hubbard
Stolen by Spirits   Gordon Hillman
The Kiss in the Dark   Rose Byron
The Ghost of the Sideshow
    [n4/5]   Lyon Mearson
The Evil History of a
    Cupboard [ed]   Robert Napier
Spirit Tales [col]   Count Cagliostro
Were You Born in February? [col]
                                Stella King

March 1929   6/3 (33)   ?
The Specter of the Mad King [a]
                        Lee Lester Leigh
Postponed by Spirits [ts]   [no credit]
My Weird Defender   Edward E. Schiff
The Puppet That Came to Life
                        Maurice Max Stern, Jr
The Strange Trial of the
    Schoolmaster's Wife [a]   [no credit]
Magic Cymbals   Alan Hynd
*The Roll-Call of the Reef
                    Sir Arthur Quiller-Couch
The Spider [n4/8]   Grace Oursler
Partners With the Beyond [a] Stuart Palmer
Phantom Lovers [n3/5]   Grant Hubbard
The Resurrected Hand   Walter E. Jamison
Skeletons in the Closets of
    Famous Families X [a]   Gordon Hillman
Old Jim's Last Broadcast
                    Harold Standish Corbin
The Mark on the Seaman's Throat
                        Rev. Arthur Ford
The Ghost of the Sideshow
    [n5/5]   Lyon Mearson

Spirit Tales [col]   Count Cagliostro
The Mystery of the British
    Ace [ed]   Robert Napier
Were You Born in March? [col] Stella King

April 1929   6/4 (34)   ?
Coins of Doom   Urann Thayer
My Daughter Who Never Existed
                    John Miller Gregory
Did the Ghost of Bismarck
    warn the Kaiser?   Albert E. Gallin
The Apparition in the Prize
    Ring   John Taverel
The Strangest Murder Trial 'A Court Bailiff'
She Walks in Beauty   Anatole Feldman
When the Yankee Ace Came Back
                    Lieut. 'Pinky' Martin
The Spider [n5/8]   Grace Oursler
The Face in the Fog [ts] Tito Schipa
A Medium's Memoirs [a5/6] Horace Leaf
The House I Haunted   Helen Brooks
The Witch in the Next Room
    [a]   Walter Gibson
Skeletons in the Closets of
    Famous Families XI [a] Gordon Hillman
A Bad Half Hour   Walter Adolphe Roberts
Phantom Lovers [n4/5]   Grant Hubbard
Phantom Fingerprints [ed] Robert Napier
Taking Tea With a Spirit
    [ts]   Marie McGraw Robinson
Were You Born in April? [col] Stella King
The Spectral Ship [ts] J. Christy MacManus
Spirit Tales [col]   Count Cagliostro
Was This Impossible [a]   Gilbert Draper
The Ghost of the Clergyman's
    Wife [ts]   Noble Forrest
The Bride and the Open Grave
    [ts]   Dr. Robert H. Chilton
A Quaker Lady's Strange
    Experience [ts]   Dr. A. J. Fawcett

May 1929   6/5 (35)   ?
Haunted Hollywood [sn1/5] Wilbert Wadleigh
Unseen Eyes   Evelyn Bentley
Did Captain Hinchcliffe Return
    to His Wife? [a]   Emilie Hinchcliffe
Murder After the Dance [ts] Stuart Palmer
The Headless Chinaman   Frederick Swain
*The Signal-Man   Charles Dickens
My Invisible Courtship   John MacAdams
Dark and Nameless   E. F. Benson
Ghosts I Have Loved [a]
            Virginia Terhune van de Water
The Spider [n6/8]   Grace Oursler
My Five Minutes in Another
    World [ts]   Grace Phelps
What Was in the Submarine?
                    Comdt. Blaise Ryan
A Magician's Strange Revenge
                    Russell Allen Hoke
Bucking the Stock Market With
    Supernatural Aid [ts] Samuel C. Appleby
Spirits in the Laboratory [a]
            George Sylvester Viereck
Phantom Lovers [n5/5]   Grant Hubbard
Silent Watchers at the Ford
                    Alvin F. Harlow
A Medium's Memoirs [a6/6] Horace Leaf
Guarded by Phantoms [ed] Robert Napier
Were You Born in May? [col] Stella King
Spirit Tales [col]   Count Cagliostro

June 1929   6/6 (36)   ?
My Friend in the Next World
                    John C. Fletcher
The Thing That Paid the Rent
    [ts]   Arthur Samuel Howe
The Chateau of Laughing
    Phantoms   George A. Scott
*The Hand   Theodore Dreiser
Jealous Ghost   Dorothy Venner
How a Spirit Corrected the
    Standard Dictionary [ts] Stuart Palmer
The Invisible Man at the Helm Win Brooks
The Wraith in the Picture
    [ts]   William H. Crawford
A Crystal Gazer's Crime   Paul Ernst
*The Ghost of Doctor Harris
    [ts]   Nathaniel Hawthorne
Can the Dead Help the Living [a]
                    Samri Frikell
Haunted Hollywood [sn2/5] Wilbert Wadleigh
The Mystery of the Spirit
    Painters   Arnold Fountain
The Room of Yellow Shadows William Stevens
Marked With a Curse 300 Years
    Old   Rita Martinez
The Spider [n7/8]   Grace Oursler
Dictated by Spirits [ed] Robert Napier
Were You Born in June? [col] Stella King
Spirit Tales [col]   Count Cagliostro

July 1929   7/1 (37)   ?
The Angel of the Marne Capt. Albert Sewell
A Phantom Battles For Her
    Child   Barbara Kenworthy
The Man With the Sabre Cut
    [sn1/4]   Alan Schultz
*The Specter That Asked For
    a Kiss   Algernon Blackwood
A Reckoning With the Dead A. M. Thompson
Garden of Enchantment   Archie Binns
The Bewitched Coffee Pot [ts]
                    Gordon Hillman
A Ghost Who Dictates Novels
    [ts]   John L. Spivak
Haunted Hollywood [sn3/5] Wilbert Wadleigh
*The Mysterious Sketch   Erckman-Chatrian
Ghosts of the Living [ts] Howard Thurston
One Flash into the Future Ross A. Bancroft
The Spider [n8/8]   Grace Oursler
The Clue of the Vanished
    Bride   Lowell Ames Norris
Spirit Tales [col]   Count Cagliostro
Who Believes in Ghosts? [ed] Robert Napier
Were You Born in July? [col] Stella King
The Phantom of the Bonnet
    Woman [ts]   Mrs Elizabeth Longnecker

August 1929   7/2 (38)   ?
My Phantom Pal   Nick Sanford
The Woman at Seven Brothers
                    Wilbur Daniel Steele
Kidnapped by a Wraith   Gilbert Draper
The Specter in the New Hotel
    [ts]   Stuart Palmer
Vengeance of the Dead   Hugh Wallace
My Strange Adventure With a
    Vampire   W. Adolphe Roberts
*The Inexperienced Ghost H. G. Wells
A Cloud of Witnesses   Francis Gilbert
Haunted Hollywood [sn4/5] Wilbert Wadleigh
David Keeps His Word   Thelma Johnson

Were You Born in January?
  [col]   Stella King
Spirit Tales [col]   Count Cagliostro

February 1930   8/2 (44)   ?
Stronger Than Death [sn1/4]
                      Wilbert Wadleigh
Ghost in the Lightning   Joseph M. Brown
Twice Born   Bessie J. Certo
The Radio Mind [a2/2]   Upton Sinclair
"My Favorite Ghost Story": S. L. Rothafel
  2.*Inn of the Two Witches Joseph Conrad
I Have Been a Specter [ts]
                      Sylvan J. Muldoon
*The Mask   Robert W. Chambers
Life Secrets of a Spirit
  Medium [a3/4]   [no credit]
Phantom Dancer of Times Square
  [a]   Stuart Palmer
*Between the Minute and the
  Hour   A. M. Burrage
My Experiences Among the
  Voodoos [a]   Mary Willis Shuey
The Violated Shrine   Robert D. Rudolph
Did They Live Before? [ed]   Robert Napier
Spirit Tales [col]   Count Cagliostro
Were You Born in February?
  [col]   Stella King

March 1930   8/3 (45)   ?
The Specter in the Bronx   O'Connor Stacy
*The Screaming Skull [nt1/2]
                      F. Marion Crawford
"My Favorite Ghost Story": Fulton Oursler
  3.*The Shadowy Third   Ellen Glasgow
*Houdini's Last Escape [a]
                  Sir Arthur Conan Doyle
When the Devil Played the Market
                      Conrad Talbot
Told By a Mute   J. F. Houghton
Stronger Than Death [sn2/4]
                      Wilbert Wadleigh
Radio Ghost   Ben Conlon
Veiled Phantoms   Capt. R. Du Chaliou
Whose Was the Hand? [a]
                  Hereward Carrington
*The Eighth Lamp   Roy Vickers
The Fatal Mummy Case [ts]   'Cheiro'
When the Voices Told Us What
  to Do [ts]   Mrs A. P. Hammerbacher
Life Secrets of a Spirit
  Medium [a4/4]   [no credit]
Were You Born in March? [col] Stella King
Spirit Tales [col]   Count Cagliostro
Electrically Controlled
  Seances [ed]   Robert Napier

April 1930   8/4 (46) Dalton Stevens
Flight of the Silver Star   H. B. H. Fortune
The House of the Sinister
  Shadows [sn1/4]   Samri Frikell
Between Two Worlds [ts]   Stuart Palmer
The Room Behind Walls   W. R. Davis
Paul Vargas - A Mystery   Hugh Conway
The Secret of Sagan [a]   Heinrich Torgau
What Men Call Miracles [a] Peter M. Wise
Shelley - The Living Ghost [a]
                      Stanley Horton
The Mystery Express   Capt. Neil Gow
Stronger Than Death [sn3/4]
                      Wilbert Wadleigh

Wraiths of Port Arthur Prison [a]
                      Horace Leaf
Were You Born in April? [col] Stella King
*The Yellow Curtains   A. M. Burrage
*The Screaming Skull [nt2/2]
                      F. Marion Crawford
The Famous 'Newspaper Tests'
  [ed]   Robert Napier
Spirit Tales [col]   Count Cagliostro

May 1930   8/5 (47) Dalton Stevens
San Francisco's Mystery Manse   Nell Kay
Who Played the Fourth Act? Edwin A. Goewey
Master of Darkness [sn1/4]
                      Arthur T. Jolliffe
Can These Things Be? [a]
                  Hereward Carrington
*The Flint Knife   E. F. Benson
The House of Sinister Shadows
  [sn2/4]   Samri Frikell
"My Favorite Ghost Story": Howard Thurston
  4.*The Dream Woman   Wilkie Collins
Summoned From the Dead   John Randall
The Master Stroke   Guy Fowler
Gambler's Gold   Jack D'Arcy
Spirit Tales [col]   Count Cagliostro
How to Read Your Husband's Mind [a]
          Norman Frescot & Bebe Stanton
Stronger Than Death [sn4/4]
                      Wilbert Wadleigh
Were You Born in May? [col]   Stella King

June 1930   8/6 (48) Dalton Stevens
The Elephant and the Honeymoon
                      Pauline de Silva
The Thing in the Laboratory   Perry Paul
Why Are They Dying?   Charles Stewart
Justice in Lost Lady Swamp   Rose Ross
I Heard the Sunken Bell [ts]
                  Theodore Orchards
The Mystery of the Jealous Queen
                  Mary Tarver Carroll
Keeping Faith With Dusty   Guy Fowler
The Ghost Master of Berlin [a]
                  Ruprecht von Sturm
Master of Darkness [sn2/4]
                      Arthur T. Jolliffe
Spirit Tales [col]   Count Cagliostro
Black Magic in Java   Mabel Lockman
The House of Sinister Shadows
  [sn3/4]   Samri Frikell
Can a Dog Have a Soul?   Walter B. Gibson
"My Favorite Ghost Story":   'Cheiro'
  5. The Moving Finger Writes 'Cheiro'
Haunted Harvard [a]   Gordon Hillman
Were You Born in June? [col] Stella King

July 1930   9/1 (49) Dalton Stevens
Park Avenue Vampire [sn1/4] Ramon Dawson
The Ghost of a Burning Ship   Nell Kay
Bucto Ghost-Haven   Theodore Orchards
The Miser's Return   Harold S. Corbin
Hun Poy Remembers the Code Edwin Goewey
"My Favorite Ghost Story":   Lon Chaney
  6.*Pollock and the Porroh Man
                      H. G. Wells
The Scotland Yard of Ghostland
  [a]   Capt. Neil Gow
Were You Born in July? [col]   Stella King
Spirit Tales [col]   Count Cagliostro
What the Organist Saw   C. S. Hawthorne

March 1931   10/3 (57) Dalton Stevens
The Man With Four Arms [nt1/2]
                              Stanley Moore
The Psychic Detective [a]
                              Sylvan J. Muldoon
By Rope and Fire   Jack D'Arcy
*Mummy No. 249   Sir Arthur Conan Doyle
The House of the Fog [n3/6]
                              H. Thompson Rich
The Prehistoric Phantom   Wilbert Wadleigh
None So Blind   Everil W. Murphy
A Bewitched Bow   Gledhill Hallas
The Evil Three [n4/5]   Victor Rousseau
Were You Born in March? [col]   Stella King
Devil Stone   Melvin Moffett
Spirit Tales [col]   Count Cagliostro

April 1931   10/4 (58) Dalton Stevens
This World and the Next [ed] Harold Hersey
The Phantom Menace of the
  Screen [n1/5]   Arthur T. Jolliffe
*The Captain of the Polestar
  [nt]   Sir Arthur Conan Doyle
The Man With Four Arms [nt2/2]
                              Stanley Moore
The Curse of Green Acres
                        Mary Agnew MacLean
The Evil Three [n5/5]   Victor Rousseau
Midnight Sorcery   W.H.D. Bence
Forgotten Harbor   Gordon Hillman
The House of the Fog [n4/6]
                              H. Thompson Rich
Were You Born in April? [col] Stella King
Ten-Ton Ghosts of Baraboo [a]
                        Theodore Orchards
Spirit Tales [col]   Count Cagliostro

May 1931   10/5 (59) Dalton Stevens
The Affair of the Clutching
  Hand   Hugh B. Cave
The Haunted Bridge of Pasadena
  [ts]   Stuart Palmer
The Man Who Outwitted the
  Devil   'Signor Bellini'
Footsteps in the Dark   Owen Fox Jerome
The Phantom Menace of the
  Screen [n2/5]   Arthur T. Jolliffe
Did Old Hughie Come Back?
                        Lillian Averne Clark
From Out the Vasty Deep   George Tibbetts
The House of the Fog [n5/6]
                              H. Thompson Rich
A Chinese Web of Mystery [ts]   'Cheiro'
Were You Born in May? [col]   Stella King
Find Your Life Numbers [col]
                        Florence Campbell
The Specter of Notre Dame   Lloyd Owen
Spirit Tales [col]   Count Cagliostro
The Crime of the Third Chamber
  [a]   Herbert Wall Taylor
True Ghost Story Corner [col]
                        Hereward Carrington

June 1931   10/6 (60)   George Wren
When Fear Rides [na1/4]   Donald Wylie
Talisman of Fate   Jack D'Arcy
Your Destiny in Your Scribble
  [col]   Louise Rice
Chicago's Flying Horror [ts] Stuart Palmer
True Ghost Story Corner [col]
                        Hereward Carrington

The Phantom Menace of the Screen
  [n3/5]   Arthur T. Jolliffe
There is No Medicine For This
                        Dr Paul Bronson
The Toad Man Specter   Conrad Richter
Find Your Life Numbers [col]
                        Florence Campbell
*Who Was the Strangler?   E. & H. Heron
The House of the Fog [n6/6]
                              H. Thompson Rich
Were You Born in June? [col] Stella King
Spirit Tales [col]   Count Cagliostro
What Do Your Dreams Mean? [a]
                        Margaret Rowan

July 1931   11/1 (61)   George Wren
The Thing That Limped   Gordon Hillman
How to Be a Ghost [ts] Sylvan J. Muldoon
Find Your Life Numbers [col]
                        Florence Campbell
When Fear Rides [na2/4]   Donald Wylie
Drum Beats of Terror Preston Kennard Mears
Demon of the Sickle   W.H.D. Bence
What Do Your Dreams Mean?
  [col]   Margaret Rowan
Not For a Million Dollars
                        James Howard Hull
Is Bear Mountain Haunted?
  [a]   E. Irvine Haines
Your Destiny in Your Scribble
  [col]   Louise Rice
White Witch of Stonington   Stuart Palmer
The Phantom Menace of the
  Screen [n4/5]   Arthur T. Jolliffe
Spirit Tales [col]   Count Cagliostro
Your Stars [col]   Evangeline Day
The True Ghost Story Corner
  [col]   Hereward Carrington

Aug/Sep 1931   11/2 (62)   Carl Pfeufer
The Pinecrest Ghost   Lillian Averne Clark
The Strange Case of Dick
  Tredennis [na1/3]   Marie Van Vorst
My Own Phantom [ts]
                Archbishop Frederick E. J. Lloyd
Salt is Not For Slaves   E. W. Hutter
Requickened Dust   Mildred Cram
Your Stars [vol]   Evangeline Day
Little Brown Dwarf [ts]
                        Herbert Hall Taylor
What Do Your Dreams Mean?
  [col]   Margaret Rowan
When Fear Rides [na3/4]   Donald Wylie
Out of the Shadow of Madness   Edith Ross
Your Destiny in Your Scribble
  [col]   Louise Rice
The Phantom Menace of the Screen
  [n5/5]   Arthur T. Jolliffe
Find Your Life Numbers [col]
                        Florence Campbell
Spirit Tales [col]   Count Cagliostro

Oct/Nov 1931   11/3 (63)   Stuart Leach
Traveller of the Shadows   L. V. Jefferson
House of Fire   Aubrey Feist
The Strange Case of Dick
  Tredennis [na2/3]   Marie Van Vorst
Mwaba's Amulet   Preston K. Mears
When Fear Rides [na4/4]   Donald Wylie
Not on the Passenger List Eleanor Clarage

***

GHOSTS & SCHOLARS

A British small press magazine published annually by the Haunted Library, 11b Cote Lea Square, Southgate, Runcorn, Cheshire. Editor/Publisher: Rosemary A. Pardoe. Originally a one-off tribute to M. R. James, the booklet spawned a sequel, entitled More Ghosts & Scholars, *and thereafter became an annual.*

[Spring] 1979   [No.1]   Stephen Jones
Shadows of the Master   [a]   Mike Ashley
The James List   [bib]   Hugh Lamb
Old Johannes   Peter Shilston
A Serious Call   George Hay
An Incident in the City   A. F. Kidd
M.R. James: A Portfolio   [ap] Russ Nicholson

[Summer] 1980   [No.2]   Martin Helsdon
   [entitled MORE GHOSTS & SCHOLARS]
Figures in a Landscape   A. F. Kidd
Return to the Runes   David Sutton
The Fifteenth Evening   David Rowlands
The Catacomb   Peter Shilston
All That Flies   George Hay
A Forgotten Disciple of
   M. R. James   [a]   Richard Dalby
The James List: Addendum
   [bib]   [various]

[Summer] 1981   No.3   Russ Nicholson
The Burning   Ramsey Campbell
The Uncommon Salt   David G. Rowlands
Old Hobby Horse   A. F. Kidd
The Abysmal   Stephen Gresham
*Letters to a Child   [ltrs]   M. R. James

[May] 1982   No.4   David Lloyd
The Poor Nun of Burtisford
        William Fairlie Clarke
Come, Follow!   Sheila Hodgson
The Executor   David G. Rowlands
Amyas Northcote: A Forgotten
   Master of the Ghost Story
   [a]   Richard Dalby
The Unfinished Ghost Stories
   of M.R. James   [a]   Rosemary Pardoe

[Summer] 1983   No.5   Wendy Adrian Wees
Conkers   David G. Rowlands
The Gravedigger and Death   Mary Ann Allen
The Alabaster Bowl   Kelvin I. Jones
Mawnan Rectory   Dave Reeder
Noel Boston: Master Antiquarian
   [a]   Mike Ashley
M.R. James: an English Humorist
   [a]   A. F. Kidd
The Manuscripts of M.R. James
   [bib]   Rosemary Pardoe

***

THE GORGON

An amateur fantasy magazine published bi-monthly by Stanley Mullen, 4936 Grove St., Denver, Colorado. Editor: Stanley Mullen. Although essentially a fannish 'zine and thus normally outside the purview of this Index, it did, in later issues publish some significant items of and about fantasy by some fledgeling big-name writers. In this Index the run-of-the-mill fannish items have been omitted. The Gorgon was hectographed for the first six issues and then printed offset thereafter.

March 1947   1/1 (1)   Roy Hunt
Caput Mortuum [v]   Stanley Mullen
Darkness   Gertrude Voorhies
Cartouche - A. Merritt [a]   Stanley Mullen
Cartoon Gallery [pic]
              Roy Hunt & Stanley Mullen
A Dero Named Clarence   Stanley Mullen

May/June 1947   1/2 (2)   Roy Hunt
A Strange View of the River Stanley Mullen
Through a Jade Glass [a] Marijane Nuttall
Goat Mask   Stanley Mullen
Ivan [gs]   Roy Hunt
Notes on Ophiolatory [a]
              Charles Ford Hansen
The Corkscrew Bug [v]   Mike Castle

July 1947   1/3 (3)   Roy Hunt
The Disappearance of Peregrine
              Nowell Chase
*The Vanguard of Venus [nt1/2]
              Landell Bartlett
The Story Behind "The Star
    Rover" [a]   Phil Rasch
Tasha - A Fragment from "Witches
    There Were"   Sophia Magafan
Cartouche - Clark Ashton Smith
    [a]   Stanley Mullen

September 1947   1/4 (4)
    [special 'Philcon Memory Book' issue]
Cartouche - Campbell [a]   Stanley Mullen
Morgan Le Fay   Virgil Utter
The Scorched Tree   Alex Saunders
Spaceport at Night [v]   Theophilus Alvor
*The Vanguard of Venus [nt2/2]
              Landell Bartlett

Literary Criticism and Off-Trail
    Literature [a]   Phil Rasch
The Ultimate Prozine [a]   Joe Kennedy
Necromancy [pic] Roy Hunt & Stanley Mullen
Dream   Lloyd Arthur Eshbach

November 1947   1/5 (5)
Death of the Wood Nymphs Marijane Nuttall
Sidelights on the Merrittales:
    1. Metalanim and Nan-Matal [a] Phil Rasch
Reprisal   Ben Singer
The Martian's Head   Michael Wigodsky
Good Eating!   Donn Brazier
World After Destruction   Marion Zimmer
The Bird of Doom [pic]
            C. R. Bunnell & Stanley Mullen
Sleuth is Stranger Than
    Fiction [a]   Forrest J. Ackerman

January 1948   1/6 (6)   Roy Hunt
The Shadow Woman   Shan Nosgorov
Storms of Night   Marijane Nuttall
The Killer   David H. Keller
Sidelights on the Merrittales:
    2. The Rrrllya [a]   Phil Rasch
Deserted House   Genevieve K. Stephens
Haunted Mines [a]   Lee Beecher
Prospector's Cabin   Archie Musick

Mar/April 1948   1/7 (7)   Roy Hunt
Operation Venus   Landell Bartlett
Sidelights on the Merrittales:
    3. Ys and Carnac [a]   Phil Rasch
Druid Stones [pic]   Roy Hunt
Vampire Horde [v]   Lloyd Arthur Eshbach
The Immoral Storm [spf]   Joe Kennedy
Tchaka [v]   Shan Nosgorov

[Fall] 1948   2/1 (8)   Howard Miller
Sidelights on the Merrittales:
4. The Kraken [a]   Phil Rasch
Trapped [v]   Joseph B. Baker
This Will Flay You   William Walrich
Hiroshima Dawn [v]   Alvin A. Laney
Hogurth Hill [v]   R. Flavie Carson
The Ultimate Fanzine [a]   'Astra' Zimmer
Walpurga's Night [v]   Virgil Utter
The Light Master [v]   Theophilus Alvor
Truth Gas   Alex Saunders
Campbell Checklist [bib]   Jack Riggs
Lemuria [v]   Justin Herman

[January] 1949   2/2 (9)   Roy Hunt
Under the Anaesthetic [v] Theophilus Alvor
Ghost Town Siding [v]   Archie Musick
The Paisley Shawl   Cynthia Carey
On This Night [v]   Genevieve Stephens
Adana [v]   Lee Beecher
Sidelights on the Merrittales:
5. The Face in the Abyss [a]   Phil Rasch
Ex Aqua [v]   Con Pederson
Beyond Ka-ree [v]   Albert Toth
Lafcadio Hearn [a]   Paul O'Connor
The Flight / The Landing [v] Gordon Kull

March 1949   2/3 (10)   Roy Hunt
Those Martin Boys   William Wallrich
Some Notes on Hearn [a]   Paul O'Connor
Unholy Street   Stanley Mullen
Sonnet to Palomar [v]   Justin Herman
Lost Destiny   George R. Cowie
The Sorceress   Marion Zimmer
Sidelights on the Merrittales:
6. Alice in Wonderland [a]   Phil Rasch
The Night [v]   Robert Flavie Carson
The Silent Horde   Philip Gray
The Fantast [v]   Lin Carter
A Page of Space [ss]   John Grossman
A Space Hazard   Jack Riggs

[May] 1949   2/4 (11)   Roy Hunt
The Perfumed Garden   David H. Keller
The Saga of Professor Jameson
   [a]   Neil R. Jones
Red Star [v]   Virgil Utter
Suspended Animate [v]   G. A. Kull
Oil [v]   Howard Haynes
More Notes on Lafcadio Hearn
   [a]   Paul O'Connor
The Last Bachelor   Larry O'Neill
The Flying Discs   Phil Rasch
We Stand in Crumbled Room   Erik Margrave
Two Poems [2v]   Michael Wigodsky
Night [v]   Jack Marsh
There Will Be Darkness [v] Justin Herman
Coma Berenices   Landell Bartlett
Memory Bridge [v]   Lawrence Howard
The Poet [v]   Lin Carter

[The above data was supplied by Howard DeVore and Steve Miller]

***

GOTHIC

A scholarly magazine relying strongly on critical articles analysing all aspects of gothic/weird fiction. Published twice yearly by Gothic Press, 4998 Perkins Road, Baton Rouge, Louisiana. Editor: Gary William Crawford. As the reviews serve as a springboard for further analyses they are incorporated within the index. Gothic is a large-format printed magazine with no cover or interior art.

June 1979   1/1 (1)
Daylight Nightmares [a]
                    Pamela J. Shelden & Kurt Paul
The Dead Field   David Sutton
Stevenson's "Silent Symbols" of
   the "Fatal Cross Roads" in
   Dr Jekyll and Mr Hyde [a]
                    Mark M. Hennelly,Jr
Entombed   Robert Keefe
Lovecraft: The Dissonance Factor
   in Imaginative Literature [a]
                    Dirk W. Mosig
Oregon Gothic   Ardath Mayhar
Two Views of St. Armand's Lovecraft
   [rv]   Donald R. Burleson & John McInnis
Best-Selling Horror [rv]
                Benjamin Franklin Fisher IV
The English Ghost Story [rv]
                Benjamin Franklin Fisher IV

December 1979   1/2 (2)
The Exile [nt]   Galad Elflandsson
Faith and Doubt in the Castle
   of Otranto [a]   Syndy McMillen Conger
The Fifth Door   John Bovey
The 1978 Bibliography of Gothic
   Studies [bib]   Frederick S. Frank,
                    Gary William Crawford,
            & Benjamin Franklin Fisher IV
Horror by the Bucket - and the
   Fingerbowel [rv] Benjamin F. Fisher IV
Romantic Gothicism [rv]   Bette B. Roberts
The Cult of the Occult [rv]
                    Mark M. Hennelly,Jr

June 1980   2/1 (3)
The Voice of Blood   Jean Muno
Beyond Mystery: Emergence from
   Delusion as a Pattern in

Gothic Fiction [a]   Paul Lewis
The Lady in Darkness   Lee Weinstein
The Narrow House   Phillip C. Heath
Party, Last Tuesday [v] Roberta Ventsias
Two-Thirds of Ketterer's
   Trilogy [rv]   Kent Ljungquist
A Recent Gothic Study [rv] John A. Stoler
Dark World Enough and Time [rv]
                    Mark M. Hennelly, Jr
The Modern Weird Tale and the
   Gothic Tradition [rv]William E. Coleman

December 1980   2/2 (4)
Later Victorian Ghost Stories:
   The Literature of Belief [a]
                    Daniel Sheridan
Poe's 'Ligeia' and the Pleasures
   of Terror [a]   Terry Heller
The 1979 Bibliography of Gothic
   Studies [bib]   Frederick S. Frank,
                    Gary William Crawford,
            & Benjamin Franklin Fisher IV
The German Gothic Novel [rv]
                Benjamin Franklin Fisher IV
A Critical Biography of Le Fanu
   [rv]   Randy L. DeJaynes
MacAndrew's Gothic Study [rv]
                    Devendra P. Varma
Mary Shelley's *Frankenstein* [rv]
                Benjamin Franklin Fisher IV
Lovecraft Criticism [rv]   Stephen Eng

***

H

THE HAUNT OF HORROR

A digest magazine of 'terror and the macabre', published bi-monthly by the Marvel Comics Group, 575 Madison Avenue, New York. Editor: Gerard Conway.

***

HOR-TASY

A small press fantasy magazine, duplicated in octavo format and published irregularly by Ansuda Publications, Harris, Iowa. Editor/Publisher: Daniel R. Betz. Pledged to publish only original treatments of horror and fantasy.

1980	No.1	Dan Mayorga
Lady Latanya		H. J. Baker
When Edward Comes		B. F. Watkinson
The Old Stone Hut		D. Richard Bud
The Basement [play]		Laurel Speer
Grandather Tuppa's Story or,		
The Vanishing Trolls of		
Norway		Gaird Wallig
The Moon Maid		Lari Davidson
The Garden of Death [v]		Mark McLaughlin

1982	No.2	Geraldine M. Ward
The Raid on Spider Walkins		
		Richard Zaccaro
Faith in the Family		Tracy Deaton
Beneath Trees Green and Wide		
		Sharon Pisacreta
One Tale of Thumpin		Gaird Wallig

***

120

H. P. L.

A one-shot magazine limited to an edition of 1000 copies (of which 35 were hard-bound) and a tribute to the life and work of H. P. Lovecraft. Published and edited by Meade & Penny Frierson, Crestline Hts., Birmingham, Alabama in 1972 in large quarto format.

***

I

IMPULSE

A British fantasy/sf magazine published monthly in pocketbook format by Roberts & Vinter, 42/44 Dock Street, London. Editor: Kyril Bonfiglio (until issue 7), thereafter Keith Roberts (with Editor-in-Chief, Harry Harrison). Technically a continuation of Science Fantasy *it had a complete change of volume numbering and, to some extent, a change of editorial policy.*

Make Room! Make Room! [n3/3] Harry Harrison

November 1966   1/9   Keith Roberts
Guest Editorial [ged]   Judith Merril
The Ice Schooner [n1/3] Michael Moorcock
The Simple for Love   Keith Roberts
Stop Seventeen   Robert Wells
The Eyes of the Blind King Brian W. Aldiss
The Roaches   Thomas M. Disch
SF Film Festival [a] Francesco Biamonti
Pasquali's Peerless Puppets Edward Mackin

December 1966   1/10   Keith Roberts
Inside Out Kenneth Bulmer & Richard Wilson
Three Points of a Demographic
   Curve   Thomas M. Disch
The Familiar   Keith Roberts
Hell Revisited: An Interview
   with Kingsley Amis [in] Thomas M. Disch
The Real Thing [nt]   Eric C. Williams
The Plot Sickens [spf]   Brian W. Aldiss
The Ice Schooner [n2/3] Michael Moorcock
The Voice of the CWACC   Harry Harrison

January 1967   1/11   Keith Roberts
Mantis [nt]   Chris Boyce
Green Eyes   Richard Wilson
*The Shrine of Temptation   Judith Merril
Coincidence   Chris Hebron
Grutch   Pete Hammerton
The Ice Schooner [n3/3] Michael Moorcock

February 1967   1/12   Agosta Morol
The Bad Bush of Uzoro   Chris Hebron
Just Passing Through   Brian W. Aldiss
Inconstancy   Brian M. Stableford
The Number You Have Reached
                    Thomas M. Disch
The Pursuit of Happiness   Paul Jents
It's Smart to Have an English
   Address   D. G. Compton
Impasse   Chris Priest
See Me Not [nt]   Richard Wilson
Keith Roberts Re-reads the
   'True History' of Lucian
   of Samosata [a]   Keith Roberts

***

J

JEET

A small press sf/fantasy digest published and edited quarterly by Ken Hahn, Auburn, New York.

April 1977 No.1	Ken Hahn
A Boy and his Monkey [spf]	
	Birdwhanger Cord
Hipsterama [v]	John Thiel
The Debt	Brad Bronson
False Gods [ss]	John DiPrete
Swamp Jinny	John Thiel
Cassandra's Song	A. B. Clingan
Monster of the Faith [v]	Neal Blaikie
'Ozymandias' by Perzine	
Shelley Beans [v]	Bill Bridget
Jonos [cs]	John Thiel
	[art: Ken Hahn]
The Sword of the Blue Atom	C. C. Clingan
The Crossing Over	Ken Hahn
Final Analysis	John DiPrete
The Dump [v]	Stephanie Stearns
The Night's Last Walk	A. K. Molnar
Masquerade	Gordon Linzner

Summer [July] 1977 No.2	Ken Hahn
Time For Love	Mark Jacobs
Hudson and Company	Brad Bronson
The Last Little Boy	C. C. Clingan
Mother Goose's Closet Nursery	
Rhymes [v]	Bill Bridget
Dream a Little Dream of Me	
	Stephanie Stearns
Heresy of Llorf	John DiPrete
Sunshine and Shadow	A. B. Clingan
Jewel [v]	Neil Selmer Kvern

* * *

K

KADATH

A small press fantasy magazine published and edited annually by Lin Carter, 100-15 195th St., Hollis, Queens, New York. High printing costs killed the magazine after only one issue although the first was barely distributed. Not even all of the advance subscribers (at $5 a copy) received it. It is one of the rarest of the more recent magazines and should not be confused with the Italian Kadath which is also included in this Index.

[Summer] 1974	No.1	*John Allan
*The Birth of Art [v]		A. Merritt
Jewel Quest		Hannes Bok
*On Reading Lord Dunsany's		
'Book of Wonder' [v]		H. P. Lovecraft
Dear Ech-Pi-El [ltr]	Clark Ashton Smith	
A Word From the Outer Dark		
[v]		Robert E. Howard
The City of Pillars		Lin Carter
*The Black Tower		Robert H. Barlow

***

KADATH

An Italian small press weird fantasy magazine published irregularly in slick format by the Kadath Press, Corso Aurelio Saffi 5/9, Genova. Publisher/Editor: Francesco Cova. Although initially in Italian it contained an English-language section which grew so that by issue No.4 the magazine was entirely in English. The full contents are listed below with the Italian items in italics.

October 1979   1/1 (1)   *Virgil Finlay
La Situazione della letteratura
  dell'orrore e di fantasy in
  Italia [a1/2]   *Francesco Cova*
Una visita al K... Museen *Enrico Daghino*
"I Have a Heart of a Little
  Boy..." [a]   *Enrico Daghino*
The Situation of Weird and
  Fantasy Fiction in Italy
  [a]   Francesco Cova
I grandi illustratori di
  Weird Tales [a]   *Monica Petitti*

May 1980   1/2 (2)   *Howard Brown
La situazione della letteratura
  dell'orrore e di fantasy in
  Italia [a2/2]   *Francesco Cova*
*Demoniacal   *David Sutton*
**Lovecraft su 'Astounding*
  Stories' [a]   *Robert Weinberg*
Il Collezionista e la Grand
  Inquisizione   *Adalberto Cersosimo*
Collector's Piece   Adrian Cole
Pezzo da collezione   *Adrian Cole*
**La Sword and Sorcery di*
  Michael Moorcock [a]   *Paul Allen*

November 1980   1/3 (3)   [photo]
   [special Brian Lumley issue]
**Zack Phalanx E' Vlad l'Impalatore*
              Brian Lumley
**La Cosa al chiaro di luna*
      H.P. Lovecraft & Brian Lumley
**Il bacio di Bugg-Shash*   *Brian Lumley*
Brian Lumley: A Bibliography
  [bib]   Brian Lumley & Francesco Cova
Too Much Monkey Business   Brian Lumley
The Man Who Got Slotted   Brian Lumley

An Interview with Brian Lumley
  [in]   Francesco Cova
The House of the Temple [nt] Brian Lumley
Kadath [v]   Brian Lumley

July 1981   1/4 (4)   Jim Pitts
   [special Weird Tales issue]
Arimetta   Manly Wade Wellman
The Sweet Grapes of Autumn
            Frances Garfield
H. Warner Munn: A Bibliography
  [bib]   Mike Ashley
*The Affair of the Cuckolded
  Warlock   H. Warner Munn
Weird Tales Today [a] Darrell Schweitzer
Lamia   Manly Wade Wellman

July 1982   1/5 (5)   Jim Pitts
   [special Occult Detectives issue]
Echo of Thunder   Ardath Mayhar
Rouse Him Not Manly Wade Wellman
Dylath-Leen [v]   Brian Lumley
The Affair at Durmamnay Hall Brian Mooney
The Death-Wish Mandate   Mike Chinn
Name and Number [nt]   Brian Lumley

***

127

L

LEAVES

*An amateur fantasy magazine published and edited by Robert H. Barlow at
Leavenworth, Kansas. Described by Sam Moskowitz as "among the finest journals
ever to be turned out by the fan field" the magazine is extremely rare with
100 copies of the first issue printed and even less of the second. Barlow
also produced the non-fiction* Dragon Fly *which is covered in the Appendices.*

Summer 1937   1/1   [R. H. Barlow?]
*The Story of the Princess
   Zulkais and the Prince
   Kalilah   William Beckford
Conclusion to William Beckford's
   Story of Princess Zulkais and
   Prince Kalilah   Clark Ashton Smith
With a Set of Rattlesnake
   Rattles [a]   Robert E. Howard
Cats and Dogs [a]   Lewis Theobald, Jr
Mist [v]   E. Toldridge
Dead Houses [a]   Edith Miniter
*Sandalwood [v]   Clark Ashton Smith
The Beautiful City [v]
                      Frank Belknap Long, Jr
*The People of the Pit   A. Merritt
H. P. Lovecraft [v]   E. Toldridge
Ephemera [v]   E. Toldridge
*The Panelled Room   August Derleth
It Will Be Thus [v]   Arthur Goodenough
The Twilight of Time   Donald Wandrei
On the Threshold of Eternity
                          Donald Wandrei
A Legend of Yesterday   Donald Wandrei
Autumnus - and October [v]
                      Arthur Goodenough

Winter 1938/39   1/2   [R. H. Barlow?]
Werewoman   C. L. Moore
Winter Night [v]   Vrest Teachout Orton
The Woman at the Window   Donald Wandrei
From a Letter [ltr]   H. P. Lovecraft
Collapsing Cosmoses   [R. H. Barlow?]
Haunted [v]   Howard Davis Spoerl
The Faun   Samuel Loveman
Flower of War [v]   Henry George Weiss
Azathoth [v]   H. P. Lovecraft
The Descendant   H. P. Lovecraft
The Book [v]   H. P. Lovecraft
O is there Aught in Wine and
   Ships! [v]   Frank Belknap Long, Jr
Futility [v]   Frank Belknap Long, Jr
The Demons of the Upper Air
   [v]   Fritz Leiber, Jr
In Defense of 'Dagon' [a] H. P. Lovecraft
The Unresisting [v]   Jonathon Lindley
March [v]   Jonathon Lindley
*The Tree-Man   Henry S. Whitehead
Thule [v]   Th. Weelkes
A Checklist of the Published
   Weird Stories of Henry S.
   Whitehead [bib]   [R. H. Barlow?]
Origin Undetermined   R. H. Barlow
The Manuscript   R. H. Barlow

***

128

M

MACABRE

A small press weird magazine published and edited by Joseph Payne Brennan in New Haven, Connecticut. Printed in digest format it was launched to fill the gap produced with the folding of Weird Tales. *Originally twice yearly it became irregular. Every issue was identified by roman numerals and that style is repeated here.*

June 1957   No. I
Delivery of Erdmore Street
                    Joseph Payne Brennan
Contrary to the Sun [v]
                    Bonnie Elizabeth Parker
The Wind of Time [v] Joseph Payne Brennan
The White Huntress [v]
                    Joseph Payne Brennan

Winter 1957   No. II
Nemesis   Phyllis Flood
As Through a Glass, Darkly
                    Elizabeth Potter
In an Upstairs Room [v]   Marijane Allen
Where?   Virginia Reid
Do Unto Others   Sandra Blake
The Department of the Navy
  Regrets to Inform [v]   Marijane Allen
The Hitch-Hiker   W. E. Dan Ross
Silver Death   Joseph Payne Brennan
The Mad Wild Angel [v]   Lilith Lorraine

Summer 1958   No. III
The Dream Thing   John Spade
Return [v]   Joseph Francis Murphy
A Room For Rent   Gene Tipton
The Pearls [v]   William J. Noble
Pawn of the Reign of Terror
  [v]   Donna Dickey Guyer
Election Incident   Joseph Payne Brennan
Black October [v]   Joseph Payne Brennan

Winter 1958   No. IV
Dance With the Dead   Robert F. Young
Misalliance [v]   Anne Marx
Rhapsody of Death   Lois Allen
Universe [v]   Alfred Leland Mooney
Shadows in the Dusk   Clarence Alva Powell
Invasion From the Swamp   Gene Tipton

Nocturne Macabre [v] Joseph Payne Brennan
Ghosts [v]   'Jeanette'
Night Landing   Jean Marie Tyson
Mount Helicon [v]   Alfred Dorn

Summer 1959   No. V
Judgement   Kit Reed
Voodoo [v]   Richard Dunwich
Revenants [v]   August Derleth
Occurrence on Kelvin's Bluff   Gene Tipton
Two Loves [v]   Jeanne Marie Tyson
Danse Macabre [v]   Violet M. Cobb
Lines to H. P. Lovecraft [v]
                    Joseph Payne Brennan
Apprehension   Joseph Payne Brennan
Lovecraft's 'Brick Row' [a]
                    Joseph Payne Brennan
The Smell of Danger [v]
                    Sydney King Russell
The Way of Our Going [v]   Alice M. Swaim
Homecoming [v]   Charles Shaw

Winter 1959   No. VI
Das Zeichen   Mildred Hughes
The Room   Patricia Brittigan
Trapped [v]   Charles Shaw
I, Too, Cassandra   Lee Priestley
Day of the Snake   Margaret Lee Johnson
Extermination   Joseph Payne Brennan
The Span [v]   Dorothy Gordon
One Day of Rain [v] Joseph Payne Brennan

Summer 1960   No. VII
We Meet Again   E. M. Nightingale
Time and H.P.L. [a] Joseph Payne Brennan
Heat Wave   Gene Tipton
The Bargain Hunter   Don Clark Bush
The Death Baby   Jeanette Brown Mackenzie
In My Garden [v]   William J. Noble

1973   No. XXII
Ice People   George Dendrinos
To Life [v]   Robert Casper
Lovecraft on the Subway
   [a]   Joseph Payne Brennan
Wildlife [v]   Leslie Nelson Jennings
The Floating Coffin [ts]   John Perry
Summons [v]   Helen T. Hill
My Love [v]   Lawrence A. Trissel
Dark Meeting [v]   Joseph Francis Murphy
The Deceased [v]   Violet Hiles Ringer
Sole Survivor [v]   Joseph Francis Murphy
Remembering Wind [v] Joseph Payne Brennan
The Watcher [v]   Joseph Payne Brennan

1976   No. XXIII
Day of Departure   Frank Sherry
1st World Fantasy Convention
   [a]   Joseph Payne Brennan
The Sun Worshipper [v]   Mary Winter
Vocation [v]   Lee E. Keebler
To All Cemetery Visitors
   [v]   Joseph Francis Murphy
Advent of Autumn [v] Joseph Payne Brennan
Ecce Homo [v]   Joseph Francis Murphy
Nightmare [v]   Doris Philbrick Brennan
Collector's Item [v]   Phoebe Solomon
When the Stars are Right [v]
                            W. Paul Ganley
Farrison [v]   Joseph Payne Brennan
Gulf of Day [v]   Joseph Payne Brennan
Lovecraft and the O'Brien
   Annuals [a]   Joseph Payne Brennan
In Memoriam: A.N.L. Munby
   [obit]   Joseph Payne Brennan
The Ancient Meadow   Joseph Payne Brennan

***

MAGAZINE OF HORROR

A weird fantasy digest published irregularly (for a period bi-monthly) by Health Knowledge Inc., 140 Fifth Ave., New York. Editor: Robert A. W. Lowndes. Relied heavily on reprints, especially from Strange Tales. *See also companion titles* Startling Mystery Stories, Weird Terror Tales *and* Bizarre Fantasy Tales.

August 1963   (1/1) 1   -
*The Man With a Thousand Legs
                    Frank Belknap Long
A Thing of Beauty   Wallace West
*The Yellow Sign   Robert W. Chambers
The Maze and the Monster   Edward D. Hoch
*The Death of Halpin Frayser
                    Ambrose Bierce
Babylon: 70 M.   Donald A. Wollheim
*The Inexperienced Ghost   H. G. Wells
The Unbeliever   Robert Silverberg
*Fidel Bassin   W. J. Stamper
*The Last Dawn   Frank Lillie Pollock
*The Undying Head   Mark Twain

November 1963   (1/2) 2   -
*The Space-Eaters [nt] Frank Belknap Long
The Faceless Thing   Edward D. Hoch
*The Red Room   H. G. Wells
Hungary's Female Vampire [a] Dean Lipton
*A Tough Tussle   Ambrose Bierce
Doorslammer   Donald A. Wollheim
*The Electric Chair   George Waight
The Other One   Jerryl L. Keane
*The Charmer   Archie Binns
*Clarissa   Robert A. W. Lowndes
*The Strange Ride of Morrowbie
    Jukes   Rudyard Kipling

February 1964   (1/3) 3   -
*The Seeds of Death [nt]   David H. Keller
The Seeking Thing   Janet Hirsch
*A Vision of Judgement   H. G. Wells
*The Place of the Pythons Arthur J. Burks
*Jean Bouchon   S. Baring-Gould
The Door   Rachel Cosgrove Payes
*One Summer Night   Ambrose Bierce
*Luella Miller   Mary Wilkins-Freeman
They That Wait   H. S. W. Chibbett
*The Repairer of Reputations
    [nt]   Robert W. Chambers

May 1964   (1/4) 4   -
Beyond the Breakers   Anna Hunger
*What Was It?   Fitz-James O'Brien
*Last Act: October   Tigrina
*A Psychological Experiment Richard Marsh
A Dream of Falling   Attila Hatvany
*The Truth About Pyecraft   H. G. Wells
*The Mark of the Beast   Rudyard Kipling
*The Dreams in the Witch-
   House [nt]   H. P. Lovecraft

September 1964   (1/5) 5   -
*Cassius [nt]   Henry S. Whitehead
Love at First Sight   J. L. Miller
Five-Year Contract   J. Vernon Shea
*The House of the Worm   Merle Prout
*The Beautiful Suit   H. G. Wells
A Stranger Came to Reap Stephen Dentinger
The Morning the Birds
   Forgot to Sing   Walt Liebscher
*Bones   Donald A. Wollheim
*The Ghostly Rental [nt]   Henry James

November 1964   (1/6) 6   Fred Wolters
*Caverns of Horror [nt] Laurence Manning
Prodigy   Walt Liebscher
*The Mask   Robert W. Chambers
The Life-After-Death of Mr.
   Thaddeus Warde   Robert Barbour Johnson
The Feminine Fraction   David Grinnell
*Dr. Heidegger's Experiment
                    Nathaniel Hawthorne
*The Pacer   August Derleth
*Lovecraft and "The Pacer" [ex]
                       August Derleth
*The Moth   H. G. Wells
*The Door to Saturn   Clark Ashton Smith

January 1965   (2/1) 7   *Fred Wolters
*The Thing From - Outside
                    George Allan England

*Back Before the Moon   S. Omar Barker
*The Road to Nowhere [nt]
                    Robert A. W. Lowndes

Fall 1970   (6/4) 34   *Virgil Finlay
*The Headless Miller of
   Kobold's Keep [nt]   Irvin Ashkenazy
Bride of the Wind   Stephen Goldin
A Song of Defeat [v]   Robert E. Howard
*The Emergency Call   Marion Brandon
Feminine Magic   David H. Keller, M.D.
*The Whistling Corpse [nt] G. G. Pendarves

February 1971   (6/5) 35   ?
*The Altar of Melek Taos [nt]
                       G. G. Pendarves
The Chenoo   Stephen Goldin
*Old City of Jade   Thomas H. Knight
*A Rendezvous in Averoigne
                    Clark Ashton Smith
*The Mystery in Acatlan
       Rachael Marshall & Maverick Terrell
*In the Lair of the Space
   Monsters [nt]   Frank Belknap Long

April 1971   (6/6) 36   ?
*Dread Exile   Paul Ernst
*The Testament of Athammaus
                    Clark Ashton Smith
The Vespers Service   William R. Bauer
*The Artist of Tao   Arthur Styron
*The Key to Cornwall David H. Keller, M.D.
The Executioner   Rachel Cosgrove Payes
*The Settlement of Dryden
   vs Shard   W. O. Inglis
*The Grisly Horror [nt] Robert E. Howard

                 ***

MARVEL TALES

A small press magazine published irregularly by Fantasy Publications, Everett, Pennsylvania. Editor/Publisher: William L. Crawford. An important publication, it was the first attempt at a newsstand semi-professional magazine, and also the first digest magazine in the fantasy field (it went large size with the last issue). See also the companion title Unusual Stories.

May 1934   1/1 (1)   L. A. Eshbach?
The Man With the Hour Glass   L. A. Eshbach
Antares [v]   Natalie H. Wooley
The Cossacks Ride Hard   August W. Derleth
*Celephais   H. P. Lovecraft
Binding Deluxe   David H. Keller, M.D.

Jul/Aug 1934   1/2 (2)   [FVC]
The Dark Beasts   Frank B. Long, Jr
The Garden of Fear   Robert E. Howard
Synthetic   Harl Vincent
From the Log of the Space-
  Ship Flammarian [v] Manly Wade Wellman
Antidote   Robert M. Hyatt
Conquest [v]   H. Donald Spatz
The Torch of Life   Joe W. Skidmore
A Horror in Profile Wilfred Blanch Talman

Winter 1934   1/3 (3)   Guy L. Huey
The Second Step   Orris M. Kellar
The Ferryman [v]   Timothy H. Loft
Lilies   Robert Bloch
The Ship [v]   Duane W. Rimel
On Board the Space Ship Terra
                            L. A. Eshbach
The Golden Bough   David H. Keller, M.D.
The Titan [na1/4]   P. Schuyler Miller

Mar/Apr 1935   1/4 (4)   ?
The Creator [nt]   Clifford D. Simak
*The Doom That Came to
   Sarnath   H. P. Lovecraft
The Cathedral Crypt   John Beynon Harris
Sanctuary [v]   Natalie H. Wooley
The Titan [na2/4]   P. Schuyler Miller
Masters of Matter   Amelia Reynolds Long
Haunted House [v]   Lovell Hert
*The Nebulae of Death
   [n1/?]   George Allen England

Summer 1935   1/5 (5)   C. Ferguson,Jr
Mars Colonizes   Miles J. Breuer
Man From Makassar   Carl Jacobi
The Titan [na3/4]   P. Schuyler Miller
Annabel Reeves   Ralph Milne Farley
Witch's Bercuese [v]   Emil Petaja
The Elfin Lights   Anders W. Drake
*The Nebula of Death
   [n2/?]   George Allan England
Forrest J. Ackerman,
   Scientifictionist [a]   [no credit]

                    ***

THE MASTER THRILLER SERIES

A series of adventure pulp magazines published erratically during the 1930s by The World's Work, Ltd., Kingswood, Surrey, England. The editor has not been iden-tified. Not all of the magazines were fantasy and the contents are listed below for the fantasy titles only. However, for the sake of completeness, the titles of the entire series are listed, as this information is published nowhere else. The issues were undated (except for No.32), so the dates used are those recorded upon receipt by the British Museum Library, although the run there is incomplete. The series had two distinct incarnations. The First Series, launched in 1934, ran roughly quarterly at first, then bi-monthly until the end of 1935. Thereafter the British Library run is lost, but the issues appeared erratically until No.25 when it was revived on a regular monthly basis until the War. Several issues subsequently became separate publications such as Mystery and Detection *the first issue of which is listed here, although later issues (of which there are believed to be three) do not form part of the series. Two other titles,* Fireside Ghost Stories *and* Ghosts & Goblins, *were not, so it seems, numbered as part of the series but are believed to belong roughly where indicated below.* Tales of Wonder, *treated here as No.19 (though unnumbered), was the first trial issue of a subsequent regular sf magazine. A companion series was* Mystery Stories, *which is included in part elsewhere in this Index.*

No.1 TALES OF THE FOREIGN LEGION [Jul 33]

No.2 TALES OF THE NORTH-WEST MOUNTIES
                                    [Nov 33]

No.3 TALES OF THE SEVEN SEAS   [Mar 34]

No.4 TALES OF MYSTERY AND DETECTION (1)
June 1934   [No.1]   ?
*The Horror at Staveley Grange   'Sapper'
*The Moth   H. G. Wells
*The Pikestaffe Case [nt]
                        Algernon Blackwood
*The Queen's Square   Dorothy L. Sayers
*The Token   May Sinclair
*An Echo   H. R. Wakefield
*The Fugitive of Delphi Terrace
                        E. Phillips Oppenheim
*The Accident   Oliver Onions
*The Seventh Man Sir Arthur Quiller-Couch
*The Naturalist at Law   R. Austin Freeman
*The Honour of Israel Gow G. K. Chesterton

No.5 TALES OF THE FOREIGN LEGION (2)
                                    [Sep 34]

No.6 TALES OF THE UNCANNY   [Dec 34]
*The Willows [na]   Algernon Blackwood
*The Inexperienced Ghost   H. G. Wells
*Honolulu   Somerset Maugham
*The Wind in the Portico   John Buchan
*A Pair of Hands Sir Arthur Quiller-Couch
*Mrs. Lunt   Hugh Walpole
*The Smell in the Library   Michael Arlen
*Old Man's Beard   H. R. Wakefield
*Mint   Mrs. Belloc-Lowndes
*Rooum   Oliver Onions

No.7 TALES OF AFRICAN ADVENTURE [Jan 35]

No.8 TALES OF THE ORIENT   [Mar 35]

No.9 TALES OF THE JUNGLE   [May 35]

No.10 TALES OF THE FOREIGN LEGION 3
                                    [Jul 35]

No.11 TALES OF THE SEA   [Sep 35]

No.12 TALES OF VALOUR   [Dec 35]

No.13 TALES OF THE LEVANT   [Jul 36]

No.14 TALES OF THE AIR   [Sep 36?]

137

***

MIDNIGHT SUN

An attractive small press digest magazine published irregularly by the editor Gary Hoppenstand, 2014 Mackenzie Drive, Columbus, Ohio. Publishing fantasy, horror and science fiction Midnight Sun *slanted its issues towards a particular author. Half of the print-run of issue 4 was lost in the post and issue 5 only appeared through the dogged perseverance of the editor.*

1974   No.1   John F. Mayer
Midnight Sun [v]   Karl Edward Wagner
In the Lair of Yslsl   Karl Edward Wagner
Karl Wagner, Apostle of
  Blood [a]   Manly Wade Wellman
Killer   Karl Edward Wagner & David Drake
Lonely Places   Karl Edward Wagner
*Darkness Weaves [na1/2] Karl Edward Wagner
Lynortis Reprise [nt] Karl Edward Wagner
Death Angel's Shadow [v] Karl Edward Wagner

Sum/Fall 1975   1/2 (2) George Chastain
The Dark Muse [nt]   Karl Edward Wagner
Dragon's Teeth   David Drake
The Little Ones of the
  Hills   Robert Weinberg
The Last Wolf   Karl Edward Wagner
The House on the Borderland
  [ap]   George Chastain
*Darkness Weaves [na2/2] Karl Edward Wagner
Revenge of the Creature [v]   John Mayer
Fragment [v]   John D. Squires
Test Case   Carl Jacobi

April 1976   (2/1) 3   Andrew Smith
Arachne   H. H. Hollis
Dark Body   H. H. Hollis
Inertia   H. H. Hollis
H. H. Hollis, Biography [a]   [The Editor]

August 1976   (2/2) 4   Andrew Smith
Through All His Blood Runs
  Shadow   C. L. Grant
The Temple of the Living
  Dead   Joseph Payne Brennan
Boxes   Richard K. Lyon
Dust to Dust   Basil Copper
From All the Fields of
  Hail and Fire   C. L. Grant

1979   No.5   Mark Betcher
In the Fourth Year of the
  War   Harlan Ellison
H. H. Hollis [obit]   Gary Hoppenstand
Even Money   H. H. Hollis
The Black Revealer [a]   Robert Bloch
Forsaken Voyage   Carl Jacobi
Charles L. Grant [a] Gary Hoppenstand
What More Remains   Charles L. Grant
Needle Song   Charles L. Grant
Charles L. Grant Bibliography [bib]   –

***

MIND MAGIC

[later retitled MY SELF]

An occult fiction magazine published monthly in large pulp format by The Shade Publishing Co., 1008 West York St., Philadelphia, Pennsylvania. Editor: G. R. Bay. The first two issues published a number of anonymous editorial written articles which are listed at the end of each entry for information.

June 1931   1/1   H. S. Moskowitz
In the Second Astral [na1/4]
                                Franz Trajore
True Stories of Spirit Land
  [col]   [no credit]
From an Old Egyptian Tomb   Mont Hurst
The Grey Mists Cleared Gladys E. Dansfield
The Black Art of Eric Hampt
                         Frank Kenneth Young
The Opened Door   D. M. Coulter
The Magic of the Book of
  Psalms [col]   [no credit]
Faithful Footsteps   Manly Wade Wellman
"Don't Take That Gun!"   Courtney Hilliard
[*anonymous articles:* Using the Subconsc-
  ious; Everything is Possible; The Strong
  Man of the House; The Attracting Power;
  Overcoming 'The Blues'; Help for Diffi-
  cult Days; From the Shining Book of the
  White Magician; Thing Right For What You
  Want; When the Body Sleeps; The Mystery
  of Psychometry]

July 1931   1/2   H. S. Moskowitz
The Man From Ouija Land
  [nt1/2]   Ralph Milne Farley
Wraiths of the Sea   August W. Derleth
In the Second Astral [na2/4] Franz Trajore
The Spider That Told Rosa Zagnoni Marinoni
The Jade Woman   W. Clyde Young
At the Top of the Stairs   M. D. McFadden
Love That Did Not Die   Norris Hiatt
Bill's Other Half   Louella O. Parsons
The Babe and the Board   Helen Armstrong
The Soul-Tree   Aghara Rhamin
Secret of Dreams   Rae King
[*anonymous articles:* The Key to Mastery;
  Using Your Supermind; Birthday Guide for
  July]

August 1931   1/3   John B. Moll
Arizona Treasure   Allen Leslie Hughes
Slim Takes the Wheel   Mark T. Pattie
The House That Hated Gladys E. Dansfield
The Astral Angler   Joseph Lichtblau
The Voice in the Night Myrtle Maud Morton
Exploits of a Mystic, I   C. W. Hidden
The Avenging Ashes   Mary Vivian Kane
Pedro's Golden Dreams   Rae King
In the Second Astral [na3/4] Franz Trajore
Out of the Hurricane   Mrs J. M. Walker
The Man From Ouija Land [nt2/2]
                         Ralph Milne Farley
An Amulet From Egypt   Allen Glasser
Psychic 'Parcel Post' [a] J. C. F. Grumbine
She Used Her Head   K. Summers
The Escaping Soul   George W. Bunton
The Royal Command   Lilliace M. Mitchell

Sep/Oct 1931   1/4   J. B. Moll
The Conquering Don   Manly Wade Wellman
Gangster's Ride   Mark T. Pattie
The Whitmarsh Blood   W. Clyde Young
Exploits of a Mystic, No. II   C. W. Hidden
The White Horse   Carl Swann
"A Dead Man is Calling"
                        Helen Marr Springer
The Golden Lotus   H. P. Nicholls
The Reincarnated Eyes   Conrad Swanson
Whence the Answer? [a]   'Zerr'
In the Second Astral [na4/4] Franz Trajore
He Was a Skeptic   Jack Woodford
Best Betz Mine   Milton Goldsmith
Across the Years   Rae King
A Dead Lover's Message   Zarick Kave
Side by Side   Jane Louisa Keating
Mind Power   Eric Shantz
The Astral Menace   Ralph Milne Farley
White Men - Black Magic   Horace Watkins
The Crash   F. Norris Hiatt

retitled MY SELF MAGAZINE

<u>November 1931</u>   1/5   J. B. Moll
The Haunted House of Down
   [v]   Frank Kenneth Young
The Garden in the Desert   W. Clyde Young
See More and Get More [a] Carl M. Parrish
The Black Astral   Ed Earl Repp
The Soul Raiders [nt1/2]   Franz Trajore
Nothing But the Truth [a] Albert C. Grier
The Astral Clean-Up   Mark T. Pattie
Secret of Riches [a] Henry Thomas Hamblin
The Magic of the Book of
   Psalms [col]   Magus Albus
The Exploits of a Mystic, III   C. W. Hidden
The Hieroglyphics   Ralph Milne Farley
The Devil Himself   Mary E. Counselman
The Mysterious Pilot   Laurenz Earley
Ouija Kicks In   Joseph Lichtblau
The Interchange of Souls   Alexis Meredith
The Spirit of the Hacienda   Luis Gonzales
The Ghost Yacht   Godin V. Green
Dorothea Decides   Rae King
The Disbeliever   Sid Young
He Killed the Ghost   Donald Arthur Vance

<u>December 1931</u>   1/6   H. S. Moskovitz
Are You a Coward?   Joe W. Skidmore
Jacquelaine's Jewels   Hugh King Harris
Darn the Difference!   Robert L. Bemis
The Soul Raiders [nt2/2]   Franz Trajore
The Exploits of a Mystic, IV   C. W. Hidden
I Got a Job!   James L. Powell
Select a Far Goal [a]   Charles Sparrow
Make Your Ideas Work [a]   Albert C. Grier
Lee Fu Lin Goes Home   Ralph C. Smith
Ouija's Diamonds   Rae King
World War Aftermath   Sam Caufman, Jr
The Magic of the Psalms [col] Magus Albus
Creating Conditions [a]
    Edmund A. Youndash
An Oriental Idea   J. P. Robinson
Victim of the Chair   Maud Youngstrom
Dombroso's Power   Joseph Lichtblau
White Faces   Mark T. Pattie
The Magic Window   Thelva B. Ellis
The Shining Blade   W. Clyde Young

* * *

MONSTER PARADE

A movie monster magazine published bi-monthly in quasi-slick format by Magnum Publications, 1250 Camden Ave., S.W., Canton, Ohio, with Editorial Offices at 11 West 42nd St., New York. Editor: Larry Shaw. The first issue evidently took over from an earlier non-fantasy magazine by retaining the volume numbering, a ploy to by-pass certain postal regulations. The film previews and photo features are not indexed below.

September 1958   2/6 (1)   ?
Rock Around the Tombstone
                  Robert J. Cassidy
I'll Love You to Death!   Lawrence Block
Horror Show   Kenneth Malone
Feeding Time at the Zoo Matthew Shipwreck
Revenge of the Jukebox Vampire
                  Colin Cassidy
Witch Girl!   [no credit]
The Most Horrible Story in the
   World   Barry Miles
Feed Me, Mr. Wodgett   John Jakes

November 1958   1/2 (2)   ?
The Well of the Damned   Robert Antone
Dig That Crazy Scientist   Alex Merriman
Humans, Go Home!   Matthew Shipwreck
Orgy of the Undead   Barry Miles
The Man Who Believed in
   Werewolves   Charles D. Hammer
Seven Curses of Lust   Gordon Fry
Zoot Zombie   Matthew Shipwreck

December 1958   1/3 (3)   ?
Hipster From Hell   Elliot Zucker
Secrets of the Torture Cult Hall Thornton
The Curse of Hamid   Robert Antone
Web of the Giant   Hillary Dawn
Mummy's Rumble   Gordon Fry
Curses For Sale [a]   Bill Long
Coffins Are For Corpses   David Challon
"Find Me a Victim"   Dan Malcolm
Crossroads of the Ghouls   Ralph Burke
Magician of Death [cs]   [no credit]

March 1959   1/4 (4)   ?
The Thing Behind Hell's Door
                 Alex Merriman
Demons of Cthulhu   Charles D. Hammer
Frozen Stiff   Hal Ellson
The Story of Dracula [pic] Blackie Seymour
Death Feast of the Damned   G. H. Dubrow
Curse of the Blue Man   Barry Miles
The Monster Who Came From
   Nowhere   Kenneth Malone
She Stalks at Sundown [cs]   Lou Cameron

***

MONSTERS AND THINGS

A movie monster magazine which contained a higher percentage of weird fiction than most. Published bi-monthly in quasi-slick format by Magnum Publications, 1250 Camden Ave., S.W., Canton, Ohio, with Editorial Offices at 11 West 42nd Street, New York. Editor: Larry Shaw. The film previews and photo-sections are omitted from this index.

January 1959   1/1   ?
Go, Ghoul, Go!   James Carew
Bellman's Voodoo Head   Robert J. Cassiday
Dig That Wailing Dirge   Kenneth Malone
Revenge of the Were-Thing
                            Joseph E. Kelleam
The Vampire Legion [cs]   [no credit]
The Creeping, Flying Terror   Hillary Dawn

April 1959   1/2   ?
Horror-Beasts Dine Tonight!
                            Robert J. Cassiday
The Story of Frankenstein
     [pic]   Marie Oliveri
You Can't Cheat Death's Demon
                            David Challon
The Undertaker's Sideline
                          Richard F. Watson
Low Priestess of Hell   Daneth MacAbee
Curse of the Living Crossbones
     [cs]   [no credit]

***

MOONBROTH

A small press weird fantasy magazine published irregularly by Malvern Enterprises, Portland, Oregon (originally Bellevue, Washington). Editor/Publisher: Dale C. Donaldson. A unique magazine in that it was distributed in loose-leaf format for 'self-assembly'. It was a much respected magazine and served as an inspiration to many that followed. After Donaldson's death in January 1977 a final issue was assembled by his widow in tribute to his memory.

1971   1/1 (1)
Blake's Behemoth   Frances Aldrich
Basement Workshop   Hugh Malvern

1971   1/2 (2)
Pardonable Error   William Demic
Sasquacide   Pauline McTavish
Finale [v]   Dale C. Donaldson

1971   1/3 (3)
Pisca-Musk [nt]   Hugh Malvern

1971   1/4 (4)
Spirit Transfer   Mo DeMathews
Easy Money   Renyard Kelly
Fair Exchange   Othello F. Peters
Grotesqueries [ap]   Jeff Birchill
The Fine Art of Scrying [a]   William Demic

1972   1/5 (5)
Experiment   Othello F. Peters
Eve of Sabat [v]   Adriana Gomez
Bertwold's Dragons   Frances Aldrich
Primeval Voices   P. A. Farrington
Mr Moorlahn's Castle   Rebecca Ross
Gentle Heart   Douglas Justice

1972   2/6 (6)
Centi Child   B. George Hallenbeck
Something Special   Delores Cephus
Nameless Ones [v]   Adriana Gomez
Other Man, Other Side   Richard Stooker
Immortal   Renyard Kelly
Little Son   Pauline McTavish
The Lewton Critiques [a]   Dave Lewton

1972   2/7 (7)
Creeper   Janet Fox
The Shape-Changers   William Tredinnick , Jr
... and the Curse Goes On   Rebecca Ross
Carol's Initiation   Joseph B. Wilson
Letters to the Boss   William Demic

1972   2/8 (8)
Malicious Mermaid   Douglas Justice
A Devil in Time Makes   Sol Kanemann
Angelique [v]   Adriana Gomez
Curse, Fire and Brimstone   Adriana Gomez
Realm of the Dead [v]   Bill Wolfenbarger
Apprentice   Renee Buice
... I'll Conserve You   Sol Kanemann
Legend of the Vampire
     [a]   William Tredinnick, Jr
Introduction to Witchcraft
     [a1/4]   Joseph B. Wilson
Head Man   George Hallenbeck
Snowghost   Janet Fox
What Foods These Morsels Be
     Joe R. Christopher

1973   2/9 (9)
Waiting For Fate   Sol Kanemann
Searching For Fate   Sol Kanemann
Avatar Spawning   Richard Landwehr

1973   2/10 (10)
Plumbing Scared [v]   Shannon Isbell
Introduction to Witchcraft
     [a2/4]   Joseph B. Wilson
Good Thoughts   W. Paul Ganley
Pre-Islamic Evil Jinn
     [a]   William Tredinnick, Jr

1973	2/11 (11)
Full Moon Tonight	Amos Salmonson
Dark Woodsman	B. George Hallenbeck

1973	2/12 (12)
Draught [v]	Bill Breiding
Kiss of Bast	Douglas W. Justice
The Black Stone God	Adriana Gomez
Fodder For the King [v]	G. Sutton Breiding
Jezebel	Renee Buice

1974	3/13 (13)
Accursed Glade	John Wysocki
Nantichoke	Darlene A. Chesebro

1974	3/14 (14)
Introduction to Witchcraft [a3/4]	Joseph B. Wilson
Fate Levels	Sol Kanemann
Alone With Fate	Sol Kanemann
The Square Gray Box	Elaine V. Worrel
Self Scrutiny [v]	Margaret L. Carter

1974	3/15 (15)
Shadowseed [v]	Lewis Sanders
Vampiric Madness [v]	Lewis Sanders
Through the Dark Horse	W. Fraser Sandercombe

1974	3/16 (16)
My Son, My Son! [play]	Douglas Derek Roome
The Wargamer	Gerard E. Giannattasio
The Desert Waits [v]	Bill Breiding

1974	3/17 (17)
Necromancer's Dream [v]	Michael Fantina
Faces of Fate	Sol Kanemann
The Shape of Fate	Sol Kanemann
Dance of Dawn	Mark Otter
My Rightful Place	Mo DeMathews
The Statue's Last Plea [v]	G. Sutton Breiding

1974	3/18 (18)
Demon	David C. Smith
The Litter	Ina Rae Ussack

1974	3/19 (19)
Introduction to Witchcraft [a4/4]	Joseph B. Wilson
Torso [v]	Amos Salmonson
Delivery	Fred C. Adams
Mindcrawl [v]	Bill Breiding

1975	4/20 (20)
It Will End Here	Sol Kanemann
Capo Mafioso's Fate	Sol Kanemann
God Walks	Walter Shedlofsky
There'll Be a Hot Time in the Old Mound Tonight [v]	Sol Kanemann
Breck	W. Fraser Sandercombe

1975	4/21 (21)
Fines	Merritt Clifton
Filet [v]	Sol Kanemann
The Visit	Gary Dechau
The Black Captain	H. Warner Munn
Delayed Birthday	Gahan Addams
Coyote [v]	Shannon Isbell

Squatter's Rights [v]	Karma Beck
Lonely Wanderer [v]	Bill Breiding
Nosferatu [v]	G. Sutton Breiding

1976	5/22 (22)
Perran Sands [v]	Phyllis Anne Karr
Tomb Beasts	David C. Smith

1976	5/23 (23)
Song to M'Lady [v]	G. Sutton Breiding
Black Leather Vampire	Bill Breiding
Spillt Moonbroth [v]	G. Sutton Breiding
The Ancient Centaur to the Young Satyr Spake [v]	G. Sutton Breiding
Father of Werewolves [v]	Bill Breiding
A Paean and A Requiem [v]	G. Sutton Breiding
Lamia [v]	Bill Breiding

1976	5/24 (24)
Diversion	Michael Fantina
I Saw a Little Girl Today	Daniel McGuire
Visitor	Maureen Ann Nolan
Fate's Send-Off	Sol Kanemann
Rape of the Cheechako [v]	Karma Beck
Whatever It Was	Sandra J. McHale

1976	5/25 (25)
Vampyre [v]	Susan L. Tannahill
Dead Love	W. G. Bliss
The Shadow Well [v]	Bill Wolfenbarger
Green Bank	G. Sutton Breiding
Skeleton's Grave	Rebecca Ross
For All the Pre-1950 Igors [v]	Sol Kanemann

1976	5/26 (26)
Father and Son	J. Izzo, Jr
Sisters	Merritt Clifton
O, Holy Death [v]	John DiPrete
Night Ride	Gerard Houarner

1976	5/27 (27)
The Bloodstained Prints	William Scott Home
Kobold [v]	H. Warner Munn
Casmaran	W. Fraser Sandercombe

1976	5/28 (28)
The Shape-Changers [Pts 2 and 3]	William Tredinnick, Jr
You Can't Make a Silk Bed Out of a Sow's Ear [v]	Sol Kanemann
Dread the Full Moon	E. R. Lovick
Dust Under the Bed	Jim Zychowicz

1977	6/1 (29/30)
Immortal Satan	P. A. Farrington
Last Anniversary	Bill Tredinnick
Thicker Than Blood	Gordon Linzner
Moon Terror [v]	John DiPrete
Were Eagle	Douglas Justice
Cry of the Shoggoths [v]	Lewis Sanders
Repayment	Daniel Gaultney
One Night With Fate [v]	Sol Kanemann
When Fate Summons [v]	Sol Kanemann

[The mailing for Mb29 included Donaldson's novella "The Reluctant Warlock"]

***

MYRDDIN

*A small press fantasy magazine published irregularly by Lawson Hill, 6633 N.
Ponchartrain Blvd., Chicago, Illinois (first three issues from Northbrook,
Illinois). Editor: Lawson Hill. With the fifth issue* Myrddin *changed its
name to* Night Flights.

Winter 1975   1/1 (1)   L. Howlett
A Ghost Story   Lance Howlett
*Near Avalon [v]   William Morris
The Significance of Dwarf-
   Names in the Writings of
   J. R. R. Tolkien [a]   Ken Hoglund
Delirium [v]   R. F. Caxton
The Parable of the Three   John H. Kenneth
A Journey Into Faery Land   Marc Holden
The Possession of the Ring [a]
                                Richard Hess

August 1975   1/2 (2)   Lance Howlett
The Road to Elveron [v]   H. Warner Munn
Nocturne   Linda Detambel
City of Jewels   Jessica Salmonson
Empty Rooms [v]   Joseph Payne Brennan
Road Crew [v]   Wayne Hooks
Clyde S. Kilby: an Interview [in]
                                Ken Hoglund
A Calendar for Memia   Lance Howlett
*Night of Death [v]   Fritz Leiber
Charles Dodgson and George Macdonald:
   A Friendship Observed [a] Ken Hoglund
Of Brados and the Fall of
   Sen-Krad   Charles F. Edwards
Ice Forest at Midnight [v]
                        Joseph Payne Brennan
Deep Mysteries [v]   William H. Pugmire

[March] 1976   No.3   [photos]
Hints From Lavinny Whateley's
   Kitchen #1   Darrell Schweitzer
Madness of the Oracle [v]
                        Richard L. Tierney
Shadow Over Providence [a] Dirk W. Mosig
Magic Carpet   T. E. D. Klein
A Note and an Anecdote [a]
                        Kenneth W. Faig, Jr
City Haiku [v]   Keith Richmond
[also contains an acetate 33⅓ recording of

the Worldcon speeches by Robert Bloch and
Frank Belknap Long]

[April] 1978   No.4   Jim McLeod
The Little Glass Ship [v] H. Warner Munn
*Sara's Roses   C. C. Clingan
Return [v]   Joseph Payne Brennan
Further Up and Further In [a1/2]
                                Lois Larson
The Slayer in Dreams [v] Bill Wolfenbarger
The Wings of the White Bird
                          Darrell Schweitzer
The Battery [ss]   John DiPrete
Streams of Consciousness [v] Martin Bickman

retitled NIGHT FLIGHTS

Winter 1980/81   1/1 (1)   G. Schnobrich
          [sub-headed Myrddin 5]
Writer's Curse   Ramsey Campbell
Further Up and Further In
   [a2/2]   Lois Larson
Old Worlds For New? [a]   Thomas Egan
Dawn Woman [v]   H. Warner Munn
Merlin and Nimue [v]   Carol Ann Cupitt
Message Found in a Bottle
   [v]   George Bessette
The One Great Achievement of
   Padinre Luil   Jessica Amanda Salmonson
A Strange Encounter   Darrell Schweitzer
Hang-Up / Intimidation /
   Underscape [3v]   George Bessette
Voices [v]   Bill Wolfenbarger
Fiend-Fodder [v]   Steve Eng
My True Love [v]   Joseph Payne Brennan
Mitty of the Spaceways [v]
                           John A. Haliburton
The Conquerors [v]   H. Warner Munn

                    ***

146

THE MYSTERIOUS TRAVELER MAGAZINE

A mystery/suspense digest published bi-monthly by Grace Publishing, 105 East 15th St., New York. Editor: Robert Arthur. Inspired by the weekly radio program of the same name, the magazine contained a high percentage of macabre, terror and strange stories. With the last issue was retitled The Mysterious Traveler Mystery Reader.

November 1951   1/1 (1)   [N. Saunders]
*The Other Hangman   John Dickson Carr
*Goodbye, Goodbye   Craig Rice
The Knife   Robert Arthur
*The Big Money 'The Mysterious Traveler'
*The Man With Copper Fingers
                          Dorothy L. Sayers
*Dead Man's Story   Howard Rigsby
Repeat Performance   Andrew Saxon
*Pieces of Silver   Brett Halliday
*Side Bet   Will F. Jenkins
Found Money   John West
*The Wind   Ray Bradbury
*Rum For Dinner   Lawrence L. Blochman

January 1952   1/2 (2)   [N. Saunders]
*The $1,000,000 Motive   Brett Halliday
*The Black Cabinet   John Dickson Carr
*Play With Fire   H. W. Guernsey
*Find the Woman   Kenneth Millar
Collector's Item   Roald Dahl
*The Blue Geranium   Agatha Christie
*To the Future   Ray Bradbury
The Floating Finger   Dean Evans
The Motive   A. A. Fleming
*Smart Guy   Bruno Fischer
Change of Address   Mark Williams
*Eye Witness   'The Mysterious Traveler'

March 1952   1/3 (3)   [N. Saunders]
*I'll Be Just a Minute   Cornell Woolrich
*The Man Who Knew How   Dorothy L. Sayers
*Challenge to the Reader   Hugh Pentecost
*The White Hat   Sax Rohmer
The Jokester   Anthony Morton
*D-Day   Robert Trout
Body of an Elderly Man W. Lee Herrington
*The Lonely World   Richard Sale
*Sixty Grand Missing   Robert Arthur
"Drop Dead!"   Lou Huston

*"I, Murderer - " 'The Mysterious Traveler'
*Told For the Truth   Cyril Hume

June 1952   1/4 (4)   [N. Saunders]
*His Heart Could Break   Craig Rice
*Death By Drowning   Agatha Christie
*The Case of the Murderous Mice
                             Robert Arthur
The People Next Door   Pauline C. Smith
The Vanishing Passenger   John West
*Memory Test   Samuel W. Taylor
*Welcome Home   'The Mysterious Traveler'
*The Treasure Hunt   Edgar Wallace
*Pigeon's Blood   Fredrick Wells
*A Knife in the Night   Robert Forbes
The Hint   Jay Norman
*Back There in the Grass Gouverneur Morris

retitled The Mysterious Traveler
Mystery Reader

[September] 1952   No.5   [N. Saunders]
*Red Wine   Lawrence Blochman
*Women Are Poison   Brett Halliday
*Christmas Present
                 'The Mysterious Traveler'
*The Nine-Mile Walk   Harry Kemmelman
*Midnight Visit   Robert Arthur
*The Crowd   Ray Bradbury
*Adventure of the Sotheby
  Salesman   August Derleth
*No Bath For the Browns   Margot Bennet
*Later Than You Think
                 'The Mysterious Traveler'
*The Weeping Woman   John West
*The Whistling Room William Hope Hodgson
*A Very Neat Corpse   Alan Bird

***

147

MYSTERY STORIES

A rare British pulp magazine, companion to The Master Thriller Series published by The Worlds Work Ltd., Kingswood, Surrey. No editor credited. Published at least 20 issues of which those listed below are of a known high weird fantasy content. There may be others.

[1939]   No.18   ?

The Affair of the Three Turtles
                              Walter Rippinger
Marley's Masterpiece   Henry Rawle
Extremes Meet   Percy C. Clarke
The Last Chapter   E. Burke-Roche
The Practical Joke   Herbert Nicolson
The Road to Vandricourt   Roger Ellis
Night of Terror   Judson P. Phillips
The Scarabs   George Arnold
The Doctor Gave a Verdict   G. M. Butler

[1939]   No.19   ?

To the Confusion of Ah Lee   C. V. Tench
Another Man's Poison   R. Thurston Hopkins
Murder of the Ancients   Judson Phillips
Dawn's Disciple   J. Farquharson Lawrence
The Night Hawk   F. D. Bruce
The End of the Racket   H. M. Dixon
Appointment at Tev   John Storm
Heberden's Dam   I. S. Hammond
What Happened to Mrs Stanton
                              Verne Fletcher
A Flight from Fancy on the
   Route des Alpes   [no credit]

[1939]   No.20   ?
      [subtitled 'Mainly About Ghosts']
The Toast of Death   Charlton Robertson
Spite of Thunder   Alan Griff
Tonight at Eight   E. H. Thackeray
Black Panther   Roger Graham
Death in the Mountains   George Bellairs
Twelve Years After   John Arundel
Horror in the Fog   Russell Annabel
The Immortal Voice   James MacFie
New Corner   L. T. C. Rolt
The Inca's Ruby   A. M. Tarver

* * *

MYSTIC MAGAZINE

An occult magazine published bi-monthly by Palmer Publications, Evanston, Illinois. Editor: Raymond A. Palmer. Originally a fiction magazine the stories were gradually squeezed out by tales of 'true experiences'. After the seventh issue the non-fiction outweighed the fiction to the extent that the magazine ceased to be of relevance to the weird fantasy field. With the seventeenth issue in October 1956 the title was changed to Search *and the magazine continued featuring non-fiction only.*

November 1953   No.1   J. Allen St. John
The Hidden Kingdom [nt]   Ray Palmer
Go Visit Your Grave   Rog Phillips
I Travelled in a Flying
   Saucer   Paul M. Vest
League of the Living Dead Randall Garrett
The Astral Exile   Chester S. Geier
Searching for the Elixir of
   Life [a]   Drew Ames

January 1954   No.2   Robert G. Jones
Invasion of the Dark Ones [nt] Hal Annas
The Strange Case of Monica
   Lilith   Robert Barbour Johnson
Doppelganger   Lyn Venable
The Devil's Empire [nt]   Ray Palmer
Death in Peru   Joseph Payne Brennan
A Bishop's Hunch [ts]   Mrs Lawton Riley
The Purple Light [ts]   Lulu Bradley Cram
The Terrible Mouse [ts]   Drew Ames

March 1954   No.3   Malcolm Smith
Assignment to Life   Sanandana Kumara
The Kid With the Beautiful
   Hands   Melva Rogers
Winter Scene   William Campbell Gault
Earthbound   Charles Lee
The Devil's Dollhouse   Rog Phillips
The Demon That Stole My Wife [ts] Pat Fox
Mark Probert, the Famous Medium
   [a]   Roger Graham
Are the Saucers our Friends?
   [a]   William B. Nash
Uplift, Inc. [a]   Len Guttridge

May 1954   No.4   Malcolm Smith
I Meet the Flying Saucer Man Paul M. Vest
I Carried a Witch on My Back

[ts]   Louis Sztrokay
The Moon That Rose Twice in
   One Night [ts]   James Samuel Stemons
A Voice Saved My Life [ts] Carol McKinney
Mistress of the Kama-Loka   Peter Worth
Ming Cha   Milton Mann
...Lest Ye Be Judged   Sanandana Kumara
Mental Projection [a]   Walter G. Smith
Do Etheric Armies Exist [a] Robert Rowan

August 1954   No.5
Venusians Walk Our Streets   Paul M. Vest
The Ghost of Granada [ts]
                   Arthur Darrell Hucherby
A Funeral Before it Happened
   [ts]   Lillian M. Slayton
The Man in My Bed [ts]   Mrs Pearl McKay
In the Twinkling of an Eye
                        Sanandana Kumara
Strange Children [a] Millicent X. Horton
Your Handwriting [a]   Prof. J. S. Maxwell

October 1954   No.6
My Awakening on Another Planet Paul M. Vest
Wings and a Vision [ts]   Waldo T. Boyd
Joan Fontaine and the Palmist
   [ts]   W. E. Farbstein
How To Make a Magic Mirror [a] Ray Starr
Bloody Macbeth   Converse E. Nickerson
The Holy Man   Sanandana Kumara
What is to Be   Melva Rogers

December 1954   No.7
The Exposer Exposed [a]   Dr W. D. Chesney
Extraterrestrial Visitor
   [ts]   Miriam Teel Clarke
Firewalking [a]   D. C. McGowan
The Phantom Jeep   Bobette Gugliotta
The Golden Kitten   Charles Lee
God is In the Mountain   Peter Worth

***

149

N

THE NEKROMANTIKON

A small press magazine published quarterly by Manly Banister, 1905 Spruce Ave., Kansas City, Missouri. Editor: Manly Banister. A quarto duplicated magazine (with printed front matter) The Nekromantikon was a serious attempt to provide a market for the fan writer as a stepping-stone to the paying magazines.

Spring 1950	1/1	Manly Banister
Cry Wolf!		Manly Banister
The Abydos Tablet [a]		Eva Firestone
Two Gentlemen in Black		Edward W. Ludwig
Fear [a]		Manly Banister
Lonesome Journey [v]		M. Houston
The Humling		M. Houston
Songs of the Galaxy [v]		Rory Faulkner
Haunt		George Hart
The Dryad [v]		Emili A.
The Green Thing		Gregg Powers
Hymeneal [v]		Val Seanne

Summer 1950	1/2	Ralph R. Phillips
Ralph Rayburn Phillips [a]		
		[Manly Banister]
Fen-Wer		Manly Banister
Moon-Calf [v]		Rory Faulkner
Doomsroad		Wilkie Conner
Rainbow Cities [v]		Emili A.
Rainbow City of Antarctica		C. H. Spaulding
Mr Hodgett's Quick Conversion		
		Battell Loomis
Innsmouth: Dread City By the		
Sea [v]		R. Flavie Carson
The House of Shadows		Herman Stowell King
The Tall Terrible Women [v]		
		Lilith Lorraine
Metamorphosis		J. A. McKee
The Haunted Street [v]		
		Astara Zimmer Bradley
Oculus Penetrans		M. Houston
David H. Keller, M.D. [v]		Tom Carter

Autumn 1950	1/3	Manly Banister
Twilight Fell at Camelot [na]		M. Houston
Lilith Lorraine and the Avalon		
World Arts Academy [a]		[Manly Banister]
Avalon [v]		Lilith Lorraine
Why Abdul Alhazred Went Mad		D. R. Smith

Winter 1950/51	1/4	[Manly Banister]
King of the Golden City		Lin Carter
The Chinese Curse		Battell Loomis
The Doom of Cassandany		Stanton A. Coblentz
Janie		G. M. Carr
Dianetics: A Critical Appraisal		
[a]		D. C. Montgomery Jr, M.D.
Spaceman's Song [v]		Marion Zimmer Bradley
Future Man [v]		F. Anton Reeds
*Medallion in Quicksilver [v]		T. Heywood
Waiting For the Call [v]		Olive Morgan
Moon Secrets [v]		Andrew Duane
The Hungarian Music Shop		C. O. Betancourt
You Who Have Slain Me —		Manly Banister
Poetic Vendetta		John E. Blyler
Mis Majesty at Midnight [v]		
		Thomas H. Carter
Laptoumi Araptoumi [a]		S. R. Sheedy
Inquest in Kansas [v]		Hyacinthe Hill

Midyear 1951	No.5	Ralph R. Phillips
Changeling's Choice		Vernon L. McCain
The Undead [v]		R. Flavie Carson
Wellington Varney, V.V.		William G. Weston
Ring Around the Black Star		Frederick Gayle
Red Sand [v]		Walt Klein
Voices at Night [ss]		Wilson Tucker
Helping Hand ...		Cedric Walker
"Remembrance of Things Past..."		
		Terry Jeeves
The Pink Umbrella		David R. Bunch
Second Hand Wings		Alice Bullock
Isis Faces Crisis [a]		S. R. Sheedy
Fern Seed [v]		Isabelle E. Dinwiddie
Incorporeal Invitation [v]		Orma McCormick
The Stalker		Edward W. Ludwig
In Strange Remembering [v]		
		James E. Warren, Jr
The Spirit of Earth		James E. Warren, Jr
Ju Ju Magic		Edwin L. Brooks

The Gourmet	D. C. Montgomery, Jr
Two of Us Lie [v]	Genevieve K. Stephens
Said the Spider	Charles E. Fritch
Nova [v]	Astara Zimmer Bradley
I'll Never Leave You	Clive Jackson
Witch [v]	Lilith Lorraine
Death-Wish [v]	F. Anton Reeds
Old Man of the Moors	F. Anton Reeds & Charles Newton Briggs
The Romans Encounter the Nervii	Evan H. Appelman
Sic Transit [v]	Charlotte Todd
The Wind Blows, Mother ...	Antony Borrow
Contemplation of an Amoeba [v]	Richard Elliot
The Visitors [ss]	Wilson Tucker
Afternoon	E. C. Tubb
The Call	Alan Hunter
The Big Game	M. C. Rodman
Come, My Sweet	Steve Benedict
Here Comes the Bogyman!	Michael Tealby
Shadow Queen [v]	Emili A.
The Vortex Telescope	Battell Loomis
For the First or Last Fantast [v]	Forrest C. Davis
Weather Report From Mercury [v]	Dorothea M. Faulkner
Stranger In a World [v]	C. O. Betancourt
Nightriders [v]	G. M. Carr
Under Scorpio (Noctuary) [v]	Terence Heywood

***

[THE] NEW FANTASY JOURNAL

A small-press magazine edited and published by Irvin L. Wagner, Bronson, Michigan. A neatly mimeographed quarto magazine it laid a greater emphasis on non-fiction but is included because of its link between Wyrd *and its direct successor* Wax Dragon.

Summer 1976   No.1   Brian Pavlac
The Coming of the Philosopher
                  Darrell Schweitzer
So Come, Amyrillis   Phyllis Ann Karr
The Black Desert of Gomba-Mo
            Jessica Amanda Salmonson
The Four Branches [a]   Dale Nelson
Of Chocolate Covered Conans
   [a]   Charles R. Saunders
Reality in Zelazny Fantasy [a]   Mark Rich

1977   No.2   Randy Holmberg
Beneath the Golden Hill   Ron Nance
The Stuff of Legend [a]   Jim Allen
Fear: the Short Story [a]   David Madison
The Bight of Benin [a] Charles R. Saunders

***

NIGHT VOYAGES

A small press magazine published irregularly in slick format by Raconteur Publications, Freeburg, Illinois. Editors: Gerald J. Brown & Charles Pitts. Originally described as a 'Magazine of Creative Images' the early issues were devoted almost entirely to graphic art/comic strips. By issue No.6, however, the emphasis had shifted toward full text stories and the shift continued thereafter. The final issue appeared in spring 1984 (see note).

Fall 1977   1/1   J. A. Richardson
Star Wars II [suggested
    sequel]   [Gerald J. Brown]
Alienation [gs]   [F. Newton Burcham]
Creative Images [ap]   Charles Pitts,
        Paul M. Cordel & F. Newton Burcham
Consummation [gs]   Paul M. Cordel
Tumblins [gs]   Charles Pitts

Summer 1978   1/2   F. Newton Burcham
Sunslayer [gs]   Gerald Brown
                      [art:Charles Pitts]
Alwaysland   Paul M. Cordel
The Dream is Alive [ap] F.Newton Burcham,
            Bruce Conklin & Charles Pitts
The Richardson Interview [in] Charles Pitts
Ted, Red and Willie
    [gs.ex]   John Adkins Richardson

Winter 1978   1/3   Joan Hanke Woods
Songbringer [gs1/2]   Gerald J. Brown
            [art: Don Secrease & Paul Daly]
Creative Images [ap]   F. N. Burcham,
    Charles Pitts,Jerry Sutberry & Don Secrease
Yours Truly, Robert Bloch
    [in]   Gerald J. Brown
... And Never to Cry   Wayne Hooks
The Alien and the Elf [cs]
            F. N.Burcham & Paul M. Cordel

Summer 1979   1/4   Bruce Conklin
A Jocund Jaunt ...: Profile
    of C.L. Moore [a]   Patricia Jackson
Chrysalis [gs]   Paul Cordel
                  [art: F. Newton Burcham]
Frog Wars! [spf]   [Gerald J. Brown]
Creative Images [ap]   Charles Pitts,
            B. C. Boyer & Dan Day

Songbringer [cs2/2]   Gerald Brown
            [art: Don Secrease & Paul Daly]
The Puppet of Fate [gv]   Larry Gay
                  [art: F. Newton Burcham]
Willy   Wayne Hooks
Anne McCaffrey [in]   Karen Haber

Fall 1979   1/5   Randal Spangley
Tony and the Tribe [in]   Gerald Brown
    *[an interview with Tony de Zuniga
    compiled by Brown following a general
    discussion along with Charles Pitts,
    F. Newton Burcham, Paul Daly and Don
    Secrease. Mary de Zuniga also cont-
    ributed to the interview]*
Leda's Last Child   Della Colantone
Sunslayer: Willow at the
    World's End [gs1/3]   Gerald Brown
            [art: Don Secrease & Rick Burchett]
Catherine and L. Sprague
    de Camp [a/in]   Patricia Jackson
Charles L. Grant: In The
    Shadows [a]   Michael Bracken
Portfolio [ap]   F. Newton Burcham
... And Die, and Die   Rick Wilber
Artmaster [cs]   Dave Tipton

Summer 1980   1/6   Hans-Peter Werner
        [special All-Pro edition]
Raising Kane: Interview with
    Karl Edward Wagner, M.D. [in]
                            Gerald Brown
Mwanzo   Charles R. Saunders
Portfolio [ap]   Brad Foster
The Tim Kirk Interview [in] Gerald Brown
Sunslayer: Confrontation
    [gs2/3]   Gerald Brown
            [art: Don Secrease & Rick Burchett]

153

***

[Note: Vol.1,No.10, the final issue, was
released in Spring 1984, and thus beyond
the cut-off date of this Index. For the
record, it contained fiction: "The Last
Leg" Scott Edelman, "The Day After To-
morrow" Jan Bee Landman, "The Case of the
Crazy Cartoonist" Fred Singer, "Chamel-
eon" Gene O'Neill, "Fine Print" Michael
Bracken, "Les Bals des Victimes" James
Anderson, "Five Cents a Look" Jessica A.
Salmonson, "Rex" Gerald Brown, "The Book-
shop at the Corner" Janet Fox, "Would
Smell as Sweet" Shari Prange, "Through the
Padded Door" Ardath Mayhar, "The CornWolf"
Bill Hopkins, "Non-Fiction" Keith W.
Strandberg, "The Last Frame" Phillip C.
Heath, "The Janissaries of Rimini" David
Nalle, "I Want to be Like You" Frank Pod-
gajny, "Dragonwood" Charles de Lint.]

NOVEMBER

A small press weird fantasy magazine published quarterly in octavo format by Mathematical Shapes, Seattle, Washington. Publisher/Editor: Lawrence J. Dickson.

Autumn 1980	1/1	Carol Bevilacqua
Mechanthropy		Janet Fox
Afghan Blood		Faizullah Kakar
Three Fires of God [a]		John F. Bolek
Math Anxiety [a]		N. W. Barcus

Winter 1981	1/2	Carol Bevilacqua
Detente		Richard Bowman
The Sleeper/Savannah [v]		Jeffrey Goddin
A Realistic Goal		B. F. Watkinson
The Actuarial Fallacy [a]		
		Lawrence J. Dickson

Spring 1981	1/3	Carol Bevilacqua
A Passing Stranger		H. J. Cording
Time Travel?		Gene O'Neill
Weaver of the Dark		Janet Fox

***

NYCTALOPS

An amateur magazine published and edited irregularly by Harry O. Morris, 500 Wellesley S.E., Albuquerque, New Mexico. Dedicated to the memories of H.P. Lovecraft and August Derleth it consists primarily of non-fiction (an early fiction companion being From Beyond the Dark Gateway), but after the initial issues it became one of the major publications in the field and will be of interest to the users of this Index. The fiction content has increased in recent issues. Format changes have been frequent and it is now a neatly printed quarto sized annual.

May 1970   1/1 (1) Harry O. Morris
Clark Ashton Smith [a]   Harry O. Morris
  [all other contents are reviews]

October 1970   1/2 (2) Harry O. Morris
H. P. Lovecraft did not Write
  SF - By His Own Standards
  [a]   Eddy C. Bertin
Robert E. Howard and the
  Cthulhu Mythos [a]   Robert Weinberg
H. P. Lovecraft: A Story
  Listing [bib]   Harry O. Morris

February 1971   1/3 (3) Harry O. Morris
H. P. Lovecraft: The Critics
  [a]   Eddy C. Bertin
Further Addenda to HPL Story
  Listing [bib]   E. P. Berglund
H. P. Lovecraft: A Story
  Listing II [bib] Harry O. Morris
A Listing of Some Lovecraft
  Manuscripts [bib]   [no credit]
The Walkers [v]   Eddy C. Bertin

June 1971   1/4 (4) Harry O. Morris
The Cthulhu Mythos: A Review
  and Analysis [a]   Eddy C. Bertin
Red-Litten Yoth [v] Walter C. DeBill, Jr
R'lyeh [v]   Walter C. DeBill, Jr
You Can't Tell the Players
  Without a Program [a]   Ken Scher
Addenda to HPL Story Listing
  II [bib]   E. P. Berglund
H.P.Lovecraft: A Story
  Listing III [bib]   Harry O. Morris
Perhaps the Elder Gods James H. Lawson IV

October 1971   1/5 (5) Harry O. Morris
H. P. Lovecraft and Pseudo-
  mathematics [a]   Robert Weinberg
In the Trail of Lovecraft:
  The Followers of Cthulhu
  [a]   Eddy C. Bertin
Addenda to HPL Story
  Listing III [bib]   E. P. Berglund
Something's Eating My Brain
  [v]   Eddy C. Bertin
The Well [v]   George Laking
The Elder Fear [v]   John Bredon
The Frog at Midnight [v]   Dave Szurek
The Garret-Room [v] Richard L. Tierney
What Scared Professor
  Peaslee [a]   Daniel K. Shenandoah
"And When Blood Touches
  Blood..."   John Jacob
The Lovecraft Fiction
  Manuscripts [bib] Kenneth W. Faig, Jr
Foreign Publication of Howard
  Phillips Lovecraft [bib] E. P. Berglund

February 1972   (1/6) 6   Denis Tiani
The (bastard) Children of
  Hastur [a]   Marion Zimmer Bradley
Night Oath [v]   Dave Szurek
Fomalhaut Rising [v]   George Laking
The Colour Out of Cygnus [a]
             Alan D. Gullette
Innsmouth Map [map]   Eric Carlson
*The Sign of the Dragon-Fly
  [a]   Glenn Lord
Summons From R'lyeh [v] Gary Harrison
Lovecraft on Television [a]
           Darrell Schweitzer

156

Evil Dreams: Sonnets of the
    Outer Dark [v]   Richard L. Tierney
[I. In Evil Dreams; II. The Hills; III. The
Volcano; IV. Demon-Star; V.The Pinnacles;
VI. Zarria]
Homecoming   Walter C. DeBill, Jr
The Lovecraft Fiction
    Manuscripts, 2 [bib] Kenneth W. Faig, Jr

August 1972   (1/7) 7   Tim Kirk
    [Special Clark Ashton Smith issue]
Nyctalops [v]   Clark Ashton Smith
Five Approaches to the
    Achievement of Clark
    Ashton Smith: Cosmic
    Master Artist [a]   Marvin R. Hiemstra
Through Space and Time
    with CAS [a]   Mike Glyer
CAS: A Note on the Aesthetics
    of Fantasy [a]   Charles K. Wolfe
*Where Fantasy Meets Science
    Fiction [ltr]   Clark Ashton Smith
*The Last Romantic [a]   S. J. Sackett
The Fading Red Sun of
    Zothique [a]   Roger Bryant
The Artist: an Adulation [v]
                        Alan D. Gullette
Clark Ashton Smith: Natal
    Horoscope [a]   E. Hoffman Price
Drugs and Clark Ashton
    Smith [a]   Dennis Rickard
Eroes and the Ghoul: Necrophilia
    in the Prose and Poetry of
    Clark Ashton Smith [a]
                    Charles Richard Grose
Fulfillment [v]   Richard L. Tierney
In Zstharan [v]   Darrell Schweitzer
Opium and Sake: Prose Poems [v] Gary Drake
[I. Exordium; II. Sunset in Atlantis;
    III. Skulls of Purple; IV. The Caravan of
    Seven Camels. V. The Elephant of Onyx;
    VI. The Throne of Cthulhu]
The Oldest Dreamer   Walter C. DeBill
Tsathoggua [v]   Charles Richard Grose
                        [art: Steve Riley]
CAS: Portfolio [ap]   Herb Arnold,
    Mike Scott, Randall Spurgin & Rah Hoffman
Some Bibliographic Notes on
    CAS [bib]   T. G. L. Cockcroft
The Fiction of Clark Ashton
    Smith: When He Wrote It
    and What Remains Unpublished
    [a]   Roy A. Squires
In Search of a Smith Library
    [a]   Stuart David Schiff
Memories of Klarkash-Ton [a]George F. Haas
A Visitor From Averoigne [a] Robert Bloch
The Poetry of Clark Ashton
    Smith [a]   Frank Belknap Long
The Arcana of Arkham-Auburn
    [a]   Rah Hoffman
The Philosophy of the Weird Tale
    [note]   Clark Ashton Smith
Excerpts From the Black Book
    [ex]   Clark Ashton Smith
The Mime of Sleep [v] Clark Ashton Smith
Amor [v]   Clark Ashton Smith
Prose Pastels   Clark Ashton Smith
[6. To the Daemon; 7. The Forbidden Forest;
    8. The Mithridate]

Richard L. Tierney: His Book
    [a]   Richard L. Tierney
The Seventh Wine of Xalamundo
                    Charles Richard Grose
The City of Outcasts   Alan D. Gullette
Three Prose Poems [v]   Stanley Wiater
[Harunonn's Madness; The Ill-Fated Lovers;
    Confession to Ccathaii]
The Conquest of Yondo   Robert Weinberg
*Correspondence from Robert E.
    Howard to Clark Ashton Smith
    [ltr]   Robert E. Howard
*To Clark Ashton Smith [v]
                    Donald Sidney-Fryer

April 1973   (2/1) 8
Howard Phillips Lovecraft: The
    Early Years 1890-1914
    [a1/3]   Kenneth W. Faig, Jr
H.P. Lovecraft and the Science
    of Poe [a]   Graham Pryor
Pesh-Tlen [v]   Brian Lumley
Night Dancers [v]   Lewis Sanders
A Lovecraft Profile [a]   George Wetzel
Random Notes [col]   T. G. L. Cockcroft
'Hastur Is a Place'!!
                    Darrell Schweitzer
The Death of a Gentleman: The
    Last Days of H.P. Lovecraft
    [a]   R. Alain Everts
Waiting in the Dark [v]   Eddy C. Bertin
The Evil House [v]   Richard L. Tierney
H. Wenske: a Portfolio [ap] Helmut Wenske
A Report From Clark Ashton
    Smith Country [a] Donald Sidney-Fryer
The Ghost of H.P.L. [v] L. Sprague de Camp
Arthur Machen: Forgotten
    Master of Fantasy [a]   James Taylor
The Witchery of Robert Bloch
    [a]   Bruce Walker
Mrs Howard Phillips Lovecraft
    [a]   R. Alain Everts
The Search For Lovecraft's
    Outsider [a]   David J. Brown
The Paintings of Hieronymous
    Bosch [v]   T. E. D. Klein
The Father of the Witch [v] T. E. D. Klein
The Terror From Out of Time:
    I. The Shadow From Yith
    [rr]   Alan D. Gullette
Le Voyageur [v]   R. Alain Everts

July 1974   (2/2) 9   Denis Tiani
The Four Faces of the Outsider
    [a]   Dirk W. Mosig
In Search of Yig [a]   John J. Koblas
The Terror Out of Time:
    II. The Horror From Yith
    [rr]   Walter C. DeBill, Jr
*Howard Phillips Lovecraft and
    Sex [a]   R. Alain Everts
Artfolio by Helmut Wenske [ap]
                        Helmut Wenske
Artfolio by Mike Garcia [ap] Mike Garcia
Howard Phillips Lovecraft:
    Photographs [pic]   R. Alain Everts
HPL: The Early Years [a2/3]
                    Kenneth W. Faig, Jr
Homesickness [v]   Richard L. Tierney
Rain Magic [v]   Billy Wolfenbarger
The White Peacocks [v] G. Sutton Breiding
Changeling   Darrell Schweitzer

*＊＊

O

OUT OF THIS WORLD

*A British weird fantasy digest magazine published bi-monthly by John Spencer &
Co., 24 Shepherds Bush Road, London. No editor credited but issues assembled by
the publishers Sol Assael and Michael Nahum. A few of the later issues of the
companion magazine* Supernatural Stories *were also subtitled 'Out of This World'.
All of the stories indexed below were written by John S. Glasby.*

[October 1954]   1/1   [Ray Theobald]
A Place of Madness   A. J. Merak
The Nightmare Road   Ray Cosmic
Angel of the Bottomless Pit
                               Michael Hamilton
The Seventh Image   Randall Conway
The Devil At My Elbow   Max Chartair

[January 1955]   1/2   [Roland Turner]
Coven of Thirteen   Michael Hamilton
The Unseen   A. J. Merak
Time to Die   Randall Conway
A Little Devil Dancing   Max Chartair
The Stairway   Ray Cosmic

***

OUTLANDS

A British small press sf/fantasy magazine published quarterly by Outlands Publications, 19 Richmond Ave., Liverpool. Editor: Leslie J. Johnson, 16 Rockville Road, Liverpool.

Winter 1946	No.1	[E. Gabrielson]
Pre-Natal		John Russell Fearn
Strange Portrait		Sydney J. Bounds
Frustration [v]		Hilda M. Crossen
Bird of Time		John Gabriel
Undying Faith		Charnock Walsby
H. G. Wells [obit]		Leslie V. Heald
Rival Creators		Geo. C. Wallis
Psychic Scents [a]		A. Hastwa
The Opaque Word [ss]		Anthony Cotrion
Mystery Power [a]		Leslie V. Heald

***

P

PHANTASY DIGEST

A small press fantasy digest published irregularly by Hall Publications, Perryville, Maryland. Editor: Wayne Warfield, Aberdeen, Maryland.

1976	1/1	John Stewart
The Place of Stones		Charles Saunders
At World's End [a]		Brian Earl Brown
*The Graveyard Rats		Robert E. Howard
Fantasy Fragment [v]		James A. Cox
The Final Solution		Wayne Hooks
*The Undying Druids [a]		Andrew J. Offutt
The Beast of Time		John Bredon
Heritage [v]		John Bredon

1977	1/2	Dave Sim
*The Mirror of Wizardry [nt]		John Jakes
The John Jakes Interview [in]		
		Wayne Warfield
*Fangs of Gold		Robert E. Howard
Solomon Kane Portfolio [ap]		Marcus Boas

1977	1/3	Clyde Caldwell
Menagerie		Wayne Hooks
Slaves of the Vampire Queen		
[nt]		Michael Shea
While the Moonlight Dances		
[v]		Bernie Englum
The Blade of Serazene		Andrew J. Offutt

***

PHANTOM

A British weird fantasy magazine published monthly in large digest format by, initially, Vernon Publications (Bolton) Ltd., a separate imprint of the subsequent publisher Dalrow Publications, Dalrow House, Church Bank, Bolton, Lancashire. Editor: Leslie Syddall, assisted increasingly by art editor Cliff Lawton.

[April] 1957	1/1	R.W.S.
The Thing That Bites		Bernard L. Calmus
The Permanent Tenant		Primrose Townson
The Ginger Kitten		George Burnside
Another Man's Fear		Gavin Williams
The Best Bedroom		Mrs. J. O. Arnold
The Tenth Knotch		Terence Kitchen
The Hungarian Wine Bottle		Barney Gunn
The Cupboard		Cecilia Bartram
The Howl of the Werewolf		Bernard L. Calmus
The Tank		Thomas Narsen
Her Eye on the Shadows		
		Pat & Peter Craig-Raymond
I Wore a Black Ring		Alan Crooper
The Empty Platform		F. J. Taylor
River Mist		K. S. Choong
*Witches' Song [v]		'Tiberius'

May 1957	1/2	R.W.S.
House of Evil		H. Halton-Carr
The Old Mill		Robert Corkin
The Turn of the Tide		Florence Allen
The Undead		Greta Briggs
Shadow on the Sand		F. J. Taylor
The Unlikely Story of Mason		D. G. Howcroft
None Can Explain These Phantoms		
[a]		Allan Kent
Two Eyes For an Eye		L. B. Gordon
The Haunted House		Thomas Maddock
Simply Explained		Gerard Hewson
Call From Beyond		Andrew Armour
Mr. Chunky		David Eames
The Fiftieth Reunion		Edgar Godwin
The Grip of Justice		Gertrude Johnson
The Strange Trapdoor		H. S. Savage
The Mystery of Peg-leg Pete		Marian Baines
The Ghost Runs		Martin Thomas
The Visitor		L. Rose
Come Back to Me		Robert Corkin
Victims Live – But It's Murder [a]		
		Allan Kent

June 1957	1/3	R.W.S.
The Captain's Ship		Ewing Cowell
The Cat and the Chickens		Barbara Crabtree
The Hanged Hangsman		Robert Corkin
Off Balance		Alastair Frame
Mulligan's Treasure		Thomas Maddock
Strange Animal Phantoms [a]		
		Nora I. A. Robinson
Artist's Model		F. J. Taylor
The Mirror		Matthew Saunders
Shadow of a Hindu		Coulson Kernahan
The Appointment		Judith Morgenstern
The Cottage Down the Lane		A. B. Palmer
Travelling Companions		Thomas Edwards
Spook Feet		Samuel Forsythe
From Beyond the Wall		Thomas Maddock
Strange Companions		Sidney Norling
Red Scarf		Edgar Godwin
The 13th Cat		John Wakefield
The Letter		Robert Corkin
Needs a Long Spoon		Vera Clacton
No Way Out		Andrew Armour

July 1957	1/4	R.W.S.
The Chamber of Horrors		R. F. Thompson
*The Last Grave of Lill Warren		
		Manly Wade Wellman
The Will to Die		L. B. Gordon
Snowmaid		Zachary Cox
*The Undertaker		Alexandre Pushkin
The Genuine Article		Martin Thomas
The Smuggler		Alan Holmes
Horace		Charles de Gaur
Royal Phantoms [a]		Nora I. A. Robinson
Testament in Oils		Martin Thomas
The Clock		Eve Spelman Lyon
Harvest		Mavis Heath Miller
The Man Who Knew Better		Martin Thomas
The House By the Sea		M. Billing
The Stone That Died		B. M. Kellier

***

PRELUDE TO FANTASY

A small press magazine published irregularly in digest format by Hans-Peter Werner, Route 3, Richland Center, Wisconsin. Xeroxed.

Summer 1978   1/1   Hans-Peter Werner
Is Fantasy & Science Fiction
  a Significant Literature?
    [a]   Peter Werner
Go Down Moses   Wayne Hooks & Peter Werner
Nightmare Land of Ancient
  Colours [v]   Joey Froehlich
*The Broken Towers   Peter Werner
The Fountain   Peter Werner
*Obituary 2000 [v]   Raymond DiZazzo
*Back on the Ranch [v]   Raymond DiZazzo
*2020 [v]   Raymond DiZazzo
*Men [v]   Raymond DiZazzo
*A99 Spyrlon [v]   Raymond DiZazzo
*Pre-Release [v]   Raymond DiZazzo

Fall 1979   No.2   Hans-Peter Werner
Yon Damsel [v]   William R. Barrow
Timeless [v]   Dwight E. Humphries
Hostile Accord [v]   Dwight E. Humphries
Sessinahn   B. Richard Parks
The Wings of Liriathel   Ardath Mayhar
In Realms of Dreams [v] Carol Ann Cupitt
Pegasus: Night Myth [v] Carol Ann Cupitt
The Wind Against Wood [v] Carol Ann Cupitt
In the Waves [v]   Joey Froehlich
Dark Quatrains [v]   Mark McLaughlin
Prime Evil [v]   Denise Dumars
Edible Abstract: Woman [v] Raymond DiZazzo
The Interview [v]   Raymond DiZazzo
The Dance   Galad Elflandsson
Ghost [v]   Nancy Sue Pistorius
The Bounty Hunter [v]   Denise Dumars
Barred [v]   Dwight E. Humphries
Ship of the Witch [v]   Joey Froehlich
Flight to the Golden Mountain
    [v]   Peter Werner
S.F. = Serious Fiction? [a] Robert E. Moore

***

PRIZE GHOST STORIES

A neo-pulp supernatural magazine published by League Publications, 205 East 42nd St., New York. No editor credited but may have been Helen Gardiner. Reprinted from Ghost Stories, though abridged and retitled. No authors were credited, except for H.G.Wells, but the following includes the original by-lines. See also True Twilight Tales.

[Spring] 1963
*Stay Dead! Stay Dead! Stay Dead!
                              [A. Hughes Neupert]
*My Haunted Half Dollar   [Paul R. Milton]
*The Woman Who Took Off Her
    Body   [Lyon Mearson]
*Case of the Laughing Coffin
                              [Carol Lansing]
*The Man Who Died Twice   [Harold S. Corbin]
*Seduced By an Invisible
    Lover   [Lawrence G. Bailey]
*Specter at the Wheel   [Guy Fowler]
*"Yes, Honey Man, I am Coming!"
                              [A. M. Church]
*Phone Call From the Dead   [Wayne Drummond]
*Phantom Knockouts   [W. J. Rapp]
"Dear God, Let Me Die!" [pic] [Herb Flatow]
*Voodoo and the Virgin [Julia Tait Shearon]
*Our Weekend in the Other
    World   [Wilbert Wadleigh]
*The Late Mr.Elvesham   H. G. Wells
*Picture, Picture on the Wall
                              [Eustache Rops]
*Monkey-Face and Mrs. Thorpe
                           [Victor Rousseau]
*Tiger Woman [nt]   [Allen Van Hoesen]

                    * * *

R

ROD SERLING'S *THE TWILIGHT ZONE* MAGAZINE

A quasi-slick fantasy magazine published monthly (bi-monthly from 1983) by TZ Publications Inc., 800 Second Ave., New York. Editor: T. E. D. Klein. Gives a certain emphasis to coverage of fantasy on television and at the cinema.

April 1981	1/1 (1)	Jim Warren

Rod Serling, First Citizen of
  the Twilight Zone [a]
                        Marc Scott Zicree
Stephen King: "I Like to go
  For the Jugular" [in] Charles L. Grant
Grail [nt]   Harlan Ellison
Remembering Melody   George R. R. Martin
Author's Query   Fred C. Shapiro
The Rose Wall   Joyce Carol Oates
Escape From New York [a]   [no credit]
The Death Runner   Thomas Sullivan
The Next Side Show   Ramsey Campbell
Absolute Ebony [nt]   Felice Picano
Three Cautionary Tales Robert Sheckley
 [The Helping Hand; The Man Who Loved;
  The Wish]
Groucho   Ron Goulart
America Enters the Twilight
  Zone [col]   Marc Scott Zicree
*Walking Distance [tp]   Rod Serling

May 1981	1/2 (2)	*Rene Magritte

Peter Straub [in]   Jay Gregory
In the Sunken Museum   Gregory Frost
Blood Relations   Lewis Shiner
And I Only am Escaped to Tell
  Thee   Roger Zelazny
Chronic Offender   Spider Robinson
Seven and the Stars   Joe Haldeman
The Hand [a]   [no credit]
Drum Dancer George Clayton Johnson
Brief Encounter   Michael Garrett
How They Pass the Time in
  Pelpel   Robert Silverberg
Magritte's Secret Agent [nt] Tanith Lee
TV's Twilight Zone: 2 [col]
                  Marc Scott Zicree
*The Monsters Are Due on
  Maple Street [tp]   Rod Serling

June 1981	1/3 (3)	Darrelyn Wood

Robert Bloch: Society as Insane
  Asylum [in]   Tom Collins
The Jaunt [nt]   Stephen King
*Summer's Cloud   Anthony Boucher
*The Way I Heard It Anthony Boucher
100 Years of Fantasy
  Illustration [ap]   Stephen DiLauro
The Assignment   Mitch Potter
The Dreamshattering Mary Kittredge
Outland [in]   Robert Martin
The Fireman's Daughter Phyllis Eisenstein
Waiting For the Papers   Alan Ryan
The Inn of the Dove   Gordon Linzner
Deadline   Mel Gilden
Scenicruiser and the Silver
  Lady   Peter S. Alterman
TV's Twilight Zone: 3 [col]
                  Marc Scott Zicree
*The After Hours [tp]   Rod Serling

July 1981	1/4 (4)	Linda Lippa

Camouflage   Stanley Schmidt
Smiley   Steve Rosse
Corn Dolly   Eileen Roy
Papa Gumbo   Ron Goulart
Silver   Charles L. Grant
Luna   G. W. Perriwils
Richard Donner: TZ Alumnus
  Makes Good [in]   Robert Martin
Donner as Filmmaker: A Flair
  for the Larger-Than-Life
  [a]   [Robert Martin]
A Thousand Paces Along the
  Via Dolorosa [nt] Robert Silverberg
The Dump   Joe Lansdale
Escape   John Keefauver
The Swamp [ss]   Robert Sheckley
Summer Heat   Carmen C. Carter
The Rules of the Game Jack Ritchie

TV's Twilight Zone: 4 [col]
Marc Scott Zicree
*The Eye of the Beholder [tp] Rod Serling

August 1981   1/5 (5)   Tito Salomoni
George Romero: Revealing the
Monsters Within Us [in]   Tom Seligson
Swing Low, Sweet Chariot Reginald Bretnor
Tiger of the Mind   Ron Wolfe
A Friend in Need   Lisa Tuttle
Four   Douglas Jenmac
Midas Night   Sam Wilson
Writing For 'The Twilight
Zone' [a]   George Clayton Johnson
Hollywood Cries Wolf! [ins] Robert Martin
The Hidden Laughter   David Morrell
The Artisan   Lori Allen
Identity Crisis   James Patrick Kelly
Dr. Van Helsing's Handy Guide
to Ghost Stories [a1/4]
Kurt Van Helsing
*The Tale the Hermit Told [ss]
Alastair Reid
The Man Who Couldn't Remember David Curtis
The Next Time Around   Paul J. Nahin
TV's Twilight Zone: 5 [col]
Marc Scott Zicree
*The Odyssey of Flight 33 [tp] Rod Serling

September 1981   1/6 (6)   Ralph Mercer
Matinee at the Flame   Christopher Fahy
Premonition   Jack Wodhams
Forerunners of 'The Twilight
Zone' [a]   Allan Asherman
Stroke of Mercy   Parke Godwin
Richard Matheson on 'The Honorable
Tradition of Writing' [in1/2]
James H. Burns
Matheson in the Movies [a] Robert Martin
When the Cat's Away   John Alfred Taylor
Roderick Goes to School [ex] John Sladek
Dr. Van Helsing's Handy Guide to
Ghost Stories [a2/4] Kurt Van Helsing
The Loaner   Gary Brandner
Chameleon Junction   Hal Hill
TV's Twilight Zone: 6 [col]
Marc Scott Zicree
*Time Enough at Last [tp]   Rod Serling

October 1981   1/7 (7)   Tito Salomoni
Richard Matheson: Spinning Fantasy
from Daily Life [in2/2] James H. Burns
Out of Place   Pamela Sargent
Shootout in the Toy Shop Robert Sheckley
Zeke   Timothy Robert Sullivan
The Burden of Indigo   Gene O'Neill
Sea Change   George Clayton Johnson
The Beast Within [a]   Robert Martin
Dr. Van Helsing's Handy Guide to
Ghost Stories [a3/4] Kurt Van Helsing
Offices   Chet Williamson
The Tear Collector   Donald Olson
The Great Elvis Presley Look-
Alike Murder Mystery   Mick Farren
Paintjob   Jay Rothbell
Twilight Zone: The Third Season
[a]   Marc Scott Zicree
TV's Twilight Zone: 7 [col]
Marc Scott Zicree
*The Big, Tall Wish [tp]   Rod Serling

November 1981   1/8 (8)   C. Campbell
John Saul: 'Remember, it's only
a story' [in]   Laura Kramer
Because Our Skins Are Finer   Tanith Lee
Carousel   Thomas Disch
Heimlich's Curse   Evan Eisenberg
The Specialist   Clark Howard
Wishing Will Make it So Melissa Mia Hall
Moshigawa's Homecoming   Gordon Linzner
Halloween II [a]   Robert Martin
Again   Ramsey Campbell
Dr. Van Helsing's Handy Guide to
Ghost Stories [a4/4] Kurt Van Helsing
The Old Man's Room   Juleen Brantingham
Tweedlioop   Stanley Schmidt
TV's Twilight Zone: 8 [col]
Marc Scott Zicree
*Death's Head Revisited [tp] Rod Serling

December 1981   1/9 (9)   Peter Frommig
Harlan Ellison on the Art of
Making Waves [in]   Tom Staicar
Age of Reason   David St. Marie
Forest God   Jaspar Witco
Handyman   Kenneth Goodman
The Pasture   Joe R. Lansdale
All a Clone by the Telephone
Haskell Barkin
The Quest For Fire [a]   Ed Naha
M. R. James [a]   Mike Ashley
*The Ash-Tree   M. R. James
On 202   Jeff Hecht
The Emerson Effect   Jack McDevitt
TV's Twilight Zone: 9 [col]
Marc Scott Zicree
*The Midnight Sun [tp]   Rod Serling

January 1982   1/10 (10)   Carl Chaplin
Frank Belknap Long on Literature,
Lovecraft, and the Golden Age
of Weird Tales [in]   Tom Collins
Influencing the Hell out of Time
and Teresa Golowitz   Parke Godwin
Miss Mouse and the Fourth
Dimension   Robert Sheckley
Dream Along With Me   Reginald Bretnor
*My Most Memorable Christmas [a]
Rod Serling
Lost and Found   Connie Willis
Ghost Story [a]   Robert Martin
J. Sheridan Le Fanu [a]   Mike Ashley
*An Account of Some Strange
Disturbances in Aungier
Street [nt]   J. Sheridan LeFanu
Of Sleds and Forty Winters   Vic Johnson
The Autumn Visitors Frank Belknap Long
Final Version   John Morressy
TV's Twilight Zone: 10 [col]
Marc Scott Zicree
*The Night of the Meek [tp]   Rod Serling

February 1982   1/11 (11) *John Oberdorf
Playing the Game
Gardner Dozois & Jack Dann
Essence of Charlotte   Charles L. Grant
"Other"   Jor Jennings
My Old Man   George Alec Effinger
The Other Train Phenomenon Richard Bowker
Wes Craven ... Who's Made Nightmares
Come True [in]   Tom Seligson
Swamp Thing [a]   Jim Verniere

September 1982   2/6 (18)   James Nazz
The 'Unhappy Is He' Quiz
   [quiz]   William Fulwiler
Paul Schrader: Embracing
   the Beast [in]   James Verniere
The Red-Eyed Thing   Jere Cunningham
MTA Announces New Plan to Ease
   Subway Congestion   Gordon Linzner
Cruising   Donald Tyson
The Long Ride   John Skipp
Behind the Doors   Susan Johnson
The Jane Fonda Room   Jonathan Carroll
Creepshow [a]   Robert Martin
Something Wicked This Way Comes [a] Ed Naha
The Reaper   Jim Cort
Arthur Machen [a]   Mike Ashley
*A Machen Sampler [ex]   Arthur Machen
TV's Twilight Zone: 18 [col]
   Marc Scott Zicree
*A Machine to Answer the
   Question [play]   Rod Serling

October 1982   2/7 (19)   Rob Sauber
The 'So Saying He Vanished' Quiz
   [quiz]   Chet Williamson
Summer of Monsters   Dale Hammell
Mexican Merry-Go-Round   Avram Davidson
Five Minutes Early [ss]   Robert Sheckley
The Silly Stuff   Al Sarrantonio
Nicholas Meyer [in]   Mark Denis Shepard
Star Trek: The Great American
   Love Story [a]   Richard Matturro
Broken Walls, Shattered Dreams
   [pic]   Duncan McLaren
In a Green Shade   Melissa Mia Hall
One Small Change   Gary Brandner
Alive and Well In ... [ss] Michael S. Smith
Pigs Are Sensitive   Jon Wynne-Tyson
Saratoga Winter   Jeff Hecht
TV's Twilight Zone: 19 [col]
   Marc Scott Zicree
*In Praise of Pip [tp]   Rod Serling

November 1982   2/8 (20)   *Bruce Heapps
The 'Heroes & Heavies' Quiz
   [quiz]   Kathleen Murray
War in Fantasyland [a]   Baird Searles
The Evil Dead [a]   Stephen King
John Carpenter: Doing His Own
   'Thing' [in]   James Verniere
Hell Is Murky   John Alfred Taylor
*Levitation   Joseph Payne Brennan
The Opening   Bruce Boston
Halloween III [a]   James Verniere
Country of the Dead [pic]   John Bensink
Night Cry   Katherine M. Turney
The Spook Man   Al Sarrantonio
The Circle   Lewis Shiner
Halloween Girl   Robert Grant
The Screenplay   Joseph Cromarty
The Smell of Cherries   Jeffrey Goddin
TV's Twilight Zone: 20 [col]
   Marc Scott Zicree
*A Quality of Mercy [tp]   Rod Serling

*[There is no Vol.2 Issue 9 as that number
was allocated to the Annual Great Stories
from Rod Serling's 'The Twilight Zone'
Magazine which, for completeness, is
listed at the end of this entry.]*

December 1982   2/10 (21)   D. Christiana
The 'Unhappy Is He' Quiz Revisited
   [quiz]   William Fulwiler
Ridley Scott: 'A Visual Person'
   [in]   James Verniere
The Shrine   Pamela Sargent
Altenmoor, Where the Dogs Dance Mort Castle
Jockeying For Time   David Shifren
Magic For Sale [pic]   Mathew Kovary
The Translator   John David Sidley
XTRO [a]   James Verniere
L. P. Hartley [a]   Jack Sullivan
*W.S.   L. P. Hartley
Three Timely Tales [3ss]   Rick Norwood
What Really Happened to Uncle
   Chuckles?   Ron Wolfe
Creative Writing   Sandre Charbonneau
Pulpmeister   David J. Schow
TV's Twilight Zone: 21 [col]
   Marc Scott Zicree
*Living Doll [tp]   Charles Beaumont

February 1983   2/11 (22)   Walter Velez
Dice-Wielding Warriors [a]
   Lawrence Schick
Crossing Over   Jack McDevitt
Optoshock! [pic]   Christopher Hoffman
Personality Problem   Joe R. Lansdale
Tommy's Christmas   John R. Little
Recollections of Annie   Charles L. Grant
There's A Man Goin' Round
   Takin' Names   Robert S. Reiser
Fantasy Films '82: A Critical
   Guide [a]   James Verniere
Below Zero   John Kessel
Echoes   Lawrence C. Connolly
A Chance Affair   Mignon Glass
Roald Dahl [in]   Lisa Tuttle
*Royal Jelly   Roald Dahl
The 'So Saying, He Vanished'
   Quiz Revisited [quiz] Chet Williamson
Rod Serling's Lost 'Christmas
   Carol' [a]   Sam Frank
TV's Twilight Zone: 22 [col]
   Marc Scott Zicree
*One For the Angels [tp]   Rod Serling

April 1983   3/1 (23)   Kari Brayman
The 'Heroes & Heavies' Quiz
   Revisited [quiz]   Kathleen Murray
A Weird Jubilee [a]   Mike Ashley
Colin Wilson [in]   Lisa Tuttle
*A Colin Wilson Sampler [ex]Colin Wilson
The Journey   Abbie Herrick
Critique   Brian Ferguson
Evening in the Park   Susan Rooke
Say Goodbye to Judy   William B. Barfield
5th Dimension   Scott Edelman
Nightbears   Juleen Brantingham
The Hunger [a]   James Verniere
Notes For a 'Twilight Zone'
   Movie [ex]   Rod Serling
The Last Adam & Eve Story
   Bruce J. Balfour
Dakota Safari   Gene O'Neill
Murchison's Dream   Byron Marshall
And Now I'm Waiting   Richard Matheson
*A World of His Own [tp]Richard Matheson
TV's Twilight Zone: 23 [col]
   Marc Scott Zicree

*The Night of the Meek [tp]   Rod Serling
*Sea Change   George Clayton Johnson
*The Gargoyles of Gotham [pic]
                          Stephen DiLauro
*Carousel   Thomas Disch
*Grail [nt]   Harlan Ellison
*Groucho   Ron Goulart
*The Father of the Bride   Connie Willis
*The River Styx Runs Upstream Dan Simmons
*I'll Be Seeing You   W. G. Norris
*The Story Behind Richard Matheson's
    "The Doll" [a]   Marc Scott Zicree
*The Doll [tp]   Richard Matheson
*Rod Serling: The Facts of
    Life [in]   Linda Brevelle
*The Swamp [ss]   Robert Sheckley
*Again   Ramsey Campbell
*Not Our Brother   Robert Silverberg

* * *

S

SCIENCE FANTASY

British sf/fantasy magazine. Published originally in digest format (for a period as a large digest) by Nova Publications, 25 Stoke Newington Road, London (with several address changes) until Issue 64 (April 1964). Thereafter published in pocketbook format by Roberts & Vinter, 44 Milkwood Road, London (later 42/44 Dock Street, London). Editors: Walter Gillings, Nos. 1-2; John Carnell, Nos. 3-64; Kyril Bonfiglioli, Nos. 65-81. The magazine was originally a continuation of Gillings's Fantasy *which, despite the title, was an all-sf publication, and the first few issues of* Science Fantasy *continued that bias. Under Carnell the magazine gradually included more and more outright fantasy until, by Issue 15, it was the major flavor. Under Bonfiglioli there was an initial switch to more science fiction, but subsequently the balance remained about even. After issue 81 the magazine changed its name to* Impulse *(see separate entry).*
  Because Science Fantasy *is usually known by its sequential issue number (regardless of volume) the volume number is shown in brackets thus: [1] 1, being Volume 1, Number 1.*

Summer 1950 [1] 1		Powell
The Belt [nt]		J. M. Walsh
Time's Arrow		Arthur C. Clarke
Monster		Christopher Youd
The Battle of the Canals [a]		
		Thomas Sheridan
The Cycle		P. E. Cleator
Advent of the Entities [nt]		E. R. James
The Jinn in the Test Tube [a]		
		Herbert Hughes
Winter 1950/51 [1] 2		Harry Turner
The Ark [nt]		F. G. Rayer
Black-Out		John Russell Fearn
Silence, Please!		Charles Willis
Bogy in the Sky [a]		Thomas Sheridan
History Lesson		Arthur C. Clarke
Martian Mandate		Norman C. Pallant
The Dawn of Space-Travel [a]		
		Valentine Parker
Winter 1951/52 [1] 3		Reina M. Bull
The Time Is Not Yet ... [ged]		
		Walter Gillings
Pawley's Peepholes		John Wyndham
The Undying Enemy		F. G. Rayer
Double Trouble		William F. Temple
Then There Were Two		J. T. M'Intosh
The Moving Hills		E. R. James

Grounded		E. C. Tubb
Loser Take All		N. K. Hemming
Spring 1952 [2] 4		Reina M. Bull
Things Are On the Move ...		
[ged]		H. J. Campbell
Resurrection [na]		John Christopher
Next in Line		A. Bertram Chandler
The Treasure of Tagor		Sydney J. Bounds
Plimsoll Line		F. G. Rayer
Outworlder		Peter Hawkins
Autumn 1952 [2] 5		Gerard Quinn
The Last Fifty Years and the		
Next [ged]		J. M. Walsh
Stitch in Time [nt]		J. T. M'Intosh
Was Not Spoken		E. E. Evans
Circus [nt]		Peter Hawkins
Not As We Are [nt]		E. R. James
Enemy in Their Midst		Alan Barclay
Spring 1953 [2] 6		Gerard Quinn
The Volunteers [nt]		J. T. M'Intosh
Mr. Kowtshook		John Christopher
Confessional		E. C. Tubb
Traders' Planet		Francis G. Rayer
One in Every Port		Richard Lawrence
Insurance Policy		Lan Wright
Time to Gome Home		J. F. Burke

[Spring] 1954   [3] 7   Gerard Quinn
The Pattern of Science
    Fiction [ged]   John Wyndham
Seek Earthmen No More [nt]   F. G. Rayer
Death Sentence   John Christopher
Stranger From Space   Gene Lees
Beggars All   J. T. M'Intosh
The Trojan Way   Francis Richardson
Detective Story   J. F. Burke
Unfortunate Purchase   E. C. Tubb

May 1954   [3] 8   Gerard Quinn
Science Into Fantasy [ged]   Wilson Tucker
Tomorrow [nt]   E. C. Tubb
The Shimmering Tree   Margaret Lowe
Space Prize   Francis G. Rayer
Once Upon a Time   Jonathan F. Burke
Take a Letter   P. W. Cutler
Dawn of Peace Eternal   John Ashcroft
The Conquerors   Lan Wright

July 1954   [3] 9   Gerard Quinn
Something New Wanted ... [ged]
                              J. T. McIntosh
This Precious Stone [na]   H. J. Murdoch
Criminal Record   Brian W. Aldiss
Six of One ...   A. Bertram Chandler
Occupational Hazard   E. C. Tubb
Last Man on Mars   W. P. Cockcroft
Family Secret   Arthur Coster
Haven   Peter Hawkins

September 1954   [3] 10 Norman Partridge
Five Into Four [nt]   J. T. McIntosh
Bitter Sweet   E. C. Tubb
Zone of Youth   Martin Jordan
The Chronoclasm   John Wyndham
Dark Summer   Francis G. Rayer
Stone and Crystal   John Ashcroft
Unborn of Earth [nt]   Les Cole

December 1954   [4] 11   Gerard Quinn
Standard Style [ged]   William F. Temple
Live For Ever [nt]   J. T. McIntosh
Where's The Matter?   Richard Rowland
I Hear You Calling   Eric Frank Russell
*The Tooth   G. Gordon Dewey
The Enemy Within Us   E. C. Tubb
The Mailman   Joseph Slotkin
Co-Efficiency Zero   Francis G. Rayer
First Trip   Sydney J. Bounds
Dimple   John Kippax

February 1955   [4] 12   Gerard Quinn
What's The Difference? [ged] Alfred Bester
The Wrong Track [nt] A. Bertram Chandler
    [as by George Whitley on story]
The Dragon   Alan Barclay
The Last Day of Summer   E. C. Tubb
Auto-Fiction Ltd.   Wanless Gardener
Eternity [nt]   William F. Temple
Free Will   Dal Stivens
Breathing Space   Brian W. Aldiss

April 1955   [5] 13   Gerard Quinn
Ever Been to Uranus? [ged] Jonathan Burke
In a Misty Light [na]   Richard Varne
Late   A. Bertram Chandler
Poor Henry   E. C. Tubb
Smoothies Are Wanted   E. R. James

Mossendew's Martians   John Kippax
The Adjusters   Jonathan Burke
Pass the Salt   Helen M. Urban

June 1955   [5] 14   Gerard Quinn
Follow My Leader [ged]   E. C. Tubb
Sheamus [nt]   Martin Jordan
Special Delivery   John Kippax
Reluctant Hero   Gavin Neal
Agent   E. C. Tubb
Psi No More   Kenneth Bulmer
*Hilda   H. B. Hickey
    [misprinted as W. B. Hickey in issue]
*My Brother's Wife   Wilson Tucker
Double Act   Howard Lee McCarey

September 1955   [5] 15   Gerard Quinn
The Talisman [nt]   John Brunner
The Dogs of Hannoie   Douglas West
*The Job is Ended   Wilson Tucker
Dear Ghost   Alan Guthrie
No Future in It   Keith Woodcott
Birthday Present   Charles E. Fritch
The Predators [nt]   E. C. Tubb
Dynasty of One   James White

November 1955   [6] 16   Gerard Quinn
The Wager [nt]   E. C. Tubb
Death Do Us Part   John Brunner
Hounded Down   John Kippax
*The Mindworm   C. M. Kornbluth
The Editor Regrets   Duncan Lamont
Heart's Desire   Niall Wilde
Uncle Buno   William F. Temple
*It's a Good Life   Jerome Bixby

February 1956   [6] 17   Gerard Quinn
Non-Stop [nt]   Brian W. Aldiss
Proof Negative   Trevor Staines
*Connection Completed   Judith Merril
Uncle Clem and Them Martians John Mantley
Louey   Alan Barclay
The Biggest Game   Keith Woodcott
To Touch the Stars   Joseph Slotkin
Syllabus   Len Shaw
The Man Who Played the Blues John Brunner

May 1956   [6] 18   'Terry'
This Rough Magic [na]   John Brunner
Wishes Three   Lan Wright
*Guinevere For Everybody Jack Williamson
Fair Weather Friend   John Kippax
The Failed Men   Brian W. Aldiss
Beast of the Field   Dan Morgan
First Man in the Moon   Peter Phillips
Head First   Julian Frey

August 1956   [7] 19   Gerard Quinn
*The Climbing Wave [na]
                      Marion Zimmer Bradley
The Unharmonious Word Bertram Chandler
When Gabriel ...   John Brunner
*Stair Trick   Mildred Clingerman
Too Perfect   E. R. James
Tiles   Mike Nevard
Breathing Space [nt]   Alan Guthrie
The Coffee Pot   Joseph Slotkin

December 1956   [7] 20   Gerard Quinn
A Time to Rend [na]   John Brunner

June 1959   [12] 35   Brian Lewis
200 Years to Christmas [na] J. T. McIntosh
*Space-Time for Springers   Fritz Leiber
Fortune's Fool   Brian W. Aldiss
Atlantis - A New Theory [a] Arthur R. Weir
*The Songs of Distant Earth [nt]
                            Arthur C. Clarke

August 1959   [12] 36   Brian Lewis
Echo in the Skull [sn]   John Brunner
The Long Eureka   Arthur Sellings
*Arthur Conan Doyle [a]   Sam Moskowitz
Somebody Wants You   E. C. Tubb

November 1959   [13] 37   Brian Lewis
Castle of Vengeance [na]   Kenneth Bulmer
Time Trap   Edward Mackin
*H. G. Wells [a]   Sam Moskowitz
The Window   E. C. Tubb
Curse Strings   John Rackham
Strokie   Alan Anderson

December 1959   [13] 38   Brian Lewis
Enchanter's Encounter [nt]   E. C. Tubb
Magic Ingredient [nt]   William F. Temple
Now : Zero   J. G. Ballard
Who Was Here?   Alan Barclay
*Edgar Allan Poe [a]   Sam Moskowitz
*Warm Man   Robert Silverberg

February 1960   [13] 39   'Jarr'
The Sound-Sweep [nt]   J. G. Ballard
The Ship From Home [nt]   J. T. McIntosh
Not a Sparrow Falls   W. T. Webb
Suspect Halo   Clifford C. Reed
*Cyrano de Bergerac   Sam Moskowitz

April 1960   [14] 40   Brian Lewis
Strange Highway [na]   Kenneth Bulmer
Faceless Card   Brian W. Aldiss
Trading Post   Edward Mackin
*The Marvellous A.Merritt [a] Sam Moskowitz
Too Bad   E. C. Tubb

June 1960   [14] 41   Brian Lewis
The Gaudy Shadows [na]   John Brunner
*Counterpart [nt]   Robert Silverberg
Stage-Struck!   Brian W. Aldiss
*Edgar Rice Burroughs [a]   Sam Moskowitz

August 1960   [14] 42   Brian Lewis
Planet on Probation [nt]   J. T. McIntosh
Imprint of Chaos [nt]   John Brunner
Deities, Inc.
        Leroy B. Haugsrud & Dale R. Smith
The Dryad-Tree   Thomas Burnett Swann

October 1960   [15] 43   Brian Lewis
Beyond the Silver Sky [na] Kenneth Bulmer
Stardust [v]   Alan Lindsey
The Last World of Mr.Goddard J. G. Ballard
*Jules Verne [a]   Sam Moskowitz
Expectations   Richard Graham
The First Decade [a]   Kenneth Johns

December 1960   [15] 44   'Jarr'
        [special Weird-Story issue]
All the Devil's in Hell [na] John Brunner
The Black Cat's Paw [nt]   John Rackham
The Painter   Thomas Burnett Swann
*H. P. Lovecraft   Sam Moskowitz

February 1961   [15] 45   Brian Lewis
The Map Country [na]   Kenneth Bulmer
Studio 5, the Stars [nt]   J. G. Ballard
*Fitz-James O'Brien [a]   Sam Moskowitz

April 1961   [16] 46   Brian Lewis
*Need [na]   Theodore Sturgeon
Behind the Cloud   Edward Mackin
Displaced Person   Lee Harding
*Karel Capek [a]   Sam Moskowitz

June 1961   [16] 47   Brian Lewis
The Dreaming City [nt] Michael Moorcock
Blood Offering   John Kippax
Valley of the Rainbirds   W. T. Webb
*Stanley G.Weinbaum [a]   Sam Moskowitz
The Veil of Isis [nt]   John Rackham

August 1961   [16] 48   Brian Lewis
The Analysts [nt]   John Brunner
Mr. F is Mr. F   J. G. Ballard
*Olaf Stapledon   Sam Moskowitz
Sacrificial   Lee Harding
The Food Goes in the Top Will Worthington
Parky   David Rome

October 1961   [17] 49   Gerard Quinn
While the Gods Laugh [nt]Michael Moorcock
Reflection of the Truth   John Kippax
The Seventh Stair [nt]   Frank Brandon
*Philip Wylie [a]   Sam Moskowitz
Heinrich   Wallace West

December 1961   [17] 50   Gerard Quinn
Ankh [na]   John Rackham
Still Centre   Edward Mackin
A Cure For Mr.Kelsy   Leroy B. Haugsrud
*Shiel and Heard   Sam Moskowitz

February 1962   [17] 51   Gerard Quinn
The Stealer of Souls [nt]Michael Moorcock
The Legend [na]   W. T. Webb
The Big Sound   P. F. Woods
Ouef du Coq   John Brunner

April 1962   [18] 52   Gerard Quinn
        [special Fantasy issue]
Father of Lies [na]   John Brunner
Where Is the Bird of Fire?
        [na]   Thomas Burnett Swann
The Problem   Claude & Rhoda Nunes

June 1962   [18] 53   Gerard Quinn
The Eternal Champion [na]Michael Moorcock
The Watch-Towers [nt]   J. G. Ballard
Under the Lemonade Hat   Edward Mackin
The Man Who Knew Grodnik
                    Theodore R. Cogswell

August 1962   [18] 54   Gerard Quinn
Perilous Portal [na]   Frank Brandon
Kings in Darkness [nt] Michael Moorcock
Hat Trick   Colin Denbigh
Beginner's Luck   Steve Hall

October 1962   [19] 55   Jim Cawthorn
Matrix [nt]   Brian W. Aldiss
The Flame Bringers [nt] Michael Moorcock
The Sudden Wings   Thomas Burnett Swann
Weekend Trip   Steve Hall
Love is a Relative Thing   Stephen Cook

Housel   Alan Burns
Vashti [nt]   Thomas Burnett Swann
Timmy and the Angel   Philip Wordley

June 1965   [24] 73   Keith Roberts
The Impossible Smile [sn2/2]   Jael Cracken
Great and Small   G. L. Lack
Ploop   Ron Pritchett
Peace on Earth   Paul Jents
Deterrent   Alistair Bevan
A Pleasure Shared   Brian W. Aldiss
Prisoner   Patricia Hocknell
In Reason's Ear [nt]   Pippin Graham
Xenophilia   Thom Keyes

July 1965   [24] 74   Keith Roberts
The Furies [n1/3]   Keith Roberts
A Distorting Mirror   R. W. Mackelworth
The Door   Alistair Bevan
The Criminal   Johnny Byrne

August 1965   [24] 75   Keith Roberts
The Desolator   Eric C. Williams
Chemotopia   Ernest Hill
Idiot's Lantern   Keith Roberts
Paradise for a Punter   Clifford C. Reed
A Way With Animals   John Rackham
Grinnel [ss]   Dikk Richardson
The Furies [n2/3]   Keith Roberts

September 1965   [24] 76   ?
Instead of an Editorial [ged]
                            Brian W. Aldiss
Boomerang   E. C. Tubb
Coming-of-Age Day   A. K. Jorgensson
Temptation for the Leader R.W. Mackelworth
At Last, the True Story of
   Frankenstein   Harry Harrison
Sule Skerry   Rob Sproat
The Jobbers   Johnny Byrne
Omega and Alpha   Robert Cheetham
The Furies [n3/3]   Keith Roberts

October 1965   [24] 77   Agosta Morol
The Weirwoods [n1/2] Thomas Burnett Swann
Ragtime   Pamela Adams
Green Goblins Yet   W. Price
State of Mind   E. C. Tubb
The Foreigner   Johnny Byrne
Goodnight, Sweet Prince   Philip Wordley

November 1965   [24] 78   Keith Roberts
The Day of the Doomed King   Brian Aldiss
The Saga of Sid   Ernest Hill
Beyond Time's Aegis [nt]   Brian Craig
The Wall   Josephine Saxton
Yesterdays' Gardens   Johnny Byrne
The Weirwoods [n2/2] Thomas Burnett Swann

December 1965   [24] 79   ?
Plague From Space [n1/3]   Harry Harrison
As Others See Us   E. C. Tubb
A Question of Culture   Richard A. Gordon
Democratic Autocracy   Ernest Hill
Cleaner Than Clean   R. W. Mackelworth
Passenger   Alan Burns

January 1966   [24] 80   Keith Roberts
The God-Birds of Glentallach
  [nt]   John Rackham
Sealed Capsule   Edward Mackin
"In Vino Veritas"   E. C. Tubb
The Satyrian Games   D. J. Gibbs
For One of These   Daphne Castell
Plague From Space [n2/3]   Harry Harrison

February 1966   [24] 81   Keith Roberts
Ballad From a Bottle   Hugh Simmonds
The Warp and the Woof-Woof   John Brunner
Marina   John Harrison
Our Man in 1900   Paul Jents
Sing Me No Sorrows   E. C. Tubb
Plague From Space [n3/3]   Harry Harrison

***

Continued as IMPULSE

***

SCREEN CHILLS AND MACABRE STORIES

One of the earliest 'monster' movie magazines, published in Britain in small pulp format by Pep Publishers, Croydon, Surrey. No editor credited, though may have been Leslie Syddall or Cliff Lawton of Phantom. *Contained only one genuine story, plus two adaptations of film scenarios and eight film reviews.*

[November 1957]	1/1	–
Dead That Walk		[no credit]
*Them Ones		Robert Bloch
I Was a Teenage Werewolf		[no credit]

***

180

SEX TALES

A set of four pornographic fantasy slick magazines published by Gallery Press,
West Los Angeles, California. No editor was credited. Included for complete-
ness though not recommended to the general weird fantasy fan!

HORROR SEX TALES

[Jun/Jul] 1972   1/1   -
Gore in the Alley   Shirle Lane
Scream Your Bloody Head Off
                          Edward D. Wood, Jr
Domain of the Undead   Kip Gebakken
Bums Rush Terror   Ann Gora
Transylvanian News [a]   [no credit]
The Case of Albert Fish [a] [no credit]
Hellfire   Edw. D. Wood
Cease to Exist   T. G. Denver
Witches of Amau Ra   Dick Trent
Rue Morgue Revisited   Dick Trent

WEIRD SEX TALES

Jul/Aug 1972   1/1   -
Fornicator 101   Waldo Q. Vadis
Ant Hell   Alvin Tostig
Queen of the Martian Women Milika Sualee
News Read-Out   Norman Bates V
The Perversions of Gilles de
   Laval [a]   [no credit]
A Call From the Future   Rusty McWharf
Illusionary Rebound   Franklin Furter
Rapist From Outer Space   Cornelius Castor
38 Generations in Space   Dudley McDonley

MONSTER SEX TALES

Aug/Sep 1972   1/1   -
The Birth of Frankenstein   Kip Gebakken
Castle of Dracula   Chester Winfield
A Perfect Crime   Jonah Krumholtz
Monster Sex Club [a]   [no credit]
Frankenstein: Raging Sex
   Monster   Lorna Dunn
The Voyage of Dracula   Roy Hemp
Igor   Enoch Roengarten
Lust of the Vampire   Dudley McDonley
Night of the Moon   Jason Streek

LEGENDARY SEX TALES

Sep/Oct 1972   1/1   -
The Escape of Monte Christo Kip Gebakken
Robin Hood and his Merry Men
                            William Bends
The Taming of Hercules   Hong Sui Gai
The Forging of Genghis Khan Patrick Carey
Strangest Sex Customs of
   History [a]   [no credit]
Cleopatra's Sex Slave   Dudley McDonley
Legendary Hall of Fame [a]   [no credit]
D'Artagnan Meets the Three
   Musketeers   Wally Kief
Captain Larsen: the Sea Wolf Reevo Saint
Julius Caesar: Lustful
   Dictator   Gretchen Lansky

***

181

SHAYOL

A small press magazine published irregularly in slick format by Flight Unlimited, Inc., 8435 Carter, Overland Park, Kansas. Publisher: Arnie Fenner. Editor: Patricia Cadigan. The successor to Chacal it aimed at a wider audience with all aspects of fantasy and sf. It is also one of the most attractive of the small press magazines. The final issue is mooted to appear in 1984.

November 1977   1/1 (1)   Roger Stine
    [the indicia is dated August 1977]
Dr. Hudson's Secret Gorilla   Howard Waldrop
*The Once and Future Kane
    [a]   Karl Wagner
A Piece of Rope   Lisa Tuttle
Good-Bye to All of That   S. Dale
On Reviewing and Being Reviewed
    [a]   Michael Bishop
My Lady Sleeping [v]   Steve Utley
Tailltu: A Progressive Folio
    [ap]   Jim Fitzpatrick
The Genie-us of Tom Reamy
    [in]   Pat Cadigan
The Hobbit [ap]   Jeff Easley
Wonder Show [ex]   Tom Reamy
Mr. Wyatt in Darkest Africa   Bruce Holt
Spawn of the Ruins   Marc Laidlaw

February 1978   1/2 (2)   Robert Haas
Walk the Walk [a]   Harlan Ellison
Opium   Harlan Ellison
Sport   Terry Matz
Rex and Regina [v]   Steve Utley
Beauty and the Beast [ap]   Robert Haas
        [text by Pat Cadigan]
Waiting for Billy Star   Tom Reamy
Tom Reamy [obit]   Pat Cadigan
Thick Thews and Busty Babes
    [a]   Phil Bolick
Dreams of the Dreamer: an
    Interview with Tim Kirk
    [in]   Jan Schwab, Vikki Marshall,
        Pat Cadigan, Bob Haas & Arnie Fenner
Death From Exposure [nt]   Pat Cadigan
The Mare   William Wallace
Shayol [ap]   Vikki Marshall

Summer 1979   1/3 (3)   T. Blackshear
At a Time Very Near the End   Lisa Tuttle
Love's Heresy   Michael Bishop
Blue Eyes   Tom Reamy
Abaddon   Steve Utley
A Hero at the Gate   Tanith Lee
That's Entertainment   Lee Lacy
Sorcery! [v]   Gordon Larkin
Flash Gordon Flunked Physics
    [a]   Phil Bolick
Shine of the Times: an Inter-
    view with Stephen King
    [in]   Lewis Shiner, Marty Ketchum,
                Pat Cadigan & Arnie Fenner
Portfolio [ap]   Stephen Fabian
Horror, We Got   Howard Waldrop
"... Homecoming ..."   C. J. Cherryh

Winter 1980   1/4 (4)   Roger Stine
The Change   Ramsey Campbell
Evangels of Hope [a]   Michael Bishop
Community Property   Lisa Tuttle
Report to Montezuma [v]   S. Dale
Portfolio [ap]   Hank Jankus
The Twa Corbies   Gordon Larkin
All About Strange Monsters
    of the Recent Past   Howard Waldrop
For the Lady of a
    Physicist No.2 [v]   Michael Bishop
Sugarfang [a]   Marta Randall
In Silvered Shadows Are
    Born the Screams   Charles L. Grant
The Art of Leo & Diane
    Dillon [a/ap]   Jeff Levin
Kings of the Afternoon   Lewis Shiner
Leather Hobbits of Gor [a]   Phil Bolick

Winter 1982   2/1 (5)   Ezra Tucker
The Alien, The Child, The
    Princess [v]   Melissa Mia Hall
Green Brother   Howard Waldrop
Rover [cs]   Richard Corben
14 Questions: Michael Whelan
    [in]   Arnie Fenner & Pat Cadigan
The Secret to Being a Sci-Fi
    Guy [a]   George R. R. Martin
Fantasy (Heroic & Otherwise)
    [ap]   [six artists]
At the City Limits of Fate Michael Bishop
Checking in With C. J.
    Cherryh [in]   Ken Keller
Freezing to Death   Edward Bryant
Blackshear is Here!! [ap] Thomas Blackshear
    [Profile by Arnie Fenner]
Dog in the Manger   Steve Utley
The Flower Thief   Ken Doggett

Winter 1982   2/2 (6) Michael Whelan
The Last Communication [v]
                       Melissa Mia Hall
Prince Myshkin, and Hold
    the Relish   Harlan Ellison
Middle Earth [ap]   Robert Haas, Kim Eide,
         Thomas Blackshear, Richard Corben
[text uncredited but probably by Fenner]
Has Success Spoiled Stephen
    King? [in] Pat Cadigan, Marty Ketchum &
                            Arnie Fenner
Punchatz: A Barnstormer in
    Texas [a/ap]   Don Ivan Punchatz
    [Profile by Arnie Fenner]
"... The World As We Know't."
                       Howard Waldrop
The Ultimate Spy   Ken Doggett
A Perfect Night for Vampires [v] Alan Ryan
Nightflying with George   Pat Cadigan &
    R. R. Martin [in]   Arnie Fenner
Patriots   Michael Bishop

***

SHOCK

A weird fantasy digest magazine published bi-monthly by Winston Publications, 157 West 57th Street, New York. No editor credited. Sub-titled 'The Magazine of Terrifying Tales' the first three issues were edited in a light-hearted but serious vein and presented many good fantasy stories. The magazine then ceased publication and was purchased by Pontiac Publishing, 1546 Broadway, New York which converted it into a sado-mystery magazine with minimal fantasy interest. The four issues as Shock Mystery Tales are excluded from this Index.

May 1960	1/1	?
Feast Day		Matthew Lynge
*Bianca's Hands		Theodore Sturgeon
The Band Played On		Gene Dilmore
*Graveyard Rats		Henry Kuttner
*The Crowd		Ray Bradbury
Parlor Game		Reginald Rose
*The Monkey's Paw		W. W. Jacobs
Forever After		Jim Thompson
*The Empty Man		Anthony Boucher
Crickets		Richard Matheson
*Specialty of the House		Stanley Ellin
*Green Thoughts		John Collier
The Tenant		Avram Davidson

July 1960	1/2	?
*Bright Segment		Theodore Sturgeon
Mean Mr. Murray		Avram Davidson
*The House Party		Stanley Ellin
Pin-Up Girl		Will Folke
*9-Finger Jack		Anthony Boucher
*The Emissary		Ray Bradbury
Baby Picture		Mort Golding
Laughing Moths		Miriam Allen deFord
*Sredni Vashtar		'Saki'
*The Frog Prince		John Collier
*Our Feathered Friends		Philip MacDonald
The Doll		Pat Gibbons
*Yours Truly, Jack the Ripper		Robert Bloch

September 1960	1/3	-
Final Performance		Robert Bloch
The Witch		Ralph E. Hayes
*Open House		Charles Beaumont
The Man Who Knew Everything		
		Edward D. Hoch
*The Skeleton		Ray Bradbury
Cold Case		Ed Ritter
*Skin		Roald Dahl
Chanceyville		John Anthony West
*Johnson Looked Back		Thomas Burke
Beautiful Dreamer		R. A. Lafferty
*A Bottomless Grave		Ambrose Bierce
*Moon-Face		Jack London
*The Kennel		Maurice Level
Prison Ball		John Rublowsky
Cat Killers		Donald E. Westlake

* * *

SOMETHING ELSE

*A British small press magazine published in large slick format by Pan Visuals,
Legh Street, Patricroft, Manchester. (Current address, 11-15 Fennel Street,
Manchester.) Publisher/Editor: Charles Partington. A late descendant of the
'new wave' speculative fiction magazines (like* New Worlds, Other Times *and*
Interzone*), it also contains sf, but concentrates more on the weird and the
bizarre. Despite the long hiatus between issues, No.3 appeared in the spring
of 1984.*

Spring 1980   No.1 Michael J. Garner
Three Evolutionary Enigmas Brian W. Aldiss
 1. The Fall of Species B
 2. In the Halls of the Hereafter
 3. The Ancestral Home of Thought
Dinosaur Destruction Day
                          Andrew J. Ellsmore
The Sudden Embodiment of Benedict
   Paucemanly [ex]   M. John Harrison
Dream of a Doomed Lord [ill]
                          James Cawthorn
The Russian Intelligence
   [ex]   Michael Moorcock
Wonderful Discovery of Eng-Lan
   by Ingenious Koreans [pic]
      Robert Meadley & Richard Glyn Jones
Nosferatu's Ape [nt]   Charles Partington
Providence [a]   Tony Williams

Winter 1980   No.2   *Franz Stuck
The Man Who Saw Cliff Richard
                          Brian W. Aldiss
Old Worlds   Charles Platt
Three Nightmares in Brown   John Brunner
 1. The Great Man [ss]
 2. The Supreme Commander [ss]
 3. The Elderly Scientist [ss]
Escape to Reality [a]   Tony Williams
The Strange Events Leading to
   the Suicide of Sebastian Lumm [cs]
      Phillip Meadley & Richard Glyn Jones
Everything Blowing Up   Hilary Bailey
The Double Archetype [a]   Robert Holland

***

185

SPACE AND TIME

A small press fantasy/sf magazine published in digest format by Gordon Linzner, 138 West 70th Street, New York. Editor: Gordon Linzner. The longest running regular amateur fiction fanzine in the fantasy field it turned semi-professional with issue no. 23 (March 1974). The first few issues are of minor interest, and the magazine can be considered as entering adolescence with issue 12 (June 1971) and maturing steadily but most noticeably from issue 45 (November 1977). Originally quarterly, S&T was bi-monthly from May 1973 - January 1978, quarterly until July 1981, and now bi-annual.

Spring 1966	No.1	John Eiche
Carol For Another Christmas		Lawrence Lee
Friedman's Folly		Gordon Linzner
The Best-Laid Plans		Gordon Linzner
Archeological Discovery		Alice Bazylewsky
The Galactic Guard [s1/2]		Nestor Jaremko

Fall 1967	No.2	Alex Saviuk
Prisoner in Space		Robert Murnick
The Galactic Guard [s2/2]		Nestor Jaremko
Butterball		Irene Anfleming
Time		John Nelson
Edgar vs The Tree [cs]		Larry Lee
The Key		Gordon Linzner
Hate		Jeff Anderson
The Calendar		[Gordon Linzner]
Valgart of Zandar [s1/2]		Willie White

Spring 1968	No.3	Alex Saviuk
Battle of the Wizards		Gordon Linzner
The Man and the Mountain		Nestor Jaremko
Superedgar [cs]		[Gordon Linzner]
Valgart of Zentor [s2/2]		Willie White
The Glass Harp [v]		Lenni Sedlak
12 Noon Under the Weeping Willow [v]		Lenni Sedlak
5 A.M. Half Dream [v]		Reef Freeman
Nastasi of the Apes Returns [cs]		Larry Lee
Shadows Dim Candle and Not Even the Rain [v]		Lenni Sedlak

Winter 1968	No.4	Alex Saviuk
The Two Roads		Nestor Jaremko
Kaleidoscope in 3 Dimensions [v]		Lenni Sedlak
Hobbit [v]		Lenni Sedlak

The Hellsman [cs]		Alex Saviuk
Pottery		Esther Klemens
60 Second Happening [v]		Reef Freeman
Cthark		Gordon Linzner

Spring 1969	No.5	Steve Coronel
Encounter		Gordon Linzner
The Dawn of Time [cs]		Al Saviuk

Summer 1969	No.6	Alex Saviuk
A Capsule History		Gordon Linzner
The Hellsman [cs]		Al Saviuk

August 1969	No.7	Alex Saviuk
The Revenge of Nolfur		Gordon Linzner
A Hasty Passage [cs]		Gordon Linzner
		[art: Al Saviuk]
Beacon		Nestor Jaremko
Cross and Double-Cross [a]		Kenneth Scher
The Stranger [cs]		Fred Appel
		[art: Al Saviuk]

February 1970	No.8	Dan Osterman
The Wind in the Ruins [v]		Nestor Jaremko
Fourth Planet from Another Sun		T. C. Blatz
The Wizard [cs]		Kevin McColl
		[art: Larry Lee]
Project 37940-J		Gordon Linzner
Memories, Just Memories		Darrell Schweitzer

July 1970	No.9	Mark Gelotte
Invention		Gordon Linzner
Iron Drums		Nestor Jaremko
The Dawn of Time [cs]		Alex Saviuk
Life		Leon Taylor

186

Fifty Years [v]   John Bredon
A Tale of Allsorts   Douglas Roome

July 1977   No.43   Alex Saviuk
Sighted Justice
          Eric Vinicoff & Marcia Martin
The Perfect Counterspell
               Robert D. Sans Souci
Coffin Song [v]   Chet Gottfried
Near the End of the World   Greg Stafford
She Only Nicked Him [v]   Neal Wilgus

September 1977   No.44   Randall Spurgin
     ['Harvest of Horrors' issue]
The Feaster from the Stars   E. P. Berglund
The Thing in the Glen   William H. Pugmire
   [in ToC title is "The Final Manuscript
        of Desmond Peters"]
Haitian Lullaby [v]   Karma Beck

November 1977   No.45   Gary Kato
Mai-Kulala   Charles R. Saunders
Walk in the Rain   A. K. Molnar
Gulliver Redux   Ed Newby
The Beast Within   George C. Diezel II
Just Plain Clumsy [v]   Gary Hall
Creepogs   Phillip C. Heath
Dance Programme [ss]   Steve Eng
The Blood-Ransom of Ikribu   David C. Smith
Little Change in Temp [v]   Neal Wilgus

January 1978   No.46   James E. Hunt
A Guilt-Edged Priority
          Eric Vinicoff & Marcia Martin
Homecoming   Wayne Hooks
Foliage [v]   Steve Eng
Good Will and Foreign Shade S. Diane Bogus
The Neuro-Generation   Jon Inouye
Abdul Alhazred [v]   Steve Behrens
Through the Dark Past   Howard E. Day &
                          Charles R. Saunders
Kiss of Fire [ss]   I. E. Steele
The Ring of Confidence   Steve Sneyd

April 1978   No.47   Fran Trevisani
III   Johannes Ney
Coven [v]   Brent Webber
The Candle Man   Wayne Tryhuk
Screamer   Randall D. Larson
Metallic Face [v]   Gary Hall
Straight From the Comet's Mouth
                               John Taylor
The Passing of B-------- [ss] Steve Eng
Kidnaped on Mars [spf]   Andrew J. Offutt
The Flowers of the Ebon
   Mountains   Richard Landwehr
The Elf Connection   Neal Wilgus
Under the Night Star   G.Arthur Rahman
Barriers [v]   K. Allan Daniels

July 1978   No.48   Charles Vess
Trick or Treat   Stephen Barnes
Smith on Mars!?! [a]   Andrew J. Offutt
The Phantom   Alex Kernaghan
Mask of Evil   Wayne Hooks
Dreams in the Dungeon [v] Joey Froehlich
Arthur Rampant   Douglas Derek Roome
The Lotus-Eaters of Ozymandias
                       Andrew Darlington
X: Effervescent #4 (Wet With God)
   [v]   Michael Vance

Demons Are Forever   Gordon Linzner

October 1978   No.49   John Charette
Reflections in the Jirga G. Arthur Rahman
The Sea Spook [v]   George J. Bessette
The Teddy Bear   Darrell Schweitzer
Goddess of the Stone [v] Joey Froehlich
Botwinick's Soul   John Kelly
The Hounds of Persephone   John Taylor
Victor's Loot [v]   Steve Eng
An Elemental [cs]   Douglas Roome
                         [art: Gary Kato]
Knitting   Harry Bose
The Locked Saucer Mystery B. F. Watkinson
Starspider [v]   K. Allen Daniels
Night of the Valkings   Charles de Lint
A Wanderer Without Time [v]
                       Frederick J. Mayer

January 1979   No.50   R. G. Harrison
Duty   Eric Vinicoff & Marcia Martin
O Christmas Tree   William H. Pugmire &
                 Jessica Amanda Salmonson
Necromancy [v]   Brent Webber
Arthur's Contest   Douglas Derek Roome
The Man With the Silver Stake
                           Gordon Linzner
Castle of Light   David Madison
Payment [v]   Steve Eng

April 1979   No.51   Gary Kato
The Last Zeppelin [nt1/2]   Jon Inouye
The Collection   Blythe Ayne
Triptych   Chet Gottfried
The Mandruv Effect   Brad Cahoon & John Lee
Beauty Unkind [v]   Dwight E. Humphries
The Old Book-Shop   Steve Eng
Save the Savage!   B. F. Watkinson
And Still the Waters [v]   N. S. Thompson
The Toads of Ghorem [v]   Steve Sneyd

July 1979   No.52   Stephen Schwartz
The Last Zeppelin [nt2/2]   Jon Inouye
Curse of the Dragon Sword   Brad Cahoon
In Zeth [v]   Mark McLaughlin
Dennis and the Snail   John Kelly
A Song of Archaic Sorcery [v]
                           Joey Froehlich
In Deep   Eric Vinicoff & Marcia Martin
Questionnaire [v]   Steve Eng

October 1979   No.53   Dan Day
Celebration   Susan Anne Santo
The Human Solution   Ken Hahn
Where Are We Now?   George W. Smyth
Mercurius Speaks   Stanley Morner
Golden Opportunity [v]   Neal Wilgus
The Giant's Frosted Daughter
                       Darrell Schweitzer
The Angel of Death Uses Raid
   Roach Killer [v]   Owen Jay Korman
The Skin of Our Teeth   Eileen Kernaghan
Old Accounts / Necrobiblia /
   Follow Me [3v]   Steve Eng

January 1980   No.54   Allen Koszowski
Darkdays, Deathdays   J. J. Miller
Upon Retiring [v]   D. M. Vosk
Creatures [v]   Joey Froehlich
The Plant-Stealers of Sram   Earl Kennedy &
                            Adrian Chadwick

The Sea's Barren Faces   Gerard Houarner
A Hashish Dream [v]   Billy Wolfenbarger
Remote   Robert Medcalf, Jr
Field Work [v]   Steve Sneyd
Fishtail   M. A. Washil
Cthulhu [v]   Denise Dumars
Advice to the New Mother
  (Night Feeding Dreams) [v] Marion Cohen
Wee, Tim'rous Beastie   G. E. Coggshall
Quotidian [v]   Roger Bower
Where There's No Smoke   C. Dell Turney
Purple Lensman [spf]   Allan A. Lucas
The Cat-Woman [v]   Mark McLaughlin
Lupo [v]   Morris Liebson
Rat Children [v]   Terry L. Persun
Rune   Jennifer H. Orr
Grave Matters   Joel Henry Sherman
The Argia [v]   John Gregory Betancourt
Drug Abuse [v]   Lois Wickstrom
How Jaquerel Learned to Let
  Sleeping Gods Lie   Janet Fox
Mind-Flight [v]   Steve Eng
The Galactic Blues   Chet Gottfried
Pet Mate   Steve Martin
Ballad of the Blue Maid [v]
                                Esther M. Leipar
Signal Red for Jasper Snead
                                George Bessette
Dompadry Owes One More Year
                                Laura E. Campbell

Winter 1982/83   No.63   Bruce Conklin
Small Favors   Jack D. Ribber
Dream, 1976 [v]   Marion Cohen
The Silent Ghosts   Charles R. Saunders
The Ones Who Pickaback Away
  With Omelets   Ruth Berman
The Valley of the Swastika Joe R. Lansdale
Parallel Designs   Joel Henry Sherman
Luck of the Draw   Kevin J. Anderson
An Alien's Lament [v]   Fred W. Wright,Jr
Kedward's Box   John Alfred Taylor
He Dreamed of Dragons   Jeffrey Goddin
Critter Fritters [v]
             Robert Randolph Medcalf, Jr
The Unicorn and the Whore   Scott Edelman
Bad Timing   Mark Worden
I Am Blood [v]   Stephanie Stearns
Evening of the Dreamer   J. J. Miller
Justice [v]   Betty Nolley

Summer 1983   No.64   Allen Koszowski
The Windela Man   Mary C. Aldridge
Atlas [v]   Mary Groneman
The Golden Apple   Ken Doggett
Rejuvenation [v]
             Robert Randolph Medcalfe, Jr
A Rose in Amber [v]   Neal Wilgus
Gone   Steve Games
Punkin' Head   Bruce G. Hallenbeck
The Stones of Moel Hebog Cooper McLaughlin
Three Songs From *Dracula*
  [3v]   Michael R. Collings
  [A Threnody of Wolves; Renfield's Litany;
   The Bloofer Lady]
The Eyes of Omod   Ron Tackett
Don't Laugh [v]   John Gregory Betancourt
In Steerage [v]   Susan Packie
Turncoat [v]   Lee Barwood
Winner Take All   John Alfred Taylor

The Whitleys Have the Innsmouth
  Look [v]   Denise Dumars
Innsmouth's Trade [v]   Joey Froehlich
G-Men in Action [v]   Gordon Linzner

Winter 1983/84   No.65   Iain Byers
The Tapestry   Joan Garrison
Rest and Relaxation [v]   Roger Bower
Cogs   Chris Estey
The World of the Future [v] Marion Cohen
Bezeball - 2082 [pic]   David J. Sheskin
Floater   Scott Edelman
Abandon the Poet, Deliver the
  Night   Michael Bogue
The Mad Dance at Twilight [v]
                                Dana K. Allen
Superior Graphics   M. Lindholm
A Shorter History   L. A. Taylor
Moon of Legend [v]   Caroline D. Henry
The Spacer Walks   M. William Tiedemann
Andromeda [v]   Blair H. Allen
Past Murders   Robert Reppert
Druid Dance [v]   D. Lauretta Henderson
Galactic Gothic [v]   Steve Eng
First Rights   Steve Rasnic Tem

                    ***

SPOOR ANTHOLOGY

A small press weird fiction magazine published by the Strange Company, Madison Wisconsin on behalf of editor Fred C. Adams, Lemont Furnace, Pennsylvania. Issue 2 guest edited by E. Paul Berglund. Dedicated predominantly to stories of the Cthulhu Mythos it grew out of the non-fiction companion Spoor.

[Spring] 1974   [1]   Jude Fulkerson
Memory   W. Paul Ganley
After Reading Lovecraft's "The
    Statement of Randolph
    Carter" [v]   S. L. Tannahill
Eyes   Frank Balazs
And Beowulf Rides Again [v]
    Robert E. Howard
Feast With a Few Strangers   E. P. Berglund
Wander   Amos Salmonson
Azathoth [v]   David E. Schultz
Coup   Jason Sharpe
When Dreams Come True   Llewellyn M. Cabos
When the Gods Were King [v]
    Robert E. Howard
The Hunter Out of Chaos   Robert Weinberg

[Fall] 1974   No.2   Randall Spurgin
Casket of the Sea Queen   Richard Landwehr
The Hutch [v]   John Pocsik
The Release of Sclotha   Richard Blackmon
Born of Woman   David J. Brown
He Who Creeps   F. C. Adams
Lure to Darkness   Arthur Aspromatis
The Shunned Ship   Gerard E. Giannattasio
The Lurkers Beneath   Llewellyn M. Cabos
The Thing in the Library
    Crispin Burnham & Edward P. Berglund
Lineage of the Empty Dead
    William Scott Home

***

SPWAO SHOWCASE

An occasional volume produced by the Small Press Writers and Artists Organization (current address c/o Janet Fox, Secretary/Treasurer, 519 Ellinwood, Osage City, Kansas). Editor: No.1, David R. Warren; No.2, James A. Anderson. Published in digest format it contains a mixture of fantasy, sf and horror.

1980	1/1 (1)	
Starfall [v]		Ken Raney
		Wendelessen
The Buzzsaw Reunion [v]		Joey Froehlich
The One Left Behind		Stephen Gresham
No Green Pastures		Albert J. Manachino
Makeweight		Ron Nance
Voices [v]		David Warren
The Curse of Set		James Anderson
The Show		Phillip C. Heath
The Gallery [ap]		Michael Roden,
	Ted Guerin & Ken Raney	
The Face of Noguchi		Lois Wickstrom
Lo! Death [v]		Jerry Baker
Elf-Tune [v]		Steve Eng
The Ballad of Thumpertree		
Mountain [v]		B. F. Watkinson
The White Indians		G. Arthur Rahman
Woods and Waters Wild		Charles de Lint
Hammerapi and I [v]		Ed Lesko
A Web for Demons		Bruce Boston
Far Bright Star [v]		Stephanie Stearns

1982	II/2 (2)	
Ghouls [v]		Ken Raney
		Janet Fox
The Winter Consort		Sharon Lee
Love Song From Capella IV	[v]	Betty Nolley
Die Spinnen		David Sutton
Tide Song [v]		Lee Barwood
Something Wrong at the Castle		Bruce Boston
Tea Time [v]		A. Shulla Sannella
The Ugliness Without		Paula Freda
A Poesque Poem [v]		Jerry Baker
The Complaint		Thomas Wiloch
The Wood [v]		Thomas M. Egan
Bluemoon and the Master Thief		
		Cord Silverbird
On a Chill October's Eve	[v]	Valerie Tiley
Horror Story		Joey Froehlich
Dream-Builded [v]		Billy Wolfenbarger
Possession of Amy		Albert J. Manachino
Blood [v]		Stephanie Stearns

***

STARTLING MYSTERY STORIES

A weird mystery digest magazine published quarterly by Health Knowledge Inc., 119 Fifth Avenue, New York. Editor: Robert A.W. Lowndes. A companion title to Magazine of Horror *it also relied heavily on material reprinted from* Weird Tales *and* Strange Tales.

* * *

STIRRING FANTASY FICTION

A magazine within a magazine - a self-contained section (with its own editorial departments) within the pulp magazine Stirring Science Stories; *published bi-monthly by Albing Publications, New York. Editor: Donald A. Wollheim. The magazine folded after three issues but was revived in large pulp format by the same company, renamed Manhatten Fiction Publications, for just one issue.*

February 1941   1/1 (1)   Leo Morey
Thirteen O'Clock   Cecil Corwin
Bones   Donald A. Wollheim
*Old Trinity Churchyard [v]   A. Merritt
Key to Cornwall   David H. Keller
Out of the Jar   Charles R. Tanner
*Devotee of Evil   Clark Ashton Smith
The Abyss   Robert W. Lowndes
*Always Come Evening   Robert E. Howard

April 1941   1/2 (2)   Hannes Bok
Black Flames   Lawrence Woods
Calypso's Island   David H. Keller
The Other   Robert W. Lowndes
The Wind From the River [v]
                           Richard Morrison
The Burrowers Beneath [v]Wilfred O. Morley
The Touching Point   Edward J. Bellin
Ghost Story   [no credit]
The Coming of the White Worm
                          Clark Ashton Smith
The Doll Master   Paul Dennis Lavond
Swing Low   Elmer Perdue

June 1941   1/3 (3)   Hannes Bok
Mr. Packer Goes to Hell   Cecil Corwin
The Grey One   Robert W. Lowndes
The Words of Guru   Kenneth Falconer
The Silence   Venard McLaughlin
Kazam Collects   S. D. Gottesman
*The Moon Artist   David H. Keller
Forbidden Books [v]   Wilfred Owen Morley

March 1942   2/1 (4)   Hannes Bok
The Golden Road   Cecil Corwin
The Goblins Will Get You   Hugh Raymond
Masquerade   Kenneth Falconer
Fear of Sleep [v]   Emil Petaja
The Long Wall   Wilfred Owen Morley
The Unfinished City   Martin Pearson

                   ***

STRANGE FANTASY

A digest fantasy magazine published by Ultimate Publishing Co., Oakland Gardens, Flushing, New York. No edited credited, but issues assembled by publisher Sol Cohen. A reprint magazine it drew its contents almost totally from Fantastic. *Due to publishing arrangements with companion sf titles,* Strange Fantasy *started with issue number 8 and retained that sequential numbering. There are, therefore, no issues 1 to 7.*

Spring 1969   No.8   *Frank Bruno
*Some Fabulous Yonder [nt]
                          Philip Jose Farmer
*Dr. Adams' Garden of Evil   Fritz Leiber
*Nine Starships Waiting [nt] Roger Zelazny
*Suicide World [nt]   Harlan Ellison

Summer 1969   No.9   *Gray Morrow
*The Casket Demon   Fritz Leiber
*The Spawn of the Dark One Robert Bloch
*Saucer! Saucer!   Henry Slesar
*Neosho's Choicest   James E. Gunn
*The Crib of Hell   Arthur Pendragon
*Bright Eyes   Harlan Ellison
*A Museum Piece   Roger Zelazny
*Psychoanalysis by Telepathy
  [a]   Ellery Lanier
*The Creeping Coffins of
  Barbados [a]   Eric Frank Russell
*Cornie on the Walls   Sidney van Scyoc

Fall 1969   No.10   *?
*The Girl Who Played Wolf   Gordon Dickson
*Giants of the Earth [a]   Lee Owens
*Satan's Footprints [a] Eric Frank Russell
*The Mind Spider   Fritz Leiber
*Egyptian Festival For Ares
  [a]   Kay Bennett
*The Gift   Ray Bradbury
*And the Rains Came ...   Dan Corliss
*Candlesticks   Dean Evans
*The Odyssey of Henry Thistle Vern Fearing
*April in Paris   Ursula K. LeGuin
*Sacred Crocodile [a]   Peter Bogg
*The House   Frederic Brown
*The Devil's Due   Donald Moffitt
*Miranda   John Jakes

Spring 1970   No.11   *Barr/Kramer/Adragna
*The Shrine of Temptation   Judith Merril
*The Soft Woman   Theodore L. Thomas
*The Sudden Afternoon   J. G. Ballard
*The Mermaid and the Archer
                          Barry P. Miller
*Planet of Change [nt]   J. T. McIntosh
*Daughter of the Clan   Wilton G. Beggs
*Keepers in Space   Rog Phillips
*Hear a Pin Drop   Edward Wellen
*Victim of the Year   Robert F. Young
*Sword of Flowers   Larry M. Harris

Summer 1970   No.12   *R. Frankenberg
*Rogue Psi [nt]   James H. Schmitz
*Measureless to Man [nt]
                        Marion Zimmer Bradley
*Drunkboat [nt]   Cordwainer Smith
*Man Made   Albert R. Teichner
*Unauthorized   Harold Calin
*The Premiere   Richard Sabia
*The Trigger   Henry Slesar

Fall 1970   No.13   *Jack Gaughan
*Physician to the Universe
  [nt]   Clifford D. Simak
*Midnight in the Mirror World Fritz Leiber
*Elixir For the Emperor   John Brunner
*Thelinde's Song   Roger Zelazny
*The Man Who Painted Tomorrow Kate Wilhelm
*The Word of Unbinding   Ursula K. LeGuin
*The Recurrent Suitor   Ron Goulart
*Genetic Coda   Thomas M. Disch

***

197

STRANGE STORIES

A weird fantasy pulp published bi-monthly by Better Publications, 22 West 48th Street, New York. No editor credited but probably Mort Weisinger under Leo Margulies. When the magazine folded the balance of stories held in its inventory was used in the companion Thrilling Mystery.

February 1939   1/1 (1)   [R. Belarski?]
The Singing Shadows [nt] Vincent Cornier
The Curse of the House   Robert Bloch
Eyes of the Serpent   August W. Derleth &
                               Mark Schorer
The Invaders   Keith Hammond
Changeling   Manly Wade Wellman
The Sorcerer's Jewel   Tarleton Fiske
Major McCrary's Vision Ralph Milne Farley
The Frog   Henry Kuttner
Servant of Satan   Otis Adelbert Kline

April 1939   1/2 (2)   [R. Belarski?]
Death Has Five Guesses   Robert Bloch
Logoda's Heads   August W. Derleth
Cursed Be the City   Henry Kuttner
Lord of Evil   Tally Mason
The Box From the Stars
                    Amelia Reynolds Long
*The Dead Woman   David H. Keller
The Vengeance of Ai   Mark Schorer
The Creeper in the Darkness
                      Frank Belknap Long
Miracle in Three Dimensions   C. L. Moore
A Question of Identity   Tarleton Fiske
The Bottomless Pool   Ralph Milne Farley
Fulfillment   Will Garth
Bells of Horror   Keith Hammond

June 1939   1/3 (3)   ?
For Fear of Little Men Manly Wade Wellman
Double Ring   Will Garth
Chameleon Eyes   John Clemons
The Toad God   Dr. David H. Keller
The Man Who Was Death   Norman A. Daniels
Bride of the Antarctic   Mordred Weir
Man in the Dark   August W. Derleth
The Flying Head   A. Hyatt Verrill
Unheavenly Twin   Robert Bloch
The Hunt   Henry Kuttner

The Seal of the Satyr   Tarleton Fiske
The Great Release   Maria Moravsky
The Body and the Brain   Keith Hammond

August 1939   2/1 (4) Earle K. Bergey
Snake Goddess   E. Hoffman Price
The Bohemian   Heydorn Schley
Pink Elephants   Robert Bloch
Mrs. Elting Does Her Part   Tally Mason
A Sentence of Death   John L. Benton
Silent is the Clock   Fenton W. Earnshaw
Sagasta's Last   Carl Jacobi
Memoir for Lucas Payne August W. Derleth
Flowers From the Moon   Tarleton Fiske
Death Bridge   John Clemons
The Curse of the Crocodile
                       Bertram W. Williams
Sea Vision   Will Garth
The Citadel of Darkness [nt] Henry Kuttner

October 1939   2/2 (5) Earle K. Bergey
Death is Forbidden   Don Alviso
The Cult of the Dead   Gabriel Wilson
Kaapi   Marian Stearns Curry
Let Me Out!   Maria Moravsky
The Master   Shelton Goodall
He Waits Beneath the Sea   Tarleton Fiske
A Message For His Majesty
                       August W. Derleth
Half Bull   Manly Wade Wellman
The Ghostly Vengeance   A. Hyatt Verrill
The Geist of the Jungle R. R. Winterbotham
The Light Must Burn Capt.George J. Rawlins
House of the Griffin   Will Garth
Spawn of Blackness   Carl Jacobi

December 1939   2/3 (6) Earle K. Bergey
The Crawling Corpse   Eli Colter
The Bottle From Corezzi   Mark Schorer
The Man Who Looked Beyond   Carol Boyd

Vigil	Hampton Wells
The Soul of the Cello	Maria Moravsky
For Love of a Witch	Manly Wade Wellman
A Gift For Uncle Herman	August W. Derleth
The Grip of Death	Robert Bloch
Voices in the Wind	Robert Emerick
Passing of Eric Holm	Will Garth
He Who Spoke	Bernard Breslauer
Dread Command	David Bernard
The Room on the Annex	Tally Mason

February 1940   3/1 (7)   Earle K. Bergey

The Mask of the Marionette	Don Alviso
The Immortal Voice	James Macfie
The Man Who Knew Everything	Ray Cummings
Vengeance By Proxy	John Beynon
Me and My Shadow	Eric Frank Russell
The Day I Die	Hal G. Vermes
The Djinn of El Mohrab	Charles S. Strong
The Bag of Skin	Dorothy Quick
Ghost Knife	Bernard Breslauer
Hound of the Haunted Trail	
	George J. Rawlins
Singing Blades	Lloyd Arthur Eshbach
*The Man from Dark Valley	August W. Derleth
Dirge	Thorp McClusky

April 1940   3/2 (8)   R. Belarski

One Man's Hell [nt]	Eli Colter
I Killed Him! Remember?	
	C. William Harrison
The Gallows Geist	Earle Dow
Kanaima	Arthur J. Burks
The Slanting Shadow	August W. Derleth
The Cauldron	Lloyd Arthur Eshbach
Spider Woman	Maria Moravsky
Seance	Olga L. Rosmanith
His Name On a Bullet	Manly Wade Wellman
Path to Perdition	John Clemons
Joliper's Gift	Eldon Heath
The Thirteenth Boat	George J. Rawlins
Song of the Sun	Bernard Breslauer

June 1940   3/3 (9)   Earle K. Bergey

The Hunchback of Hanover	Don Alviso
The Vengeance of Hanuman	Hamilton Craigie
Time to Kill	Henry Kuttner
Soldier, Rest	Robert D. Price
The Panting Beast	John Clemons
The Sailor Quits the Sea	Earle Dow
The Terror Mummy	Jack B. Creamer
The Four Who Came Back	Tally Mason
Tiger! Tiger!	O. M. Cabral
The Hydroponic Monster	Maria Moravsky
After You, Mr. Henderson	August W. Derleth
Power of the Druid	Robert Bloch
The Room of Souls	Keith Hammond

August 1940   4/1 (10)   [E. K. Bergey]

The Seal of Sin	Henry Kuttner
The Dead Know All	Norman A. Daniels
The House of Stanley	George J. Rawlins
The Tapestry Gate	Leigh Brackett
Satan's Sideshow	Carson Judson
Birkett's Twelfth Corpse	August W. Derleth
I Am Going to Cracow!	Maria Moravsky
The Dead Shall Rise Up	Will Garth
Design For Doom	Eli Colter

October 1940   4/2 (11)   [E. K. Bergey]

The Evil Ones [nt]	
	August W. Derleth & Mark Schorer
To Boatl and Back	Henry Kuttner
The Bald-Headed Man	Don Tracy
The Lesser Breathren Mourn	Seabury Quinn
Be Yourself	Robert Bloch
Beast of the Island	Paul Selonke
Astral Newspaper	Will Garth
I've Got to Believe It	Bruce Walker
Jessamin's Death	Oscar J. Friend

December 1940   4/3 (12)   Earle K. Bergey

The Manci Curse [nt]	Dorothy Quick
Adventure in Valhalla	Joseph H. Hernandez
The Missing Mirage	Don Alviso
The Wine of Hera	Norman A. Daniels
Shadows	Arch Carr
Doomed	Seabury Quinn
Misty Island	Alexander Samalman
The Third Life of Nine	George J. Rawlins

February 1941   5/1 (13)   Earle K. Bergey

The Band of Death [nt]	Eli Colter
One More River	E. Hoffman Price
Ithaqua	August W. Derleth
The Shadow of Nirvana [nt]	
	Earl Pierce, Jr
Appointment With a Lady	Wyatt Blassingame
Some Day I'll Kill You	Seabury Quinn
Death, I Want to Dance!	Arthur J. Burks
Hate's Handiwork	Will Garth

* * *

STRANGE TALES

OF MYSTERY AND TERROR

A weird fantasy pulp published bi-monthly (later quarterly) by Clayton Magazines Inc., 80 Lafayette St., New York. Editor: Harry Bates. Regarded by many as the best of the weird magazines, superior even to Weird Tales. *Most of the contents, except for the final issue, will be found reprinted in* Magazine of Horror *and its companion titles. The anonymous filler articles in the following are listed at the end of each entry.*

September 1931   1/1 (1)   'Wesso'
The Dead Who Walk [na]   Ray Cummings
The Place of Pythons   Arthur J. Burks
The Dark Castle   Marion Brandon
Dr. Muncing, Exorcist [nt] Gordon MacCreagh
The Dog Who Laughed Charles Willard Diffin
The Return of the Sorcerer
    Clark Ashton Smith
Nasturtia   Capt. S. P. Meek
A Cry From Beyond   Victor Rousseau
The Awful Injustice   S. B. H. Hurst
[Fillers: The Death of Bolster; Death
  Tokens; West England's Little Folk.]

November 1931   1/2 (2)   'Wesso'
The Black Mass   Capt. S. P. Meek
Webbed Hands   Ferdinand Berthoud
Guatemozin the Visitant   [na]
    Arthur J. Burks
After Sunset   Philip Hazleton
When Dead Gods Wake   Victor Rousseau
The Thirteenth Floor   Douglas M. Dold
Cassius [nt]   Henry S. Whitehead
[Fillers: A Remarkable Mirage; Science and
  Old Magic; Specter of the Brocken; The
  Dancing Stones of Burian½]

January 1932   1/3 (3)   'Wesso'
Dead Legs   Edmond Hamilton
Wolves of Darkness [sn]   Jack Williamson
The Moon Dial [nt]   Henry S. Whitehead
The Black Laugh   W. J. Makin
The Shadow on the Sky   August W. Derleth
The Door to Saturn   Clark Ashton Smith
The Smell   Francis Flagg
The Door of Doom   Hugh B. Cave
[Fillers: An Unusual Ghost; "Hauntings" and

the Trivial; Voices from Hell; Cormoran
  and Cormelian; The Legend of the Castle Lock]

March 1932   2/1 (4)   'Wesso'
The Feline Phantom   Gilbert Draper
The Duel of the Sorcerers [sn] Paul Ernst
By the Hands of the Dead   Francis Flagg
The Trap [nt]   Henry S. Whitehead
Tiger   Bassett Morgan
Back Before the Moon   S. Omar Baker
The Case of the Sinister
  Shape   Gordon MacCreagh
The Veil of Tanit   Eugene de Rezske
[Fillers: The Oracle of Delphi; The Wizard
  Merlin; Primitive Astronomy.]

June 1932   2/2 (5)   'Wesso'
Stragella [nt]   Hugh B. Cave
Dread Exile   Paul Ernst
The Great Circle [na] Henry S. Whitehead
The House in the Magnolias
    August W. Derleth & Mark Schorer
People of the Dark   Robert E. Howard
The Emergency Call   Marion Brandon
The Golden Patio   Aubrey Feist
The Nameless Offspring Clark Ashton Smith
[Fillers: The Sleep-Bringers of Weeng; The
  Ghost of Agrippina; The Departing Soul;
  Superstitions.]

October 1932   2/3 (6)   'Wesso'
The Hunters From Beyond Clark Ashton Smith
The Curse of Amen-Ra [na] Victor Rousseau
Sea Tiger   Henry S. Whitehead
The Dead Walk Softly [nt]
    Sewell Peaslee Wright
Bal Macabre   Gustav Meyrink

The Infernal Shadow   Hugh B. Cave
The Artist of Tao   Arthur Styron
In the Lair of the Space
    Monsters [nt]   Frank Belknap Long, Jr
Strange Tales and True [a]
                        Robert W. Sneddon
[Fillers: Speaking Heads; Injustice Tri-
  umphant; Odd Superstitions; Ghost Veng-
  eance; Bird Spirits; Indian Guardian
  Spirits; Fairies of Folkore; An Incant-
  ation.]

January 1933   3/1 (7)   'Wesso'
The Second Interment   Clark Ashton Smith
The Thing That Walked on
    the Wind   August W. Derleth
The Terror by Night Charles Willard Diffin
White Lady   Sophie Wenzel Ellis
Murgunstruum [nt]   Hugh B. Cave
The Napier Limousine   Henry S. Whitehead
The Cairn on the Headland Robert E. Howard
[Fillers: Human Embers; Powwows of John
  George Hohman; The Legend of Gogmagog's
  Leap; Albertus Magnus; Headless Ghosts.]

***

STRANGE TALES

of the Mysterious and Supernatural

British weird fantasy magazine published in digest format by Utopian Publications, London. Editor: Walter Gillings (though credited to Benson Herbert, the Publisher). Because of war-time restrictions the magazine was issued as a book, with no issue identification on the first number and the sub-title 'Second Selection' on the last.

[February 1946]	[No.1]	H. W. Perl	[March 1946]	No.2	Alva Rogers
*Non-Stop to Mars	[nt]	Jack Williamson	*The Moon Devils		John Beynon Harris
*Pink Elephants		Tarleton Fiske	*The Nameless Offspring		
*The Brain of Ali Khan					Clark Ashton Smith
		Lloyd Arthur Eshbach	*The Sorcerer's Jewel		Tarleton Fiske
*The Hunters From Beyond			*The Song From the Dark Star		
		Clark Ashton Smith			Richard Tooker
*Experiment in Murder		John Russell Fearn	*Cool Air		H. P. Lovecraft
*The Tombstone		Ray Bradbury	*The Mannikin		Robert Bloch

***

THE STRANGEST STORIES EVER TOLD

A weird fantasy digest magazine published by Ultimate Publishing Co., Oakland Gardens. Flushing, New York. No editor credited but issue assembled by Sol Cohen. Reprinted stories from Fantastic Adventures *and* Amazing Stories.

***

SUPERNATURAL STORIES

British pocketbook series that originated as a digest magazine. Originally published bi-monthly during 1954/55 by John Spencer & Co., 24 Shepherds Bush Rd., London, it was suspended during a publishing hiatus in 1956 then revived in 1957 as a paperback by the same publisher (then at 131 Brackenbury Road, London) under the Badger Books imprint. Editor pseudonymously identified in early issues as John S. Manning, though issues assembled by the publishers Sol Assael and Michael Nahum. Sixty percent of the contents were written by R. Lionel Fanthorpe under various pen names, whilst the balance was written almost entirely by John S. Glasby. Later issues were accompanied by a complete novel numbered sequentially as part of the series and though not technically magazine issues are included below for completeness.

[May 1954]   1/1   Ray Theobald
The Gods of Fear   Randall Conway
Lycanthrope   Ray Cosmic
Vengeance of Set   Michael Hamilton
The Cloak of Darkness   Max Chartair
The Devil's Canvas   A. J. Merak

[July 1954]   1/2   Ray Theobald
Frog   Max Chartair
Things of the Dark   A. J. Merak
Hunter's Moon   Randall Conway
The Incredulist   John Raymond
    [as by Lionel Roberts on cover]
...And Very Few Get Out   Lionel Fanthorpe

[September 1954]   1/3   Gerald Facey
The Crystal Skull   A. J. Merak
Haunt of the Vampire   Max Chartair
The Other Seance   Michael Hamilton
Something From the Sea   Ray Cosmic
    [misprinted as by Ray Cormic throughout]
Will O' the Wisp   Randall Conway

[November 1954]   1/4   Gerald Facey
They Fly By Night   Randall Conway
The Zegrembi Bracelet   Max Chartair
House of Unreason   A. J. Merak
    [misprinted as by H. J. Merak throughout]
The Weird Lovers   A. A. Glynn
The Chair   Ray Cosmic

[January 1955]   1/5   Gerald Facey
Lurani   Max Chartair

Somewhere in the Moonlight
                                 Michael Hamilton
The Whisper of the Wind   Randall Conway
The Dark Ones   Ray Cosmic
My Name is Satan   A. J. Merak

[March 1955]   1/6   Roland Turner
The Hungry House   Randall Conway
Voice of the Drum   Michael Hamilton
Without a Shadow of Doubt   Max Chartair
The Supernaturalist   A. J. Merak
Lorelei   Ray Cosmic

[May 1955]   1/7   Gerald Facey
The Crystal Fear   Michael Hamilton
Shadow Over Endor   Ray Cosmic
Moonbeast   A. J. Merak
Mask of Asmodeus   Max Chartair
The Hungry Gods   Randall Conway

[August 1955]   1/8   Roland Turner
A Place of Meeting   Michael Hamilton
The Ugly Ones   Max Chartair
The Reincarnate   A. J. Merak
The Golden Scarab   Ray Cosmic
The Man Who Lost Thursday   Randall Conway

[Spring 1957]   1/9   Ray Theobald
The Devil's Dictionary   Edward Richards
    [as by James S. Stanton on cover]
The Ancient Alchemist   John Mason
The Artist's Model   Robert D. Ennis
The Witch of Peronia   L. C. Powers

The Dolmen	Raymond L. Burton
Snake Vengeance	Andrew Sutton

[June 1957]   1/10   J. Pollack
Nightmare   Randall Conway
The Three Green Sisters   A. J. Merak
The Midnight Walkers   Michael Hamilton
Witch-Water   Max Chartair
Mr. Pilkington's Ghost   J. J. Hansby
*The Cloak of Darkness   H. K. Lennard

[August 1957]   1/11   H. Fox
The Night Creatures   Michael Hamilton
Lord of the Necromancers   Max Chartair
The Lonely Things   Peter Laynham
It Came by Appointment   Randall Conway
The Haunter   A. J. Merak

[October 1957]   1/12   [H. Fox]
Fang   Pel Torro
Resurgam   R. L. Fanthorpe
The Uncanny Affair at Greycove
                             Lionel Roberts
I've Been Here Before   Leo Brett
The Sorcerer's Cave   Trebor Thorpe

[December 1957]   1/13   [Ray Theobald]
        [entitled OUT OF THIS WORLD]
Secret of the Snows [nt]   R. L. Fanthorpe
The Spectre of the Tower   Lionel Roberts
The Black Hound   Pel Torro
Ghost Ship   Trebor Thorpe
Sky Herd   Bron Fane

[February 1958]   1/14   [Ray Theobald]
Song of the Banshee   Trebor Thorpe
The Creature   Pel Torro
The Old House   Lionel Roberts
The Seance   Bron Fane
Flight of the Valkyries   R. L. Fanthorpe

[April 1958]   1/15   H. Fox
        [entitled OUT OF THIS WORLD]
Watchers of the Forest   R. L. Fanthorpe
Out of the Vault   Lionel Roberts
Voodoo Vengeance   Bron Fane
Black River Mill   Pel Torro
The Earthen Vessel   Trebor Thorpe

[June 1958]   1/16   H. Fox
Guardians of the Tomb   Lionel Roberts
The Creatures From Below   R. L. Fanthorpe
The Iron Oven   Trebor Thorpe
Last Bus to Llangery   Pel Torro
The Effigy   Leo Brett

[August 1958]   1/17   [Ray Theobald]
        [entitled OUT OF THIS WORLD]
The Dancing Wraiths   Lionel Roberts
Call of the Werwolf   R. L. Fanthorpe
The Secret Room   Bron Fane
The Screaming Skull   Pel Torro
The Phantom Hand   Trebor Thorpe

[October 1958]   1/18   [Ray Theobald]
Dark Kith and Kin   Peter Laynham
The Tunnel of Fear   J. J. Hansby
The Hungry Ones   Michael Hamilton
The Chalice of Circe   A. J. Merak
Something About Gargoyles   Randall Conway

[November 1958]   1/19   [Ray Theobald]
        [entitled OUT OF THIS WORLD]
Invisible Witness   R. L. Fanthorpe
The Kraken   Leo Brett
The Golden Warrior   Lionel Roberts
Night of the Ghoul   Bron Fane
The Phantom of the Goodwins Trebor Thorpe

[December 1958]   1/20   [Ray Theobald]
The Death Note [nt]   R. Lionel Fanthorpe
Sinister Strangers   Lionel Roberts
Valley of the Vampire   Bron Fane
The Other Driver   Pel Torro
The Spawn of Satan   Leo Brett

[January 1959]   1/21   [Ray Theobald]
The Silent Stranger   Bron Fane
The Haunted Pool   Trebor Thorpe
[misprinted as Trevor Thorpe throughout]
The Lamia   Leo Brett
Unknown Realms   Lionel Roberts
The Stone Crusader   R. L. Fanthorpe

[February 1959]   1/22   [Ray Theobald]
Take the Last Train   A. J. Merak
Somewhere the Devil Hides   Peter Laynham
The Serpent Ring   Max Chartair
Hexerei   Michael Hamilton
Out of the Shadows   Randall Conway

[March 1959]   1/23   [Ray Theobald]
Mermaid Reef [nt]   R. L. Fanthorpe
The Unrealistic Theatre   Leo Brett
The Other Line   Bron Fane
The Swan Mae   Lionel Roberts
The Clock That Struck Thirteen
                             Trebor Thorpe

[April 1959]   1/24   [Ray Theobald]
The Poltergeist   Pel Torro
The Hypnotist   Lionel Roberts
The Green Cloud   Bron Fane
The Drud   Leo Brett
Quest for Atlantis   R. L. Fanthorpe

[May 1959]   1/25   [Ray Theobald]
The Guide and the God [nt] R. L. Fanthorpe
The Man Within   Trebor Thorpe
The Return   Leo Brett
Charlatan   Pel Torro
Pursuit   Bron Fane

[June 1959]   1/26   [Ray Theobald]
The Dark Possessed   Michael Hamilton
Ebb Tide   Max Chartair
Doorway to Darkness   A. J. Merak
The Crimson Evil   J. J. Hansby
The Shadows of Terror   Randall Conway

[July 1959]   1/27   [Ray Theobald]
The Man Who Was Nothing   Trebor Thorpe
The Ghost Rider   R. L. Fanthorpe
White Wolf   Leo Brett
Jungle of Death   Bron Fane
Gestalt   Lionel Roberts

[September 1959]   1/28   [Ray Theobald]
The Creature in the Depths
  [nt]   J. J. Hansby
The Pipes of Pan   Michael Hamilton

[January 1962]   1/53   H. Fox
Chariot of Apollo   R. Lionel Fanthorpe
*The North Cloister   Noel Bertram
Fly, Witch, Fly   Leo Brett
The Room With the Broken Floor   Pel Torro
Forbidden Island   Bron Fane

[March 1962]   No.54   [H. Fox]
Nightmare [n]   Leo Brett

[March 1962]   1/55   H. Fox
Vampire Castle [nt]   Pel Torro
Moonlight Island   Leo Brett
Storm God's Fury   Bron Fane
The Mountain Thing   R. L. Fanthorpe
Return of Lilith   Trebor Thorpe

[April 1962]   No.56   H. Fox
The Eye of Karnak [n]   John E. Muller

[April 1962]   1/57   H. Fox
Hell Has Wings [nt]   R. Lionel Fanthorpe
The Eldritch Chair   Trebor Thorpe
Vengeance of the Poltergeist   Bron Fane
*The Barrier   Noel Bertram
The Frozen Claw   Pel Torro
The Phantom Schooner   Leo Brett

[June 1962]   No.58   H. Fox
Face in the Night [n]   Leo Brett

[June 1962]   No.59   H. Fox
Graveyard of the Damned
    [nt]   R. Lionel Fanthorpe
The Dream of Camelot   Trebor Thorpe
The Voice   Pel Torro
Temple of Quetzalcoatl   Leo Brett
The Persian Cavern   Bron Fane
The Whisperer   Deutero Spartacus

[July 1962]   No.60   H. Fox
Vengeance of Siva [n]   John E. Muller

[July 1962]   No.61   H. Fox
Chasm of Time [nt]   Bron Fane
The Unfinished Chapter   Pel Torro
The Snarling Shadow   Trebor Thorpe
The Darker Drink   R. Lionel Fanthorpe
The Bevelled Casket   Leo Brett
*Scraping the Barrel   Noel Bertram

[September 1962]   No.62   H. Fox
The Immortals [n]   Leo Brett

[September 1962]   No.63   H. Fox
The Lonely Shadows   A. J. Merak
The Beckoning Shade   Max Chartair
Dark Conquest   Randall Conway
To Suffer a Witch   Peter Laynham
And Midnight Falls   Michael Hamilton

[October 1962]   No.64   H. Fox
Gods of Darkness [n]   Karl Zeigfreid

[October 1962]   No.65   [Rainey]
Curse of the Totem   R. Lionel Fanthorpe
Vengeance of Thor   Leo Brett
The Voice in the Wall   Bron Fane
Wokolo   Pel Torro
Secret of the Shaman   Trebor Thorpe

[November 1962]   No.66   H. Fox
Legion of the Lost [n]   Pel Torro

[November 1962]   No.67   [Rainey]
The Frozen Tomb [nt]   Leo Brett
Sleeping Place   R. Lionel Fanthorpe
Strange Country   Trebor Thorpe
Cry in the Night   Bron Fane
The Thing From Boulter's Cavern   Pel Torro
The Coveters   Deutero Spartacus

[January 1963]   No.68   H. Fox
They Never Come Back [n]   Leo Brett

[January 1963]   No.69   H. Fox
Lilith - Goddess of Night
                      R. Lionel Fanthorpe
The Nine Green Men   Bron Fane
The Swing of the Pendulum   Trebor Thorpe
Ventriloquist   Pel Torro
The Silent Fleet   Leo Brett

[February 1963]   No.70   H. Fox
The Strange Ones [n]   Pel Torro

[February 1963]   No.71   H. Fox
The Gliding Wraith [nt]   Leo Brett
Twilight Ancestor [nt] R. Lionel Fanthorpe
The Man Who Never Smiled   Bron Fane
Fangs in the Night   Pel Torro
An Eye For an Eye   Trebor Thorpe

[April 1963]   No.72   H. Fox
The Forbidden [n]   Leo Brett

[April 1963]   No.73   H. Fox
Spirit of Darkness [nt]   Trebor Thorpe
Sands of Eternity   R. Lionel Fanthorpe
The Friendly Stranger   Pel Torro
Return Ticket   Bron Fane
    [as "Return Fare" on Contents Page]
The Comedians   Deutero Spartacus
House of Despair   Leo Brett

[May 1963]   No.74   H. Fox
From Realms Beyond [n]   Leo Brett

[May 1963]   No.75   H. Fox
The Phantom Crusader [nt]   Leo Brett
The Room That Never Was [nt]   Bron Fane
The Tunnel   Olaf Trent
Stranger in the Skull   Trebor Thorpe
The Stockman   Deutero Spartacus
The Stone Tablet   Neil Thanet
Footprints in the Sand   Pel Torro

[June 1963]   No.76   H. Fox
The Timeless Ones [n]   Pel Torro

[June 1963]   No.77   H. Fox
Moon Wolf   R. L. Fanthorpe
The Zombie   Erle Barton
The Walker   Bron Fane
Old Man of the Snow   Neil Thanet
Blurred Horizon   Phil Nobel
The Grip of Time Unending   Leo Brett
The Tragedians   Deutero Spartacus

[July 1963]   No.78   H. Fox
The Unseen [n]   Lee Barton

Corporal Death   Lee Barton
Stranger in the Shadow   Elton T. Neef
Au Pair   Rene Rolant
The Reluctant Corpse   R. Lionel Fanthorpe

[Summer 1966]   No.104   H. Fox
The Shadow Man [n]   Lee Barton

[Autumn 1966]   No.105   H. Fox
Curse of the Khan [nt] R. Lionel Fanthorpe
Chimney Piece   Peter O'Flinn
Uncle Julian's Typewriter   Elton T. Neefe
The Resurrected Enemy   Bron Fane
Lord of the Crags   Oben Lerteth

[Spring 1967]   No.106   H. Fox
Dark Legion [n]   John Crawford

[Spring 1967]   No.107   H. Fox
Body and Soul   Randall Conway
That Deep Black Yonder   A. J. Merak
Dust   Max Chartair
Where Dead Men Dream   Peter Laynham
The Keeper of Dark Point Michael Hamilton
The Visitors   J. J. Hansby

[Summer 1967]   No.108
*this issue has never been sighted and
it is believed not to have been published.*

[Summer 1967]   No.109   H. Fox
The Thing in the Mist   Max Chartair
Older Than Death   A. J. Merak
The Dark Time   Peter Laynham
The Haunting of Charles
  Quintain   Michael Hamilton
The Black Mirror   Randall Conway
The Night-Comer   J. J. Hansby

***

SUSPENSE

A digest magazine published quarterly by Farrell Publishing Corporation, 350 East 22nd Street, Chicago, Illinois, with editorial offices at 420 Lexington Ave., New York. Editor: Theodore Irwin. Inspired by the CBS radio and television series of the same name Suspense *divided its contents into such categories as science fiction, mystery, crime, fantasy, the macabre, adventure, chiller-thriller and even dread dilemma!*

Spring 1951   1/1   [Ken Rice?]
The Deathless Ones
                    John Chapman & Oliver Saari
*Voice in the Night   William Hope Hodgson
A Most Amazing Murder   A. B. Shiffrin
Obviously Suicide   S. Fowler Wright
*The Eye-Witness Who Wouldn't
    See   James A. Kirch
*Small Assassin   Ray Bradbury
The Quick and the Bomb   William Tenn
She Didn't Bounce   Peter Phillips
*Jeannie With the Light Brown
    Cure   Alexander Samalman
*Ghost of a Chance   Theodore Sturgeon
*Honeymoon Terror [play] John Dickson Carr
Faces Turned Against Him   John Gearson

Summer 1951   1/2   [Docktop?]
Operation Peep   John Wyndham
Blood Will Tell   Nathaniel Weyl
The Nightmare Face   Walter Snow
Survival   Thomas Gilchrist
Criminal at Large   Larry Holden
Elusive Witness   Georges Simenon
Black Death   John Krill
Fatal Mistake   John Basye Price
*Penny Wise, Fate Foolish
                    Mary Elizabeth Counselman
World Within   Thomas A. Coffee
Pardon My Terror   Irving Burstiner
Evil is the Night   Edith Saylor Abbott
*Maiden Beware [play]   Richard Lewis
The Perfectly Calm Murder F. Hugh Herbert
*A Horseman in the Sky   Ambrose Bierce

Fall 1951   1/3   [Docktop?]
The Saboteur   William Sambrot
My Favorite Corpse   Dorothy F. Horton
Love Ethereal   Horace L. Gold
The Thing on the Snow Waldo Carlton Wright
*Dear Automaton   A. E. van Vogt
Rip Tide   Russell Branch
*Wall of Fear   Will F. Jenkins
You Can't Run Away   Philip Weck
Not a Leg to Stand On   Don Mardick
Terror in the Sun   Talmage Powell
How Can You Be Reading This?
                    Charles S. Gesner
*The Seventh Man Sir Arthur Quiller-Couch
Pattern For Dying   Morris Cooper
Dark Vengeance   Fritz Leiber, Jr

Winter 1952   1/4   [Ed Emsh?]
Threat of Violence   R. J. Burrough
*The Screaming Woman   Ray Bradbury
And Never Come Back Dorothy Marie Davis
The Third Degree   Charles Lenart
Ask No Quarter   Duane Yarnell
Find the Witness   Ted Stratton
Hot Eyes   Dean Evans
*You Killed Elizabeth   Brett Halliday
*Give Back the Dead James Robbins Miller
Murder Town [nt]   Raymond Drennen
The Way Out [ss]   Lorrie McLaughlin

                    ***

210

SWAN WEIRD MAGAZINES

A variety of weird fiction magazines and pocketbooks published in varying formats at irregular intervals during the Second World War and after by Gerald G. Swan, 17 Chapel Street, London. These publications exist in different states and printings as well as reprintings dependant upon war-time paper restrictions and distribution problems. Most of the stories were purchased at around the same time and in essence the publications represent a single series. To demonstrate some of the problems associated with these publications, a number of copies of Gang Shorts *No.1 were printed with the cover from* Weird Shorts *No.1. Later Swan combined four of his magazines as a paperback entitled* Four-in-One Weird and Occult Shorts *even though two of the titles included* Racing Shorts *and* Detective Shorts *contained no weird fiction at all.*

WEIRD STORY MAGAZINE

August 1940	No.1	?
Doctor Doom, Ghost Detective		
		William J. Elliott
A Witch's Charm Against Witchcraft [a]		[no credit]
The Village in the Mist		Basil Herbert
The Chained Terror		Henry Retlaw
Description of a Warlock [a]		[no credit]
Dale Vernon, Ghost Investigator [cs]		[no credit]
The Dead Hand Grips		James Bruce
The Last Word		W. E. Tillot
Witch's Lullaby [v]		W.J.E.
In An Old Graveyard [v]		W.E.
So This is Death		Leopold J. Wollett
The Were Wolf [v]		E. L. Lowitt
Weird Story in Brief [ss]		L. T. J. Wilte

YANKEE WEIRD SHORTS

[Three issues in a series of 'Yankee' Magazines representing various genres]

[March 1942]	No.6	?
The Death of Julian Morton		W. P. Cockroft
Spider Fire		Kay Hammond
Forbidden Waters		George Scott
The Horror at Castle Droon		Colin Robertson
The Merry-Go-Round		Ronald Brett

[May 1942]	No.14	?
A Seance in Hell		Gregg Burlison
Cats Are Uncanny!		John Maxwell
Shadow Worlds		W. P. Cockroft

[June 1942]	No.19	?
Devil's Disciple		F. W. Murray
The Devil of Dwr Ddu		Ann Elliott
An Amazing Adventure		J. R. Gregg
Pebbles of Dread		Gerald Evans

WEIRD POCKET LIBRARY

[1943]	No.1	?
The Dark City [nt]		Kay Hammond
"Milky Throws a Boomerang"		
		Trevor Dudley-Smith

[this last story is non-fantasy]

WEIRD SHORTS

[1944]	No.1	?
In Alien Valleys		Henry Rawle
The Immortal Guardians		Trevor Dudley-Smith
Sigrid's House		Dallas Kirby
Night of Terror!		E. A. Cross
The Demon and the Dictator		David Alun
The Revenge of Arnul		W. P. Cockroft
The Kraken		I. O. Evans

OCCULT

[1945]	No.1	?
The Guide		Irene Amesbury
Call of the Pool Goddess		John C. Craig
The Room Without Windows		W. P. Cockroft
The Bride of Yum-Chac		Henry Rawle
The Fulfilment		Alexander O. Pearson
Sir Rodney Keeps a Date		Andrew Ringwood
The Window		Winifred M. Carnegie
Binker's Ghost		A. C. Bailey

retitled OCCULT SHORTS

[1946]	No.2	?
The Sack	Winifred M. Carnegie
The Dancing Dolls	John Body
The Black Caduceus	S. G. J. Ouseley
The Hands	V. J. Hanson
Self and Shadow	A. C. Bailey
The Forbidden Village	W. P. Cockroft
Flashback	Henry Rawle
Far Enough	Ian Avon
Brain Storm	[no credit]

WEIRD STORY MAGAZINE

[1946]	No.1	?
The Secret of Clare Church	Hadyn Perry
The Kiss of Lilith	Sam Bate
The Mind of a Murderer	John Body
Ghost Dogs [a]	A. C. Bailey
Gruenaldo	Henry Rawle
Four Gold Teeth	Christopher Harmon
John Raike's Model	Sutro Miller
Hands in a Mirror	Meredith Huntley
Vampires Work at Night	Shelley Smith
Royal Ghosts [a]	A. C. Bailey
The Stain	Hedley H. Gore

[1946]	No.2	?
Death Was His Hobby	Tom Lawrence
The Incident is Closed	[no credit]
The Horror Undying	W. P. Cockroft
The Invisible Filament	Bertha Lou
Obscene Parade	N. Wesley Firth
Floating Hearse	R. Gilmour
Arachne	Christine Gittings
Prisoner	Rex Ernest

WEIRD AND OCCULT MISCELLANY
[strictly speaking a paperback anthology, but included here for completeness]

[April 1949]	[-]	?
The Monk	Winifred Carnegie
The Black Mamba	Herbert J. Brandon
The Pit of Acheron	S. G. J. Ouseley
A God of One's Own	T. R. Lawrence
A Sacrifice to Pan	A. C. Bailey
The Woman Who Hated Cats	
	Margaret St. J. Bathe
The Dawn and Then	Nancy Davies
The Intruder	Henry Rawle
Death in the Tower	Fred Robins
N'Zamba's Gift	Frank C. Brooke
The Howl of a Dog	W. P. Cockroft
The Doll	Winifred M. Carnegie
It's a Lovely Morning	Norman C. Pallant
The Singular Sequel to the Case	
of the Montrose Diamond	F. G. Rayer
Dead on Time	Eugene Campbell
The Black Room	John Theydon
A Queer Guardian	Frank C. Brooke
'D' For Death	Clifford Lewis
The Secret of the Vault	S. G. J. Ouseley
Dream-Child	A. C. Bailey
Captain Jenkins and Amadeo	
Smith	Shelley Smith
The Dummy	Francis Lynne
One Wild Dark Night	Iris Weigh
The House in the Quarry	John Body
Delayed Action	Bernard Whall
The Lady in Red	Evyn Thomas
The Dance of Death	A. C. Bailey

WEIRD AND OCCULT LIBRARY
[issued ten years later from material ac-quired during the forties]

[Spring 1960]	No.1	?
Vashtarin	Kay Hammond
Twenty-Five Years	Herbert J. Brandon
Cause or Effect	Maurice Grove
Dr. Kranzer's Masterpieces	S. G. J. Ouseley
The Horsehair Chair	Winifred M. Carnegie
The Case of Eva Gardiner	A. M. Burrage
In the Dark Temple	Norman C. Jallant
Green Eyes For Evil	Leslie Bussey
Scuttled	Christine Douglas
The Sins of the Fathers	Tom Lawrence
So Near - So Far	Philip Glyde

[Summer 1960]	No.2	?
The Voice of Amalzzar	Henry Rawle
Skulls That Cannot Be Shifted	
[a]	A. C. Bailey
His Second Chance	A. C. Bailey
The Cat and the Occult [a]	F. Thomas
*Death Mates	Hugh J. Gallagher
Come, Brother, Come!	Dallas Kirby
A Court Martialled Ghost [a]	A. C. Bailey
Where That Dark Water Is	Chas. H. Bradford
Beneath the Mountain	Christine Gittings
Judgement Bell	John Russell Fearn
Made of Sand	M. E. Orman

[Autumn 1960]	No.3	?
The Incredible Awakening	Norman C. Pallant
Black-Man's Magic	Frank C. Brooke
Labyrinth of Zekor	S. G. J. Ouseley
Silvester's Oasis	Henry Rawle
The Hill of Worms [ss]	A.S. Quilter Palmer
As White as Snow	Ian Mercer
*A Guest of Vanderdecken	Ernest L. McKeag
The Last Word	A. E. Crawley
The Yellow Mask	John Body
Corner Cottage	A. M. Burrage
A Lot of Gammon	[no credit]

***

SWORD & SORCERY ANNUAL

A one-shot fantasy digest published by Ultimate Publishing Co., Oakland Gardens, Flushing, New York as a companion to Fantastic. *No editor credited but issue assembled by Sol Cohen.*

[Winter 1974] 1975   [1]   Stephen Fabian
*Queen of the Black Coast
   [nt]   Robert E. Howard
*L. Sprague de Camp: Sword
   and Satire [a]   Sam Moskowitz
*The Pillars of Chambalor   John Jakes
*Master of Chaos   Michael Moorcock
*The Mirror of Cagliostro
   [nt]   Robert Arthur
*The Cloud of Hate   Fritz Leiber
*The Masters   Ursula K. LeGuin
*Horseman!   Roger Zelazny

***

213

T

TALES OF MAGIC AND MYSTERY

A weird fiction/occult pulp magazine published monthly by Personal Arts Company, Camden, New Jersey with editorial offices at 931 Drexel Bldgs., Philadelphia, Pennsylvania. No editor credited but issues assembled by Walter Gibson.

December 1927   1/1   [Earle Bergey?]
Strange Personalities of the
   Past and Present [col] Alfred Maurice
The Story of the Werewolves   [no credit]
The Black Well of Wadi   Frank Owen
The Miracle Man of Benares
   [ts]   Howard Thurston
The Adventure of the Mummy's
   Hand   Jack Hazlitt
Bullet Catching [a1/2]   Bernard Perry
The Devil's Darling   Eric Jules
The Ghost-Maker [a]   [no credit]
Rahman Bey, After His Famous
   Test [pic]   [no credit]
The Black Pagoda [nt1/3]   Peter Chance
Houdini [a]   Walter B. Gibson
Slave of the Poppy   N.W. Jenkins
John Halliday in 'The Spider'
   [ill]   'Hawls'
Easy Magic You Can Do [col]   [no credit]

January 1928   1/2   [Earle Bergey?]
Tomorrow's Paper Charlton Lawrence Edholm
History of Chiromancy [a]   [no credit]
*Ghostly Hands   Miriam Allen deFord
Two Magic Words [a]   [no credit]
The Temple of Fire [a]   [no credit]
The Haunts of Ghosts [a]   A.W. Jarvis
The Black Pagoda [nt2/3]   Peter Chance
Strange Personalities [col] Alfred Maurice
A Burmese Adventure [ts] Howard Thurston
The Comic Mask   Howard Winton Stokes
Number Magic [a]   'Astro'
Bullet Catching [a2/2]   Bernard Perry
*The Yellow Pool   Frank Owen
Houdini in Europe [a] [Walter B. Gibson]
The Story of the Magi [a]   [no credit]
Easy Magic You Can Do [col]   [no credit]

February 1928   1/3   [Earle Bergey?]
Strange Personalities [col] Alfred Maurice
The Dead of Egypt [a]   Arthur Neale
The Magic Cart   Archie Binns
The Athenian Ghost   [no credit]
Magic Pictorial [pic]   [no credit]
Further Adventures in India
   [ts]   Howard Thurston
The Onyx Vase   Carl M. Rosenquist
Mechanical Men [a]   [no credit]
The Soul That Could Leave Its
   Body   Ludwig Haupt
Daring Exploits of Houdini
   [a]   Walter B. Gibson
The Black Pagoda [nt3/3]   Peter Chance
Easy Magic You Can Do [col]   [no credit]

March 1928   1/4   [Earle Bergey?]
Strange Personalities [col] Alfred Maurice
Adventures of Astro, Seer of Secrets:
   I: The Unaccountable Disappearance
   of John Hanson   ['Astro']
Further Famous Escapes of Harry
   Houdini [a]   Walter B. Gibson
Magic Pictorial [pic]   [no credit]
Adventures in Mind-Reading
   [a]   Bernard Perry
Cool Air   H.P. Lovecraft
The Girl Who Was Burned Alive
   [ts]   Howard Thurston
Something About Black Cats [a] [no credit]
The Mystery of Handwriting [a] N.M. Bunker
The Nerve Specialist   Newton Fuessle
The Famous Japanese Decapitation
   Mystery [a]   [no credit]
The Evil Eye of Superstition
   [a]   [no credit]
Easy Magic You Can Do [col]   [no credit]

April 1928   1/5   [Earle Bergey?]
Strange Personalities [col] Alfred Maurice
The Flowers of Enchantment
                    Robert Leslie Bellem
Tibet - Land of Mystery [a]   Arthur Neale
Magic Pictorial [pic]   [no credit]
The Dance of Death   W. Clyde Young
The Aims of Alchemy [a]   [no credit]
Among the Head-Hunters of
  Java [ts]   Howard Thurston
Adventures of Astro:
  II. The Fanshawe Ghost   ['Astro']
Houdini's Rendition of Mazeppa's
  Ride [a]   Walter B. Gibson
Alectryomancy [a]   [no credit]
The Lure of the Shrivelled Hand Frank Owen
Easy Magic You Can Do [col]   [no credit]

                  ***

TALES OF TERROR FROM THE BEYOND

A large-size neo-pulp weird fiction magazine published by Charlton Publications, Division Street, Derby, Connecticut.   Editor: Patrick Masuli.

Summer 1964	1/1	?
The Bronze Plaque		Julian Lash
Horror of the Blood Monster		Dick Kahn
At Pixie's Pool ...	Stanton A. Coblentz	
Angelica		Richard Ignatius
*The Dog Who Came Back	Stanton A. Coblentz	
*Daughter of Urzun	Stanton A. Coblentz	
*The Round Tower	Stanton A. Coblentz	
Heart's Dimension		Monet Green
*The Grotto of Cheer	Stanton A. Coblentz	
*Immanuel Predicts	Stanton A. Coblentz	
The Game		Lionel Olay
*The Mysterious Miss Maltra		
	Stanton A. Coblentz	
One Minute Past Noon	Stanton A. Coblentz	
Night of Terror		Ernest H. Hart
"Specialty of the House		Stanley Ellin

***

216

TALES OF THE FRIGHTENED

A weird fantasy digest magazine published irregularly (intended schedule was bi-monthly) by Republic Features Syndicate, 39 West 55th Street, New York. Editor credited as Lyle Kenyon Engel but work actually carried out by Michael Avallone. Spin-off of the radio series "The Frightened" narrated by Boris Karloff.

Spring 1957   1/1
The Curse of Cleopatra   Michael Avallone
The Malignant Jewel   Sidney Porcelain
The Glass Thread   Elsie Milnes
Incident in a Flying Saucer   James Harvey
Cat Woman   Gerald Gordon
The Stop at Nothing   Mark Dane
Alias Napoleon   John Jakes
Faith Killer   Winston Marks
Mistaken Identity   Ralph Williams
Old Snagglebuck   William G. Weston
Scorpion   Hal Ellson
But a Kind of Ghost   John Wyndham
The Gardener   John Christopher
The Unwatched Door [ss] Richie McPherson
The Frightened ["Say Goodnight
   to Mr Sporko"]   Boris Karloff
The Singular Occurrence at Styles
                             Alan Henry

August 1957   1/2   -
The Queen's Bedchamber   Ledru Baker, Jr
The Man Who Thought He Was
   Poe   Michael Avallone
The Man Who Stole His Body   Mark Mallory
Mr. Tiglath   Poul Anderson
The Black Spot   William B. Hartley
White Legs   Mark Dane
The Lucky Coffin   C. B. Gilford
Wise Beyond His Years   Claude Ferrari
Span Trap   Sidney Porcelain
Duty   Tristan Roberts
Dead End   Mack Reynolds
The Window   A. Bertram Chandler
Miss Bard's Lover   Elizabeth Luna
The Frightened ["The Man in
   the Raincoat"]   Boris Karloff

***

217

THRESHOLD OF FANTASY

A small press weird fantasy digest magazine published irregularly by Fandom Unlimited Enterprises, 3378 Valley Forge Way, San Jose, California. Editor & Publisher: Randall D. Larson.

***

THE THRILL BOOK

A semi-monthly adventure magazine published by Street & Smith, 79/89 Seventh Ave., New York. Editor: Harold Hersey (first eight issues), then Ronald Oliphant. The first eight issues appeared in dime novel booklet format, then publication switched to standard pulp format.

March 1, 1919   1/1 (1)   S.H. Reisenberg
Wolf of the Steppes   Greye La Spina
Ivory Hunters   Will Gage Carey
The Jeweled Ibis [nt1/2]   J.C. Kofoed
The Man Who Met Himself   Donovan Bayley
In the Shadows of Race [na1/3]
                          J. Hampton Bishop
Lilith [v]   Roy LeMoyne
The Twisted Papers [v]   Larrovitch

March 15, 1919   1/2 (2)   S.H. Reisenberg
The Web of Death   Clare Douglas Stewart
A Hooting, Tooting Son-of-a-Gun
                    Howard Dwight Smiley
The Broken Idol   Isra Putnam
Miladi [v]   Charles Kiproy
My Lovely [v]   Albert Owens
The Jeweled Ibis [nt2/2]   J.C. Kofoed
In the Shadows of Race [na2/3]
                          J. Hampton Bishop

April 1, 1919   1/3 (3)   S.H. Reisenberg
The Hank of Yarn   Perley Poore Sheehan
Captain Georges Guynemeer [v]
                          Harold Hersey
Courage   Andrew Soutar
Flowerlight [v]   Philip Kennedy
The Clasp of Rank   S. Carlton
At the End of the Wires Athelstane Hicks
The Living Dead   Seymour LeMoyne
The Death of Columbine [v]   Roy LeMoyne
In the Shadows of Race [na3/3]
                          J. Hampton Bishop

April 15, 1919   1/4 (4)   S.H. Reisenberg
Down the Coast of Shadows
    [nt1/2]   Perley Poore Sheehan
The Thing That Wept Charles Fulton Oursler
Profit By Loss   Clarence L. Andrews
The Haunted House [v]   Harry Kemp

Alpheus Bings, Thrill Hound:
    1. Death's Head Mystery [v1/3]
                          Ronald Oliphant
The Hidden Emperor   George C. Hull
The King [v]   Vail Vernon
Freedom [v]   Arnold Tyson

May 1, 1919   1/5 (5)   S.H. Reisenberg
The Inefficient Ghost   Isra Putnam
Down the Coast of Shadows
    [nt2/2]   Perley Poore Sheehan
The Devil's Own [nt1/2] Chester L. Saxby
The Dummy and the Ventriloquist
    [v]   Harold Hersey
Life [v]   Roy LeMoyne
The Stone Image   Seabury Grandin Quinn
The Battle [v]   Arnold Tyson
Alpheus Bings, Thrill Hound:
    2. The Inanition Cure [v2/3]
                          Ronald Oliphant
Nothing But Dust   Frederick Booth
The One-Man Log Drive Raymond S. Spears

May 15, 1919   1/6 (6)   S.H. Reisenberg
Crawling Hands [nt1/2]   P.A. Connolly
After [v]   Charles Kiproy
The Devil's Own [nt2/2] Chester L. Saxby
Magic in Manhattan   Robert W. Sneddon
Marsa [v]   Carl Buxton
Out of Our Hands' Reach [v]   Roy LeMoyne
When Basset Forgot   Harcourt Farmer
From Over the Border   Greye La Spina
The Rim of the World   Duffield Osborne
Alpheus Bings, Thrill Hound:
    3. The Purple Fear Ray [v3/3]
                          Ronald Oliphant
Romance [v]   Roy LeMoyne

June 1, 1919   1/7 (7)   S.H. Reisenberg
Strasbourg Rose [n1/4]   John R. Coryell

At the Hands of the Master   Everett McNeil
The Escape   Mordaunt Hall
Violets?   Harold de Polo
Crimson Flowers   Tod Robbins
The Song From the Dead   Pearl Bragg
Love's Silence [v]   Arnold Tyson
Such Beauty [v]   Roy LeMoyne
A Thousand Miles [v]   Charles Kiproy
Dim Unknown [v]   Carl Buxton
One Like Yourself [v] Alphonse de la Ferte
The Distant Stars [v] Francois de Vallient
Beyond a Single Day [v]   Philip Kennedy

October 15, 1919   3/2 (16)   James Reynolds
Juju [nt]   Murray Leinster
Hands Invisible   William H. Kofoed
The Gift Wife [n3/4]   Rupert Hughes
The Heads of Cerberus [n5/5]Francis Stevens
The Ultimate Ingredient   Greye La Spina
Amaratite   Ralph Roeder
The Mystery of the Timber Tract
                            Francis Metcalfe
Like Princes   Eugene A. Clancy
Figure Nine   Horatio Winslow
A Recruit for the Lambs   L. R. Ridge
Concerning the Pithecanthropus
    Erectus [v]   W. B. Horner
A Ballad of Morgan [v]   William van Wyck
Blind and Lame   E. C. Beckwith

***

THRILLER

A neo-pulp fantasy magazine published by-monthly by Tempest Publications, 2 West 45th St., New York. Editor: Harry Schreiner. Like Adventures in Horror, Thriller relied on quasi-pornographic stories illustrated with stills from movies. A low quality magazine at best. Covers are photographs.

February 1962   1/1
The Vampire Was a Sucker   'Siral'
Fiend of the Future   John Baskerville
The Werewolf Lover   Geoffrey Van Loan, Jr
Bored to Death   Sir John Catalpa
Dream-Time, Scream Time   Sir David Leeds
Why Did They Let Him Live?   [no credit]
Fact or Fiction? [col] Sir Gustav Mannheim
The Damned Spot   Harry Schreiner
The Secret Horror of Dr.Hyde Sandor Szabo
The Girl and the Monster   'Hugo'
A Case of Mistaken Identity Thomas Beecham
Her Blood Ran Hot   Count Igor Karloff II
Dance of Death   [no credit]

May 1962   1/2
The Monster Who Ate Candy   Harry Van
Murder in a Cat's Eye   Louis de Calvella
Death Calls on the Phone   Renee St. Hahn
The Jelly Monster From Hell Thomas Beecham
Girl in the Solid Gold Coffin
                           Gloria Forrester
Fact or Fiction? [col]   [no credit]
Lay Me in My Grave   Lisa Baron
The Skeleton's Kiss   Harry Schreiner
The Mummy Who Wanted a Daddy   [no credit]
Song of the Slasher   'Siral'
True Horror Thrillers [col]
                     Dr. Gustav Mannheim
Ghouls You May Know [pic]   [no credit]
True Weird Tales [a]   [no credit]
How To Spot a Vampire   [no credit]

July 1962   1/3
Half-Girl - Half-Man   Eve Loesseur
Werewolves are Furry   Sandor Szabo
Monster For Hire   Peter Fel
The Real Thing   Sir Basil Charteris
Kiss My Cold Lips   Dolores M. Pennerman
Creatures From Outer Space   [no credit]
True Terror Thrillers [col]
                       Dr. Gustav Mannheim
Fact or Fiction [a]   Jonas T. Wainwright
The Headless Gunslinger of
  Dodge City   [no credit]
The Feeder   Lorenzo Drake
The Thing That Loved Girls -
  to Death   Harry   Van
The Hospital Horror   H. V. Schreiner
Quips From the Crypt [pic]   [no credit]

***

TOADSTOOL WINE

A one-shot magazine composed of samples from six small press publications and published in large-size format by Weirdbook Press, Amherst Branch, Buffalo, New York. The individual sections compiled by the respective editors but the whole assembled by W. Paul Ganley from an idea suggested by C. C. Clingan.

[October] 1975	Lee Brown Coye
The Literature of Cosmic Dread [a]	Fritz Leiber
Fantasy & Terror	
Ithtidzik	David C. Smith
The Sword That Sings [v]	Stephanie Stearns
"Die, Black Dog!" [a]	Charles R. Saunders
Moonbroth	
Dragons, Snakes and Wiverns [a]	Bill Tredinnick
Scra	Douglas Justice
Spellbound [v]	Gahan Addams
Lover's Parting [v]	Margaret L. Carter
Space & Time	
Death of a Unicorn	Michael M. Levy
Pleasure	Frederic Croft
Transmutation [v]	John Bredon
Icarus 2000 [cs]	Gene Day
Weirdbook	
The Shaman's Head	Jack Wysocki
Clover and Mushrooms [v]	Alixandra Lee
The Black Footprints	William Scott Home
Sorcerer's Web [v]	Joseph Payne Brennan
How Ranthes Yin Sailed a Boat on the Waters of the River Time	Darrell Schweitzer
Drowned [v]	Robert E. Howard
Ache of an Ancient Avatar [v]	Walter Shedlofsky
Whispers	
*The Bait	Fritz Leiber
*Story-Writing [ltr]	H. P. Lovecraft
*The Inglorious Rise of the Catsmeat Man	
	Robin Smyth
Wyrd	
The Last Battle	Brian Howard Crist
White Bear and Red Moon [ap]	Steve Swenston
St Columba and the Monster of Loch Ness	
	Phyllis Ann Karr
The Genesis [ap]	Jim Garrison

***

TRUE TWILIGHT TALES

A neo-pulp supernatural magazine published by League Publications, 205 East 42nd St., New York. Editor: Helen Gardiner (first issue), John M. Williams (second). Reprinted from Ghost Stories, *though stories were abridged and retitled. See also* Prize Ghost Stories.

Fall 1963   [No.1]   ?
*Case of the Passionate Ghost
                          Cordelia Makarius
*The Thing   Virgil Dane
*Curse of the Violated Virgin   Jack D'Arcy
*What Was in the Upper Berth?
                          Marion Crawford
*My Murdered Wife's Eyes
   Still Live   C. Young, Jr
*The Night Death Pitched a
   No-Hitter   Peter Hemming
*Town of Terror   Gordon Hillman
*Banquet For 11 Corpses   Walter G. Proctor
*The Perfect Strangler   E. and H. Heron
*The Phantom Whistler   Gordon Hillman
*Five Minutes to Live   Ace Baker
*I'm Dead - and it's Beautiful
                          Everil W. Murphy
*Interrupted Wedding   Reginald Denton
*The Corpse That Wouldn't Die
                          Sylvan J. Muldoon
*The Invisible Scratcher
                          Mary Agnew McLean

Spring 1964   [No.2]   ?
*That Night the Dead Took Over
                          Thelma Johnson
*Taxi to Hell - and Back!   Harry A. Bemis
*"Till Death do Us Wed"   Arthur Leslie
*The Skull That Screamed
   "Murder!"   Gordon Hillman
*Nightmare!   Nora Lilienthal
*The Devil Doctor Wanted Me
   For His Patient!   Philip Wolfe
*Case of the Premature Funeral
                          Harold Dillon
*Return of the Ghost Ship   Gordon Hillman
*Ghost Who Begged "Kiss Me!
   Love Me!"   Algernon Blackwood
*Child or Demon - Which Was
   She?   Eugene Branscombe
*The Corpse Wanted Company   Dr. Henry Leigh
*Ghost Story - Written by the
   Ghost Itself   John L. Spivak
*The Spirit That Got Spanked
                          Sophie W. Ellis
*Death Crashed the Party   Archie Binns
*Portrait of a Murder   Erckmann-Chatrian

***

224

U

UNCANNY STORIES

A weird/sf pulp published by Manvis Publications, 4600 Diversity Ave., Chicago with editorial offices at RKO Building, Radio City, New York. Editor not credited, but Robert O. Erisman.

April 1941   1/1   [N. Saunders?]
Coming of the Giant Germs [nt]
                                  Ray Cummings
The Earth-Stealers
                   Frederic Arnold Kummer, Jr
Beyond Hell [nt]   R. DeWitt Miller
The Man From the Wrong Time-
   Track   Denis Plimmer
*Speed Will Be My Bride   David H. Keller
Meet My Brother - Mr. Ghost
                       Wayne D. Overholser

                    ***

UNCANNY TALES

A weird menace pulp published irregularly by Manvis Publications, 4600 Diversity Ave., Chicago, with editorial offices at RKO Building, Radio City, New York. No editor credited but issues assembled by Robert O. Erisman. Volume numbering is correct as the magazine is believed to be a retitling of an earlier detective/ mystery pulp. It is possible that the issues for October/November 1938 and February 1939 also qualify for this Index, but it has not proved possible to trace them. This magazine should not be confused with the Canadian fantasy pulp of the same title which is also included in this Index.

April/May 1939   2/6 (1?)   [Saunders?]
Take Me, and Die!   Arthur J. Burks
Horror Owns My Heart   Omar Gwinn
Nameless Brides of Forbidden
  City   Frederick C. Davis
Revelry in Hell   Donald Graham
Agony in Clay   Mindret Lord
Mortician For Satan's Other
  World   Donald Dale
Stalked by Terror's Mate   George E. Clark
Keepsake From the Corpse   Blackstone Clay

August 1939   3/1 (2?)   [N. Saunders]
The Gargoyles of Madness   Russell Gray
Hell's Hangman   George E. Clark
...And the Blood of a Maiden   Donald Dale
The Thing in the Shaft
                    Robert Leslie Bellem
Open the Dead Door   Alexander Faust
Honeymoon in Hell   Allan K. Echols
Blood is My Bride   Cyril Plunkett
Cavern of Sin   John Wallace

November 1939   3/2 (3?)   [Saunders?]
Lovely Bodies For the Butcher
                            Russell Gray
Satan is My Lover   William A. Rossi
Dance With My Bride and Die
                        Arthur J. Burks
Debutantes for the Damned   Brent North
The Blood and the Girl   Allan K. Echols
When Terror Beckons   Gabriel Wilson
Pawn of Hideous Desire   Ray Cummings
Wooed by a Werewolf   Robert Leslie Bellem
The Dead White Thing   Ray King

March 1940   3/3 (4?)   [Saunders?]
Where Beauty Dwelt With Terror
                        Donald Graham
Sin-Slaves for Sale   Brent North
The Flesh-Hungry Phantoms   Arthur J. Burks
Blood-Brides of the Lusting
  Corpse   Gabriel Wilson
Mates For Horror's Half-Men   Russell Gray
Curse of the Lovely Torso   Robert L. Bellem
Satan is my Master   Allan K. Echols
Goddess of the Ghouls
                    Frederic Arnold Kummer, Jr

May 1940   3/4 (5?)   [Saunders?]
Fresh Blood For My Bride   Ray King
Monster of the Marsh   Gabriel Wilson
The Thing Thirsts for Three   Lon Cordot
The Claw Will Come to Caress Me!
                            Brent North
Satan Lives For My Love   Donald Graham
Cult of the Lusting Carcase
                        Holden Sanford
House Where Evil Lived   Russell Gray

***

UNCANNY TALES

Canadian fantasy/sf pulp published by the Adam Publishing Company, 455 Spadina Ave., Toronto (from issue 15, 28 Wellington Street West, Toronto) until issue 17, thereafter, Norman Book Company, 95 King Street East, Toronto (address 78 Wellington Street West, Toronto on last issue). Editor: Melvin R. Colby (not credited). The first four issues were in large digest format, changing to standard pulp with issue 5.

November 1940	No.1	?
Murder in the Graveyard	Thomas P. Kelley
Sharks	William Weldin
The Lover and the Beam [ts]	
	Anne, Lady Selsdon
U Day Zaung: An Oriental	
Mystery	C. Harcourt Robertson
The Talking Heads [n1/5]	Thomas P. Kelley

December 1940	No.2	*?
Voice of Conscience	Halton James
Cleopatra Lives Again	Roy P. Devlin
Frisco Fog	Ethel Preszatore
The God Moloch	C. Harcourt Robertson
One Way Ticket	Valentine Worth
Camera Phobia	Calford Drew
Voice of Space	Larry Comstock
Stupor	[no credit]
The Talking Heads [n2/5]	Thomas P. Kelley

January 1941	No.3	*?
The Mummy	Valentine Worth
Flaming Phantasm	John Hollis Mason
Terrible Crimes of the Past:	
The Black Hole of Calcutta	
[a]	Thomas P. Kelley
The Phantom Train	Leslie A. Croutch
Tim's Tree	Al Fredd
The Talking Heads [n3/5]	Thomas P. Kelley

March 1941	No.4	?
Death Has My Body	Gregory James
Lorelei	G. Wallace
Little Priestess of Murder	Roger Gleason
Terrible Crimes of the Past:	
Salome [a]	Thomas P. Kelley
The Talking Heads [n4/5]	Thomas P. Kelley

May 1941	No.5	Ted Steele
The Wine Siren	D. N. Kane
Escape - To Hell	Roy Danyer
The Shaggy God	Thomas P. Kelley
The Thing Creeps	Geoffrey Myers
The Talking Heads [n5/5]	Thomas P. Kelley
Isle of Madness [na1/2]	Thomas P. Kelley
Fenton Lied ... Or	George Huntley
The Emperor Heard	Clifford Barnes
Uncanny Facts: Ghosts Heard	
in Old Castles [a]	[no credit]

June 1941	No.6	Walter Leslie
Beyond the Veil [nt]	Gene Bannerman
Death Meteor	Oliver Saari
Dancing Partner	Leslie A. Croutch
The Man Who Killed Hitler	Valentine Worth
Isle of Madness [na2/2]	Thomas P. Kelley
*The Thought Monsters	Donald A. Wollheim

July 1941	No.7	Walter Leslie
*I Found Cleopatra [n1/3]	Thomas P. Kelley
Lady of the Tomb	Wagner Hall
Mark of the Cloven Hoof	Pierre Janley
*Bones	Donald A. Wollheim
Restless Souls	Wallace Bennett
*The Strange Return	Lawrence Woods
The Phantom Voice	George Grant
*The Grey One	Robert W. Lowndes
*Cosmophobia	Millard Verne Gordon
*Fog [v]	Mary C. Shaw

August 1941	No.8	Walter Leslie
The House of Crawling Death	Pierre Janley
The Germ Creator	Allen Lake
The Swamps Come Back	Nadine Booth Brumell
Myrrha - A Mystery	Rolland Jones

227

*Blueprint   Donald A. Wollheim
*I Found Cleopatra [n2/3] Thomas P. Kelley
*!!!   X
*The Doll Master   Paul Dennis Lavond

September 1941   No.9   Walter Leslie
Cycles of an Ego [nt]   C. Lamont Turner
Doomed by the Dead   Allen Lake
*I Found Cleopatra [n3/3] Thomas P. Kelley
The Mine of the Moon Men   Callan Edmunds
Flowers of Death   Rolland Johns
*The Other   Robert W. Lowndes

October 1941   No.10   Wilf Long
Science of Satan   J. B. Gardner
Disintegration   C. Lamont Turner
*The Abyss   Robert W. Lowndes
*Castle on Outerplanet   S. D. Gottesman
Listening, Listening   Lawton Fenson
The Perfumed Death   Wallace Bennett
Doctors of Evil   Niel Perrin
Death in the Sun   Than Dorier
Black Castle of Hate   Valentine Worth
*An Empty House at Night [v]
                           Cristel Hastings

November 1941   No.11   Wilf Long
Expedition No. 1   James Francis Redshaw
*The Coming of the White
  Worm   Clark Ashton Smith
*A Million Years in the
  Future [n1/5]   Thomas P. Kelley
The Dream   John R. Brooks
Strong Fingers of Death   D. H. Fairley
The Skeleton in Armor   Howard Callahan
The Hat   Donald A. Wollheim
Strange Tree   Leslie Merle
*The Touching Point   Edward J. Bellin
*Forbidden Books [v] Wilfred Owen Morley
*Rocket of 1955   Cecil Corwin
Monkey Language [a]   J.G.

December 1941   No.12   Wilf Long
The Coming of Darakk   Denis Plimmer
City of the Centaurs   Gene Bannerman
Bury Me Deep   John R. Brooks
Mystery of the Missing
  Ships   James Francis Redshaw
*A Million Years in the
  Future [n2/5]   Thomas P. Kelley
*Compensation   C. V. Tench
Earthlight on the Moon [v] Lilith Lorraine

January 1942   No.13   Bick
Lure of the Lily   Robert W. Lowndes
*Doctor of Doodling   Frederick Traff
The Stolen God   Denis Plimmer
Fire Out of Space   Chester B. Conant
*The Growing Terror   Donald A. Wollheim
*A Million Years in the
  Future [n3/5]   Thomas P. Kelley

February 1942   No.14   Wilf Long
*The Way Back [nt]   Sam Moskowitz
The Magic Touch of Mozart
                      John Victor Peterson
*Spokesman For Terra   Hugh Raymond
The Man Who Remembered   Thos. S. Gardner
Drums of Reig Rawan   Donald A. Wollheim
*A Million Years in the
  Future [n4/5]   Thomas P. Kelley

Magician of Space   James V. Taurasi
The Channelers   Denis Plimmer
Kill I Must   Harry Walton

March 1942   No.15   K. P. Ainsworth
*Dimension of Darkness   S. D. Gottesman
*The Lightning's Course
                      John Victor Peterson
*170 Miles a Minute   Ward Skeen
The Strange Case of Julian
  Rayne   Denis Plimmer
*A Million Years in the
  Future [n5/5]   Thomas P. Kelley
*The City in the Sofa   Cecil Corwin

April 1942   No.16   K. P. Ainsworth
*After 12,000 Years [n1/4]
                      Stanton A. Coblentz
The Green Invasion   Denis Plimmer
*Thirteen O'Clock   Cecil Corwin
*Kazam Collects   S. D. Gottesman

May 1942   No.17   G. M. Rae
*Mr Packer Goes to Hell   Cecil Corwin
*The Words of Guru   Kenneth Falconer
The Soul Eater   Thomas P. Kelley
The Kiss of Bohaana   C. V. Tench
*Forgotten Tongue   Walter C. Davies
*After 12,000 Years [n2/4]
                      Stanton A. Coblentz
*The Man From the Future Donald A. Wollheim
Blacklist   Robert W. Lowndes

July 1942   No.18   G. M. Rae
*Dead Center   S. D. Gottesman
*Power   Hugh Raymond
*No Place to Go   Edward J. Bellin
*After 12,000 Years [n3/4]
                      Stanton A. Coblentz
*What Sorghum Says   Cecil Corwin

September 1942   No.19   K. P. Ainsworth
*When Half-Worlds Meet   Hugh Raymond
The Unborn   Denis Plimmer
*Interference   Walter C. Davies
*Transitory Island   Richard Wilson
*After 12,000 Years [n4/4]
                      Stanton A. Coblentz
*The Reversible Revolutions Cecil Corwin

December 1942   No.20   K. P. Ainsworth
*The Goblins Will Get You   Hugh Raymond
*Mechanica   Frank Edward Arnold
The Brain Conscription   Zan Savage
*Blind Flight   Millard Verne Gordon
Portrait of the Artist's Mother
                           Denis Plimmer
The Coming of the Comet Donald A. Wollheim
*The Long Wall   Wilfred Owen Morley
Ambition [v]   Wilfred Owen Morley
The God of OO   Allen Warland
*Fire-Power   S. D. Gottesman
Whither Canadian Fantasy?
  [a]   Donald A. Wollheim

Sep/Oct 1943   No.21   K. P. Ainsworth
*The Last Viking   Hugh Raymond
Louisiana Night   Denis Plimmer
The Unholy Glass   Millard Verne Gordon
The Land of Living Death Robert W. Murphy
*The Riddle of Tanye   W. P. Cockroft

*The Martians Are Coming
                        Robert W. Lowndes
The Plane Equator   Stanley Whiteside
The Curse of Huitzil
                    Leonard B. Rosborough
The Golden Weapon   Zan Savage
*Always Comes Evening [v]
                       Robert E. Howard
The Spot of Blood   C. V. Tench

                    ***

UNIQUE TALES

UNIQUE

Two distinct magazines both published by Shroud Press carried virtually the same title. UNIQUE TALES, issued from 5652 Vineland Ave., North Hollywood, California in 1974 was certainly unique in its format (11 x 3 inches). UNIQUE, issued under the Valcour & Krueger imprint, 1020 Eighth Ave., San Diego, California, in 1978, was in a more traditional slick format and, to some extent, was a continuation of the Fantasy Classics series.

UNIQUE TALES

1974   1/1   Dante Volpe
The Mad Merger Meets the Gorn
    From Sucker ... [spf]   David Andrews
*Death, the Friend [v]
                      George Allan England
Mashing the Groovies   Lalt Weibscher
The Sorcerer's Shop   Robert Silverberg
Strange Sister [v]   Robert E. Briney
Hi, Whattya Know? [a]   Jack Woodford
Inathotep's Tale   Fred C. Adams
The Little Bird   David A. English

UNIQUE

January 1978   1/1   F.D. McSherry, Jr
*Monster of the Tarn   Nelson Kent
*Black Curtains   G. Frederick Montefiore
*The Marble Virgin   Kennie McDowd
*The (Really) Old Fogies
    Column [col]   [no credit]

***

UNKNOWN/
UNKNOWN WORLDS

A fantasy pulp published monthly (later bi-monthly) by Street & Smith, 79 Seventh Avenue, New York. Editor: John W. Campbell. This legendary magazine treated weird fantasy on a rather more serious level than Weird Tales, with the paradoxical consequence that it published rather more humorous fantasy stories than any of the other pulps. The British edition achieved a sufficiently autonomous existence to warrant a separate entry in this Index.

March 1939   1/1 (1)   H.W. Scott
Sinister Barrier [n]   Eric Frank Russell
Who Wants Power?   Mona Farnsworth
Dark Vision   Frank Belknap Long
Trouble With Water   H.L. Gold
"Where Angels Fear - "   Manly Wade Wellman
Closed Doors   A.B.L. Macfadyen, Jr
Death Sentence   Robert Moore Williams

April 1939   1/2 (2)   Graves Gladney
The Ultimate Adventure [sn] L. Ron Hubbard
You Thought Me Dead   William G. Bogart
The Changeling [nt]   Arthur J. Burks
Death Time   D.M. Bricker
Strange Gateway   E. Hoffman Price
Divide and Rule [sn1/2] L. Sprague de Camp

May 1939   1/3 (3)   H.W. Scott
Returned From Hell [na]   Steve Fisher
The Missing Ocean   H.W. Guernsey
Danger in the Dark   L. Ron Hubbard
The Cloak   Robert Bloch
The Piping Death   Robert Moore Williams
Whatever   Mona Farnsworth
Divide and Rule [sn2/2] L. Sprague de Camp

June 1939   1/4 (4)   H.W. Scott
Flame Winds [n]   Norvell W. Page
The Right Ear of Malchus   J. Allan Dunn
Don't Go Haunting [nt]   Robert Coley
The Summons   Don Evans
The Gnarly Man   L. Sprague de Camp
Parole   Thomas Calvert McClary
The Hexer   H.W. Guernsey

July 1939   1/5 (5)   H.W. Scott
Slaves of Sleep [n]   L. Ron Hubbard
The Elemental   Frank Belknap Long

Nothing in the Rules [nt]
                      L. Sprague de Camp
Way Station   .   Herb Weiss
The Joker   Mona Farnsworth

August 1939   1/6 (6)   Graves Gladney
The Ghoul [n]   L. Ron Hubbard
Don't Dream   Donald Wandrei
Forsaking All Others   Lester del Rey
Two Sought Adventure [nt]   Fritz Leiber
The Misguided Halo   .   Henry Kuttner

September 1939   2/1 (7)   H.W. Scott
None But Lucifer [n]
                  H.L. Gold & L. Sprague de Camp
Danger: Quicksand   H.W. Guernsey
Caliph of Yafri [nt]   Silaki Ali Hassan
The Coppersmith   Lester del Rey
Portrait   Ray Cummings
Over the Border [a]   Eric Frank Russell

October 1939   2/2 (8)   Modest Stein
The Elder Gods [sn]   Don A. Stuart
The Dawn of Reason [v]   James H. Beard
Dreams May Come   H. Warner Munn
A God in a Garden   Theodore Sturgeon
Anything   Philip St. John
Blue and Silver Brocade   Dorothy Quick
The Enchanted Week End [sn]
                            John MacCormac

November 1939   2/3 (9)   Graves Gladney
Sons of the Bear God [n]   Norvell W. Page
Day Off   Horace L. Gold
The Bronze Door   Raymond Chandler
The Monocle [nt]   H.W. Guernsey
The Question is Answered   Stewart Toland
  [as by 'Stewart Todd' on contents page]

June 1941   5/1 (25)   –
The Fountain [sn]   Nelson S. Bond
Not According to Dante   Malcolm Jameson
The Crest of the Wave   Jane Rice
The Howling Tower   Fritz Leiber
The Shape of Desire   Cleve Cartmill
Yesterday Was Monday   Theodore Sturgeon
Joshua   R. Creighton Buck
Nightmare Island [nt]   E. Waldo Hunter

August 1941   5/2 (26)   –
The Case of the Friendly Corpse
   [n]   L. Ron Hubbard
The Road Beyond   Norman A. Daniels
The Devil We Know   Henry Kuttner
Mr. Jinx   Robert Arthur
Armageddon   Fredric Brown
Take My Drum to England   Nelson S. Bond
The Golden Egg [nt]   Theodore Sturgeon
Even the Angels   Malcolm Jameson

retitled UNKNOWN WORLDS

October 1941   5/3 (27)   –
The Land of Unreason [n]
         L. Sprague de Camp & Fletcher Pratt
No News Today   Cleve Cartmill
A Good Knight's Work   Robert Bloch
Prescience   Nelson S. Bond
Finger! Finger!   Margaret Ronan
Borrowed Glory   L. Ron Hubbard
On a Limb [a]   Anthony Boucher
Smoke Ghost   Fritz Leiber
A Gnome There Was [nt]   Henry Kuttner
The Dolphin's Doubloons   Silaki Ali Hassan

December 1941   5/4 (28)   –
Bit of Tapestry [n]   Cleve Cartmill
Occupation: Demigod   Nelson S. Bond
Brat   Theodore Sturgeon
Snulbug   Anthony Boucher
The House   Jane Rice
"With a Blunt Instrument"
                            Eric Frank Russell
Hereafter, Inc.   Lester del Rey
Czech Interlude   Vic Phillips
Mr. Arson [nt]   L. Sprague de Camp

February 1942   5/5 (29)   –
The Undesired Princess [n]
                            L. Sprague de Camp
Etaoin Shrdlu   Fredric Brown
The Shoes   Robert Bloch
He Didn't Like Cats   L. Ron Hubbard
The Refugees   Frank Belknap Long
The Sunken Land   Fritz Leiber
In His Own Image   Malcolm Jameson
Design For Dreaming [nt]   Henry Kuttner

April 1942   5/6 (30)   –
Prelude to Armageddon [n]   Cleve Cartmill
Jesus' Shoes   Allan R. Bosworth
The Compleat Werewolf [nt] Anthony Boucher
The Room   L. Ron Hubbard
Census Taker   Frank Belknap Long
Pobby [nt]   Jane Rice

June 1942   6/1 (31)   –
Solomon's Stone [n]   L. Sprague de Camp
Grab Bags Are Dangerous
                            Frank Belknap Long

Tomorrow   Robert Arthur
The Ghost of Me   Anthony Boucher
The Idol of the Flies   Jane Rice
The Old Ones Hear   Malcolm Jameson
Al Haddon's Lamp [nt]   Nelson S. Bond

August 1942   6/2 (32)   –
Hell is Forever [sn]   Alfred Bester
The Jumper   James Beard & Theodore Sturgeon
The Hill and the Hole   Fritz Leiber
Everything's Jake   John Hawkins
The Ghost [nt]   A. E. van Vogt
Fighters Never Quit   Malcolm Jameson
The Wisdom of the East   L. Sprague de Camp
Step Into My Garden   Frank Belknap Long
The Bargain   Cleve Cartmill
Though Poppies Grow [nt]   Lester del Rey
Sine Pace [v]   Edith Borden Greer

October 1942   6/3 (33)   –
The Unpleasant Profession of
   Jonathan Hoag [sn]   John Riverside
The Frog   P. Schuyler Miller
Magician's Dinner   Jane Rice
Letter to an Invisible Woman   Hannes Bok
Are You Run-down, Tired –
                            Babette Rosmond Lake
The New One   Fredric Brown
And I, One Life Too Late [v]
                            Ruth Stewart Schenley
The Lie   Richard Louis
The Goddess' Legacy   Malcolm Jameson
Contemplation [v]   Marvin Miller
The Darkest Path [v]   Arte Harbison
Compliments of the Author
   [nt]   Henry Kuttner

December 1942   6/4 (34)   –
The Sorcerer's Ship [n]   Hannes Bok
Transients Only   Mary Macgregor
The Golden Age   Elmer Ransom
The Wall   Robert Arthur
The Hag Seleen
         Theodore Sturgeon & James H. Beard
Watch Dog [v]   Frances Hall
It Will Come to You   Frank Belknap Long
The Elixir [nt]   Jane Rice

February 1943   6/5 (35)   –
Wet Magic [na]   Henry Kuttner
The Ka of Kor-Sethon [v]   Hannes Bok
Thieves' House [nt]   Fritz Leiber
The Angelic Angleworm [nt] Fredric Brown
The Ultimate Wish   E. M. Hull
No Graven Image [nt]   Cleve Cartmill
Guardian   Michael Corbin
The Hat Trick   Felix Graham
The Witch   A. E. van Vogt

April 1943   6/6 (36)   –
Conjure Wife [n]   Fritz Leiber
The Golden Bridle   Jane Rice
The Giftie Gi'en   Malcolm Jameson
No Greater Love [nt]   Henry Kuttner

June 1943   7/1 (37)   –
Wheesht [na]   Cleve Cartmill
The Wishes We Make   E. M. Hull
Blind Alley [nt]   Malcolm Jameson
A Bargain in Bodies   Moses Schere
Sriberdegibit   Anthony Boucher

The Rabbit and the Rat   Robert Arthur
The Devil is Not Mocked Manly Wade Wellman
Eight Ball   Hugh Raymond
The Green-Eyed Monster   Theodore Sturgeon
The Hounds of Kalimar [nt]
                          P. Schuyler Miller

August 1943   7/2 (38)   -
Hell Hath Fury [n]   Cleve Cartmill
Conscience Ltd.   Jack Williamson
Heaven is What You Make It
  [nt]   Malcolm Jameson
The Bones
    James H. Beard & Theodore Sturgeon
One Man's Harp   Babette Rosmond
They Bite   Anthony Boucher
Greenface   James H. Schmitz

October 1943   7/3 (39)   -
The Book of Ptath [n]   A. E. van Vogt
The Refugee   Jane Rice
The Patient   E. M. Hull
Fido   Chester S. Geier
Change   Roby Wentz
Clean-Up   Cleve Cartmill

FROM UNKNOWN WORLDS

*A retrospective sampling of fiction issued
by Street & Smith under the editorship of
John W. Campbell, Jr., after the War to test
the market for a possible revival of Unknown which, in the event, did not occur.*

1948   [-]   Edd Cartier
*The Enchanted Week-End [sn] John MacCormac
*The Refugee   Jane Rice
*Nothing in the Rules [nt]
                          L. Sprague de Camp
*The Cloak   Robert Bloch
*Yesterday Was Monday   Theodore Sturgeon
*Fiction [v]   Allan Grant
*Trouble With Water   H. L. Gold
*Lurani [v]   Paul Dennis Lavond
*Anything   Philip St. John
*The Compleat Werewolf [nt]
                          Anthony Boucher
*One Man's Harp   Babette Rosmond
*Black Cats [v]   Cristel Hastings
*The Devil We Know   Henry Kuttner
*The Psychomorph   E. A. Grosser
*The Hexer   H. W. Guernsey
*The Summons   Don Evans
*The Dawn of Reason [v]   James H. Beard
*Jesus' Shoes   Allan R. Bosworth

✳ ✳ ✳

UNKNOWN /

UNKNOWN WORLDS

British reprint of the US fantasy pulp magazine just indexed. Published by The Atlas Publishing & Distributing Co., 18 Bride Lane, London. No UK editor identi- fied, but issues probably assembled by Paul Imbush. The first volume of the UK edition was imported directly by Atlas and was thus identical to the US edition. With the outbreak of World War II, however, Atlas printed their own edition which was to outlive the US original. All stories, bar one, were reprinted from the US edition, some twice. Atlas also published the subsequent sampler volume From Unknown Worlds *which differs slightly from the US original.*

[March to August 1939, Vol.1, identical to
        US edition]

September 1939   2/1 (7)   H.W. Scott
*None But Lucifer [n]
            H. L. Gold & L. Sprague de Camp
*Danger: Quicksand   H. W. Guernsey
*Portrait   Ray Cummings

October 1939   2/2 (8)   Modest Stein
*The Elder Gods [sn]   Don A. Stuart
*Dreams May Come   H. Warner Munn
*A God in a Garden   Theodore Sturgeon
*Anything   Philip St. John
*Blue and Silver Brocade   Dorothy Quick

November 1939   2/3 (9) Graves Gladney
*Sons of the Bear-God [n] Norvell W. Page
*Day Off   H. L. Gold

December 1939   2/4 (10)   Edd Cartier
*Lest Darkness Fall [n]L. Sprague de Camp

January 1940   2/5 (11)   H. W. Scott
*Soldiers of the Black Goat
    [n]   Marian O'Hearn
*On the Knees of the Gods
    [n1/3]   J. Allan Dunn
*Doubled in Brass   Lester del Rey

February 1940   2/6 (12)   Edd Cartier
*Death's Deputy [sn]   L. Ron Hubbard
*Call of Duty   Laurence Bour, Jr
*On the Knees of the Gods
    [n2/3]   J. Allan Dunn

March 1940   3/1 (13)   Edd Cartier
*Philtered Power   Malcolm Jameson
*The Black Farm [nt]   H. W. Guernsey
*The Living Ghost   E. A. Grosser
*Gateway   Robert Arthur
*Derm Fool   Theodore Sturgeon
*On the Knees of the Gods
    [n3/3]   J. Allan Dunn

April 1940   3/2 (14)   Edd Cartier
*The Indigestible Triton [n]
                          Rene Lafayette
*The African Trick   H. W. Guernsey
*All is Illusion   Henry Kuttner

May 1940   3/3 (15)   M. Isip
*The Roaring Trumpet [n]
         L. Sprague de Camp & Fletcher Pratt
*Mad Hatter   Winston K. Marks
*Well of the Angels   E. Hoffmann Price

June 1940   3/4 (16)   Edd Cartier
*But Without Horns [n]   Norvell W. Page
*The Kraken   Frederick Engelhardt
*The Man From Nowhere
                    Frank Belknap Long, Jr

July 1940   3/5 (17)   -
*Fear [n]   L. Ron Hubbard
*The Dream   Jane Rice
*The Flayed Wolf   P. Schuyler Miller

August 1940   3/6 (18)   -
*The Mathematics of Magic [n]
         L. Sprague de Camp & Fletcher Pratt
*Tombi Sink   J. Vale Downie
*It [nt]   Theodore Sturgeon

*Sine Pace [v]   Edith Borden Greer

Autumn 1945   3/5 (35)   -
*Pobby [nt]   Jane Rice
*The Compleat Werewolf [nt]
                          Anthony Boucher
*The Ultimate Wish   E. M. Hull
*Guardian   Michael Corbin
*Even the Angels   Malcolm Jameson

Winter 1945   3/6 (36)   -
*The Road Beyond   Norman A. Daniels
*The Devil We Know   Henry Kuttner
*The Shoes   Robert Bloch
*The Wisdom of the East L. Sprague de Camp
*Step Into My Garden   Frank Belknap Long
*The Giftie Gien   Malcolm Jameson
*The Firing Line [nt]   George O. Smith
[this was reprinted from ASTOUNDING SF]

Summer 1946   3/7 (37)   -
*The Unpleasant Profession of
    Jonathan Hoag [sn]   John Riverside
*Mr. Jinx   Robert Arthur
*The Darkest Path [v]   Arte Harbison
*Jesus' Shoes   Allan R. Bosworth

Winter 1946   3/8 (38)   -
*The Land of Unreason [n]
         L. Sprague de Camp & Fletcher Pratt
*Finger! Finger!   Margaret Ronan

Spring 1947   3/9 (39)   -
*The Case of the Friendly
    Corpse [n]   L. Ron Hubbard
*Take My Drum to England Nelson S. Bond
*No News Today   Cleve Cartmill
*The Dolphin's Doubloons Silaki Ali Hassan

Summer 1947   3/10 (40)   -
*The Fountain [sn]   Nelson S. Bond
*Not According to Dante   Malcolm Jameson
*The Howling Tower   Fritz Leiber, Jr
*The Shape of Desire   Cleve Cartmill
*Yesterday Was Monday   Theodore Sturgeon
*Joshua   R. Creighton Buck

Winter 1947   3/11 (41)   -
*Swamp Train   Harry Walton
*The Sea Thing [nt]   A. E. van Vogt
*The Crest of the Wave   Jane Rice
*Nightmare Island   E. Waldo Hunter
*The Wisdom of An Ass [nt]
                        Silaki Ali Hassan

Spring 1948   3/12 (42)   -
*He Shuttles   Theodore Sturgeon
*The Psychomorph   E. A. Grosser
*When It Was Moonlight Manly Wade Wellman
*Well of the Angels   E. Hoffmann Price
*The Pipes of Pan   Lester del Rey
*The Kraken   Frederick Engelhardt
*Transparent Stuff   Dorothy Quick

Summer 1948   4/1 (43)   -
*Bit of Tapestry [n]   Cleve Cartmill
*Occupation: Demigod   Nelson S. Bond
*"With a Blunt Instrument"
                        Eric Frank Russell

Winter 1948   4/2 (44)   -
*The Enchanted Week-End [sn]
                          John MacCormac
*Caliph of Yafri [nt]   Silaki Ali Hassan
*The Dawn of Reason [v]   James H. Beard
*The Coppersmith   Lester del Rey
*The House   Jane Rice
*Snulbug   Anthony Boucher
*Lurani [v]   Paul Dennis Lavond

Spring 1949   4/3 (45)   -
*The Golden Bridle   Jane Rice
*No Greater Love [nt]   Henry Kuttner
*A Good Knight's Work   Robert Bloch
*Sine Pace [v]   Edith Borden Greer
*Mr. Arson   L. Sprague de Camp
*Hereafter, Inc.   Lester del Rey
*Brat   Theodore Sturgeon
*Czech Interlude   Vic Phillips

Summer 1949   4/4 (46)   -
*Solomon's Stone [n] L. Sprague de Camp
*Fisherman's Luck   Frank Belknap Long
*Prescience   Nelson S. Bond

Winter 1949   4/5 (47)   -
*The Ultimate Egoist   E. Hunter Waldo
*The Crossroads   L. Ron Hubbard
*Carillon of Skulls   Philip James
*They   Robert Heinlein
*The Forbidden Trail [nt]   Jane Rice
*The Hexer   H. W. Guernsey
*The Summons   Don Evans

FROM UNKNOWN WORLDS

[For background details see US listing]

1952   [-]   Edd Cartier
*The Enchanted Week-End [sn]
                          John MacCormac
*The Refugee   Jane Rice
*Nothing in the Rules [nt]
                        L. Sprague de Camp
*The Cloak   Robert Bloch
*Yesterday Was Monday   Theodore Sturgeon
*Fiction [v]   Allan Grant
*Trouble With Water   H. L. Gold
*Lurani [v]   Paul Dennis Lavond
*Anything   Philip St. John
*The Compleat Werewolf [nt]
                          Anthony Boucher
*Black Cats [v]   Cristel Hastings
*The Devil We Know   Henry Kuttner
*The Psychomorph   E. A. Grosser
*The Hexer   H. W. Guernsey
*The Summons   Don Evans
*Jesus' Shoes   Allan R. Bosworth
*The Dawn of Reason [v]   James H. Beard

* * *

UNUSUAL STORIES

The earliest attempt at a serious small press fantasy fiction magazine. Published and edited by William L. Crawford, Everett, Pennsylvania an incomplete 'Advance Issue' was followed by a new companion magazine Marvel Tales *(also included in this Index) and it was over a year before two slim digest-sized issues appeared.*

March 1934   1/1 (1)   -
          [Advance Issue]
When the Waker Sleeps   Cyril G. Wates
Richard Tooker [a]   [no credit]
Tharda, Queen of Vampires   Richard Tooker
       [this story incomplete]

May/June 1935   1/1 (1)   -
Waning Moon   Robert A. Wait
A Resume of Rays   Forrest J. Ackerman
The Jewels of Charlotte   Duane W. Rimel
The Experiment   R. H. Barlow
Dawn-Shapes [v]   Kenrad Leister
The White Gulls Cry   P. Schuyler Miller

Winter 1935   1/2 (2)   -
A Diamond Asteroid [s1/?]
                Lowell H. Morrow
The Black Lotus   Robert Bloch
The River Dwellers   Lionel Dilbeck
The Two Doors   E. Theodore Pine
Derelict [v]   Robert W. Lowndes

            ***

V

THE VORTEX

A bold attempt at a 'slick'-style digest magazine by the small press imprint of Fansci Pubafi, 70 Mirabel, San Francisco. Editors: Gordon M. Kull & George R. Cowie. Although intended as a bi-monthly the second issue was delayed and was of a considerably poorer appearance as funds were depleted.

[Spring] 1947 No.1   [photo]
Demobilization   George R. Cowie
Doubt [v]   Jim Reid
Eniac, One [a]   James Levelle
Dreams Can Be Dangerous Lon Nichaelous
Vital Potion   Gordon M. Kull
Hell, Yes! [ss]   Ed S. Heyman
The World and Science Fiction
 [a]   Gordon M. Kull
The Fisherman of Mars Robert Sader

[Fall] 1947 No.2   [photo]
Perfection   E. E. Evans
Allons [v]   Gordon M. Kull
Synopsis   Forrest J. Ackerman
The Cosmic Reporter [a] James Taurasi
Burg Frankenstein [pic] Gordon M. Kull
Heredity   David H. Keller, M.D.
Said the Dreamer [v] Clark Ashton Smith
The Night Watchman Stanley Mullen

***

W

WAX DRAGON

A small press fantasy magazine published irregularly in octavo format by New Fantasy Publications, 123 S. Ruggles St., Bronson, Michigan. Publisher/Editor: Irvin L. Wagner. In reality it was a continuation of New Fantasy Journal *incorporating some of the elements of another Wagner magazine* Forum on Fantasy *(not covered in this Index).*

1977   No.1 M. Littlejohn
The Spirit Duplicator Darrell Schweitzer
The Bight of Benin [a]
        Charles R. Saunders

1980   No.2 William Church
Blackelven [a] Charles R. Saunders
Specter in the Buried
 Chamber Jessica Amanda Salmonson
First of the Litter Irvin L. Wagner
The Half-Scalan   An-Clovis

1980   No.3 Randy Holmberg
Ding-Dong Bell Brenda F. Watkinson
Feast of the Gods Al D. Cockrell
Is It True What They Say
 About Leopard Men? [a]
        Charles R. Saunders

     ***

WEIRD ADVENTURES

*A small press magazine published irregularly by the editor, Robert F. Fester,
Carbondale, Illinois.*

May 1978	1/1	Rod Whigham
At the Beach		Andrew J. Offutt
R.E.H.: College Fictioneer [a]		Bill Celis
The Bohemian Road		Robert F. Fester
Sweeter Even Than Honey		Wayne Hooks

[Fall] 1978	1/2	Gene Day
Sentinel of Kahel		Howard E. Day
The Essence of the Cimmerian [a]		Andrew J. Offutt
The Story of Obbok		Darrell Schweitzer
Oktober 31st [v]		Robert F. Fester
The City of Mists		Ken Huff & Charles R. Saunders
The Demise of Vlad		Robert F. Fester

***

WEIRDBOOK

One of the leading small press weird fiction magazines published irregularly by Weirdbook Press, Amherst Branch, Buffalo, New York. Editor: W. Paul Ganley. See also companion magazine Eerie Country *and sampler* Toadstool Wine.

[April] 1968   No.1   *R. R. Phillips
The Cobra in the Dream   Robert E. Howard
The Dark Ones [v]   A. Arthur Griffin
The Dunes of Death   Joseph Payne Brennan
The Gates   Walter Quednau
Out of the Night   H. Warner Munn
*Eine Kleine Nachtmusik [v]   Walt Klein
*Aftermath From Angle Two
                        Allan G. Leverentz
*From a Runestone [v] Michael De Angelis
I Am Human   Oliver Ward
*Sea Encounter [v]   Edd Roberts
*The Wizard Stone [v]   Andrew Duane
*Dread Huntress   Andrew Duane
Cold November Night [v]
                        Joseph Payne Brennan
Love Philter [v]   H. Warner Munn

[March] 1969   No.2   G. M. Farley
In the Rose Garden [v]   A. Arthur Griffin
City of the Seven Winds
                        Joseph Payne Brennan
*The Spell of Night [v]   Andrew Duane
Return of the Spy   H. Warner Munn
*Variations on a Theme by Heine
   [v]   Walt Klein
Terror From the Ages   Ray Jones
Like Father   Leo P. Kelley
The Wanderer [v]   H. Warner Munn
Courts of the Mourning [ss]
                        Michael F. Knight
The Son of Time   Walter Quednau
No Stone Unturned   Charlene James
To Fade in Silence   Timothy R. Allison
Weird Tales [v]   Walter Shedlofsky
In the Mask Shop [v]   Janet Fox
The Spaceship Game [ss]   Larry Dworin
*The Entity   George T. Wetzel
The Haunted Hut   Robert E. Howard

[February] 1970   No.3   G. M. Farley
Usurp the Night   Robert E. Howard
Messenger of Death [v]
                        W. Fraser Sandercombe
Doom Season [v]   A. Arthur Griffin
Liebestraum   Marie-Louise
Time and Falling Snow [v]
                        Joseph Payne Brennan
The Wavemaker [ss]   W. Fraser Sandercombe
Pterodactyls [v]   Janet Fox
The Town [2s]   Daniel W. Preston
   [1. To Attempt Escape; 2. The Essence of
   Terror]
Summons [v]   Darrell Schweitzer
Ode to Maldronah [v]   Tim Powers
Body and Soul   Walter Quednau
Incantation   David Anthony Kraft
Lullabye [v]   Linda-Susan Miller
Nocturne [v]   James Wade
Say it With Spiders   Janet Fox
The Creeping Shadows [v]   E. Bertin
The Throwaway Man   Steve Chapman
Cryptic Summons [v]   Wade Wellman
The Well   Ray Jones
The Temple [v]   Andrew Duane

[January] 1971   No.4   G. M. Farley
The Fruits of Yebo's Sins
                        William Scott Home
Poems in an Oriental Style
   [v]   David Winges
Picnic   Eddy C. Bertin
A Sip of Crimson   Daniel W. Preston
A Death Song [v]   W. Fraser Sandercombe
The Sandals of Sargon
                James Wade & Sotireos Vlahopoulos
The Changeling [v]   H. Warner Munn
Come to Mother   Darrell Schweitzer
The Acts of Hours   [v] Joseph Payne Brennan
Alien Words [v]   Joseph Payne Brennan
High Moon   Gregory Francis

***

WEIRD MYSTERY

A weird fantasy digest magazine published quarterly by Ultimate Publishing Co., Oakland Gardens, Flushing, New York. No editor credited, but issues assembled by Sol Cohen. Relied heavily on reprints from Fantastic Adventures and Fantastic.

Fall 1970   No.1   *L. R. Summers
*The Soul Snatchers [na]   Lee Francis
*Death's Double   Grover Kent
*Who Sups With the Devil   S. M. Tenneshaw
*Make Yourself a Wish   Geoff St. Reynard
*The Curse of Ra [nt]   H. B. Hickey
*Astral Rhythm   Bernie Kamins
*The Cat-Snake   Frances Deegan
*Mr. Jones' Eternal Camera
                       Berkeley Livingston

Winter 1970   No.2   *Ed Valigursky
*Call Me Monster [nt]   G. L. Vandenberg
*Darkness Box   Ursula K. LeGuin
*A Night With Hecate   Edward W. Ludwig
*Solomon's Demon   Arthur Porges
*The Idol   A. Bertram Chandler
*No Harm Done   Jack Sharkey
*Hungarian Rhapsody   Wilson Kane
*A Lesson For the Teacher   Robert Bloch
*The Mating Season   Wilton G. Beggs

Spring 1971   No.3   *Ed Valigursky
*Morpheus in Hades!   E. Bruce Yaches
*Rest in Agony [na]   Ivar Jorgensen
*The Arm of Enmord   Jack Sharkey
*The Furies of Zhahnoor   H. B. Fyfe
*The Mirror   William Lawrence Hamling
*Piercing the Future [a] Gary Lee Horton
*The Convention   Ede Witt
*The Hungry Eye   Robert Bloch
*The Labyrinth [a]   Sandy Miller
*A Dozen of Everything
                      Marion Zimmer Bradley
*Death Trap For Giants [a] Mildred Murdoch

Summer 1971   No.4   *Robert G. Jones
*The Dead Don't Die [na]   Robert Bloch
*Too Good To Be Used [a]   Pearl Miller
*The Traveling Brain   William P. McGivern
*Planet of the Dead   Rog Phillips
*The Magic Transformation [a]
                          E. Bruce Yaches
*Malayan Superstitions [a]   H. R. Stanton
*The Gloves of Gino   P. F. Costello
*Without Incident [a]   Leslie Phelps
*The Haunted House   Guy Archette
*The Fate Changer   Richard O. Lewis
*Mighty Mouse [a]   June Lurie

***

WEIRD TALES

The longest-running and most legendary of all fantasy pulps, the first series running for 279 issues. It has since been revived twice, with a third revival planned at time of writing. Publisher: March 1923 – May/Jun/July 1924, Rural Publishing Corporation, 854 N. Clark St., Chicago, Illinois; November 1924 – October 1938, Popular Fiction Co., 2457 E. Washington St., Indianapolis, Indiana; November 1938 – September 1954, Weird Tales (a subsidiary of Short Stories, Inc.), 9 Rockefeller Plaza, New York. The editorial offices were initially at Baldwin Building, Indianapolis, moving to Holliday Building, Indianapolis in 1925, to 3810 N. Broadway, Chicago in 1926, and then to 840 N. Michigan, Chicago from 1928 till the move to New York. Editors: March 1923 – April 1924, Edwin Baird; November 1924 – March 1940, Farnsworth Wright; May 1940 – September 1954, Dorothy McIlwraith. The May/Jun/July issue was assembled by J. C. Henneberger from stories selected by Baird and Otis Adelbert Kline. The magazine was in pulp format for all issues except May 1923 – May/July 1924 which were large pulp, and September 1953 – September 1954 which were digest.

The magazine was revived in 1973 in neo-pulp format under the Weird Tales imprint, published by Leo Margulies, 8230 Beverly Boulevard, Los Angeles, California. Editor: Sam Moskowitz.

The magazine was revived again in 1980 in pocketbook format published by Kensington Publishing Corporation, 21 East 40th St., New York, under the Zebra Books imprint. Editor: Lin Carter. Both revivals lasted for only four issues each.

A Canadian edition was published by the American News Company, 474 Wellington St. West, Toronto, Ontario. The first series, from June 1935 – July 1936, was identical to the US. The second series, May 1942 – November 1951, was substantially the same but featured new covers and interior art (until January 1948) plus story changes as noted on the respective issues below. Unfortunately it was not possible to check every Canadian issue until late in the production of this Index, and I would refer you to page 286 for further notes.

Three different British editions exist. The first was published by Gerald G. Swan, Edgware House, Burne St., Marylebone, London, and consisted of three undated issues released during 1942, corresponding in part to the US September 1940, November 1940 and January 1941. The second series was a single issue released in 1946 from William C. Merritt, 335 City Road, London with stories selected from the US October 1937 issue. The third series was distributed by Thorpe & Porter, East Street, Oadby, Leicester. Undated (and unnumbered until issue 10), they were released irregularly between November 1949 and July 1954, corresponding to the US July 1949 – May 1954, but omitting September 1949 and July 1953. Full details of the variant editions are inserted after the relevant issues below.

4. A Strange Manifestation [ts]
Matt. Byrne ap'Rhys, C.E.

September 1923   2/2 (6)   R. M. Mally
The People of the Comet
[nt1/2]   Austin Hall
The Black Patch   Julian Kilman
The Soul of Peter Andrus   Hubert La Due
The Case of Dr. Johnstone
Burton Peter Thom
The Dead-Naming of Lukapehu   P. D. Gog
The Cup of Blood   Otis Adelbert Kline
*Black Magic [a]   Alphonse Louis Constant
[credited to the translator C. P. Oliver]
The Devil's Cabin   Vance Hoyt
The Old Burying Ground Edgar Lloyd Hampton
Sunfire [na2/2]   Francis Stevens
The Gorilla   Horatio Vernon Ellis
The Talisman   Nadia Lavrova
The Autobiography of a Blue
Ghost   Don Mark Lemon
*The Damned Thing   Ambrose Bierce
The Teakwood Shrine   Farnsworth Wright
The Money-Lender   Vincent Starrett
The Bloodstained Parasol James Ravenscroft
The Cauldron [col] Preston Langley Hickey
1. Pat McClosky's Ghost [ts]
J. P. Cronister
2. The Velvet Death [ts]   Henry Trefon
3. Arthur Armstrong's
Predicament [ts]   D. G. Prescot, Jr

October 1923   2/3 (7)   R. M. Mally
The Amazing Adventure of Joe
Scranton [nt1/2]   Effie W. Fifield
The Phantom Farmhouse   Seabury Quinn
*Dagon   H. P. Lovecraft
The Man Who Owned the World   Frank Owen
Gray Sleep   Charles Horn
The People of the Comet
[nt2/2]   Austin Hall
The Sign From Heaven   A. Havdal
The Inn of Dread   Arthur Edwards Chapman
The Hairy Monster   Neil Miller
Devil Manor   E. B. Jordan
The Case of the Golden Lily
Francis D. Grierson
Weird Crimes: Bluebeard [a] Seabury Quinn
An Adventure in the Fourth
Dimension   Farnsworth Wright
*The Pit and the Pendulum Edgar Allan Poe
After the Storm   Sarah Harbine Weaver
The Cauldron [col] Preston Langley Hickey
1. After I Was Dead   John W. Walton
2. Mysterious Radio   Maxwell Levey

November 1923   2/4 (8)   Washburn
Draconda [n1/6]   John Martin Leahy
The Crawling Death [nt]   P. A. Connolly
The Closed Room   Maebell McCalment
The Phantom Violinist Walter F. McCanless
Lucifer   John D. Swain
The Spider   Arthur Edwards Chapman
The Amazing Adventure of Joe
Scranton [nt2/2]   Effie W. Fifield
The Iron Room   Francis D. Grierson
Prisoners of the Dead   Paul Suter
The Death Pit [nt]   Oscar Schisgall
The Wax Image   Burton Harcourt
Poisoned   Farnsworth Wright

The Magic Mirror   Mary S. Brown
The Invisible Monster   Sonia H. Greene
The Pebble Prophecy   Valens Lapsley
*The Tell-Tale Heart   Edgar Allan Poe
Weird Crimes:
The Grave Robbers [a]   Seabury Quinn
The Survivor   Edwin G. Wood

January 1924   3/1 (9)   R. M. Mally
The Abysmal Horror [sn1/2]   B. Wallis
Black Sorcery   Paul Annixter
The Hand of Fatma   Harry Anable Kniffin
The Man Who Banished Himself
Ferdinand Berthoud
Hope [v]   Prestone L. Hickey
A Game of Chance   Henry Lieferant &
Sylvia B. Saltzberg
Solution [v]   Clark Ashton Smith
The Open Window   Frank Owen
The Cat Called Carlos   H. F. Leslie
The Cataleptic [v]   Charles Layng
*The Picture in the House H. P. Lovecraft
Draconda [n2/6]   John Martin Leahy
The Hook of Death Mrs. Harry Pugh Smith
The Monstrosity   George W. Crane
The Cobra Lily   Ledyard M. Bailey
Weird Crimes: The Magic
Mirror Murders [a]   Seabury Quinn
*The Black Cat   Edgar Allan Poe
Snake   Galen C. Colin

February 1924   3/2 (10)   R. M. Mally
Planet Paradise [nt] Dick Presley Tooker
The Tap   Arthur Edwards Chapman
The Thing That Should Not Be
Burton Peter Thom
The Ghost [v]   Mary Sharon
The Guilty Man   Marion Carrere
The Transparent Ghost [na1/3]
Isa-Belle Manzer
Coils of Darkness [na1/3]   Sybla Ramus
Carved in the Flesh Tom Rawson Hilbourne
The Hall Bedroom   W. Elwyn Backus
The Door of Doom   Mary Sharon
The Abysmal Horror [sn2/2]   B. Wallis
The Hound   H. P. Lovecraft
Draconda [n3/6]   John Martin Leahy
The Ghost of Silent Smith
C. Franklin Miller
Doctor DeBruce   Earl Leaston Bell
The Hater   B. W. Wilson
Weird Crimes:
Swiatek the Beggar [a]   Seabury Quinn
The Killer   Harold Ward

March 1924   3/3 (11)   R. M. Mally
The Spirit Fakers of
Hermannstadt [nt1/1]   Harry Houdini
The Hermit of Ghost Mountains
C. Franklin Miller
Justice in the Foothills   Clement White
Zillah   Valma Clark
Hunger [v]   Leonard Fohn
The Fine Art of Suicide   Howard Rockey
The Melancholy Pool [v] Clark Ashton Smith
Ashes   C. M. Eddy, Jr
The Crystal Globe [v] Prestone L. Hickey
The Rats in the Walls   H. P. Lovecraft
The Voice of Euphemia
Eudora Ramsay Richardson

November 1925   6/5 (26)   A. Brosnatch
*The Stolen Body   H. G. Wells
The Return of the Undead   Arthur Leeds
*Lukundoo   Edward Lucas White
Vale of the Corbies   Arthur J. Burks
Midnight Realism   William Sanford
The Acid in the Laboratory
                    Gordon Philip England
Candle-Light   Louise Garwood
The Man-Trap   Hamilton Craigie
The Seventh Devil   F. Douglas McHenry
Ghostly Lovers [v]   William James Price
Under the Hau Tree   Katherine Yates
The Headless Spokesman   Irvin Mattick
The Waning of a World [sn1/4]
                        W. Elwyn Backus
The Gargoyle [sn3/3]   Greye La Spina
*The Young King   Oscar Wilde
The Fiends of the Seine   Dick Heine
*Whispers of Heavenly Death [v]
                        Walt Whitman
*The Conqueror Worm [v]   Edgar Allan Poe

December 1925   6/6 (27)   Joseph Doolin
The Tenants of Broussac [nt] Seabury Quinn
When the Graves Were Opened
                    Arthur J. Burks
The Sea Thing   Frank Belknap Long, Jr
The Fan   Frank Owen
The Black Box   H. Thompson Rich
The Ghost Girl [v]   William James Price
*The Valley of Spiders   H. G. Wells
Sir Rupert's Treasure   James Cocks
The Deadly Amanita   Eli Colter
*What Was It?   Fitz-James O'Brien
The Consul's Bones   W. J. Stamper
Retribution   George T. Spillman
The Last Man   Douglas Oliver
The Hour of Death   Grover Brinkman
*The Haunted Palace [v]   Edgar Allan Poe
The Waning of a World [sn2/4]
                        W. Elwyn Backus

January 1926   7/1 (28)   A. Brosnatch
Stealer of Souls [nt] Charles Hilan Craig
On the Dead Man's Chest [na1/4] Eli Colter
The Dead Soul   Raoul Lenoir
The Black Crusader   Alicia Ramsey
McGill's Appointment   Elsie Ellis
The Mystery Under the Sea
                    Donald Edward Keyhoe
Adam, to Lilith [v]   E. Hoffmann Price
The Avenger   H. Thompson Rich
The Fair Pastie Pye Arthur Edwards Chapman
*The Sands of Dee [v]   Charles Kingsley
*Wandering Willie's Tale   Walter Scott
The Gong Ringers   Hasan Vokine
The Waning of a World [sn3/4]
                        W. Elwyn Backus
The Tomb   H. P. Lovecraft
*Lenore [v]   Edgar Allan Poe

February 1926   7/2 (29)   C.B. Petrie,Jr
Red Ether [nt1/2]   Petterson Marzoni
The Isle of Missing Ships
   [nt]   Seabury Quinn
The Word of Santiago   E. Hoffmann Price
The Avenging Hand   Roy Wallace Davis
Phantom Billiards   Frank E. Walker
*The White Dog   Feodor Sologub

The Thing in the Glass Box
                    Sewell Peaslee Wright
Italian Love [v]   William James Price
The Kidnapper's Story   Walter G. Detrick
On the Dead Man's Chest [na2/4]
                        Eli Colter
The Other Half   Edwin L. Sabin
*The Twa Corbies [v]   [no credit]
*The Cats of Ulthar   H. P. Lovecraft
*Spleen [v]   Charles Baudelaire
The Waning of a World [sn4/4]
                        W. Elwyn Backus

March 1926   7/3 (30)   A. Brosnatch
Lochinvar Lodge   Clyde Burt Clason
The Jungle Monsters   Paul S. Powers
A Message from Space   J. Schlossel
Something Toothsome   Arthur J. Burks
Dead in Three Hours   Elwin J. Owens
*A Dream of Armageddon   H. G. Wells
The Evening Star [v]   Francis Hard
The Music of Madness   William E. Barrett
*The Mask of the Red Death Edgar Allan Poe
The Inland Sea [v] Frank Belknap Long, Jr
The Luster of the Beast
                Charles Christopher Jenkins
Dr. Jerbot's Last Experiment
                    Granville S. Hoss
On the Dead Man's Chest [na3/4] Eli Colter
Swamp Horror   Will Smith & R. J. Robbins
The Curse   Charles Hilan Craig
*Death Carol   Walt Whitman
Red Ether [nt2/2]   Petterson Marzoni
Astarte [v]   E. Hoffmann Price

April 1926   7/4 (31)   E. M. Stevenson
Wolfshead   Robert E. Howard
The Outsider   H. P. Lovecraft
The Contra-Talisman George Ballard Bowers
The Hooded Death   Joel Martin Nichols
Out of the Mists of Time
                    William Benton Frazier
Knights of the Red Owl   Elwin J. Owens
The Derelict Mine [sn1/3] Frank A. Mochnant
Teeth   Galen C. Colin
The Vengeance of India   Seabury Quinn
The Phantom Drug   A. W. Kapfer
The House in the Willows
                    Sewell Peaslee Wright
Duval's Weird Experiment F. William Sarles
*The Mummy's Foot   Theophile Gautier
*Tiger [v]   William Blake
The Things That Are God's
                    C. Franklin Miller
The Yellow Specter   Stewart Van der Veer
The Glacier Lode   Strickland Gillilan
On the Dead Man's Chest [na4/4] Eli Colter

May 1926   7/5 (32)   Andrew Bensen
The Ghosts of Steamboat Coulee
                    Arthur J. Burks
The Devil-Ray [nt1/3]
                    Joel Martin Nichols, Jr
The Dead Hand   Seabury Quinn
The Silent Trees   Frank Owen
The Man Who Was Saved   B. W. Sliney
Bat's Belfry   August W. Derleth
Queen of the Vortex   F. William Sarles
*The Werewolf   Frederick Marryat
*Horreur Sympathique [v]
                    Charles Baudelaire

The Isle of the Fairy Morgana
                        John Martin Leahy
The Barnacle Goose [a]   Alvin F. Harlow
The Mist Monster   Granville S. Hoss
The Dream Snake   Robert E. Howard
*Clarimonde   Theophile Gautier

March 1928   11/3 (54)   C. C. Senf
The Strange People [sn1/3] Murray Leinster
The Eighth Green Man   G. G. Pendarves
Night Trees [v]   Frank Belknap Long, Jr
The Tenant   August W. Derleth
Flames of Destiny   Arlton Eadie
The Vampire [a]   Alvin F. Harlow
The Twin Soul   Amelia Reynolds Long
The Poet [v]   A. Leslie
Ebony Magic   Stella Wynne
The Curse of a Song   Eli Colter
*Epigraphe Pour un Livre
  Condamne [v]   Charles Baudelaire
The Black Angel   C. Ed Rowley
The Tree-Man Ghost   Percy B. Prior
The Giant World [sn3/3]   Ray Cummings
The Hyena   Robert E. Howard
*The Legend of the Moor's
  Legacy   Washington Irving

April 1928   11/4 (55)   C. C. Senf
The Haunted Castle [v] Lilla Price Savino
The Jewel of Seven Stones [nt]
                        Seabury Quinn
The Magic of Chac-Mool   Clyde Criswell
The Time Will Come   Will MacMahon
The Phantom [v]   Cristel Hastings
Whispers   Robert S. Carr
Remembrance [v]   Robert E. Howard
The Strange People [sn2/3] Murray Leinster
Medusa   Royal W. Jimerson
From Beyond   Everil Worrell
The Spectral Lover   R. Anthony
The Familiar [a]   Alvin F. Harlow
The Fantasmal Terror   Willis Overton
The Chain   H. Warner Munn
*The Legend of St. Julian Gustave Flaubert

May 1928   11/5 (56)   C. C. Senf
The Bat-Men of Thorium [sn1/3]
                        Bertram Russell
The Skeleton Under the Lamp Bassett Morgan
The Hand of the Invisible E. Irving Haines
Sea Curse   Robert E. Howard
Riders in the Sky   Mark R. Schorer &
                        August W. Derleth
A Wager in Candlesticks
                        Robert T. Greibling
Three Coffins   Arthur J. Burks
The Basilisk [a]   Alvin F. Harlow
The Doomed Treveans   G. G. Pendarves
Through the Veil   Anne M. Bilbro
Sonnets of the Midnight Hours:
 1. The Hungry Flowers [v] Donald Wandrei
 2. Dream Horror [v]   Donald Wandrei
The Strange People [sn3/3] Murray Leinster
The Black Madonna   A. W. Wyville
Malchior Makes Magic
                Charles Henry Mackintosh
*Rappaccini's Daughter Nathaniel Hawthorne
Clair de Lune [v]   Minnie Faegre Knox

June 1928   11/6 (57)   C. C. Senf
*The Devil's Martyr   Signe Toksvig
The Serpent Woman   Seabury Quinn
The Elemental Law   Everil Worrell
The Hate   Wilford Allen
The Dimension Terror   Edmond Hamilton
*The Lurking Fear   H. P. Lovecraft
The Philosopher's Stone August W. Derleth
The Bat-Men of Thorium [sn2/3]
                        Bertram Russell
Wild Horses [v]   Eugene C. Dolson
The Phantom Fiddler   Arlton Eadie
The Blue Lizard   Fiswoode Tarleton
Sonnets of the Midnight Hours:
 3. Purple [v]   Donald Wandrei
The Last Laugh   C. Franklin Miller
The White Road [v]   Manly Wade Wellman
*The Specter Bridegroom Washington Irving
The Fad For Relics [a]   Alvin F. Harlow

July 1928   12/1 (58)   C. C. Senf
The Witches' Sabbath [nt1/2] Stephen Bagby
The Green Monster   Arthur Macom
Tony the Faithful   W. K. Mashburn, Jr
The Three-Storied House August W. Derleth
Weird Recipes [a]   Alvin F. Harlow
The Space-Eaters [nt]
                        Frank Belknap Long, Jr
Sonnets of the Midnight Hours:
 4. The Eye [v]   Donald Wandrei
On a Far World   Wilford Allen
The Gates of Nineveh [v] Robert E. Howard
The Bat-Men of Thorium [sn3/3]
                        Bertram Russell
Under the Moon [v]   Eugene C. Dolson
The Man Who Remembered Willis Knapp Jones
The Grappling Ghost   Capwell Wyckoff
The Statue of Anuta   Arthur W. Davenport
The Little Husbands   David H. Keller
Symphonic Death   Fred R. Farrow, Jr
*The Bowmen   Arthur Machen

August 1928   12/2 (59)   C. C. Senf
Black Mora [v]   A. Leslie
Red Shadows [nt]   Robert E. Howard
You Can't Kill a Ghost Frank Belknap Long
Vulture Crag   Everil Worrell
The Rose Window   Charlton Lawrence Edholm
Crashing Suns [nt1/2]   Edmond Hamilton
The Man in the Green Coat Eli Colter
Sonnets of the Midnight Hours:
 5. The Grip of Evil Dreams [v]
                        Donald Wandrei
The Witches' Sabbath [nt2/2] Stephen Bagby
Dirge [v]   Leavenworth Macnab
The Vengeance of Nitocris
                Thomas Lanier Williams
Three Poems in Prose   Charles Baudelaire
[L'Irreparable; Les Sept Vieillards;
 Une Charogne]
Wonderfully Preserved Relics
  [a]   Alvin F. Harlow
The Justice of the Czar
                George Fielding Eliot
*The Demoiselle D'Ys   Robert W. Chambers

September 1928   12/3 (60)   C. C. Senf
The Harp of Alfred [v] Robert E. Howard
The Devil-Plant   John Murray Reynolds
Invisible Threads [nt1/2] Arthur J. Burks

The Dance of the Dead [v]   Robert B. Gray
Ubbo-Sathla   Clark Ashton Smith
The Man on the Ground   Robert E. Howard
*Green Tea   J. Sheridan Le Fanu

August 1933   22/2 (116)   M. Brundage
The Chosen of Vishnu   Seabury Quinn
Ashes of Eden [v]   Kirk Mashburn
The Vampire Airplane   Arlton Eadie
Dead Men Walk   Harold Ward
The House by the Sea [v] Frances Elliott
The Superior Judge   J. Paul Suter
Golden Blood [n5/6]   Jack Williamson
The Owl   F. A. M. Webster
A Pair of Swords   Carl Jacobi
An Elegy For Mr. Danielson
                        August W. Derleth
The Green Sea [v]   Hung Long Tom
*The Door   Henry S. Whitehead

September 1933   22/3 (117)   M. Brundage
The Slithering Shadow   Robert E. Howard
Nostalgia [v]   Mary Elizabeth Counselman
The Horror on the Asteroid Edmond Hamilton
Malay Horror   Seabury Quinn
The Return of Andrew Bentley
           August W. Derleth & Mark Schorer
Golden Blood [n6/6]   Jack Williamson
The Watcher in the Green Room Hugh B. Cave
The Dead Man's Story   Julius Long
Ballade of Creatures Abroad
   by Night [v]   Wilfred Blanch Talman
*Death Waters   Frank Belknap Long, Jr
Deserted House [v]   Marion Doyle
A Vintage From Atlantis Clark Ashton Smith
Rain [v]   Hung Long Tom

October 1933   22/4 (118)   M. Brundage
The Vampire Master [n1/4] Hugh Davidson
The Mansion of Unholy Magic
   [nt]   Seabury Quinn
The Pool of the Black One Robert E. Howard
The House of the Worm   Mearle Prout
The Plutonian Terror   Jack Williamson
The Seed of the Sepulcher
                        Clark Ashton Smith
The Black, Dead Thing   Frank Belknap Long
The Cat-Woman   Mary Elizabeth Counselman
The Ultimate Word [v]   Marion Doyle
*The Festival   H. P. Lovecraft

November 1933   22/5 (119)   M. Brundage
Shambleau   C. L. Moore
The War of the Sexes   Edmond Hamilton
Ghost Town [v]   Cristel Hastings
Lord of the Fourth Axis E. Hoffmann Price
The Holiness of Azedarac
                        Clark Ashton Smith
On Top   Ralph Allen Lang
Sic Transit Gloria [v]   Brook Byrne
The Accursed Isle
                 Mary Elizabeth Counselman
The Vampire Master [n2/4] Hugh Davidson
The Man Who Saw Red   J. Wilmer Benjamin
*The Premature Burial   Edgar Allan Poe

December 1933   22/6 (120)   M. Brundage
King Cobra   Joseph O. Kesselring
A Dead House [v]   Clarence Edwin Flynn
Red Gauntlets of Czerni   Seabury Quinn

The Ox-Cart   Frank Owen
Abd Dhulma, Lord of Fire   G. G. Pendarves
Old Garfield's Heart   Robert E. Howard
Monkeys   E. F. Benson
The Vampire Master [n3/4] Hugh Davidson
The Closed Door   Harold Ward
The Lady in Gray   Donald Wandrei
*Secret of the Growing Gold   Bram Stoker

January 1934   23/1 (121)   M. Brundage
The Solitary Hunters [sn1/3]
                        David H. Keller
The Red Knife of Hassan   Seabury Quinn
Place Names [v]   Katherine van der Veer
Invaders of the Ice World Jack Williamson
Too Late [v]   Alfred I. Tooke
A Phantom in the Sky   Dale Clark
Rogues in the House   Robert E. Howard
The Weaver in the Vault Clark Ashton Smith
The Vampire Master [n4/4] Hugh Davidson
In the Triangle   Howard Wandrei
Candles [v]   Dorothy Quick
*The Woman of the Wood   A. Merritt
Possession   Julius Long

February 1934   23/2 (122)   M. Brundage
The Sapphire Goddess [nt] Nictzin Dyalhis
The Virus of Hell   William H. Pope
The Valley of the Worm   Robert E. Howard
Tarbis of the Lake   E. Hoffmann Price
The Man Who Returned   Edmond Hamilton
The Place of Hairy Death   Anthony Rud
To a Bullet-Pierced Skull
   [v]   Alfred I. Tooke
The Solitary Hunters [sn2/3]
                        David H. Keller
The Witchcraft of Ulua   Clark Ashton Smith
Nocturne [v]   Herbert Kaufman, Jr
*The Sixth Tree   Edith Lichty Stewart
The Star-Gazer Climbs [v]   Hazel Burden
The Lantern [v]   Hung Long Tom

March 1934   23/3 (123)   M. Brundage
The Black Gargoyle   Hugh B. Cave
Gray World   Paul Ernst
Winged Death   Hazel Heald
The Charnel God   Clark Ashton Smith
Thundering Worlds   Edmond Hamilton
Remembrance [v]   Mary C. Shaw
The Clenched Hand   Stuart Strauss
The Solitary Hunters [sn3/3]
                        David H. Keller
Ghouls of the Sea   J. B. S. Fullilove
The Nightmare Road   Florence Crow
The Late Mourner   Julius Long
*Why Weird Tales? [ed]
                    [Otis Adelbert Kline]

April 1934   23/4 (124)   M. Brundage
Satan's Garden [nt1/2] E. Hoffmann Price
Black Thirst [nt]   C. L. Moore
Corsairs of the Cosmos   Edmond Hamilton
Shadows in the Moonlight Robert E. Howard
The Death of Malygris Clark Ashton Smith
Behind the Screen   Dale Clark
The Cane   Carl Jacobi
*Bells of Oceana   Arthur J. Burks
In Mayan Splendor [v]
                     Frank Belknap Long, Jr

Wharf Watchman [v]   Edgar Daniel Kramer
Death in Twenty Minutes
                    Charles Henry Mackintosh
*The Supreme Witch   G. Appleby Terrill

February 1935   25/2 (134)   M. Brundage
The Web of Living Death [nt]
                    Seabury Quinn
The Grisly Horror   Robert E. Howard
The Body-Masters   Frank Belknap Long, Jr
Murder in the Grave   Edmond Hamilton
Rulers of the Future [nt2/3]   Paul Ernst
The Silver Bullet   Phyllis A. Whitney
Listening [v]   Cristel Hastings
The Metronome   August W. Derleth
Anything Could Happen   Kurt Barle
The Dinner Set   Fanny Kemble Johnson
*The Fireplace   Henry S. Whitehead
Witches [v]   Donna Kelly

March 1935   25/3 (135)   M. Brundage
The Lord of the Lamia [nt1/3]
                    Otis Adelbert Kline
Sonnet of the Unsleeping Dead
    [v]   Parker White
Clutching Hands of Death   Harold Ward
Jewels of Gwahlur   Robert E. Howard
Julhi   C. L. Moore
Rulers of the Future [nt3/3]   Paul Ernst
Drums of the Congo [v]
                    Katherine van der Veer
What Waits in Darkness   Loretta Burrough
The Sealed Casket   Richard F. Searight
*The Judge's House   Bram Stoker

April 1935   25/4 (136)   M. Brundage
The Man Who Was Two Men
                    Arthur William Bernal
The Hand of the O'Mecca   Howard Wandrei
Shadows of Blood   Eando Binder
Dear Ghosts [v]   Clarence Edwin Flynn
Lord of the Lamia [nt2/3]
                    Otis Adelbert Kline
The Last Hieroglyph   Clark Ashton Smith
The New World [v]   Richard F. Searight
Dream-Stair [v]   Robert Nelson
Out of the Eons   Hazel Heald
The Aztec Ring   John Flanders
The Man Who Could Not Go Home L. E. Frailey
An Empty House at Night [v]
                    Cristel Hastings
*The Canal   Everil Worrell

May 1935   25/5 (137)   M. Brundage
The Death Cry [nt]   Arthur B. Reeve
Yellow Doom   Robert H. Leitfred
Under the Tomb [v]   Robert Nelson
The Bronze Casket   Richard H. Hart
Beyond the Black River [nt1/2]
                    Robert E. Howard
Lord of the Lamia [nt3/3]
                    Otis Adelbert Kline
The Flower Women   Clark Ashton Smith
On Hangman's Hill [v]   Robert Avrett
Muggridge's Aunt   August W. Derleth
The Secret of the Tomb   Robert Bloch
*Arthur Jermyn   H. P. Lovecraft
Tea-Drinking [v]   Hung Long Tom

June 1935   25/6 (138)   M. Brundage
The Horror in the Studio   Dorothy Quick
Satan in Exile [sn1/4]
                    Arthur William Bernal
Flapping Wings of Death
                    Amelia Reynolds Long
The Destroying Horde   Donald Wandrei
Dominion [v]   Clark Ashton Smith
The Spider's Web   John Scott Douglas
Beyond the Black River [nt2/2]
                    Robert E. Howard
The Suicide in the Study   Robert Bloch
The Woman in Gray   Walker G. Everett
Together   Ida M. Kier
*The Cup of Blood   Otis Adelbert Kline
Autumn Leaves [v]   A. Leslie
[Canadian edition identical]

July 1935   26/1 (139)   M. Brundage
The Avenger From Atlantis Edmond Hamilton
Waiter No. 34   Paul Ernst
Why Was My Dream So Real?
    [v]   June Power Reilly
Jirel Meets Magic   C. L. Moore
There Is a Might [v]   Elma Dean
Satan in Exile [sn2/4]
                    Arthur William Bernal
The Curse of the Valedi   Capt. S. P. Meek
A Grave Must Be Deep   Aalla Zaata
*On a Train With a Madman   Pan-Appan
[credited to translator Roy Temple House]
The Honor of Don Pedro   Wallace J. Knapp
*The Violet Death   Gustav Meyrink
*The Wondersmith   Fitz-James O'Brien
[Canadian edition identical]

August 1935   26/2 (140)   M. Brundage
Doctor Satan   Paul Ernst
The Drome of the Living Dead
                    John Scott Douglas
Ghost [v]   Leona Ames Hill
The Black Orchid   Seabury Quinn
The House Party at Smokey
    Island   L. M. Montgomery
Once in a Thousand Years
                    Frances Bragg Middleton
Satan in Exile [sn3/4]
                    Arthur William Bernal
The Treader of the Dust Clark Ashton Smith
Old Salt [v]   Edgar Daniel Kramer
*The Idol and the Rajah   Claude Farrere
*In Amundsen's Tent   John Martin Leahy
[Canadian edition identical]

September 1935   26/3 (141)   M. Brundage
The Blue Woman   John Scott Douglas
Night Song [v]   Hung Long Tom
The Carnival of Death [sn1/4]
                    Arlton Eadie
The Man Who Chained the Lightning
                    Paul Ernst
Vulthoom   Clark Ashton Smith
Satan in Exile [sn4/4]
                    Arthur William Bernal
Vampires [v]   Dorothy Quick
The Shambler From the Stars   Robert Bloch
One Chance   Ethel Helene Coen
The Toad Idol   Kirk Mashburn
*The Monster-God of Mamurth
                    Edmond Hamilton

Green Horror H. Thompson Rich
The Black Drama [na3/3] Gans T. Field
Dead Dog Manly Wade Wellman
Three Gentlemen in Black August W. Derleth
*The Tree H. P. Lovecraft
*Invaders From Outside J. Schlossel
In November Only [v] Marion Doyle

September 1938 32/3 (176) M. Brundage
Israfel [pic] Virgil Finlay
As 'Twas Told to Me Seabury Quinn
The Magic Mirror Algernon Blackwood
The Wreck [v] Alfred I. Tooke
The White Rat
Earl Peirce, Jr. & Bruce Bryan
A Thunder of Trumpets Robert E. Howard & Frank Thurston Torbett
The Mandarin's Canaries Robert Bloch
*The Wood [v] H. P. Lovecraft
The Fire Princess [sn2/3] Edmond Hamilton
The Prophet Speaks [v] Clark Ashton Smith
The Witch in the Fog Alexander Faust
The Cavern Manly Wade Wellman & Gertrude Gordon
The Eyes of Ustad Isa
Charles Henry Mackintosh
*A Witch's Curse Paul Ernst
The Jolly Hangman [v] Edgar Daniel Kramer

October 1938 32/4 (177) M. Brundage
The Horns of Elfland [pic] Virgil Finlay
Beyond the Phoenix Henry Kuttner
Black Moon Seabury Quinn
*Death [v] William Shakespeare
The Isle of Abominations Kadra Maysi
Jekal's Lesson David Bernard
The Fire Princess [sn3/3] Edmond Hamilton
*The Maze of Maal Dweb Clark Ashton Smith
The Black Monk G. G. Pendarves
*The Other Gods H. P. Lovecraft
Witches on the Heath [v] Leah Bodine Drake
Up Under the Roof Manly Wade Wellman
*The Oldest Story in the World Murray Leinster

November 1938 32/5 (178) A. R. Tilburne
I Found Cleopatra [n1/4] Thomas P. Kelley
Fothergill's Jug Thorp McClusky
The Hound of Pedro Robert Bloch
The Thing in the Trunk Paul Ernst
Lynne Foster is Dead Seabury Quinn
*The Nameless City H. P. Lovecraft
Recompense [v] Robert E. Howard
*Leonora Everil Worrell

December 1938 32/6 (179) Ray Quigley
More Lives Than One Seabury Quinn
I Found Cleopatra [n2/4] Thomas P. Kelley
The Sin-Eater [nt] G. G. Pendarves
The Blessed Damozel [pic] Virgil Finlay
The Snowman Loretta Burrough
Beetles Robert Bloch
The Ghost Kings [v] Robert E. Howard
*Passing of a God Henry S. Whitehead

January 1939 33/1 (180) Virgil Finlay
[misdated January 1938 on contents page]
Waxworks Robert Bloch
"Hence, Loathed Melancholy!" [pic] Virgil Finlay
Medusa's Coil Z. B. Bishop
The Fifth Candle Cyril Mand
The Warrior [v] Emil Petaja
Bride of the Lightning Edmond Hamilton
Othello Time [v] Vincent Starrett
I Found Cleopatra [n3/4] Thomas P. Kelley
And Thus I Knew [v] Dorothy Agard Ansley
The Silver Coffin Robert Barbour Johnson
These Doth the Lord Hate Gans T. Field
Date in the City Room Talbot Johns
*A Rendezvous in Averoigne
Clark Ashton Smith

February 1939 33/2 (181) Virgil Finlay
The King and the Oak [v] Robert E. Howard
Death is an Elephant Nathan Hindin
The City of Death [v] Edith Hurley
The Poltergeist of Swan Upping
Seabury Quinn
*The Double Shadow Clark Ashton Smith
Fearful Rock [na1/3] Manly Wade Wellman
Crazy Nell [v] Edgar Daniel Kramer
The Drifting Snow August W. Derleth
Giant-Plasm Donald Wandrei
I Found Cleopatra [n4/4] Thomas P. Kelley
The Transgressor Henry Kuttner
"Shapes of Men That Were" [pic] Virgil Finlay
*The Last Horror Eli Colter
Two Sonnets:
*1. The Lamp [v] H. P. Lovecraft
*2. Zaman's Hill [v] H. P. Lovecraft

March 1939 33/3 (182) Virgil Finlay
The Metal Chamber Duane W. Rimel
The Swine of Æaea Clifford Ball
The House Where Time Stood Still Seabury Quinn
The Return of Hastur August W. Derleth
Fearful Rock [na2/3] Manly Wade Wellman
Desert Dawn [v] Robert E. Howard
"Satan, Yawning on his Brazen Seat" [pic] Virgil Finlay
Comrades of Time Edmond Hamilton
Introduction to a Stranger [v] David Wright O'Brien
*The Quest of Iranon H. P. Lovecraft
The Stratosphere Menace Ralph Milne Farley
Smoke Fantasy Thomas R. Jordan
*The Devils of Po Sung Bassett Morgan

April 1939 33/4 (183) Virgil Finlay
The Red God Laughed Thorp McClusky
Trinities [v] Edgar Daniel Kramer
"Their Eyes Upturned and Begged and Burned" [pic] Virgil Finlay
Susette Seabury Quinn
Hellsgarde C. L. Moore
Armies From the Past Edmond Hamilton
The Red Swimmer Robert Bloch
In an Old Street [v] Vincent Starrett
Hydra Henry Kuttner
Fearful Rock [na3/3] Manly Wade Wellman
The High Places Frances Garfield
Mommy Mary Elizabeth Counselman
Will-o'-the-Wisp [v] Charles Sloan Reid
The Wicked Clergyman H. P. Lovecraft
Special News Bulletin Vincent Gaddis
*The Curse of Yig Z. B. Bishop

May 1939   33/5 (184)   Harold DeLay
The Hollow Moon   Everil Worrell
The Dark Isle   Robert Bloch
Washington Nocturne   Seabury Quinn
The Thinking Machine   J. J. Connington
The Plumed Serpent [v]   Howell Calhoun
Almuric [n1/3]   Robert E. Howard
The Dead Host's Welcome [v]   John Fletcher
The Face at Death Corner   Paul Ernst
Witch's Hair   Mearle Prout
In a Dark Wood [v]   Marion Doyle
The Phantom Island   Arlton Eadie
Cross of Fire   Lester del Rey
"Where Crafty Gnomes" [pic]   Virgil Finlay
The Watcher at the Door   Henry Kuttner
*Harbor Whistles [v]   H. P. Lovecraft
"Not Both!"   Frances Garfield
*The Dead Soul   Raoul Lenoir
Dust [v]   Edgar Daniel Kramer

June/July 1939   34/1 (185)   Virgil Finlay
Giants of Anarchy   Eando Binder
Far Below   Robert Barbour Johnson
They Run Again [v]   Leah Bodine Drake
Lens-Shy   W. M. Clayton
The Sitter in the Mound   Bruce Bryan
The Hills of Kandahar [v] Robert E. Howard
The Man Who Came Back
                  Frederic Arnold Kummer, Jr
The Stroke of Twelve   Earl Peirce, Jr
*The Howler [v]   H. P. Lovecraft
Mansions in the Sky   Seabury Quinn
Circe [v]   Edgar Daniel Kramer
The Phantom Werewolf [ts]   [no credit]
*The Willow Landscape   Clark Ashton Smith
Almuric [n2/3]   Robert E. Howard
Headache   Paul Ernst
The Death Watch   Hugh B. Cave
"We Are No Other Than a Moving
   Row" [pic]   Virgil Finlay
*Celephais   H. P. Lovecraft
*Imprisoned With the Pharaohs
   [nt]   Harry Houdini

August 1939   34/2 (186)   Virgil Finlay
The Valley Was Still   Manly Wade Wellman
Apprentice Magician   E. Hoffmann Price
Spawn   P. Schuyler Miller
Voice in a Veteran's Ear [v] Gans T. Field
The Little Man   Clifford Ball
Return From Death   Bruce Bryan
The Fisherman's Special   H. L. Thomson
The House of Three Corpses   Seabury Quinn
Giants in the Sky   Frank Belknap Long, Jr
Dupin and Another [v]   Vincent Starrett
Almuric [n3/3]   Robert E. Howard
The Laugh   Richard H. Hart
The Totem-Pole   Robert Bloch
My Tomb [v]   James E. Warren
I Can Call Spirits [pic]   Virgil Finlay
*The Fall of the House of
   Usher   Edgar Allan Poe
*The Gardens of Yin [v]   H. P. Lovecraft

September 1939   34/3 (187)   Virgil Finlay
While Zombies Walked   Thorp McClusky
Spanish Vampire   E. Hoffmann Price
The Door Without a Key   Seabury Quinn
King of the World's Edge [n1/4]
                  H. Warner Munn

Spawn of the Maelstrom
          August W. Derleth & Mark Schorer
*Cool Air   H. P. Lovecraft
*A Night in Malneant   Clark Ashton Smith
*Gray Ghouls   Bassett Morgan

October 1939   34/4 (188)   Harold Delay
The Mystery of the Missing
   Magnate   Ralph Milne Farley
The Witch's Cat   Gans T. Field
*The Sorcerer's Apprentice [a]   Lucian
The Lady of the Bells [nt]   Seabury Quinn
In the Walls of Eryx [nt]
          H. P. Lovecraft & Kenneth Sterling
King of the World's Edge [n2/4]
                  H. Warner Munn
The Dead Speak [v]   Vivian Stratton
Finished Game   Harry Buttman
*Worms of the Earth [nt] Robert E. Howard
The Dream [v]   Edith Hurley
The Hashish Eater [pic]   Virgil Finlay

November 1939   34/5 (189)   Virgil Finlay
The Man Who Died Twice   Eli Colter
Towers of Death   Henry Kuttner
Bogey-Man [v]   Charles Sloan Reid
Uncanonised   Seabury Quinn
The Withered Heart   G. G. Pendarves
The Web of Silence
          Mary Elizabeth Counselman
The Haunted Car   David Bernard
The Hunch   Gene Lyle III
King of the World's Edge [n3/4]
                  H. Warner Munn
*The Phantom Drug   A. W. Kapfer
Is That the Wind Dying? [pic]
                  Virgil Finlay

December 1939   34/6 (190)   Hannes Bok
Glamour   Seabury Quinn
The Considerate Hosts   Thorp McClusky
Lords of the Ice   David H. Keller
Nymph of Darkness
          C. L. Moore & Forrest J. Ackerman
*Night Gaunts [v]   H. P. Lovecraft
Escape From Tomorrow
                  Frank Belknap Long, Jr
Mannikins of Horror   Robert Bloch
"Deep Night, Dark Night" [pic]
                  Virgil Finlay
Dead Man's Schooner   Andre Linville
Bacchante [v]   Clark Ashton Smith
King of the World's Edge
   [n4/4]   H. Warner Munn
Weird Things [v]   Vivian Stratton
*The Copper Bowl   George Fielding Eliot

January 1940   35/1 (191)   Virgil Finlay
Spotted Satan   Otis Adelbert Kline &
                  E. Hoffmann Price
Mortmain   Seabury Quinn
A Million Years in the Future
   [n1/4]   Thomas P. Kelley
Twister   Mary Elizabeth Counselman
Realization [v]   Harry Warner, Jr
Portrait of a Bride   Earl Peirce, Jr
Forbidden Cupboard   Frances Garfield
The Unveiling   Alfred I. Tooke
Up From the Earth's Center
   [pic]   Virgil Finlay
*Lips of the Dead   W. J. Stamper

The Case of Charles Dexter
    Ward [abr.n1/2]   H. P. Lovecraft
By What Mystic Mooring   Frank Owen
Drifting Atoms   Mary Elizabeth Counselman
The Phantom Pistol   Carl Jacobi
The Ghost of a Chance   A. B. Almy
Beauty's Beast   Robert Bloch
Altimer's Amulet   August W. Derleth
Futility [v]   Marvin Miller
The Ballad of Lalune [v] Leslyn MacDonald
Superstitions and Taboos
    [pic]   Irwin J. Weill

July 1941   35/10 (200)   Hannes Bok
The Robot God [nt]   Ray Cummings
Song Without Words [nt]   Seabury Quinn
The Enchantress of Sylaire
                        Clark Ashton Smith
First Night   Mindret Lord
The Believers   Robert Arthur
The Case of Charles Dexter
    Ward [abr.n2/2]   H. P. Lovecraft
I Killed Hitler   Ralph Milne Farley
It All Came True in the
    Woods   Manly Wade Wellman
The Devil's Tree [v]   Dennis Plimmer
Shadows of Han [v]   Gerald Chan Seig
Superstitions and Taboos
    [pic]   Irwin J. Weill

September 1941   36/1 (201)   M. Brundage
Beyond the Threshold [nt]
                         August W. Derleth
Birthmark [nt]   Seabury Quinn
Where are You, Mr. Biggs?   Nelson S. Bond
The Man Who Lived   Raymond F. O'Kelly
Unhallowed Holiday   O. M. Cabral
A Sorcerer Runs for Sheriff   Robert Bloch
The Half-Haunted   Gans T. Field
The Music From Infinity   Thorp McClusky
The Lost Gods   Dorothy Quick
Reincarnation [v]   Gerald Chan Seig
Witch Dance [v]   Clark Ashton Smith
Superstitions and Taboos
    [pic]   Irwin J. Weill

November 1941   36/2 (202)   Hannes Bok
Dreamer's Worlds [nt]   Edmond Hamilton
Core of the Purple Flame
    [nt]   Robert H. Leitfred
The Spirits of the Lake   Alonzo Deen Cole
The Werewolf Howls   Clifford Ball
The Mystery of Uncle Alfred   Mindret Lord
The Liers in Wait   Manly Wade Wellman
Chameleon Man   Henry Kuttner
Compliments of Spectro   August W. Derleth
The Book of the Dead   Frank Gruber
Haunted Hour [v]   Leah Bodine Drake
*The Owls [v]   Charles P. Baudelaire
Superstitions and Taboos
    [pic]   Irwin J. Weill
It Happened to Me:
    The Guardian Angel [ts] Sigmond Miller

January 1942   36/3 (203)   [Etta]
*The Shadow Over Innsmouth
    [abr.nt]   H. P. Lovecraft
Parasite Mansion [nt]
                Mary Elizabeth Counselman
Who Can Escape?   Seabury Quinn

The White Lady   Dorothy Quick
Death Thumbs a Ride   Robert Arthur
The Ghost of Lancelot Biggs Nelson S. Bond
The Phantom Slayer   Fritz Leiber, Jr
Table For Two   Arthur Leo Zagat
The Curse [v]   Page Cooper
Superstitions and Taboos
    [pic]   Irwin J. Weill
[Canadian edn.36/3,May 42. See Note p.286]

March 1942   36/4 (204)   Hannes Bok
Hell on Earth [nt]   Robert Bloch
Tibetan Vengeance [nt]   Stafford Aylmer
The Superfluous Phantom   Malcolm Jameson
The March of the Trees   Frank Owen
Child's Play   Alice Mary Schnirring
The Rat Master   Greye La Spina
The Treasure of the Red
    Ash Desert   Stanton A. Coblentz
*Herbert West: Reanimator
    1. From the Dark   H. P. Lovecraft
Death of the Kraken   David H. Keller
Here, Daemos!   August W. Derleth
Garden at Lu [v]   Gerald Chan Seig
Wood Wife [v]   Leah Bodine Drake
Hunger [v]   Page Cooper
Superstitions and Taboos
    [pic]   Irwin J. Weill
[Canadian ed. 36/4, Jul 42; see note p.286]

May 1942   36/5 (205)   Ray Quigley
Stoneman's Memorial [nt]   Seabury Quinn
The Enchanted River   Dorothy Quick
Ghost for a Night   Robert Arthur
Masquerade   Henry Kuttner
The Deadly Theory   Greye La Spina
Black Bargain   Robert Bloch
The Giant in a Test Tube
                     George Armin Shaftel
The Concrete Phantom   Weston Parry
Crystal Vision   Alice Mary Schnirring
The Gypsy's Hand   Alonzo Deen Cole
Vengeance in Her Bones   Malcolm Jameson
The Dreamer in the Desert [v]
                           Francis Flagg
Superstitions and Taboos
    [pic]   Irwin J. Weill
[Canadian ed. 37/1, Sep 42,see note p.286]

July 1942   36/6 (206)   M. Brundage
Coven [nt]   Manly Wade Wellman
Is the Devil a Gentleman?
    [nt]   Seabury Quinn
Lansing's Luxury   August W. Derleth
The Gun   Frank Gruber
For Tomorrow We Die   Frank Owen
Dead Silence   Leonard Lee Charlot
The High Tower   Everil Worrell
Poor Little Tampico   Hannes Bok
*Herbert West: Reanimator
    2. The Plague-Demon   H. P. Lovecraft
The Redoubtable Horace
    Goppendyke   John Broome
*Moonlight [v]   Paul Verlaine
    [credited to translator Timæus Gaylord]
A Mangrove Swamp [v]   William de Lisle
Superstitions and Taboos
    [pic]   Irwin J. Weill
[Canadian ed. 37/1, Nov 42,see note p.286]

Great Pan is Here   Greye La Spina
A Thin Gentleman With Gloves
                                 August Derleth
On Lake Lagore   [v]   Dorothy Gold
Hammer of Cain   James Causey &
                                 Bill Blackbeard
*Herbert West, Reanimator:
   6. The Tomb-Legions   H. P. Lovecraft
[Canadian ed. 36/14, Mar 44, omits Weill;
new cover, adds "The Fisherman's Special"
by H.L.Thomson; see note p.287]

January 1944   37/3 (215)   Harold DeLay
Bon Voyage, Michele [nt]   Seabury Quinn
Dimensional Doors [nt]   Hannes Bok
The Master of Cotswold [nt] Nelson S. Bond
The Golden Goblins   Manly Wade Wellman
House of Hate   Allison V. Harding
He Came at Dusk   Frank Belknap Long
The Hidden Player   Roger S. Vreeland
The Sea Shell   Ray Bradbury
Superstitions and Taboos
   [pic]   Irwin J. Weill
[Canadian ed. 36/15, May 44, see note p.287]

March 1944   37/4 (216)   John Giunta
The Trail of Cthulhu [nt]   August Derleth
The Unbeliever   Seabury Quinn
Hoofs   Manly Wade Wellman
The Shoes of Judge Nichols
                          Stanton A. Coblentz
From the House of the Rat
   Catcher   H. Bedford-Jones
The Peeper   Frank Belknap Long
The Marmot   Allison V. Harding
Reunion   Ray Bradbury
Tragic Magic   Hannes Bok
Ghouls Feeding [v]   Damon Knight
Superstitions and Taboos
   [pic]   Irwin J. Weill
[Canadian ed. 36/15, Jul 44, new cover;
omits Weill; adds "The Totem Pole" Bloch,
(US Aug 39),"The Laugh" Hart (US Aug 39),
"On Lake Lagore"[v] Gold (US Nov 43)]

May 1944   37/5 (217)   M. Brundage
Iron Mask [nt]   Robert Bloch
The Day the World Stood Still
   [nt]   Allison V. Harding
The Letters of Cold Fire
                          Manly Wade Wellman
Man in a Hurry   Alan Nelson
Unpublished Story   H. Bedford-Jones
The Dear Departed   Alice Mary Schnirring
The Lake   Ray Bradbury
The Gothic Window   Dorothy Quick
Fungi From Yuggoth [5v]   H. P. Lovecraft
[Evening Star; St. Toads; The Well; The
             Window; Homecoming]
Superstitions and Taboos
   [pic]   Irwin J. Weill
[Canadian ed. 37/5, Sep 44, see note p.287]

July 1944   37/6 (218)   A. R. Tilburne
Death's Bookkeeper [nt]   Seabury Quinn
The Beasts of Barsac [nt]   Robert Bloch
John Thunstone's Inheritance
                          Manly Wade Wellman
Plane and Fancy   P. Schuyler Miller
Stranger in the Mirror   George N. Laws

Guard in the Dark   Allison V. Harding
The Spare Room   Crawford Sullivan
There Was an Old Woman   Ray Bradbury
The Man Who Wouldn't Hang
                          Stanton A. Coblentz
Lady Macbeth of Pimley Square
                               August Derleth
A Charm [v]   Page Cooper
Weirditties [pic]   Bok & Nichol
Superstitions and Taboos
   [pic]   Irwin J. Weill
[Canadian ed. 37/6, Nov 44, see note p.287]

September 1944   38/1 (219)   A. R. Tilburne
The Shadow Folk [nt]   Edmond Hamilton
The Long Still Streets of
   Evening   Frank Owen
The Seven Seas Are One Allison V. Harding
Bang! You're Dead!   Ray Bradbury
The Devil's Ticket   Robert Bloch
Pacific 421   August Derleth
Sorcery From Thule   Manly Wade Wellman
The Wayward Skunk   Harold Lawlor
The Weirds of the Woodcarver
                               Gardner F. Fox
Monsieur Bluebeard   Emil Petaja
The Path Through the Marsh
   [v]   Leah Bodine Drake
Rats [v]   Glen Ward Dresbach
To the Moon [v]   Stanton A. Coblentz
Superstitions and Taboos
   [pic]   Irwin J. Weill
[Canadian ed. 38/1, Jan 45, omits Coblentz
and Weill; new cover; adds "The Ghost
Punch" Bok (US Nov 44), "Desert Dawn" [v]
Howard (US Mar 39)]

November 1944   38/2 (220)   Matt Fox
The Dweller in Darkness [nt]
                               August Derleth
Ride the El to Doom [nt]
                          Allison V. Harding
The Bat is My Brother [nt]   Robert Bloch
A Gentleman From Prague   Stephen Grendon
The Jar   Ray Bradbury
Dark Mummery   Thorp McClusky
The Dead Man's Hand   Manly Wade Wellman
The Ghost Punch   Hannes Bok
Superstitions and Taboos
   [pic]   Irwin J. Weill
[No Canadian ed., but stories scattered
through other issues, often under false
by-lines]

January 1945   38/3 (221)   M. Brundage
Priestess of the Labyrinth
   [nt]   Edmond Hamilton
Revolt of the Trees [nt]
                          Allison V. Harding
The Green God's Ring [nt]   Seabury Quinn
Ship-in-a-Bottle   P. Schuyler Miller
The Inverness Cape   August Derleth
Thorne on the Threshold Manly Wade Wellman
The Poems   Ray Bradbury
Tatiana   Harold Lawlor
Grave Robbers [v]   Marvin Miller
The Castle [v]   Glen Ward Dresbach
Superstitions and Taboos
   [pic]   Irwin J. Weill
[Canadian ed. 38/3, Mar 45, omits Miller

*and Weill; same cover; adds "The King and
the Oak" [v] Howard (US Feb 39), "Witches
on the Heath" [v] Drake (US Oct 38)]*

March 1945   38/4 (222)   A. R. Tilburne
Lords of the Ghostlands [nt] Seabury Quinn
In the Beginning   H. Bedford-Jones
A Birthday Present for Tommy   Charles King
The Peripatetic Corpse   Harold Lawlor
The Shonokins   Manly Wade Wellman
Please Go 'Way and Let Me
  Sleep   Helen W. Kasson
Alannah   Stephen Grendon
The Tombstone   Ray Bradbury
Second Childhood   Jack Snow
A Sip With Satan   Roger S. Vreeland
Quest Unhallowed [v]   Page Cooper
Bewitched [v]   Willard N. Marsh
Wind Walks Not Alone [v]   Dan Kelly
Superstitions and Taboos
  [pic]   Irwin J. Neill
*[Canadian ed. 38/3, May 45, omits Kelly and
Weill; same cover; adds "Handmade Hero" Lee
Tilburne (US Short Stories Feb 10, 1944)]*

May 1945   38/5 (223)   Pete Kuhlhoff
The Man Who Cried 'Wolf' [nt] Robert Bloch
The Shining Land [nt]   Edmond Hamilton
The Watchers   Ray Bradbury
The Legend of 228   Harold Lawlor
The Lost Day   August Derleth
The Ultimate Paradox   Thorp McClusky
The Music-Box From Hell   Emil Petaja
Blood From a Stone   Manly Wade Wellman
Welcome Home!   Charles King
The Witch [v]   William DeLisle
Superstitions and Taboos
  [pic]   Irwin J. Weill
*[Canadian ed. 38/3, Jul 45, omits Petaja and
Weill; same cover; adds "The Jar" Edward
Banks" (= Bradbury, US Nov 44), "Wind Walks
Not Alone" [v] Kelly (US Mar 45), "Evening
Star" [v] Lovecraft (US May 44)]*

July 1945   38/6 (224)   *L. B. Coye
The Watcher From the Sky [nt]
                            August Derleth
Devil Dog [nt]   Manly Banister
Fog Country   Allison V. Harding
The Dai Sword   Manly Wade Wellman
One Way to Mars   Robert Bloch
The Inn Outside the World Edmond Hamilton
Carnaby's Fish   Carl Jacobi
Quaking Providence   Reeder Gould
The Dead Man   Ray Bradbury
Superstitions and Taboos
  [pic]   Irwin J. Weill
*[Canadian ed. 38/3, Sep 45, now sighted,
see note page 287]*

September 1945   39/1 (225)   Pete Kuhlhoff
The Skull of the Marquis de
  Sade [nt]   Robert Bloch
Take Back That Which Though
  Gavest [nt]   Seabury Quinn
The God-Box   August Derleth
Night of Impossible Shadows
                          Allison V. Harding
Skeleton   Ray Bradbury

Votaress   Emil Petaja
The Dark Brothers   Harold Lawlor
Mr. Lupescu   Anthony Boucher
Outbound   Paul Ernst
The Thing From the Barrens Jim Kjelgaard
Remorse [v]   Page Cooper
The Sorcerer to His Love [v]
                          Clark Ashton Smith
Superstitions and Taboos
  [pic]   Irwin J. Weill
*[Canadian ed. 38/3, Nov 45, omits Weill; same
cover; adds "The Music Box From Hell" by
H. J. Swanza (=Petaja, US May 45)]*

November 1945   39/2 (226)   L. B. Coye
Lost Elysium [nt]   Edmond Hamilton
The Murderous Steam Shovel
  [nt]   Allison V. Harding
The Mad Dancers [nt]   Roger S. Vreeland
Mrs. Lannisfree   August Derleth
The Cranberry Goblet   Harold Lawlor
The Fangs of Tsan-Lo   Jim Kjelgaard
Soul Proprietor   Robert Bloch
The Mirror   Charles King
Midnight Moon [v]   Stanton A. Coblentz
Superstitions and Taboos
  [pic]   Irwin J. Weill
*[Canadian ed. 38/3, Jan 46, omits Weill; same
cover; adds "Ride the El to Doom" Alice
B. Harcraft (=Harding, US Nov 44), "Home-
coming" [v] Lovecraft (US May 44)]*

January 1946   39/3 (227)   A. R. Tilburne
Kurban [nt]   Seabury Quinn
Chariots of San Fernando [nt]
                           Malcolm Jameson
Sin's Doorway   Manly Wade Wellman
Seed   Jack Snow
Mr. Bauer and the Atoms   Fritz Leiber
Satan's Phonograph   Robert Bloch
Pikeman   August Derleth
The Diversions of Mme. Gomorra
                            Harold Lawlor
All the Time in the World   Charles King
*Recapture [v]   H. P. Lovecraft
Superstitions and Taboos
  [pic]   Irwin J. Weill
*[Canadian ed. 38/4, Mar 46, same cover; omits
Weill; adds "The Bat is My Brother" R. J.
Comber (=Bloch, US Nov 44)]*

March 1946   39/4 (228)   L. B. Coye
Twice Cursed [nt]   Manly Wade Wellman
The Man in Crescent Terrace
  [nt]   Seabury Quinn
The Bogy Man Will Get You   Robert Bloch
Dead Man's Shoes   Stephen Grendon
Chanu   Jim Kjelgaard
The Jonah   Emil Petaja
Tunnel Terror   Allison V. Harding
The Traveller   Ray Bradbury
Tree Woman [v]   Dorothy Quick
Forgetful Hour [v]   Yetza Gillespie
Superstitions and Taboos
  [pic]   Irwin J. Weill
*[Canadian ed. 38/4, May 46; same cover; adds
"The Dead Man's Hands" T. K. Whitely
(=Wellman, US Nov 44)]*

May 1946   39/5 (229)   Ronald Clyne
The Valley of the Gods [nt]
                                Edmond Hamilton
Three in Chains [nt]   Seabury Quinn
Midnight   Jack Snow
The Man in Purple   Dorothy Quick
The Smiling People   Ray Bradbury
†Once There Was an Elephant   R. H. Phelps
Rain, Rain, Go Away!   Gardner F. Fox
The Silver Highway   Harold Lawlor
†Frozen Fear   Robert Bloch
†The Haunted Stairs [v]   Yetza Gillespie
†The Nixie's Pool [v]   Leah Bodine Drake
†Superstitions and Taboos
   [pic]   Irwin J. Weill
*[Canadian ed. 38/4, Jul 46, omits those
marked †;same cover; adds "The Dweller
in Darkness" Derleth (US Nov 44)]*

July 1946   39/6 (230)   Matt Fox
Shonokin Town [nt]   Manly Wade Wellman
Catspaws [nt]   Seabury Quinn
The Night   Ray Bradbury
The Wings   Allison V. Harding
The Man Who Told the Truth
          Jim Kjelgaard & Robert Bloch
I'll Be Glad When I'm Dead   Charles King
The Cinnabar Redhead   Harold Lawlor
The Shingler   E. L. Wright
For Love of a Phantom   Stanton A. Coblentz
Ghost   P. Schuyler Miller
Moon Phantoms [v]   Dorothy Haynes Madle
Long Watch [v]   Dorothy Quick
Superstitions and Taboos
   [pic]   Irwin J. Weill
*[Canadian ed. 38/4, Sep 46, omits King; adds
"Once There Was an Elephant" Phelps & "The
Nixie's Pool" [v] L.B.Drake (both US May 46)]*

September 1946   39/7 (231)   Pete Kuhlhoff
Lotte [nt]   Seabury Quinn
Day of Judgement   Edmond Hamilton
Enoch   Robert Bloch
Alice and the Allergy   Fritz Leiber
Not Human   Bert David Ross
The Horn   Charles King
The Machine   Allison V. Harding
Six Flights to Terror   Manly Banister
Polar Vortex   Malcolm M. Ferguson
Threshold of Endurance   Betsy Emmons
Xerxes' Hut   Harold Lawlor
*The Port [v]   H. P. Lovecraft
Superstitions and Taboos
   [pic]   Irwin J. Weill
*[Canadian ed. 38/4, Nov 46, omits Emmons;
adds "Frozen Fear" R.T.Bowen (=Bloch, US
May 46)]*

November 1946   39/8 (232)   Boris Dolgov
Spawn of the Green Abyss
   [nt]   C. Hall Thompson
Mayaya's Little Green Men   Harold Lawlor
Superstitions and Taboos
   [pic]   Irwin J. Weill
Let's Play "Poison"   Ray Bradbury
A Collector of Stones   August Derleth
The Door [v]   Harriet A. Bradfield
Eyes in the Dark   Seabury Quinn
Lizzie Borden Took an Axe   Robert Bloch
Shipmate   Allison V. Harding

Heard on the Roof at Midnight
   [v]   Leah Bodine Drake
Frogfather   Manly Wade Wellman
*[Canadian ed. 38/4, Jan 47, omits Bloch and
Weill;same cover; adds "I'll Be Glad When
I'm Dead" King (US Jul 46), "A Gentleman
From Prague" Grendon (US Nov 44), "Thresh-
old of Endurance" Emmons (US Sep 46), "The
Extra Passenger" Grendon (US Jan 47)]*

January 1947   39/9 (233)   A. R. Tilburne
The Hog [nt]   William Hope Hodgson
The King of Shadows [nt] Edmond Hamilton
The House Beyond Midnight
   [nt]   Allison V. Harding
Shadow of Melas [nt]   Roger S. Vreeland
The Final Hour   Chester S. Geier
†The Extra Passenger   Stephen Grendon
Cellmate   Theodore Sturgeon
†There Was an Old Woman   Charles King
The Handler   Ray Bradbury
†The Seal-Woman's Daughter
   [v]   Leah Bodine Drake
†Superstitions and Taboos
   [pic]   Irwin J. Weill
*The Familiars [v]   H. P. Lovecraft
The Pigeon Flyers [v]   H. P. Lovecraft
*[Canadian ed. 38/4, Mar 47, omits those
marked †;same cover; adds "The Nameless
City" Lovecraft (US Nov 38), "Leonora"
Worrell (US *Nov 38)]*

March 1947   39/10 (234)   Boris Dolgov
Mr. George [nt]   Stephen Grendon
*Venturer of the Martian
   Mimics [nt]   Eric Frank Russell
The Terror in Teakwood [nt] Harold Lawlor
Fluffy   Theodore Sturgeon
Hoodooed   Seabury Quinn
The Immortal Lancer   Allison V. Harding
Sweets to the Sweet   Robert Bloch
On a Weird Planet [v] Stanton A. Coblentz
†*Continuity [v]   H. P. Lovecraft
†A Memory [v]   H. P. Lovecraft
†Superstitions and Taboos
   [pic]   Irwin J. Weill
*[Canadian ed. 38/4, May 47, omits those
marked †;same cover; adds "Lizzie Borden
Took an Axe" Herbert Scanlon (= Bloch, US
Nov 46)]*

May 1947   39/11 (235)   Matt Fox
The Place With Many Windows
   [nt]   Allison V. Harding
Masked Ball [nt]   Seabury Quinn
The Corbie Door [nt]   Carl Jacobi
Mistress Sary   William Tenn
The Lifted Veil   Ray Cummings
The Black Madonna   Harold Lawlor
Loup-Garou   Manly Banister
The Trap   Walter Harwood
Superstitions and Taboos
   [pic]   Irwin J. Weill
*[Canadian ed. 38/4, Jul 47, omits Weill;
same cover; adds "There Was An Old Woman"
King (US Jan 47), "The Haunted Stairs" [v]
Yetza Gillespie (US May 46), "Continuity"
[v]Lovecraft (US*Mar 47)]*

To the Chimera [v]   Clark Ashton Smith
Death's Bouquet   Peter Phillips
The Devil's Lottery
          Mary Elizabeth Counselman
[Canadian edition identical]

November 1948   41/1 (244)   John Giunta
The Perfect Host [nt]   Theodore Sturgeon
The House on Forest Street
    [nt]   Allison V. Harding
The Indian Spirit Guide   Robert Bloch
Blessed Are the Meek   Stephen Grendon
Incident at the Galloping
    Horse   Carl Jacobi
Tryst Beyond the Years
          Malcolm Kenneth Murchie
Such Stuff as Dreams   Seabury Quinn
The Ponderer   Eric Frank Russell
The Ghostlings [v]   Dorothy Quick
Weirdisms [pic]   Lee Brown Coye
[Canadian edition identical]

January 1949   41/2 (245) Lee Brown Coye
Four From Jehlam [nt] Allison V. Harding
Our Fair City [nt]   Robert Heinlein
Food for Demons   E. Everett Evans
The Thirteenth Floor   Frank Gruber
Open Season on the ... Bottoms
          Snowden T. Herrick
The Great Stone Death   John D. MacDonald
Lover in Scarlet   Harold Lawlor
The Sorcerer's Apprentice   Robert Bloch
The Big Shot   Eric Frank Russell
Balu   Stephen Grendon
The Bonan of Baladewa
          Mary Elizabeth Counselman
The Heads on Easter Island
    [v]   Leah Bodine Drake
A Curse [v]   Page Cooper
Weirdisms [pic]   Lee Brown Coye
[Canadian edition identical]

March 1949   41/3 (246)   Matt Fox
The Testament of Claiborne
    Boyd [nt]   August Derleth
The Martian and the Moron
    [nt]   Theodore Sturgeon
The Strange Island of Dr.
    Nork [nt]   Robert Bloch
The Holiday [nt]   Allison V. Harding
The Wizard of Bird-in-Hand
    [nt]   Arthur J. Burks
The Will of Raminchantra
          Stanton A. Coblentz
The Other Santa   Thorp McClusky
Weirdisms [pic]   Lee Brown Coye
[Canadian edition identical]

May 1949   41/4 (247)   John Giunta
The Damp Man Again [nt]
          Allison V. Harding
The Inner Man [nt]   Arthur J. Burks
Vampire Kith and Kin [nt] Seabury Quinn
Matthew South and Company   Carl Jacobi
The Door Beyond   Harold Lawlor
The Scrawny One   Anthony Boucher
Phoebe   Malcolm Kenneth Murchie
The Antimacassar   Greye La Spina
But Not to Dream   John D. MacDonald
Kingsridge 214   August Derleth
[Canadian edition identical]

July 1949   41/5 (248)   Matt Fox
Come and Go Mad [nt]   Fredric Brown
The Masher [nt]   Ewen Whyte
From the Vasty Deep H. Russell Wakefield
The Blue Spectacles   Stephen Grendon
How Strange My Love   Russell Branch
The Ubiquitous Professor
    Karr   Stanton A. Coblentz
In the X-Ray   Fritz Leiber, Jr
The Previous Incarnation   Harold Lawlor
Floral Tribute   Robert Bloch
Dark O' the Moon   Seabury Quinn
[Canadian edition identical]
[UK edition, unnumbered/undated (Nov 49)]

September 1949   41/6 (249)   M. Labonski
One Foot and the Grave [nt]
          Theodore Sturgeon
The Deep Drowse [nt] Allison V. Harding
The Rainbow Jade [nt]   Gardner F. Fox
Country House   Ewen Whyte
The Slayers and the Slain August Derleth
The Shot-Tower Ghost
          Mary Elizabeth Counselman
Blindman's Buff   Seabury Quinn
Thinker   Malcolm Kenneth Murchie
The Woman on the Balcony   Dorothy Quick
Weirdisms [pic]   Lee Brown Coye
[Canadian edition identical]
[No UK edition]

November 1949   42/1 (250)   Matt Fox
The Underbody [nt]   Allison V. Harding
These Debts Are Yours [nt] Arthur J. Burks
Conscience Maketh Cowards   Seabury Quinn
Out of the Wrack I Rise
          H. Russell Wakefield
Murder Man   Ewen Whyte
Twilight Play   August Derleth
The Green Window Mary Elizabeth Counselman
Stranger at Dusk   Malcolm Kenneth Murchie
The Barren Field   Yves Theriault
Skydrift   Emil Petaja
Terror Under Eridu   Malcolm M. Ferguson
Demon Lure [v]   Harriet A. Bradfield
Forest God [v]   Dorothy Quick
Weirdisms [pic]   Lee Brown Coye
[Canadian edition identical]
[UK edition (No.2), undated (Jan 50)]

January 1950   42/2 (251)   Matt Fox
Black Harvest of Moraine
    [nt]   Arthur J. Burks
The Ormolu Clock   August Derleth
In That Same Moment   Manly Wade Wellman
The Smiling Face Mary Elizabeth Counselman
The Urbanite   Ewen Whyte
The Mysterious Miss Maltra
          Stanton A. Coblentz
The Last Train   Fredric Brown
The Mask of Don Alfredo   Mal Bissell
Outside of Time   Carroll John Daly
The Family   Margaret St. Clair
The Cactus   Mildred Johnson
Dark Rosaleen   Seabury Quinn
Sea King's Daughter [v]   Dorothy Quick
The Vision [v]   Leah Bodine Drake
[Canadian edition identical]
[UK edition (No.3), undated (May 50)]

September 1951   43/6 (261) Lee Brown Coye
*Gimlet Eye Gunn [nt]   H. Bedford-Jones
The Metamorphosis of
    Earth [nt]   Clark Ashton Smith
Rapport   Mary Elizabeth Counselman
The Ring of Bastet   Seabury Quinn
Camel Vengeance   Garnett Radcliffe
Church in the Jungles   Arthur J. Burks
*A Square of Canvas   Anthony M. Rud
Sleepers [v]   Dorothy Quick
[Canadian edition identical]
[UK edition, No.13, undated (Jan 52)]

November 1951   44/1 (262)   Kelly Freas
Hideaway [nt]   Everil Worrell
*Pigeons From Hell [nt]   Robert E. Howard
The Brides of Baxter Creek   C. J. Barr
*Dagon   H. P. Lovecraft
The Bird   Margaret St. Clair
Hector   Michael West
The Night They Crashed the
    Party   Robert Bloch
Fling the Dust Aside   Seabury Quinn
*Was it Murder?   H. C. McNeile
When the Night Wind Howls
        L. Sprague de Camp & Fletcher Pratt
Hallowe'en Candle [v]   Yetza Gillespie
Unexpiated [v]   Harriet A. Bradfield
[Canadian edition identical - last issue]
[UK edition, No.14, undated (Mar 52)]

January 1952   44/2 (263)   Jon Arfstrom
The Black Island [nt]   August Derleth
Lucy Comes to Stay   Robert Bloch
The Seamstress   E. Everett Evans
*The Guard of Honor   Paul Suter
Lover's Meeting   Harold Lawlor
Cat's Cradle   E. W. Tomlinson
Cat-Eyes [v]   Harriet A. Bradfield
The Iron Hands of Katzaveere
    David Lewis Eynon
Not Altogether Sleep [v]
    Clark Ashton Smith
Sonnet for the Psychoanalysts
    [v]   Clark Ashton Smith
*Ooze [nt]   Anthony M. Rud
[UK edition, No.15, undated (Apr 52)]

March 1952   44/3 (264)   Joseph Eberle
Morne Perdu [nt]   Alice Drayton Farnham
*The Horror at Red Hook [nt]
    H. P. Lovecraft
The Monkey Ship   Garnett Radcliffe
The Mask   Curtis W. Casewit
The Scarred Soul   Seabury Quinn
The Prism   Mary Elizabeth Counselman
The Place of Desolation   August Derleth
*Jungle Beasts   William P. Barron
O Golden-Tongued Romance [v]
    Clark Ashton Smith
The Bride of Death [v]
    Joseph Howard Krucher
[UK edition, No.16, undated (Aug 52)]

May 1952   44/4 (265)   Virgil Finlay
The Lamia in the Penthouse
    [nt]   Thorp McClusky
Rhythmic Formula   Arthur J. Burks
A Bit of Moss   Suzanne Pickett
*The Eighth Green Man   G. G. Pendarves

She Wore a Black Rose   Frederick Sanders
Dark Laughter   Garnett Radcliffe
*The Fifth Candle   Cyril Mand
The Little Tree   C. F. Birdsall
The Night Road   August Derleth
The Devil of Maniara   Douglas Leach
Father's Vampire   Alvin Taylor &
    Len J. Moffatt
Double Haunt [pic] Joseph Howard Krucher
Out of Space [v]   Dorothy Quick
Ghost Port [v]   Pauline Booker
[UK edition, No.17, undated (Oct 52)]

July 1952   44/5 (266)   Jon Arfstrom
Hell's Bells   Duncan H. Munroe
Which's Witch   Harold Lawlor
The Emperor's Letter   David Eynon
Elmer Bittersnitt and the
    Three Bears   Harry Botsford
There Was Soot on the Cat Suzanne Pickett
The Green Parrot   Joseph P. Brennan
*The Temple of Servants   Paul Ernst
The Plaid   Abrach
Live Evil   Emil Petaja
The Lakes of Nai Loodie   Donald F. Vieweg
*Alethia Phrikoides [v]   H. P. Lovecraft
Black Candles [v]   Yetza Gillespie
A Weirdutation [pic] Joseph Howard Krucher
[UK edition, No.18, undated (Jan 53)]

September 1952   44/6 (267) Virgil Finlay
*Hallowe'en in a Suburb [v] H. P. Lovecraft
Island of the Hands   Margaret St. Clair
Table Number Sixteen   Curtis W. Casewit
One Fantastic Day   Frederick Sanders
A Habit Out of History   David Eynon
The Archive [v]   Henry T. Simmons
Where To, Please?   L. Sprague de Camp &
    Fletcher Pratt
*The Phantom Express   H. Thompson Rich
Sa'antha   E. Everett Evans
The Lost Path   August Derleth
The Singing Shadow [v]   Yetza Gillespie
*The Sin-Eater [nt]   G. G. Pendarves
[UK edition, No.19, undated (Feb 53)]

November 1952   44/7 (268) A. Di Giannurio
Black as the Night   Alice Farnham
The Unicorn   Frank Owen
Astra   Arthur J. Burks
The Artist and the Door   Dorothy Quick
The Japanese Tea Set   Francis J. O'Neil
Fermentation   Curtis W. Casewit
*The Chapel of Mystic Horror
    [nt]   Seabury Quinn
The Mermaid [v]   Leah Bodine Drake
*The Chain   Hamilton Craigie
[UK edition, No.20, undated (Apr 53)]

January 1953   44/8 (269)   Kelly Freas
Once There Was a Little Girl
    [nt]   Everil Worrell
The Phantom Soldier at
    Ticonderoga   Dr. Cyrus Macmillan
I Can't Wear White   Suzanne Pickett
The Gloves   Garnett Radcliffe
*The Werewolf of Ponkert [nt]
    H. Warner Munn
Wet Straw   Richard Matheson
Red Ghosts in Kentucky [v] Leah Bodine Drake

Spring 1981   48/2 (285)   Tom Barber
[both these issues bear the same date]
*The Night Ocean [nt]
                H. P. Lovecraft & Robert H. Barlow
Boy Blue   Steve Rasnic Tem
Fear   Joseph Payne Brennan
Valse Triste   Ray Faraday Nelson
The Song of the Gallows
  Tree [v]   Robert E. Howard
*The Feast in the Abbey   Robert Bloch
The Lamashtu Amulet
                 Mary Elisabeth Counselman
Something in the Moonlight   Lin Carter
Trick or Treat   Ramsey Campbell
*Liberation [v]   Robert A. W. Lowndes
*The Guardian [v]   Robert A. W. Lowndes
The Descent Into the Abyss
            Clark Ashton Smith & Lin Carter
*The Sapphire Siren [nt]   Nictzin Dyalhis
The Sombrus Tower   Tanith Lee

Fall 1981   48/3 (286)   Tom Barber
The Chinese Woman [na] Evangeline Walton
The Messenger   Steve Rasnic Tem
*To the Nightshade [v] Clark Ashton Smith
The Opposite House [nt]
                 John & Diane Brizzolara
The Guardian of the Idol
          Gerald W. Page & Robert E. Howard
The Black Garden   Carl Jacobi

*The House of the Temple [nt] Brian Lumley
*The Red Brain   Donald Wandrei
*The Summons [v]   Robert A. W. Lowndes
*The Viola [v]   Robert A. W. Lowndes
Nobody Ever Goes There   Manly Wade Wellman
The Summons of Nuguth-Yug
                 Gary Myers & Marc Laidlaw
*The Wind That Tramps the World   Frank Owen
The Winfield Inheritance   Lin Carter

Summer 1983   48/4 (287)   Tom Barber
The Next Glade [nt]   Robert Aickman
Crocuses   Charles Sheffield
The Belfrey   James Anderson
There Are No Ghosts in
  Catholic Spain [v]   Ray Bradbury
Homecoming   Frank Belknap Long
Compliments of the Season John Brizzolara
The City of Dread [nt] Lloyd Arthur Eshbach
The Doom Chant of Than-Kul
  [v]   Robert E. Howard
Save the Children!   Steve Rasnic Tem
The Sea Gods [v]   Clark Ashton Smith
*Ooze [nt]   Anthony M. Rud
Late Night Final   Stuart H. Stock
The Vengeance of Yig   Lin Carter

                    ***

==
NOTES REGARDING THE CANADIAN EDITION
==

   The notes appended to the 1942-47 issues regarding the Canadian edition were based
on numerous but incomplete details supplied by Grant Thiessen and the Toronto Spaced-
Out Library. Attempts to obtain a full file of notes were thwarted until, at the last
minute, I was delighted to receive from Chester Cuthbert a full and very complete listing of the contents. Too late to amend the details above it at least allows me this
chance to provide full addenda and corrigenda to the notes. The dates first given below
relate to the US edition, as listed.

January 1942 *[Canadian 36/3, May 1942]*
New Cover: artist Edmond Good.
*[Note: it is possible, though not certain,
that Good painted all the Canadian covers
for the issues May 42-Jan 45]*

May 1942 *[Canadian 37/1, September 1942]*
New cover; omits Arthur, La Spina & Cole;
adds "Never the Twain" Leonard White [=
Seabury Quinn(US Sep 42)],"Inheritance"
[v] S.S.Hager (US Jul 40),"The Book and the
Beast" Robert Arthur (new, not in US WT
until Mar 43),"Ears of the Dead"[v]James
Arthur (US Jul 40),"Bad Company"[v]L.B.Drake
(US Mar 41),"Lover of Caladiums"[v]Maria
Moravsky (new, US WT May 43),"Realization"
[v] W.Parry (US Jan 40),"The Dream"[v] no
credit (= Edith Hurley,US Oct 39),"The Plumed Serpent"[v]H.Calhoun (US May 42).

July 1942 *[Canadian 37/1, November 1942]*
New cover; omits [v] de Lisle; adds "Dreamer" [v] C.S.Youd (US Mar 41).

September 1942 *[Canadian 36/7, January 1943]*
New cover. Omits Quinn and Weill. Adds
"Fear: A Fantasy"[v]W.D.Vermilyea(US Feb 36)

"The Gipsy's Hand"A.D.Cole (US May 42),
"Salvage"[v:US Feb 36]and "Haunted" [v:US
Mar 36]both A.I.Tooke,"Ghost For a Night"
R.Arthur (US May 42),"The Devil's Swamp"
[v]R. Avrett (US Mar 36),"Flight of Time"
[v]J.M.Barnard (US Mar 41),"Winter Night"
[v]A.Olsen (US May 40),"Painted Cave"[v]J.B.
Green.

November 1942 *[Canadian 36/8, March 1943]*
New cover. Omits Flynn, Moravsky & Weill.
Adds "Ol' Sancho"[v]& "Judge Bean's Bear"
[v] both S.Omar Barker (from US *Short Sto-
ries* Jul 10,1941 and Mar 25,1942), "The
Deadly Theory" G.La Spina (US May 42), "A
Weird Prophecy" K.Gary (US May 40).

January 1943 *[Canadian 36/9, May 1943]*
New cover. Omits Weill. Adds "The Sui-
cide's Awakening"[v] G.Wright (US May 25),
"Edge of the Cliff" D.Quick (US Mar 41).

March 1943 *[Canadian 36/10, July 1943]*
New cover. No omits. Adds "On Pell Street"
F.Owen (US Jul 40),"Return"[v]L.M.Ames (US
Nov 31). ["The Book and the Beast"R.Arthur
is in this issue and the Can.Sep 42]

May 1943   *[Canadian 36/11,September 1943]*
New cover. Omits Weill and Moravsky. Adds
"Portrait of a Bride" E.Peirce,Jr.(US Jan
40), "Forbidden Cupboard" F.Garfield (US
Jan 40), "Twister" M.E.Counselman(US Jan 40)

July 1943   *[Canadian 36/12, November 1943]*
New cover. Omits Quick, Smith & Weill.
Adds "Realization" [v] H.Warner,Jr.(US Jan
40), "The Little Man" C.Ball, "My Tomb"[v]
J.E.Warren,Jr., "Dupin and Another" [v] V.
Starrett and "Return From Death" B. Bryan
(all US Aug 39)

September 1943   *[Canadian 36/13,January 44]*
New cover. Omits Drake and Weill. Adds
"Spawn" P.S.Miller (US Aug 39).

November 1943 *[Canadian 36/14, March 1944]*
As noted. Also adds "Voice in a Veteran's
Ear" [v] G.T. Field (US Aug 39) and omits
[v] by L.B. Drake.

January 1944   *[Canadian 36/15, May 1944]*
As noted, but omits Weill.

May 1944   *[Canadian 37/5, September 1944]*
New cover. Omits Lovecraft and Weill.
Adds "Trinities" [v: US Apr 39] & "Crazy
Nell" [v: US Feb 39] both E.D.Kramer; "The
Ghost Kings" [v] R.E.Howard (US Dec 38).

July 1944   *[Canadian 37/6, November 1944]*
New cover. Omits Cooper,Bok, Nichol and
Weill. Adds "In an Old Street" [v] V.Star-
rett (US Apr 39), "Recompense" [v] R.E. Howard (US Nov 38), "To the Moon" [v] S.A. Coblentz (US Sep 44), "Lips of the Dead" W.J.
Stamper (US*Jan 40)

September 1944 - May 1945 *[Canadian 38/1*
January 1945 - 38/3 July 1945]
Details as noted.

July 1945   *[Canadian 38/3, September 1945]*
Omits Weill. Adds "The Window" [v] H.P.
Lovecraft (US May 44), "St.Toads" [v] J.H.
Brownlow (= H.P.Lovecraft,US May 44), "The
Ghost Punch" H.Bok (US Nov 44; Can Jan 45)

September 1945 - November 1951 *[Canadian*
38/3 November 1945 - 44/1 November 1951]
Details as noted.

* * *

WEIRD TERROR TALES

*A weird fantasy digest magazine published quarterly by Health Knowledge Inc.,
140 Fifth Ave., New York. Editor: Robert A.W. Lowndes. See also companion
Magazine of Horror and other titles.*

Winter 1969/70   1/1   *Virgil Finlay
*Dead Legs   Edmond Hamilton
*The House and the Brain
                    Edward Bulwer-Lytton
*Ms.Found in a Bottle   Edgar Allan Poe
*He   H. P. Lovecraft
*The Beast of Averoigne Clark Ashton Smith
*The Whispering Thing   Eddy C. Bertin
*The Dead-Alive [nt]
            Nat Schachner & Arthur L. Zagat

Summer 1970   1/2   *Virgil Finlay
*The Dead Walk Softly [nt]
                    Sewell Peaslee Wright
*The Shadow on the Sky   August Derleth
The Laundromat   Dick Donley
*The Man Who Never Came Back
                        Pearl Norton Swet
*The Web of Living Death [nt]
                        Seabury Quinn

Fall 1970   1/3   Richard Schmand
*Stragella [nt]   Hugh B. Cave
*The Girdle   Joseph McCord
*The Trap [nt]   Henry S. Whitehead
*The Church Stove at Raebrudafisk
                        G. Appleby Terrill
The Cellar Room   Steffan B. Aletti
*The Wheel   H. Warner Munn

                   ***

WEIRD WINDOW

A British small press magazine duplicated in quarto format and published by David A. Sutton, King's Norton, Birmingham. Editor: James D. Oddey (a pseudonym for Sutton).

* * *

WEIRD WORLD

A British weird fantasy small pulp magazine published by Gannet Press, 77 Claughton Road, Birkenhead, Cheshire. No editor credited.

[Winter 1955]   1/1   Roger Davis
White Zombie   Ricky Drayton
Vengeance of the Snake   James O'Connelly
Jonathan Elder's Letter   Lilian Kirby
Woman Running   Justin Croome
There Are Harps in Hell, Too
                                Charles E. Price
The Dreamer   Hecate Muller
The Man Who Loved Cats   Konstantin Faber
On Information Received   Hamilton Park

[Spring 1956]   1/2   Roger Davis
Man Wanted   Richard James
Creatures of the Blitz   Henry Carter
The God From the Machine   Andy Jenks
The Charlady Who Travelled
    Faster Than Light   Anthony Righton
The Great Zimilcof   Barry Pearson
*The Fall of the House of
    Usher   Edgar Allan Poe
The Kiss of Death   John Leonards
The Jewelled Dagger   Alistair Wallace
Witches' Song [v]   'Tiberius'
A Dream [v]   [no credit]

***

290

WHISPERS

A small press weird fantasy magazine published irregularly by Whispers Press, currently of 70 Highland Ave., Binghamton, New York. Publisher/Editor: Stuart David Schiff. The leading small press magazine, it was originally intended as Whispers From Arkham *serving as a continuation of Derleth's* The Arkham Collector. *Early issues carried an extensive coverage of news and developments in the fan-press and in August 1976 Schiff issued a mini-*Whispers *which consisted entirely of news and thus does not feature in the following.*

<u>July 1973</u>   1/1 (1)   Tim Kirk
Renunciation of the Right of
  First Option to Buy Arkham
  House [announcement]   Donald Wandrei
Outsider [v]   Walter Shedlofsky
The House of Cthulhu   Brian Lumley
Toward a Greater Appreciation
  of H. P. Lovecraft: The
  Analytic Approach [a]
                    Prof. Dirk W. Mosig
The Urn   David Riley
Robert Howard and the Stars
  [a1/2]   E. Hoffmann Price
The Cats of Anubis [v]   Robert E. Howard
The Willow Platform   Joseph Payne Brennan
The Altar [v]   Richard L. Tierney
Cradle Song For a Baby
  Werewolf [v]   H. Warner Munn
Guillotine [v]   Walter Shedlofsky

<u>December 1973</u>   1/2 (2)   Steve Fabian
The Way to Casm's Place   Henry Hasse
The Story of Obbok   Darrell Schweitzer
The Prophet From Providence
  [a]   Prof. Dirk W. Mosig
About *Gather, Darkness!* and
  Conjure Wife [a]   Fritz Leiber
The Song of the Bone   Dave Drake
Robert E. Howard and the Stars
  [a2/2]   E. Hoffmann Price
The Bait   Fritz Leiber
In Halls of Fantasy [v] Richard L. Tierney
The Vampire in America [a]
                    Manly Wade Wellman
Egypt [v]   Robert E. Howard
A Weather Report From the Top of
  the Stairs   James Sallis & David Lunde

<u>March 1974</u>   1/3 (3) Lee Brown Coye
          [special Lee Brown Coye issue]
The Shortest Way   Dave Drake
Lee Brown Coye: An Appreciation
  [a]   Gahan Wilson
Lee Brown Coye: An Appreciation
  [a]   Stuart David Schiff
Lee Brown Coye: A Folio [ap]
                          Lee Brown Coye
*Chips and Shavings [ts] Lee Brown Coye
Elizabeth, My Love ....   G. E. Symonds
Sticks   Karl Edward Wagner

<u>July 1974</u>   1/4 (4)   Tim Kirk
*The Inglorious Rise of the
  Catsmeat Man   Robin Smyth
The Sea Girl [v]   Robert E. Howard
The Sails of Fancy [a]   Fritz Leiber
The White Ship [ap]   [various]
*The White Ship [holograph
  manuscript]   H. P. Lovecraft
They Will Not Hush
            James Sallis & David Lunde
To Gorice XII, King in Carce
  [v]   Richard L. Tierney
The Farmhouse   David Riley
The Abandoned Boudoir [v]
                    Joseph Payne Brennan
Ice Forest at Midnight [v]
                    Joseph Payne Brennan
The Soft Wall   Dennis Etchison
The Demoniac Footsteps [pic] Steve Fabian

<u>November 1974</u>   2/1 (5) Vincent DiFate
Take Me, For Instance   Hugh B. Cave
Zukala's Jest [v]   Robert E. Howard
Reflections   Pemle K. Ennis

Old Woman   Joel Hagen
Carib Grotesques [ap]   John Stewart
The House at Evening   Frances Garfield
Beyond Any Measure [nt] Karl Edward Wagner

August 1982   5/1-2 (17-18) John Stewart
On The Shining and Other
   Perpetrations [a]   Stephen King
Before the Play [nt]   Stephen King
Return of the Curse of the
   Son of Mr King: Book Two [a]
                               David J. Schow
It Grows on You   Stephen King
Gunslinger Folio [ap]   John Stewart
Preparations For the Game   Steve Rasnic
Lovey's Rival   Juleen Brantingham
In Quest of Something   Robert Chilson
Red-Cloak   Ellen Kushner
The Other Room   Lisa Tuttle
Mort in Bed   Richard A. Lupoff
A Posthumous Bequest   David Campton
An End to Dreaming   Janet E. Morris
The Dancer in the Flames   David Drake
A Night on the Docks   Freff

October 1983   5/3-4 (19-20)   K. Johnson
The Shadow's Edge: an Interview
   with Whitley Strieber [in]
                               Paul R. Gagne
Perverts   .   Whitley Strieber
Catmagic [ex]   Whitley Strieber
The Legend of Santa Claus C. Bruce Hunter
When I Grow Up   Charles L. Grant
The Masai Witch   Stephen Goldin
Danse Macabre   Phillip C. Heath
Ray Bradbury: Literature as
   Lark [in]   Robert W. Smith
The Phantom Knight   Darrell Schweitzer
The Ventriloquist's Daughter
                           Juleen Brantingham
One for the Horrors   David J. Schow
A Lovecraftian Art Folio [ap]
               Roman Scott, Richard Huber,
      Dave Carson, John Goodier, Earl Geier
In the Kingdom of the Thorn   Janet Fox
Let No One Weep for Poor Sally
   Karnes   Charles L. Grant
Give Me a Little Whistle   Michael Bishop
The Hollow Grave   Gerald W. Page
Pulling the Hagen   Kevin Egan
Along About Sundown   Manly Wade Wellman
Final Game   Hugh B. Cave
Home Call   Dennis Etchison & CC Palaski

***

WITCHCRAFT & SORCERY

A neo-pulp fantasy magazine published irregularly (originally bi-monthly) by Fantasy Publishing Co. Inc., 1855 West Main St., Alhambra, California. Editor: Gerald W. Page. Although a continuation of the magazine Coven 13 *(hence the issue numbering) W&S had a totally different format, nature of content and editorial approach, let alone name, and as such can to all intents be regarded as a different magazine.*

Jan/Feb 1971   1/5   Jerry Burge
*The Great Pyramid of Giza
  [v]   L. Sprague de Camp
Welcome as Love Come [v]   Anthony Sandor
The Dark Door   Leo P. Kelley
Musings [v]   Robert E. Howard
House of Evil   Pauline C. Smith
The Momentary Ghost   Carleton Grindle
Portrait of Things to Come   Leon Zeldis
The Ideas   Edith Ogutsch & Ross Rocklynne
*Four Letters to Clark Ashton
  Smith [ltr]   H. P. Lovecraft
Ghost Tour [a]   Andre Norton
Mistress of Death   Robert E. Howard &
                          Gerald W. Page
Wind Magic   Edmund Shirlan
*The Forgotten [v]   Lin Carter
The Hate   Terri Pinckard
Jade Pagoda [col]   E. Hoffmann Price
The Rat and the Snake   A. E. van Vogt
Department of Pointed Tales:
  1. Bruce [ss]   Saliitha Grey
  2. Embarkation of Evil [ss] W. S. Cobun, Jr
  3. Smoke [ss]   Leo Tifton
Tower of Blood [nt]   David A. English
Were-Creature   Kenneth Pembrooke

May 1971   1/6   Steve Fritz
Flight [v]   Robert E. Howard
A Garland of Three Roses From
  Atlantis [3v]   Donald Sidney-Fryer
  [O Ebon-Colored Rose; Rose Verdastre;
  Song]
Dragon's Daughter [nt]   E. Hoffmann Price
Mother Love   Brian Lumley
Ghost Lake   August Derleth
Witch Ways [pic]   R. Edwards Jennings
Silverheels   Glen Cook

Department of Pointed Tales:
  1. Dragon Saga [ss]   Saliitha Grey
  2. The Lorn of Toucher   Ross Rocklynne
Tomorrow's Mask   Emil Petaja
Jade Pagoda [col]   E. Hoffmann Price
Circe's Laughter   Carleton Grindle
The Grimoire [col]   Gerald W. Page
Fire Master   Edmund Shirlan
Hungry Ghosts   David A. English

[Winter] 1972   No.7   Bob Maurus
Hopes of Dreams [v]   Robert E. Howard
Thirst [nt]   Gerald W. Page
Price of a Demon   Gary Brandner
Witch Ways [pic]   R. Edwards Jennings
Department of Pointed Tales:
  1. In the Sorcerer's Garden
    [ss]   Susan M. Patrick
  2. Appointment in Samarkand [ss] Glen Cook
  3. The Dancing Girl of
    Isphatam [ss]   Leo Tifton

[Summer] 1972   No.8   Jerry Burge
The Castle at the World's
  Edge [nt]   Carleton Grindle
Gola's Hell   Emil Petaja
Sergi   Dale C. Donaldson
Jade Pagoda [col]   E. Hoffmann Price

[Summer] 1973   No.9   Stephen E. Fabian
Yesterday's Witch   Gahan Wilson
Today's Witch   Dale C. Donaldson
Tomorrow's Witch   Carleton Grindle
A Witch For All Seasons   Gans T. Field
Yuggoth Comes to Providence
  [v]   L. Sprague de Camp
The Archangeli Syndrome Deane Dickensheet
Jade Pagoda [col]   E. Hoffmann Price

294

Death God's Doom [nt]   E. C. Tubb

[Fall] 1974   No.10   Jeff Jones
Othuum [rr]
 1. The Last Rite   Brian Lumley
 2. Out of the Darkness   David Gerrold
 3. The White Magician   Emil Petaja
 4. The Gate Cracks Wider
                              Miriam Allen deFord
 5. The Doom That Came to
     Blagham   Ross Rocklynne
Jade Pagoda [col]   E. Hoffmann Price
Into the Blue Forest   Leo Tifton
The Man With the Aura   R. A. Lafferty
Purr   Len Wilburn
Restless Waters   Robert E. Howard

                    ***

THE WITCH'S TALES

A weird fantasy magazine published monthly in large pulp format by the Carwood Publishing Co., New York. Editor: Tom Chadburn. Inspired by the radio series of the same name each issue featured a story by the series writer Alonzo Deen Cole, but thereafter relied heavily on reprints from turn-of-the-century periodicals. As not all of these have been identified there may be more reprints than are indicated here.

November 1936	1/1	Elmer C. Stoner
The Madman		Alonzo Deen Cole
*The Fountain of Youth		
	William Hamilton Osborne	
*The Phantom of the Links		
	John Campbell Haywood	
Castle of Death		Laurence D. Smith
The Striker		P. C. Macfarland
A Sheaf of Ghost Stories [5ts]		
		[no credit]

December 1936	1/2	Elmer C. Stoner
The Return of Oliver Manton		
		Fletcher Robinson
Mrs. Hawker's Will		Alonzo Deen Cole
[adapted from radio by Laurence D. Smith]		
Phantom Fingers		Val McNamara
*The Death-Trap		George Daulton
A Presentiment		Lionel Jervis
*The Monster of Lake LaMetrie		
		Wardon Allan Curtis
The Pig of the Patio		Robert Findlay
The Dog With the Woman's Eyes		
		Arthur Applin
My Opinion [a]	Mrs Bertha L. Darling	
Strange Experiences [a]		Sam D. Cohn

***

296

WORLDS BEYOND

A fantasy/sf digest published monthly by Hillman Periodicals Inc., 4600 Diversey Ave., Chicago, Illinois, with editorial offices at 535 Fifth Ave., New York. Editor: Damon Knight.

December 1950	1/1	Paul Calle
Six-Legged Svengali		
	Mack Reynolds & Fredric Brown	
*An Epistle to the Thessalonians		
	Philip Wylie	
Simworthy's Circus	Larry Shaw	
*The End of the Party	Graham Greene	
The Big Contest	John D. MacDonald	
*The Hunter Gracchus	Franz Kafka	
The Mindworm	C. M. Kornbluth	
*The Smile of the Sphinx [nt]		
	William F. Temple	
Invasion Squad	Battell Loomis	
*Wow	William Seabrook	
The Loom of Darkness	Jack Vance	

January 1951	1/2	H. R. van Dongen
March Hare Mission [nt]	Ford McCormack	
Tree of Wrath	John Christopher	
The Tourist Trade	Bob Tucker	
*Ghost of Mr Kitcat	Rumer Godden	
Survival Ship	Judith Merril	
*"Naam"	R. E. Morrough	
The Green Cat	Cleve Cartmill	
*The Supremacy of Uruguay	E. B. White	
The Fittest	Katherine MacLean	
*A Matter of Fact	Rudyard Kipling	
Null-P	William Tenn	

February 1951	1/3	H. R. van Dongen
Brain of the Galaxy [nt]	Jack Vance	
The Deadliest Female	Lester del Rey	
Like a Bird, Like a Fish	H. B. Hickey	
*The Old Brown Coat	Lord Dunsany	
The Acolytes	Poul Anderson	
*Forgotten Tongue	Walter C. Davies	
Clothes Make the Man	Richard Matheson	
*The Rocket of 1955	C. M. Kornbluth	
Rock Diver	Harry Harrison	
*Valley of Doom	Halliday Sutherland	

***

297

WORLDS OF FANTASY

The short-lived fantasy companion to Galaxy SF Magazine, *published irregularly by Universal Publishing & Distributing Corp., 235 East 45th Street, New York. An early trial issue had been issued by Galaxy Publishing Corp., 421 Hudson St., New York. Editor: Lester del Rey (first two issues), Ejler Jakobsson (last two).*

[September] 1968   1/1   Jack Gaughan
The Mirror of Wizardry [nt]   John Jakes
Death is a Lonely Place   Bill Warren
As Is   Robert Silverberg
What the Vintners Buy   Mack Reynolds
Conan and the Cenotaph
    Lin Carter & L. Sprague de Camp
After Armageddon   Paris Flammonde
A Report on J.R.R. Tolkien [a]
    Lester del Rey
The Man Who Liked   Robert Hoskins
Delenda Est   Robert E. Howard
However [nt]   Robert Lory

[August] 1970   1/2   Jack Gaughan
Walker Between the Planes
    [nt]   Gordon R. Dickson
The Crayfish   Helen Arvonen
Oh Say, Can You See?   Erik van Lhin
Unmistakably Henry   Jean Cavrell
Long Live Lord Kor! [na]   Andre Norton
Call Me Million   Frederik Pohl
Teddy Bear   James E. Gunn
Last Night and Every Night
    James Tiptree, Jr

Winter 1970/71   1/3   Jack Gaughan
What Do You Mean - Fantasy?
  [ged]   Theodore Sturgeon
The Tombs of Atuan [abr.n]
    Ursula K. LeGuin
Me - Too   Sonya Dorman
Death of a Peculiar Boar Naomi Mitchison
Santa Titicaca   Connie Willis
A Ship Will Come   Robert F. Young
In the Cards   Robert Bloch
Funny Place   Naomi J. Kahn
The Man Doors Said Hello To
    James Tiptree. Jr
If a Flower Could Eclipse [nt]
    Michael Bishop

Spring 1971   1/4   Jack Gaughan
Search For the Plynck [ged]
    Theodore Sturgeon
Reality Doll [n]   Clifford D. Simak
The Passing of Auntie Mat Ross Rocklynne
Kerman Widens Lead in Poll
    Frank S. Robinson
The Garden
    M. L. Brannock Lunde & David Lunde
Hunt With the Rain   S. C. Beck
Ptolemaic Hijack   Ruth Berman

***

WYRD

An erratic and irregular small press magazine of weird fantasy published originally by Wyrd Publications, Colon, Michigan transferring, with issue 4, to 324 Candy Lane, Santa Rosa, California. From issue 6 it was published by The Chaosium, Albany, California, and with issue 8 by Tintagel, Berkeley, California. Editors: Al D. Cockrell & Irvin L. Wagner (issues 1-3), Brian Crist (issue 4), Greg Stafford (issues 5-7) and Robert Nycroft Abercrombie (issue 8). Format varied between octavo and quarto.

June 1973	No.1	Jim Erskine
Cul-de-Sac		Ron Nance
For We Are Men No More		Richard Landwehr
The Inn of the Arrows		Al D. Cockrell
Bus Ride		Brett Martell
The Gambler's Demon		Brian Crist
The Seven Steps to Salvation		
		Irvin L. Wagner
Robbie [v]		Theodore Kriner
Wind		Anna Crownfield
Fall 1973	No.2	Jim Erskine
The Golden Mask		David Madison
The Basement		Theodore Kriner
The Golden Rin of Xama		Brian Crist
Table Discussion	Charles Collier, Jr &	
		Steve Swenston
The Stone That Fell From		
the Sky		William H. Stout
How Slygar the Barbarian Became		
Slygar the One True Prophet		Ron Nance
Spring 1974	No.3	Steve Swenston
Along the Ancient Way		Al D. Cockrell
The Disintigration of Snailbrass		
		Greg Stafford
Tale of Three Tasks		George Duck
Who Writes Your Horoscope?		
		JeanPaul Jenack
Poems [v]		Theodore Kriner
December 1974	No.4	Steve Oliff
Never Argue With Antique		
Dealers		Darrell Schweitzer
Hotline		C. L. Ballentine
A Rain of Spiders		
	Jessica Amanda Salmonson	

The Funeral of Thamyris the		
Warlock [s1/2]		David Madison
[Summer] 1975	No.5	Gene Day
The Unicorns, or Beasts of		
Mystery		Ron Nance
. . . .		Brian Crist
The Funeral of Thamyris the		
Warlock [s2/2]		David Madison
Cad Goddeu, the Battle of the		
Trees [gs]		Gene Day
A Winged Shadow		Chet Gottfried
Translation of an Ogham Stick		
(with Footnotes)		Greg Stafford
Winter 1976/77	No.6	Tom Clark
Norman's Intended		Jack Goodstein
A Sudden Storm in Spring [v]		
		Paul Edwin Zimmer
Speaking Out [v]		Phillip Corwin
Gunfighter [gs]		Steve Oliff
Ballad of Borrell		Gordon Linzner
Manabozho and the Lacrosse Game		
[gs]	Greg Stafford [art: Mark Roland]	
Weird, Weirder [2v]		Deirdre Evans
Adventures of Mr. Moon [cs]		Al Cox
The Experiment		John DiPrete
A Fable [v]		Chet Gottfried
A Foolish/Ghoulish Mistake [v]		
		Sol Kanemann
Terror Across Time [gs] Stephanie Stearns		
	[art: Mel Laybourne]	
Movie Review: Conan the		
Barbarian [spf]		[Greg Stafford]
Taken / Nocturnal Nemesis [2v]		
		Stephanie Stearns
The Wolves of Severtatis	Phyllis Ann Karr	

***

Author Index

A

A., EMILI
The Dryad [v]   Nek 1,Spr 50
Rainbow Cities [v]   Nek 2,Sum 50
Shadow Queen [v]   Nek 5,mid 51

ABARTIS, CEJARIJA
US writer and English teacher
The Dreamhouse   TZ Aug 82

ABBOT, EDITH SAYLOR
Evil is the Night   Sus Sum 51

ABDULLAH, ACHMED [1881-1945]
*Russian-born, English-educated, US writer
of adventure stories, most noted for The
Thief of Bagdad*
Renunciation   GS Sep 29

ABE, MASAKI [1951-]
Japanese librarian and active fantasy fan
Robert E. Howard: Checklist of
  Books Available in Japanese
  [bib]   FCr 4/5,Aug 75

ABERNATHY, ROBERT [1924-]
US linguist and occasional sf writer
Tag   BFF Jan 54

ABRACH
The Plaid   WT Jul 52

ABRASH, MICHAEL
True Romance   S&T 61,Win 81/2

ACKERMAN, FORREST J [1916-]
US sf agent, writer, editor & bibliophile
Profile   *MT 5,Sum 35*
Interview   *Gam 4,Feb 65*
A Basic Science Fiction Library
  [sym]   ArkS Win 49
*Brave Nude World [a]   Ftc May 68
  [*American Sunbather, 1961]
College of Scientifictional
  Knowledge [quiz]   FF Nov 50

A Resume of Rays   UnS May/Jun 35
Sleuth is Stranger Than Fiction
  [a]   Ggn 5,Nov 47
Synopsis   Vor 2,1947

  as Dr. Acula
*Terror From Transylvania [a]   BWT 1960
  [*Famous Monsters of Filmland, 1958]

  as J. E. Tomerlin
Alienation of Affection   SFy 21,Feb 57

  + C. L. Moore
Nymph of Darkness   WT Dec 39

  + Tigrina & William F. Nolan, by-lined
  as by Ackerman only
*The Girl Who Wasn't There   Gam 1,1963
  [*rev'd;orig. "The Lady Takes a Powder"
  Inside, 1953]

  + Donald A. Wollheim
*Great Gog's Grave   FB Dec 81
  [*pub'd in an Avon comic-book in 40s]

ACKERMAN, WENDAYNE [1912-]
Interview   *Div 26/7,May/Jul 78*

ACKERMAN, WILL
Palindromophobia   FB Feb 83

ACULA, DR.
  Pseud: see Forrest J ACKERMAN

ADAMS, EVANGELINE
Selected: My Favorite Ghost Story
  1."Gem of Ill-Omen" Cheiro   GS Jan 30

ADAMS, F[RED(erick)] C.
US small-press writer, poet, editor
At the Foot of the Oak   EC 4,1980
Curiosity [v]   Div 16,Sep 76
Delivery   Mb 19,1974
The Feast of Argatha   FyT 2,Win 77
Green Temple   F&T 5,1974
He Who Creeps   Spoor 2,1974
Inathotep's Tale   UnT 1,1974
The Mask of Zeng [Cth]   S&T 22,Jan 74
Medusa [v]   Div 13,Mar 76

Never Kill a Fly!   F&T 2,1973
Revelation [v]   Div 13,Mar 76
The Still Ones [Cth]   DMR 1,1975
Translations From the Book of
  Yng:
  1.The Debt of the Summoner
     [Cth]   FBDG 3,Apr 74
  2.The Punishment of Igharta
     [Cth]   FBDG 3,Apr 74
  3.The Fleece of Yaggar [Cth]
                                 FBDG 3,Apr 74
  (4)The Temple of Bones [Cth]
                                 FBDG 4,Oct 77
  (5)The Son of Nisharga [Cth]
                                 FBDG 4,Oct 77
[Cth - Cthulhu Mythos]

ADAMS, H'AMY
I Told Their Fortunes to Three
  Kings [a]   GS Aug 30

ADAMS, PAMELA
Ragtime   SFy 77,Oct 65

ADAMS, SAMUEL HOPKINS [1871-1958]
US novelist and screenwriter
Isle of Blight   Ftc Jan/Feb 53

ADAMS, VIDA TAYLOR
"Whoso Diggeth a Pit -"   WT May/Jul 24

ADCOCK, A. ST. JOHN [1864-1930]
UK editor of The Bookman
*Of William Hope Hodgson [ex]
                                 ArkC 5,Sum 69
  [*from Introduction to The Calling
  of the Sea Hodgson,1920]

ADDAMS, GAHAN
Delayed Birthday   Mb 21,1975
Spellbound [v]   TW 1975

ADDIS, H. A. NOUREDDIN
Doctor Grant's Experiment   WT May/Jul 24

ADDIS, MARGUERITE LYNCH
Sorcery Past and Present [a]   WT Jun 27

AICKMAN, ROBERT [Fordyce] [1914-81]
UK writer, film and opera critic and
Inland Waterways enthusiast
Obituary   Eld 2,1982
Profile & Bibliography   Nyc 18,Apr 83
Le Miroir   Whsp 10,Aug 77
The Next Glade [na]   WT 4,Sum 83
*The Waiting Room   ArkC 9,Spr 71
  [*The Sketch Christmas 1956]

AIKEN, JOAN [1924-]
UK novelist noted for her children's books
Old Fillikin   TZ Apr 82
Picnic Area   TZ Jul 82

AINSLEE, ROBERT
The House That Ghosts Built   GS Jan 29

AIRTH, FRANK
Havoc For Sale   EM Apr/May 39
Time Takes a Holiday   EM Feb 39

AKI, TANUKI
  Pseud: see Charles DE LINT

ALBERT, LINCOLN
Believed pseud. of Greg Benford & Laurence
Littenberg, but unconfirmed
Treaty   Ftc Aug 70

ALBRIGHT, ROBERT CHOATE
The Flame of the Ages   WT Nov 28

ALBUQUERQUE SCIENCE FICTION SOCIETY
  by Roy Tackett, Bob Vardeman, Sal Di-
  Maria, Mike Kring, Walter Williams,
  Dick Patten, Kathy Patten, Robin Patten
  Carol Alsup & Brian Pharos
An Exquisite Corpse SF Story I
  [rr]   Nyc 13,May 77

ALBUS, MAGUS
The Magic of the Psalms [col]
                                 MM Jun-Dec 31

ALCOCK, FRANCIS
The Letter From Home   TU 2(1937)

ALDISS, BRIAN W[ilson] [1925-]
UK author, reviewer and anthologist
Are You An Android [spf]   SFy 34,Apr 59
Blighted Profile   SFy 29,Jun 58
Breathing Space   SFy 12,Feb 55
Cardiac Arrest [nt   Ftc Dec 70
The Carp That Once [spf]   SFy 28,May 58
The Circulation of the Blood
  [nt]   Imp 1,Mar 66
Criminal Record   SFy 9,Jul 54
The Day of the Doomed King
  [Vuk]   SFy 78,Nov 65
The Eyes of the Blind King
  [Vuk]   Imp 9,Nov 66
Faceless Card   SFy 40,Apr 60
The Failed Men   SFy 18,May 56
Flowers of the Forest   SFy 24,Aug 57
Fortune's Fool   SFy 35,Jun 59
Frankenstein Unbound [n2] Ftc Mar-May 74
Intangibles, Inc.   SFy 33,Feb 59
Instead of an Editorial [ged]
                                 SFy 76,Sep 65
Judas Danced   SFy 27,Feb 58
Just Passing Through   Imp 12,Feb 67
Let's Be Frank   SFy 23,Jun 57
Man In His Time [nt]   SFy 71,Apr 65
The Man Who Saw Cliff Richard SE 2,Win 80
Matrix [nt]   SFy 55,Oct 62
No Gimmick   SFy 21,Feb 57
Non-Stop [nt]   SFy 17,Feb 56
*The Oh in Jose   Imp 5,Jul 66
  [*Cad 3,Mar 66]
Pink Plastic Gods   SFy 65,Jun/Jul 64
A Pleasure Shared   SFy 73,Jun 65
The Plot Sickens [spf]   Imp 10,Dec 66
Skeleton Crew [sn]   SFy 62,Dec 63
Smile, Please! [a]   SFy 30,Aug 58
Stage Struck!   SFy 41,Jun 60
Three Evolutionary Enigmas   SE 1,Spr 80
With Esmond in Mind   SFy 20,Dec 56

  as Jael Cracken
The Impossible Smile [sn2]
                            SFy 72-73,May-Jun 65

Lazarus   SFy 65,Jun/Jul 64

  as John Runciman
No Moon Tonight! [nt]   SFy 66,Jul/Aug 64
Unauthorised Persons [nt]
                           SFy 65,Jun/Jul 64
[Vuk - Prince Vukasan]

ALDRICH, FRANCES
  Pseud: see Dale DONALDSON

ALDRICH, THOMAS BAILEY [1836-1907]
US poet,editor,dramatist & novelist
*Poe [v]   ArkC 3,Sum 68

ALDRIDGE, MARY C.
The Windela Man   S&T 64,Sum 83

ALETTI, STEFFAN B.
The Castle in the Window   MoH 22,Jul 68
The Cellar Room   WTT 3,Fal 70
The Eye of Horus   MoH 24,Nov 68
The Last Work of Pietro of
  Apono   MoH 27,May 69

ALEXANDER, DAVID [1907-73]
US writer and newspaperman
The Other Ones   FM Aug 53

ALEXANDER, GATES
Virgins of the Stone Death ES Aug 37

ALI HASSAN, SILAKI
  Pseud: see Ulysses G. MIHALAKIS

ALLEN, A. LEWIS
She Heard the Reaper Coming
  [ts]   GS Oct 26

ALLEN, BLAIR H.
Andromeda [v]   S&T 65,Win 83/4

ALLEN, DANA K.
The Mad Dance at Twilight [v]
                           S&T 65,Win 83/4

ALLEN, DAVID
From Outside   DFy 19,Feb 79

ALLEN, ERIC
Dead Men Do Tell Tales   TU 2(1937)

ALLEN, FLORENCE
The Turn of the Tide   Phtm 2,May 57

ALLEN, IRWIN [1916-]
US film-maker
Profile   Chl Nov 81

ALLEN, JIM
The Stuff of Legend [a]   NFJ 2,1977

ALLEN, L. HARPER
The Blood Veins of the Robot
                           WT Jun/Jul 31

ALLEN, LOIS
Rhapsody of Death   Mac 4,Win 58

ALLEN, LORI
The Artisan   TZ Aug 81

ALLEN, MARIJANE
The Department of the Navy Regrets
  to Inform [v]   Mac 2,Win 57
In an Upstairs Room [v]   Mac 2,Win 57

ALLEN, MARY ANN
  Pseud: see Rosemary PARDOE

ALLEN, PAUL C.
US fan, founder of Fantasy Newsletter
Of Swords and Sorcery [col]
                           FCr 8-15,May 76-Jan 79
*La Sword & Sorcery di Michael
  Moorcock [a]   Kad 2,May 80
  [*from above column]

ALLEN, STEVE [1921-]
US writer,actor,musician & humorist
*The Late Mr. Adams   Gam 5,Sep 65
  [*Fourteen For Tonight,1955]

ALLEN, WILFORD
The Arctic Death   WT Jun 27
The Bone-Grinder   WT Jan 28
The Hate   WT Jun 28
Night-Thing   WT Jul 29
On a Far World   WT Jul 28
The Planet of Horror   WT Jun 30
The Swooping Wind   WT Dec 27

ALLERTON, J.J.
Probable Ziff-Davis house name
The Typewriter   Ftc Jun 55

ALLISON, TIMOTHY R.
Fragmentation   Wbk 5,1972
Precession   Wbk 8,1974
To Fade in Silence   Wbk 2,1969

ALLISTONE, B. WILMOT
The Ghost House   G&G(1938)

ALLWAYS, ROBERT
A Suicide Complex   WT Nov 24

ALMEDINGEN, EDITH M.
An Examination in Diplomacy WT Aug 29

ALMY, A.B.
The Ghost of a Chance   WT May 41

ALPAJPURI
  Pseud: see Paul NOVITSKY

ALSUP, CAROL

  + Albuquerque SF Society
The Exquisite Corpse SF Story I
                           Nyc 13,May 77

ALTER, ROBERT EDMOND [1925-65]
US mystery writer
Comrade Vukashin's Clock   BMM Nov 65
Coup de Grace   BMM Oct 65
A Sense of Crawling   MoH 17,Fal 67

  as Robert Retla
The Marinus Ghost   BMM Nov 65

ALTERMAN, PETER S.
Scenicruiser and the Silver Lady
                           TZ Jun 81

ANDERSON, RALPH PARKER
The Purple Light   WT Nov 24

ANDREWS, CLARENCE L.
May be either Clarence Leroy Andrews(1862-
1952) or Clarence Ladelle Andrews (1882-
1962)
Burnt Bridges   TB Sep 1,19
Profit By Loss   TB Apr 15,19
Vanishing Gold   TB Jul 1,19

ANDREWS, DAVID
The Mad Merger Meets the Gorn
   From Sucker... [spf]   UnT 1,1974

ANDREWS, JOHN W.
The Parable of Keys: an Allegory
   [ss]   Anu 1,Aut 66

ANDREWS, JOHN J.
Translator: see Vsevolod IVANOV

ANDREWS, PETER J.
The Collected Poems of Xirius
   Five [ss]   Ftc Oct 78

ANDREWS, V[irginia] C[leo] [1933-]
US author and former comercial artist
Interview   TZ Jun 83

ANDREYEFF, LEONID [1871-1919]
Russian lawyer, painter and writer
*Lazarus   WT Mar 27
*Lazarus   MoH 16,Sum 67
   [*first published in 1906]

ANFLEMING, IRENE
Pseud: see Gordon LINZNER

ANNABEL, RUSSELL
Horror in the Fog   MyS 20(1939)

ANNAS, HAL
Invasion of the Dark Ones [nt]
                                    Mystic Jan 54

ANNEMANN, THEO
Inside Secrets of False Mediums
   and Their Marvels [a2]   GS Jan-Feb 31

ANNIXTER, PAUL
Pseud: see Howard A. STURTZEL

ANSELL, ROBIN
   + 'Karen Young'[Dave Reeder]
   Jungle Breath, Jungle Death FyM 4,Jul 83

ANSLEY, DOROTHY AGARD
And Thus I Knew [v]   WT Jan 39

ANSPACH, MARK
Limerick [v]   FCw 1,Jan 77

ANTHONY, ARDEN
Mr. Justice Sits In   EM Feb 39
Tomb of Torment   EM Apr/May 39

ANTHONY, PIERS [1934-]
US-naturalised UK-born sf/fantasy writer;
full name Piers Anthony Dillingham Jacob.
*Alf Laylah Wa Laylah [a]   Ftc Dec 69
   [*Niekas, 1966]
Encounter   Ftc Oct 64
Hasan [n2]   Ftc Dec 69-Feb 70
The Life of the Stripe   Ftc Feb 69
Phog   Ftc Jun 65
Possible to Rue   Ftc Apr 63

ANTHONY, R.
Pseud: see Anthony M. RUD

ANTONE, ROBERT
The Curse of Hamid   MP Dec 58
The Well of the Damned   MP Nov 58

ANVIL, CHRISTOPHER
US sf writer; real name Harry C. Crosby
High Road to the East   Ftc May 68
Merry Christmas From Outer
   Space   Ftc Dec 64
The New Way   BI Nov/Dec 67
A Sense of Disaster   Ftc Jan 79

AP'RHYS, MATT BYRNE
A Strange Manifestation [ts]
                                    WT Jul/Aug 23

APPEL, FRED
The Stranger [cs:art Al Saviuk]
                                    S&T 7,Aug 69

APPELMAN, EVAN H.
The Romans Encounter the Nervii
                                    Nek 5,mid 51

APPLEBY, SAMUEL C.
Bucking the Stock Market with
   Supernatural Aid [ts]   GS May 29

APPLIN, ARTHUR [G.T.] [1883-1949]
UK Author, film critic & producer
*The Dog With the Woman's Eyes Wtch Dec 36
   [*probably from UK mag.like Pearson's
   at the turn of the century]

AQUINO, MICHAEL A.
Lovecraftian Ritual: Ceremony of the
   Nine Angles, The Call to Cthulhu
   [a]   Nyc 13,May 77

ARBOGAST, DONALD K.
Pseud: see Ted WHITE

ARCHER, LEE
Ziff-Davis house-name; real author unknown
Peter Merton's Private Mint   Ftc Oct 56

ARCHER, REXTON
Red Circle house-name; real author unknown
The Pain Master's Bride   ES Aug 37
Thirsty Steel   EM Aug 38
The Three From Nowhere   EM Nov 38

ARCHETTE, GUY
Pseud: see Chester S. GEIER

ARDEN, RICE
Pseud.of US writer Maurice Arden Weekly
Necromansaur   Phtm 16,Jul 58

as Boris Karloff
The Frightened:
[The Man in the Raincoat]   TF Aug 57
[Say Goodnight to Mr.Sporko]   TF Spr 57

AVON, IAN
Far Enough   OS 2(1946)

AVRETT, ROBERT
The Devil's Swamp [v]   WT Mar 36
On Hangman's Hill [v]   WT May 35

AYCOCK, ROGER D[ee] [1914-]

    as Roger Dee
Guest Artist [nt]   Ftc May/Jun 53
The Springbird   BFF Jul 53

AYLMER, STAFFORD
[Probably same as UK occasional writer
Arthur Stafford Aylmer]
Tibetan Vengeance [nt]   WT Mar 42

AYNE, BLYTHE
The Collection   S&T 51,Apr 79

                B

BAARDSON, W. A.
The Mound of Yig? [a]   E&O 1,1973

BABCOCK, NATHANIEL T.
*The Man With the Brown Beard   WT Sum 73
  [*Argosy Feb 1896]

BACKUS, W. ELWYN
Behind the Moon [nt3]   WT Dec 29-Feb 30
The Hall Bedroom   WT Feb 24
The Phantom Bus   WT Sep 30
Subterranea [nt]   WT Nov 31
The Waning of a World [sn4]
                          WT Nov 25-Feb 26
The Youth-Maker   WT Apr 27

BACON, JONATHAN [1948-]
[See also Editor Index]
"Conan the Barbarian" Checklist
  [bib]   FCr 1,Nov 74
Eisner and The Spirit [in] FCr 1,Nov 74
Interview with Stephen R.
  Donaldson [in]   FCr 15,Jan 79
Jack Kirby: Myth Maker [in] FCr 1,Nov 74
"Kull the Conqueror" Checklist
  [bib]   FCr 2,Feb 75
Robert E.Howard Editors'/Pub-
  lishers' Roundtable [sym2]
                 FCr 9-10/11,Aug 76-Mar 77

  + Mike Hodge
A Conversation with A.J.Hanley
  [in]   FCr 2,Feb 75

[Note: also adapted "Ancient Sorceries" by
Algernon Blackwood as cs FCr4/5,Aug 75]

BAER, STAN
Nite File   Ftc Oct 54

BAGBY, ROSS F.
The Arctic Stone   [Cth]   Eld 7,1980
The Horror in the Blue Glass
  Bottle   [Cth]   FBDG 4,Oct 77
[Cth - Cthulhu Mythos]

BAGBY, STEPHEN
[Pseud. of Charles M.Stephens]
The Rosicrucian Lamp   WT Jun 29
Whispering Tunnels [nt]   WT Feb 25
The Witches' Sabbath [nt2] WT Jul-Aug 28

BAIL, GRACE SHATTUCK
Witchcraft [v]   Wbk 13,1978

BAILEY, A[lice] C[ooper]
Binker's Ghost   OS 1(1945)
A Court-Martialled Ghost [a] WOL 2(1960)
The Dance of Death   WOM(1949)
Dream Child   WOM(1949)
Ghost Dogs [a]   WSM 1(1946)
His Second Chance   WOL 2(1960)
Royal Ghosts [a]   WSM 1(1946)
A Sacrifice to Pan   WOM(1949)
Self and Shadow   OS 2(1946)
Skulls That Cannot be Shifted
  [a]   WOL 2(1960)

BAILEY, DANIEL
The Fearful Fane [v]   EvM Win 75

BAILEY, HARRY
The Wolf of the Campagna   WT Feb 25

BAILEY, HILARY   [1936-]
Everything Blowing Up   SE 2,Win 80
[see also pseud. Pippin GRAHAM]

BAILEY, LAWRENCE G.
The Dog With a Man's Eyes   GS Nov 27
*Seduced By an Invisible Lover
  [retitling of above story,
  reprinted anonymously]   PGS 1963

BAILEY, LEDYARD M.
The Cobra Lily   WT Jan 24

BAILLIE, PETER
Grave Mistake   Phtm 7,Oct 57
Inheritance   Phtm 5,Aug 57

BAINES, MARIAN
The Mystery of Peg-Leg Pete
                         Phtm 2,May 57

BAIRD, EDWIN [1886-1957]
US detective fiction writer and first
editor of Weird Tales
Anton's Last Dream   WT May 37

BAKER, ACE
    Pseud: see Paul R. MILTON

BAKER, DENYS VAL [1917-]
UK author, anthologist and raconteur
*The Inheritance   FyT 3,Sum 78
  [*The Face in the Mirror,1971]

BAKER, DOUG
Deliverance [v]   EvM Sum 76

BAKER, [H(erbert)] J[ERRY]   [1953-]
US restaurant manager
Curse of Ler-Ku Nasthur [v]
                              Nyc 18,Apr 73
Lady Latanya   Hor 1,1980
Lo! Death [v]   SPWAO 1,1980
A Poesque Room [v]   SPWAO 2,1982
The Skull of Gur'la-ya   Eld 7,1980

BAKER, JOSEPH B.
Trapped [v]   Ggn(8) 1948

BAKER, Jr., LEDRU
The Queen's Bedchamber   TF Aug 57

BAKER, R. RAY
Back to Earth   TB Jul 15,19

BALAZS, FRANK L.
Eyes   Spoor 1,1974
The Last Day of Illilium   ToF 1,Spr 82

BALCH, DAVID ARNOLD
Mind Over Matter   GS Dec 31/Jan 32

BALDWINSON, JOHN
Mary, Mary   Ftc Mar 65

BALFORT, NEIL
     Pseud: see R. L. FANTHORPE

BALFOUR, BRUCE J.
The Last Adam & Eve Story   TZ Apr 83
Some Days Are Like That [ss] TZ Jun 82

BALL, B[RIAN] N[eville]   [1932-]
UK writer and lecturer in English
The Excursion [nt]   SFy 71,Apr 65

BALL, CLIFFORD   [1896-1947]
Duar the Accursed   WT May 37
The Goddess Awakes [nt] [Rald] WT Feb 38
The Little Man   WT Aug 39
The Swine of Aeaea   WT Mar 39
The Thief of Forthe   [Rald] WT Jul 37
The Werewolf Howls   WT Nov 41
*[Rald - note, "Duar the Accursed" is set
in the same background]*

BALLARD, J[ames] G[raham]   [1930-]
UK author of 'speculative' fiction
The Last World of Mr Goddard
                              SFy 43,Oct 60
Minus One   SFy 59,Jun 63
Mr. F is Mr. F   SFy 48,Aug 61
Mobile   [VS]   SFy 23,Jun 57
Now: Zero   SFy 38,Dec 59
Prima Belladonna   [VS]   SFy 20,Dec 56
A Question of Re-entry [nt]   Ftc Mar 63
Say Goodbye to the Wind [VS] Ftc Aug 70
The Screen Game [nt] [VS]   Ftc Oct 63
The Singing Statues   [VS]   Ftc Jul 62
The Sound-Sweep [nt]   SFy 39,Feb 60
Studio 5, the Stars [nt]   [VS]
                              SFy 45,Feb 61
The Sudden Afternoon   Ftc Sep 63
*The Sudden Afternoon   StF 11,Spr 70
Time of Passage   SFy 46,Feb 64
The Watch-Towers [nt]   SFy 53,Jun 62
You and Me and the Continuum Imp 1,Mar 66
[VS - Vermilion Sands]

BALLENTINE, C. L.
Hotline   Wyrd 4,Dec 74

BALSLEY, LORNE
The Carnivorous Bubble   EM Nov 38
The Corpse Symphony   EM Apr/May 39

BALZAC, HONORE DE
     see under Honore DE BALZAC

BANCROFT, ROSS A.
One Flash Into the Future   GS Jul 29

BANGS, JOHN KENDRICK   [1862-1922]
US editor, writer and humorist
*The Water Ghost of Harrowby Hall
                              AFR 16,1951
     [*The Water Ghost of Harrowby Hall,1894]

BANISTER, MANLY [Miles]   [1914-]
US writer [see Editor Index]
Cry Wolf!   Nek 1,Spr 50
Cursed Awakening   WT Sep 43
Devil Dog [nt]   WT Jul 45
Eena   WT Sep 47
Fear [a]   Nek 1,Spr 50
Fen-Wer   Nek 2,Sum 50
Loup-Garou   WT May 47
Magnanthropus [sn2]   Ftc Sep-Oct 61
Room Without Windows   BFF Sep 54
Satan's Bondage [nt]   WT Sep 42
Seed of Eloraspon [sn2]   Ftc Oct-Nov 64
Six Flights to Terror   WT Sep 46
Song in the Thicket [nt]   WT May 47
You Who Have Slain Me -   Nek 4,Win 50/1

  uncredited
Lilith Lorraine and the Avalon
  World Arts Academy [a]   Nek 3,Aut 50
Ralph Rayburn Phillips [a]   Nek 2,Sum 50

BANKS, EDWARD
     Pseud: see Ray BRADBURY

BANKS, JEFF
  as Jack D. Ribber
Small Favors   S&T 63,Win 82/3

BANKS, RAYMOND E.   [1918?-]
US writer and science editor
Buttons   Gam 3,1964
More Like Home   Ftc May 59

BANNERMAN, GENE
     Likely pseud. of Thomas P. KELLEY

BANNISTER, CHRISTOPHER
When Ghosts Walked   TB Jul 1,19

BANSTEAD, ARTHUR
The Kindly Ghost of Westfield
  Close   Phtm 16,Jul 58

BARCLAY, ALAN
     Pseud: see George B. TAIT

BARCUS, N. W.
Math Anxiety [a]   Nov 1,Aut 80

The Opium Ship [n4]   TB Jul 1-Aug 15,19
*The Singing Sands of Prester
  John   [TFO]   Ftc Sep 63
  [*Blue Book Feb 39]
The Sleeper   WT Oct 34
Unpublished Story   WT May 44
The Wife of the Humorous
  Gangster [APC]   WT Nov 40
*The Wolf-Woman   [TFO] Ftc Oct 63
  [*Blue Book Aug 39]

  as Gordon Keyne
The Kings Do Battle Again   WT Sep 40
[APC - Adventures of a Professional Corpse;
TFO - Trumpets From Oblivion]

BEECH, DAVID
  Building Blocks   SFy 66,Jul/Aug 64

BEECHAM, THOMAS   (pseud)
  A Case of Mistaken Identity   Thrl Feb 62
  The Jelly Monster From Hell   Thrl May 62

BEECHER, LEE
  Adana [v]   Ggn[9] 1949
  Haunted Mines [v]   Ggn Jan 48

BEESTON, L. J.
British writer, mostly of adventure and
children's stories
  The Tenth Crisis   TB Jul 1,19

BEGGS, WILTON G.
  Adjustment   Ftc Sep 63
  Daughter of the Clan   Ftc Nov 64
  *Daughter of the Clan StF 11,Spr 70
  The Mating Season   Ftc Oct 63
  *The Mating Season   WM 2,Win 70

BEHRENS, STEVE
  Abdul Alhazred [v]   S&T 46,Jan 78
  A Walk Over Darkling Snow [v] Wbk 14,1979

BEILIN, JONATHAN
  Mara [nt]   EC 9,1982

BEINE, ROBERT
  See Me in Black   BFF Sep 54

BEINING, GUY R.
  The Corners Falling Into One
    [v]   Wyrd 8,1980

BELFLOWER, JAMES A.
  Error: see Guy FOWLER

BELITT, BEN
  Tzo-Lin's Nightingales   WT Feb/Mar 31

BELL, EARL LEASTON
  Doctor DeBruce   WT Feb 24
  The Land of Lur   WT May 30

BELL, E. N.
  Sister Gage   Mac 17,Sum 65

BELL, JOHN
British writer
  A Hot Summer's Day   Imp 5,Jul 66

BELL, JOHN
Canadian collector and small press editor
  *Coils [v]   DFd 4,Win 83
    [*Journal Fantome No.4,1980]
  Crossroads   DFy 23,Nov 80
  The Day Frank Schoonover Died CT 4,May 78
  Duel [v]   DFd 4,Win 83
  A Fitting Place   DFy 17,Jul 78
  *Illuminations [v]   DFd 4,Win 83
    [*Journal Fantome No.4,1980]

BELL, MICHAEL J.
  Advice of a Friend   AD 4,Fal 76
  Nothing Gained But Faith
    [SphW]   S&T 27,Nov 74
  Nothing Gained But Friendship
    [SphW]   Div 5,Oct 74
  Nothing Gained But Honor
    [SphW]   S&T 18,May 73
  Passengers   Div 7,Feb 75
  Quest of the Blade [SphW]   S&T 25,Jul 74
  A Secular Quest   S&T 37,Jul 76
[SphW - Sphereworld]

BELL, THORNTON
Personal pseud. for R. L. FANTHORPE, used
once on a story by H. O. MANSFIELD

BELLAIRS, GEORGE
Pseud. used by UK banker and mystery
novelist HAROLD BLUNDELL [1902-]
  Death in the Mountains   MyS 20(1940)

BELLEM, ROBERT LESLIE
Prolific US mystery pulp writer
  Curse of the Lovely Torso   UT Mar 40
  The Flowers of Enchantment   TMM Apr 28
  *Nameless Dread of the Savage
    Sirens   BoT Dec 49
    [*one of the Spicy pulps,1930s]
  The Thing in the Shaft   UT Aug 39
  Wooed By a Werewolf   UT Nov 39

BELLIN, EDWARD J.
House pseud. used in magazines edited by
Donald A.Wollheim
    by Henry Kuttner
  The Touching Point   SFF Apr 41
  *The Touching Point   UTC 11,Nov 41

    author unknown, possibly John Michel
  *No Place to Go   UTC 18,Jul 42
    [*Cosmic SF May 41]

BELLINI, SIGNOR
  Pseud: see Joshua SMITH

BELLOC-LOWNDES, Mrs
  See under Mrs Belloc-LOWNDES

BEMIS, HARRY A.
  Other-World Taxi   GS Dec 29
  *Taxi to Hell - and Back! [retitle
    of above story]   TTT Spr 64

BEMIS, ROBERT L.
  Darn the Difference!   MM Dec 31

BENCE, W. H. D.
  Demon of the Sickle   GS Jul 31
  Midnight Sorcery   GS Apr 31

BENDS, WILLIAM
Robin Hood and His Merry Men
                          LST 1,Sep/Oct 72

BENEDICT, STEVE
Come, My Sweet   Nek 5,mid-51

BENET, STEPHEN VINCENT [1898-1943]
US poet and author
*The Gold Dress   AFR 5,1947
  [*Saturday Evening Post 1942]
*Johnny Pye and the Fool-Killer
                          Ftc May/Jun 53
  [*Saturday Evening Post Sep 18,1937]

BENFORD, GREG[ORY Albert] [1941-]
US Professor of Physics & sf writer
The Movement   Ftc Oct 70

  + Laurence Littenberg
The Prince of New York   Ftc Jun 70
[see also pseud. Lincoln ALBERT]

BENFORD, JAMES [1941-]
US scientist & engineer, twin brother of
Greg Benford
Pulse   Ftc Aug 71

BENJAMIN, JAY WILMER
Drowned Argosies   WT Jul 34
Eric Martin's Nemesis   WT Mar 37
Homecoming Day   WT Mar 36
The Man Who Saw Red   WT Nov 33

BENNETT, GERTRUDE [Barrows] [1884-1939?]
US pulp writer best known as follows
  as Francis Stevens
The Heads of Cerberus [n5]
                          TB Aug 15-Oct 15,19
Sunfire [na2]   WT Jul/Aug-Sep 23

BENNETT, HARRIET
*The Jewels of Vishnu   MoH 19,Jan 68
  [*The Strand Magazine Dec 1903]

BENNETT, H. M.
The Case of the Greigson Brothers
                          TU 3(1938)

BENNETT, JAMES W.

  + Soong Kwen-Ling
Flight   WT Mar 32
*Flight   MoH 26,Mar 69
The Soul-Catching Cord   WT Apr 25

BENNETT, KAY
*Egyptian Festival for Ares
  [a]   StF 10,Fal 69

BENNETT, K. W.
The Seventeenth Summer [na]
                          SFy 58,Apr 63

BENNETT, MARGOT [1903-]
Scottish writer, mostly of mysteries
*No Bath For the Browns   MysT 5,1952
  [*Lilliput Magazine,1945]

BENNETT, WALLACE
[May be pseud. of Thomas P. Kelley]
The Perfumed Death   UTC 10,Oct 41
Restless Souls   UTC 7,Jul 41

BENSINK, JOHN
Country of the Dead [pic] TZ Nov 82
Midtown Bodies   TZ Aug 82

BENSON, E[dward] F[rederic] [1867-1940]
Prolific UK novelist and story writer
The Bed By the Window   WT Nov 29
Dark and Nameless   GS May 29
The Flint Knife   GS May 30
The Hanging of Alfred Wadham WT Aug 29
James Lamp   WT Jun 30
Monkeys   WT Dec 33
The Shuttered Room   WT Dec 29
The Wishing-Well   WT Jul 29
The Witch-Ball   WT Oct 29
[these stories would have appeared in UK
magazines at about the same time, most
notably 'Hutchinson's Mystery Magazine']

BENTLEY, EVELYN
Unseen Eyes   GS May 29

BENTON, DAVID B.
The Dream Fear [v]   Eld 2,1981

BENTON, JOHN L.
  Pseud: see Norman A. DANIELS

BENTON, PAUL
The Beast   WT Dec 26

BERES, MICHAEL
Prairie Path   TZ Dec 83

BERESFORD, LESLIE
Popular British writer of adventure stories
The Uncanny Four   GS Jan 30

BERGER, ARTHUR ASA
Thinking of Frankenstein [a] Ariel 2,1977

BERGLUND, E[DWARD] P[AUL] [1942-]
US military officer [see Editor Index]
Feast With a Few Strangers Spoor 1,1974
The Feaster From the Stars
  [Cth]   S&T 44,Sep 77
Foreign Publications of H.P.
  Lovecraft [bib]   Nyc 5,Oct 71
Homecoming   WW 2,Mar 71
*Homecoming   E&O 1973
H.P.Lovecraft - Addenda to Story
  Listing [bib3]   Nyc 3-5,Feb-Oct 71
Rude Awakening [ss]   S&T 26,Sep 74
The Sand Castle [Cth]   Eld 2,1981
Sword of the Seven Suns   Eld 3,Mar 78
Wings in the Night [Cth] DMR 1,1975

  + Crispin Burnham
The Thing in the Library Spoor 2,1974

  + Walter C. DeBill,Jr. as 'Drs. Eric von
  Konnenberg & Pierre de Hammais'
The History of the Great Race
  [spf]   FBDG 3,Apr 74

  + Robert E.Weinberg
The Dark Stairway   FBDG 1,Apr/May 72

[Cth - Cthulhu Mythos]

BERMAN, RUTH   [1942-]
US teacher and poet
The Ones Who Pickaback Away With
  Omelets [spf]   S&T 63,Win 82/3
Ptolemaic Hijack   WoF 4,Spr 71

BERMEL, ALBERT
Bourbon on a Champagne Carpet Fear Jul 60

BERNAL, A[RTHUR] W[ILLIAM]
The Man Who Played With Time   WT Mar 32
The Man Who Was Two Men   WT Apr 35
Satan in Exile [sn4]   WT Jun-Sep 35
So Very Strange!   WT Apr 37
Vampires of the Moon [sn3] WT May-Jul 34

BERNARD, DAVID
Dread Command   StS Dec 39
The Haunted Car   WT Nov 39
Jekal's Lesson   WT Oct 38
The Piper From Bhutan   WT Feb 38
Wedding Hells   EM Apr/May 39

BERNARD, MICHAEL
US sports reporter and book critic
It Ain't Missed Yet   FB Dec 81

BERTHOUD, FERDINAND
The Man Who Banished Himself   WT Jan 24
Webbed Hands   ST Nov 31
*Webbed Hands   SMS 9,Sum 68

BERTIN, EDDY C[harly]   [1944-]
Belgian writer and collector
Profile   DH 10,Aut/Win 74
And the Darkness Never Answers
  [v]   E&O 1973
The Ashley Premiere   BFT 2,Mar 71
Behind the White Wall   Wbk 12,1977
Catherine Duval: Modern Master
  of Gothic Horror [a]   E&O 1973
The Creeping Shadows [v]   Wbk 3,1970
The Cthulhu Mythos: A Review
  and Analysis [a]   Nyc 4,Jun 71
*The Fear Dimensions of Oswald
  Kielemoes [a]   DH 12,Aut/Win 75
  [*Ambrosia II,1973]
A House With a Garden   Wbk 5,1972
*H.P.Lovecraft Did Not Write SF
  - By His Own Standards [a] Nyc 2,Oct 70
  [*Shadow 7,Sep 69]
*H.P.Lovecraft: The Critics [a]
                            Nyc 3,Feb 71
  [*Shadow 7,Sep 69]
I Hate You   Wbk 12,1977
*In the Trail of Lovecraft:
  The Followers of Cthulhu [a]
  [*Shadow 9,Jan/Feb 70] Nyc 5,Oct 71
The Lovecraftian Works of
  Colin Wilson [a]   DH 2,1972
The Lover [ss]   Wbk 11,1977
The Man Who Collected Eyes SMS 16,Sum 70
*Marcel Bealu, the Water Spider [a]
  [*Shadow 11,Jul/Aug 70] Nyc 14,Mar 78
A Matter of Competition   F&T 4,1973
Never Touching   Wbk 15,1981
Night [v]   WW 2,Mar 71
Picnic   Wbk 4,1971

*The Price to Pay   FyT 1,Sum 77
  [*a Dutch anthology, details unknown]
*Roland Topor [a]   Nyc 14,Mar 78
  [*Shadow 12,Nov/Dec 70]
The Sea is My Bed   DDH Dec 78
Something Small, Something
  Hungry [nt]   Wbk 13,1978
Something's Eating My Brain [v]
                            Nyc 5,Oct 71
A Song For the Living, a Song
  For the Dead [v]   E&O 1973
A Taste of Rain and Darkness WW 1,Jun 70
*A Taste of Rain and Darkness BFT 1,Fal 70
To Save the World [v]   ArkS Sep 83
Waiting in the Dark [v]   DH 5,1973
*Waiting in the Dark [v]   Nyc 8,Apr 73
The Walkers [v]   Nyc 3,Feb 71
The Way Back Home   Wbk 14,1979
Where Are Yesterday's Castles
  [v]   E&O 1973
A Whisper of Leathery Wings FCr 9,Aug 76
*The Whispering Thing   WTT 1,Win 69
  [*The 9th Pan Book of Horror Stories
  ed. Herbert van Thal,1968 as "The
  Whispering Horror"]
*The Writer in Fandom: Eddy C.
  Bertin [a]   DH 10,Aut/Win 74
  [*rev'd from Shadow 13,May/Jun 71]

BERTRAM, NOEL
Pseud: see Noel BOSTON

BESSETTE, GEORGE J[ules]   [1928-]
US occasional writer
Barbecue [v]   Arg 9,Fal 83
Bruncheon Interlude   Arg 8,Fal/Win 81
Dog Meat [v]   S&T 58,Jan 81
Hang Up [v]   NF 1,Win 80/1
Intimidation [v]   NF 1,Win 80/1
Message Found in a Bottle [v]
                             NF 1,Win 80/1
The Sea Spook [v]   S&T 49,Oct 78
Signal Red For Jasper Snead S&T 62,Sum 82
The Telecommander   S&T 55,Apr 80
Underscape [v]   NF 1,Win 80/1

BESTER, ALFRED   [1913-]
*US author and travel writer, best known
for his sf*
Hell is Forever [sn]   UW Aug 42
The Roller Coaster   Ftc May/Jun 53
What's The Difference? [ged]
                            SFy 12,Feb 55

BETANCOURT, C. O.
The Hungarian Music Shop   Nek 4,Win 50/1
Stranger in a World [v]   Nek 5,mid-51

BETANCOURT, JOHN [G(REGORY)]   [1963-]
US student and writer
The Argia [v]   S&T 62,Sum 82
Don't Laugh [v]   S&T 64,Sum 83

BETKER, LENORE
Of Brides and Brimstone   Cov Sep 69

BETTERLEY, EVA JOY
Am I the Victim of Hallucination
  [ts]   GS Dec 27
How Could it Happen - Like That? GS Jun 28

BISHOP, MICHAEL   [1945-]
US writer of sf and fantasy
At the City Limits of Fate
  [Kudzu]   Shyl 5,Win 82
Evangels of Hope [a]   Shyl 4,Win 80
For the Lady of a Physicist
  No.2 [v]   Shyl 4,Win 80
Give Me a Little Whistle
                           Whsp 19/20,Oct 83
If a Flower Could Eclipse [nt]
                                  WoF 3,70/1
Love's Heresy   Shyl 3,Sum 79
On Reviewing and Being
  Reviewed [a]   Shyl 1,Nov 77
Patriots   Shyl 6,Win 82
Within the Walls of Tyre [nt] Wbk 13,1978

BISHOP, ZEALIA B[rown]   [?1895-?]
*Married name of US writer of confessions
and historical stories, born Zealia Brown
and married first as Zealia B.Reed
    stories revised by H.P.Lovecraft*

    as Zealia B.Reed
The Curse of Yig *[Cth]*   WT Nov 29

    as Zealia B.Bishop
*The Curse of Yig   *[Cth]*   WT Apr 39
*The Curse of Yig   *[Cth]*   AFR 14,1950
Medusa's Coil   *[Cth]*   WT Jan 39
The Mound [abr.na] *[Cth]*   WT Nov 40
[Cth - Cthulhu Mythos]

BISSELL, MAL
The Mask of Don Alfredo   WT Jan 50

BITNER, WILLIAM
A Drop of Water   S&T 25,Jul 74
An Evening in the Wood   DFy 8,May 76
It's Nothing   S&T 58,Jan 81
The Platinum Box   S&T 40,Jan 77

BIXBY, [Drexel] JEROME [Lewis] [1923-]
US writer; former magazine editor
Angels in the Jets   Ftc Fal 52
Can Such Beauty Be?   BFF Sep 53
*The Draw   Ftc Mar 67
  [*Amazing Stories* Mar 54]
The Good Dog   Ftc Jan/Feb 54
Halfway to Hell   BFF Jan 54
*It's a *Good* Life   SFy 16,Nov 55
  [*Star SF 2* ed.Frederik Pohl,1953]
The Monsters   Ftc Sep/Oct 53
The Murder-Con [nt]   Ftc Oct 54
The Young One   Ftc Apr 54
*The Young One   Ftc Jan 67

    as Jay B.Drexel
For Little George   Ftc Aug 54

    + Joe E.Dean
Share Alike   BFF Jul 53

BIXBY, NEWELL
The Girl Who Was God   Fear May 60

BLACK, BRANTON   (pseud)
Devil's Brew   ES Aug 37

BLACK, JULES
Only For You   BMM Nov 65

BLACK, Jr., R.JERE
Lyonesse [v]   WT Dec 28
Masquerade [v]   WT Mar 30
The Pirate [v]   WT Aug 30

BLACKBEARD, BILL   [1926-]
US author, researcher and bibliophile
  + James Causey
Hammer of Cain   WT Nov 43

BLACKMON, RICHARD
The Release of Sclotha   Spoor 2,1974

BLACKMON, ROBERT C.
*According to R.K.Jones this is a pseud.of
Roger Howard Norton,but according to Will
Murray,who has inspected the S&S files,it
is a real name.*
The Devil's Nightmare   Ace Jul 36
Fangs of the Soul   EM Feb 39

BLACKWOOD, ALGERNON [Henry]   [1869-1951]
*British mystic, novelist and short story
writer*
*Ancient Sorceries [nt] *[JS]*   FC 4,1973
  [*John Silence*,1908]
*Ancient Sorceries [adapted as a cs
  by Jonathan Bacon]   FCr 4/5,Aug 75
*Ghost Who Begged "Kiss Me! Love
  Me!"   TTT Spr 64
  [*orig."The Woman's Ghost Story" *The
  Listener*,1907; see also "The Specter
  That Asked For a Kiss"]
The Magic Mirror   WT Sep 38
*The Nemesis of Fire [na] *[JS]*
                                 BFT 2,Mar 71
  [*John Silence*,1908]
*The Other Wing   AFR 8,1948
  [*McBride's Magazine* Nov 15]
*The Pikestaffe Case [nt]   TMD(1934)
  [*Tongues of Fire*,1924]
*A Psychical Invasion [na2]
  [JS]   MoH 21-22,May-Jul 68
  [*John Silence*,1908]
Roman Remains   WT Mar 48
*Secret Worship [nt] *[JS]* FCr 4/5,Aug 75
  [*John Silence*,1908]
*Smith: an Episode in a Lodging
  House   FFy Jun 71
  [*The Empty House*,1906]
*The Specter That Asked For a Kiss
                                 GS Jul 29
  [*orig."The Woman's Ghost Story" *The
  Listener*,1907; see also "Ghost Who
  Begged "Kiss Me! Love Me!"]
*A Victim of Higher Space *[JS]* AFR 18,1952
  [*The Occult Review* Dec 14]
*The Willows [nt]   TU 1(1934)
  [*The Listener*,1907]
[*The Woman's Ghost Story - see "Ghost Who
  Begged 'Kiss Me! Love Me!'" and "The
  Specter That Asked For a Kiss"]

BLADE, ALEXANDER
*Ziff-Davis house name used by many writers;
following story's author unidentified*
The Cheat   Ftc May 58

BLAIKIE, NEAL R.
Monster of the Faith [v]   Jeet 1,Apr 77

BOUNDS, SYDNEY J[ames] [1920-]
UK writer, mostly of short stories
Borden Wood   FyT 2,Win 77
First Trip   SFy 11,Dec 54
Random Power   SFy 20,Dec 56
Scissors   SFy 63,Feb 64
The Solution   Div 28/9,Feb/Mar 79
Strange Portrait   Out Win 46
The Treasure of Tagor   SFy 4,Spr 52

BOUR, Jr., LAURENCE
Black Was the Night   WT May 40
Call of Duty   Unk Feb 40
*Call of Duty   UnkB Feb 40

BOURGOYNE, JAMES
My $250,000 Ghost   GS Dec 28

BOUSFIELD, H[enry] T[homas] W[ishart]
UK writer   [1891-?]
The Impossible Adventure   WT Nov 40

BOVA, BEN[jamin William] [1932-]
US sf & technical writer and editor
Talk to Me, Sweetheart   BI Nov/Dec 67

BOVEY, JOHN
The Fifth Door   Gothic Dec 79

BOWEN, R. T.
   Pseud: see Robert BLOCH

BOWER, ROGER
Grandfather's Table Talk [v]
                            S&T 61,Win 81/2
Quotidien [v]   S&T 62,Sum 82
Rest and Relaxation [v] S&T 65,Win 83/4

BOWERS, Dr EDWIN F[rederick] [1871-?]
US physician and medical/occult writer
My First Encounter With a Ghost
   [a]   GS Aug 30

BOWERS, GEORGE BALLARD
The Charm That Failed   WT Jun 26
The Contra-Talisman   WT Apr 26
A Gaddaan Alaad   WT Mar 25
That White Superiority   WT Feb 25

BOWIE, ROBERT G.
   + Robinson H. Harsh
Crossed Lines   WT Feb 25

BOWKER, RICHARD
The Other Train Phenomenon   TZ Feb 82

BOWLES, O. J.
A Dream That Lasted a Century   GS May 28

BOWMAN, EARL WAYLAND
Senorita Serpente   WT Jul/Aug 23

BOWMAN, RICHARD
Detente   Nov Win 81

BOYCE, CHRIS [1943-]
*Scottish writer; newspaper research
librarian*
George   Imp 4,Jun 66
Mantis [nt]   Imp 11,Jan 67

The Rig [nt]   Imp 7,Sep 66

BOYD, CAROL
The Man Who Looked Behind   StS Dec 39

BOYD, LYLE G.
   *Wife of William C. BOYD, whom see for
   details.*

BOYD, THOMAS
*The Bibliophile   MoH 18,Nov 67
   [*The Bookman Jan 28]

BOYD, WALDO T.
Wings and a Vision [ts]   Mystic Oct 54

BOYD, WILLIAM C[louser] [1903-83]
US Professor of Immunochemistry
   + Lyle G. Boyd as Boyd Ellanby
House...Wife [nt]   BFF Nov 53

BOYETTE, PAT
UFOs [cs]   FCr 4/5,Aug 75

BRABY, JAMES
Nightmare   TCP(1937)

BRACKEN, MICHAEL
Charles L. Grant: In the Shadows
   [a]   NV 5,Fal 79
The Monteleone Connection [in] NV 7,Spr 81
More Than Amazing [a]   NV 8,Fal 81

   + Wayne W. Martin
Game of Chance   NV 9,Win/Spr 83

BRACKETT, LEIGH [Douglas] [1915-78]
US author and screenwriter
Return to Wonder [a]   FCr 8,May 76
The Tapestry Gate   StS Aug 40

BRADBURY, RAY[mond Douglas] [1920-]
US writer, poet and playwright
Interviews   Div 25,Mar 78
                            Whsp 19/20,Oct 83
*Asleep in Armageddon   AFR 11,1949
   [*Planet Stories Win 48]
Bang! You're Dead! [JC]   WT Sep 44
The Black Ferris   WT May 48
*The Burning Man   Ariel 2,Win 77
   [*Long After Midnight,1976]
The Candle   WT Nov 42
   [story completed by Henry Kuttner]
*A Careful Man Dies   Gam 5,Sep 65
   [*New Detective Nov 46]
The Crowd   WT May 43
*The Crowd   MysT 5,1952
*The Crowd   Shk May 60
The Dead Man   WT Jul 45
Death in Mexico [v]   Gam 1,1963
The Ducker   [JC]   WT Nov 43
The Dwarf   Ftc Jan/Feb 54
*The Emissary   Shk Jul 60
   [*Dark Carnival,1947]
Fever Dream   WT Sep 48
The Gift   Ftc Jul 59
*The Gift   StF 10,Fal 69
The Handler   WT Jan 47
Holiday   ArkS Aut 49
*Homecoming   AFR 3,1947
   [*Dark Carnival,1947]

BRANDON, FRANK
    Pseud: see Kenneth BULMER

BRANDON, HERBERT J.
The Black Mamba   WOM(1949)
Twenty-Five Years   WOL 1(1960)

BRANDON, MARION
The Dark Castle   ST Sep 31
*The Dark Castle   SMS 6,Fal 67
The Emergency Call   ST Jun 32
*The Emergency Call   MoH 34,Fal 70

BRANE, REGINALD
    Pseud: see Michael AMBROSE

BRANIN, JEFF
Third Tramp Stuff [v]   Wyrd 8,1980
Whadya Mean My Poems Have No
    Utility? [v]   Wyrd 8,1980

BRANSCOMBE, EUGENE
    Pseud: see Victor ROUSSEAU

BRANSON, BRANLEY ALLAN
Weird of the Bald   EC 2,1979

BRANSTON, A. J.
Can One Live Again? [a]   Phtm 8,Nov 57
Vampire - Fact or Fiction?
    [a]   Phtm 5,Aug 57

BRANTINGHAM, JULEEN
Lovey's Rival   Whsp 17/18,Aug 82
Nightbears   TZ Apr 83
The Old Man's Room   TZ Nov 81
The Ventriloquist's Daughter
                                    Whsp 19/20,Oct 83

BRASINGTON, A. LARRY
    as Stephen Cross
The Shadow in the Valley   Eld 8,1982
The Temple in the Swamp   FBDG 4,Oct 77

BRAUNBECK, GARY
Sleep [v]   Eld 9,1983
Voyeurs   Eld 9,1983

BRAZIER, DONN
Fat Chance [a]   Div 6,Dec 74
Good Eating   Ggn 5,Nov 47

BREDON, JOHN
    Pseud: see Steve ENG

BREED, B. S.
Ghosts Started Murder Trials
    [a]   Phtm 6,Sep 57
The Highway Phantoms [a]   Phtm 8,Nov 57

BREEN, JON L.
US writer, mostly of crime fiction
The Ballad of Lookhma [spf]   FB Oct 81

BREESE, EDWARD Y.
All in the Game   Ftc Feb 69

BREIDING, BILL
Black Leather Vampire   Mb 23,1976
Death Without a Funeral [v] Div 4,Sep 74

The Desert Waits [v]   Mb 16,1974
Draught [v]   Mb 12,1973
Father of Werewolves [v]   Mb 23,1976
The Golden Key [v]   Nyc 14,Mar 78
Lamia [v]   Mb 23,1976
Lonely Wanderer [v]   Mb 21,1975
Mindcrawl [v]   Mb 19,1974
Repulsion [v]   Div 11,Oct 75

BREIDING, G. SUTTON   [1950-]
US poet and writer
The Ancient Centaur to the Young
    Satyr Spake [v]   Mb 23,1976
Arkham House [v]   Div 20,May 77
Babylonian Suite [v]   Nyc 15,Jan 80
Farewell [v]   Div 4,Sep 74
Flowers for Kolleen [v]   Div 10,Aug 75
Fodder For the King [v]   Mb 12,1973
For Lovecraft [v]   Div 14,May 76
Green Bank [ss]   Mb 25,1976
Halloween Arcane [v]   Nyc 13,May 77
I Am the Favoured Prince [v]Nyc 18,Apr 83
Invitation to a Shy Satyr
    [v]   Div 28/9,Feb/Mar 79
Lawbooks of Necrophilia [a] Div 5,Oct 74
Love Song [v]   Nyc 10,Jan/Feb 75
Lovesong to a Woodnymph [v]
                                    Div 26/7,May/Jul 78
Nosferatu [v]   Mb 21,1975
A Paean and a Requiem [v]   Mb 23,1976
Post Card 1 [v]   Nyc 17,Jun 82
San Francisco [v]   Nyc 11/12,Apr 76
The Smith-Daemon and the
    Samurai   Div 11,Oct 75
Song to M'Lady [v]   Mb 23,1976
Spillt Moonbroth [v]   Mb 23,1976
The Statue's Last Plea [v]   Mb 17,1974
Untitled [v]   Nyc 10,Jan/Feb 75
[untitled]   Nyc 14,Mar 78
The White Peacocks [v]   Nyc 9,Jul 74
Windghost [v]   Div 7,Feb 75

    + Harry O. Morris
December Childhood [v]   Nyc 15,Jan 80
Dejected Prayer [v]   Nyc 16,Mar 81
Lampshade Wounds [v]   Nyc 16,Mar 81
Soft Darling [v]   Nyc 16,Mar 81

BRENNAN, DORIS PHILBRICK
Nightmare [v]   Mac 23,1976

BRENNAN, JOSEPH PAYNE   [1918-]
*US writer, poet and technical services
specialist at Yale University Library*
Interview   ToF 1,Spr 82
The Abandoned Boudoir [v] Whsp 4,Jul 74
Absence [v]   Wbk 12,1977
The Acts of Hours [v]   Wbk 4,1971
Advent of Autumn [v]   Mac 23,1976
Age [v]   Wbk 11,1977
Alien Words [v]   Wbk 4,1971
The Ancient Meadow [v]   Mac 23,1976
Apparition in the Sun [LL]Mac 13,Sum 63
Apprehension   Mac 5,Sum 59
Arkham Episode [v]   HPL 1972
Atavism [v]   Mac 11,Sum 62
The Autumn Sign [v]   Mac 20,1968
Better Oblivion's Leaf [v]   EC 4,1980
Bird Unseen [v]   Wbk 16,1982
Black October [v]   Mac 3,Sum 58
Black Thing at Midnight   MoH 7,Jan 65

BROOKE, FRANK C.
Black Man's Magic   WOL 3(1960)
N'Zamba's Gift   WOM(1949)
A Queer Guardian   WOM(1949)
[all three have a connected background]

BROOKHART, GEORGE
The Affair of the Dancing
  Coffins   GS Feb 27

BROOKS, EDWIN L.
Ju Ju Magic   Nek 5,mid-51

BROOKS, HELEN
The House I Haunted   GS Apr 29
Whispering Walls   GS Jun 28

BROOKS, JOHN R.
Bury Me Deep   UTC 12,Dec 41
The Dream   UTC 11,Nov 41

BROOKS, TERRY   [1944-]
US attorney, author of Sword of Shannara
Interview   BFWK Aut 78

BROOKS, WIN
The Invisible Man at the Helm   GS Jun 29

BROOME, JOHN
*The Pulsating Planet   [nt]   Ftc Apr 70
  [*Fantastic Adventures Sep 41]
The Redoubtable Horace
  Goppendyke   WT Jul 42

BROWER, JOSEPH E.
The Way of the Reaper   [v]   DFy 22,Mar 80

BROWN, BILL
Medicine Dancer   FM Nov 53

BROWN, BRIAN EARL
REH Zebra Cover Blurbs vs
  Reality [a]   FCr 10/11,Mar 77

  + Wayne Warfield
At World's End [a]   PD 1,1976

BROWN, DAVID J.
Born of Woman   Spoor 2,1974
No Balm in Gilead [a]   ArkS 2,Sep 83
The Search For Lovecraft's
  Outsider [a]   Nyc 8,Apr 73

BROWN, FREDRIC [William]   [1906-72]
US mystery and sf writer
The Angelic Angleworm [nt]   UW Feb 43
*The Angelic Angleworm [nt]   UWB May 43
Armageddon   Unk Aug 41
*Armageddon   UWB Aut 44
Come and Go Mad [nt]   WT Jul 49
Double Whammy:
  Naturally [ss]   BFF Sep 54
  Voodoo [ss]   BFF Sep 54
Etaoin Shrdlu   UW Feb 42
*Etaoin Shrdlu   UWB Mar 42
The Geezenstacks   WT Sep 43
The House   Ftc Aug 60
*The House   StF 10,Fal 69
*Imagine [ss]   TZ Dec 83
  [*Mag. F & SF May 55]

*Keep Out   Ftc Mar 66
  [*Amazing Stories Mar 54]
The Last Train   WT Jan 50
The New One   UW Oct 42
*The New One   UWB Oct 42

  + Mack Reynolds
*Dark Interlude   Div 25,Mar 78
  [*Galaxy SF Jan 51]
Six-Legged Svengali   WB Dec 50

  as Felix Graham
The Hat Trick   UW Feb 43
*The Hat Trick   UWB May 43

BROWN, GERALD J.   [1950-]
*US public relations officer [see also
Artist and Editor indices]*
Raising Kane [in]   NV 6,Sum 80
Songbringer [cs2]   NV 3-4,Win 78-Sum 79
Sunslayer [cs]   NV 2,Sum 78
The Tim Kirk Interview [in]   NV 6,Sum 80
Tony and the Tribe [in]   NV 5,Fal 79
Willow at the World's End
  [cs3]   NV 5-7,Fal 79-Spr 81
Yours Truly, Robert Bloch [in] NV 3,Win 78

  as Paul M. Cordel
The Alien and the Elf [cs]   NV 3,Win 78
Alwaysland   NV 2,Sum 78
Chrysalis [cs]   NV 4,Sum 79

  uncredited
Frog Wars [spf]   NV 4,Sum 79
Star Wars II [suggested
  sequel]   NV 1,Fal 77
*[The cs under Brown's name are all part of
the Sunslayer sequence]*

BROWN, MARY S.
The Magic Mirror   WT Nov 23

BROWN, PAUL CAMERON
Homuncular Forms [v]   Wyrd 8,1980

BROWN, RICH[ARD W.]   [1942-]
The Adventures of Jack, and That
  Which Befell Him   Ftc Jun 75
Dear Ted   Ftc Oct 72

BROWN, ROBERT H.   [1960-]
Person to Person   Ftc Jan 80

BROWN, ROSEL GEORGE   [1926-67]
US writer, mostly of sf and fantasy
And a Tooth   Ftc Aug 62
David's Daddy   Ftc Jun 60
There's Always a Way   Ftc Jul 60
Visiting Professor   Ftc Feb 61

BROWN, WALTER C.
Death Wore an Astrakhan Hat   WT Mar 41

BROWNE, A. R.
The Ghost Who Reformed   GS Jul 27

BROWNE, DULCIE
Ghost Farm [ts]   WT Nov 40

BROWNE, GORDON
The Empathic Man   Ftc Jan 62

BURNHAM, Jr., ROBERT
Bramryd the Brave and the Third
Wish   FB Aug 83

BURNS, ALAN   [1926-]
UK chemist
Housel   SFy 72,May 65
Passenger   SFy 79,Dec 65

BURNS, GORDON
Deep Calleth   WT May/Jul 24

BURNS, JAMES H.
Richard Matheson [in2]   TZ Sep-Oct 81

BURNS, WALTER
The Ghost of Liscard Manor   WT Nov 24

BURNSIDE, GEORGE
The Ginger Kitten   Phtm 1,Apr 57

BURRAGE, A[lfred] M[cLelland] [1889-1956]
UK novelist & short story writer
*Between the Minute and the
  Hour   GS Feb 30
The Case of Eva Gardiner   WOL 1(1960)
Corner Cottage   WOL 3(1960)
*Nobody's House   GS Dec 31/Jan 32
*Yellow Curtains   GS Apr 30
  [*all from *Some Ghost Stories*,1927]

BURROUGH, LORETTA G.
At the Time Appointed   WT Feb 37
Creeping Fingers   WT Aug 31
Person or Persons Unknown   WT Jan 41
The Snowman   WT Dec 38
A Visitor From Far Away   WT Feb 36
What Waits in Darkness   WT Mar 35
The Will of the Dead   WT Aug 37

BURROUGH, R. J.
Threat of Violence   Sus Win 52

BURROUGHS, E. S.
Mother Love   EC 2,1979

BURROWES, GEORGE
The Mirror   WT Feb 33

BURSTINER, IRVING
Pardon My Terror   Sus Sum 51

BURTON, RAYMOND L.
  Pseud: see E. C. TUBB

BURUS, WALTER NOBLE
The Man The Law Forgot   WT Jun 23

BUSBY, Jr., F. M.   [1921-]
US writer, former Digital-Communications
Engineer
I'm Going to Get You   Ftc Mar 74
Once Upon a Unicorn   Ftc Apr 73
The Puiss of Krrlik   Ftc Apr 72
The Real World   Ftc Dec 72

BUSH, DON CLARK
The Bargain Hunter   Mac 7,Sum 60

BUSH, LAURENCE C.
Surrealism and Modern Horror
  Literature [a]   Nyc 18,Apr 83

BUSSEY, LESLIE
Green Eyes For Evil   WOL 1(1960)

BUTLER, ELLIS PARKER   [1862-1937]
US essayist and humorist
*"Dey Ain't No Ghosts"   GS Oct 29
  [*Humorous Ghosts* ed. Dorothy
   Scarborough,1921]

BUTLER, G. M.
The Doctor Gave a Verdict   MyS 18(1939)

BUTLER, IRA T.
Conglomerate [v]   Arg 8,Fal/Win 81

BUTLER, RON
Too Tough to Bury   Ftc Jun 55
What Number Are You Calling? Ftc Oct 55

BUTT, ELIZABETH
Am I Six Thousand Years Old?
  [a]   GS Nov 30

BUTTMAN, HARRY
Finished Game   WT Oct 39

BUTTS, ED
A Meeting of Hunters   EC 9,1982

BUTZ, C. A.
Dream Sepulture [v]   WT Jul 36
Swamp Demons [v]   WT Aug/Sep 36

BUXTON, CARL
House name used by Harold Hersey & others
    by Harold Hersey
Marsa [v]   TB May 15,19

    by Clark Ashton Smith
The Love That Stirs Me So [v] TB Sep 15,19

    by poets unknown (may be Hersey)
Dim Unknown [v]   TB Oct 1,19
Living Memories [v]   TB Sep 15,19

BYE, JON
The Green Man Speaks [v]   DH 23,Sum 81
The Promise [v]   DH 26,Spr 83
Revelations [v]   DH 25,Sum 82

BYRNE, BROOK
Sic Transit Gloria [v]   WT Nov 33
The Werewolf's Howl   WT Dec 34

BYRNE, JOHNNY   [1937-]
Irish short story/screenwriter
The Criminal   SFy 74,Jul 65
The Foreigner   SFy 77,Oct 65
Harvest   SFy 69,Jan/Feb 65
The Jobbers   SFy 76,Sep 65
Love Feast   SFy 67,Sep/Oct 64
Yesterday's Gardens   SFy 78,Nov 65

BYRON, ROSE
The Kiss in the Dark   GS Feb 29

C

CABOS, LEW[ELLYN] M.
The Adventures of Doc Savage
[a]   Div 12,Jan 76
Ancestral Memory and Reincarnation
in Robert E.Howard's Fiction
[a]   E&O 3,1983
Beneath the Sleeping City [Cth] DMR 1,1975
Candles Burning Blue [Cth] FBDG 4,Oct 77
The Color From Beyond [Cth] Eld 4,Oct 78
Curse of the Black One [Cth] Div 4,Sep 74
Dr. Dexter   [Cth]   ToF 1,Spr 82
The Eye of Atcha-Talan
[Amer]   Div 10,Aug 75
The Hour of Demons   E&O 2,1983
Howl of the Wolves [Cth]   S&T 23,Mar 74
The Lurkers Beneath   Spoor 2,1974
The Man From Blood [a]   Div 19,Mar 77
The Nameless Isle [Cth]   S&T 31,Jul 75
The Sword of God [JS]   DFy 19,Feb 79
The Thing in the Abyss [Cth] Eld 5,Apr 79
Thundering Drums [JS]   DFy 11,Jan 77
The Valley of the Dead
[Amer]   S&T 37,Jul 76
When Dreams Come True   Spoor 1,1974
Wreck of the Alatair   S&T 20,Sep 73

    as C.H. Mallory
Mad Eyes in Darkness   [Cth] DMR 1,1975
[Amer - Amergon; Cth - Cthulhu Mythos;
JS - John Smith]

CABRAL, O[lga] M.
Mirage   WT Jan 41
Tiger! Tiger!   StS Jun 40
Unhallowed Holiday   WT Sep 41

CADIGAN, PAT[ricia]   [1953-]
US commercial writer [see Editor Index]
Beauty and the Beast [a]   Shyl 2,Feb 78
Death From Exposure [nt]   Shyl 2,Feb 78
The Genie-Us of Tom Reamy
[in]   Shyl 1,Nov 77
Last Chance For Angina Pectoris
at Miss Sadie's Saloon, Dry
Gulch   Chac 2,Spr 77
Tom Reamy [obit]   Shyl 2,Feb 78

    + Arnie Fenner
14 Questions: Michael Whelan
[in]   Shyl 5,Win 82
Night-Flying With George
R.R.Martin [in]   Shyl 6,Win 82

    + Arnie Fenner & Marty Ketchum
Has Success Spoiled Stephen
King? [in]   Shyl 6,Win 82

    + Arnie Fenner, Marty Ketchum &
Lewis Shiner
Shine of the Times [in]   Shyl 3,Sum 79

    + Arnie Fenner, Bob Haas, Vikki
Marshall & Jan Schwab
Dreams of the Dreamer [in] Shyl 2,Feb 78

CADOR, C[ARODAC] A.
Keeper of the Wood   DFd 3,Sum 80

*Payment in Kind   FyT 7,Spr 81
[*Gnostica Aug 75]

CAFFREY, NICK
    + David A. Riley
The Artist in Fandom: Jim Pitts
[in]   DH 9,Sum 74

CAGLIOSTRO, COUNT   (House pseud)
Spirit Tales [col] GS Feb 27-Aug/Sep 31
[this col appeared regularly from the
first issue, but with no by-line]

CAHILL, LAURENCE J.
Charon   WT Jan 35
They Called Him Ghost   WT Jun 34
*They Called Him Ghost   MoH 22,Jul 68

CAHOON, BRAD
Curse of the Dragon Sword   S&T 52,Jul 79
Dead Run   S&T 55,Apr 80

    + John Lee
The Mandruv Effect   S&T 51,Apr 79

CAILLOU, ALAN
    Pseud: see Alan LYLE-SMITH

CAIN, M. J.
The Tryst in the Tomb   WT Nov 28

CAIRN, SILVESTER
The Silver Button   Phtm 15,Jun 58

CALDER, A. W.
Song of Death   WT Jun 38
The Thought-Devil   WT Jul 32

CALHOUN, HOWELL [Vincent]   [1921-]
The Lost Temple of Xantoos [v] WT Oct 36
Omega [v]   WT Jan 37
The Plumed Serpent [v]   WT May 39

CALIN, HAROLD
*Unauthorized   StF 12,Sum 70
[*Amazing Stories Oct 59]

CALLAHAN, HOWARD
The Skeleton in Armor   UTC 11,Nov 41

CALLOWAY, ARTEMUS
Jungle Death   WT Apr 23

CALMUS, BERNARD L.
The Howl of the Werewolf   Phtm 1,Apr 57
The Thing That Bites   Phtm 1,Apr 57

CAMNER, HOWARD
Mystical Lady [v]   Div 22,Sep 77

CAMOIN, FRANCOIS
Centaur   TZ Dec 83

CAMPBELL, E. D.
The Hybrid Queen   SFy 22,Apr 57

CAMPBELL, EUGENE   [1922-]
Dead on Time   WOM(1949)

CAMPBELL, FLORENCE
  Find Your Life Numbers
    [col]   GS May-Aug/Sep 31

CAMPBELL, GRACE M.
  The Law of the Hills   WT Aug 30

CAMPBELL, HANNAH BAIRD
  At Eventide [v]   WT Feb 30
  Ballade of Wandering Ghosts [v] WT Mar 29

CAMPBELL, H[erbert] J.
  UK research chemist; former sf editor and
  writer
    Things Are on the Move [ged]
                            SFy 4,Spr 52

CAMPBELL, Jr., JOHN W[ood] [1910-71]
  US writer; editor of sf magazine Analog
  (formerly Astounding) from 1937-71.
    Profile   Div 25,Mar 78
    To Write - Be Wrong! [a]   Biz Jan 41
      rewrite of story by Arthur J.Burks
      run under by-line Don A.Stuart
    The Elder Gods [sn]   Unk Oct 39
    *The Elder Gods [sn]   UnkB Oct 39

CAMPBELL, LAURA E.
  Atomic Slippage   Div 23,Nov 77
  Dompadry Owes One More Year S&T 62,Sum 82

CAMPBELL, [John] RAMSEY [1946-]
  UK writer, mostly of horror fiction.
    Interview   Whsp 15/16,Mar 82
    Accident Zone   FyT 2,Win 77
    Again   TZ Nov 81
      [also in *GSTZ,1982]
    Among the Pictures Are These
                            Nyc 16,Mar 81
    Bait   DH 26,Spr 83
    Bergman and the Horror Film:
      Some Observations [a]   DH 9,Sum 74
    The Burning   G&S 3,1981
    The Change   Shyl 3,Win 80
    Conversion   Whsp 15/16,Mar 82
    Cthulhu in Celluloid [a]   ArkC 3,Sum 68
    *Cthulhu in Celluloid [a;
      revised version]   DH 25,Sum 82
    Derleth As I Knew Him [a2]
                            DH 7-8,Dec 73-Apr 74
    Down There   WT 1,Spr 81
    The Drowned Car [v]   Mac 21,1970
    Eye of Childhood   Whsp 15/16,Mar 82
    *The Face in the Desert [Cth]FBDG 4,Oct 77
      [*Mirage 7,1965]
    Heading Home   Whsp 11/12,Oct 78
    Jack in the Box   DH 26,Spr 83
    Just Waiting   TZ Dec 83
    A Madness From the Vaults [Cth] HPL 1972
    *A Madness From the Vaults
      [Cth]   FyT 1,Sum 77
    The Next Side Show   TZ Apr 81
    Night Beat   HoH Jun 73
    Out of Copyright   Whsp 15/16,Mar 82
    *Reflections on 'The Face in the
      Desert' [a]   FBDG 4,Oct 77
      [*Weird Fantasy 1,Win 69]
    *Reply Guaranteed   Whsp 5,Nov 74
      [*Tandem Horror 2 ed.Richard Davis,1968]

    The Scar   SMS 13,Sum 69
    The Shadows in the Barn DH 12,Aut/Win 75
    Smoke Kiss   Whsp 8,Dec 75
    Snakes and Ladders   TZ Apr 82
    To Wake the Dead: Prologue DH 20,1979
    Trick or Treat   WT 2,Spr 81
    The Voice of the Beach [Cth]
                            FyT 10,Sum 82
    Wrapped Up   FyT 7,Spr 81
    Writer's Curse   NF 1,Win 80/1

      as Montgomery Comfort
    The Stages of the God   Whsp 5,Nov 74
  [Cth - Cthulhu Mythos]

CAMPION, THOMAS
  The Ghost Wanted My Heart   AH Apr 71

CAMPTON, DAVID   [1924-]
  UK playwright and radio dramatist
    Alderman Stratton's Fancy
                            Whsp 13/14,Oct 79
    At the Bottom of the Garden Whsp 9,Dec 76
    *Goat   Whsp 8,Dec 75
      [*New Writings in Horror & the
       Supernatural ed.David Sutton,1971]
    A Posthumous Bequest   Whsp 17/18,Aug 82

CANNING, DERMOT
  Ghost With a Mission [a]   Phtm 6,Sep 57

CANNING, PHILIP
  Colloquy on a Field of Skulls
    [ss]   Anu 4,Aut 68
  Eine Kleine Nachtmusik [v]   Anu 4,Aut 68
  From the Diary of a Corpse
    [v]   Anu 4,Aut 68
  Illumination [v]   Anu 2,Spr 67
  Irem [v]   Anu 2,Spr 67
  A Knight of Uthar-Pent   Anu 2,Spr 67
  My Lords, a Fretful Spirit
    Speaks... [v]   Anu 2,Spr 67
  The Perfumed Room   Anu 4,Aut 68
  Vanished Hunters [v]   Anu 3,1968

CANNON, PETER
  Fantasy Acrostic No.1 [quiz]   TZ Jun 83
  H.P.Lovecraft [in]   TZ Aug 83
  Lovecraft's Old Men   Nyc 16,Mar 81
  "You Have Been in Providence,
    I Perceive" [a]   Nyc 14,Mar 78

      "+ H.P.Lovecraft"
  The Madness Out of Space [nt2]
    [Cth]   Eld 8-9,1982-83
  [Cth - Cthulhu Mythos]

CAPELLA, RAY/RAUL GARCIA   [1933-]
  Puerto Rican born writer;former fan artist
    Arquel of Argos [a]   FB Nov 82
    *Caravan to Kuthchemes [nt]   FB Nov 82
      [Arquel;*an earlier version appeared
       in Anduril 7,Feb 79]
    *The Leopard of Poitain [Arquel] FB May 83
      [*Amra 53,1970]
    Look Behind Me   FB Feb 82

CAPOBIANCO, MICHAEL
  The October Pumpkins
                            Div 28/9,Feb/Mar 79

CEDAR, LARRY
Interview   TZ Oct 83

CELIS, BILL
R.E.H.: College Fictioneer [a]
                                   WA 1,May 78

CEPHUS, DELORES
Pseud: see Dale C. DONALDSON

CERSOSIMO, ADALBERTO
Il Collezionista e la Grand
  Inquisizione   Kad 2,May 80

CERTO, BESSIE J.   [1896-]
Twice Born   GS Feb 30

CHADWICK, ADRIAN
Pseud: see A. Bruce CLINGAN

CHADWICK, PAUL
Mistress of the Snarling Death Ace Jul 36

CHALLIS, GEORGE
Pseud: see Frederick FAUST

CHALLON, DAVID
Coffins Are For Corpses   MP Dec 58
You Can't Cheat Death's Demon M&T Apr 59

CHAMBERLAIN, Lieut. E. W.
Deserter   WT Dec 31

CHAMBERS, ROBERT W[illiam] [1865-1933]
US novelist and short story writer
*Cassilda's Song [v]   MoH 8,Apr 65
*The Demoiselle D'Ys   WT Aug 28
*The Fatal Messenger   GS Nov 29
  [*The Mystery of Choice,1897]
*In the Court of the Dragon   AFR 5,1947
*In the Court of the Dragon   MoH 10,Aug 65
*The Mask   GS Feb 30
*The Mask   MoH 6,Nov 64
*Passeur   MoH 8,Apr 65
  [*The Mystery of Choice,1897]
*The Repairer of Reputations   MoH 3,Feb 64
*The Sign of Venus   WT Sum 73
  [*The Tree of Heaven,1907]
*The Splendid Apparition   WT Win 73
  [*In Search of the Unknown,1904]
*The Yellow Sign   AFR 2,1947
*The Yellow Sign   MoH 1,Aug 63
  [*all other stories from The King
  in Yellow,1895]

CHAMPION, D. L.
US pulp adventure and mystery writer
  as Jack d'Arcy
The Bowery Wraith   GS Aug 30
By Rope and Fire   GS Mar 31
*Curse of the Violated Virgin TTT Fal 63
  [*see "Talisman of Fate"]
Dead Man's Courage   GS Oct 30
Frozen Vengeance   GS Dec 30
Gambler's Gold   GS May 30
The Gospel of a Gangster's Ghost GS Nov 30
Talisman of Fate   GS Jun 31
  [see rep. as "Curse of the
  Violated Virgin]

CHANCE, PETER
The Black Pagoda [na3] TMM Dec 27-Feb 28

CHANDLER, A[rthur] BERTRAM [1912-]
UK-born Australian Ship's Master and sf
writer
The Converts   SFy 27,Feb 58
Female of the Species   Ftc Sep 59
The Genie   Ftc Sep 61
Ghost   SFy 26,Dec 57
Gold Is Where You Find It
  [a]   Div 25,Mar 78
The Hairy Parents   Ftc Oct 78
How to Win Friends   SFy 25,Oct 57
The Idol   Ftc Aug 59
*The Idol   WM 2,Win 70
The Key [nt]   [JG]   Ftc Jul 59
Late   SFy 13,Apr 55
The Magic,Magic Carpet [nt]   Ftc Oct 59
The Maze   SFy 21,Feb 57
Next in Line   SFy 4,Spr 52
The Principle   SFy 22,Apr 57
Six of One...   SFy 9,Jul 54
Spartan Planet [n2] [JG] Ftc Mar-May 68
The Trouble With Them   SFy 24,Aug 57
The Underside   SFy 32,Dec 58
The Unharmonious Word   SFy 19,Aug 56
The Window   TF Aug 57
The Wrong Track [nt]   SFy 12,Feb 55
  [as by 'George Whitley' on story]

    as George Whitley
Can Do   SFy 34,Apr 59
Castaway   WT Nov 47
*Change of Heart   Ftc May 62
  [*also in New Worlds 110,Sep 61]
The Tie That Binds   SFy 26,Dec 57
[JG - John Grimes and the Rim Worlds]

CHANDLER, LAWRENCE
Ziff-Davis house name used original by
Howard Browne, then by various writers
  by W. P. McGivern
Death's Bright Angel   Ftc Jun 54

  by Henry Slesar
Tool of the Gods   Ftc Nov 57

  by authors unknown (may be Paul Fairman)
The Day After Eternity [nt]   Ftc Feb 55
*The Day After Eternity [nt]   Ftc Feb 59
Death Has Strong Hands   Ftc Apr 55
Hello, Young Lover   Ftc Oct 58
The Vicar of Skeleton Cove   Ftc Dec 54

CHANDLER, RAYMOND   [1888-1959]
US detective story writer
The Bronze Door [nt]   Unk Nov 39
*Professor Bingo's Snuff [nt] Ftc Sum 52
  [*Park-East Magazine,1951]

CHANEY, LENORE E.
White Man's Madness   WT Jan 25

CHANEY [Sr.], LON   [1883-1930]
US silent movie star
Selected: My Favorite Ghost Story:
  6."Pollock and the Porroh Man"
    by H. G. Wells   GS Jul 30

CHANT, [Eileen] JOY[ce]   [1945-]
UK librarian and writer
Spring, the Young Warrior [v] BFWK Aut 78
White Are the Horns of the
   Horses [v]   DFd 3,Sum 80

CHAPIN, ANNA ALICE
When Dead Lips Speak   TB Aug 1,19

CHAPMAN, ARTHUR EDWARDS   [1898-]
*Apparently a UK writer, not to be confused
with the US historical novelist*
The Borgia Ring   WT Oct 32
The Fair Pastie Pie   WT Jan 26
The Inn of Dread   WT Oct 23
The Spider   WT Nov 23
The Tap   WT Feb 24
Was it the Devil's Work [a]   GS Dec 26

CHAPMAN, GAYNOR
Ultramarine   DH 13,Spr 76

CHAPMAN, JOHN L.
   + Oliver Saari
The Deathless Ones   Sus Spr 51

CHAPMAN, STEVE   [1951?-]
US theatre actor/playwright
The Throwaway Man   Wbk 3,1970

CHARBONNEAU, SANDRE
Creative Writing   TZ Dec 82

CHARLOT, LEONARD LEE
Dead Silence   WT Jul 42

CHARTAIR, MAX
   Pseud: see John S. GLASBY

CHARTERIS, Sir BASIL   (pseud)
The Real Thing   Thrl Jul 62

CHASE, ADAM
   Pseud: see Stephen MARLOWE

CHASE, FRANKLIN
Trapped Without Hope on the
   Ship of the Dead   AH Aug 71

CHASE, NOWELL
The Disappearance of Peregrine Ggn Jul 47

CHASE, ROBERT
Last Laughter   Ftc Jan 59

CHATER, LEE
The Thing on the Stairs   Cov Mar 70

CHAUVIN, CY
British and American SF:
   'Waves' Apart? [a]   BL 4/5,Jan 78

CHECKLEY, Jr., JAMES W.
A Switch in Time   Div 7,Feb 75

CHEETHAM, ROBERT
Omega and Alpha   SFy 76,Sep 65

CHEIRO
   Pseud: see Louis HAMON

CHENEY, L. STANLEY
Midnight Encore of Edgar Allan Poe
   [v]   Mac 20,1968

CHERNA, HOWARD
Devil of Denham Swamp   AH Oct 70

CHERRYH, C[arolyn] J[anice]   [1942-]
US novelist, mostly of sf & fantasy
Interview   Shyl 5,Win 82
"...Homecoming..."   Shyl 3,Sum 79

CHESEBRO, DARLENE A.
Nantichoke   Mb 13,1974

CHESNEY, Dr. W. D.
The Exposer Exposed [a]   Mystic Dec 54

CHESTERTON, G[ilbert] K[eith] [1874-1936]
UK author, poet, artist & essayist
*The Honour of Israel Gow   TMD 1(1934)
   [*orig."The Strange Justice" *Cassell's
   Magazine* Apr 11; as above in *The
   Innocence of Father Brown*,1911]
*The Noticeable Conduct of Professor
   Chadd   AFR 17,1951
   [*The Club of Queer Trades,1905, from
   The Idler during 1904]

CHIBBETT, H[arold] S[tanley] W[alter]
UK civil servant   [1900-78]
They That Wait   MoH 3,Feb 64
They Worked the Oracle   WT Nov 50

   as A. Hastwa
Psychic Scents [a]   Out Win 46

CHILSON, ROBERT   [1945-]
US clerk and writer
In Quest of Something   Whsp 17/18,Aug 82

CHILTON, Dr ROBERT H.
The Bride and the Open Grave [ts]
                              GS Apr 29

CHINN, MIKE   [1954-]
UK laboratory technician
But the Stones Will Stand   FyT 10,Sum 82
The Death-Wish Mandate   Kad 5,Jul 82
The Pistol and the Sword   DH 20,1979
The Second Dragons [s3]
             DH 10,12,14,Aut/Win 74-Sum 76
Sic Transit   FyT 8,Sum 81

CHOONG, K. S.
River Mist   Phtm 1,Apr 57

CHRISTIE, AGATHA [Mary Clarissa]
UK mystery novelist/playwright [1890-1976]
*The Blue Geranium *[MM]*   MysT Jan 52
   [**The Thirteen Problems*,1932]
*Death By Drowning *[MM]*   MysT Jun 52
   [**Mystery Magazine*,1926]
The Woman Who Stole a Ghost   GS Nov 26
   [better known as "The Last Seance"]
[MM - Miss Marple]

CHRISTOPHER, HUGH
The Mind of Young Crandle   SFy 58,Apr 63

The Curse of a Song   WT Mar 28
The Dark Chrysalis [nt3]   WT Jun-Aug 27
The Deadly Amanita   WT Dec 25
Design For Doom   StS Aug 40
Farthingale's Poppy   WT Jul 25
The Golden Whistle   WT Jan 28
The Greatest Gift   WT Mar 27
The Last Horror   WT Jan 27
*The Last Horror   WT Feb 39
The Man in the Green Coat   WT Aug 28
The Man Who Died Twice   WT Nov 39
On the Dead Man's Chest [na4]
                           WT Jan-Apr 26
One Man's Hell [nt]   StS Apr 40
The Vengeance of the Dead [nt2]
                           WT Feb-Mar 29

COLVIN, JAMES
    Pseud: see Michael MOORCOCK

COMFORT, MONTGOMERY
    Pseud: see Ramsey CAMPBELL

COMPTON, D. G.   [1930-]
UK novelist, mostly of sf
It's Smart to Have an English
    Address   Imp 12,Feb 67

COMPTON, F. T.
Three Flowers [ts]   WT Jul 40

COMPTON, PAUL
The Diary of Philip Westerly
                          WT Aug/Sep 36

COMSTOCK, LARRY
Voice of Space   UTC 2,Dec 40

CONANT, CHESTER B.
    Pseud: see Chester COHEN

CONDER, WILLIAM A[ndrew] [1957-]
US industrial engineer
Al Azif [v]   E&O 2,1983
The Babysitter [v]   Arg 6,Sum/Fal 79
The Bard of Auburn [v]   FCr 6,Nov 75
Coquette [v]   S&T 37,Jul 76
Cthulhu Speaks [v] [Cth]   E&O 2,1983
The Dream [v]   E&O 2,1983
The Dreamer [v]   DFy 9,Sep 76
The Experience   [Cth]   Div 14,May 76
Genesis [v]   Arg 5,Win/Spr 79
Hell's Artist [v]   FCw 1,Jan 77
Hide and Seek   Div 19,Mar 77
Hymn to Apollo [v]   FCw 1,Jan 77
Invocation [v]   EC 4,1980
Love at First Sight [v]   E&O 2,1983
Love Unveiled [v]   Eld 3,1978
*Love Unveiled [v]   E&O 2,1983
Lycanthrope [v]   FCw 1,Jan 77
Macabre [v]   FCw 1,Jan 77
Mike Hammer: Redneck Superman
    [a]   Div 23,Nov 77
My Love, My Wedding [v]   Div 13,Mar 76
Nocturnal Goddess [v]   E&O 2,1983
Ode to the Pulps [v]   FCr 8,May 76
The Shadow [v]   E&O 2,1983
Sonnet to Howard [v]   FCr 6,Nov 75
The Strange Boy [v]   E&O 3,1983
This Man From Providence [v]
                          Nyc 11/12,Apr 76

To Lovecraft, the Second Master
    [v]   E&O 2,1983
To Poe, the Master [v]   E&O 2,1983
Tryst [v]   Arg 5,Win/Spr 79
Twilight Calling [v]   Wyrd 8,1980
Ulysses [v]   FCw 1,Jan 77

CONGDON, HENRY
Love - Beyond the Border   GS Jan 30

CONGER, SYNDY McMILLEN
Faith and Doubt in the Castle
    of Otranto [a]   Goth Dec 79

CONLON, BEN   [1892-?]
Dead Men's Eyes   GS Apr 28
Radio Ghost   GS Mar 30
The Varsity Murder [n5] GS Sep 29-Jan 30

CONNELL, KARL KIM
    Translator; see Jean MUNO

CONNER, J. H.
Into the Valley of Whispering
    Shadows   GS Sep 26

CONNER, WILKIE
Doomsroad   Nek 2,Sum 50

CONNINGTON, J. J.
    Pseud: see Alfred W. STEWART

CONNOLLY, LAWRENCE C.
US printer,writer and folk-singer
Echoes   TZ Feb 83
Mrs.Halfbooger's Basement   TZ Jun 82
Rope the Hornet   Ftc Jul 80

CONNOLLY, P. A.
Crawling Death [nt]   WT Nov 23
The Crawling Hands [nt2]
                        TB May 15-Jun 1,19

CONNOLLY, PATRICK
At the End of the Road   FyT 3,Sum 78

CONNOR, WILL
The Road in Back   Mac 10,Win 61/2

CONNORS, SCOTT
*The Riddle of the Black
    Seal [a]   Nyc 10,Jan/Feb 75
    [*Esoteric Order of Dagon mailing Oct 74]

CONOVER, Jr., WILLIS   [1920-]
US radio broadcaster on VoA in Europe
Awakening [v]   WT May 40
Introduction to "Supernatural
    Horror in Literature" [a] WT Fal 73

CONRAD, CHARLES
Dreadful Heritage   GS Nov 29

CONRAD, GREGG
    Pseud: see Roger P. GRAHAM

CONRAD, JOSEPH   [1857-1924]
Polish born UK novelist
*The Inn of the Two Witches   GS Feb 30
    [*Metropolitan Magazine May 1913;
    also in Within the Tides,1915]

The Universe is Mine [mt]   Ftc Apr 58

COSTER, ARTHUR
    Pseud: see Richard DE MILLE

COSTIKYAN, GREG
    Games Fen Will Play [col] Ftc Apr-Oct 80

COTRION, ANTHONY
    Pseud: see Ernest L. GABRIELSON

COTTRELL, WILLIAM D.
    In Beulah Land, the Pipes That
      Play   FB May 83

COULSON, JUANITA   [1933-]
US writer and noted fan editor
    The Dragon of Tor-Nali [Clar] Ftc Feb 75
    Wizard of Death   [Clar]   Ftc Feb 73
    [Clar - Clarique]

COULTER, D. M.
    The Opened Door   MM Jun 31

COUNCIL, J. O.
    The Rabbit Box   BMM Jan 66

COUNSELMAN, MARY ELIZABETH   [1911-]
US writer and poet
    The Accursed Isle   WT Nov 33
    African Wood-Carving [a] Whsp 6/7,Jun 75
    The Black Stone Statue   WT Dec 37
   *The Black Stone Statue   ASFR 3,1952
    The Bonan of Baladewa   WT Jan 49
    The Breeze and I   WT Jul 47
    The Cat Woman   WT Oct 33
   *The Cat Woman   AFR 8,1948
    Cellini's Pitchfork   FB May 82
    Chinook   WT Jul 51
    Cordona's Skull   WT Jul 50
    A Death Crown For Mr Hapworthy WT May 48
    The Devil Himself   MM Nov 31
    The Devil's Lottery   WT Sep 48
    Drifting Atoms   WT May 41
    Echidna [v]   WT Jul 32
   *The Fay-Child [v]   Div 18,Jan 77
      [*The Delineator during 1926]
    Gentle Reader   Div 23,Nov 77
    The Girl With the Green Eyes WT May 33
    The Green Window   WT Nov 49
    Healer   WT 1,Spr 81
    The House of Shadows   WT Apr 33
   *The House of Shadows   AFR 13,1950
    In Loving Tribute: I Remember
      Seabury [a]   E&O 2,1983
    The Lamashtu Amulet   WT 2,Spr 81
    The Lens   WT Nov 47
    Madman's Song [v]   WT Apr 32
   *Madman's Song [v]   E&O 2,1983
    Mommy   WT Apr 39
   *Mommy   AFR 15,1951
    The Monkey Spoons   WT May 50
    Night Court   WT Mar 53
    Nostalgia [v]   WT Sep 33
    Parasite Mansion   WT Jan 42
   *Penny Wise, Fate Foolish   Sus Sum 51
      [*see "The Three Marked Pennies"]
    The Prism   WT Mar 52
    Pyramid   E&O 3,1983
    Rapport   WT Sep 51

Ring Eclipse [v]   WT Jan 41
Seventh Sister   WT Jan 43
The Shot-Tower Ghost   WT Sep 49
The Smiling Face   WT Jan 50
Something Old   WT Nov 50
*Something Old   Phtm 13,Apr 58
The T'ang Horse   FB May 83
The Three Marked Pennies   WT Aug 34
   [see also "Penny Wise, Fate Foolish]
The Tree's Wife   WT Mar 50
Twister   WT Jan 40
The Unwanted   WT Jan 51
Voodoo Song [v]   WT Jul 33
Way Station   WT Nov 53
The Web of Silence   WT Nov 39
Witch-Burning [v]   WT Oct 36

'A COURT BAILIFF'
    Pseud: see Dan O'BRIEN

COURTENAY, BRYCE
    A Ghost of a Chance   Phtm 15,Jun 58

COVA, FRANCESCO
Italian fan publisher [see Editor Index]
    An Interview with Brian Lumley
      [in]   Kad 3,Nov 80
    The Situation of Weird and
      Fantasy Fiction in Italy
      [a]   Kad 1,Oct 79
    [also in Italian in two parts,
      Oct 79 - May 80]

    + Brian Lumley
    Brian Lumley: A Bibliography
      [bib]   Kad 3,Nov 80

COVER, ARTHUR BYRON   [1950-]
    Pelican's Claws   HoH Aug 73

COVINGTON, BRADLEY
    Wraith of Rannigan's Reef
                            GS Dec 31/Jan 32

COWELL, EWING
    The Captain's Ship   Phtm 3,Jun 57

COWIE, GEORGE R.
    [see Editor Index]
    Demonilization   Vor 1,1947
    Lost Destiny   Ggn Mar 49

COWLES, Rev. COWLEY
    My Wreath of Death   GS Nov 27

COWLEY, KEN[neth Woodford]   [1928-]
UK advertising director
    Ad Infinitum   DH 21.1980
    Dracula Reflects [Drac]   DH 18,1978
    Ghost Writer   DH 22,Spr 81
    Second Chance   DH 19,1979
    Wish   DH 17,Sum 77
[Drac - Dracula series]

COWPERTHWAITE, DAVID
    Incident in a Graveyard [v] FyM 4,Jul 83
    To Innsmouth [v]   FyM 3,Jun 82
    To R'lyeh [v]   FyM 3,Jun 82

*The Dead Who Walk [na]   MoH 8,Apr 65
Explorers Into Infinity [nt3]
                                WT Apr-Jun 27
The Giant World [sn3]   WT Jan-Mar 28
The Lifted Veil   WT May 47
*The Man Who Discovered Nothing ASFR 2,1951
  [*All-Story Weekly Jan 10,1920]
The Man Who Knew Everything   StS Feb 40
Pawn of Hideous Desire   UT Nov 39
Portrait   Unk Sep 39
*Portrait   UnkB Sep 39
The Robot God [nt]   WT Jul 41
*The Science of Time-Travel [a] AMF Feb 50
  [*Super Science Stories (Can) Jun 44]
They Hanged a Phantom For Murder
                                GS Jan 27
*The Three-Eyed Man   AFR 14,1950
  [*Argosy/All-Story Jul 7,1923]

  as Ray King
  [not to be confused with Rae King]
The Dead White Thing   UT Nov 39
Fresh Blood For My Bride   UT May 40

  + Mrs Ray Cummings as Gabriel Wilson
Blood Brides of the Lusting
Corpse   UT Mar 40
The Cult of the Dead   StS Oct 39
Monster of the Marsh   UT May 40
When Terror Beckons   UT Nov 39

CUNNINGHAM, JERE
The Red-Eyed Thing   TZ Sep 82

CUPITT, CAROL ANN
Gods and Children of Gods [v] Eld 7,1980
In Realms of Dreams [v]   PtF 2,1979
Merlin and Nimue [v]   NF 1,Win 80/1
Pegasus: Night Myth [v]   PtF 2,1979
Swans in the Morning [v]   S&T 56,Jul 80
Twig-Fingers [v]   S&T 61,Win 81/2
We Walked These Hills But
  Never Knew [v]   DFd 4,Win 83
The Wind Against Wood [v]   PtF 2,1979

CURRAN, ROBERT J.
The Burial   WW 1,Jun 70
The Dog   WW 2,Mar 71
Walker   S&T 35,Mar 76

CURRIER, HARRY W.
The Man Upstairs [nt]   WT Nov 53

CURRY, MARIAN STEARNS
Kaapi   StS Oct 39

CURTIS, DAVID
The Man Who Couldn't Remember TZ Aug 81

CURTIS, ROBERT H.
Harry's Story   TZ Jun 83

CURTIS, WARDON ALLAN   [1867-1940]
*The Fate of the 'Senegambian
  Queen'   WT Fal 73
  [*The Black Cat Nov 1900]
*The Monster of Lake LaMetrie Wtch Dec 36
  [*Pearson's Magazine Sep 1899]

CURTISS, FRANCISCO
A Mystery Downstairs   TB Sep 1,19

CUTLER, P. W.
Take a Letter   SFy 8,May 54

CZAPLA, CATHY YOUNG
Nemesis [v]   DFd 4,Win 83
Weathering the Storm [v] S&T 61,Win 81/2

CZECH, K[ENNETH] P[AUL]
The Snow Maiden   FB Feb 83

                    D

DAGGAN, JOHN
The Last Weapon   S&T 16,Aug 72
The Sack of Berondan   S&T 19,Jul 73

DAGHINO, ENRICO
"I Have a Heart of a Little
  Boy..." [a]   Kad 1,Oct 79
Una visita al K... Museen   Kad 1,Oct 79

DAHL, ROALD   [1916-]
US novelist and writer for children
Interview   TZ Feb 83
Profile   Nyc 18,Apr 83
Collector's Item   MysT Jan 52
*Royal Jelly   TZ Feb 83
  [*Kiss, Kiss, 1960]
*Skin   Shk Sep 60
  [*Someone Like You,1953]

DAINGERFIELD, FOXHALL
The Ghost Girl From Under the
  Cedars [ts]   GS Apr 28

DALBY, RICHARD   [1949-]
UK bookdealer and fantasy specialist
Amyas Northcote: A Forgotten Master
  of the Ghost Story [a]   G&S 4,1982
A Forgotten Disciple of M.R.
  James [a]   G&S 2,1980

DALE, DONALD
  Pseud: see Mary Dale BUCKNER

DALE, PETER
The Legacy   Phtm 6,Sep 57

DALE, S[EPTIMUS]
  Pseud: see Stephen UTLEY

DALEY, JOHN BERNARD
The Gun   Ftc Feb 55

DALLAS, GUS
US newspaperman
The Ones That Got Away   Ftc Oct 79

DALLAS, PAUL [V.]
Figurex   Ftc Oct 58
Gas!   Ftc Jul 57
Hell's Own Parlor   Ftc May 57
Operation Female   Ftc Jun 57
Time Squeeze   Ftc Sep 58

Happiness [v]   F&T 5,1974
The Hardwood Pile   Unk Sep 40
*The Hardwood Pile   UnkB Sep 40
Howard and the Races [a]   FCr 10/11,Mar 77
[H.P.Lovecraft: Mosig vs de Camp -
  see Lovecraft: A Review]
Lest Darkness Fall [n]   Unk Dec 39
*Lest Darkness Fall [n]   UnkB Dec 39
The Little Green Men [v]   FCr 7,Feb 76
Lovecraft: A Review [a]   FCr 4/5,Aug 75
  [a review by Dirk Mosig de Camp's
  Lovecraft: A Biography which led to
  a continuing exchange of correspond-
  ence in the next two issues]
 - H.P.Lovecraft: Mosig vs de Camp
  [a]   FCr 6,Nov 75
 - De Camp Responds [a]   FCr Jan 76
Magus Imperitus [v] [Cth]   FBDG 3,Apr 74
Mr. Arson   Unk Dec 41
*Mr Arson   UWB Spr 49
My Uglies [v]   Wbk 10,1976
Night [v]   ArkC 3,Sum 68
Nothing in the Rules [nt]   Unk Jul 39
  [also in *FUW,1948 and *FUWB,1952]
The Octopus [v]   Whsp 6/7,Jun 75
Pratt and His Parallel Worlds
  [a]   Ftc Dec 72
Priapus   [WN]   Ftc Dec 77
Psyche [v]   HPL 1972
Savages and Scriveners [a]
                             Div 26/7,May/Jul 78
Sesquithoughts on Lovecraft
  [a]   Nyc 14,Mar 78
Sierran Shaman [a]   Ftc Oct 72
Sirrush [v]   SMS 12,Spr 69
Skald in the Post Oaks [a]   Ftc Jun 71
Solomon's Stone [n]   UW Jun 42
*Solomon's Stone [n]   UWB Sum 49
The Stone of the Witch Queen
  [nt]   [Psd]   Wbk 12,1977
The Stronger Spell   [Psd]   FM Nov 53
Superman in a Derby [a]   Ftc Nov 74
Tintagel [v]   ArkC 1,Sum 67
Two Men in One [a]   Ftc Feb 72
The Undesired Princess [n]   UW Feb 42
The Wheels of If [sn]   Unk Oct 40
*The Wheels of If [sn]   UnkB Oct 40
White Wizard in Tweeds [a]   Ftc Nov 76
William Morris: Jack of All
  Arts [a]   Ftc Sep 74
The Wisdom of the East   UW Aug 42
*The Wisdom of the East   UWB Aug 42
Yuggoth Comes to Providence
  [v]   W&S 9,1973

   + Lin Carter
Black Sphinx of Nebthu [nt]   Ftc Jul 73
Conan and the Cenotaph   WoF 1,1968
Red Moon of Zembabwei [nt]   Ftc Jul 74
Shadow in the Skull [nt]   Ftc Feb 75
The Witch of the Mists [nt]   Ftc Aug 72
[these five are all Conan stories]

   + H. L. Gold
None But Lucifer [n]   Unk Sep 39

   comp.of fragments by Robert E. Howard
The Black Stranger [na] [Con] FM Feb 53
  [aka "The Treasure of Tranicos"]
The Frost Giant's Daughter [Con] FM Aug 53
  [orig."Gods of the North" by Howard,
  The Fantasy Fan Mar 34]

   + Fletcher Pratt
The Castle of Iron [sn] [HS] Unk Apr 41
*The Castle of Iron [sn] [HS] UnkB Jul 41
Caveat Emptor   [Gav]   WT Mar 53
The Green Magician [na] [HS]
                                  BFF 9,Oct 54
The Land of Unreason [n]   Unk Oct 41
*The Land of Unreason [n]   UWB Win 46
The Mathematics of Magic [n]
  [HS]   Unk Aug 40
*The Mathematics of Magic [n]
  [HS]   UnkB Aug 40
The Roaring Trumpet [n] [HS]   Unk May 40
*The Roaring Trumpet [n] [HS]   UnkB May 40
The Wall of Serpents [na] [HS] FM Jun 53
When the Night Wind Howls [Gav] WT Nov 51
"Where To, Please?"   [Gav]   WT Sep 52
[Con - Conan the Cimmerian; Cth - Cthulhu
Mythos; Gav - Gavagan's Bar; HS - Harold
Shea; Psd - Pusad/Poseidonis; WN - Willy
Newbury]

DE CASTRO, ADOLPHE   [1859-1959]
Common form of name used by US consul,
poet & writer Gustaf Danziger
Edgar Allan Poe [v]   WT May 37

   stories rev'd by H. P. Lovecraft
The Electric Executioner   WT Aug 30
The Last Test [nt]   WT Nov 28

DE CROUET, HENRI
   + Hasan Vokine
The Revenge of Philippe Auguste WT Aug 25

DE GARIS, EDITH
The Dragon Girl   WT Jan 32

DE GAUR, CHARLES
Horace   Phtm 4,Jul 57

DE GEORGE, EDWARD
The Carrot of Doom   FB Feb 82

DE HAMMAIS, Dr. PIERRE
   Pseud: see Edward Paul BERGLUND

DE HEREDIA, JOSE-MARIA
Oblivion [v]   ArkS Sum 49

DE HINDESONE, Dr. C. AVELASQUEZ
The Beloved Specter   GS Dec 28

DE JAYNES, RANDY L.
A Critical Biography of Le Fanu
  [rv]   Goth Dec 80

DE KREMER, JEAN-RAYMOND   [1887-1964]
Belgian journalist and writer
   as John Flanders
The Aztec Ring   WT Apr 35
The Graveyard Duchess   WT Dec 34
The Mystery of the Last Guest   WT Oct 35
Nude With a Dagger   WT Nov 34

DE LA FERTE, ALPHONSE
One Like Yourself [v]   TB Oct 1,19

DE LA REE, GERRY
US bookdealer and specialist publisher
An Unknown HPL Artist [a]   HPL 1972

DEAN, ERIC
  Leave It to Umpax   Ftc Feb 56

DEAN, GERALD
  The Devil-Bed   WT Sep 25

DEAN, JOE E.
  + Jerome Bixby
  Share Alike   BFF Jul 53

DEATON, TRACY
  Faith in the Family   Hor 2,1982

DECHAU, GARY
  The Visit   Mb 21,1975

DECKER, ALBERT
  The Demonic Apocalypse   Div 22,Sep 77

DEE, ROGER
  Pseud: see Roger D. AYCOCK

DEEGAN, FRANCES M.
Ziff-Davis house-name. Following author
unknown, but may be William Hamling
*The Cat-Snake   WM 1,Fal 70
  [*Fantastic Adventures* Apr 48]

DEES, SYLVIA [1939-]
  Policy Conference   Gam 5,Sep 65

DEFOE, DANIEL [1659?-1731]
British novelist and journalist
*The Apparition of Mrs Veal WT Dec 26
  [*orig.1706]
*The Friendly Demon   MoH 14,Win 66/7
  [*orig.1726]

deFORD, MIRIAM ALLEN [1888-1975]
US journalist and mystery writer
  The Cats of Rome   WT Win 73
  The Dreaming Eyes   Ftc Jan 61
*Ghostly Hands   TMM Jan 28
*Ghostly Hands   WT Win 73
  [*orig."The Neatness of Ann Rutledge"
  Westminster Magazine during 1924]
  Henry Martindale, Great Dane BFF Mar 54
  Inside Story   Gam 3,1964
  Laughing Moths   Shk Jul 60
  Never Stop to Pat a Kitten WT Jul 54
  Othuum: The Gate Cracks Wider
  [rr:Chap.4]   W&S 10,1974

DEL REY, LESTER [Ramon Alvarez] [1915-]
US author and editor, now publisher
  The Coppersmith   Unk Sep 39
*The Coppersmith   UWB Win 48
  Cross of Fire   WT May 39
*Cross of Fire   MoH 30,Dec 69
  The Deadliest Female   WB Feb 51
  Doubled in Brass   Unk Jan 40
*Doubled in Brass   UnkB Jan 40
  Forsaking All Others   Unk Aug 39
  Hereafter, Inc   UW Dec 41
*Hereafter, Inc   UWB Spr 49
*Little Jimmy   SFy 30,Aug 58
  [*Mag.F & SF* Apr 57]
*No Head For My Bier   Ftc Aug 68
  [*Fantastic Adventures* Sep 50]
*No Strings Attached   SFy 31,Oct 58

[*If* Jun 54]
  The Pipes of Pan   Unk May 40
*The Pipes of Pan   UWB Spr 48
  A Report About J.R.R.Tolkien
  [a]   WoF 1,1968
  Though Poppies Grow [nt] UW Aug 42

    as Philip St.John
  Anything   Unk Oct 39
*Anything   UnkB Oct 39
  [also in *FUW,1948 and *FUWB,1952]

    as Erik van Lhin
  Oh Say, Can You See?   WoF 2,1970

    + James H.Beard as Philip James
  Carillon of Skulls   Unk Feb 41
*Carillon of Skulls   UWB Win 49

    + Frederik Pohl as Charles Satterfield
  No More Stars [nt]   BFF Jul 54

DELANO, FARFAL
  Black Heath   WT Jan 54

DELLINGER, PAUL [1938-]
US newspaper reporter
  The Cliffhanger Sound [MrL] Ftc Jan 80
  Girl of My Dreams   Ftc Oct 80
  Rat Race   Ftc Jan 62
[*MrL - Mr. Lazarus*]

DEMIC, WILLIAM
  Pseud: see Dale C. DONALDSON

DEMING, RICHARD
  The Afterlife of Reilly   BFF May 54
  The Helpful Haunt   BFF Nov 53
  Too Gloomy For Private Pushkin
                  FM Feb/Mar 53

DEMMON, CALVIN W. [1942-]
  Who's Afraid   Ftc Dec 72

DENBIGH, COLIN
  Hat Trick   SFy 54,Aug 62

DENBROOK, BARBARA
  The Pictures   EC 1,Jul 76

DENDRINOS, GEORGE
  Ice People   Mac 22,1973

DENMARK, HARRISON
  Pseud: see Roger ZELAZNY

DENTINGER, STEPHEN
  Pseud: see Edward D. HOCH

DENTON, REGINALD
  House pseud: see C.S. HAWTHORNE

DENVER, T. G.
  Cease to Exist   HST 1,1972

DEREVANCHUK, GORDON
Canadian fan and writer
  Bride of the Vodyanyk CT 5,Jan 79
  Lord of the Lightning DFy 12,Apr 79

    as Gordon Derry
  Perchance to Dream   DFy 9,Sep 76

DETRICK, WALTER G.
Dead Hands   WT Jun 25
The Kidnapper's Story   WT Feb 26
Through the Horn Gate   WT Apr 25

DEVLIN, ROY P.
  Probably pseud. of Thomas P. KELLEY

DEWEY, [G.] GORDON
*The Collectors   Ftc Dec 68
  [*Amazing Stories Jun/Jul 53]
*The Tooth   SFy 11,Dec 54
  [*Mag. F & SF Aug 52]

DEXTER, LON
Earthworms of Karma [sn3] WT Jul-Sep 30

DI PRETE, JOHN   [1952-]
US freelance writer [see Editor Index]
The Battery [ss]   Myrd 4,Mar 76
The Experiment   Wyrd 6,Win 76/7
False Gods [ss]   Jeet 1,Apr 77
Final Analysis   Jeet 1,Apr 77
Heresy of Llorf   Jeet 2,Sum 77
Moon Terror [v]   Mb 29,1977
O, Holy Death [v]   Mb 26,1976
Starllorn the Philosopher
  [gs]   BL 1-3,Aug 76-Mar 77
When the Universe Imploded [v]BL 1,Aug 76
*Work Break   BL 1,Aug 76
  [*Sunrise Mar 76]

DIAZ, PEDRO
In the Borderland   WT Jun 30

DICK, PHILIP K[indred]   [1928-82]
US writer, mostly of sf.
Interview   TZ Jun 82
*Breakfast at Twilight   Ftc Nov 66
  [*Amazing Stories Jul 54]
The Cookie Lady   FM Jun 53
The King of the Elves   BFF Sep 53
Novelty Act [nt]   Ftc Feb 64
Out in the Garden   FM Aug 53
The Unteleported Man [sn]   Ftc Dec 64
Upon the Dull Earth   BFF 9,1954

DICKENS, CHARLES [John Huffam] [1812-70]
UK novelist and editor
*The Bagman's Story   WT Oct 26
  [*The Pickwick Papers,1836/7]
*A Child's Dream of a Star   WT Jul 30
  [*Household Words Apr 6,1850]
*The Signal-Man   GS May 29
*The Signalman   WT Apr 30
*The Signalman   FGS(1938)
  [*All the Year Round Christmas 1866]
*The Silent Prison [ex]   BC Win 70/1
  [*American Notes,1842]

  + Charles A.Collins
*The Trial For Murder   SMS 3,Win 66/7
  [*All the Year Round Christmas 1865]

DICKENSHEET, DEANE
The Archangeli Syndrome   W&S 9,1973

DICKENSON, MAY FREUD
The Mate   TB Jul 15,19

DICKINSON, DANIEL N.
The Sex Shop   Div 19,Mar 77
Twilight Games   S&T 15,May 72

DICKSON, GORDON R[upert] [1923-]
US author, mostly of sf and fantasy
After the Funeral   Ftc Apr 59
The Girl Who Played Wolf   Ftc Aug 58
*The Girl Who Played Wolf   StF 10,Fal 69
IT, Out of Darkest Jungle
  [play]   Ftc Dec 64
The Seats of Hell [nt]   Ftc Oct 60
The Summer Visitors   Ftc Apr 60
Walker Between the Planes [nt] WoF 2,1970

DICKSON, KEN
The Chinese Box   FyT 4,Spr 79
His Winter Hobby   DH 18,1978
We Three [v]   DH 16,Spr 77

DICKSON, LAWRENCE J.
The Actuarial Fallacy [a]   Nov Win 81

DIEZEL II, GEORGE C.
The Beast Within   S&T 45,Nov 77
Chant Ye All of Xmas [v]   Div 6,Dec 74
The Cosmic Specter [v]   E&O 2,1983
Dark Pursuer [v]   Div 5,Oct 74
Lost [v]   Div 3,Aug 74
Moon Over Xingu   DFy 10,Dec 76
Red Men Know [v]   E&O 2,1983
Slumber's Lost Ship [v]   Div 2,Jul 74
That Dark Gateway [v]   FBDG 4,Oct 77
When Ages Call   Div 10,Aug 75

  + Gordon Linzner
Spawn of the North   S&T 33,Nov 75

DIFFIN, CHARLES WILLARD
The Dog That Laughed   ST Sep 31
*The Dog That Laughed   MoH 16,Sum 67
*The Power and the Glory   AFR 13,1950
  [*Astounding Stories Jul 30]
The Terror By Night   ST Jan 33

DILAURO, STEPHEN
The Gargoyles of Gotham [pic] TZ Feb 82
  [also in *GSTZ,1982]
A Glimpse of Ghostly Britain
  [pic]   TZ Jul 82
One Hundred Years of Fantasy
  Illustration [pic]   TZ Jun 81

DILBECK, LIONEL
The River Dwellers   UnS Win 35

DILLON, HAROLD
*Case of the Premature Burial TTT Spr 64
  [*retitle of following story]
Your Soul is Not Your Own!   GS Dec 29

DILLON, WALTER
Woman of Compassion   Mac 15,Sum 64

DILMORE, GENE
The Band Played On   Shk May 60

DIMARIA, SAL
  + Albuquerque SF Society
An Exquisite Corpse SF Story Nyc 13,May 77

DIMEO, STEVE[N]
  Adapting Ursula Le Guin's "The
    Lathe of Heaven"as a Public
    Television Movie [a]   Ftc Jul 80
  The Martian Chronicles [a]   Ftc Jan 80
  Shadows of a Dream   Wbk 9,1974

DINWIDDIE, ISABELLE E.
  Fern Seed [v]   Nek 5,mid-51

DIOMEDE, JOHN K.
  Pseud: see Geo.Alec EFFINGER

DIRK, JAN
  Clay-Covered Justice   WT Jul 25
  Radio V-Rays   WT Mar 25

DISCH, THOMAS M[ichael] [1940-]
  US writer, poet and critic
  book reviews   TZ May-Jul,Sep 82
  Carousel   TZ Nov 81
    [also in *GSTZ,1982]
  Dangerous Flags   Ftc Aug 64
  Descending   Ftc Jul 64
  The Double-Timer   Ftc Oct 62
  Fables of the Past and Future:
    The Enchanted Prince, 1963   Ftc Aug 63
    Master Said-and-Done   Ftc Aug 63
    The Return of the Medusæ   Ftc Aug 63
  Final Audit   Ftc Jul 63
  Genetic Coda   Ftc Jun 64
  *Genetic Coda   StF 13,Fal 70
  Hell Revisited [in]   Imp 10,Dec 66
  Leader of the Revolution   Biz Oct 65
  Music Box   TZ Dec 83
  The Number You Have Reached   Imp 12,Feb 67
  102 H-Bombs [nt]   Ftc Mar 65
  The Roaches   Imp 9,Nov 66
  A Thesis on Social Forms and
    Social Controls in the U.S.A.
    [spf]   Ftc Jan 64
  13 All-Time Classics of Fantasy
    [list]   TZ Jun 83
  13 Great Works of Fantasy From
    the Last 13 Years [list]   TZ Aug 83
  Three Points on the Demographic
    Curve   Imp 10,Dec 66
  *"Utopia? Never!"   Ftc Apr 79
    [*Amazing Stories Aug 63]
  The Vamp   Ftc Feb 65
  X-Yes   Ftc Dec 69

    as Dobbin Thorpe
  Death Before Dishonor   Ftc Feb 64
  Minnesota Gothic   Ftc Jan 64
  *Now is Forever   Ftc Jul 79
    [*Amazing Stories Mar 64]

    + John Sladek
  The Way to a Man's Heart   BMM Jan 66

DIXON, C. A.
  The Moose That Talked [ts]   FF May 50

DIXON, H. M.
  The End of the Rackett   MyS 19(1940)

DIXON, V[ERNA] L[EE]
  sister of C.C.Clingan
  Angels Wings [v]   Div 17,Nov 76
  Dissecting the Gothic Novel

  [a]   Div 18,Jan 77
  The Monument   Div 1,Jun 74
  Slowly, Slowly, Wheels the
    Midnight Star [v]   Div 2,Jul 74

DiZAZZO, RAYMOND   [1947-]
  US telephone engineer and poet
  *A99 Spyrlon [v]   PtF 1,Sum 78
  *Back on the Ranch [v]   PtF 1,Sum 78
  Edible Abstract:Woman [v]   PtF 2,1979
  The Interview [v]   PtF 2,1979
  *Men [v]   PtF 1,Sum 78
  .*Obituary 2000 [v]   PtF 1,Sum 78
  *Pre-Release [v]   PtF 1,Sum 78
  *2020 [v]   PtF 1,Sum 78
    [*all from Clovin's Head,1976]

DOBEY, CHARLES
  The Ghost is Coming to Take
    me to Hell   AH Feb 71

DOENIM, SUSAN
  Psued: see Geo.Alec EFFINGER

DOGGETT, KEN
  The Flower Thief   Shyl 5,Win 82
  The Golden Apple   S&T 64,Sum 83
  The Ultimate Spy   Shyl 6,Win 82

DOHERTY, G[eoffrey] D[onald] [1927-]
  UK English and drama instructor
  Fantasy and the Nightmare [a]
                                  Imp 8,Oct 66

DOLD, DOUGLAS M.
  US pulp magazine editor
  Prisoners of Fear   GS Feb 31
  The Thirteenth Floor   ST Nov 31
  *The Thirteenth Floor   MoH 23,Sep 68

DOLPHIN, REX
  UK writer of mysteries & boys' fiction
  Off the Map   WT Jul 54

DOLSON, EUGENE C.
  Under the Moon [v]   WT Jul 28
  Wild Horses [v]   WT Jun 28

DONALDSON, DALE C.   [1923-77]
  US social worker; fan editor & writer
  Finale [v]   Mb 2,1971
  Mythconception [v]   F&T 5,1974
  Not So Strange [col]   Div Oct 75-Mar 76
  Pia   Cov Nov 69
  Sergi   W&S 8,1972
  Today's Witch   W&S 9,1973

    as Frances Aldrich
  Bertwold's Dragons   Mb 5,1972
  Blake's Behemoth   Mb 1,1971

    as Delores Cephus
  Something Special   Mb 6,1972

    as Mo DeMathews
  My Rightful Place   Mb 17,1974
  Spirit Transfer   Mb 4,1971

    as William Demic
  The Fine Art of Scrying [a]   Mb 4,1971
  Letters to the Boss   Mb 7,1972
  Pardonable Error   Mb 2,1971

DOZOIS, GARDNER   [1947-]
US writer and anthologist
Mainstream SF and Genre SF [a]   Ftc Nov 73
  [speech given at DisClave,Memorial
  Day,1973]
Wires   Ftc Dec 71

  + Jack Dann
Playing the Game   TZ Feb 82
  [also in *GSTZ,1982]

DRAKE, ANDERS W.
The Elfin Lights   MT Sum 35

DRAKE, DAVID A[llen]   [1945-]
US attorney
The Barrow Troll   Whsp 8,Dec 75
The Dancer in the Flames Whsp 17/8,Aug 82
Dragon's Teeth   MS 2,Fal 75
The Master of Demons   DH 11,Win/Spr 75
Nemesis Place   Ftc Apr 78
No Limit on Hippogrifs [v]   ArkC 2,Win 68
The Shortest Way   Whsp 3,Mar 74
The Song of the Bone   Whsp 2,Dec 73
The World Fantasy Convention
  [a]   Whsp 8,Dec 75

  + Karl Edward Wagner
Killer   MS 1,1974

DRAKE, GARY
Opium and Sake   [6 prose-poems]
    I: Exordium
   II: Sunset in Atlantis
  III: Skulls of Purple
   IV: The Caravan of Seven Camels
    V: The Elephant of Onyx
   VI: The Throne of Cthulhu
                        (all) Nyc 7,Aug 72

DRAKE, KEITH A.
The Game of the Bowl   S&T 42,May 77

DRAKE, LEAH BODINE   [1914-64]
US poet and Pulitzer Prize-winner
Abracadabra [a]   ArkS Aut 49
Bad Company [v]   WT Mar 41
Changeling [v]   WT Sep 42
Foxy's Hollow   FM Aug 53
Haunted Hour [v]   WT Nov 41
The Heads on Easter Island [v] WT Jan 49
Heard on the Roof at Midnight
  [v]   WT Nov 46
A Hornbook For Witches [v]   ArkS Win 48
In the Shadows [v]   WT Oct 35
The Mermaid [v]   WT Nov 52
Mop-Head   WT Jan 54
The Nixie's Pool [v]   WT May 46
Old Wives' Tale [v]   ArkS Sum 48
Out! [v]   WT Mar 54
The Path Through the Marsh [v] WT Sep 44
Red Ghosts in Kentucky [v]   WT Jan 53
Revenant [v]   WT Mar 51
The Saints of Four-Mile Water
  [v]   ArkS Spr 49
Sea Shell [v]   WT Sep 43
The Seal-Woman's Daughter [v] WT Jan 47
Six Merry Farmers [v]   WT Sep 53
The Steps in the Field [v]   WT Nov 47
The Stranger [v]   WT Sep 47
Swan Maiden [v]   WT May 51

They Run Again [v]   WT Jun/Jul 39
Unhappy Endings [v]   ArkS Spr 48
The Unknown Land [v]   ArkS Aut 48
A Vase From Araby [v]   WT Mar 43
The Vision [v]   WT Jan 50
*The Vision [v]   ArkS 2,Sep 83
Whisper Water [v]   WT May 53
The Witch Walks In Her Garden
  [v]   WT Apr 37
Witches on the Heath [v]   WT Oct 38
*Witches on the Heath [v] WT(Can) Mar 45
Wood Wife [v]   WT Mar 42

DRAPER, GILBERT
The Feline Phantom   ST Mar 32
*The Feline Phantom   SMS 14,Win 69
Kidnapped By a Wraith   GS Aug 29
Was This Impossible? [a]   GS Apr 29

DRAYTON, RICKY
Pseud. of UK gangster writer Michael Barnes
White Zombie   WWd 1(1955)

DREISER, THEODORE   [1871-1945]
US novelist
*The Hand   GS Jun 29
  [*Munsey's Magazine May 19]

DRENNEN, RAYMOND
Murder Town [nt]   Sus Win 52

DRESBACH, GLENN WARD
The Castle [v]   WT Jan 45
Rats [v]   WT Sep 44

DRESSER, DAVIS   [1904-]
US detective writer, creator of Mike Shayne
      as Brett Halliday
*The $1,000,000 Motive   MysT Jan 52
  [*orig.1945]
*Pieces of Silver   MysT Nov 51
  [*Argosy Jul 30,1938]
*Women Are Poison   MysT 5,1952
  [*orig.1936]
*You Killed Elizabeth   Sus Win 52
  [*London Mystery Magazine Feb/Mar 51]

DREW, CALFORD
Camera Phobia   UTC 2,Dec 40

DREXEL, JAY B.
    Pseud: see Jerome BIXBY

DRUMMOND, WAYNE
The Phone Call From the Dead   GS Jul 27
*Phone Call From the Dead   PGS,1963
  [reprinted anonymously]

DU CHALIOU, Capt. R.
Veiled Phantoms   GS Mar 30

DU PONT, LEON
Curse of a Thousand Cats   EM Aug 38
Mate of the Beast   ES Aug 37

DUANE, ANDREW
    Pseud: see Robert E. BRINEY

DUANE, DIANE   [1952-]
The Mdaha   FB Aug 82

[ex. from *The Door Into Shadow*]

DUBIOUS, GARDNER
Pseud: see Mike GLICKSOHN

DUBROW, G. H.
Death Feast of the Damned   MP Mar 59

DUCK, GEORGE
The Black Gauntlet   DFy 6,Jan 75
Tale of Three Tasks   Wyrd 3,Spr 74

DUDLEY-SMITH, TREVOR
see Elleston TREVOR

DUERR, Dr. HOWARD J.
Walpurgisnacht [v]   Wbk 13,1978

DUGAN, SEAN
Droite de Signeur [v]   Wyrd 8,1980

DULING, ENNIS
Huggins' World   TZ Aug 83

DUMARS, DENISE [Diane]   [1956-]
US writing instructor
And the Dead [v]   Div 26/7,May/Jul 78
The Ark Ham [v]   Nyc 16,Mar 81
At the Foot of the Bed [v] FyM 3,Jun 82
The Bounty Hunter [v]   PtF 2,1979
Cthulhu [v]   S&T 62,Sum 82
A Druid Prayer Translated
    [v]   Div 26/7,May/Jul 78
The Freeway Up Ramp   S&T 61,Win 81/2
Paragraph Poem No.2 [v]   Nyc 15,Jan 80
Prime Evil [v]   PtF 2,1979
She [v]   S&T 60,Jul 81
Surely [v]   S&T 55,Apr 80
Toward the Elflight [v]   FB Feb 83
The Whitleys Have the Innsmouth
    Look [v]   S&T 64,Sum 83

    + Marshall Watts
Pirating Each Glance [v]   Nyc 17,Jun 82

DUMAS, ALEXANDRE   [1802-70]
French novelist and dramatist
*The Wolf-Leader [n8]   WT Aug 31-Mar 32
    [*trans. by Alfred Allinson from
    book, pub'd. in Paris in 1857]

DUNCAN, ARTHUR
The Ghost of Drumlochy Castle   TU 2(1937)

DUNLAPPE, WILLIAM
The Blood-Drenched Corpse of the
    Priestess of Satan   AH Dec 70
The Naked Slaves of the Master
    of Hell   AH Oct 70

DUNN, CLETTIS
Whispering Fingers   GS Jun 27

DUNN, DENNIS
A Strange Meeting in Greece   Wbk 8,1974

DUNN, J[oseph] ALLAN [Elphinstone]
US pulp novelist   [1872-1941]
On the Knees of the Gods [n3]
          Unk Jan-Mar 40

*On the Knees of the Gods   [n3]
          UnkB Jan-Mar 40
The Right Ear of Malchus   Unk Jun 39

DUNN, LORNA
Frankenstein: Raging Sex Monster
          MST Aug/Sep 72

DUNSANY, LORD   [1878-1957]
*Irish poet, dramatist, author, Edward
John Moreton Drax Plunkett.*
*The Hoard of the Gibbelins   AFR 4,1947
    [*The Book of Wonder,1912]
*The Madness of Andelsprutz   AFR 9,1949
    [*A Dreamer's Tales,1910]
*The Old Brown Coat   WB Feb 51
    [*Tales of Three Hemispheres,1919]
*The Rebuff   [Jorkens]   ASFR 2,1951
    [*The 4th Book of Jorkens,1948]
*The Sign   [Jorkens]   ArkS Aut 48
    [*Jorkens Has a Large Whiskey,1940]
*The Slugly Beast [Jorkens]   AFR 7,1948
    [*Jorkens Remembers Africa,1934]
*The Three Infernal Jokes   AFR 1,1947
    [*Tales of Wonder,1916]
*True History of the Hare and
    the Tortoise   FC 3,1973
    [*Fifty-One Tales,1915]
*When the Gods Slept   FFy Dec 70
    [*Time and the Gods,1906]
*The Wonderful Windows   AFR 12,1950
    [*The Book of Wonder,1912]

DUNWICH, RICHARD
Voodoo [v]   Mac 5,Sum 59

DUPUY, R. ERNEST
The Edge of the Shadow   WT Jul 27

DURHAM, RALPH
Out of a Gleaming Tomb   GS Jan 27

DURWOOD, THOMAS
[see Editor Index]
Hogarth's Last Tarzan [in] Ariel 1,Aut 76

    uncredited
Barry Windsor-Smith [in]   Ariel 3,Apr 78
John Berkey [in]   Ariel 4,Oct 78
Michael Hague [in]   Ariel 4,Oct 78

DUVAC, PATRICE
Parameters   FB Dec 83

DWIGHT, JOHN
The Fates   WT Sep 28
The Thing in the Pyramid   WT Oct 25

DWORIN, LARRY
The Spaceship Game [ss]   Wbk 2,1969

DWYER, BERNARD AUSTIN
Ol' Black Sarah [v]   WT Oct 28

DWYER, JAMES F[rancis]   [1874-1952]
Australian traveler and adventure writer
*The Cave of the Invisible   AFR 14,1950
    [*Blue Book Apr 39]
*The Phantom Ship of Dirk van
    Tromp   AFR 18,1952
    [*Breath of the Jungle,1915]

Snowbound in Glimmerwhite Hall
  [nt] *[Bj]*   CT 6/7,Jul 79
A Tapestry of Dreams   BFWK Aut 78
The Virgins of Po   CT 4,May 78
The Way of Wizards *[Bj]* DFd 3,Sum 80
[Bj - Blackjack Davy]

ELIOT, [Major]GEORGE FIELDING [1894-1971]
  The Copper Bowl   WT Dec 28
*The Copper Bowl   WT Dec 39
  His Brother's Keeper   WT Sep 31
  The Justice of the Czar WT Aug 28

ELLANBY, BOYD
  Pseud: see William C. BOYD

ELLIN, STANLEY [Bernard]   [1916-]
US mystery writer
*The House Party   Shk Jul 60
  [*Ellery Queen's Mystery Magazine* May 54]
*Specialty of the House   Shk May 60
*Specialty of the House   TTFB Sum 64
  [*Ellery Queen's Mystery Magazine* May 48]

ELLIOT, Dr.JEFFREY N.   [1947-]
US political scientist,writer & editor
Interviews with:
  Robert Bloch   Div 26/7,May/Jul 78
  Ray Bradbury   Div 25,Mar 78
  Ramsey Campbell   Whsp 15/16,Mar 82
  C.L. Moore   Div 28/9,Feb/Mar 79
  William F.Nolan   NV 9,Win/Spr 83
  A. E. van Vogt   NV 8,Fal 81

ELLIOTT, ANN
  The Devil of Dwr Ddu   YWS 19(1942)

ELLIOTT, BRUCE   [1914?-73]
  "So Sweet as Magic..." [na]   FM Aug 53

ELLIOTT, FRANCES
  The Beggar [v]   WT Feb 37
  The Hill Woman [v]   WT Oct 34
  The House By the Sea [v] WT Aug 33

ELLIOTT, H[arold] CHANDLER   [1909-]
Canadian-born US physician & lecturer
  A Brush With the Enemy   BFF Jul 54

ELLIOTT, RICHARD
  Contemplation of an Amoeba
  [v]   Nek 5,mid-51

ELLIOTT, WILLIAM J[ames]   [1886-?]
UK novelist and thriller writer
  Doctor Doom, Ghost Detective   WSM Aug 40

  as W.E./W.J.E.
  In An Old Graveyard [v]   WSM Aug 40
  Witch's Lullaby [v]   WSM Aug 40

  as E. L. Lowitt
  The Werewolf [v]   WSM Aug 40

  as W. E. Tillot
  The Last Word   WSM Aug 40

  as L.T.J.Wilte
  Weird Story in Brief [ss]   WSM Aug 40

  as Leopold J.Wollett
  So This is Death   WSM Aug 40

ELLIS, ELSIE
  McGill's Appointment   WT Jan 26

ELLIS, HORATIO VERNON
  The Gorilla   WT Sep 23

ELLIS, JEREMY
  Silver Bullets   WT Apr 30

ELLIS, MOLLIE FRANK
  Case No.27   WT May 23

ELLIS, PETER BERESFORD   [1943-]
UK journalist and writer
  as Peter Tremayne
  The Imshee   Wbk 18,1983
  In Memoriam: Dave McFerran
  [obit]   Agd 1,Aut 80
  The Kelpie's Mask   FyM 4,Jul 83
  [title should be "The Kelpie's Mark"]
  The Plowing of Pras-a-Ufereth
  [L-K]   FyM 3,Jun 82
  Reflections of a Dark Eye FyT 7,Spr 81
  Snake Fright!   Eld 9,1983
  The Storm Devil of Lan-Kern
  [L-K]   FyT 11,Win 82
[L-K - Lan-Kern]

ELLIS, ROGER
  The Road to Vandricourt MyS 18(1939)

ELLIS, SOPHIE [Louise] WENZEL
  The Dwellers in the House WT Jun 33
  The Lily Garden   Phtm 16,Jul 58
  The Spirit in the Garden GS Nov 29
*The Spirit That Got Spanked TTT Spr 64
  [*ret.of "The Spirit in the Garden"]
  White Lady   ST Jan 33
  The White Wizard   WT Sep 29

  as Sophie Louise Wenzel
  The Unseen Seventh   TB Jun 15,19

ELLIS, THELVA B.
  The Magic Window   MM Dec 31

ELLISON, HARLAN   [1934-]
*US writer and columnist most noted for his
teleplays and offtrail short stories*
  Interview   TZ Dec 81
  Profile   FCr 4/5-6,Aug-Nov 75
  The Abnormals   Ftc Apr 59
*Along the Scenic Route [gs]Ariel 3,Apr 78
  [*adapted from "Dogfight on 101"
  Adam Aug 69; art: Al Williamson]
  The Big Trance   DW Aug 57
*Blank   FCr 3,May 75
  [*Infinity SF* Jun 57]
  Bright Eyes   Ftc Apr 65
*Bright Eyes   StF 9,Sum 69
  A Bucketful of Diamonds DW Feb 57
  The Cave of Miracles [nt] Ftc Sep 57
  Djinn, No Chaser   TZ Apr 82
  Eggsucker   Ariel 2,Win 77
  [sequel to "A Boy and His Dog"]
  Grail [nt]   TZ Apr 81
  [also in *GSTZ,1982*]
  In the Fourth Year of the War MS 5,1979
*Knox   FCr 4/5,Aug 75
  [*Crawdaddy* Mar 74]

Neon   HoH Jun 73
  [corrected version pub'd in HoH Aug 73]
Opium   Shyl 2,Feb 78
Paingod   Ftc Jun 64
Phoenix Treatment   Ftc Aug 57
Prince Myshkin, and Hold the
  Relish   Shyl 6,Win 82
Rain, Rain, Go Away   SFy 20,Dec 56
*Reaping the Whirlwind   FCr 4/5,Aug 75
  [*Introduction to *Approaching
  Oblivion*,1974]
Revolt of the Shadows   Ftc Dec 57
Rock God   Cov Nov 69
Satan is My Ally   Ftc May 57
Suicide World [nt]   Ftc Oct 58
*Suicide World [nt]   StF 8,Spr 69
Walk the Walk [a]   Shyl 2,Feb 78
World of Women [nt]   Ftc Feb 57

    as Ellis Hart
Damn the Metal Moon   Ftc Sep 57
A Furnace For Your Foe   Ftc Jan 58
March of the Yellow Death   Ftc Oct 57
Mourners For Hire   Ftc May 57
Pot-Luck Genii   Ftc Dec 57

    as E. K. Jarvis (house name)
If This Be Utopia   Ftc Dec 57
The Moon Stealers [nt]   Ftc Oct 57

    as Clyde Mitchell (house name)
The Wife Factory [nt]   Ftc Nov 57

ELLSMORE, ANDREW J.
Dinosaur Destruction Day   SE Spr 80

ELLSON, HAL
Fear   BMM Nov 65
Frozen Stiff   MP Mar 59
The Rainy Night   Fear May 60
Scorpion   TF Spr 57

ELY, DAVID [1927-]
US newspaperman and novelist
Court of Judgement   Ftc Oct 61
The Last Friday in August   Ftc Dec 61

EMANS, ELAINE V.
Terza Rima for Weasel [v]
                               Arg 7,Fal/Win 80

EMANUEL, VICTOR R.
  see pseud Victor ROUSSEAU

EMERICK, ROBERT
Voices in the Wind   StS Dec 39

EMERSON, JIN
Unnamed [v]   DH 19,1979

EMERSON, ORVILLE R.
The Grave   WT Mar 23

EMMONS, BETSY
The Ghost of the Model 'T'   WT Nov 42
Threshold of Endurance   WT Sep 46
*Threshold of Endurance   WT(Can) Jan 47

EMMONS, E. THAYLES
Two Hours of Death   WT May 23

EMPRINGHAM, DOUGLAS R.
US poet, playwright and film-maker
  as Douglas (Derek) Roome
The Apprentice Avenger
  [AGP]   FBDG 4,Oct 77
Arthur Rampant [AGP]   S&T 48,Jul 78
Arthur's Contest [AGP]   S&T 50,Jan 79
Cat's Paw! Cat's Paw![AGP]   S&T 54,Jan 80
An Elemental [gs]   S&T 49,Oct 78
My Son, My Son! [play]   Mb 16,1974
The New Subscriber [AGP]   FBDG 3,Apr 74
A Novice Conductor   Eld 5,Apr 79
The Root   S&T 16,Aug 72
Seekers Are Pure [v]   S&T 57,Oct 80
A Tale of Allsorts [AGP]   S&T 42,May 77
[AGP - Arthur Graf Pell]

ENDORE, [Samuel] GUY [1900-70]
US author and screenwriter
*The Day of the Dragon   AFR 2,1947
  [*Blue Book Jun 34]

ENG, STEVE/STEPHEN [1940-]
*US property manager; fantasy poet, poetry
bibliographer and scholar*
As Always [v]   Wyrd 8,1980
At the Window [v]   S&T 61,Win 81/2
Balanced Books [v]   S&T 54,Jan 80
Beyond [v]   Wyrd 8,1980
Blast! [v]   Arg 6,Sum/Fal 79
Bone-Yowl [v]   FyT 6,Sum 80
*Crimson-Witch [v]   CT 5,Jan 79
  [*see orig. under John Bredon pseud.]
Dance Programme [ss]   S&T 45,Nov 77
Dead-March [v]   S&T 54,Jan 80
Dinner [v]   Div 24,Jan 78
Earth-Arson [v]   S&T 61,Win 81/2
Elf-Tune [v]   SPWAO 1,1980
Farewell, Lyrista [v]   S&T 61,Win 81/2
Feast [v]   Wyrd 8,1980
The Festival [v]   Eld 6,1979
Fiend-Fodder [v]   NF 1,Win 80/1
Foliage [v]   S&T 46,Jan 78
Follow Me [v]   S&T 53,Oct 79
*Foreseen [v]   Eld 8,1982
  [*The American Poet,Stella Craft
   Tremble,1973; see also under Bredon]
Friend's Fate [v]   S&T 54,Jan 80
Galactic Gothic [v]   S&T 65,Win 83/4
Garden Guests [v]   EC 3,1980
Ghosts [v]   EC 3,1980
*Ghosts [v]   Eld 7,1980
Ghoul-Reader [v]   Eld 4,Oct 78
Ghoul-Treat [v]   S&T 54,Jan 80
Green Bride [v]   CT 5,Jan 79
Grimoire [v]   CT 5,Jan 79
Haven [v]   Wyrd 8,1980
Haven in the Head [v]   E&O 3,1983
Heard! Heard! Heard! [v]   Nyc 17,Jun 82
H.P.Lovecraft: Friend Out
  of Time [v]   Eld 2,1981
In Lieu of Applause [v]   FyT 9,Spr 82
Incarnation [v]   DFd 4,Win 83
Inn of the Dutchman   CT 6/7,Jul 79
Justice [v]   Arg 6,Sum/Fal 79
Kingsport Christmas [v]   Nyc 15,Jan 80
Knife-Thirst [v]   DFy 19,Feb 79
Latest Oasis [v]   DFy 23,Nov 80
Lovecraft Criticism [rv]   Goth Dec 80
May-Eve [v]   ArkC 9,Spr 71

EVANS, E[dward] EVERETT   [1893-1958]
US sf writer and noted fan
Flame Birds of Angala   WT Jul 51
Food For Demons   WT Jan 49
Perfection   Vor 2,1947
Sa'antha   WT Sep 52
The Seamstress   WT Jan 52
The Shed   ASFFR Jan 53
The Undead Die   WT Jul 48
Was Not Spoken   SFy 5,Aut 52

EVANS, GERALD   [1910-]
Welsh Telecommunications Traffic Officer
Pebbles of Dread   YWS 19(1942)

EVANS, I[drisyn] O[liver]   [1894-1977]
Welsh civil servant,writer & editor
The Kraken   WS 1(1944)

EVANS, KEN[DALL]
The Day I Lost It   Ftc May 76
The Haircut   EC 8,1982
Metamorphosis   Ftc May 74

EVANS, ROSALIE
Because Their Bones Were
  Unburied [ts]   GS Oct 27

EVERETT, Mrs H[enrietta] D[orothy]
UK author   [1851-1923]
*The Death Mask   MoH 23,Sep 68
  [*The Death Mask,1920, though most
  likely had earlier magazine pub'n]

EVERETT, WALKER G.
The Woman in Gray   WT Jun 35
*The Woman in Gray   BFT 2,Mar 71

EVERTS, R[andolph] ALAIN
US researcher and specialty publisher
The Death of a Gentleman: The Last
  Days of H.P.Lovecraft [a] Nyc 8,Apr 73
Howard Phillips Lovecraft [pic]
                                ArkS 3,Dec 83
*Howard Phillips Lovecraft and
  Sex [a]   Nyc 9,Jul 74
  [*Esoteric Order of Dagon apa, 2nd
  Mailing, Aug 73]
Howard Phillips Lovecraft:
  Photographs [pic]   Nyc 9,Jul 74
Ira A. Cole and Howard Phillips
  Lovecraft:a Brief Friendship
  [a]   HPL 1972
Jon D. Arfstrom [in]   E&O 3,1983
The Man Who Was W.Paul Cook
  [a]   Nyc 16,Mar 81
Margaret Brundage [a/in]   E&O 2,1983
Mrs Howard Phillips Lovecraft
  [a]   Nyc 8,Apr 73
Olive Grafton Owen - Forgotten
  Poet [a]   ArkS 1,Jun 83
The Original Cover for "The
  Purcell Papers" [a]   E&O 3,1983
Poem en Prose:I [v]   HPL 1972
Le Voyageur [v]   Nyc 8,Apr 73

'AN EX-CONVICT'   (pseud)
Whispering Darkness   GS Feb 28

EYLES, F. A. H.
Crime and the Crystal   GS Dec 29

EYNON, DAVID [LEWIS]
L'Affaire Verenekin   WT Jul 53
The Cuckoo Clock   WT May 51
The Emperor's Letter   WT Jul 52
A Habit Out of History   WT Sep 52
I'll Be Back   WT May 53
The Iron Hands of Katzareere   WT Jan 52
Make Me a Child Again   WT Mar 54
The Priceless Polescu   WT Jul 51
The Sixth Gargoyle   WT Jan 51
A Very Special Quality   WT Jan 54

F

FABER, KONSTANTIN
The Man Who Loved Cats   WWd 1(1955)

FAFARA, D. L.
The Inheritance   EC 6,1982

FAGAN, WILLIAM
H.P.Lovecraft [v]   ArkC 2,Win 68

FAHY, CHRISTOPHER
Matinee at the Flame   TZ Sep 81

FAIG, Jr., KENNETH W.
A.W.D. [v]   Wbk 5,1972
Howard Phillips Lovecraft: The
  Early Years 1890-1914 [a3]
                       Nyc 8-10,Apr 73-Jan/Feb 75
The Lost Man [v]   E&O 1,1973
The Lovecraft Fiction Manuscripts
  [bib2]   Nyc 5-6,Oct 71-Feb 72
A Note and an Anecdote [a] Myrd 3,1976

FAIRFIELD, HENRY W. A.
Pseud: see Harold Standish CORBIN

FAIRLEY, D. H.
Strong Fingers of Death   UTC 11,Nov 41
*Strong Fingers of Death   BrFT 1(1950)

FAIRMAN, PAUL W.   [1916-77]
US author and editor [see Editor Index]
All Walls Were Mist [nt]   Ftc Dec 55
Beyond the Black Horizon [nt] Ftc Jun 55
Black Blockade [nt]   Ftc Feb 56
The Body Hunters [nt]   Ftc Feb 59
Give Me My Body! [nt]   Ftc Jun 59
The Smashers [nt]   Ftc Aug 55
"Some Day They'll Give Us Guns"
                                Ftc Sum 52
This is My Son   Ftc Oct 55

  as Ivar Jorgensen
*(a house name though used almost ex-
clusively by Fairman. Those marked + are
suspected as Fairman's but unconfirmed)*
+And Then He Was Two   Ftc Jun 57
+Dark Miracle   Ftc Jul 57
+"Madam, I Have Here"   Ftc Dec 55
The Missing Symbol   Ftc Nov/Dec 52
+Operation Graveyard [nt]   Ftc Oct 57

FARMER, HARCOURT
When Basset Forgot   TB May 15,19

FARMER, PHILIP JOSE   [1918-]
US writer of sf & fantasy
The God Business [na]   BFF Mar 54
Some Fabulous Yonder [nt]   Ftc Apr 63
*Some Fabulous Yonder [nt]   StF 8,Spr 69

FARNHAM, ALICE DRAYTON
Black as the Night   WT Nov 52
Morne Perdu [nt]   WT Mar 52

FARNSWORTH, MONA
All Roads   Unk Aug 40
*All Roads   UnkB Nov 40
Are You There?   Unk Nov 40
*Are You There?   UnkB Nov 40
The Joker   Unk Jul 39
Whatever   Unk May 39
Who Wants Power?   Unk Mar 39

FARREN, MICK   [1943-]
UK writer and former rock musician
The Great Elvis Presley Look-Alike
  Murder Mystery   TZ Oct 81

FARRERE, CLAUDE   [1876-1957]
*Pseud. of French writer Charles Edouard
Bargone*
    translator unknown
The Idol and the Rajah   WT Aug 35

    trans. by Roy Temple House
The Keen Eyes and Ears of Kara
  Kedi   WT Dec 37
The Passing of Van Mitten   WT Feb 38

FARRINGTON, P. A.
    Pseud: see Dale C. DONALDSON

FARROW, Jr., FRED H./J.
The Bed of Shadows   WT May 29
Symphonic Death   WT Jul 28

FAULCONER, FOREMAN
A Feather From Lucifer's Wing
  [v]   ArkS Spr 49

FAULKNER, BRIAN
A Man [v]   S&T 61,Win 81/2

FAULKNER, DOROTHEA M.
Weather Report From Mercury
  [v]   Nek 5,mid-51

FAULKNER, RORY
Moon-Calf [v]   Nek 2,Sum 50
Songs of the Galaxy [v]   Nek 1,Spr 50

FAULKNER, WILLIAM   [1897-1962]
US novelist and Nobel Prize winner
*The Kid Learns   Gam 2,1963
  [*Picayune May 31,1925]

FAUS, JOSEPH
Because the Cat Remembered   GS Jan 28

    + James Bennett Wooding
The Extraordinary Experiment of
  Dr Calgroni   WT Mar 23

FAUST, ALEXANDER
    Pseud: see Harry ALTSHULER

FAUST, FREDERICK   [1892-1944]
*Prolific US pulp writer, novelist & war
correspondent; creator of 'Dr.Kildare'*
    as Max Brand
*The Strange Loves of Beatrice
  Jervan   FF May 50
  [*orig."John Ovington Returns"
  All-Story Weekly Jun 8,1918]

    as George Challis
*The Smoking Land [n]   AMF Feb 50
  [*Argosy* May 29-Jul 3,1937]

FAWCETT, Dr. A. J.
A Quaker Lady's Strange
  Experience [ts]   GS Apr 29

FAWCETT, E[dward] DOUGLAS   [1866-1960]
UK writer and philosopher
*Hartmann the Anarchist [n2 -
  incomplete]   FFy Jun 71
  [*book, Edward Arnold, London:1893]

FAWCETT, RICHARD
US teacher and specialty publisher
A Greater Darkness   FyM 2,Apr 81

FEARING, VERN
Dr.Schpritzer's Island [nt]   Ftc Aug 54
The Odyssey of Henry Thistle
                              Ftc Jan/Feb 54
*The Odyssey of Henry Thistle
                              StF 10,Fal 69
You'll Never Know   Ftc Jun 54

FEARN, JOHN RUSSELL   [1908-60]
Prolific UK writer, editor & playwright
Black-out   SFy 2,Win 50/1
*Experiment in Murder   STB 1(1946)
  [*ret. of "Portrait of a Murderer"]
Judgement Bell   WOL 2(1960)
Portrait of a Murderer   WT Dec 36
  [see rep. as "Experiment in Murder"]
Pre-Natal   Out Win 46

    as Philip Glyde   (unconfirmed)
So Near - So Far   WOL 1(1960)

    as Alex O. Pearson   (unconfirmed)
The Fulfilment   OS 1(1945)

FEIST, AUBREY
The Golden Patio   ST Jun 32
*The Golden Patio   SMS 18,Mar 71
House of Fire   GS Oct/Nov 31

FEIST, RAYMOND E.
Profit and the Grey Assassin FB May 82

FEL, PETER
Monster For Hire   Thrl Jul 62

FELDMAN, ANATOLE
She Walks in Beauty   GS Apr 29

FELGENHAUER, H. R.
Star Picker [v]   EC 8,1982

FISCHER, BRUNO   [1908-]
US mystery/suspense writer
*Smart Guy   MysT Jan 52
    [*Avon Books,1945]

    as Russell Gray
The Gargoyles of Madness   UT Aug 39
House Where Evil Lived   UT May 40
Lovely Bodies for the Butcher   UT Nov 39
Mates for Horror's Half-Men   UT Mar 40

FISCHER, HARRY   [1910-]
    + Fritz Leiber
The Lords of Quarmall [sn2]
    [F&GM]   Ftc Jan-Feb 64
[F&GM - Fafhrd & the Gray Mouser]

FISCHER, MICHAEL
Minister Without Portfolio   Ftc Oct 54

FISHER IV, BENJAMIN FRANKLIN
Best-Selling Horror [rv]   Goth Jun 79
The English Ghost Story [rv]   Goth Jun 79
The German Gothic Novel [rv]   Goth Dec 80
Horror by the Bucket - and
    the Fingerbowl [rv]   Goth Dec 79
Mary Shelley's Frankenstein
    [rv]   Goth Dec 80

    + Frederick S. Frank & Gary W. Crawford
The 1978 Bibliography of Gothic
    Studies [bib]   Goth Dec 79
The 1979 Bibliography of Gothic
    Studies [bib]   Goth Dec 80

FISHER, LOUIS
Enough Rope   Ftc Dec 58

FISHER, Jr., PHILIP M.
*The Ship of Silent Men [nt]
                            SMS 11,Win 68/9
    [*All-Story Weekly Jan 3,1920]
*The Strange Case of Lemuel
    Jenkins [nt]   AFR 2,1947
    [*All-Story Weekly Jul 26,1919]

FISHER, STEVE[n Gould] [1912-]
US mystery and script writer
Returned from Hell [na]   Unk May 39
Satan's Faceless Henchmen   Ace May 36

FISKE, TARLETON
    Pseud: see Robert BLOCH

FITE, LEN C.
Another Country [v]   S&T 58,Jan 81
The Flagellants [v]   Eld 2,1981
Lilith [v]   S&T 60,Jul 81

FITZGERALD, ANITA
    + Mark Mellen
In the Grip of Edgar the Great GS Aug 26

FITZGERALD, GREGORY
All in the Appearance [v]   DDH Dec 78
A Halloween Story   DDH Dec 78

FITZPATRICK, DONOVAN G.
The Toad   WT Mar 24

FITZPATRICK, ROBERT FLEMING
*"I Paint From Death" [nt]   SSET Sum 70
    [*Amazing Stories Aug 49]

FLAGG, FRANCIS
    Pseud: see George Henry WEISS

FLAGG, RONALD
Song of the Spectre   EM Nov 38
The Soul-Scorchers' Lair   ES Aug 37
Tomb Treachery   EM Aug 38

FLAMEL, NICHOLAS   (pseud)
The Shrieking Curse of the
    Voodoo God   AH Jun 71

FLAMMONDE, PARIS
After Armageddon   WoF 1,1968

FLANAGAN, RICHARD P.
The Postman Always...   Cov Sep 69

FLANDERS, JOHN
    Pseud: see Jean-Raymond DE KREMER

FLAUBERT, GUSTAV   [1821-80]
*The Legend of St.Julian the
    Hospitaller   WT Apr 28
    [*Trois Contes,1877]

FLEMING, A. A.
The Motive   MysT Jan 52

FLEMING, BRANDON
The Ruby   WT Jan 33

FLEMING-ROBERTS, G. T.
Prolific US pulp writer
Satan's Forge   Ace Sep 36

FLETCHER, HARRY
*Possible, though unconfirmed pseud. of
Harry Walton*
A Star Falls on Broadway   Ftc Mar/Apr 53

FLETCHER, JO[anna Louise Gould] [1958-]
*UK journalist;sf/fantasy reviewer and
columnist*
    as Charlotte Dean
Death Wish [v]   FyT 10,Sum 82
A Lady's Retribution [v]   FyT 11,Win 82

FLETCHER, JOHN
"The Dead Host's Welcome" [v]   WT May 39

FLETCHER, JOHN C.
    Error: see Harold Standish CORBIN

FLETCHER, VERNE
What Happened to Mrs.Stanton?
                            MyS 19(1939)

FLINK, HARVEY WAGNER
A Dream of Bubastis [v]   WT Dec 30
Lilith in the Red Land [v]   WT Sep 29
Transformation [v]   WT Oct 29

FLINT, TERRENCE
Rehearsal With Doom   ES Aug 37

FOX, GARDNER F[rancis] [1911-]
US sf/fantasy & historical novelist
*Heart of Light   Ftc Mar 68
  [*Amazing Stories* Jul 46]
The Holding of Kolymar   Ftc Oct 72
Rain, Rain, Go Away!   WT May 46
The Rainbow Jade   WT Sep 49
The Weirds of the Woodcarver   WT Sep 44

FOX, JANET [1940-]
US writer; former high-school teacher
Arkham by Moonlight [v]   Eld 5,Apr 79
Bedtime Story   NV 8,Fal 71
Creeper   Mb 7,1972
Daemon-Tree [v]   Eld 7,1980
Death [v]   FyM 4,Jul 83
Demon and Demoiselle [Arc]   Ftc Oct 78
Garage Sale   TZ Aug 82
Ghouls [v]   SPWAO 2,1982
How Jaquerel Fell Prey to
  Ankarrah   [Jaq]   S&T 55,Apr 80
How Jaquerel Learned to Let
  Sleeping Gods Lie [Jaq]   S&T 62,Sum 82
How Jaquerel Was Slain By the
  God Brann   [Jaq]   Wbk 16,1982
Humanchange [v]   E&O 3,1983
In the Kingdom of the Thorn
                    Whsp 19/20,Oct 83
In the Mask Shop [v]   Wbk 2,1969
Innsmouth Update [v]   E&O 3,1983
Kingdoms of Night [v]   Eld 9,1983
Lillith [v]   E&O 3,1983
The Lord Loved Little People
                    S&T 17,Nov 72
Materialist   MoH 32,May 70
Mechanthropy   Nov Aut 80
The Miraculous God Machine   S&T 12,Jun 71
Moldword [v]   Wbk 5,1972
Nothing to be Frightened About
  [v]   Eld 6,1979
Only Toys   EC 1,Jul 76
Pterodactyls [v]   Wbk 3,1970
Say It With Spiders   Wbk 3,1970
Screaming to Get Out   Wbk 12,1977
Seventy Steps [v]   Eld 8,1982
She-Bear   [Arc]   Ftc Jan 74
Snowghost   Mb 8,1972
The Song the Brahmin Sings
                    Div 28/9,Feb/Mar 79
Weaver of the Dark   Nov Spr 81
Winewind [v]   Arg 8,Fal/Win 81
A Witch in Time   [Arc]   Ftc Sep 73
The Wrong Kind of Silence [v] Wbk 5,1972
[Arc - Arcana; Jaq - Jaquerel]

FOX, PAT
The Demon That Stole My Wife
  [ts]   Mystic Mar 54

FOX, PAUL HERVEY
The Strange Case of Dr.Fell
  [sn4]   GS Apr-Jul 28

FRAILEY, L. E.
The Man Who Could Not Go Home WT Apr 35

FRAME, ALASTAIR
Off Balance   Phtm 3,Jun 57

FRAME, J. A.
The Settlement [ss]   EC 7,1982

FRANCIS, GREGORY
  Pseud: see Frank H. PARNELL

FRANCIS, LEE
*Ziff-Davis house name used originally by
Leroy Yerxa. Following story unidentified
by may be by Paul Fairman or W.L.Hamling*
*The Soul-Snatchers [na]   WM 1,Fal 70
  [*Fantastic Adventures* May 52]

FRANK, FREDERICK S.
  +Gary W.Crawford & Benjamin Fisher IV
The 1978 Bibliography of Gothic
  Studies [bib]   Goth Dec 79
The 1979 Bibliography of Gothic
  Studies [bib]   Goth Dec 80

FRANK, SAM
Rod Serling's Lost 'Christmas
  Carol' [a]   TZ Feb 83

FRANKOS, STEVEN
Clover and Clover Again   FB Aug 82
Toadally Ridiculous   FB May 83

FRANZ, ALDEN
The Mad Monster Strikes Again AH Feb 71

FRASER, BRIAN M.
Prophet of Doom and Gloom
  [in: Frederik Pohl]   Ftc Jul 80
Putting the Past Into the
  Future [in: Andre Norton]   Ftc Oct 80

FRAZEE, [Charles] STEVE   [1909-]
Dragon Fires [nt]   FM Feb/Mar 53

FRAZIER, ROBERT
Flash Sleep [v]   NV 8,Fal 81
Rendezvous 2062 [v]   FB Nov 82

FRAZIER, WILLIAM BENTON
Out of the Mists of Time   WT Apr 26

FREDA, PAULA
The Ugliness Without   SPWAO 2,1982

FREDD, AL
  Pseud: see Leslie A. CROUTCH

FREDERICK, CHARLES L.
The Pelican   WT Nov 24

FREDERICK, ORLIN
  Pseud: see F. Orlin TREMAINE

FREELAND, CLAUDE E.
A Child's Guardian Angel [ts] GS Nov 29
The Flaming Wraith [ts]   GS Oct 29
The Invisible Rider [ts]   GS Aug 29

FREEMAN, CHARLES A.
  + Col.George Warburton Lewis
The Night of a Thousand Eyes GS Jul 27

FREEMAN, FRANK
Wish It Away   Ftc Jan/Feb 54

FRY, J. M.
The Ring   WT Jan 32

FRYE, ESTELLE
The Face in the Mask   Ftc Jun 61

FRYER, DONALD SIDNEY
    see under Donald SIDNEY-FRYER

FUESSLE, NEWTON A.
The Nerve Specialist   TMM Mar 28
*A Perfect Melody   TB Oct 1,19
    [*New Magazine Nov 1910]

FULLER, ALICE T.
The Tomb-Dweller   WT Feb 25

FULLER, GEORGE
Yellow and White   WT Mar 24

FULLER, HOWARD ELSMERE
Wolfgang Fex, Criminal   WT Aug 25

FULLILOVE, J.B.S.
Ghouls of the Sea   WT Mar 34

FULWILER, WILLIAM
R'lyeh Rises [v]   DFy 14,Sep 77
The Scroll [v]   DFy 17,Jul 78
Short Cut   Eld 9,1983
The 'Unhappy Is He' Quiz [quiz]   TZ Sep 82
The 'Unhappy Is He' Quiz
   Revisited [quiz]   TZ Dec 82
Whippoorwills [v]   DFy 14,Sep 77

FUNNELL, AUGUSTINE
Andrea   DFy 2,Fal 73
A Cut Above   DFy 2,Fal 73
Sundown   DFy 1,Sum 73
White Room   DFy 1.Sum 73

FURMAN, AVIS
Incantation   GS Feb 31

FURTER, FRANKLIN   (pseud)
Illusionary Rebound   WST Jul/Aug 72

FYFE, H[orace] B[rown] [1918-]
The Clutches of Ruin [nt]   Gam 4,Feb 65
The Furies of Zhahnoor   Ftc Oct 60
*The Furies of Zhahnoor   WM 3,Spr 71
Koenigshaufen's Curve   FM Aug 53

                G

GABBARD, G[REG(ory)] N. [1941-]
US warehouse clerk; fantasy poet & artist
The Great Sardine of Sardis   CT 5,Jan 79
In the Slums of Slumberland   CT 3,Jan 78
Nocturne [v]   CT 5,Jan 79
Robb   DFy 17,Jul 78
Rune of the Elder Gods [v]   DFy 11,Jan 77
Yog-Sothoth 'a Go-Go [spf]
                              Arg 7,Fal/Win 80

GABRIEL, JOHN
    Pseud: see Ernest L. GABRIELSON

GABRIELSON, ERNEST L[ouis] [1891-1978]
   as Anthony Cotrion
The Opaque Word [ss]   Out Win 46

   as John Gabriel
Bird of Time   Out Win 46

GADDIS, VINCENT H[ayes] [1913-]
US authority on psychic phenomena
Arizona's Lost Death Trap [a]
                              Anu 2,Spr 67
Shadows Out of the White
   House [a]   Ftc Oct 58
Special News Bulletin   WT Apr 39

GAGNE, PAUL R.
The Shadow's Edge: an Interview
   With Whitley Strieber [in]
                              Whsp 19/20,Oct 83

GAI, HONG SUI
The Taming of Hercules   LST Sep/Oct 72

GALLAGHER, HUGH J.
*Death Mates   WOL 2(1960)
   [*orig."Death Mates for the Lust
   Lost" Yankee Mystery Shorts 2,1941]

GALLEGHER, CARLA
Sibling   S&T 55,Apr 80

GALLIN, ALBERT E.
Did the Ghost of Bismarck
   Warn the Kaiser? [a]   GS Apr 29

GALOUYE, DANIEL F[rancis] [1920-76]
US journalist and writer
The Big Blow-Up   Ftc Mar 61
*The Big Blow-Up   Ftc Jul 79
Centipedes of Space [nt]   Ftc Apr 64
Descent Into the Maelstrom [nt]Ftc Apr 61
The Reality Paradox   Ftc Jan 61
A Silence of Wings [nt]   Ftc Feb 62
Spawn of Doom [nt]   Ftc Dec 61
Summons of the Void   Ftc Dec 60
The Trekkers   Ftc Sep 61

GALUS, SUSAN
Let the Earth Quake   Wbk 5,1972

GALUSHA, TOM
Regin and Sigurd [v]   Wyrd 8,1980

GAMES, STEVE
Gone   S&T 64,Sum 83

GAMMELL, LEON L. [1936-]
The Horror Out of Time   FCw 3,Feb 77
The Scarlet Sigil   FCr 7,Feb 76
The Shadow Vampire   Eld 4,Oct 78
Tomb of the Black Ape   Eld 7,1980

GANLEY, W. PAUL [1934-]
US Associate Professor of Physics;
specialty publisher [see Editor Index]
Atlantic City: 5.30 P.M. [v] ArkC 9,Spr 71
Balthor the Dreamer   Mac 21,1970
Forerunners of Doom   Eld 7,1980
Ghost Story   S&T 42,May 77
Good Thoughts   Mb 10,1973
The Guardian [v]   Mac 20,1968

The Price of Eggs   Ftc Dec 59
Quick Cure   Ftc Feb 56
Random Choice [nt]   Ftc Mar 61
The Savage Machine [nt]   Ftc Nov 58
The Sixteen Keys [nt] [D]   Ftc May 76
The Trouble With Magic [nt]   Ftc Mar 59
The Vengeance of Kyvor [na2]
                                  Ftc Apr-May 57
Woman Driver [nt]   Ftc Jun 54
You Too Can Win a Harem   DW May 57

  + Robert Silverberg as Clyde Mitchell
The Mummy Takes a Wife [nt]   Ftc Dec 56

  + Robert Silverberg as Robert Randall
The Slow and the Dead [nt]   Ftc Aug 56
[D - Lord Darcy]

GARRISON, JOAN
The Cenote   E&O 3,1983
Its Master's Keeper   Div 18,Jan 77
The Specimen   Div 12,Jan 76
The Tapestry   S&T 65,Win 83/4

GARSON, CLEE
Ziff-Davis house name used by David Wright
O'Brien, Paul Fairman and others.
  by William P. McGivern (unconfirmed)
Scavengers of Space [nt]   Ftc Oct 55

GARSON, PAUL
Mammoths [v]   EC 2,1979

GARTH, WILL
Standard Magazines house name
  by Norman A. Daniels
Double Ring   StS Jun 39

  by August Derleth
The Dead Shall Rise Up   StS Aug 40
Passing of Eric Holm   StS Dec 39

  by authors unknown
Astral Newspaper   StS Oct 40
Fulfillment   StS Apr 39
Hate's Handiwork   StS Feb 41
House of the Griffin   StS Oct 39
Sea Vision   StS Aug 39

GARVER, JAMES
Untitled Centrepiece [v]   FCr 13,Jun 78

GARWOOD, LOUISE
Candle-Light   WT Nov 25
Fayrian   WT Feb 25
Ghost [v]   WT Dec 31
Ghosts [v]   WT Jul 26
The Living [v]   WT Sep 29

GARY, KEN
A Weird Prophecy [ts]   WT May 40

GARY, ROMAIN   [1914-80]
Russian (Georgia) born French writer, real
name Romain Kacewgari
*The Living Statue   BMM Oct 65
  [*Hissing Tales,1964]

GASKELL, ELIZABETH [Cleghorn] [1810-65]
UK Victorian novelist
*The Old Nurse's Story   WT Oct 27
  [*Household Words Christmas 1852]

GATTO, JOHN TAYLOR
Lovecraft and the Grotesque
  Tradition [a]   Nyc 13,May 77
Whispering in the Dark [a]
                                  Whsp 11/12,Oct 78

GAULDING, LYLE
The Altar of Flame   Anu 3,1968
The Beast From Baalazz [Cth]   Anu 1,Aut 66
[Cth - Cthulhu Mythos]

GAULT, WILLIAM CAMPBELL   [1910-]
US writer of crime & sports fiction
Winter Scene   Mystic Mar 54

GAULTNEY, DANIEL
Repayment   Mb 29,1977

GAUTIER, THEOPHILE   [1811-72]
French poet, critic and novelist
*Clarimonde   WT Feb 28
  [*orig."La Morte Amoreuse",1839]
*The Mummy's Foot   WT Apr 26
*The Mummy's Foot   GS Oct/Nov 31
  [*orig."La Pied de Momie",1863]
  [versions used trans.by Lafcadio Hearn
  in One of Cleopatra's Nights,1882]

GAY, LARRY
The Black Sword [v]   DFy 12,Apr 79
The Puppet of Fate [v]   NV 4,Sum 79
Winner Takes All? [v]   DFy 21,Oct 79

GAYLE, FREDERICK
Ring Around the Black Star   Nek 5,mid-51

GAYLORD, MYRTLE LEVY
The Wish   WT Apr 23

GAYLORD, TIMEUS
  Pseud: see Clark Ashton SMITH

GEARON, JOHN
Faces Turned Against Him   Sus Spr 51

GEBAKKEN, KIP
The Birth of Frankenstein   MST Aug/Sep 72
Domain of the Undead   HST 1972
The Escape of Monte Christo
                                  LST Sep/Oct 72

GEIER, CHESTER S.   [1921-]
US author and magazine editor
The Astral Exile   Mystic Nov 53
Fido   UW Oct 43
*Fido   UWB May 44
The Final Hour   WT Jan 47
A Length of Rope   Unk Apr 41
*A Length of Rope   UnkB Jul 41

  as Guy Archette
*The Haunted House   WM 4,Sum 71
  [*Fantastic Adventures Jun 49]

GELOTTE, MARK
  [see Artist Index]
A Bride of the Darkness   S&T 14,Feb 72

GEMIGNANI, PEGGY
The Beauty and the Beast   EvM Sum 76

GILLINGS, WALTER   [1912-79]
UK newspaperman and pioneer sf editor
The Time is Not Yet [ged] SFy 3,Win 51/2

   as Herbert Hughes
The Jinn in the Test Tube
  [a]   SFy 1,Sum 50

   as Valentine Parker
The Dawn of Space Travel
  [a]   SFy 2,Win 50/1

   as Thomas Sheridan
The Battle of the Canals [a] SFy 1,Sum 50
Bogy in the Sky [a]   SFy 2,Win 50/1

GILLMORE, NELLIE CRAVEY
The White Scar   WT Apr 25

GILMORE, MICHAEL
Odysseus and Penelope Before
  Breakfast : [v]   Arg 9,Fal 83

GILMOUR, R.
Floating Hearse   WSM 2(1946)

GITTENS, ALLEN J.
Escape to Eden [v]   DH 22,Spr 81

GITTINGS, CHRISTINE
Arachne   WSM 2(1946)
Beneath the Mountain   WOL 2(1960)

GLAD, VICTORIA
Each Man Kills   WT Mar 51

GLADHILL, ELIZABETH
Death's Shadow [ts]   GS Sep 30

GLANYIL, JOSEPH
The Death Dance of the
  Fisherman's Devil   AH Jun 71

GLASBY, JOHN S[tephen] [1928-]
UK research chemist and author
   as Max Chartair
The Beckoning Shade   SN 63(1962)
The Cloak of Darkness   SN 1(1954)
  [see rep.as by H. K. Lennard]
The Devil at My Elbow   OTW 1(1954)
*The Devil at My Elbow   SN 34(1960)
Dust   SN 107(1967)
Ebb Tide   SN 26(1959)
Frog [nt]   SN 2(1954)
Haunt of the Vampire   SN 3(1954)
The Lady Labyrinth   SN 28(1959)
A Little Devil Dancing   OTW 2(1955)
*A Little Devil Dancing   SN 36(1960)
Lord of the Necromancers [nt] SN 11(1957)
Lurani   SN 5(1955)
Mask of Asmodeus   SN 7(1955)
Mythos   [Cth]   SN 45(1961)
Nightmare on Ice   SN 79(1963)
The Phantom Wakes   SN 31(1960)
The Serpent Ring   SN 22(1959)
The Thing in the Mist [Cth] SN 109(1967)
The Ugly Ones   SN 8(1955)
Witch-Water   SN 10(1957)
Without a Shadow of a Doubt SN 6(1955)
The Zegrembi Bracelet   SN 4(1954)

   as Randall Conway
The Black Mirror   SN 109(1967)
Body and Soul   SN 107(1967)
Dark Conquest   SN 63(1962)
Dark of the Dawn   SN 28(1959)
The Gods of Fear   SN 1(1954)
The Hungry Gods   SN 7(1955)
The Hungry House   SN 6(1955)
Hunter's Moon   SN 2(1954)
It Came By Appointment   SN 11(1957)
The Man Who Lost Thursday SN 8(1955)
Nightmare [nt]   SN 10(1957)
Not Without Sorcery   SN 45(1961)
Out of the Shadows   SN 22(1959)
A Place of Shadows   SN 79(1963)
The Seventh Image   OTW 1(1954)
*The Seventh Image   SN 34(1960)
The Shadow of Terror   SN 26(1959)
Something About Gargoyles SN 18(1958)
Strange Company   SN 31(1960)
They Fly By Night   SN 4(1954)
Time to Die   OTW 2(1955)
*Time to Die   SN 36(1960)
The Whisper of the Wind   SN 5(1955)
Will o' the Wisp   SN 3(1954)

   as Ray Cosmic
The Chair   SN 4(1954)
The Dark Ones   SN 5(1955)
The Golden Scarab   SN 8(1955)
Lorelei   SN 6(1955)
Lycanthrope   SN 1(1954)
The Nightmare Road   OTW 1(1954)
*The Nightmare Road   SN 34(1960)
Shadow Over Endor   SN 7(1955)
Something From the Sea   SN 3(1954)
  [see rep.as "The Sea Thing" by
   John Morton]
The Stairway   OTW 2(1955)
*The Stairway   SN 36(1960)

   as John Crawford
Dark Legion [n]   SN 106(1967)

   as Michael Hamilton
And Midnight Falls   SN 63(1962)
Angel of the Bottomless Pit OTW 1(1954)
*Angel of the Bottomless Pit SN 34(1960)
Coven of Thirteen   OTW 2(1955)
*Coven of Thirteen   SN 36(1960)
The Crystal Fear   SN 7(1955)
The Dark Possessed   SN 26(1959)
The Haunting of Charles Quintain
                           SN 109(1967)
Hexerei   SN 22(1959)
The Hungry Ones   SN 18(1958)
The Keeper of Dark Point [Cth]
                           SN 107(1967)
The Midnight Walker   SN 10(1957)
Never Look Behind You   SN 31(1960)
The Night Creatures   SN 11(1957)
The Other Seance   SN 3(1954)
The Pipes of Pan   SN 28(1959)
A Place of Meeting   SN 8(1955)
Solitude   [Cth]   SN 79(1963)
Somewhere in the Moonlight SN 5(1955)
Vengeance of Set   SN 1(1954)
Voice of the Drum   SN 6(1955)
When Darkness Falls   SN 45(1961)

   as J. J. Hansby
The Creature in the Depths [nt]
                           SN 28(1959)

GODWIN, TOM   [1915-]
US occasional sf writer
Empathy [nt]   Ftc Oct 59

GOEWEY, EDWIN A.
Crooked Ghosts   GS Nov 28
The Curse of the House of
  Gables   GS Jul 26
The Ghost Who Wore Handcuffs   GS Jun 27
Hun Poy Remembers the Code   GS Jul 30
Johnny Kelly's Christmas Ghost   GS Jan 27
The Man Who Killed a Ghost   GS Aug 26
My Yuletide Phantom   GS Jan 29
The Phantom Ace [na2]   GS Feb-Mar 27
Phantom Drums   GS Aug 27
The Phantom in Armor [nt2] GS Jan-Feb 28
The Phantom of the Sawdust
  Ring   GS Oct 29
The Riddle of Thornley Towers   GS Mar 28
The Specter Cuts the Ace   GS Oct 27
The Specter in the Night Club   GS Feb 29
A Specter Locked in Steel   GS Apr 28
When the Red Gods Call [n6]
                                  GS May-Oct 28
Who Played the Fourth Act?   GS May 30
"Who's Afraid of a Ghost?"   GS Jul 27
A Witness From the Bottom of
  the Lake   GS Dec 27
Written in Sand   GS Sep 27

GOG, P. D.
  Pseud: see Charles E. LAUTERBACH

GOLD, DOROTHY
On Lake Lagore [v]   WT Nov 43
*On Lake Lagore [v]   WT(Can) Jul 44

GOLD, H[orace] L[eonard] [1914-]
Canadian-born US author and editor
And Three to Get Ready   Ftc Sum 52
Day Off   Unk Nov 39
*Day Off   UnkB Nov 39
Don't Take it to Heart   Ftc Jul/Aug 53
Love Ethereal   Sus Fal 51
*No Charge For Alterations   Ftc Sep 67
  [*Amazing Stories Apr/May 53]
Notes From the Journal of
  H.L.Gold [a]   FB May 83
Trouble With Water   Unk Mar 39
  [also in *FUW,1948 and *FUWB,1952]
*Trouble With Water   FB May 83
Warm, Dark Places   Unk Oct 40
*Warm, Dark Places   UnkB Oct 40
*Warm, Dark Places   FB Oct 81

  + L.Sprague de Camp
None But Lucifer [sn]   Unk Sep 39
*None But Lucifer [sn]   UnkB Sep 39

GOLDBERG, BEVERLY
A Nice Home   HoH Jun 73

GOLDEN, HARRY
A Step and a Half   TB Oct 1,19

GOLDIN, STEPHEN [Charles] [1947-]
US writer, mostly of sf
Bride of the Wind   MoH 34,Fal 70
The Chenoo   MoH 35,Feb 71
For Services Rendered   MoH 31,Feb 70
The Masai Witch   Whsp 19/20,Oct 83

  + Kathleen Sky
The Devil Behind the Leaves   FB Oct 81

GOLDING, MORT[on Jay] [1925-]
US free-lance writer
Baby Picture   Shk Jul 60

GOLDMAN, NATHAN
Apology to the Red Planet [v]
                                  Arg 9,Fal 83

GOLDSMITH, HOWARD   [1943-]
US writer, mostly of juvenile fiction
Homecoming   Chl Jul 81

GOLDSMITH, MILTON
Best Betz Mine   MM Sep/Oct 31

GOLDSTEIN, EVELYN
Days of Darkness   Ftc Jan 60
Man Under Glass [nt]   Ftc Aug 59
The Vandal   Fear May 60

GOMEZ, ADRIANA
Angelique [v]   Mb 8,1972
The Black Stone God   Mb 12,1973
Curse, Fire and Brimstone   Mb 8,1972
Eve of Sabat [v]   Mb 5,1972
Nameless Ones [v]   Mb 6,1972

GONZALES, LUIS
The Spirit of the Hacienda   MM Nov 31

GOODALL, SHELTON
The Master   StS Oct 39

GOODENOUGH, ARTHUR
Autumnus - and October [v] Lvs 1,Sum 37
It Will Be Thus [v]   Lvs 1,Sum 37

GOODMAN, BLANCHE
The Haunted Dagger   GS May 27
The Man To Whom Pictures Talk   GS Jan 28

GOODMAN, HAL
Why the Traveling Salesman From
  Aldebaran Doesn't Stop in
  Omaha Anymore   TZ Jul 82

GOODMAN, KENNETH
Handyman   TZ Dec 81

GOODSTEIN, JACK
The Learning Experience   EC 7,1982
Norman's Intended   Wyrd 6,Win 76/7
PastDue!   S&T 25,Jul 74

GORA, ANN   (pseud)
Bums Rush Terror   HST 1972

GORDON, DOROTHY   (deceased)
Dark [v]   Mac 12,Win 62/3
The Span [v]   Mac 6,Win 59

GORDON, GERALD
Cat Woman   TF Spr 57

GORDON, GERTRUDE
  + Manly Wade Wellman
The Cavern   WT Sep 38

as Craig Browning
*Spawn of Darkness   Ftc May 68
   [*Fantastic Adventures May 50]

as Gregg Conrad
*The Mental Assassins   Ftc Dec 68
   [*Fantastic Adventures May 50]

as Sanandara Kumara
Assignment to Life   Mystic Mar 54
The Holy Man   Mystic Oct 54
In the Twinkling of an Eye   Mystic Aug 54
— Lest Ye Be Judged   Mystic May 54

as Charles Lee
Earthbound   Mystic Mar 54
The Golden Kitten   Mystic Dec 54

as Milton Mann
Ming Cha   Mystic May 54

as D. C. McGowan
Firewalking [a]   Mystic Dec 54

as Inez McGowan
In This Dark Mind   Ftc Sep 58

as Rog Phillips
...But Who Knows Huer or Huen?
   [LB]   Ftc Nov 61
The Creeper in the Dream [nt]   Ftc Feb 59
The Devil's Dollhouse   Mystic Mar 54
From This Dark Mind   Ftc Nov/Dec 53
*From This Dark Mind   Ftc Jul 67
Go Visit Your Grave   Mystic Nov 53
*In What Dark Mind   SSET Sum 70
   [*Fantastic Adventures Apr 51]
*Incompatible   Ftc Mar 68
   [*Fantastic Adventures Sep 49]
It's Better Not to Know   Ftc Apr 58
Jason's Secret   Ftc Sep 58
Keepers in Space   Ftc Apr 59
*Keepers in Space   StF 11,Spr 70
The Lurker   Ftc Jun 59
The Only One That Lived   Ftc May 59
*Planet of the Dead   WM 4,Sum 71
   [*Fantastic Adventures Oct 49]
*The Supernal Note   Ftc Aug 68
   [*Amazing Stories Jul 48]
*The Unthinking Destroyer   Ftc Oct 69
   [*Amazing Stories Dec 48]
World of Traitors   Ftc Nov 57
*The World of Whispering Wings Ftc Apr 79
   [*Amazing Stories May 52]
[LB - Lefty Baker]

as Melva Rogers
The Kid With the Beautiful
   Hands   Mystic Mar 54
What Is To Be   Mystic Oct 54

as Gerald Vance   (house name)
The Cosmic Trap   Ftc Nov 57

as Peter Worth   (house name)
God is in the Mountain   Mystic Dec 54
Mistress of the Kama-Loka   Mystic May 54

GRAHAME, REX   (pseud)
Wolf Vengeance   Ace May 36

GRANDFIELD, JOHN
   [see Artist Index]
Morvenna [v]   FyT 1,Sum 77

GRANGER, DARIUS JOHN
   Pseud: see Stephen MARLOWE

GRANT, ALAN
   Pseud: see Gerald CLARKE

GRANT, BRUCE
Feline   WT May 23

GRANT, CHARLES L.   [1942-]
US writer & anthologist; former high-school
teacher
   Interview   NV 5,Fal 79
   Bibliography   MS 5,1979
Benny, Kind and Gentle   Wbk 14,1979
But the Other Old Man Stopped
   Playing   Ftc Apr 73
Essence of Charlotte   TZ Feb 82
From a Single Word   FB Aug 82
From All the Fields of Hail
   and Fire   MS 4,Aug 76
In Silvered Shadows Are Born
   the Screams   Shyl 4,Win 80
Knock and See What Enters   Ftc Dec 77
The Last Ambition   Whsp 13/14,Oct 79
Let No One Weep For Poor
   Sally Karnes   Whsp 19/20,Oct 83
Needle Song   MS 5,1979
Recollections of Annie   TZ Feb 83
Red River Lies Drowning   Ftc Feb 77
Silver   TZ Jul 81
Stephen King [in]   TZ Apr 81
Through All His Blood Runs
   Shadow   MS 4,Aug 76
To Be a Witch, in Three-Quarter
   Time   Ftc Feb 75
What More Remains   MS 5,1979
When I Grow Up   Whsp 19/20,Oct 83

GRANT, DAVID J.
Middle Earth and the Bible
   [a]   FCr 4/5,Aug 75

GRANT, DONALD M[etcalf]   [1927-]
US specialty publisher
   Interview   FCr 10/11,Mar 77

GRANT, FULTON T.
*The Devil Came to Our Valley   Ftc Apr 64
   [*Bluebook Jan 37]

GRANT, GEORGE
Horror in the Dungeon   ET Jul 41
The Phantom Voice   UTC 7,Jul 41

GRANT, LEE
Signal Thirty-Three [nt]   Ftc Oct 55

GRANT, ROBERT
Halloween Girl   TZ Nov 82

GRANVILLE, AUSTYN W.
*His Natal Star   Ftc Mar 63
   [*Chicago Journal, turn of the century]

GRAVES, FREDERICK
Arachne   G&G(1938)
The Trophy   TCP(1937)
Vampyr   TU 3(1938)

GRAY, CLIFFORD
Lust For Blood   ES Aug 37

GRAY, PHILIP
The Silent Horde   Ggn Mar 49

GRAY, ROBERT B.
The Dance of the Dead [v]   WT Jul 33

GRAY, ROBERTA
Not Your Philosophy, Horatio!
  [nt4]   DH 2-5,1972-73

GRAY, RUSSELL
  Pseud: see Bruno FISCHER

GRAY, STEVEN S.
When He Awakens   Ftc Mar 60

GREATRAIKES, A. and H.
The Ticking of the Clock   WT Dec 29

GREEN, GODIN V.
The Ghost Yacht   MM Nov 31

GREEN, JOHN H.
Seven Men in a Tank   WT Mar 25

GREEN, JULIA BOYNTON
Painted Cave [v]   WT Apr 36
The Return [v]   WT Sep 34

GREEN, MONET
Heart's Dimension   TTFB Sum 64

GREEN, SCOTT E.   [1951-]
US writer, editor and bookdealer
The City on No Map [v]   S&T 58,Jan 81
The Motel Room   FyT 10,Sum 82
Ripple Across Time [v]   S&T 61,Win 81/2
Visiting the Zoo [v]   S&T 59,Apr 81
The Weapon Waits [v]   NV 8,Fal 81

GREEN, SIMON R.
In the Labyrinth   FyT 12,Win 83
Manslayer!   Agd Aut 80
Soulhunter   FyM 3,Jun 82

GREEN, TERENCE M.   [1947-]
Interview With Robertson Davies:
  Beyond the Visible World [in] TZ Jul 82

GREENBERG, DORIS
The Unemployed   Ftc Apr 57

GREENE, GRAHAM   [1904-]
UK novelist
*The End of the Party   WB Dec 50
  [*Nineteen Stories,1947]

GREENE, SONIA HAFT   [1883-1972]
Ukrainian-born US-resident saleswoman and
milliner, born Sonia Shifirkin. Married
in 1924, as her second husband, H. P.
Lovecraft
Profile   Nyc 8,Apr 73
  revised by H. P. Lovecraft
The Invisible Monster   WT Nov 23

  as Sonia Haft Lovecraft Davis
Memories of Lovecraft: I [a] ArkC 4,Win 69

GREENFIELD, WILL H.
The Mouse and the Cheese   TB Oct 1,19

GREENHOUGH, TERRY   [1944-]
UK writer of sf & historical novels
Once Upon a Midnight   Wbk 18,1983

GREENIER, ALAN
Could You Be Next? [cs]   S&T 12,Jun 71

GREENING, RHONDI
Archives of Fear   F&T 4,1973
Of Sorcerers and Salamanders F&T 7,1975

GREENWALD, A. J.
Bottled in Russia   BFF May 54

GREER, EDITH BORDEN
Sine Pace   [v]   UW Aug 42
*Sine Pace   [v]   UWB Spr 45
*Sine Pace   [v]   UWB Spr 49

GREER, LLOYD
"I'll Come Back to Haunt You!" GS Sep 29

GREER, RICHARD
Ziff-Davis house name used by Randall
Garrett, Robert Silverberg and others.
Following author unknown.
The Secret of the Shan   Ftc Jun 57

GREGG, J. R.
An Amazing Adventure   YWS 19(1942)

GREGORY, FRANKLIN [Long] [1905?-]
US journalist and author
The Big Breeze   BFF Nov 53
Earth Shaker   BFF Sep 54
Purdy's Circus   Ftc Mar 60
Stop on the Red   Ftc Mar/Apr 53

GREGORY, JAY
Peter Straub [in]   TZ May 81

GREGORY, JOHN
Terror's Tomb   ES Aug 37

GREGORY, JOHN MILLER
My Daughter Who Never Existed GS Apr 29
Spirit Fingers   GS Oct 27
Talking Glass   GS Apr 27

GREGORY, STEPHEN
  Pseud: see Stephen JONES

GREIBLING, ROBERT T.
A Wager in Candlesticks   WT May 28

GRENDON, STEPHEN
  Pseud: see August DERLETH

GRENFELL, GITA
Despair [v]   Mac 18,Win 65/6

GRESHAM, STEPHEN   [1947-]
US Associate Professor of English
The Abysmal   G&S 3,1981
The Coming Out   Eld 2,1981
The Drabbletails   Eld 7,1980
  [sequel to Robert Bloch's "Yours

HAHN, GEORGE R.
+ Richard Levin as Cyril Mand
The Fifth Candle   WT Jan 39
*The Fifth Candle   WT May 52

HAHN, KEN
An Afternoon Off   EvM Sum 77
Black Market Tape   BL 4/5,Jan 78
Charlie of Shrall   EvM Spr 77
The Crossing Over   Jeet 1,Apr 77
For Their People   BL 3,Mar 77
The Human Solution   S&T 53,Oct 79
Light : Lost   DFy 15,Jan 78
Lord Tremaine and Squig the
  River Rat   AD 5,Win 77
The Night Keeper   EvM Win 77/8
Shallay   Div 22,Sep 77
Stalemate   EvM Fal 76

  as Birdwhanger Cord
A Boy and His Monkey [spf] Jeet 1,Apr 77

HAIBLUM, ISIDORE   [1935-]
US writer
Confessions of a Free-Lance
  Fantasist [a3]   TZ Jun-Dec 83
                                [not in Oct]

HAINER, L. M.
Dick Severin Came Back   GS Sep 30
Sign of the Cobra   GS Nov 30

HAINES, E. IRVINE
The Hand of the Invisible   WT May 28
Is Bear Mountain Haunted? [a]   GS Jul 31

HADJU, JACK
Revelation [v]   ArkC 3,Sum 68

HALBERT, HAL
The Devil Bird   WT Apr 24

HALDEMAN II, JACK C.   [1941-]
US writer
Chang Bhang   Ftc Nov 73
  [misprint for "Ghang Bhang"]
The End of the World Rag   Ftc Dec 77
Garden of Eden   Ftc Dec 71
Laura's Theme   Ftc Jun 75
Open Frame   TZ Aug 83
What I Did on My Summer Vacation
                                Ftc Jul 73
What Weighs 8000 Pounds and
  Wears Red Sneakers?   Ftc Jul 78

  + Jack Dann
Limits   Ftc May 76

HALDEMAN, JOE W[illiam]   [1943-]
US author, noted for his sf
Interview   DH 21,1980
The Devil His Due   Ftc Aug 75
  [tp version of "I of Newton"]
I of Newton   Ftc Jun 70
Seven and the Stars   TZ May 81

HALIBURTON, JOHN A.
Mitty of the Spaceways [v] NF 1,Win 80/1

HALL, AUSTIN   [1882?-1933]
US pulp writer of sf and westerns
*Almost Immortal [nt]   MoH 13,Sum 66
  [*All-Story Weekly Oct 7,1916]
The People of the Comet
  [nt2]   WT Sep-Oct 23

HALL, DESMOND W.
Has admitted to having had a story
published in WT under an undisclosed
pseud.

HALL, ETHEL
Atmospherics   Phtm 8,Nov 57

HALL, FRANCES
After the Absence [v]   EC 6,1982
Prowler [v]   Unk Oct 40
*Prowler [v]   UnkB Oct 40
Watch Dog [v]   UW Dec 42
*Watch Dog [v]   UWB May 44

HALL, GARY
Just Plain Clumsy [v]   S&T 45,Nov 77
Metallic Face [v]   S&T 47,Apr 78
Shadows [v]   S&T 60,Jul 81

HALL, JOY
The Still Waters   Ftc Apr 55

HALL, LOAY H.
Dunsany: The Man and the
  Influence [a]   BFWK Aut 78

  + Randall Larson
"The Horror in the Garden"   Eld 9,1983

HALL, MELISSA MIA
The Alien, the Child, the
  Princess [v]   Shyl 5,Win 82
In a Green Shade   TZ Oct 82
The Last Communication [v] Shyl 6,Win 82
Wishing Will Make It So   TZ Nov 81

HALL, MERRILEE
Conversation [v]   Wbk 14,1979

HALL, MORDAUNT
The Escape   TB Oct 1,19

HALL, PAUL
Dr.Blenheim Operates   GS Sep 27

HALL, REX
Down Through the Ages   WT Apr 24

HALL, STEVE
Beginner's Luck [MC]   SFy 54,Aug 62
Hole in the Dyke [MC]   SFy 58,Apr 63
Out of Character [nt]   SFy 57,Feb 63
Party Piece [MC]   SFy 60,Aug 63
Three of a Kind [nt]   SFy 61,Oct 63
Week-End Trip [MC]   SFy 55,Oct 62

  as Russ Markham
Discontinuity   SFy 56,Dec 62
[MC - The Midnight Club]

HALL, WAGNER
  [May be a pseud. of Thomas P. Kelley]
Lady of the Tomb   UTC 7,Jul 41

HARD, FRANCIS
    Pseud: see Farnsworth WRIGHT

HARDING, ALLISON V.
City of Lost People [nt]	WT May 48
The Coming of M. Alkerhaus	WT Mar 48
The Damp Man [DM]	WT Jul 47
The Damp Man Again [DM]	WT May 49
The Damp Man Returns [DM]	WT Sep 47
The Day the World Stood Still	WT May 44
Death Went That Way	WT Nov 43
The Deep Drowse	WT Sep 49
Fog Country	WT Jul 45
The Follower	WT Sep 48
Four From Jehlam [nt]	WT Jan 49
The Frightened Engineer	WT Jan 48
Guard in the Dark	WT Jul 44
*Guard in the Dark	AFR 14,1950
The Holiday [nt]	WT Mar 49
The House Beyond Midnight [nt]	WT Jan 47
House of Hate	WT Jan 44
The House on Forest Street	WT Nov 48
The Immortal Lancer	WT Mar 47
The Inn By Doomsday Falls	WT Nov 47
Isle of Women [nt]	WT Jul 48
The Machine	WT Sep 46
The Marmot	WT Mar 44
The Murderous Steam Shovel	WT Nov 45
Night Must Not Come	WT Sep 43
Night of Impossible Shadows	WT Sep 45
The Place With Many Windows	WT May 47
Revolt of the Trees [nt]	WT Jan 45
Ride the El to Doom	WT Nov 44
[see rep. as by Alice B. Harcraft]	
Scope	WT Jan 51
The Seven Seas Are One	WT Sep 44
Shipmate	WT Nov 46
Take the Z Train	WT Mar 50
Tunnel Terror	WT Mar 46
The Underbody [nt]	WT Nov 49
The Unfriendly World	WT Jul 43
The Wings	WT Jul 46

    as Alice B. Harcraft
| *Ride the El to Doom | WT (Can) Jan 46 |
[DM - The Damp Man]

HARDING, LEE   [1937-]
Australian writer
All My Yesterdays	SFy 59,Jun 63
Displaced Person	SFy 46,Apr 61
Sacrificial [nt]	SFy 48,Aug 61

HARDING, RALPH STEPHEN
The Actual Alienation of Jacob Johnston	S&T 56,Jul 80
Ancient Warrior [v]	DFy 19,Feb 79
Baby Laura's Little White Casket [v]	Eld 7,1980
Creature [v]	Eld 9,1983
Day of the Skeleton, Night of the Pumpkin	CT 6/7,Jul 79
I Am the Corpse [v]	EvM Win 77/8
Revenge [v]	Eld 6,1979
Revolver, Rationale IV [v]	S&T 55,Apr 80
The Song	DFy 19,Feb 79

HARDING, ROBERT COSMO
| First Degree | WT May/Jul 24 |

HARDINGHAM, L. H.
    as Bertram Russell
The Bat-Men of Thorium [sn3]	WT May-Jul 28
The Scourge of B'Moth [nt]	WT May 29
*The Scourge of B'Moth [nt]	SMS 2,Fal 66

HARE, AUGUSTUS [John Cuthbert][1834-1903]
UK essayist, biographer and traveler
| *The Vampire of Groglin Grange | Chl Nov 81 |
    [*The Story of My Life,1896/1900]

HARKER, CARL SCOTT
Farewell Kiss	Div 21,Jul 77
Reasons [v]	Arg 5,Win/Spr 79
To Mankind [v]	Arg 5,Win/Spr 79

HARLOW, ALVIN F[ay]   [1876-1963]
US Popular historian.
[Note: all WT articles below belong in the series "Folks Used to Believe"]
The Barnacle Goose [a]	WT Feb 28
The Basilisk [a]	WT May 28
The Cockatrice [a]	WT May 29
Conceptions of Deity [a]	WT Jan 28
The Dragon and His Kinsmen [a]	WT Dec 27
The Fad for Relics [a]	WT Jun 28
The Fairy Court [a]	WT Nov 28
The Familiar [a]	WT Apr 28
The Indestructible Bone [a]	WT Sep 27
Lilith [a]	WT Dec 28
May Dew [a]	WT Mar 29
The Mouse Legend [a]	WT Jun 29
The Murderer's Touch [a]	WT Aug 29
The Phoenix [a]	WT Oct 28
Pope Joan [a]	WT Feb 29
The Resurrecting Snake [a]	WT Jan 29
The Roc [a]	WT Oct 29
The Salamander [a]	WT Sep 29
Salty Superstitions [a]	WT Jul 29
The Serpent in Eden [a]	WT Sep 28
Silent Watchers at the Ford	GS May 29
Some 'Old Masters' [a]	WT Oct 27
The Unicorn [a]	WT Apr 29
The Vampire [a]	WT Mar 28
Weird Recipes [a]	WT Jul 28
The Werewolf [a]	WT Nov 27
Wonderfully Preserved Relics [a]	WT Aug 28

HARMON, CHRISTOPHER
| Four Gold Teeth | WSM 1(1946) |

HARNESS, CHARLES L[eonard]   [1915-]
US patents lawyer
| The Call of the Black Lagoon | ASFFR Jan 53 |

HARPER, RORY
| M-M-Magic | FB Dec 81 |

HARPER, THOMAS DEV.
| The Hermit of Chemeketa Mountain | WT Apr 29 |

HARRIET, SIDNEY
| Eats! | Cov Mar 70 |

HARRINGTON, JOHNS
| The Teakwood Box | WT Mar 38 |

HARRINGTON, M. R.
    see pseud. Ramon DE LAS CUEVAS

HARTL, JOHN
Artist of the Impossible [a]   F&T 7,1975

HARTLEY, L[eslie] P[oles]   [1895-1972]
UK novelist and short story writer
Profile   TZ Dec 82
*W.S.   TZ Dec 82
  [*The Second Ghost Book ed. Cynthia
  Asquith, 1952]

HARTLEY, WILLIAM B.
The Black Spot   TF Aug 57

HARTWELL,Ph.D., DAVID G.
US editor and publisher
Howard Phillips Lovecraft [a]
                               Whsp 5,Nov 74

HARVEY, JAMES
Confession   Fear Jul 60
Incident in a Flying Saucer   TF Spr 57

HARVEY, JON M.
  [see Editor Index]
Fantasy in the Theatre [a]   DH 14,Sum 76
A Vampire By Any Other
  Name [a]   DH 22,Spr 81

HARVEY, WILLIAM FRYER   [1885-1937]
UK physician, educator and author
*Sambo   AFR 5,1948
  [*The Beast With Five Fingers,1928]
*The Traveller [v]   E&O 3,1983

HARWOOD, WALTER
The Trap   WT May 47

HASFORD, GUSTAV
Cezanne,Dying in the Rain   Wbk 11,1977
Twilight   S&T 16,Aug 72

HASSAN, SILAKI ALI
  Pseud: see Ulysses G. MIHALAKIS

HASSE, HENRY   [1913-77]
US sf/fantasy author
The Ensorcelled   Whsp 6/7,Jun 75
The Guardian of the Book [Cth] WT Mar 37
The Violin String   Ftc Apr 61
The Way to Casm's Place   Whsp 2,Dec 73
[Cth - Cthulhu Mythos]

HASTINGS, CRISTEL
Black Cats [v]   Unk Dec 40
*Black Cats [v]   UnkB Dec 40
  [also in *FUW,1948 and *FUWB,1952]
Empty House   WT Aug 38
The Empty House [v]   WT Nov 31
An Empty House at Night [v]   WT Apr 35
*An Empty House at Night [v] UTC 10,Oct 41
Fear [v]   WT Jul 26
Fog [v]   WT Apr 32
Ghost Town [v]   WT Nov 33
The Haunted House [v]   WT May 29
The Haunted Room [v]   WT Aug 32
The Jungle [v]   WT Dec 27
Listening [v]   WT Feb 35
Mystery [v]   WT May 32
Neptune's Neighbours [v]   WT Apr 29
An Old House [v]   WT Nov 27

Painted Dragons [v]   WT May 27
Penalty [v]   WT Nov 32
The Phantom [v]   WT Apr 28
The Swamp [v]   WT Aug 27
Swamp Symphony [v]   WT Mar 30

HASTINGS, MARY WILHELMINA
*The Attribute of Fools   BC Win 70/1
  [*a turn of the century magazine]

HASTWA, A.
  Pseud: see H.S.W. CHIBBETT

HASTY,Jr., W. L.
The Elder Gods   WT Oct 35
The Haunted Castle   WT Dec 35

HATFIELD, LEON N.
The Flying Fury   GS Dec 28
How a Reporter Interviewed a
  Ghost [ts]   GS Sep 28

HATVANY, ATTILA
A Dream of Falling   MoH 4,May 64

HAUFF, WILHELM   [1802-27]
German writer and folklorist
*The Severed Hand   WT Oct 25
  [*orig.c 1824]

HAUGEN, GENEVIEVE
Attic For Rent   Ftc Jun 57
The Illegitimate Egg   Ftc May 58
The Ugly Beauty   Ftc Oct 57

HAUGHT, JIM
Transient and Immortal   MoH 18,Nov 67

HAUGSR(A)UD, LEROY B.
A Cure For Mr.Kelsy   SFy 50,Dec 61

        + Dale R.Smith
Dieties, Inc.   SFy 42,Aug 60

HAUPT, LUDWIG
The Soul That Could Leave Its
  Body   TMM Feb 28

HAVDEL, A.
The Sign From Heaven   WT Oct 23

HAW, ALFRED
Consider the Lilies   Phtm 9,Dec 57
Hagbury Hill   Phtm 14,May 58
The Whistled Overture   Phtm 7,Oct 57

HAWES, CHRIS W.
Lost in Villefere [v]   Div 6,Dec 74

HAWES, JAMES CARY
The Crystal Ball   TB Aug 1,19

HAWKINS, JOHN
Everything's Jake   UW Aug 42

HAWKINS, PETER   [1926-]
UK bank clerk
Circus [nt]   SFy 5,Aut 52
The Daymakers [nt]   SFy 23,Jun 57
Haven [nt]   SFy 9,Jul 54
Outworlder   SFy 4,Spr 52

HERBERT, FRANK   [1920-]
US writer, best known for his sf
Interview   Ariel 3,Apr 78
Occupation Force   Ftc Aug 55
The Priests of Psi [na]   Ftc Feb 60

HERBERT, F. HUGH
US playwright for radio, cinema & theatre
The Perfectly Calm Murder   Sus Sum 51

HERBERT, GEORGE
    Pseud: see Charles T. Smith

HERMAN, IRA H.
    as Mitya Kornedeplov
Palapagos [nt15] S&T 25-39,Jul 74-Nov 76
    (last two episodes appeared under
    Herman's own name)

HERMAN, JUSTIN
Lemuria [v]   Ggn (8) 1948
Sonnet to Palomar [v]   Ggn Mar 49
There Will Be Darkness [v]   Ggn (11) 1949

HERNANDEZ, JOSEPH H.
Adventure in Valhalla   StS Dec 40

HERNDON, BEN
Douglas Heyes [in]   TZ Aug 82

HERNHUNTER, AL
Of Mice and Monsters   FB Dec 81

HERON, E. & H.
    Pseud: see Kate & Hesketh PRICHARD

HERRICK, ABBIE
The Journey   TZ Apr 83

HERRICK, SNOWDEN T.
The Hidden Talent of Artist
    Bates   WT Sep 48
Open Season on the - Bottoms WT Jan 49

HERRINGTON, W. LEE
Body of an Elderly Man   MysT Mar 52

HERRON, DON
The Blades of Hell [v]   FyT 6,Sum 80
Bran Mak Morn [a]   DFd 3,Sum 80
A Key to "The Little Booke"
    [a]   Nyc 11/12,Apr 76
Magic [v]   Div 26/7,May/Jul 78
Re-enter the Dragon [a]   Div 5,Oct 74

HERRON, VENETTE
*Toean Matjan   WT Jan 38

HERSEY, HAROLD   [1892-1953?]
US pulp magazine editor & publisher
Captain George Guynemeer [v] TB Apr 1,19
The Dead Book   TB Jul 15,19
The Dummy and the Ventriloquist
    [v]   TB May 1,19
The Street Without a Name   TB Jun 1,19
This World and the Next [ed] GS Apr 31

    as Carl Buxton
Marsa [v]   TB May 15,19

    as Philip Kennedy
Flowerlight [v]   TB Apr 1,19

    as Charles Kiproy
After [v]   TB May 15,19
The Dance [v]   TB Jul 1,19
Miladi [v]   TB Mar 15,19

    as Larrovitch
The Twisted Tapers [v]   TB Mar 1,19

    as Roy LeMoyne
The Death of Columbine [v] TB Apr 1,19
Life [v]   TB May 1,19
Lilith [v]   TB Mar 1,19
Out of Our Hands' Reach [v] TB May 15,19
Romance [v]   TB May 15,19
Shafts of Light [v]   TB Jun 15,19

    as Albert Owens
Hidden Pathways [v]   TB Aug 1,19
My Lovely [v]   TB Mar 15,19
The Old Lovers [v]   TB Jun 1,19

    as Arnold Tyson
Aglaia [v]   TB Jun 15,19
The Battle [v]   TB May 1,19
Freedom [v]   TB Apr 15,19

    as Vail Vernon
The King [v]   TB Apr 15,19
    (Hersey may have written other poems
    under these house names. See entries,
    also those for Francois de Vallient,
    Harry Kemp and Seymour LeMoyne)

HERT, LOVELL
Haunted House [v]   MT Mar/Apr 35

HESS, LEONARD
John Shard Comes Back   GS Mar 27
"To the Dead, All Things Are
    Clear"   GS Feb 27

HESS, RICHARD
The Possession of the Ring
    [a]   Myrd 1,Win 75

HEWELCKE, GEOFFREY
    as Hugh Jeffries
The Dust of Death [nt]   WT Apr/May 31

HEWSON, GERARD
Simply Explained   Phtm 2,May 57
Stony Dykas   Phtm 15,Jun 58

HEYDRON, VICKI ANN
    [Mrs Randall Garrett]
The Sacrifice [v]   Wyrd 8,1980

HEYES, DOUGLAS
Interview   *TZ Aug 82*

HEYMAN, ED S.
Hell, Yes! [ss]   Vor 1,1947

HEYWOOD, D. R.
Hunt a Wild Dream [s2]
                        SFy 70-71,Mar-Apr 65

HEYWOOD, TERENCE
*Medallion in Quicksilver [v]Nek 4,Win 50/1
    [*Quicksilver* (date unknown)]
Under Scorpio(Noctuary) [v] Nek 5,mid-51

*The Skull That Screamed
   'Murder!' [Cran]   TTT Spr 64
   [*orig."The Headless Shadow"]
Stolen By Spirits [a]   GS Feb 29
The Thing That Limped [Cran]   GS Jul 31
*Town of Terror   TTT Fal 63
   [*orig."Forgotten Harbor"]
What Happened Aboard the Old
   'Memphis Queen'   GS Jul 30
   [see rep.as "The Phantom Whistler"]
[Cran - Cranshawe, Psychic Investigator]

HILLYARD, JOHN
   + Wallace West
The Disenchanted   Ftc Jan/Feb 54
*The Disenchanted   Ftc Dec 68

HINCHCLIFFE, EMILIE
Did Captain Hinchcliffe Return
  to His Wife? [ts]   GS May 29

HINDIN, NATHAN
US musician and former law student
  written by Robert Bloch from ideas
  supplied by Hindin and published as
  by Hindin
Death is an Elephant   WT Feb 39
Fangs of Vengeance   WT Apr 37

HINDS, ROY W.
  Recoiling Sparks   TB Oct 1,19

HINTON, JOSEPH W.
  He Who Laughs   FCw 2,Feb 77

HIPWELL, HERBERT
  The Madman   WT Jun 23

HIRSCH, JANET
  The Seeking Thing   MoH 3,Feb 64

HJORT, JAMES WILLIAM
US writer and artist
Along For the Ride   Wbk 12,1977
Graveyard Jestering   Wbk 11,1977
Yhagni's Priest   Wbk 16,1982

HOAR, ROGER SHERMAN
  see pseud: Ralph Milne FARLEY

HOCH, EDWARD D[entinger] [1930-]
Prolific US mystery/crime writer
The Empty Zoo   MoH 11,Nov 65
The Faceless Thing   MoH 2,Nov 63
Funeral in the Fog   [Ark]   WT Sum 73
*The Man From Nowhere [Ark] SMS 5,Sum 67
   [*Famous Detective Stories,1956]
The Man Who Knew Everything   Shk Sep 60
The Maze and the Monster   MoH 1,Aug 63
*A Sword For a Sinner [nt]
   [Ark]   SMS 12,Spr 69
   [*Saint Mystery Magazine Oct 59]
*The Vicar of Hell [Ark]   SMS 17,Fal 70
   [*Famous Detective Stories Aug 56]
*The Village of the Dead [Ark] SMS 1,Sum 66
   [*Famous Detective Stories,1955]
*The Witch is Dead   [Ark]   SMS 2,Fal 66
   [*Famous Detective Stories,1956]
[Ark - Simon Ark]

HOCKNELL, PATRICIA
  Only the Best   SFy 69,Jan/Feb 65
  Prisoner   SFy 73,Jun 65

HODEL, MIKE
US writer and radio host
Negotiations at a Lower Level FB Nov 82
Second Chance   FB Feb 82

HODGE, MIKE
  + Jonathan Bacon
A Conversation with A.J.Hanley
  [in]   FCr 2,Feb 75

HODGENS, RICHARD M.
  One By One   MoH 23,Sep 68

HODGSON, SHEILA
UK author and radio/television playwright
Come, Follow!   G&S 4,1982

HODGSON, WILLIAM HOPE   [1877-1918]
UK writer, seaman and physical educator
Profiles   WT Sum-Win 73; TZ Apr 82
*The Derelict [nt]   AFR 4,1947
   [*Red Magazine Dec 1,1912]
*Eloi, Eloi, Lama Sabachthani   WT Fal 73
   [*orig."The Baumoff Explosion" Nash's
   Weekly Sep 17,1919]
*The Finding of the Graiken   WT Sum 74
   [*Red Magazine Feb 15,1913]
*The Haunted Jarvee [Car]   AFR 18,1952
   [*Carnacki the Ghost-Finder,1948]
The Hog [nt]   [Car]   WT Jan 47
*Lost [v]   ArkC 5,Sum 69
*The Mystery of the Sargasso   AFR 17,1951
   [*orig."The Mystery of the Derelict"
   Story Teller Jul 1907]
*The Riven Night   E&O 3,1983
   [*Shadow 19,Apr 73]
The Room of Fear   E&O 2,1983
*Shoon of the Dead [v]   ArkC 5,Sum 69
*The Stone Ship   AFR 9,1949
   [*Red Magazine Jul 1,1914]
*The Terror of the Water-Tank   WT Win 73
   [*Blue Book Sep 1907]
*A Tropical Horror   WT Sum 73
   [*Grand Magazine Jun 1905]
Two Letters From William Hope
  Hodgson [ltrs]   ArkS 2,Sep 83
*The Voice in the Night   AFR 1,1947
*The Voice in the Night   Sus Spr 51
*The Voice in the Night   TZ Apr 82
   [*Blue Book Nov 1907]
*The Whistling Room [Car]   Myst 5,1952
*The Whistling Room [Car]   MoH 9,Jun 65
   [*The Idler Mar 1910]
*Who Make Their Bed in Deep
  Waters [v]   FCr 12,Nov 77
[Car - Carnacki]

HOFFMAN, CHARLES
Conan the Existential [a]   Ariel 1,1976

HOFFMAN, CHARLES F[enno]   [1806-84]
US author, journalist and editor
*The Boiler   Imp 8,Oct 66
   [*orig."Ben Blower's Story"]

Blackwood [v]   DFy 5,Oct 74
The Dream [v]   DFy 7,Sep 75
Keepers of the Dark [v]   DFy 10,Dec 76
Last of the Caravans [v]   DFy 6,Jan 75
Looking to the Sun   CT 2,Jul 77
An Obstacle Grotesque [v]   DFy 4,Jul 74
Payment [v]   DFy 1,Sum 73
A Pillow of Wind [v]   DFy 9,Sep 76
Roundstones and Sunchild   CT 2,Jul 77
Synthetic Realm [v]   DFy 8,May 76
There Used to be a Time [v]   DFy 4,Jul 74
Tomorrow is Such a Long
  Time [v]   DFy 1,Sum 73
United [v]   DFy 2,Fal 73

    + Gene Day
Proxy   CT 2,Jul 77

JACK, GEOFFREY
The Night the Zombies Walked   AH Apr 71

JACKSON, CLIVE G.B.
I'll Never Leave You   Nek 5,mid-51
*The Still,Small Voice   AFR 14,1950
  [*Slant 2,Sum 49]

JACKSON, DAVID
Walking Cane   F&T 7,1975

JACKSON, MARGARET [1895-?]
The Sign on the Chinese
  Rug [ts]   GS Nov 28
The Thing on the Roof   GS Dec 28

JACKSON, PATRICIA
A Jocund Jaunt with Jirel of
  Joiry... [a]   NV 4,Sum 79
Catherine and L.Sprague de
  Camp [a/in]   NV 5,Fal 79

JACKSON, PETER
A Hero Lives in Brooklyn [a] Ariel 1,1976
Jim Crocker, Prince of
  Atlantis [a]   Ariel 3,Apr 78

    + Michael Sollars
The Night of Mozatlan   Ariel 3,Apr 78

JACKSON, SHIRLEY   [1919-65]
US novelist & short story writer
Root of Evil   Ftc Mar/Apr 53
*Root of Evil   Ftc Jun 69

JACOB, JOHN [1950-]
"And When Blood Touches Blood..."
                                 Nyc 5,Oct 71
Canons I and II [2v]   E&O 1,1973
Final Call [v]   HPL 1972
The Left Behind [Cth]   E&O 1,1973
*Mushroom   [Cth]   FBDG 3,Apr 74
  [*Comic Courier 3,Jan 70]
The Rynlaerth Megaliths [Cth]
                                 FBDG 1,Apr/May 71
Totem   HPL 1972
[Cth - Cthulhu Mythos]

JACOBI, ABEL
The Emperor's Dogs   BMM Nov 65

JACOBI, CARL [Richard] [1908-]
US author, newspaper reporter & editor
Interview   E&O 1,1973
The Aquarium   [Cth]   FCr 7,Feb 76
  [original version; an edited version
  appeared in Dark Mind,Dark Heart
  ed. August Derleth,1962]
The Black Garden   WT 3,Fal 81
The Cane   WT Apr 34
Carnaby's Fish   WT Jul 45
The Cocomacaque   ArkC 8,Win 71
The Corbie Door [nt]   WT May 47
The Devil Deals   WT Apr 38
The Digging at Pistol Key   WT Jul 47
The Face in the Wind   WT Apr 36
Forsaken Voyage   MS 5,1979
Hamadryad   Whsp 6/7,Jun 75
The Haunted Ring   GS Dec 31/Jan 32
Incident at the Galloping Horse WT Nov 48
The La Prello Paper   WT Mar 48
The Last Drive   WT Jun 33
The Lorenzo Watch   WT Jan 48
Man From Makassar   MT Sum 35
Matthew South and Company   WT May 49
Mive   WT Jan 32
The Music Lover   WT Sum 74
A Pair of Swords   WT Aug 33
The Phantom Pistol   WT May 41
The Pit   WT 1,Spr 81
Portrait in Moonlight   WT Nov 47
Rambling Memoirs [a]   Div 21,Jul 77
The Random Quantity   AFR 5,1948
Revelations in Black   WT Apr 33
Sagasta's Last   StS Aug 39
The Satanic Piano   WT May 34
Some Correspondence [a]   E&O 2,1983
The Spanish Camera   WT Sep 50
Spawn of Blackness   StS Oct 39
The Syndicate of the Snake   E&O 2,1983
Test Case   MS 2,Sum/Fal 75
[Cth - Cthulhu Mythos]

JACOBS, MARK
The Brain Death   AD 1,Win 75
The Death Toller   AD 1,Win 75
The Drug   AD 1,Win 75
No Place Like Home   AD 2,Win 75/6
Not the Nova Said Seven   AD 2,Win 75/6
The Pleasure Stones of Karina   AD 3,Spr 76
A Shadow Review [a]   AD 3,Spr 76
Spiders Are Harmless   AD 2,Win 75/6
Teacher   AD 4,Fal 76
Time For Love   Jeet 2,Sum 77
To View and Eagle   AD 3,Spr 76

JACOBS, PAUL
The Flaming Curse of Belden
  Hall   GS Oct 26

JACOBS, W[illiam] W[ymark] [1863-1943]
UK civil service accountant & writer
*The Monkey's Paw   Shk May 60
*The Monkey's Paw   SMS 15,Spr 70
  [*Harper's Magazine Sep 1902]

JACOBSON, JERRY
Funeral In Another Town   WT Fal 73

JACQUES, EDWIN M.
Twilight [v]   Mac 21,1970

A Thousand Degrees Below Zero
  [nt]   TB Jul 15,19
Tyrants Need to be Loved   Ftc Feb 60

    + Poul Anderson, Isaac Asimov, Robert
    Bloch & Robert Sheckley
The Covenant [rr]   Ftc Jul 60
[MoD - Master of Darkness]

JENKS, ANDY
  The God From the Machine   WWd 2(1956)

JENKS, GEORGE C.
  The Vengeance of Vishnu   TB Jun 15,19

JENKS, TUDOR   [1857-1922]
US author and editor
*A Lost Opportunity   FFy Jun 71
  [*Imaginotions,1894]

JENMAC, DOUGLAS
  Four   .   TZ Aug 81

JENNINGS, JOR
  "Other"   TZ Feb 82

JENNINGS, LESLIE NELSON
  Wildlife [v]   Mac 22,1973

JENNINGS, R[obert] EDWARDS   [1918-]
US PC worker [see Artist Index]
  Fulfillment   Anu 2,Spr 67

JENTS, PAUL
  Clay   Imp 4,Jun 66
  Our Man in 1900   SFy 81,Feb 66
  Peace on Earth   SFy 73,Jun 65
  The Pursuit of Happiness
    [nt]   Imp 12,Feb 67
  Unto All Generations   SFy 66,Jul/Aug 64

JEROME, OWEN FOX
    Pseud: see Oscar J. FRIEND

JERVIS, LIONEL
  A Presentiment   Wtch Dec 36

JIMERSON, ROYAL W.
  Medusa   WT Apr 28
  *Medusa   WT May 38

JOHNS, KENNETH
    Pseud: see Kenneth BULMER & John NEWMAN

JOHNS, ROLLAND
    [see also Rolland JONES]
  Flowers of Death   UTC 9,Sep 41

JOHNS, TALBOT
  Date in the City Room   WT Jan 39
  *Date in the City Room   WT Jul 51

JOHNS, VICTOR
  The Hideous Face   WT Apr 23

JOHNSON, ERNEST
  The Light at Curry's Point EC 2,1979

JOHNSON, FANNY KEMBLE
  The Dinner Set   WT Feb 35

JOHNSON, GEORGE CLAYTON
US author, screenwriter & former architect
  All of Us Are Dying   TZ May 82
  The Birth   Gam 3,1964
  Drum Dancer   TZ May 81
  The Freeway   Gam 1,1963
*Kick the Can [tp]   TZ Oct 83
    [*first bdcst CBS-TV Feb 9,1962;
    presented with a newly-written
    Afterword]
  Lullabye and Goodnight   Gam 5,Sep 65
  Sea Change   TZ Oct 81
    [also in *GSTZ,1982]
  Writing For "The Twilight Zone"
    [a]   TZ Aug 81

JOHNSON, GERTRUDE
  The Grip of Justice   Phtm 2,May 57

JOHNSON, LESLIE J.   [1914-]
UK local government Education Officer
    + Eric Frank Russell
  Eternal Rediffusion   WT Fal 73

JOHNSON, LESLIE N.
  With the Coming of Dawn   WT Jul 26

JOHNSON, MARGARET LEE
  Day of the Snake   Mac 6,Win 59

JOHNSON, MILDRED
  The Cactus   WT Jan 50
  The Mirror   WT Sep 50

JOHNSON, ROBERT BARBOUR   [1909?-]
*Charles Fort and a Man Named
  Thayer [a]   Anu 2,Spr 67
    [*Rhodomagnetic Digest Oct/Nov 51]
  Far Below   WT Jun/Jul 39
  Lead Soldiers   WT Dec 35
  The Life-After-Death of Mr.
    Thaddeus Ward   MoH 6,Nov 64
  Lupa   WT Jan 41
  Mice   WT Nov 36
*The Pet of Mrs.Lilith   SMS 7,Win 67/8
    [see "The Strange Case of Monica
    Lilith"]
  The Silver Coffin   WT Jan 39
  The Strange Case of Monica
    Lilith   Mystic Jan 54
*The Strange Case of Monica
    Lilith   Phtm 16,Jul 58
    [see further reprint under the orig.
    title "The Pet of Mrs.Lilith"]
  They   WT Jan 36

JOHNSON, ROGER
  The Relic [v]   ArkC 9,Spr 71
  To His Mistress, Dead and
    Darkly Returned [v]   ArkC 8,Win 71
  To My Masters [v]   ArkC 10,Sum 71

JOHNSON, SUSAN
  Behind the Doors   TZ Sep 82

JOHNSON, THELMA E.
  David Keeps His Word   GS Aug 29
    [see "That Night the Dead Took Over"]
  Fate [v]   WT Oct 29
*That Night the Dead Took Over TTT Spr 64
    [*orig. "David Keeps His Word"]

JOHNSON, TIM K.
Epitaph For Michael [v]   Div 15,Jul 76

JOHNSON, VIC
Of Sleds and Forty Winters   TZ Jan 82

JOHNSON, VICTORIA BEAUDIN
Disillusionment [v]   WT Dec 35

JOHNSON, WILL
August Evening [v]   EC 7,1982
Ghoul's View [v]   Wbk 16,1982
Some Lines After Brennan [v]   EC 8,1982

JOLLIFFE, ARTHUR T.
The Living Dead Man   GS Jan 31
Master of Darkness [sn4]   GS May-Aug 30
The Phantom Menace of the
  Screen [n5]   GS Apr-Aug/Sep 31
Through the Wall   GS Sep 27
Where None Could Live   GS Feb 31

JONES, ALAN
Fruit   WW 1,Jun 70
The Terror Film Career of
  Pete Walker [a]   DH 23,Sum 81

JONES, ALICE ELEANOR
Recruiting Officer   Ftc Oct 55

JONES, BRUCE
The Maiden and the Dragon   Ariel 3,Apr 78

JONES, IDWAL
The Third Interne   WT Jan 38

JONES, KELVIN I.
The Alabaster Bowl   G&S 5,1983
The Corruption of the
  Innocents [a]   DH 20(1979)
The Green Man   FyT 12,Win 83
The Weird of Caxton   DH 26,Spr 83

JONES, K. L.   [1946-]
US lawyer
Herbie Feamster, Lord of
  Dimensions   FB Dec 81
Oops!   Ftc Apr 79
A Spider For Sandra   FB Nov 82
A Visit With Lenny   [MSS]   Ftc Jul 80
[MSS - The Man in the Silver Suit]

JONES, LANGDON   [1942-]
UK writer and musician
The Empathy Machine   SFy 69,Jan/Feb 65

JONES, LESLIE
Behind the Curtain   SMS 5,Sum 67

JONES, NARD
Nomadic Skull   WT May 33

JONES, NEIL R[onald]   [1909-]
US insurance claims executive and games
inventor; noted early pulp sf writer
The Saga of Professor Jameson
  [a]   Ggn (11) 1949

JONES, RAY
Breath of Ages   EC 2,1979

Terror From the Ages   Wbk 2,1969
The Walls   EC 3,1980
The Well   Wbk 3,1970

JONES, RAYMOND F.   [1915-]
US writer, best known for his sf
Death Eternal   Ftc Oct 78

JONES, ROGER
Hurry Down Sunshine   Imp 5,Jul 66
The Island   SFy 69,Jan/Feb 65

JONES, ROLLAND
  [see also Rolland JOHNS]
Myrrha - A Mystery   UTC 8,Aug 41

JONES, STEPHEN/STEVE [Gregory] [1953-]
UK tv producer/director; sf/fantasy
illustrator, designer, editor & columnist
Brooding on Success: David
  Cronenberg [in]   DH 25,Sum 82
Good Omens: an Interview With
  Richard Donner [in]   DH 24,Win 81
The Space Merchant: an Interview
  with Frederik Pohl [in]   DH 19(1979)
The Writer in Fandom: David
  Sutton [in]   DH 12,Aut/Win 75

  as Steven Gregory
The Dreamer [v]   DH 11,Win/Spr 75
Midnight [v]   DH 26,Spr 83

  + Carl Hiles
The Forever Man [in]   DH 21,1980

JONES, SUSAN CARLETON
  see pseud: Susan CARLETON

JONES, VINCENT
To Him Who Waits [ts]   GS Nov 29

JONES, WILLIS KNAPP
The Beast of the Yungas   WT Sep 27
Bright Eyes of Adventure   WT Mar 25
The Fading Ghost   WT Oct 25
The Green Scarab   WT Aug 25
The Man Who Remembered   WT Jul 28
The Other Vera   WT Aug 26
Return to Earth   WT Jun 37

JONES, YVONNE
Whichever Be First [v]   DH 17,Sum 77

JORDAN, CHARLES T.
The Borderland Bridge   TB Jun 15,19

JORDAN, E. B.
Devil Manor   WT Oct 23

JORDAN, [Richard Arthur] MARTIN [1913-]
UK civil servant
Sheamus [nt]   SFy 14,Jun 55
Zone of Youth   SFy 10,Sep 54

JORDAN, THOMAS R.
Smoke Fantasy   WT Mar 39

JORGENSEN, IVAR
Ziff-Davis house name used predominantly
by Paul W. Fairman
  by Howard Browne
The 7th Bottle [nt]   Ftc Aug 54

KEENE, DAY
Dead Man's Shoes   WT Mar 50

KELLAR, LINDA
The Five Horns of Artaius
  [v]   DFd 4,Win 83

KELLAR, MICHAEL
Lamia [v]   Div 19,Mar 77
Love Call From the Darkness
  [v]   Div 22,Sep 77
To Une Undead [v]   Div 20,May 77

KELLAR, ORRIS M.
The Second Step   MT Win 34

KELLEAM, JOSEPH E[veridge] [1913-]
US civil servant
From the Dark Waters   AFR 6,1948
The Last Druid   Ftc Oct 61
The Red Flowers of Tulp   Ftc Feb 62
Revenge of the Were-Thing   M&T Jan 59

KELLER,[M.D.], [Dr.] DAVID H[enry]
US physician & psychiatrist; [1880-1966]
noted early sf/fantasy & medical writer
  Bibliography   FyM 2-3,Apr 81-Jun 82
  Obituary   ArkC 1,Sum 67
*The Abyss [sn2]   MoH 23-24,Sep-Nov 68
  [*The Solitary Hunters & The Abyss,1948]
*The Ambidexter   [WL]   Ftc Jan 67
  [*Amazing Stories Apr 31]
A Basic Science Fiction Library
  [sym]   ArkS Win 49
The Battle of the Toads [TFC]   WT Oct 29
*The Battle of the Toads [TFC]
                                MoH 30,Dec 69
Binding De Luxe   MT May 34
*Bindings De Luxe   WT Jan 43
The Bride Well   [TFC]   WT Oct 30
*The Bride Well   [TFC]   MoH 33,Sum 70
The Bridle   WT Sep 42
Calypso's Island   SFF Apr 41
[The Chestnut Mare - see Speed Will Be
  My Bride]
Creation Unforgiveable   WT Apr 30
The Damsel and Her Cat   WT Apr 29
*The Dead Woman   StS Apr 39
  [*Fantasy Magazine Apr 34]
Death of the Kraken   WT Mar 42
The Dogs of Salem   WT Sep 28
The Door   ArkS Sum 49
Dust in the House   WT Jul 38
Feminine Magic   [TFC]   MoH 34,Fal 70
The Goddess of Zion   WT Jan 41
The Golden Bough   MT Win 34
*The Golden Bough   WT Nov 42
*Granny's Last Meal   FyM 3,Jun 82
  [*Peon 5,Dec 48]
Heredity   Vor 2,1947
*Heredity   MoH 13,Sum 66
The House Without Mirrors   WT 1,Spr 81
*The Ivy War [nt]   Ftc Sep 67
  [*Amazing Stories May 30]
The Jelly-Fish   WT Jan 29
The Key to Cornwall   [TFC]   SFF Feb 41
*The Key to Cornwall [TFC]   MoH 36,Apr 71
The Killer   Ggn 6,1948
The Last Magician   WT May 32
The Little Husbands   WT Jul 28

Lords of the Ice   WT Dec 39
*The Metal Doom [n2]   Ftc Nov 67-Jan 68
  [*Amazing Stories May-Jul 32]
*The Moon Artist   SFF Jun 41
  [*Cosmic Tales Sum 39]
*The Mother   Ftc Oct 61
  [*Fantascience Digest 2,Jan/Feb 38]
*No More Tomorrows   Ftc Sep 66
  [*Amazing Stories Dec 32]
No Other Man   [TFC]   WT Dec 29
*No Other Man   [TFC]   MoH 32,May 70
The Oak Tree   [TFC]   MoH 26,Mar 69
The Perfumed Garden   Ggn (May) 49
Raymond the Golden [TFC]   MoH 28,Jul 69
The Seeds of Death [nt]   WT Jun/Jul 31
*The Seeds of Death [nt]   MoH 3,Feb 64
The Solitary Hunters [sn3]   WT Jan-Mar 34
*Speed Will Be My Bride   UnS Apr 41
  [*orig."The Chestnut Mare"Scienti-
  Snaps Sum 40]
*Stenographer's Hands   AFR 2,1947
  [*Amazing Stories Quarterly Fall 28]
The Sword and the Eagle [TFC]
                                 MoH 27,May 69
The Tailed Man of Cornwall [TFC] WT Nov 29
*The Tailed Man of Cornwall
  [TFC]   MoH 31.Feb 70
The Temple of Death [T]   SMS 16,Sum 70
The Thing in the Cellar   WT Mar 32
*The Thing in the Cellar   AFR 6,1948
*The Thirty and One [TFC]   MoH 29,Sep 69
  [*Marvel Science Stories Nov 38]
Tiger Cat   WT Oct 37
The Toad God   StS Jun 39
The Typewriter   FT Fal 36
*Unto Us a Child is Born   Ftc Apr 79
  [*Amazing Stories Jul 33]
The Valley of Bones   WT Jan 38
*Wolf Hollow Bubbles [T]   SMS 11,Win 68/9
  [*booklet, Arra Publishers,1934]
*The Worm   Ftc Sep 65
*The Worm   Ftc Jul 79
  [*Amazing Stories Mar 29]
*The Yeast Men   AFR 14,1950
  [*Amazing Stories Apr 28]
[T - Taine of San Francisco; TFC - Tales
From Cornwall; WL - Wing Loo]

KELLER, KEN
Checking In With C. J. Cherryh
  [in]   Shyl 5,Win 82

KELLEY, GEORGE
The Night of the Hanged Men   F&T 7,1975

KELLEY, LEO P[atrick] [1928-]
US freelance writer
Any Questions?   Ftc Oct 62
The Dark Door   W&S 5,Jan/Feb 71
Generation Gap   WT Sum 74
Like Father   Wbk 2,1969
To the Victor   Ftc May 64

KELLEY, MICHAEL J.
A Therapeutic Success   BMM Jan 66

KELLEY, THOMAS P. [1904-82]
Canadian pulp writer and former boxer
The Black Hole of Calcutta
  [a]   UTC 3,Jan 41

The Hound   ET Jul 41
I Found Cleopatra [n4] WT Nov 38-Feb 39
*I Found Cleopatra [n3] UTC 7-9,Jul-Sep 41
Isle of Madness [na2] UTC 5-6,Mar-Jun 41
The Last Pharaoh [n4]   WT May-Aug 37
A Million Years in the
  Future [n4]   WT Jan-Jul 40
*A Million Years in the
  Future [n5]   UTC 11-15,Nov 41-Mar 42
Murder in the Graveyard   UTC 1,Nov 40
Salome [a]   UTC 4,Mar 41
The Shaggy God   UTC 5,May 41
The Soul-Eater   UTC 17,May 42
The Talking Heads [n5]
                     UTC 1-5,Nov 40-May 41
The Weird Queen [n?;1 part only
  published]   ET Jul 41

  as Gene Bannerman
Beyond the Veil [nt]   UTC 6,Jun 41
City of the Centaurs   UTC 12,Dec 41

  as Roy P. Devlin
Cleopatra Lives Again   UTC 2,Dec 40

  as Valentine Worth
Black Castle of Hate   UTC 10,Oct 41
The Man Who Killed Hitler   UTC 6,Jun 41
The Man Who Killed Mussolini   ET Jul 41
The Mummy   UTC 3,Jan 41
One Way Ticket   UTC 2,Dec 40

*[Although it is known that Kelley wrote
other stories for UTC his pseudonyms are
not known. Likely candidates, though
not confirmed, are:
  Wallace Bennett, Wagner Hall, Halton
  James, D.N. Kane, Allen Lake, Scott
  Malcolm and Neil Perrin
for which see individual entries]*

KELLIER, B. M.
The Stone That Died   Phtm 4,Jul 57

KELLY, DAN
Wind Walks Not Alone [v]   WT Mar 45
*Wind Walks Not Alone [v] WT(Can)Jul 45

KELLY, DONNA
Witches [v]   WT Feb 35

KELLY, ELLA BLANCHE
The Eye of the Camera   GS Jan 28
The Specter at the Feast   GS Aug 28
A Spirit Danced for Me   GS Nov 27

KELLY, JAMES PATRICK
Identity Crisis   TZ Aug 81

KELLY, JOHN D.
Botwinick's Soul   S&T 49,Oct 78
The City at Night   DFy 22,Mar 80
The Courage   EvM Win 77/8
Dennis and the Snail   S&T 52,Jul 79
In Transit   Div 23,Nov 77
Manifest Destiny   Arg 6,Sum/Fal 79

KELLY, RENYARD
  Pseud: see Dale C. DONALDSON

KELLY, T. CHRISTOPHER
The Hidden Traitor   S&T 38,Sep 76

To Sacrifice a Pawn   S&T 57,Oct 80

KELLY, T[homas] HOWARD   [1895-?]
Guided By a Spirit Hand   GS Sep 26
The Ha'nts of Amelia Island   GS Aug 26

KELTY, M.
The Evil That Grows   G&G(1938)

KEMMELMAN, HARRY
*The Nine-Mile Walk   MysT 5,1952
  [*Ellery Queen's Mystery Magazine Apr 47]

KEMP, ERNEST
  as Trebor Thorpe
Travellers' Rest   SN 83(1963)
[consists of "Spawn of Death" and "Curse
of the Witch" by Kemp reworked as a
single story sequence by R.L. Fanthorpe]

KEMP, HARRY
*Apparently a real poet whose name was also
used as a house pseud. in TB*
  by Harry Kemp
The Haunted House [v]   TB Apr 15,19
Let Them Tip Tables [v]   TB Sep 15,19
Theophany [v]   TB Aug 15,19

  possibly by Harold Hersey
The Ballad of the Living Dead
  [v]   TB Jul 15,19

KEMP, LYSANDER
Boil One Cat   Ftc Aug 54
Silent Night   Ftc Apr 55

KEMPE, JOSEPH C.
Abandoned Bog [v]   WT Apr 38
Frost Demons   [v]   WT Mar 43

KEMPER, RACHAEL
The Dancing Shoes   EC 7,1982
Quiet Evening at Home   Wbk 4,1971

KEMPER, VIKTOR R.
The Hour of the Wolf [v] ArkC 6,Win 70

KEMPH, OBADIAH
Fangs of a Fiend for the Girl
  Who Died Twice   AH Aug 71
It Takes Two for Terror   AH Dec 70
Long Night in the Hellfire
  Mansion   AH Jun 71
Revenge From Hell   AH Apr 71

KENDALL, CARLTON W.
The Fear   TB Sep 1,19

KENEBORUS, GEORGE
The Hidden Ones [v]   Anu 1,Aut 66

KENNEDY, JIM
The Mad Arab [ss]   S&T 20,Sep 73

KENNEDY, JOE
The Immoral Storm [spf] Ggn 7,Mar/Apr 48
The Ultimate Prozine [a]   Ggn 4,Sep 47

KENNEDY, LIAM
The Mirror   WT Nov 40

The Well   WT Jun 23

KIMBERLY, GAIL
  Requiem   Chl Jul 81

KIMBLE, CAROLINE
  Night Drive   CT 6/7,Jul 79

KIMMEL, ERIC A.
  The Ghoul of Herat   EC 6,1982

KING, CHARLES
  All the Time in the World   WT Jan 46
  A Birthday Present For Tommy   WT Mar 45
  The Horn   WT Sep 46
  I'll Be Glad When I'm Dead   WT Jul 46
  *I'll Be Glad When I'm Dead   WT(Can)Jan 47
  The Mirror   WT Nov 45
  There Was An Old Woman   WT Jan 47
  *There Was An Old Woman   WT(Can)Jul 47
  Welcome Home!   WT May 45

KING, FORREST L.
  "Never Touch a Ghost!"   GS Feb 27

KING, HERMAN STOWELL
  The House of Shadows   Nek 2,Sum 50
  Nocturne [v]   ArkC 1,Sum 67

KING, OWEN
  The Ghost of Death [ts]   WT Jun 23

KING, RAE
  Across the Years   MM Sep/Oct 31
  Dorothea Decides   [Dor]   MM Nov 31
  Ouija's Diamonds   [Dor]   MM Dec 31
  Pedro's Golden Dreams   MM Aug 31
  Secret of Dreams   MM Jul 31
  [Dor - Dorothea]

KING, RAY
  Pseud: see Ray CUMMINGS

KING, STELLA
  Were You Born In— [col] GS Jan 27-Jun 31
  [as by 'Stella' from Jan 27-Jun 28]

KING, STEPHEN   [1946-]
  US best-selling horror writer
  Interviews   Shyl 3,Sum 79; Shyl 6,Win 82
                TZ Apr 81; Chl Nov 81
  Profiles   DH 25,Sum 82; Whsp 17/18,Aug 82
  Before the Play [nt]   Whsp 17/18,Aug 82
  Digging the Boogens [a]   TZ Jul 82
  The Evil Dead [a]   TZ Nov 82
  The Glass Floor   SMS 6,Fal 67
  It Grows On You   Whsp 17/18,Aug 82
  The Jaunt [nt]   TZ Jun 81
    [also in *GSTZ,1982]
  On 'The Shining' and other
    Perpetrations [a]   Whsp 17/18,Aug 82
  *The Raft [nt]   TZ Jun 83
    [*Gallery Nov 82]
  The Reaper's Image   SMS 12,Spr 69

KING, TAPPAN [Wright]
  US; grandson of Austin Tappan Wright, the
  author of Islandia
  Will the Real Bruce Wayne Please
    Stand Up? [a]   Ariel 1,1976

KINGERY, LAWRENCE
  Snake Pit   Ftc May 58

KINGSLEY, CHARLES   [1819-1875]
  UK parson, novelist and poet
  *The Sands of Dee [v]   WT Jan 26
    [*Alton Locke,1850]

KINGSTON, DAVE
  Gory Terror in the Night   AH Oct 70

KIPLING, [Joseph] RUDYARD [1865-1936]
  UK writer, best known for his Jungle Books
  *As Easy as A.B.C. [nt] SFy 67,Sep/Oct 64
    [*London Magazine Apr 1912]
  *The Mark of the Beast   MoH 4,May 64
    [*The Pioneer Jul 1890]
  *A Matter of Fact   WB Jan 51
    [*Many Inventions,1893]
  *The Phantom 'Rickshaw   MoH 22,Jul 68
  *The Strange Ride of Morrowbie
    Jukes   MoH 2,Nov 63
    [*these last two both from "The
    Quartet" Christmas Annual of the
    Civil & Military Gazette,1885]

KIPPAX, JOHN
  Pseud: see John HYNAM

KIPROY, CHARLES
  House pseud. used by Harold Hersey and
  others
    by Harold Hersey
  After [v]   TB May 15,19
  The Dance [v]   TB Jul 1,19
  Miladi [v]   TB Mar 15,19

    by poets unknown
  Simple Flowers [v]   TB Aug 1,19
  A Thousand Miles [v]   TB Oct 1,19
  To Spend With Ease [v]   TB Sep 1,19

KIRBY, DALLAS
  Come, Brother, Come!   WOL 2(1960)
  Sigrid's House   WS(1944)

KIRBY, LILIAN
  Jonathan Elder's Letter   WWd 1(1955)

KIRCH, JAMES A.
  *The Eye-Witness Who Wouldn't
    See   Sus Spr 51
    [*Argosy during 1949]

KIROV, IVAN   (pseud)
  Soviet Science Fiction [in]   Gam 3,1964

KIRSCH, G. S.
  + A. P. Wightman
  The Onus   Div 24,Jan 78

KISSINGER, G.
  A Spell of Desperation   Cov Sep 69

KISSLING, DOROTHY R.
  Did I Marry a Ghost?   GS Feb 28

KITCHEL, KELSEY [PERCIVAL]
  Mummy   WT Nov 29
  Was I Hypnotized?   GS Oct 30

Quest of the *Necronomicon*
[*Cth*]   FBDG 2,Dec 72
The Recital   FBDG 2,Dec 72
Resurrection   Div 9,Jun 75
A Search for Rick's Lake
[a]   Nyc 10,Jan/Feb 75

+ Eric Carlson & Joseph A. West
Carl Jacobi [in]   E&O 1,1973
[*Cth - Cthulhu Mythos*]

KOCH, ROGER
Home Visit   TZ Jun 82

KOFOED, J. C.
The Jeweled Ibis [nt2]   TB Mar 1-15,19

KOFOED, WILLIAM H.
Hands Invisible   TB Oct 15,19

KOONTZ, DEAN R[ay]   [1945-]
US writer; former school teacher
The Crimson Witch [n]   Ftc Oct 70
A Darkness in my Soul   Ftc Jan 68
The Good Ship Lookoutworld   Ftc Feb 70

KOPASKA-MERKEL, DAVID C.
Mecroniya   Eld 2,1981

+ Ronald McDowell
The Stalker   Eld 8,1982

KORAS, BINNY
For Clytie [v]   WT Nov 26

KORMAN, OWEN JAY
The Angel of Death Uses Raid
Roach Killer [v]   S&T 53,Oct 79
Gazing [v]   EC 9,1982

KORNBLUTH, CYRIL M.   [1923-58]
US writer, best known for his sf
*Kazam Collects   AFR 15,1951
[*orig. as by S. D. Gottesman]
The Mindworm   WB Dec 50
*The Mindworm   SFy 16,Nov 55
*The Rocket of 1955   WB Feb 51
[*orig. as by Cecil Corwin]
Time Bum   Ftc Jan/Feb 53
*Time Bum   Ftc Jun 69
*The Words of Guru   AFR 5,1948
[*orig.as by Kenneth Falconer]

as Cecil Corwin
*The City in the Sofa   UTC 15,Mar 42
[*Cosmic Stories* Jul 41]
The Golden Road   SFF Mar 42
Mr.Packer Goes to Hell   SFF Jun 41
*Mr.Packer Goes to Hell   UTC 17,May 42
*The Reversible Revolutions   UTC 19,Sep 42
[*Cosmic Stories* Mar 41]
*The Rocket of 1955   UTC 11,Nov 41
[*Stirring Science Stories* Apr 41;
see rep.as by Kornbluth above]
Thirteen O'Clock   SFF Feb 41
*Thirteen O'Clock   UTC 16,Apr 42
*What Sorghum Says   UTC 18,Jul 42
[*Cosmic Stories* May 41]

as Walter C. Davies
*Forgotten Tongue   UTC 17,May 42
*Forgotten Tongue   WB Feb 41

[*Stirring Science Stories* Jun 41]
*Interference   UTC 19,Sep 42
[*Cosmic Stories* Jul 41]

as Kenneth Falconer
Masquerade   SFF Mar 42
The Words of Guru   SFF Jun 41
*The Words of Guru   UTC 17,May 42
[see further rep.as by Kornbluth]

as S. D. Gottesman
*Dead Center   UTC 18,Jul 42
[*Stirring Science Stories* Feb 41]
*Dimension of Darkness   UTC 15,Mar 42
[*Cosmic Stories* May 41]
*Fire Power   UTC 20,Dec 42
[*Cosmic Stories* Jul 41]
Kazam Collects   SFF Jun 41
*Kazam Collects   UTC 16,Apr 42
[see also under Kornbluth above]

as Robert W.Lowndes
*The Martians are Coming UTC 21,Sep/Oct 43
[Lowndes supplied the idea and Donald
Wollheim the conclusion, but Kornbluth
wrote the story][*Cosmic Stories* Mar 41]

+ Frederik Pohl as S. D. Gottesman
*Castle on Outerplanet   UTC 10,Oct 41
[*Stirring Science Stories* Apr 41]

KORNBLUTH, MARY [G.]   [1920-]
[Widow of Cyril M.Kornbluth]
+ Katherine MacLean
Chicken Soup   WT Win 73

KORNEDEPLOV, MITYA
Pseud: see Ira HERMAN

KOS, JOEL
+ Richard S.Shaver
The Key to Mantong,the Ancient
Language [a]   Ftc Jul 58

KOTOWSKI,Jr., FRANCIS
I, Like Gelatine, Existed [v] Wyrd 8,1980

KOVARY, MATHEW
Magic For Sale [pic]   TZ Dec 82

KOWALEWSKI, FELIX
Death is a Woman [v]   WT Jun 37
Death of the Artist [v]   WT Mar 37

KRAFT, DAVID ANTHONY
Incantation   Wbk 3,1970

KRAMER, EDGAR DANIEL
The Black Gang [v]   WT Nov 36
Bride of Baal [v]   WT May 36
Circe [v]   WT Jun/Jul 39
City in the Sea [v]   WT Jan 37
Crazy Nell [v]   WT Feb 39
*Crazy Nell [v]   WT(Can)Sep 44
Dead Singer [v]   WT Feb 37
Dust [v]   WT May 39
The Dying Tramp [v]   Unk Jun 40
Grave-Stones [v]   WT Nov 37
Hagar [v]   WT Jul 36
The Jolly Hangman [v]   WT Sep 38
Microcosms [v]   WT Jul 38
Murder Mask [v]   WT Jun 37
Old Salt [v]   WT Aug 35

Rescued [v]   WT Mar 37
Trinities [v]   WT Apr 39
*Trinities [v]   WT(Can)Sep 44
Ultimate [v]   WT May 37
Vespers [v]   WT Dec 36
Wharf Watchman [v]   WT Jan 35

KRAMER, LAURA
John Saul: 'Remember It's Only
  a Story' [in]   TZ Nov 81

KREPPS, ROBERT W[ilson]   [1919-]
US fantasy and adventure novelist
  as Geoff St.Reynard
*Elementals of Jedar   Ftc Apr 69
  [*Fantastic Adventures May 50]
*Make Yourself a Wish   WM 1,Fal 70
  [*Fantastic Adventures Mar 48]
*The Sword of Ra [na]   SSET Sum 70
  [*Fantastic Adventures Feb 51]
*The Usurpers [nt]   Ftc Dec 68
  [*Fantastic Adventures Jan 50]

KRILL, JOHN
Black Death   Sus Sum 51

KRINER, THEODORE
The Basement   Wyrd 2,Fal 73
Last Tango on the Planet of
  the Apes [a]   S&T 26,Sep 74
Poems [v]   Wyrd 3,Spr 74
Robbie [v]   Wyrd 1,Jun 73
The Waiting Game   S&T 22,Jan 74

KRING, MIKE
  + Albuquerque SF Society
An Exquisite Corpse SF Story I
                                Nyc 13,May 77

KRIPPNER, DAVID T.
Presence of Mind [v]   DFy 3,Mar 74

KROLL, HARRY HARRISON
Bloody Man   WT Apr 25
Fairy Gossamer   WT Dec 24
The Graveyard Skunk   WT Aug 25

KRUCHER, JOSEPH HOWARD
The Bride of Death [v]   WT Mar 52
Double Haunt [pic]   WT May 52
A Weirdutation [pic]   WT Jul 52

KRUMHOLTZ, JONAH
A Perfect Crime   MST Aug/Sep 72

KUBE-McDOWELL, MICHAEL P[aul] [1954-]
US teacher and writer
Slippage   TZ Aug 82

KUBILIUS, WALTER   [1918-]
US writer & newspaper editor
*The Day Has Come   AFR 12,1950
  [*Stirring Science Stories Mar 42]

KULKARNI, VENKATESH SRINIVAS
Witness the Conestoga Wagon
  [v]   Arg 6,Sum/Fal 79

KULL, GORDON M.
Allons [v]   Vor 2,1947
Burg Frankenstein [pic]   Vor 2,1947

The Flight [v]   Ggn(9) 1949
The Landing [v]   Ggn(9) 1949
Suspended Animate [v]   Ggn(11) 1949
Vital Potion   Vor 1,1947
The World and Science Fiction
  [a]   Vor 1,1947

KUMARA, SANANDANA
  Pseud: see Roger P. GRAHAM

KUMMER, Jr., FREDERIC ARNOLD   [1912?-]
US sf/adventure writer
The Earth-Stealers   US Apr 41
Goddess of the Ghouls   UT Mar 40
The Man Who Came Back   WT Jun/Jul 39

KUNTZ, Dr. THEODORE
Long Fingers   GS Oct/Nov 31

KURTZ, KATHERINE   [1944-]
US author and technician
Camber the Heretic [ex] [Cam]   FB Dec 81
Healer's Song   [Cam]   FB Aug 82
Legacy   FB Feb 83
[Cam - Camber of Culdi]

KUSHNER, ELLEN
Red Cloak   Whsp 17/18 Aug 82

KUTTNER, HENRY   [1915-58]
US sf, fantasy and mystery writer. [Note:
although by-lined solely to Kuttner many
of the stories written after Kuttner's
marriage to C.L.Moore in June 1940 are
collaborations.]
All is Illusion   Unk Apr 40
*All is Illusion   UnkB Apr 40
Ballad of the Gods [v]   WT Feb 36
Ballad of the Wolf [v]   WT Jun 36
Beyond the Phoenix   [Elak]   WT Oct 38
The Case of Herbert Thorp   WT Nov 37
Chameleon Man   WT Nov 41
The Citadel of Darkness [nt]
  [Ray]   StS Aug 39
Compliments of the Author [nt]   UW Oct 42
*Compliments of the Author [nt] UWB Oct 42
Cursed Be the City [Ray]   StS Apr 39
Design for Dreaming [nt]   UW Feb 42
*Design for Dreaming [nt]   UWB Mar 42
The Devil We Know   Unk Aug 41
*The Devil We Know   UWB Win 45
  [also in *FUW,1948 and *FUWB,1952]
Dragon Moon [nt]   [Elak]   WT Jan 41
The Eater of Souls   WT Jan 37
*The Elixir of Invisibility [nt]Ftc Aug 70
  [*Fantastic Adventures Oct 40]
The Frog   [Cth]   StS Feb 39
A Gnome There Was [nt]   UW Oct 41
The Graveyard Rats   WT Mar 36
*The Graveyard Rats   Shk May 60
H.P.L. [v]   WT Sep 37
The Hunt   [Cth]   StS Jun 39
Hydra   [Cth]   WT Apr 39
I, the Vampire   WT Feb 37
*The Invaders   [Cth]   FCr 13,Jun 78
  [*orig.as by Keith Hammond]
It Walks By Night   [Cth]   WT Dec 36
The Jest of Droom Avista   WT Aug 37
Masquerade   WT May 42
The Misguided Halo   Unk Aug 39
No Greater Love [nt]   UW Apr 43

LAFFERTY, R[aphael] A[loysius] [1914-]
US electrical engineer & author
Beautiful Dreamer   Shk Sep 60
Been a Long, Long Time   Ftc Dec 70
Berryhill   Whsp 9,Dec 76
Calamities of the Last Pauper   FB Nov 82
The Cliffs That Laughed   MoH 26,Mar 69
Ghost in the Corn Crib   HoH Jun 73
The Man Who Never Was   MoH 16,Sum 67
The Man With the Aura   W&S 10,1975
Old Hallowe'en on the Guna
  Slopes   Ftc Aug 75
The Ultimate Creature   MoH 18,Nov 67

LAIDLAW, MARC   [1960-]
The Landlords [v]   Esc Fal 77
Spawn of the Ruins   Shyl 1,Nov 77
The Vaults of Slime [v]   Div 20,May 77

  + Gary Myers
The Summons of Nuguth-Yug   WT 3,Fal 81

LAKE, ALLEN
[Possible pseud. of Thomas P. Kelley]
Doomed by the Dead   UTC 9,Sep 41
The Germ Creator   UTC 8,Aug 41

LAKE, ARTHUR
The Street of Laughing Ghosts   GS Apr 27

LAKE, BABETTE ROSMOND
  see under Babette ROSMOND

LAKE, LEONARD M.
  + Babette Rosmond as Babette Rosmond
  Lake
Are You Run-Down, Tired -   UW Oct 42
*Are You Run-Down, Tired -   UWB Oct 42

LAKE, ZEKE
The Iron Lady in the Crypt   WT Mar 25

LAKING, GEORGE
Fomalhaut Rising [v]   Nyc 6,Feb 72
The Well [v]   S&T 13,Sep 71
*The Well [v]   Nyc 5,Oct 71
  [*poem submitted to both magazines
     at the same time]

LAMB, HUGH [Charles] [1946-]
UK journalist, proofreader & anthologist
The James List [bib]   G&S 1,1979

LAMONT, DUNCAN
The Editor Regrets...   SFy 16,Nov 55

LANDIS, ARTHUR H[arold] [1917-]
US historical & fantasy novelist
  as James R. Keaveny
Let There Be Magick [n4]
                                   Cov Sep 69-Mar 70

LANDIS, JOHN   [1950-]
US film director
Interview   TZ Oct 83

LANDON, RUFUS W.
Visions in Smoke   WT Mar 29

LANDWEHR, RICHARD [WILLIAM]
Avatar Spawning   Mb 9,1973

Casket of the Sea Queen   Spoor 2,1974
The Dance of the Devil
  Scourge   S&T 32,Sep 75
The Flowers of the Ebon
  Mountains   S&T 47,Apr 78
For We Are Men No More   Wyrd 1,Jun 73
Release of the Demon Thralls
  [v]   S&T 36,May 76
To Touch the Dark Cloud   S&T 30,May 75

LANE, JOEL
Cobweb and Clay [v]   FyM 4,Jul 83
The Face [v]   DH 24,Win 81
Invocation [v]   DH 26,Spr 83
Strange Eons and the Cthulhu
  Mythos [a]   DH 24,Win 81
The Worm [v]   FyT 11,Win 82

LANE, LOIS
The Purple Sedan   WT Aug 29

LANE, RONNIE M.
Things That Go Bump in the
  Night [v]   DDH Dec 78
Toppling [v]   DDH Dec 78

LANE, SHIRLE
Gore in the Alley   HST 1,1972

LANEY, ALVIN A.
Hiroshima Dawn [v]   Ggn (8) 1948

LANG, ALLEN KIM   [1928-]
US Blood Bank Supervisor; writer
I, Gardener   Ftc Dec 59
*I, Gardener   Ftc Apr 69

LANG, ANDREW   [1844-1912]
*Scottish literary figure, author, editor,
folklorist and anthologist*
*The Grocer's Knock   AFR 3,1947
  [*orig. "The Grocer's Cough" in *The
     Book of Dreams and Ghosts*,1897]

LANG, BRAD
The Three-Legged Chicken   Ftc Apr 78

LANG, RALPH ALLEN
On Top   WT Nov 33
The Silver Knife   WT Jan 32
The Thunderstones of Nuflo   WT Jul 34

LANHAM, C. T.
Promise For My Enemy [v]   WT Dec 28

LANIER, ELLERY
Psychoanalysis by Telepathy [a]Ftc Sep 58
*Psychoanalysis by Telepathy [a]
                                   StF 9,Sum 69
Spontaneous Generation [a]   Ftc Nov 58

LANIER, SIDNEY   [1842-1881]
US poet, musician and lecturer
*Barnacles [v]   WT Sep 26
*Song of the Hound [v]   WT Oct 25
  [*Poems*, 1877 (edition unknown)]

LANKASHIRE, JAMES
The Waters of Meron   DFy 7,Sep 75

LONG, JULIUS
US fantasy/detective writer and attorney

LONGNECKER, Mrs. ELIZABETH

LOOMIS, BATTELL

LORD, GLENN

LUCAS, ALLEN A.
Dead to the World   FyT 11,Win 82
The House Next Door to the
  House on the Borderland
  [v]   FyM 3,Jun 82
Purple Lensman [spf]   S&T 62,Sum 82

LUCIAN [c125-190 A.D.]
Greek advocate, writer and satirist
*Dialogue of the Dead   FC 4,1973
*The Sorcerer's Apprentice [a]   WT Oct 39

LUDLOW, FITZHUGH   [1836-70]
US author
*A Dose of Hasheeh [ex]   BC 1,Win 70/1
  [*The Hasheesh Eater,1857]

LUDWICK, KATHLEEN
*Dr. Immortelle [nt]   Ftc May 68
  [*Amazing Stories Quarterly Fall 30]

LUDWIG, EDWARD W[illiam] [1920-]
US bookdealer and specialty publisher;
former writer and musician
The (In)visible Man   Gam 3,1964
A Night With Hecate   Ftc Oct 63
*A Night With Hecate   WM 2,Win 70
The Stalker   Nek 5,mid-51
Two Gentlemen in Black   Nek 1,Spr 50
Woman on Fire   Ftc Oct 60

LUEPKE, ANTONIE H.
My Ghostly Burglar Alarm [ts] GS Sep 27

LUMLEY, BRIAN   [1937-]
UK author; former military officer
Interviews & DH 14,Sum 76;*Nyc 13,May 77
  Bibliography   Kad 3,Nov 80
Author! Author! [v]   AD 6,Fal 77
Billy's Oak   [TC]   ArkC 6,Win 70
Black Prayer [v]   EC 5,1981
The Burrowers Beneath [ex]   HPL 1972
City Out of Time [v]   FyT 2,Win 77
*A Cry at Night [v]   AD 5,Win 77
  [*Visions of Khroy'don ed. William
   H. Pugmire]
Cryptically Yours   Esc Fal 77
The Cyprus Shell   ArkC 3,Sum 68
Destiny [v]   Wbk 11,1977
Dylath-Leen [v]   Kad 5,Jul 82
  [not the same as Lumley's story of
   the same name]
Enough! [v]   ArkC 8,Win 71
Escape [v]   Esc Fal 77
Fantasy Crossroads [v] FCr 10/11,Mar 77
Fantasy Tales [v]   FyT 3,Sum 78
The House of Cthulhu [Th] Whsp 1,Jul 73
The House of the Temple [nt]
  [Cth]   Kad 3,Nov 80
*The House of the Temple [nt]
  [Cth]   WT 3,Fal 81
How Kank Thad Returned to
  Bhur-Esh   [Th]   Ftc Jun 77
In Pressure-Pounded Chasms
  [v]   ArkC 9,Spr 71
An Item of Supporting Evidence
                               ArkC 7,Sum 70
Kadath [v]   Kad 3,Nov 80
*Kadath [v]   Nyc 18,Apr 83
The Kiss of Bugg-Shash [Cth] Cth 3,1978

[*Il bacio di Bugg-Shash[Cth]Kad 3,Nov 80]
The Last Rite [rr]   W&S 10,1974
  [Chap.1 of rr "Othuum"]
Late Shopping   Wbk 18,1983
Lord of the Worms [na] [TC] Wbk 17,1983
Maggot [v]   Nyc 15,Jan 80
The Man Who Got Slotted   Kad 3,Nov 80
The Man Who Saw No Spiders   Wbk 13,1978
Mother-Love   W&S 6,May 71
*Mother-Love   DH 14,Sum 76
Mylakhrion the Immortal[Th] FyT 1,Sum 77
Name and Number [nt] [TC/Th] Kad 5,Jul 82
Nyctalops [v]   Nyc 13,May 77
Pesh-Tlen [v]   Nyc 8,Apr 73
*Problem Child   DH 14,Sum 76
  [*Vampires,Werewolves and Other
   Monsters ed. Roger Elwood,1974]
Recognition   Wbk 15,1981
The Skull of H.P.L. [v]   Wbk 12,1977
The Sorcerer's Dream [Th]
                              Whsp 13/14,Oct 79
The Strange Years   FyT 9,Spr 82
Survivors [v]   Nyc 17,Jun 82
Swamp Call [v]   FyT 8,Sum 81
Swordsmith and Sorcerer [rr]FCr 15,Jan 79
  [Chap.11 of rr: "Ghor, Kin-Slayer"]
Tharquest and the Lamia
  Orbiquita [Th]   Ftc Nov 76
Tindalos [v]   Nyc 14,Mar 78
Too Much Monkey Business   Kad 3,Nov 80
Treasure of the Scarlet
  Scorpion   [Th]   Wbk 16,1982
The Unbeliever   FB Aug 83
Vanessa's Voice   Whsp 11/12,Oct 78
Weirdbook [v]   Wbk 13,1978
Whistler [v]   EC 1,Jul 76
The Wind-Walker [v]   FyT 6,Sum 80
Witching Hour [v]   Wbk 16,1982
Zack Phalanx Is Vlad the
  Impaler   Wbk 11,1977
[*Zack Phalanx e' Vlad the
  Impaler   Kad 3,Nov 80]

  completion of fragment by H.P.Lovecraft
The Thing in the Moonlight ArkC 4,Win 69
*The Thing in the Moonlight FyT 5,Win 79
[*La Cosa al chiaro di luna Kad 3,Nov 80]
[Cth - Cthulhu Mythos; Th - Theem'hdra;
 TC - Titus Crow]

LUMLEY, WILLIAM
[*"An old sailor" - H.P.Lovecraft]
  rewritten by H.P.Lovecraft
The Diary of Alonzo Typer [Cth] WT Feb 38
[Cth - Cthulhu Mythos]

LUMPKIN, JIMMY
They Came From Hell   S&T 17,Nov 72

LUNA, ELIZABETH
Miss Bard's Lover   TF Aug 57

LUNDE, DAVID
  + M. L. Brannock Lunde
The Garden   WoF 4,Spr 71

  + James Sallis
They Will Not Hush   Whsp 4,Jul 74
A Weather Report From the
  Top of the Stairs   Whsp 2,Dec 73

McFARLAND, N. R.
The Depth of the Lens   WT Dec 29

MacFARLAND, P. C.
The Striker   Wtch Nov 36

McFERRAN, DAVE   [1954-1980]
Obituary   Agd 1,Aut 80
A Fevered Glimpse of Chaos
  [a]   Chac 2,Spr 77
Jim Fitzpatrick: The Early
  Years [in]   Agd 1,Aut 80

MacFIE, JAMES
The Immortal Voice   MyS 20(1939)
*The Immortal Voice   StS Feb 40

McG., W. J.
In Flanders Fields [ts]   GS May 27

McGIBENY, MONROE D.
Death-Gate [v]   WT Nov 29

McGILLIVRAY, RAY
The Forty Jars   WT Apr 23

McGIVERN, WILLIAM P[eter]   [1924-82]
*US author, originally of sf/fantasy, later
best known for his crime/thriller novels*
Amphytrion 40   Ftc Sep/Oct 53
*Fix Me Something to Eat   SSET Sum 70
  [*Fantastic Adventures May 51]
*I Love Lucifer   Ftc Mar 68
  [*Amazing Stories Dec 53/Jan 54]
Jinn and Tonic [nt]   Ftc May/Jun 53
Love That Potion   Ftc Feb 55
Mr. Dittman's Monsters   Ftc Jan/Feb 54
The Moon and Nonsense   Ftc Apr 54
Never Mind a Martian [nt]   Ftc Nov/Dec 53
Operation Mind-Pick [nt]   Ftc Jul/Aug 53
*The Traveling Brain   WM 4,Sum 71
  [*Fantastic Adventures Mar 52]

    as Lawrence Chandler   (house name)
Death's Bright Angel   Ftc Jun 54

    as P. F. Costello (house name)
For the Greater Good   Ftc Jun 55

    as Clee Garson
Scavengers of Space [nt]   Ftc Oct 55

    as E. K. Jarvis   (house name)
The Rough Rock Road [nt]   Ftc Apr 56

    as Bill Peters
The Chase   Ftc Nov/Dec 53

    as Gerald Vance (house name)
Conception: Zero [nt]   Ftc Jun 56
The Yellow Needle [nt]   Ftc Oct 54

McGOWAN, D. C.
  Pseud: see Roger P. GRAHAM

McGOWAN, INEZ
  Pseud: see Roger P. GRAHAM

MacGREGOR, JAMES M[urdoch]   [1925-]
Scottish journalist and author
    as J. T. McIntosh
*Beggars All [nt]   SFy 7(Spr 54)
  [*Mag. F & SF Apr 53]

Escape Me Never   Ftc Mar/Apr 53
Five Into Four [nt]   SFy 10,Sep 54
Live For Ever [nt]   SFy 11,Dec 54
Merlin [nt]   Ftc Mar 60
Planet of Change [nt]   Ftc Sep 64
*Planet of Change [nt]   StF 11,Spr 70
Planet of Probation [nt]   SFy 42,Aug 60
The Ship From Home [nt]   SFy 39,Feb 60
Something New Wanted [ged]   SFy 9,Jul 54
Stitch in Time [nt]   SFy 5,Aut 52
Then There Were Two   SFy 3,Win 51/2
200 Years to Christmas [na]   SFy 35,Jun 59
The Volunteers [nt]   SFy 6,Spr 53
World Without Annette [nt]   Ftc May 60

    as H. J. Murdoch
This Precious Stone [na]   SFy 9,Jul 54

MacGREGOR, LOREN
The Message   S&T 16,Aug 72

MacGREGOR, MARY
  Pseud: see Malcolm JAMESON

MacGUCKIN, Mrs. MARY
Suicide - or What? [a]   GS Feb 29

McGUIRE, DANIEL
I Saw a Little Girl Today   Mb 24,1976

McGUIRE, JOHN J[oseph]   [1917-]
US writer, teacher & radio announcer
Testing [nt]   Ftc Jun 64

McHALE, SANDRA J.
Whatever It Was   Mb 24,1976

McHANEY, DENNIS
Robert E. Howard Editors/Publishers'
  Roundtable [sym2]
                   FCr 9-10/11,Aug 76-Mar 77

MACHEN, ARTHUR [Llewelyn-Jones] [1863-
Welsh author and journalist   1947]
  Profiles: Nyc 8,Apr 73; TZ Sep 82
*The Bowmen   WT Jul 28
  [*London Evening News Sep 29,1914]
*The Lost Club   WT Oct 35
  [*orig.1890; taken from The Shining
  Pyramid,1923]
A Machen Sampler [ex]   TZ Sep 82
  [contains extracts from "The Great
  God Pan", "The Inmost Light", "The
  White People", "The Happy Children",
  "Far Off Things", "The Hill of Dreams",
  "The Great Return", "A Fragment of
  Life"]
*The Terror [sn]   FC 1,1973
  [*book, Duckworth, London: 1917]

MACHEN, HARRY EMERSON
Frog Man   BMM Jan 66

McHENRY, F. DOUGLAS
The Seventh Dial   WT Nov 25

McINNIS III, JOHN L.
Notes on Researching
  Lovecraftiana [a]   HPL 1972

    +Donald R. Burleson
Two Views of St. Armand's Lovecraft

[a]   Goth Jun 79

McINTOSH, J. T.
    Pseud: see James M. MacGREGOR

McINTOSH, PAT[ricia]
    Beruthiel [v]   FyT 3,Sum 78

McINTYRE, GEORGE A.
    Initiation [v]   FyT 9,Spr 82

McKAY, Mrs. PEARL
    The Man in My Bed [ts]   Mystic Aug 54

MacKAY, Mrs. RENE PARKS
    Demon Haunted   GS Mar 28

McKAY, TERRELL
    Burning Eyes   GS Feb 29
    The Galloping Ghost of Troop 'F'
                             GS Nov 26

McKAY, VERA
    Dancers in the Locked House   GS Nov 29

McKEAG, ERNEST L[ionel] [1896-1976]
UK writer, journalist and editor
*A Guest of Vanderdecken   WOL 3(1960)
    [*Cute Fun 29(1949)]

McKEE, J. A.
    Metamorphosis   Nek 2,Sum 50

MACKELWORTH, R[onald] W[alter] [1930-]
UK insurance sales manager
    A Cave in the Hills   SFy 70,Mar 65
    Cleaner Than Clean   SFy 79,Dec 65
    A Distorting Mirror   SFy 74,Jul 65
    Temptation for the Leader SFy 76,Sep 65
    A Visitation of Ghosts [nt] Imp 4,Jun 66

MACKENZIE, JEANETTE BROWN
    The Death Baby   Mac 7,Sum 60

McKEOWN, W.
    Well, I'll Tell You, Ma WT Nov 24

MACKEY, JOE
    The Idol   Fear Jul 60

McKILLIP, PATRICIA [Anne] [1948-]
US fantasy writer & novelist
    + Stephen R.Donaldson & Anne McCaffrey
    How We Write [sym]   NV 6,Sum 80

McKIMMEY, JAMES
    5-4-3-2-   BI Nov/Dec 67

MACKIN, EDWARD
    An Affair of Gravity   SFy 28,Apr 58
    Behind the Cloud   SFy 46,Apr 61
    Chaotics   SFy 31,Oct 58
    Criffle-Shaped   SFy 26,Dec 57
    The Diagnoser   SFy 34,Apr 59
    The Jung at Heart [nt]   SFy 61,Oct 63
    Mobius Trip   SFy 57,Feb 63
    Pasquali's Peerless Puppets Imp 9,Nov 66
    Sealed Capsule   SFy 80,Jan 66
    Still Centre   SFy 50,Dec 61
    Time Trap   SFy 37,Nov 59
    Trading Post   SFy 40,Apr 60

Under the Lemonade Hat   SFy 53,Jun 62
[all stories except "Sealed Capsule" are in
the *Hek Belov* series]

McKINNEY, CAROL
    A Voice Saved My Life [ts] Mystic May 54

MACKINTOSH, CHARLES HENRY
    Death in Twenty Minutes WT Jan 35
    The Eyes of Ustad Isa   WT Sep 38
    Guardians of the Guavas WT Sep 30
    Melchior Makes Magic   WT May 28

MACKINTOSH, CRAIG
    + Brian M.Stableford as Brian Craig
    Beyond Time's Aegis [nt] SFy 78,Nov 65

McKRACKEN, JAMES A.
    Pseud: see Glenn A. RAHMAN

McKYE, BARNEY
    Chiquita, or Going Bananas Div 12,Jan 76

MacL, C. H.
    see Cassie H. MacLAURY

McLAREN, DUNCAN
    Broken Walls,Shattered Dreams[a]TZ Oct 82

McLAREN, EDWIN
    Jack O'Mystery   WT Jun 23

MacLAREN, IAN
    The Clash of Dishes   WT Fal 73

McLAUGHLIN, COOPER
    The Stones of Moel Hebog S&T 64,Sum 83

McLAUGHLIN, LORRIE
    The Way Out [ss]   Sus Win 52

McLAUGHLIN, MARK
    As Osiris Wills   S&T 60,Jul 81
    The Cat-Woman [v]   S&T 62,Sum 82
    Dark Quatrains [v]   PF 2,1979
    Devil's Food [v]   Arg 7,Fal/Win 80
    Dreamscapes [v]   S&T 61,Win 81/2
    The Garden of Death [v] I,1980
    Grotesque [v]   Div 28/9,Feb/Mar 79
    In Zeth [v]   S&T 52,Jul 79
    Inspiration [v]   Arg 7,Fal/Win 80
    Last Kiss [v]   Arg 6,Sum/Fal 79
    The Metal Gods [v]   DFy 22,Mar 80
    Pet Show [v]   Arg 8,Fal/Win 81
    The Vampires [v]   Div 28/9,Feb/Mar 79
    A Wee Visitor [v]   Arg 6,Sum/Fal 79
    Witch-House [v]   Nyc 15,Jan 80

McLAUGHLIN, VENARD
    The Silence   SFF Jun 41

MacLAURY, CASSIE H.
    Captive Souls [nt2]   GS Sep-Oct 27
    Werewolf   GS Mar 27

    as C.H. MacL.
    The Silver Moth   GS Apr 27

McLEAN, DAVIDA
    Pseud: see David M. SKOV

McLEAN, DIANE
  Yours For Eternity   Phtm 13,Apr 58

MacLEAN, KATHERINE [Anne] [1925-]
US writer, lecturer & laboratory technician
  The Fittest   WB Jan 51

    + Harry Harrison
*Web of the Norns [na]   SFy 28,Apr 58
as Web of the Worlds [na]   FM Nov 53

    + Mary Kornbluth
  Chicken Soup   WT Win 73

MacLEAN, MARY AGNEW
  The Curse of Green Acres   GS Apr 31
*The Invisible Scratcher   TTT Fal 63
    [*retitle of first story]

MacLENNAN, J. MUNRO
  The Vicar and the Devilkins   Ftc Jun 54

MacLENNAN, PHYLLIS
  A Contract in Karasthan   Ftc Jul 63

MacLEOD, Captain JACK
  The Ghost That Stopped a Train GS Apr 28

McLOUGHLIN, JOHN
  Colour Poems   FBDG 4,Oct 77

McLOUGHLIN, PATRICK
  More Than a Woman   Phtm 13,Apr 58

McMAHON, A. P.
  Creatures of the Night   WT Mar 24

McMAHON, WILL
  The Time Will Come   WT Apr 28

MacMANUS, J. CHRISTY
  The Spectral Ship [ts]   GS Apr 29

McMASTER, W. B.
  The Flames of Hell [v]   DFy 7,Sep 75
  Oh My God! They Come Again
    [v]   DFy 3,Mar 74

MacMILLAN, Dr. CYRUS
  Atlantic Isle of Mystery   WT Jan 54
  The Phantom Soldier at
    Ticonderoga   WT Jan 53

McMURRAY, CLIFFORD
  The Different Man: Dickson's
    Donal Graeme [a]   Div 28/9,Feb/Mar 79

MacNAB, LEAVENWORTH
  Despair and the Soul [v]   WT Nov 27
  Dirge [v]   WT Aug 28
  The Hanging of Aspara   WT Jun 25
  Lake Desolation [v]   WT Aug 27
  Let Night Have Sway [v]   WT Jan 29

McNAMARA, VAL
  Phantom Fingers   Wtch Dec 36

McNEIL, EVERETT
  At the Hands of the Master   TB Oct 1,19

McNEILE, H[erman] C[yril] [1888-1937]
UK writer, best known as the creator of
Bulldog Drummond
*Was it Murder?   WT Nov 51

    as 'Sapper'
*The Horror at Staveley Grange TMD 1(1934)
    [*The Saving Clause,1927]

MacNURLEN, Dr. G. W.
  Caravan of the Lost [ts]   GS Jul 28

MACOM, ARTHUR
  The Green Monster   WT Jul 28

MACPHERSON, RICHIE
  The Unwatched Door [ss]   TF Spr 57

McQUEEN, Corporal WALDO
  The Voice in the Foxhole [ss] FF May 50

McQUIRE III, PAUL
  Shadow Shapes   Div 26/7,May/Jul 78

MacREADY, R. G.
  The Plant-Thing   WT Jul.25
*The Plant-Thing   FC 2,1973

McS., DEWI
    Pseud: see David M. SKOV

McTAVISH, PAULINE
    Pseud: see Dale C. DONALDSON

McWHARF, RUSTY
  A Call From the Future   WST Jul/Aug 72

MADDOCK, THOMAS
  From Beyond the Wall   Phtm 3,Jun 57
  The Haunted House   Phtm 2,May 57
  Mulligan's Treasure   Phtm 3,Jun 57

MADDOX, WILLIAM J.
  The Tale of the Golden Ghost   GS Jun 27

MADISON, DAVID   [1951-78]
  Memoriam   DFd 3,Sum 80
  Castle of Light   [M&D]   S&T 50,Jan 79
  The City of Silence [M&D]   DFd 3,Sum 80
  The Desolation of Yr/
    Marcus's Song [v]   DFd 3,Sum 80
  The Empress of Dreams [v]   Div 12,Jan 76
  Fear: The Short Story [a]   NFJ 2,1977
  From Under the Hills   Db 1,Spr 78
  The Funeral of Thamyris the
    Warlock [s2] [M&D] Wyrd 4-5,Dec 74-75
  The Glyphs of Doom [M&D]   S&T 42,May 77
  The Golden Mask   Wyrd 2,Fal 73
  Grass   DFy 8,May 76
  The Hunt   AD 4,Fal 76
  Inn of the Bones   [M&D]   Div 9,Jun 75
  The Red Leather Book   AD 6,Fal 77
  Shelter   S&T 61,Win 81/2
  The Tower   DFy 9,Sep 76
  Tower of Darkness [M&D]   S&T 28,Jan 75
  The Trouble With Timothy   DFy 15,Jan 78
  What Rough Beast   [M&D]   Div 19,Mar 77
  [M&D - Marcus and Diana]

MADLE, DOROTHY HAYNES
  Moon Phantoms [v]   WT Jul 46

St.George and the Mushroom
  [St.G]   CT 3,Jan 78
*St.George and the Mushroom
  [St.G]   Arg 5,Win/Spr 79
The Shadow   Arg 6,Sum/Fal 79
Tower of Babel   CT 2,Jul 77

  + Dale Hammell
Raphael de Soto [a]   CT 4,May 78
[St.G - Adrian St.George]

MAND, CYRIL
  Pseud: see George R. HAHN & Richard
  LEVIN

MANDEL, NATHANIEL
The Journey of Thomas Howell EC 7,1982

MANDEVILLE, Sir JOHN   [1300?-72?]
Name adopted by author of a noted medieval
fantasy travelogue, most likely the work of
an English (or Irish) knight who later became a French physician Jehan de Bourgogne.
*An Odd Sort of People [ex]   FC 1,1973
  [*Boke of the Voiages and Travailes of
  Sir John de Mandeville, Kt. purportedly
  written in 1355, with the earliest
  known manuscript dated to 1366]

MANIS, MIKE
Leaving Earth [v]   Div 26/7,May/Jul 78

MANN, JACK
  Pseud: see E. Charles VIVIAN

MANN, MILTON
  Pseud: see Roger P. GRAHAM

MANNERING, T. W.
Trapped in a Room of Horror
  With the Slave of Satan   AH Feb 71

MANNHEIM, Dr./Sir GUSTAV
Fact or Fiction? [col]   Thrl Feb 62
True Horror Thrillers [col] Thrl May 62
True Terror Thrillers [col] Thrl Jul 62

MANNING, LAURENCE   [1899-1974]
Canadian-born US sf writer
*The Call of the Mech-Men [nt]
  [SC]   MoH 11,Nov 65
  [*Wonder Stories Nov 33]
*Caverns of Horror [nt] [SC] MoH 6,Nov 64
  [*Wonder Stories Mar 34]
Mr.Mottle Goes Pouf   FM Aug 53
*The Moth Message [SC] MoH 14,Win 66/7
  [*Wonder Stories Dec 34]

  + Fletcher Pratt
*The City of the Living Dead AFR 2,1947
  [*Science Wonder Stories May 30]
[SC - The Stranger Club]

MANSELL, MARK
Blue Towers Against the Moon
  [v]   DFy 17,Jul 78
Panorama [v]   DFy 15,Jan 78

MANSFIELD, HARRY O[rford] [1901-]
UK writer and teacher; the following were
sold via R. L. Fanthorpe who marketed them
under his own pseuds.
  as Thornton Bell
The Lady Loves Cats   SN 91(1964)
  as Leo Brett
The Clubmen   SN 83(1963)
The Golem   SN 95(1965)
The Grip of Time Unending SN 77(1963)
  as Phil Nobel
The Chinese Lustre Vase SN 87(1964)
I'll Never Leave You   SN 89(1964)
  as Rene Rolant
Shadow of Fear [nt]   SN 99(1965)
  as Robin Tate
The Abbot's Ring   SN 85(1964)
God's Sin Eater   SN 101(1965)
In a Glass Darkly   SN 93(1964)
Spring Fever   SN 95(1965)
  as Pel Torro
The Zoologist [nt]   SN 97(1965)

MANTLEY, JOHN [Truman] [1920-]
Canadian writer and actor
The Black Crucible [nt] SFy 22,Apr 57
Uncle Clem and Them Mar.'ans
             SFy 17,Feb 56

MANZER, ISA-BELLE
The Transparent Ghost [na3]
          WT Feb-Apr 24

MARCHMONT, ROSS
  Pseud: see William Scott HOME

MARDER, ARLENE
Snow Job   S&T 29,Mar 75

MARDICK, DON
Pseud. of a US schoolteacher & author
Not a Leg to Stand On   Sus Fal 51

MARGRAVE, ERIK
We Stand in Crumbled Room Ggn(11)1949

MARICONDA, STEVE
Some Antecedents of the Shining
  Trapezohedron [a]   FB Oct 83

'MARIE-LOUISE'
  see Marie-Louise SHARE

MARINONI, ROSA ZAGNONI
  see under Rosa ZAGNONI

MARION, TIM C.
Barbarian King [v]   Div 5,Oct 74

MARKHAM, HAROLD
The Falling Knife   WT Feb 30
In a Dead Man's Shoes   WT Apr 29
The Second-Hand Limousine WT Nov 31

MARKHAM, NORMAN G.
The Horrible Effigy   Anu 1,Aut 66
Last Words [v]   Anu 1,Aut 66
The Murals   Anu 4,Aut 68
Realism [v]   Anu 1,Aut 66

The Toad Idol   WT Sep 35
Tony the Faithful   WT Jul 28
The Vengeance of Ixmal   WT Mar 32
Voodoo Vengeance   WT Nov 34
[ND - Nita Duboin]

MASON, DAVID   [?-1974]
  Account Closed   Fear Jul 60
  The Time   Ftc Jun 70

MASON, DOUGLAS R[ankine]   [1918-]
UK writer and school headmaster
  as John Rankine
  Pattern as Set   Imp 5,Jul 66
  Seventh Moon [nt]   [DF]   Imp 3,May 66
[DF - Dag Fletcher]

MASON, JOHN
  Pseud: see E. C. TUBB

MASON, JOHN HOLLIS
Canadian writer; now writes sf as John
Keith
  Flaming Phantasm   UTC 3,Jan 41

MASON, TALLY
  Pseud: see August DERLETH

MASSIE, CHRIS   (pseud) [1880-1964]
*A Fragment of Fact   TZ Jun 83

MASTERSON, ALLAN
  The Fisherman at Crescent Beach WT Jan 51

MATCHA, JACK B.   [1919-]
US author, editor and publisher
  King's Jester   Gam 2,1963

  as John Tanner
  Open Season   Gam 4,Feb 65

MATHE, DARIA
  The Dragoness and Her Slave
  [v]   Eld 2,1981

MATHESON, RICHARD [Burton] [1926-]
US screenwriter and author
  Interviews   TZ Sep-Oct 81;TZ Oct 83
  And Now I'm Waiting   TZ Apr 83
  Clothes Make the Man   WB Feb 51
  Crescendo   Gam 1,1963
  Crickets   Shk May 60
  The Curious Child   Ftc Jun 54
  Deus Ex Machina   Gam 2,1963
  The Doll [tp]   TZ Jun 82
    [script for The Twilight Zone series
     but never filmed; also in *GSTZm1982]
  Interest   Gam 5,Sep 65
  Mad House [nt]   Ftc Jan/Feb 53
 *Mad House [nt]   Ftc Jan 67
  Mother By Protest [nt]   Ftc Sep/Oct 53
  Slaughter House   WT Jul 53
  Sorry, Right Number   BFF Nov 53
  To Fit the Crime   Ftc Nov/Dec 52
 *To Fit the Crime   Ftc Aug 69
  The Wedding   BFF Jul 53
  Wet Straw   WT Jan 53
 *A World of His Own [tp]   TZ Apr 83
    [*first bdcst. CBS-TV Jul 1,1960]

MATHESON, RICHARD CHRISTIAN [1954-]
US writer, son of the preceding
  The Dark Ones [ss]   TZ Jun 82
  Graduation   Whsp 10,Aug 77
  Holiday   TZ Feb 82

MATHIESON, THEODORE
  The Black Sadhu   Fear May 60

MATHISON, VOLNEY G.
  The Death Bottle   WT Mar 25

MATTHEWS, GORDON
  The Trail of the 'Necronomicon'
  [Cth]   FBDG 1,Apr/May 72
[Cth - Cthulhu Mythos]

MATTICK, IRVIN
  The Headless Spokesman   WT Nov 25
  Red and Black   WT Jan 25

MATTURRO, RICHARD
  Star Trek: The Great American
  Love Story [a]   TZ Oct 82

MATZ, TERRY
  Sport   Shyl 2,Feb 78

MAUGHAM, HERBERT J.
  The Basket   WT Mar 23

MAUGHAM, W[illiam] SOMERSET   [1874-1965]
UK novelist and dramatist
  Honolulu   TU 1(1934)

MAUPASSANT, GUY de
  see under Guy DE MAUPASSANT

MAURER, ALLAN   [1947-]
US writer and former reporter
  Frozen Star   Ftc Jan 80

MAURICE, ALFRED
  Pseud: see Walter B. GIBSON

MAXON, H. L.
  The Ether Ray   WT Sep 25

MAXWELL, JOHN
  Cats Are Uncanny   YWS 14(1942)

MAXWELL, Prof. J. S.
  Your Handwriting [a]   Mystic Aug 54

MAY, FRANCES
  The Chain [v]   ArkC 3,Sum 68

MAYER, ALBERT E.
  Halloween   DFy 23,Nov 80

MAYER, FREDERICK J.
  Academy's Film Seerer [a]
                            Div 26/7,May/Jul 78
  Cat's Eye Marbles [v]   Nyc 14,Mar 78
  Dead [v]   Eld 7,1980
  Devil Cat [v]   Div 26/7,May/Jul 78
  Ghost Flowers [v]   Eld 9,1983
  An Interview With Donald
    Sidney-Dryer [in]   Nyc 11/12,Apr 76
  An Interview With E.
    Hoffmann Price [in]   Div 24,Jan 78

MILLER, R[ichard] DeWITT
US writer; authority on psychic phenomena
Beyond Hell [nt]   US Apr 41

MILLER, ROB HOLLIS
I Recognize... [v]   Nyc 14,Mar 78
Lovecraft and Satanism [a]
                         Nyc 10,Jan/Feb 75
Magic [v]   Nyc 16,Mar 81

MILLER, SANDY
*The Labyrinth [a]   WM 3,Spr 71

MILLER, SIGMOND
The Guardian Angel [ts]   WT Nov 41

MILLER, STEVE
An Interview With Mildred
   Broxon [in]   Div 24,Jan 78
Searching for the Magic:
   Workshops [a]   Div 22,Sep 77

MILLER, SUTRO
John Raike's Model   WSM 1(1946)

MILLER, Jr., WALTER M[ichael] [1922-]
US writer, best known for his sf
*The Little Creeps [nt]   Ftc May 68
   [*Amazing Stories Dec 51]
Six and Ten are Johnny [nt]   Ftc Sum 52
*Six and Ten are Johnny [nt] Ftc Jan 66
The Will   Ftc Jan/Feb 54
*The Will   Ftc Apr 69
Wolf Pack   Ftc Sep/Oct 53
*Wolf Pack   Ftc May 66

MILLER, WARREN SCOTT [1955?-]
From Beyond the Dark Gateway
   [Cth]   FBDG 3,Apr 74
[Cth - Cthulhu Mythos]

MILLER, WILLIAM P. [1919?-]
US novelist and mystery writer
The Towers of Kagasi   Gam 4,Feb 65

MILLS, RICHARD
Caverns of the Soul [a] Nyc 10,Jan/Feb 75

MILNES, ELSIE
The Glass Thread   TF Spr 57

MILTON, FLETCHER R.
The Flaming Eyes   WT Mar 25

MILTON, JACK
The Thousand-Dollar Wish   Ftc Sep 58

MILTON, PAUL R[obert] [1904-]
Blood Brother to a Ghost   GS Sep 28
Five Fatal Minutes   GS Dec 30
   [see "Five Minutes to Live"]
A Haunted Half-Dollar   GS Dec 27
   [see "My Haunted Half-Dollar"]
The Invisible Strangler   GS May 28
*My Haunted Half-Dollar   PGS 1963
   [*orig. "A Haunted Half-Dollar"]

   as Ace Baker
*Five Minutes to Live   TTT Fal 63
   [*orig. "Five Fatal Minutes"]

MILYER, A. V.
Mordecai's Pipe   WT Jun 36

MIMES, SAMUEL STEWART   ·
Just Bones   WT May/Jul 24

MIMMS, MARION HEIDT
The Chair   WT Oct 26

MINERS, HAROLD FREEMAN
Desert Madness [nt]   WT Jun 23

MINITER, EDITH   [1867-1934]
US amateur journalist
Dead Houses [a]   Lvs 1,Sum 37

MISH, CHARLOTTE
A Dangerous Girl [ss]   TB Aug 15,19
A Very Short Story [ss]   TB Aug 15,19

MISKE, JACK C[HAPMAN]
Prominent US sf fan of the 1940s
Characterization in Imaginative
   Literature [a]   ArkS Spr 49

MITCHELL, ALBERT PAGE
   see Edward Page MITCHELL

MITCHELL, BOB
If it Was Like it Is [a]   Div 7,Feb 75

MITCHELL, CLYDE
Ziff-Davis house name
   by Harlan Ellison
The Wife Factory [nt]   Ftc Nov 57

   by Randall Garrett & Robert Silverberg
The Mummy Takes a Wife [nt] Ftc Dec 56

   by Henry Slesar
A Kiss For the Conqueror   Ftc Feb 57

MITCHELL, DAVE
Curse of the Wizard   S&T 19,Jul 73

MITCHELL, EDWARD PAGE [1852-1927]
US writer and newspaperman
   by-lined 'Albert Page Mitchell' in error
*The Balloon Tree   WT Win 73
   [*New York Sun Feb 25,1883]
*The Devilish Rat   WT Sum 74
   [*New York Sun Jan 27,1878]

MITCHELL, J[ohn] A[mes] [1845-1918]
US artist, editor and author
*The Last American [nt]   ArkS Spr 49
   [*book, F.A.Stokes, New York,1889]

MITCHELL, LILLIACE M.
The Royal Command   MM Aug 31

MITCHELL, ROGER
What is It [v]   ArkC 5,Sum 69

MITCHELL, STEPHEN G.
Flowers of the Forest   DFy 17,Jul 78
The Garden of Old Night   FCr 14,Sep 78
Roses, Bright and Dark   DFy 14,Sep 77

MITCHISON, NAOMI [Mary Margaret] [1897-]
Scottish writer, sister of J.B.S.Haldane
Death of a Peculiar Boar   WoF 3,1970/1

MOCHNANT, FRANK A.
The Derelict Mine [sn3]   WT Apr-Jun 26

MOFFAT, J.
Honest John   G&G(1938)

MOFFATT, LEN J[ames] [1923-]
+ Alvin Taylor
Father's Vampire   WT May 52

MOFFETT, CLEVELAND [Langston] [1863-1926]
US journalist, dramatist and writer
*The Mysterious Card   WT Win 73
  [*The Black Cat Feb 1896]
*The Mysterious Card Revealed WT Win 73
  [*The Black Cat Aug 1896]

MOFFETT, MELVIN
Devil Stone   GS Mar 31

MOFFITT, DONALD
The Devil's Due   Ftc May 60
*The Devil's Due   StF 10,Fal 69

MOLARSKY, DEL
Love is a Barometer   Ftc Jan/Feb 53

MOLNAR, A[nthony] K[alman] [1950-]
US business manager and photographer
Bagpipe Murder   S&T 59,Apr 81
Ghost Food   BL 4/5,Jan 78
Grand Central Saviour   BL 1,Aug 76
A Letter   S&T 58,Jan 81
Lovestar   Div 12,Jan 76
The Martin Gorsham Case   AD 6,Fal 77
The Night's Last Walk   Jeet 1,Apr 77
Subway Suckers   S&T 55,Apr 80
Walk in the Rain   S&T 45,Nov 77

MONAGHAN, J. J. D.
Accursed [v]   Phtm 8,Nov 57
The End of the Game   Phtm 10,Jan 58
The Puzzle   Phtm 11,Feb 58
21st December 1955   Phtm 9,Dec 57

MONAGHAN, WILLIAM
An Evil Out of Krak   EvM Sum 77

MONET, LIREVE
Pseud: see Everil Worrell MURPHY

MONTANA, R. A.
Interstate 15   Ftc Apr 75

MONTEFIORE, G. FREDERICK
Black Curtains   WT Mar 25
*Black Curtains   Unq 1,Jan 78

MONTELEONE, THOMAS F. [1946-]
US writer and playwright
Interview   NV 7,Spr 81
Present Perfect   Ftc Sep 74
Taking the Night Train   NV 7,Spr 81

MONTGOMERY, Jr., D. C.
Dianetics: A Critical Appraisal
  [a]   Nek 4,Win 50/1
The Gourmet   Nek 5,mid-51

MONTGOMERY, L[ucy] M[aud] [1874-1942]
Maiden name of Canadian writer Mrs. Mac-
donald, author of Anne of Green Gables.
The House Party at Smoky Island WT Aug 35
*The House Party at Smoky Island
                           SMS 10,Fal 68

MOONEY, ALFRED LELAND
Universe [v]   Mac 4,Win 58

MOONEY, BRIAN
The Affair at Durmamnay Hall Kad 5,Jul 82
The Dream Shop   FyT 1,Sum 77
The Elevation of Theophilus
  Goatgrime   FyT 8,Sum 81
Encounter   DH 22,Spr 81
For the Life Everlasting   FyT 5,Win 79
For Whom the Ghouls Troll DH 3,1972
The Guardians of the Gates
  [nt] [Cth]   Cth 2,1977
Kenneth Grant: A New Viewpoint
  on H. P. Lovecraft [a]   DH 3,1972
Something in Wood [a]   DH 4,1972
Treasure Hunting [a]   DH 1,1971
Undead [v]   FyT 2,Win 77
The Witch of Nuide   DH 15,Win 76
[Cth - Cthulhu Mythos]

MOORCOCK, MICHAEL [John] [1939-]
UK author, editor and anthologist
Aspects of Fantasy [a4]
                           SFy 61-64,Oct 63-Apr 64
Black Sword's Brothers [nt]
  [E]   SFy 61,Oct 63
The Comic Spirit [a]   DH 17,Sum 77
  [speech given at the 2nd World Fantasy
  Convention, New York, Oct 31, 1976]
*Count Brass [n2] [DH]   Ftc Jun-Aug 75
  [*book, Granada, St. Albans, 1973]
Dead God's Homecoming [nt]
  [E]   SFy 59,Jun 63
Doomed Lord's Passing [nt]
  [E]   SFy 64,Apr 64
[The Dream of Earl Aubec - see Master of
Chaos]
The Dreaming City [nt][E] SFy 47.Jun 61
The Eternal Champion [na]
  [JD]   SFy 53,Jun 62
The Flame Bringers [nt] [E] SFy 55,Oct 62
The Greater Conqueror [nt] SFy 58.Apr 63
The Heroes in Heroic Fantasy
  [a]   DFd 3,Sum 80
The Ice Schooner [n3]
                           Imp 9-11,Nov 66-Jan 67
*Islands   Ariel 2,1977
  [*orig."Not By Mind Alone" New Worlds
  Sep 63]
Kings in Darkness [nt] [E] SFy 54,Aug 62
The Last Enchantment [E] Ariel 3,1978
*The Macabre in Heroic Fantasy
  [DH]   FCr 8,May 76
  [*very brief ex.from The Jewel in
  the Skull,1967 to serve as an art
  feature for Lee Brown Coye]
Master of Chaos   Ftc May 64
*Master of Chaos   S&S 1974
Mervyn Peake: an Appreciation
  [a]   SFy 60,Aug 63
The Nemedians [rr]   FCr 12,Nov 77
  [Chap.5 of rr."Genseric's Fifth-Born
  Son"]

[Not By Mind Alone - see Islands]
The Russian Intelligence [ex] SE 1,Spr 80
  [from *The Russian Intelligence*,1980]
Sad Giant's Shield [na] *[E]* SFy 63,Feb 64
*The Sleeping Sorceress *[E]*   Ftc Feb 72
  [*orig."The Torment of the Last Lord"
  The Sleeping Sorceress,1971]
The Stealer of Souls [nt]
  [E]   SFy 51,Feb 62
*The Stone Thing [spf]   FyT 1,Sum 77
  [*Triode* (fanzine) No.20,Oct 74]
To Rescue Tanelorn [nt]   SFy 56,Dec 62
While the Gods Laugh [nt]
  [E]   SFy 49,Oct 61

  as James Colvin
The Deep Fix [na]   SFy 64,Apr 64
[DH - Dorian Hawkmoon; E - Elric of
Melnibone (Note: "Master of Chaos" and
"To Rescue Tanelorn" share the same
background); *JD - John Daker/Erekose.*
All three series are interrelated]

MOORE, ALAN
Shrine of the Lizard   WW 2,Mar 71
To the Humfo [v]   WW 1,Jun 70

MOORE, CARL
A Nightmare of Devil-Spawned
  Mysticism   BoT Dec 49
  [probably a reprint from a 1930s
  US pulp]

MOORE, C[atherine] L[ucille] [1911-]
US author and scriptwriter. See note under
entry for Henry Kuttner.
  Interviews   Chac 1,Win 76;Div 22,Sep 77
                          Div 28/9,Feb/Mar 79
  Profile   NV 4,Sum 79
The Black God's Kiss [nt] *[J]* WT Oct 34
Black God's Shadow   *[J]*   WT Dec 34
Black Thirst [nt]   *[NWS]*   WT Apr 34
*Black Thirst [nt]   *[NWS]*   AFR 3,1947
The Cold Gray God   *[NWS]*   WT Oct 35
The Dark Land   *[J]*   WT Jan 36
Dust of the Gods   *[NWS]*   WT Aug 34
Fruit of Knowledge [nt]   Unk Oct 40
*Fruit of Knowledge [nt]   UnkB Oct 40
Hellsgarde   *[J]*   WT Apr 39
Jirel Meets Magic *[J]*   WT Jul 35
Julhi   *[NWS]*   WT Mar 35
Lost Paradise   *[NWS]*   WT Jul 36
Miracle in Three Dimensions   StS Apr 39
Scarlet Dream   *[NWS]*   WT May 34
*Scarlet Dream   *[NWS]*   AFR 5,1948
Shambleau   *[NWS]*   WT Nov 33
*Shambleau   *[NWS]*   AFR 7,1948
The Tree of Life   *[NWS]*   WT Oct 36
Werewoman   *[NWS]*   Lvs 2,1938
Yvala   *[NWS]*   WT Feb 36

  + Forrest J. Ackerman
*Nymph of Darkness   *[NWS]*   WT Dec 39
  [*Fantasy Magazine* during 1935]

  + Henry Kuttner
Quest of the Starstone *[J/NWS]* WT Nov 37
[J - Jirel of Joiry; NWS - Northwest
Smith]

MOORE, GERALD V.
Beyond Proof or Explanation   GS Jul 28

MOORE, L. A. P.
Alpha Centauri A Nine   Ftc Jan 80
Pluto and Cerberus and Mickey
                          Arg 8,Fal/Win 81

MOORE, M. J. P.
The Writing Man   Imp 7,Sep 66

MOORE, ROBERT E.
S.F.=Serious Fiction? [a]   PtF 2,1979

MOORE, ROGER E.
Coyote Awakens   FB Dec 83

MOORE, RUTH ANN
Tolkien and the Elves [a] FCr 4/5,Aug 75

MOORE, STANLEY
The Man With Four Arms [nt2]
                          GS Mar-Apr 31

MOORE, [Joseph] WARD [1903-78]
US writer
Conversation Piece   Whsp 11/12,Oct 78

  + Avram Davidson
Joyleg [sn2]   Ftc Mar-Apr 62

MORAN, JOHN C.
Observations Upon the Decline of
  Aesthetic Appreciations during
  the Present Age... [a]
                          Nyc 11/12,Apr 76

MORAND, PAUL   [1888-1976]
*Malay Love Magic   WT Sep 37
  [*East India and Company*,1927]

MORAVSKY, MARIA   [1859-1947]
Beyond the Frame   WT Jul 40
The Castle of Tamara   WT Apr 27
The Great Release   StS Jun 39
The Green Brothers Take Over WT Jan 48
The Hydroponic Monster   StS Jun 40
I Am Going to Cracow!   StS Aug 40
Into Fantasy [v]   WT Nov 42
Let Me Out!   StS Oct 39
Lover of Caladiums   WT(Can)Sep 42
*Lover of Caladiums   WT May 43
The Ode to Pegasus   WT Nov 26
The Soul to the 'Cello   StS Dec 39
Spider Woman   StS Apr 40
What Was in the Seaman's Chest? GS Nov 28

MORDTMAN, A. J.
The Ship That Committed Suicide WT Mar 36

MORE, DENNIS
  Pseud: see Keith TAYLOR

MORETTI, M. G.
The Strangling Hands   WT Feb 38

MORGAN, BASSETT   [1885-?1974]
Pseud. used on all her fiction by US
writer Mrs. Grace Jones
Bimini   WT Jan 29
*Bimini   AFR 10,1949
Black Bagheela   WT Jan 35
Demon Doom of N'Yeng Sen   WT Aug 29
The Devils of Po Sung   WT Dec 27
*The Devils of Po Sung   WT Mar 39

Edmond Hamilton "He That Hath
  Wings"   Ftc Jul 63
John Campbell Haywood "The
  Gray People"   SMS 8,Spr 68
Robert E.Howard "The Dead
  Remember"   Ftc Dec 61
Robert E.Howard "The Garden of
  Fear"   Ftc May 61
David H.Keller "The Mother" Ftc Oct 61
Murray Leinster "The Darkness
  on Fifth Avenue"   Ftc Mar 62
H.P.Lovecraft & August W.
  Derleth "The Shadow Out of
  Space"   Ftc Feb 62
Eric Frank Russell "The Cosmic
  Relic"   Ftc Jun 61
Nat Schachner "The Dragon of
  Iskander"   Ftc Jul 62
Clifford D.Simak "The Creator" Ftc Jul 61
Clark Ashton Smith "The Root
  of Ampoi"   Ftc Aug 61
A.E.van Vogt "Ship of Darkness"
                            Ftc Sep 61
Edgar Wallace "Planetoid 127" Ftc Nov 62
Jack Williamson "Nonstop to
  Mars"   Ftc Apr 62

MOSS, DUNCAN
  Pseud: see Michael AMBROSE

MOSS, F.K.
  The Death Cell   WT May 23

MOSS, ROBERT
  The Cottage   Phtm 5,Aug 57

MOSTOW, JOSHUA
  The Smell of Witchcraft   EC 1,Jul 76

MOUDREY, JOE
*Three Approaches to the Fall
  of the House of Usher [a]
                            Nyc 11/12,Apr 76
  [*Esoteric Order of Dagon 9th Mailing
   Feb 75]

MOUDY, WALTER F[rank]   [1929-73]
US Lawyer
  The Dreamer   Ftc Apr 65
  I Think They Love Me   Ftc May 65

MUDFORD, WILLIAM   [1792-1848]
UK author and journalist
*The Iron Shroud   BC Win 70/1
  [*Blackwood's Magazine Aug 1830; this
   version taken from The Scrap-Book
   Oct 1907]

MUELLER, RICHARD
  Little Axes   FB Dec 83
  Stage Magic   FB Nov 82

MULDOON, SYLVAN J[oseph]   [1903-]
US biographer and occult writer
*The Corpse That Wouldn't Die TTT Fal 63
  [*see "The Ghost of the Hydeville
   Peddler"]
  The Ghost of the Hydeville
  Peddler [see above] [ts] GS Sep 30

How to be a Ghost [ts]   GS Jul 31
I Have Been a Specter [ts]   GS Feb 30
The Psychic Detective [a]   GS Mar 31

MULLEN, SOPHIA
  as Sophia Magafan
Tasha - a Fragment from "Witches
  That Were"   Ggn 3,Jul 47

MULLEN, STANLEY   [1911-73]
US author, artist and fan publisher [see
Editor Index]
  Caput Mortuum [v]   Ggn 1,Mar 47
  Cartouche - Campbell [a] Ggn 4,Sep 47
    - Clark Ashton Smith [a] Ggn 3,Jul 47
    - A. Merritt [a]   Ggn 1,Mar 47
  The Dead Companions   Ftc Mar 57
  A Dero Named Clarence   Ggn 1,Mar 47
  Goat Mask   Ggn 2,May/Jun 47
  The Night Watchman   Vor 2,1947
  A Strange View of the
  River   Ggn 2,May/Jun 47
  Unholy Street   Ggn (10) Mar 49

    as Shan Nosgorov
The Shadow Woman   Ggn (6) Jan 48
Tchaka [v]   Ggn (7),Mar/Apr 48

[also wrote text to cartoons by Roy Hunt
and C.R.Bunnell]

MULLER, GREGG JONES
  Cymru, Ambyth [v]   DFd 4,Win 83
  Sandy Denny [v]   DFd 3,Sum 80

MULLER, HECATE
  The Dreamer   WWd 1(1955)

MULLER, JOHN E.
House pseud. used on sf/horror published by
John Spencer/Badger Books.
  by R.Lionel Fanthorpe
The Exorcists [n]   SN 94(1965)
The Eye of Karnak [n]   SN 56(1962)
Out of the Night [n]   SN 100(1965)
Return of Zeus [n]   SN 52(1962)
Spectre of Darkness [n]   SN 98(1965)
Vengeance of Siva [n]   SN 60(1962)

  by John S.Glasby
The Unpossessed [n]   SN 42(1961)

MUMFORD, ETHEL WATTS   [1878-1940]
US novelist, poet and playwright
  Phantom Perfumes   GS Dec 27
  The Specter in Red   GS Jun 27

MUNN, H[arold] WARNER   [1903-81]
US author and poet
  Obituary   Eld 2,1981
  Bibliography   Kad 4,Jul 81
  [Achsah Young of Windsor - see The Master
   Has a Narrow Escape]
*The Affair of the Cuckolded
  Warlock   Kad 4,Jul 81
  [*booklet, Lanthorne Press, WA: 1975]
  All-Hallows [v]   Whsp 6/7,Jun 75
  The Beautiful Morning   Wbk 4,1971
  The Black Captain   Mb 21,1975
  [The Bug-Wolves of Castle Manglâna -
   see The Master Fights]
  [The Cat Organ - see The Master Strikes]

Dictated by Spirits [a]   GS Jun 29
Did They Live Before? [a]   GS Feb 30
Direct Voice Messages [a]   GS Aug 28
Do Animals Comes Back? [a]   GS Oct 28
Do Animals Live After Death [a]   GS Nov 29
Eerie Children [a]   GS Oct 29
Electrically Controlled Seances
  [a]   GS Mar 30
The Evil History of a Cupboard
  [a]   GS Feb 29
The Eyesight of the Soul [a]   GS Feb 28
The Famous 'Newspaper Tests' [a]   GS Apr 30
Guarded By Phantoms! [a]   GS May 29
How a Woman Saved a Ghost [a]   GS Jan 29
Light on Telepathy [a]   GS Dec 29
The Luck of Being Mediumistic
  [a]   GS Nov 27
The Mystery of Ectoplasm [a]   GS Mar 28
The Mystery of the British Ace
  [a]   GS Mar 29
Now, Let Us Discuss Magic [a]   GS Dec 27
Phantom Finger-Prints [a]   GS Apr 29
Premonitions and Prophecies [a]   GS Jun 28
A Prison Warden's Story [a]   GS Sep 29
The Romance of the 'Supernatural'
  [a]   GS Sep 27
She Spent $15,000,000 on Ghosts!
  [a]   GS Dec 28
The Sinclair Experiments [a]   GS Jan 30
Spirits, or Mind Reading - Which?
  [a]   GS Oct 27
Spirits That Are Not Ghosts [a]   GS Nov 28
Things Brought by Ghosts [a]   GS Jul 28
Voodoo and Obeah [a]   GS Apr 28
What Has Margery Proved? [a]   GS Aug 29
What Truth is There in Witchcraft?
  [a]   GS Jan 28
Who Believes in Ghosts? [a]   GS Jul 29

NARSON, THOMAS
The Tank   Phtm 1, Apr 57

NASH, WILLIAM B.
Are the Saucers Our Friends?
  [a]   Mystic Mar 54

NATION, WINONA MORRIS
Leopard Night [v]   FCr 13, Jun 78
The Red Rain [v]   FCw 2, Feb 77

NEAL, GAVIN
Reluctant Hero   SFy 14, Jun 55

NEAL, JIM
Blood-Prayer [v]   FB Dec 83
Challenge [v]   FB Dec 81
The Hour of the Anvil [v]   FB Oct 81
Minutes of the Last Meeting of
  the Heroes' Club [v]   FB May 82
Wizard and Warrior [v]   FB Feb 83

NEALE, ARTHUR
[May be pseud. of Walter B. Gibson]
The Dead of Egypt [a]   TMM Feb 28
Tibet - Land of Mystery [a]   TMM Apr 28

NEEF(E), ELTON T.
  Pseud: see R. Lionel FANTHORPE

NEIDIGH, KIM L.
Graveyard Abomination [v]   Nyc 14, Mar 78

NELSON, ALAN   [1911-]
Man in a Hurry   WT May 44

NELSON, DALE
The Four Branches [a]   NFJ 1, Sum 76
In Carcosa [v]   Nyc 11/12, Apr 76

NELSON, GEOFFREY
Halloween [v]   DH 21, 1980

NELSON, JOHN
Time   S&T 2, Fal 67

NELSON, MAISIE
Enduring [v]   WT Sep 40

NELSON, RANNEY
But Morrison Wept   Wbk 5, 1972

NELSON, R[AY]/[Radell] [FARADAY] [1931-]
US writer
The City of the Crocodile [S] Ftc Mar 74
Food   Gam 4, Feb 65
A Song on the Rising Wind [nt] Ftc Nov 74
Valse Triste   WT 2, Spr 81
[S - Satyricon]

NELSON, ROBERT
Dream-Stair [v]   WT Apr 35
Jorgas [v]   WT Feb 36
Night of Unrest [v]   WT Sep 37
Sable Reverie [v]   WT Sep 34
Under the Tomb [v]   WT May 35

NELSON, WILL W.
Voodooism [a]   WT Jul/Aug 23

NEMEC, DAVID
Browning's Lamps   TZ Jun 82

NESBIT, EDITH   [1858-1924]
UK novelist, especially for children
*Man-Size in Marble   FFy Feb 71
  [*orig.1886; Grim Tales, 1893]

NEUPERT, A. HUGHES
The Dead Who Know No Peace   GS Aug 27
*Stay Dead! Stay Dead! Stay Dead! PGS 1963
  [*anon.rep. of first story]

NEVARD, MIKE
Tiles   SFy 19, Aug 56

NEVILLE, KRIS [Ottman] [1925-80]
US writer
Another Creator   FB Oct 81
*As Holy and Enchanted   Gam 1, 1963
  [*see as by 'Henderson Starke']
The Bull Fights   FB Aug 83
The Man With the Fine Mind Ftc Jan/Feb 53
*The Man With the Fine Mind   Ftc Jul 67
The Opal Necklace   Ftc Sum 52
*The Opal Necklace   Ftc Jun 69

  as Henderson Starke
As Holy and Enchanted   ASFFR Apr 53
  [see rep.as by Neville]

uncredited
The Gamma Interview:
   Forrest J. Ackerman [in]   Gam 4,Feb 65
   Rod Serling [in]   Gam 1,1963
   Robert Sheckley [in]   Gam 2,1963
   Soviet Science Fiction [in] Gam 3,1964

NOLLEY, BETTY
Justice [v]   S&T 63,Win 82/3
Love Song From Capella IV [v] SPWAO 2,1982

NORLING, SIDNEY
Strange Companions   Phtm 3,Jun 57

NORMAN, JAY
The Hint   MysT Jun 52

NORMENT, ANNE IRVINE
Hands in the Dark [ts]   GS Jul 26
"Ouija Never Lies"   GS May 27

NORRIS, [Benjamin] FRANK[lin] [1870-1902]
US journalist and novelist
*The Guest of Honor   WT Sum 73
   [*Pilgrim Magazine Jul/Aug 1902]

NORRIS, LOWELL AMES
The Clue of the Vanished Bride   GS Jul 29
The Invisible Tenant [ts]   GS Feb 29

NORRIS, W. G.
I'll Be Seeing You   TZ Apr 82
   [also in *GSTZ,1982]

NORSWORTHY, GEORGE
The Third Man   WT Mar 30

NORTH, BRENT   (pseud)
The Claw Will Come to Caress Me UT May 40
Debutantes for the Damned   UT Nov 39
Sin Slaves For Sale   UT Mar 40

NORTH, ERIC
   Pseud: see Bernard CRONIN

NORTH, Z. G.
Living Doll   DFy 10,Dec 76

NORTHCOTE, AMYAS   [1864-1923]
UK Magistrate and writer
   Profile   G&S 4,1982

NORTON, ALICE M[ary]
   see under pseud: Andre NORTON

NORTON, ANDRE   [1912-]
US sf/fantasy novelist; former librarian.
Real name Alice Mary Norton
By a Hair...   Phtm 16,Jul 58
Ghost Tour [a]   W&S Jan/Feb 71
Long Live Lord Kor! [na]   WoF 2,1970

NORTON, C. C.
Nightwalkers [v]   FCr 14,Sep 78

NORTON, FORREST
Mr.Milford's Magic Camera   DW Aug 57

NORWICH, DOROTHY
The Game   WT Jan 31

NORWOOD, RICK
The Other One [ss]   TZ May 82
Three Timely Tales [3ss]   TZ Dec 82

NOSGOROV, SHAN
   Pseud: see Stanley MULLEN

NOURSE, ALAN E[dward]   [1928-]
US physician, sf and medical writer
Magic Show   Ftc Dec 69
The Mirror [nt]   Ftc Jun 60

NOVITSKI, PAUL DAVID   [1950-]
The Loser of Solitaire   Ftc Jan 79

   as Alpajpuri
Asylum in the Concrete   Ftc Feb 75

NUGOR, MAX
The Indoor Safari   SMS 10,Fal 68

NUNES, CLAUDE   [1924-]
South African Government Statistician
   + Rhoda Nunes
The Problem   SFy 52,Apr 62

NUNES, RHODA [Gwylleth] [1938-]
South African writer, wife of the above
   + Claude Nunes
The Problem   SFy 52,Apr 62

NUTTALL, MARIJANE
   [Mrs. Stanley Mullen]
The Death of the Wood Nymphs   Ggn Nov 47
Storms of Night   Ggn Jan 48
Through a Jade Glass [a] Ggn 2,May/Jun 47

NYHAN, MARY
Whose Ghost?   Phtm 5,Aug 57

O

OATES, JOYCE CAROL   [1938-]
US short story writer
The Rose Wall   TZ Apr 81
   [also in *GSTZ,1982]

O'BRIEN, DAVID WRIGHT   [1918-44]
US sf/fantasy pulp writer
Introduction to a Stranger [v] WT Mar 39
*Spook For Yourself   Ftc Oct 70
   [*Fantastic Adventures Jan 42]

O'BRIEN, DEN/DAN
   as 'A Court Bailiff'
The Strangest Murder Trial   GS Apr 29

   + Gilbert Patten
Spirit Hands   GS Sep 27

O'BRIEN, FITZ-JAMES   [1828-62]
Irish poet, writer and journalist, resident
in US from 1852.
*The Diamond Lens [nt]   WT Apr 29
*The Diamond Lens [nt]   FC 2,1973
   [*The Atlantic Monthly Jan 1858]
*The Dragon Fang   WT Jul 27
   [*Harper's during 1856]

Sunset and Evening Calm [v] ArkS 1,Jun 83
  [probably all first appeared in the
  amateur press in the 1910s]

OWEN, THOMAS
  Blood Moon   Whsp 13/14,Oct 79

OWENS, ALBERT
*House pseud. used by Harold Hersey and
possibly one other*
  by Harold Hersey
  Hidden Pathways [v]   TB Aug 1,19
  My Lovely [v]   TB Mar 15,19
  The Old Loves [v]   TB Jun 1,19

  by poet unknown
  Among the Stars [v]   TB Sep 1,19

OWENS, BARBARA
  The New Man   TZ Mar 82
  Something Evil   TZ Aug 82

OWENS, ELWIN J.
  Black Temple Band   WT Dec 24
  Dead in Three Hours   WT Mar 26
  Knights of the Red Owl   WT Apr 26
  Mystery River   WT May/Jul 24
  Six Bearded Men   WT Nov 24

OWENS, LEE [see also Lee Owen]
*Giants of the Earth [a]   StF 10,Fal 69
  [*Fantastic Adventures Aug 51]

                    P

PACKARD, FRANK L[ucias] [1877-1942]
Canadian adventure writer
*The Red Lure   TB Sep 15,19
  [*New Magazine Feb 1911]

PACKIE, SUSAN
  In Steerage [v]   S&T 64,Sum 83
  Preservation of the Species [v]
                                 Wbk 18,1983

PADGETT, LEWIS
  Pseud: see Henry KUTTNER

PAGE, DEREK
  The Sixty Minute Egg   BMM Nov 65

PAGE, GERALD W. [1939-]
US writer and editor [see Editor Index]
  Chang Dree   Whsp 13/14,Oct 79
  Confession in Darkness   Wbk 14,1979
  The Dark Glass [ss]   Wbk 5,1972
  The Grimoire [col]   W&S 6,May 71
  Hallucination   Anu 3,1968
  The Hollow Grave   Whsp 19/20,Oct 83
  The Man With the Silver Eyes
    [nt]   Wbk 13,1978
  The Off-Season   SMS 1,Sum 66
  Overhill Mountain   Anu 4,Aut 68
  The Pool of the Worlds [nt]   Wbk 18,1983
  Thirst [nt]   W&S 7,1972
  The Tree   MoH 10,Aug 65
  Two Princes of Saturn   Wbk 15,1981
  The Warrior Who Did Not Know
    Fear   Whsp 15/16,Mar 82

  as Carleton Grindle
The Castle at the World's Edge
  [nt]   W&S 8,1972
Circe's Laughter   W&S 6,May 71
The Momentary Ghost   W&S 5,Jan/Feb 71
Tomorrow's Witch   W&S 9,1972
The Treason of Morn Connacht Anu 4,Aut 68

  as Kenneth Pembroke
Were-Creature   W&S 5,Jan/Feb 71

  as Leo Tifton
The Dancing Girl of Isphatam
  [ss]   W&S 7,1972
Into the Blue Forest   W&S 10,1974
Smoke [ss]   W&S 5,Jan/Feb 71

  + Jerry Burge as 'Len Wilburn'
Purr   W&S 10,1974

  completion of fragments by Robert E.
  Howard
The Guardian of the Idol   WT 3,Fal 81
Mistress of Death   W&S 5,Jan/Feb 71

PAGE, J. RICHARD
  Plain Chant [v] ·   NV 8,Fal 81

PAGE, NORVELL W.   [1904?-61]
*US publicity officer, writer and news-
paperman*
  But Without Horns [n]   Unk Jun 40
*But Without Horns [n]   UnkB Jun 40
  Flame Winds [n] [PJ]   Unk Jun 39
  Sons of the Bear God [n] [PJ] Unk Nov 39
*Sons of the Bear God [n] [PJ] UnkB Nov 39
  [PJ - Prester John]

PAIN, GUY
  The Choking of Allison Grey   WT Jun 27
  The Jonah   WT Aug 25

PAINE, ALBERT BIGELOW   [1861-1937]
US novelist and biographer
*The Black Hands   WT Sum 73
  [*Pearson's Magazine Aug 1903]

PAINTON, FRED C.
  Vampire Meat   DrD Apr 35

PALASKI, CC
  + Dennis Etchison
Home Call   Whsp 19/20,Oct 83

PALLANT, NORMAN C[harles] [1910-72]
UK journalist
  In the Dark Temple   WOL 1(1960)
    [by-line misprinted as 'Jallant']
  The Incredible Awakening   WOL 3(1960)
  It's a Lovely Morning   WOM(1949)
  Martian Mandate [nt]   SFy 2,Win 50/1

PALMER, A. B.
  The Cottage Down the Lane   Phtm 3,Jun 57

PALMER, ANDREW
  The Vampire's Fangs Were Red With
    My Woman's Blood   AH Feb 71

PALMER, A. S. QUILTER-
  see under A. S. QUILTER-PALMER

Lost Dream [v]   WT Jan 38
*The Mist   Div 21,Jul 77
   [*Phantasmagoria (fanzine) Jul 37]
Monsieur Bluebeard   WT Sep 44
The Music-Box From Hell   WT May 45
   [see rep.as by H.J. Swanza]
Only Gone Before   MoH 20,Mar 68
Skydrift   WT Nov 49
Tomorrow's Mask   W&S 6,May 71
Votaress   WT Sep 45
The Warrior   WT Jan 39
Witch's Bercuese [v]   MT Sum 35

   as E. Theodore Pine
The Two Doors   UnS Win 35

   as H. J. Swanza
*The Music-Box From Hell   WT(Can)Nov 45
   [*orig.as by Petaja]

   + Brian Lumley, David Gerrold, Miriam
   Allen deFord & Ross Rocklynne
Othuum [rr:Chap.3]   W&S 10,1974

PETERKIN, DOROTHY MARIE
The Doomed [v]   WT Jun 29

PETERS, BILL
   Pseud: see William P. McGIVERN

PETERS, I. W. D.
The Gallows   WT Mar 23

PETERS, OTHELLO F.
   Pseud: see Dale C. DONALDSON

PETERSON, DON
The White Feather Hex   WT Mar 51

PETERSON, JOHN VICTOR
*The Lightning's Course   UTC 15,Mar 42
   [*Comet Jan 41]
The Magic Touch of Mozart   UTC 14,Feb 42

PETITTI, MONICA
I grandi illustratori di Weird
   Tales [a]   Kad 1,Oct 79

PEYTON, DENNIS
How Dennis By Means of Prowess
   Gat Him Published of Caxton
   [s/v]   Wyrd 7,Fal 77

PFLOCK, KARL T.
AFC   Ftc Sep 73

PHAROS, BRIAN
   + Albuquerque SF Society
An Exquisite Corpse SF Story I
                                     Nyc 13,May 77

PHELPS, GRACE
My Five Minutes in Another
   World [ts]   GS May 29

PHELPS, LESLIE
*Without Incident [a]   WM 4,Sum 71

PHELPS, R. H.
Once There Was an Elephant   WT May 46
*Once There Was an Elephant   WT(Can)Sep 46

PHELPS, WILLIAM LYON   [1865-1943]
Selected 'My Favorite Ghost Story':
   7. "The Upper Berth" F. Marion
      Crawford   GS Aug 30

PHILIPS, GARY
The Cure [v]   CT 3,Jan 78

PHILIPS, JUDSON P[entecost] [1903-]
US mystery writer
*Murder of the Ancients   MyS 19(1939)
*Night of Terror   MyS 18(1939)
   [*US detective pulps of the 1930s]

   as Hugh Pentecost
*Challenge to the Reader   MysT Mar 52
   [*Ellery Queen's Mystery Magazine May 47]

PHILIPS, RANDY
Mr. Smith   Arg 2,Jul 72
Tormented   Arg 1,May 72
Unknown Lust   Arg 1,May 72

PHILLIFENT, JOHN T[homas] [1916-76]
UK sf/fantasy writer
Point [na]   Ftc Dec 61

   as John Rackham
Ankh [na]   [DrW]   SFy 50,Dec 61
The Black Cat's Paw [nt]
   [DrW]   SFy 44,Dec 60
Bring Back a Life   SFy 70,Mar 65
Curse Strings   SFy 37,Nov 59
Drog   SFy 27,Feb 58
Fire and Ice [na] [DrW]   SFy 56,Dec 62
The God-Birds of Glentallach
   [nt]   SFy 80,Jan 66
God Killer   SFy 66,Jul/Aug 64
A Light Feint   [F]   Imp 2,Apr 66
Nulook   SFy 34,Apr 59
Room With a Skew [F] SFy 68,Dec 64/Jan 65
The Veil of Isis [nt] [DrW]   SFy 47,Jun 61
A Way With Animals   SFy 75,Aug 65
What You Don't Know [nt]   SFy 59,Jun 63
With Clean Hands [nt]   SFy 60,Aug 63
[DrW - Dr.Wilson; F - 'Fred']

PHILLIPS, A[LEXANDER] M[oore] [1907-]
US architectural draughtsman and writer
The Extra Bricklayer   Unk Sep 40
*The Extra Bricklayer   UnkB Sep 40
Lycanthropy [v]   Wbk 18,1983
   [poem left in inventory of UW when
   it folded]
The Mislaid Charm [sn]   Unk Feb 41
*The Mislaid Charm [sn]   UnkB Feb 41
Time-Travel Happens! [a]   Unk Dec 39

PHILLIPS, GENE
Candles in Kaldesh   EC 4,1980
Chu-Tang and the Puppeteer
   [C-T]   Arg 7,Fal/Win 80
Chu-Tang at the Willow Bridge
   Inn [C-T]   Arg 5,Win/Spr 79
Eidolon [v]   Div 19,Mar 77
The Fane of Aiyapta [C-T]   Arg 9,Fal 83
Fungi and the Stars [v]   DFy 22,Mar 80
The Moon of Glass [v]   Db Spr 78
Prayer of Kadru-Sekoth [v]   EC 1,Jul 76
[C-T - Chu Tang]

PLATT, CHARLES   [1945-]
UK-born US-resident writer, editor and designer.
Old Worlds   SE 2,Win 80
One of Those Days   SFy 68,Dec 64/Jan 65
A Visit With Isaac Asimov [in]
                                 Ariel 4,Oct 78

PLIMMER, DENIS
Canadian writer
The Channelers   UTC 14,Feb 42
The Coming of Darakk   UTC 12,Dec 41
The Devil's Tree [v]   WT Jul 41
*The Devil's Tree [v]   WT(Can)Sep 47
The Green Invasion   WT Nov 40
*The Green Invasion   UTC 16,Apr 42
Louisiana Night   UTC 21,Sep/Oct 43
The Man From the Wrong Time-
   Track   US Apr 41
Portrait of the Artist's
   Mother   UTC 20,Dec 42
The Stolen God   UTC 13,Jan 42
The Strange Case of Julian
   Rayne   UTC 15,Mar 42
The Unborn   UTC 19,Sep 42

PLUNKETT, CYRIL
Blood is My Bride   UT Aug 39

POCSIK, JOHN   [1943-]
The Fiend Within   Ariel 1,Aut 76
The Hutch [v]   Spoor 2,1974
Surprise Visit   Ariel 4,Oct 78

PODOLSKY, EDWARD
The Figure of Anubis   WT Feb 25
The Masters From Beyond   WT Sep 25

POE, E. A.
[Spoof pseud. used by one or more of the editors of Gamma]
Hans Off in Free Pfall to the
   Moon [spf]   Gam 4,Feb 65

POE, EDGAR ALLAN   [1809-49]
US poet, short story writer, editor and essayist.
*Berenice   WT Apr 32
   [*Southern Literary Messenger Mar 1835]
*The Black Cat   WT Jan 24
   [*Saturday Post Aug 19,1843]
*The Cask of Amontillado   Ftc Nov/Dec 52
*The Cask of Amontillado   BC 1,Win 70/1
   [*Godey's Lady's Book Nov 1846]
*The Conqueror Worm [v]   WT Nov 25
   [*Graham's Magazine Jan 1843]
*A Descent Into the Maelstrom   WT Jan 30
   [*Graham's Magazine May 1841]
*Eldorado [v]   WT Sep 26
   [*Flag of Our Union Apr 21, 1849]
*The Fall of the House of Usher WT Aug 39
*The Fall of the House of Usher WWd 2(1956)
   [*Gentleman's Magazine Aug 1839]
*The Haunted Palace [v]   WT Dec 25
   [*American Museum Apr 1839]
*Israfel [v - ex. only]   WT Sep 38
   [*Poems 2nd. edition, 1831]
*The Lake To — [v]   Ariel 2,1977
   [*Tamerlane and Poems,1827]
*Lenore [v]   WT Jan 26

*Lenore [v - ex. only]   WT Mar 40
   [*orig."A Paean" Poems 2nd. edn.1831]
*Ligeia   WT Nov 26
*Ligeia   MoH 33,Sum 70
*Ligeia [ex. only]   S&T 42,May 77
   [*American Museum Sep 1838]
*Ms Found in a Bottle   WT 1,Win 69/70
   [*Baltimore Saturday Visitor Oct 19,1833]
*The Mask of the Red Death   WT Mar 26
   [*Graham's Magazine May 1842]
*Metzengerstein   WT Jan 28
   [*Baltimore Saturday Courier Jan 14,1832]
*Murders in the Rue Morgue   WT Jun 23
*Murders in the Rue Morgue   BC 1,Win 70/1
   [*Graham's Magazine Apr 1841]
*Never Bet the Devil Your Head WT Mar 24
*Never Bet the Devil Your Head BFT 1,Fal 70
   [*Broadway Journal Aug 16,1845]
*The Oblong Box   MoH 7,Jan 65
   [*Godey's Lady's Book Sep 1844]
*The Pit and the Pendulum   WT Oct 23
   [*The Gift 1843]
*The Premature Burial   WT Nov 33
   [*Dollar Newspaper Mar 27,1844]
*The Raven [v - ex. only]   WT Sep 39
   [*American Review Feb 1845]
*Silence - A Fable   Arg 4,Spr/Sum 77
   [*The Saturday Courier Jan 4,1840]
*The Tell-Tale Heart   WT Nov 23
*The Tell-Tale Heart   Ftc Fal 52
*The Tell-Tale Heart   SMS 1,Sum 66
   [*The Pioneer Jan 1843]
*The Thousandth-and-Second Tale WT Nov 27
   [*Godey's Lady's Book Feb 1845]
*William Wilson   WT Nov 35
   [*Gentleman's Magazine Oct 1839]

Incomplete fragment attributed to Poe
   as completed by Robert Bloch
The Lighthouse   Ftc Jan/Feb 53
*The Lighthouse   TZ Aug 82

   as completed by Richard L. Tierney
The Lighthouse   Nyc 14,Mar 78
*The Lighthouse   E&O 2,1983

POHL, FREDERIK   [1919-]
US author and former editor,mostly of sf
Interviews   DH 19,1979; Ftc Jul 80
Call Me a Million   WoF 2,1970
*Day Million   Imp 8,Oct 66
   [*Rogue Feb 66]
The Ghost Maker   BFF Jan 54

   as Paul Dennis Lavond
Lurani [v]   Unk Feb 40
*Lurani [v]   UWB Win 48
   [also in *FUW,1948 and *FUWB,1952]

   as James MacCreigh + Isaac Asimov
Legal Rites   WT Sep 50

   + Cyril Kornbluth as S.D. Gottesman
*Castle on Outerplanet   UTC 10,Oct 41
   [*Stirring Science Stories Apr 41]

   + Lester del Rey as Charles Satterfield
No More Stars [nt]   BFF Jul 54

POLLARD, JOHN X.
Ziff-Davis house-name used originally by Howard Browne. Following author unknown, but may be Paul W. Fairman
The Monarch of Mars [nt]   Ftc Apr 56

The Tree-Man Ghost WT Mar 28
When the Dead Return WT Dec 27

PRITCHARD, KENNETH B.
The Electric World FT Fal 36

PRITCHARD, MARY EUGENE
On a Haunted Piano GS May 27

PRITCHETT, RON
Ploop SFy 73,Jun 65

PROCTOR, WALTER G.
    Pseud: see Harold S. Corbin

PRONZINI, BILL   [1943-]
US sf/fantasy & mystery writer and antho-
logist
How Now Purple Cow Ftc Apr 69
The Prophecy Ftc Dec 68

    + Barry N. Malzberg
Another Burnt-out Case Ftc Oct 78

    + Jeffrey Wallman
I, Vampire Cov Mar 70

PROUT, MEARLE
Guarded WT Mar 38
The House of the Worm WT Oct 33
*The House of the Worm MoH 5,Sep 64
Masquerade WT Feb 37
Witch's Hair WT May 39

PRYOR, GRAHAM   [1948-]
The Bells FBDG 3,Apr 74
H.P. Lovecraft and the Science
of Poe [a] Nyc 8,Apr 73
The Song of Rhin FBDG 1,Apr/May 72

PUGMIRE, WILLIAM H.
Crimson and Clown White AD 6,Fal 77
Deep Mysteries [v] [Cth] Myrd 2,Aug 75
Never Steal From a Whateley
    [Cth] Div 14,May 76
The Thing in the Glen (The Final
    Manuscript of Desmond Peters)
    [Cth] S&T 44,Sep 77
The Value of Pulp Fiction [a] AD 4,Fal 76
Whispering Wires S&T 20,Sep 73

    + Jessica Amanda Salmonson
O Christmas Tree S&T 50,Jan 79
[Cth - Cthulhu Mythos]

PUMILIA, JOSEPH F.   [1945-]
US copywriter and commercial artist
As Dreams Are Made On Ftc Feb 73
The Weird Tale of Phillip Love HPL 1972

    + Bill Wallace (as 'M.M.Moamrath')
The Next to the Last Voyage of
    the Cuttle Sark [spf] Chac 2,Spr 77

PUNSHON, E[rnest] R[obertson] [1872-1956]
UK playwright and mystery writer
The Haunted Chessmen WT Mar 30

PURCELL, BRICE
Cut Out This Aztec Heart FF Nov 50

PURCELL, DICK
The Girl in Tube 14 [nt] Ftc Aug 55

PURCELL, Mrs JACK
The Crawling Specter of
    Hatfield Hall GS Feb 27

PUSHKIN, ALEXANDER   [1799-1837]
Russian writer and poet
*The Queen of Spades WT Aug 27
    [*orig.1834]
*The Undertaker Phtm 4,Jul 57
    [*also known as "The Coffin Maker";
    version taken from *Prose Tales*,1894]

PUTNAM, ISRA
    Pseud: see Greye LA SPINA

PUTNAM, NINA WILCOX
The Curtain [v] TB Jul 1,19

Q

QUEDNAU, WALTER
    Pseud: see W. Paul GANLEY

QUICK, DOROTHY   [1900-62]
US poet and writer
After an Air Raid [v] WT Jan 43
Ann Boleyn [v] WT Nov 34
The Artist and the Door WT Nov 52
The Bag of Skin StS Feb 40
Blue and Silver Brocade Unk Oct 39
*Blue and Silver Brocade UnkB Oct 39
Candles [v] WT Jan 34
The Cracks of Time WT Sep 48
The Dark Things [v] WT Sep 53
Demon Lover [v] WT Nov 53
Edge of the Cliff WT Mar 41
The Enchanted River WT May 42
For a Sea Lover [v] WT Jan 51
Forest God [v] WT Nov 49
The Ghostlings [v] WT Nov 48
The Gothic Window WT May 44
The Horror in the Studio WT Jun 35
House of Life [v] WT Jul 53
Long Watch [v] WT Jul 46
*Long Watch [v] WT Sum 74
The Lost Door WT Oct 36
The Lost Gods WT Sep 41
The Man in Purple WT May 46
The Manci Curse [nt] StS Dec 40
More Than Shadow WT Jul 54
Out of Space [v] WT May 52
Pattern [v] WT Jul 50
The River [v] WT Sep 48
Sea King's Daughter [v] WT Jan 50
Sleepers [v] WT Sep 51
Strange Music [v] WT Jul 43
Strange Orchids WT Mar 37
This Night [v] WT Sep 54
Three Men [v] WT Jul 51
*Three Men [v] Phtm 4,Jul 57
Transparent Studd Unk Jun 40
*Transparent Stuff UWB Spr 48
Tree Woman [v] WT Mar 46
Turn Over WT Nov 40
Two For a Bargain [nt] Unk Dec 40

R

RACKHAM, JOHN
    Pseud: see John T. PHILLIFENT

RADCLIFFE, GARNETT   [1899-?]
UK writer

The Fingers of Kali   G&G(1938)
The Gloves   WT Jan 53
The Monkey Ship   WT Mar 52
The Vengeance of Kali Mai   WT May 53
You Should be Careful   WT Jan 54

RADWAY, D. L.
The Room in the Tower   WT Jul/Aug 23

RAGSDALE, EDITH LYLE
The Burning Wrath of Allah   WT Mar 25
The Purple Death   WT May/Jul 24
Vials of Wrath   WT May 26

RAHMAN, G[LENN] ARTHUR
The Book of Belialon   FCw 2,Feb 77
The Dancer in the Storm   EvM Win 77/8
A Frog in Search of a Princess
                               Div 26/7,May/Jul 78
House of the Domovoi   DFy 16,Jun 78
The Lost Mind of Kerr Gulch   AD 6,Fal 77
Reflections in the Jirga   S&T 49,Oct 78
The Sun of God   Nyc 14,Mar 78
Under the Night Star   S&T 47,Apr 78
The White Indians   SPWAO 1,1980

    as James A.McKracken
The Antique Hunters   FCw 1,Jan 77

    + Ron Fortier
The Bride of Balan   S&T 60,Jul 81

    + Philip J. Rahman
*The Minneiska Incident   Eld 3,Mar 78
The Quest For Unknown Amherst
   [na4]   Eld 6-9,1979-83

    as James A.McKracken + Philip J. Rahman
The Temple of Nephrenka   FCr 10/11,Mar 77

RAHMAN, PHILIP J.
    + J.A.McKracken (Glenn A. Rahman)
The Temple of Nephrenka   FCr 10/11,Mar 77

    + Glenn A. Rahman
*The Minneiska Incident   Eld 3,Mar 78
The Quest For Unknown Amherst
   [na4]   Eld 6-9,1979-83

RAINBOW, ELIZABETH
The Masker [v]   Mac 18,Win 65/6
The Silken Skirt [v]   Mac 18,Win 65/6

RAINES, SAMUEL
US attorney
"A Little Child Shall Lead-"   GS Apr 27

RALSTON, BARBARA
She Married Her Astral Lover   GS Nov 26

RAMEY, BEN C.
   see under pseud: H.H. HOLLIS

RAMSAY, ELLEN M.
The Brimstone Cat   WT Feb 27

'RAMSAY RED'
Burglars Bewitched   GS Nov 27

RAMSEY, ALICIA
The Black Crusader   WT Jan 26

RAMUS, SYBLA
Coils of Darkness [na3]   WT Feb-Apr 24

RANDALL, FLORENCE ENGEL   [1917-]
US writer
The Boundary Beyond   Ftc Jul 64
One Long Ribbon   Ftc Jul 62

RANDALL, JOHN
Summoned From the Dead   GS May 30

RANDALL, MARTA
US writer, mostly of sf
Sugarfang [a]   Shyl 4,Win 80

RANDALL, ROBERT
   Pseud: see Randall GARRETT & Robert
   SILVERBERG

RANDOLPH, GEORGIANA ANN   [1908-57]
US mystery writer and screenwriter
   as Craig Rice
*Goodbye, Goodbye   MysT Nov 51
   [*Ellery Queen's Mystery Magazine Jun 46]
*His Heart Could Break   MysT Jun 52
   [*Ellery Queen's Mystery Magazine Mar 43]

RANEY, DEB[ORAH K.]
Antemeridiem [v]   Div 12,Jan 76
The Beginning [v]   FCw 1,Jan 77
Death of a Ghost [v]   FCw 2,Feb 77
King Clair's Defeat [v]   FCw 3,Feb 77
A Maiden's Revenge [v]   Div 18,Jan 77
Rachael and Kismet [v]   FCr 6,Nov 75
To Race a Jungle Night [v]   FCr Jan 76

RANKINE, JOHN
   Pseud: see Douglas R. MASON

RANSOM, ELMER
The Golden Age   UW Dec 42
*The Golden Age   UWB Feb 43

RAPHAEL, RICK   [1919-]
US businessman and former news director
Identity Mistaken   Ftc Mar 64

RAPLEE, ELIZABETH VIRGINIA
To a Skull on My Bookshelf [v] WT Oct 37

RAPP, W[ILLIAM] J[ORDAN]   [1895-1942]
US; Editor of True Story 1926-42
Four Sceptics - and the Prowler GS Jan 29
The Invisible Chess-Player   GS Mar 28
Invisible Knockouts   GS Dec 27
*Phantom Knockouts   PGS 1963
   [*orig. "Invisible Knockouts"]
Poisoned Paradise   GS Feb 28
When Ghost Slays Ghost   GS Jan 28

RASCH, PHIL
The Flying Discs [a]   Ggn(11)1949
Literary Criticism and Off-
   Trail Literature [a]   Ggn(4)Sep 47
Sidelights of the Merrittales:
   1.Metalanim and nan-Metal
     [a]   Ggn 5,Nov 47
   2.The Rrrllya [a]   Ggn 6,Jan 48
   3.Ys and Carnac [a]   Ggn 7,Mar/Apr 48
   4.The Kraken [a]   Ggn(8) 1948

5.The Face in the Abyss [a] Ggn(9) 1949
6.Alice in Wonderland [a]   Ggn(10)1949
The Story Behind "The Star
   Rover" [a]   Ggn 3,Jul 47

RASMUS, CARL
The Scar [nt]   WT Apr 23

RASNIC, STEVE
   see under Steve Rasnic TEM

RATH, SARA LINDSAY
The Crest of Satan   ArkC 10,Sum 71

RATHBONE, JAMES
   see under James PARKHILL-RATHBONE

RAVENSCROFT, JAMES L.
The Bloodstained Parasol   WT Sep 23

RAWLE, HENRY
Once suspected a pseud. of John Russell
Fearn but now believed a real writer. See
also note under Henry Retlaw.
   Armand's Return   G&G(1938)
   The Bride of Yum-Chac   OS 1(1945)
   Flashback   OS 2(1946)
   Gruenaldo   WSM 1(1946)
   The Head of Ekillon   G&G(1938)
   In Alien Valleys   WS(1943)
   The Intruder   WOM(1949)
   Marley's Masterpiece   MyS 18(1939)
   Revenoff's Fantasia   TGHH Dec 39
   Silvester's Oasis   WOL 3(1960)
   The Voice of Amalzzar   WOL 2(1960)

RAWKINS, WATSON
Black Man and White Witch   WT Jun/Jul 31

RAWLINS, [Capt.] GEORGE J.
Hound of the Haunted Trail   StS Feb 40
The House of Stanley   StS Aug 40
The Light Must Burn   StS Oct 39
The Third Life of Nine   StS Dec 40
The Thirteenth Boat   StS Apr 40

RAY, C. L.
The Jade Frog   GS Oct 29

RAYER, F[rancis] G[eorge] [1921-81]
UK sf and technical writer
   The Ark [nt]   SFy 2,Win 50/1
   Co-Efficiency Zero   SFy 11,Dec 54
   Dark Summer   SFy 10,Sep 54
   Plimsoll Line   SFy 4,Spr 52
   Seek Earthmen No More [nt] SFy 7(Spr 54)
   The Singular Sequel to the Case
      of the Montrose Diamond WOM(1949)
   Space Prize   SFy 8,May 54
   Trader's Planet   SFy 6,Spr 53
   The Undying Enemy [nt]   SFy 3,Win 51/2
   Wishing Stone   SFy 30,Aug 58

RAYMOND, EMIL
Arms in the Dark   GS Oct 27
Convicted by a Silent Witness GS Jul 26
The Flaming Specter of Long
   Ridge   GS Sep 26
Hidden in Hollow Men   GS Aug 26
The Shadow of Crime   GS Oct 29

Sheltered By a Shadow   GS Oct 26
The Spirit Quarterback   GS Feb 27
   [as by Ralph Barton in ToC]

RAYMOND, HARRY
Corey's Cat   WT Mar 43

RAYMOND, HUGH
   Pseud: see John B. MICHEL

RAYMOND, JOHN
   House name: see R.Lionel FANTHORPE

REAMY, TOM   [1935-77]
US printer, writer and fan editor
   Interview   Shyl 1,Nov 77
   Obituary   Shyl 2,Feb 78
   Blue Eyes   Shyl 3,Sum 79
   Mistress of Windraven   Chac 1,Win 76
   Waiting for Billy Star   Shyl 2,Feb 78
   Wonder Show [ex]   Shyl 1,Nov 77
   [an advance ex.from Blind Voices]

RECOUR, CHARLES
   Pseud: see Henry BOTT

REDD, DAVID
Nancy   Ftc Feb 71

REDSHAW, JAMES FRANCIS
[Possible pseud. of Thomas P. Kelley]
   Expedition No. 1   UTC 11,Nov 41
   Mystery of the Missing Ships
                             UTC 12,Dec 41

REDGROVE, PETER [William] [1932-]
UK writer
*The White Monument   Imp 5,Jul 66
   [*orig.bdcst BBC Third Programme]

REED, CLIFFORD C[ecil] [1911-]
South African born,UK writer & accountant
   The Misfit   SFy 31,Oct 58
   Paradise For a Punter   SFy 75,Aug 65
   A Sense of Proportion   SFy 30,Aug 58
   Suspect Halo   SFy 39,Feb 60
   Sweet Smell of Success   SFy 33,Feb 59
   What Happened to Lodwick SFy 29,Jun 58
   Who Steals My Purse   SFy 32,Dec 58

REED, DAVID V.
   Pseud: see David VERN

REED, KIT   [1932-]
Regular by-line used by US writer and
lecturer Lillian Craig Reed
   Frontiers   TZ May 82
   Judgement   Mac 5,Sum 59

REED, ZEALIA BROWN
   see under Zealia Brown BISHOP

REEDER, DAVE [1950-]
UK editor, writer & former librarian
   Albion Evening [v]   Eld 6,1979
   Away ... Away [v]   FyM 3,Jun 82
   Cae Coch   FyM 2,Apr 81
   A Gent.of Providence   FyM 1,Sep 80
   The Last Trick   FyT 6,Sum 80
   Leopard Eyes [v]   FyM 1,Sep 80
   Mawhan Rectory   G&S 5,1983

RILEY, DAVID A.
After Nightfall   WW 1,Jun 70
As Silver Dusk Suffuses Red [v] DH 5,1973
Corpse-Maker   WW 2,Mar 71
The Farmhouse   Whsp 4,Jul 74
The Feasters of the Night [v] WW 2,Mar 71
The House That Found Movement
   and Death [v]   WW 1,Jun 70
In Piece [v]   DH 6,1973
Olympiad of Ghosts [v]   DH 3,1972
Rain [v]   DH 2,1972
A Sense of Movement   FBDG 1,Apr/May 72
The Shadow By the Altar   DH 26,Spr 83
That Greater Death [v]   DH 5,1973
Thoughts in a Solitary
   Churchyard [v]   DH 5,1973
The Urn   Whsp 1,Jul 73
*The Urn   DH 11,Win/Spr 75

   + Nick Caffrey
The Artist in Fandom: Jim
   Pitts [in]   DH 9,Sum 74

RILEY, Mrs. LAWTON
A Bishop's Hunch [ts]   Mystic Jan 54

RILEY, STEPHEN T.
   [see Artist Index]
Donald Grant Interview [in]
                             FCr 10/11,Mar 77
Kenneth Smith: An Appreciation
   [a]   FCr 14,Sep 78

RIMEL, DUANE W[eldon]   [1915-]
US writer; former newspaperman
The Disinterment   WT Jan 37
The Forbidden Room   FT Fal 36
The Jewels of Charlotte   UnS May/Jun 35
The Key [v]   ArkC 1,Sum 67
The Metal Chamber   WT Mar 39
Shadow on the Wall [v]   ArkC 5,Sum 69
The Ship [v]   MT Win 34
Strange Flowers Bloom [v] ArkC 8,Win 71

RINEHART, MARY ROBERTS   [1876-1958]
US writer and novelist
*The Love-Affair of a Freak BC 1,Win 70/1
   [*orig.believed to be The Scrap Book
   during 1907]

RINGER, VIOLET HILES
The Deceased [v]   Mac 22,1973

RINGWOOD, ANDREW
Sir Rodney Keeps a Date   OS 1(1945)

RIPPINGER, WALTER
The Affair of the Three Turtles
                               MyS 18(1939)
Dying Man Wanted   ToT(1937)

RITCHIE, JACK
The Rules of the Game   TZ Jul 81

RITCHIE, RITA
A Matter of the Mind   BMM Jan 66

RITTER, ED[MOND]
Cold Case   Shk Sep 60

RITTER, ROBERT
The Cross-Town Void Maker   EC 3,1980

RIVERSIDE, JOHN
   Pseud: see Robert A. HEINLEIN

ROACH, ROBERT
   as A. K. Jorgensson
Coming-of-Age Day   SFy 76,Sep 65

ROARKE, BYRON
   [see Editor Index]
C. L. Moore [in]   Chac 1,Win 76
Robert E. Howard Editors'/Publishers'
   Roundtable [sym2]
                     FCr 9-10/11,Aug 76-Mar 77

ROARKE, JESSE
Atonement   Ftc Jan 62
Ripeness is All   Ftc May 62

ROBBINS, CLARENCE AARON   [1888-1949]
US writer
   as Tod Robbins
The Bibulous Baby   TB Jul 1,19
The Conquerors   TB Aug 15,19
Crimson Flowers   TB Oct 1,19
Fragments   TB Sep 1,19
Undying Hatred   TB Sep 15,19
A Voice From Beyond   TB Jul 15,19

ROBBINS, R. J.
   + Will Smith
Swamp Horror   WT Mar 26
Under the N-Ray   WT May 25

ROBBINS, TOD
   Pseud: see Clarence Aaron ROBBINS

ROBERTS, BETTE B.
Romantic Gothicism [rv]   Goth Dec 79

ROBERTS, EDD
Sea Encounter [v]   Wbk 1,1968

ROBERTS, JAMES P.
Disintegration of Terraplane   EC 9,1982

ROBERTS, KEITH [John Kingston]   [1935-]
UK author and commercial artist [see
Artist Index]
Anita   [A]   SFy 67,Sep/Oct 64
   [consists of two stories:"The Witch"
   and "Anita"]
Brother John [nt] [Pav]   Imp 3,May 66
The Charm   [A]   SFy 68,Dec 64/Jan 65
Corfe Gate [nt]   [Pav]   Imp 5,Jul 66
Escapism   SFy 67,Sep/Oct 64
The Familiar   [A]   Imp 10,Dec 66
Flight of Fancy   SFy 69,Jan/Feb 65
The Furies [n3]   SFy 74-76,Jul-Sep 65
The Helmet-Maker's Wife   Ariel 2,1977
Idiot's Lantern   [A]   SFy 75,Aug 65
The Jennifer   [A]   SFy 70,Mar 65
Keith Roberts re-reads the True
   History of Lucian of Samosata
   [a]   Imp 12,Feb 67
The Lady Anne [nt] [Pav] Imp 2,Apr 66
Lords and Ladies [nt] [Pav]Imp 4,Jun 66
The Middle Earth   [A]   SFy 72,May 65

Story of a Small Boy   Eld 9,1983

+ Phil Panaggio
Cleanthis Leonides (or
  Haggopain's Third Wife)   Eld 6,1979

ROSE, REGINALD
Parlor Game   Shk May 60

ROSELIEP, RAYMOND
Lorenzo's Visit [v]   ArkC 2,Win 68

ROSENBERG, WILLIAM S.   [1899-1966]
US song-writer, entertainer & showman
  as Billy Rose
*The Tourists   Ftc Mar/Apr 53
  [*from his syndicated newspaper
  column "Pitching Horseshoes",1949]

ROSENQUEST, CARL M.
The Onyx Vase   TMM Feb 28

ROSENQUEST, J. WESLEY
Return to Death   WT Jan 36
The Secret of the Vault   WT May 38

ROSMANITH, OLGA L.
Seance   StS Apr 40

ROSMOND, BABETTE
One Man's Harp   UW Aug 43
*One Man's Harp   UWB Jan 44
  [also in *FUW,1948].

+ Leonard M. Lake as Babette Rosmond
Lake
Are You Run-Down, Tired -   UW Oct 42
*Are You Run-Down, Tired -   UWB Oct 42

ROSS, BERT DAVID
The Last Adam and Eve [nt]   WT Nov 47
Not Human   WT Sep 46

ROSS, EDITH
The Leopard Woman   GS Jan 29
A Lost Soul's Vengeance   GS Oct 30
Out of the Shadow of Madness GS Aug/Sep 31

ROSS, IRWIN
The Man in the Dark   MoH 12,Win 65/6

ROSS, JIM
A Matter of Time   Ftc Nov 73

ROSS, RANDALL T.
Cross Index   Ftc Feb 55

ROSS, REBECCA
  Pseud: see Dale C. DONALDSON

ROSS, ROSE
Justice in Lost Lady Swamp   GS Jun 30

ROSS, W[illiam] E[dward] D[AN(iel)] [1912-]
Canadian-born US writer prolific in all
popular genres; former actor & journalist
The Hitch-Hiker   Mac 2,Win 57

ROSSE, STEVE
Smiley   TZ Jul 81

ROSSI, WILLIAM A.
Satan is My Lover   UT Nov 39

ROTH, ELEANOR
Embroidered Curse   EC 1,Jul 76

ROTH, I. DANIEL
J.C. in the Springtime   TZ May 82

ROTHAFEL, S[amuel] L[ionel] [1881-1936]
US Theatre Owner
Selected 'My Favorite Ghost Story':
  2."Inn of the Two Witches" by
    Joseph Conrad   GS Feb 30

ROTHBELL, JAY
Paintjob   TZ Oct 81

ROTHERA, LESLIE E.
Beliefs in Peril   Phtm 9,Dec 57

ROTHMAN, MAURICE
The Dream   WT Dec 27

ROTHOVIUS, ANDREW E.
The Gate of Diminishingness   Anu 3,1968
[A Cthulhu Mythos story]

ROTSLER, WILLIAM   [1926-]
US writer, photographer, film-maker and
cartoonist
A New Life   Ftc May 74
War of the Magicians   Ftc Nov 73

ROUSSEAU, VICTOR   [1879-1960]
Best known by-line of the London-born,US-
resident Jewish writer Victor Rousseau
Emanuel, who also wrote as H. M. Egbert
The Angel of the Marne   GS Jul 29
  [by-line shown as Capt.Albert Sewell
  on Contents Page]
The Blackest Magic of All   GS Jul 28
  [see also "Medium For Justice"]
The Case of the Jailor's Daughter
  [IB]   WT Sep 26
The Chairs of Stuyvesant Baron
  [IB]   WT Apr 27
Child or Demon - Which? [DrM]   GS Oct 26
  [see also as by 'Eugene Branscombe']
A Cry From Beyond   ST Sep 31
*A Cry From Beyond   MoH 20,Mar 68
The Curse of Amen-Ra [na]   ST Oct 32
*The Curse of Amen-Ra [na]   BWT 1960
*The Curse of Amen-Ra [na]   MoH 17,Fal 67
The Doll That Came to Life [DrM] GS Jan 27
The Dream That Came True [IB]   WT Jun 27
The Evil Three [n5]   GS Dec 30-Apr 31
The Fetish of the Waxworks [IB] WT Feb 27
Fire, Water - and What? [DrM]   GS Jun 27
The Ghost of the Red Cavalier
  [DrM]   GS Mar 27
He Told Me He Married a Ghost   GS May 27
The House of the Living Dead
  [n6] [DrM]   GS Dec 27-May 28
The Legacy of Hate [IB]   WT Dec 26
The Major's Menagerie [IB]   WT Jan 27
The Man Who Lost His Luck [IB] WT May 27
*Medium For Justice   SMS 4,Spr 67
  [*orig."The Blackest Magic of All"]
Our Astral Honeymoon   GS Jun 28

SAMSON, E. M.
It!   WT May/Jul 24

SAN SOUCI, ROBERT D.
The House of Origins   DFy 22,Mar 80
None Return From Dead Merasha
                              S&T 34,Jan 76
The Perfect Counterspell   S&T 43,Jul 77
Silver Mirror, Red War   Wbk 10,1976

SANDER, ANTHONY
Welcome as Lover, Come O
    Thunder [v]   W&S 5,Jan/Feb 71

SANDERCOMBE, W[illiam] FRASER [1949-]
Canadian free-lance writer & artist
Antique Shop   Wbk 6,1973
Breck   [Breck]   Mb 20,1975
Casmaran   [Breck]   Mb 27,1976
The Cross and the Grave   EC 3,1980
A Death Song [v]   Wbk 4,1971
Donu   Wbk 8,1974
A Flight of Shadows [v]   Wbk 4,1971
He is Satisfied [v]   EC 1,Jul 76
Ketrendel   EC 7,1982
Messenger of Death [v]   Wbk 3,1970
Scarecrow [v]   EC 5,1981
Sheena O'Meara   EC 1,Jul 76
Through the Dark House [Breck] Mb 15,1974
The Wave-Maker [ss]   Wbk 3,1970

SANDERS, FREDERICK
One Fantastic Day   WT Sep 52
The Return of Simon Carib   WT May 54
She Wore a Black Rose   WT May 52

SANDERS, LEWIS
Cry of the Shoggoths [v]   Mb 29,1977
Night Dancers [v]   Nyc 8,Apr 73
Shadowseed [v]   Mb 15,1974
Vampiric Madness [v]   Mb 15,1974

SANDISON, ROBERT C.
Burnt Things   WT Dec 30
River of Lost Souls   WT May 30
The Vrykolakas   WT Apr 32

SANFORD, HOLDEN
Cult For the Living Carcase   UT May 40

SANFORD, MURRAY
Blue Peter   WT Nov 50

SANFORD, NICK
US movie stuntman
My Phantom Pal   GS Aug 29

SANFORD, WILLIAM
Grisley's Reception   WT Apr 25
Midnight Realism   WT Nov 25
The Midnight Visitor   WT Sep 25
The Scarlet Night   WT Mar 23

SANNELLA, A. SHULLA
Tea Time [v]   SPWAO 2,1982

SANTO, SUSAN ANNE
Celebration   S&T 53,Oct 79
Prisoners   S&T 57,Oct 80

SANTORI, HELEN
A Living Doll   BMM Jan 66

'SAPPER'
Pseud: see H. C. McNEILE

SARGENT, E. N.
The Girl in the Mirror   Ftc Mar 58

SARGENT, PAMELA [1948-]
US writer and anthologist
The Broken Hoop   TZ Jun 82
Out of Place   TZ Oct 81
The Shrine   TZ Dec 82

SARGENT, Jr., SAMUEL M.
The Dane   WT Mar 25
The Death Cell [v]   WT Feb 27
Obliteration [v]   WT Oct 27
On Canton Road [v]   WT Aug 26

SARLES, F. WILLIAM
Duval's Weird Experiment   WT Apr 26
The Foe From Beyond   WT Dec 26
Queen of the Vortex   WT May 26

SARNO, LOUIS
The Legend of Denarius   WT Jun 29

SARRANTONIO, AL [1952-]
US writer and former editor
The Brick Cloud   FB Aug 82
The Quiet Ones   Wbk 18,1983
The Return of Mad Santa   FB Feb 82
The Silly Stuff   TZ Oct 82
The Spook Man   TZ Nov 82

SASSAMAN, GARY
Kung Who? [gs;illus. Mike Hodge]
                              FCr 2,Feb 75

SASSER, DAMON
Robert E. Howard Editors'/Publishers'
    Roundtable [sym2]
                    FCr 9-10/11,Aug 76-Mar 77

SATIN, JOSEPH
The Man Who Got Around   BFF Jan 54

SATTER, MARLENE Y.
as Lee Barwood
The Climbing Tree   Wbk 15,1981
Ghost Writer   S&T 57,Oct 80
Glowing Eyes in Darkness [v] FB Nov 82
Rainsong   Wbk 18,1983
Tide Song [v]   SPWAO 2,1982
Turncoat [v]   S&T 64,Sum 83

SATTERFIELD, CHARLES
Pseud: see Frederik POHL & Lester
    DEL REY

SAUL, JOHN
US horror novelist
Interview   TZ Nov 81

SAUNDERS, ALEX
The Scorched Tree   Ggn 4,Sep 47
Truth Gas   Ggn (9) 1948

The Murder of Etelven Thios
[ET]   Wbk 14,1979
My Lady of the Darkwood [J]   Esc Fal 77
Never Argue With Antique Dealers
                              Wyrd 4,1974
*Never Argue With Antique Dealers
                              Ftc Jan 80
A Night in a Haunted Wood   NV 8,Fal 81
The One True God   BL 1,Aug 76
The Other Murder of Etelven
  Thios [ET]   Wbk 15,1981
The Outcast [v]   EC 4,1980
The Phantom Knight   Whsp 19/20,Oct 83
Reflections [v]   EC 1,Jul 76
The Silent Screamers   S&T 11,Apr 71
Something Like the Hobo Bird   Esc Fal 77
The Soul of the Poet   Wbk 12,1977
A Special Purpose   FBDG 3,Apr 74
The Spirit Duplicator   WD 1,1977
The Stones Would Weep   FyT 12,Win 83
The Story of Obbok   Whsp 2,Dec 73
*The Story of Obbok   WA 2,1978
The Story of the Brown Man   FCw 1,Jan 77
*The Story of the Brown Man   FyT 6,Sum 80
A Strange Encounter   NF 1,Win 80/1
Summons [v]   Wbk 3,1970
The Teddy Bear   S&T 49,Oct 78
Tom O'Bedlam's Night Out   Ftc Sep 77
Two Lovers: Three Nights Beneath
  a Balcony [v]   F&T 7,1975
2001½ [spf.cs]   S&T 11,Apr 71
*The Veiled Pool of Mistorak
  [J]   FCw 2,Feb 77
*The Veiled Pool of Mistorak
  [J]   BFWK 1,Aut 78
  [*Void 3,1976]
A Vision of Rembathene   FCr 10/11,Mar 77
The Vision of Tseng Yuan-Li   BL 3,Mar 77
Weird Tales Today [a]   Kad 4,Jul 81
The White Isle [nt] [T&H]   Wbk 9,1975
The White Isle [sn2] [T&H] Ftc Apr-Jul 80
The Wings of the White Bird   Myrd 4,1978
Wrecking Crew   S&T 17,Nov 72

   as Artemis Vreeb
Canoe Ride   S&T 28,Jan 75
[ET - Etelven Thios; J - Sir Julian;
T&H - Throdrexon and Hamakara]

SCITHERS, GEORGE   [1929-]
US editor,writer and fan publisher
  Robert E.Howard Editors'/Publishers'
  Roundtable [sym2]
                         FCr 9-10/11,Aug 76-Mar 77

SCOBEE, BARRY
  The Idol-Chaser   WT Aug 29

SCORTIA, THOMAS N[icholas]   [1926-]
US writer; former chemist
  Broken Image [nt]   Ftc Nov 66
  The Destroyer [nt]   Ftc Jun 65
  End of the Line   Ftc Feb 55
  Morality   Ftc Dec 69

SCOTLAND, JAY
  Pseud: see John W.JAKES

SCOTT, E[ARL] W.
  Haunted [v]   WT Nov 28

  + Marion Scott
  Hurtling Horror   WT Jun 26

SCOTT, GEORGE A.
  The Chateau of Laughing Phantoms
                                GS Jun 29

SCOTT, GEORGE [Ryley]
UK medical writer
  Forbidden Waters   YWS 6(1942)

SCOTT, MAITLAND
  Pseud: see Robert T.M. SCOTT (II)

SCOTT, MARION
  + Earl W.Scott
  Hurtling Horror   WT Jun 26

SCOTT, MARTHA
  Feast Of Blood for the Girl
  Who Couldn't Die   AH Apr 71

SCOTT, PETE
  Stephen King: the Shadow
  Exploded [a]   DH 25,Sum 82

SCOTT, R[eginald] T[homas] M[aitland][1882-]
Canadian writer and novelist. There is
confusion over fiction by this Scott and
his son Robert (see below).
  Nimba, the Cave Girl   WT Mar 23

SCOTT, RIDLEY
UK film director
  Interview   TZ Dec 82

SCOTT, R[obert] T. M[aitland] [?1908-43?]
Canadian writer, son of Reginald T. M.
Scott (see above). The following is be-
lieved to be the work of the son, but is
unconfirmed.
   as Maitland Scott
  Massacre Curse   Ace Sep 36
  Priestess of Pain [nt]   Ace May 36
  Satan's Armchair   Ace Jul 36

SCOTT, Sir WALTER   [1771-1832]
Scottish historical novelist
*The Tapestried Chamber   WT Sep 26
  [*Keepsake Annual for 1829,1828]
*Wandering Willie's Tale   WT Jan 26
  [*Redgauntlet,1824]

SCOTTEN, H. F.
  The Invading Madness   WT Sep 30
  The Thing in the House [nt]   WT May 29
*The Thing in the House [nt] MoH 13,Sum 66

SEABROOK, WILLIAM   [1886-1945]
US author, reporter and explorer
*Wow   WB Dec 50
  [*orig.1921]

SEANNE, VAL
  Hymeneal [v]   Nek 1,Spr 50

SEARIGHT, FRANKLYN
  [son of Richard F.Searight]
  The Innsmouth Head [Cth]   DMR 1,1975
  Interlude at the Bridge [Cth] Pgn 1,May 80

Spawn of Darkness   WT Sep 54
The Watcher Awakes   WT Sep 53

SHAW, LARRY [Taylor]   [1924-]
US author, editor and literary agent
Simworthy's Circus   WB Dec 50

SHAW, LEN
Syllabus   SFy 17,Feb 56

SHAW, MARY C.
Fog [v]   WT Dec 34
*Fog [v]   UTC 7,Jul 41
Remembrance [v]   WT Mar 34

SHAWB, CLAY
Non-Life [v]   Nyc 11/12,Apr 76

SHAYNE, ANTON
Shadow, Shadow   Chl Sep 81

SHEA, MICHAEL   [1947?-]
US writer and fantasy novelist
Nemo Me Impune Lacessit
   [Cth]   Whsp 15/16,Mar 82
Slaves of the Vampire Queen
   [nt]   [Nifft]   PD 3,1977
[Cth - Cthulhu Mythos; Nifft - Nifft the
Lean]

SHEA, J. VERNON   [1912-81]
US laboratory technician, writer and fan
editor.
Obituary   Eld 2,1981
The Circle Manque [a]   Nyc 11/12,Apr 76
A Clerihew [v]   HPL 1972
Five Year Contract   MoH 5,Sep 64
The Flaw   MoH 15,Spr 67
HPL and Films [a]   HPL 1972
Lost in the Corridors of Time   E&O 3,1983
The Secret Member [a]   Whsp 13/14,Oct 79
Soon to be Retired   E&O 2,1983

SHEARON, Mrs. JULIA [TAIT]
The Mystery of the Vanished Bride
                                     GS May 27
*Voodoo and the Virgin   PGS 1963
   [*see "The White Leopard" below]
What a Seventh Daughter Saw   GS Dec 26
The White Leopard   GS Sep 27
   [see rep.as "Voodoo and the Virgin"]

SHECKLEY, ROBERT   [1928-]
US sf/fantasy author and lecturer
Interview   Gam 2,1963
The Altar   Ftc Jul/Aug 53
*Beside Still Waters   Ftc May 67
   [*Amazing Stories Oct/Nov 53]
The Demons   FM Feb/Mar 53
Five Minutes Early   TZ Oct 82
The Hungry   Ftc Jun 54
*The Hungry   Ftc Aug 69
Miss Mouse and the Fourth
   Dimension   TZ Jan 82
Shootout in the Toy Shop   TZ Oct 81
The Swamp   TZ Jul 81
*The Swamp   GSTZ,1982
Three Cautionary Tales   TZ Apr 81
What a Man Believes   Ftc Nov/Dec 53
*What a Man Believes   Ftc Jan 66

Wild Talents, Inc.   Ftc Sep/Oct 53
*Wild Talents, Inc.   Ftc Nov 65

   + Poul Anderson, Isaac Asimov, Robert
   Bloch and Murray Leinster
The Covenant [nt.rr]   Ftc Jul 60

   as Finn O'Donnevan
Feeding Time   FM Feb/Mar 53

SHEDLOFSKY, WALTER   [1917-]
US resident Jewish writer and poet,creator
of the 'Anachuttle' (for example see 'Vapor
Fletch' below)
Ache of an Ancient Avatar [v]   TW 1975
The Book and the Horror [v]   HPL 1972
Cromlech [v]   HPL 1972
Death From Hyades [v]   DFy 11,Jan 77
The Dream Child [v]   F&T 6,1974
The Dreamer's Knell [v]   HPL 1972
The Frightened Waltz   Esc Fal 77
The Ghost-Child [v]   FCr 13,Jun 78
The Ghost Sword [v]   DFy 8,May 76
God Walks   Mb 20,1975
Guillotine [v]   Whsp 1,Jul 73
Many Columned Iram [v]   HPL 1972
Nightmare [v]   ArkC 1,Sum 67
Outsider [v]   Whsp 1,Jul 73
Psychogeist [v]   Wbk 9,1975
The Purple Door [v]   ArkC 4,Win 69
Sitthura Waits [v]   DFy 20,Jul 79
Star Winds [v]   ArkC 6,Win 70
Strange Jewel   EC 8,1982
Vapor Fletch [v]   ArkC 7,Sum 70
Verse of Necromancy [v]   F&T 7,1975
Weird Tales [v]   Wbk 2,1969
Ylalotha [v]   Wbk 10,1976
Zothique [v]   DFy 6,Jan 75

SHEEDY, S. R.
Isis Faces Crisis [a]   Nek 5,mid-51
Laptoumi Araptoumi [a]   Nek 4,Win 50/1

SHEEHAN, PERLEY POORE   [1875-1943]
US author, newspaperman and scenarist
Down the Coast of Shadows
   [nt2]   TB Apr 15-May 1,19
The Hank of Yarn   TB Apr 1,19
*Monsieur de Guise   WT Sum 74
   [*The Scrap Book Jan 1911]

SHEFFIELD, CHARLES   [1935-]
UK-born US-resident computer businessman
Crocuses   WT 4,Sum 83
Power Failure [nt]   Ftc Apr 78
The Treasure of Odirex [nt]
   [ED]   Ftc Jul 78
We Hold These Truths to be
   Self-Evident   Ftc Dec 77
[ED - Erasmus Darwin]

SHEFFIELD, M. K.
The First Circle [v]   FBDG 3,Apr 74

SHELDEN, PAMELA J.
   + Kurt Paul
Daylight Nightmares [a]   Goth Jun 79

SHELDON, ALICE   [1916-]
US psychologist and sf writer
   as James Tiptree, Jr.
Fault   Ftc Aug 68

[Ai - Aihai(Tales set on Mars); At - Tales
of Atlantis; Av - Averoigne; Cth - Cthulhu
Mythos; Hy - Hyperborea; X - Xiccarph]
Z - Zothique]
[See also notes under Charles Baudelaire
and William Beckford]

SMITH, CORDWAINER   [1913-66]
Pseud. used on all sf by US Professor of

Asiatic Studies Paul Myron Linebarger
*Drunkboat [nt]   StF 12,Sum 70
  [*Amazing Stories Oct 63]
The Fife of Bodidharma   Ftc Jun 59

SMITH, DALE R.
Why Abdul Alhazred Went Mad
  [Cth]   Nek 3,Aut 50
  +Leroy B. Haugsrud
Deities, Inc.   SFy 42,Aug 60
[Cth - Cthulhu Mythos]

SMITH, DAVID C[laude]   [1952-]
US writer
Aliastra the Sorceress   S&T 39,Nov 76
The Apach' Curse   S&T 17,Nov 72
Aragot   Div 23,Nov 77
The Blood Ransom of Ikribu   S&T 45,Nov 77
*Come, Death   [Dev]   ToF 1,Spr 82
  [*Belial 3,1976]
Continuing the Characters of
  Robert E. Howard [col]   Db Spr 78
The Dark   [Cth]   S&T 23,Mar 74
Demon   Mb 18,1974
Descales' Skull   S&T 19,Jul 73
Dragon's Jaw and Twin Pillars
  [Dev]   S&T 41,Mar 77
The End of Days [na2]
                               Chac 1-2,Win 76-Spr 77
Ithtidzik   TW 1975
The Jewel of the Sorcerer's
  Daughter   E&O 2,1983
The Last Words of Imatus Istum F&T 6,1974
Tellus Mater   S&T 33,Nov 75
Tomb Beasts   Mb 22,1976
Tommy's Cat   S&T 37,Jul 76
Yasdis' Vengeance   Div 9,Jun 75
[Cth - Cthulhu Mythos; Dev - Dever]

SMITH, DEAN W[esley]
Bleeding Letters [v]   Div 24,Jan 78
Frankenstein Love   Div 20,May 77
Instinctive Love   Div 15,Jul 76

SMITH,Ph.D., E[dward] E[lmer] [1890-1965]
US chemist and sf author
The Open Mind [a]   Biz Jan 41

SMITH, Lady ELEANOR [Furneaux][1902-45]
UK novelist, reporter and film critic
Satan's Circus   WT Oct 31

SMITH, EVELYN E.   [1927-]
The Agony of the Leaves [nt]   BFF Jul 54
Call Me Wizard [na]   BFF Jan 54
Dragon Lady   BFF 10,1955

SMITH, GEORGE O[liver] [1911-81]
US radio engineer and sf author
*The Firing Line   UWB Win 45
  [*Astounding SF Dec 44]

SMITH, GORD
Dollars   CT 2,Jul 77

SMITH, Mrs. HARRY PUGH
The Hook of Death   WT Jan 24

SMITH, JAMES W.
Corsairs   DFy 6,Jan 75
The Gamble   DFy 3,Mar 74

SMITH, JOSHUA   [?-1930]
US stage magician
  as Signor Bellini
The Man Who Outwitted the Devil GS May 31

SMITH, JUNIUS B.
US lawyer and astrologer
An Arc of Direction   WT Jun 25
The Man Who Dared to Know   WT Apr 24
Unexpected   TB Sep 1,19
  + J.U. Giesy
Ebenezer's Casket [nt2] WT Apr-May/Jul 24

SMITH, K. E.
Incident   SFy 22,Apr 57

SMITH, LAURENCE D.
Call of the Claw   EM Apr/May 39
Castle of Death   Wtch Nov 36
[see also under Alonzo Deen Cole]

SMITH, MICHAEL S.
Alive and Well in... [ss]   TZ Oct 82

SMITH, PAULINE C[oggeshall] [1908-]
US mystery writer
House of Evil   W&S 5,Jan/Feb 71
Last Rites   Cov Jan 70
The People Next Door   MysT Jun 52

SMITH, RALPH C.
Lee Fu Lin Goes Home   MM Dec 31

SMITH, RICHARD
The Chennaut [v]   DH 23,Sum 81

SMITH, ROBERT W.
Ray Bradbury: Literature as
  Lark [in]   Whsp 19/20,Oct 83

SMITH, SHELLEY
  Pseud: see Nancy BODINGTON

SMITH, TEVIS CLYDE   [1908-]
Hindu Evil   FCr 9,Aug 76
John Bourbon [v]   FCw 2,Feb 77
On an Ancient Shore [v]   FCr 12,Nov 77
Paganini [v]   FCr 13,Jun 78
The Phantom Athlete   FCr 6,Nov 75
Rough Love Pays   FCr 8,May 76
Three Slugs of Lead   DFy 14,Sep 77
Trouble With Tezcatlipoca [v] FCw 3,Feb 77
What Robert Howard Said on
  Wednesday Night [v]   FCr 13,Jun 78
Wulfdene [v]   FCw 1,Jan 77
  + Harold Preece
Two Views of Bob Howard FCr 10/11,Mar 77

SMITH, THORNE   [1892-1934]
US novelist and humorist
*Sex, Love and Mr.Owen   DW Feb 57
  [*a chapter from Rain in the
    Doorway,1933]

SMITH, WALTER G.
Mental Projection [a]   Mystic May 54

SMITH, WARD
Tarantula   Chl Jul 81

STEELE II, ADDISON
    Pseud: see Richard A. LUPOFF

STEELE, I. E.
Kiss of Fire [ss]   S&T 46,Jan 78

STEELE, WILBUR DANIEL   [1886-1970]
US author
*The Woman at Seven Brothers   GS Aug 29
    [*Land's End & Other Stories,1918]

STEGALL, HELEN
Darkdreamer [v]   DFd 4,Win 83

STEGER, SHELBY
Stay With Me   WT Mar 50

STEICHART, A. J.
The Shaver Mystery - Dangerous
    Nonsense [a]   Ftc Jul 58

STEIGER, BRAD   [1936-]
*Pseud. used by US teacher of creative
writing and specialist on psychic pheno-
mena Eugene E. Olson*
Three Tales For the Horrid at
    Heart:
    Rapport I; Rapport II;
    Rapport III   Ftc Jan 63
Two More Tales for the Horrid
    at Heart:
    Sacrifice Play
    One Too Many   Ftc Aug 63

STEINBECK, JOHN [Ernst]   [1902-68]
US novelist and Nobel Prizewinner
*The Affair at 7 Rue de M- MoH 12,Win 65/6
    [*orig.1954]

STEINER, PAUL
Boy Meets Dream Girl [col]   DW May 57
It Sounds Fantastic, But...
    [col]   Ftc Mar-Apr 57
Windfalls [col]   DW Feb 57

STEINHAUER, R. G.
The Songs Are of Earth   Ftc Oct 80

'STELLA'
    Pseud: see Stella KING

STEMONS, JAMES SAMUEL
The Moon That Rose Twice in
    One Night [ts]   Mystic May 54

STENGREAVE, FRANCIS
The Haunted Ship [nt]   FGS(1938)

STEPHENS, CHARLES M.
    see under pseud: Stephen BAGBY

STEPHENS, GENEVIEVE K.
Deserted House   Ggn 6,Jan 48
On This Night .[v]   Ggn (9) 1949
Two of Us Lie [v]   Nek 5,mid-51

STEPHENS, MOYE E.
    + Jim Hiatt
Ghosts of the Air   WT Jun 26

STERLING, GEORGE   [1869-1926]
US poet
*Satan and Lilith [v]   WT Nov 28
    [*extract from "A Wine of Wizardry"
    Cosmopolitan Sep 1907; other lines
    were used for Virgil Finlay's pic-
    torial series in WT Dec 37, Feb 39,
    Mar 39 and May 39]

STERLING, KENNETH   [1920-]
US physician
    + H.P. Lovecraft
In the Walls of Eryx [nt]   WT Oct 39
*In the Walls of Eryx [nt]   ASFR 3,1951

STERN, Jr., MAURICE MAX
The Puppet That Came to Life . GS Mar 29

STERN, PAUL F.
    Pseud: see Paul ERNST

STEVENS, FRANCIS
    Pseud: see Gertrude BENNETT

STEVENS, HAROLD
Junkman   Ftc May 65

STEVENS, WILLIAM
The Room of Yellow Shadows   GS Jun 29

STEVENSON, ROBERT LOUIS   [1850-94]
Scottish novelist and poet
*Markheim   WT Apr 27
    [*The Merry Men & Other Fables,1887]

STEWART, ALFRED WALTER
    as J.J. Connington
The Thinking Machine   WT May 39

STEWART, CHARLES
Why Are They Dying?   GS Jun 30

STEWART, CLARE DOUGLAS
The Web of Death   TB Mar 15,19

STEWART, EDITH LICHTY
The Sixth Tree   WT May/Jul 24
*The Sixth Tree   WT Feb 34

STEWART, RICHARD ADDISON
The Preacher   EC 1,Jul 76

STILL, HENRY
Catalyst   Ftc Feb 61
Gold is Anywhere   Ftc Apr 55
The Long Forgotten   Ftc Aug 56
Operation Scrumblies   Ftc Aug 58
While My Love Waits   Ftc Feb 55

STILLMAN, GRACE
The Woods of Averoigne [v]   WT Jun 34

STINE, G[eorge] HARRY   [1928-]
US engineer and writer
    as Lee Correy
Coffin Run [nt]   Ftc Aug 57

STINE, HANK [Henry Eugene]   [1945-]
US writer, editor & former filmmaker
    + Larry Niven
No Exit   Ftc Jun 71

STYRON, ARTHUR
The Artist of Tao   ST Oct 32
*The Artist of Tao   MoH 36,Apr 71
The Clock   WT Jun 25
The Lip   WT May 25

SUALEE, MILIKA
Queen of the Martian Women WST Jul/Aug 72

SUDOL, ROBERT C. [1954-]
Threshold to Doomcrack   HPL 1972

SUGAR, ANDY
106   BMM Oct 65

SUGARMAN, LOUAL B.
The Gray Death   WT Jun 23
*The Gray Death   WT May 34

SULLIVAN, CHESTER
The Eggs of Hann   Ariel 4,Oct 78

SULLIVAN, CRAWFORD
The Spare Room   WT Jul 44

SULLIVAN, JACK
US teacher of English and Humanities
L. P. Hartley [a]   TZ Dec 82
No Light Ahead [a]   Whsp 15/16,Mar 82

SULLIVAN, J[OSEPH] P[ATRICK] D.
Ganymede [v]   DFy 9,Sep 76
Glories Lost and Won   DFy 5,Oct 74
Satan's Jest [v]   DFy 21,Oct 79
Words, Dreams and a Blade DFy 6,Jan 75

SULLIVAN, THOMAS   [1940-]
The Death Runner   TZ Apr 81

SULLIVAN, TIMOTHY ROBERT
Zeke   TZ Oct 81

SULLY, HELEN
Memories of Lovecraft: II [a]
                           ArkC 4,Win 69

SUMMERS, K.
She Used Her Head   MM Aug 31

SUPRENANT, W. J.
Guardian   WT Jul 54
The Stormcliff Papers   WT Jan 54

SURD, ABE
Pseud: see Peter SIDEBOTTHAM

SUTER, J. PAUL   [1899-?]
Abyss Under the World [s2] WT Aug-Sep 37
The Answer of the Dead   WT Mar 32
Beyond the Door   WT Apr 23
*Beyond the Door   WT Sep 30
*Beyond the Door   WT May 54
The Guard of Honor   WT Jul/Aug 23
*The Guard of Honor   WT Jan 52
A Midnight Confession   WT Aug 32
Prisoner of the Dead   WT Nov 23
The Superior Judge   WT Aug 33
The Wolf in the Dark   GS Feb 31
The Woman With Two Souls   GS Jan 27

SUTHERLAND, DONALD
Interview   TZ Oct 83

SUTHERLAND, HALLIDAY
*Valley of Doom   WB Feb 51
  [*Fantasy No.2,1939]

SUTTON, ANDREW
Pseud: see E. C. TUBB

SUTTON, DAVID A[mbrose] [1947-]
UK postal officer; small press editor and
writer. [see Editor Index]
Interview   DH 12,Aut/Win 75
Ben's Beeches   DH 18(1978)
The Cinema of Roman Polanski
  [a]   DH 22,Spr 81
The Collector   DH 15,Win 76
Corruption   FyM 1,Sep 80
The Cosmic in Fiction [a] DH 8,Apr 74
The Cosmic in Films [a] DH 10,Aut/Win 74
The Cosmic in Music [a] DH 9,Sum 74
The Dead Field   Goth Jun 79
*Demoniacal   [Cth] Cth 3,1978
*Demoniacal (in Italian) Kad 2,May 80
  [*New Writings in Horror & the Super-
  natural Vol.2 ed.Sutton,1972; see
  sequel "The Kiss of Bugg-Shash" by
  Brian Lumley]
A Dream [v]   WW 1,Jun 70
The Golden Age of British Horror
  Fanzines [a2]   DH 1-2,1971-72
In the Catacomb [v]   WW 2,Mar 71
The Invisible Prince [a] DH 23,Sum 81
The Lady in Gray [v]   WW 1,Jun 70
Paradox: The Worlds of M. C.
  Escher [a]   DH 13,Spr 76
Return to the Runes   G&S 2,1980
Die Spinnen   SPWAO 2,1982

  + Michael Barrett
Brian Lumley: Latter Day
  Lovecraftian [a/in] DH 14,Sum 76
*Brian Lumley: Latter Day
  Lovecraftian [a/in] Nyc 13,May 77

SUTTON, GERTRUDE MACAULEY
Gesture   WT Sep 30

SUTTON, PAUL FRANCIS
Ballad of Winds [v]   WT Aug 29

SWAIN, ALICE M.
The Way of our Going [v] Mac 5,Sum 69

SWAIN, DWIGHT V[reeland] [1915-]
US author and lecturer
*The Bottle Imp [nt]   Ftc Dec 70
  [*Fantastic Adventures Sep 42]

SWAIN, FREDERICK
The Headless Chinaman GS May 29

SWAIN, JOHN D.
Hunger   WT Oct 27
Lucifer   WT Nov 23
*Lucifer   WT Dec 30

SWANN, CARL
The White Horse   MM Sep/Oct 31

TANNAHILL, SUSAN L.
After Reading Lovecraft's "The
  Statement of Randolph Carter"
  [v]   Spoor 1,1974
The Elphin Knight [v]   DH 19(1979)
In the Dark and the Light of
  the Moon   Wbk 11,1977
Old Houses [v]   Wbk 8,1974
Treasure Quest [v]   F&T 6,1974
Vampyre [v]   Mb 25,1976

TANNER, CHARLES R.   [1896-1974]
Out of the Jar   SFF Feb 41
The Princess of Mars, by Edgar
  Rice Burroughs [v]   Ftc Aug 68
*Tumithak of the Corridors [na] Ftc Oct 79
  [*Amazing Stories Jan 32]

TANNER, JOHN
  Pseud: see Jack MATCHA

TARLETON, FISWOODE
The Blue Lizard   WT Jun 28

TARLETON, J. PHILIP
Love is the Color of Blood   AH Oct 70

TAROKATH, CARMUTH
  Pseud: see William TREDINNICK

TARVER, A. MALCOLM
The Curse of the Old Oak Chest TU 2(1927)
The Inca's Ruby   MyS 20(1939)
The Sea Ghost   TU 3(1938)

TATE, PETER
UK journalist and writer
The First Last Martyr   Imp 6,Aug 66
Same Autumn, in a Different
  Park   Ftc Sep 67
*The Thinking Seat [nt]   Ftc May 67
  [*New Worlds SF Nov 66]

TATE, ROBIN
  Pseud: see R. Lionel FANTHORPE and
    Harry O. MANSFIELD

TAURASI, JAMES V[incent]   [1917-]
US insulation engineer; early sf fan
The Cosmic Reporter [a]   Vor 2,1947
Magician of Space   UTC 14,Feb 42

TAVEREL, JOHN
  Pseud: see Robert E. HOWARD

TAYLOR, ALVIN
  + Len J.Moffatt
Father's Vampire   WT May 52

TAYLOR, CHUCK
Call it Complacency or Wise
  Resignation [v]   Arg 9,Fal 83

TAYLOR, F. J.
Artist's Model   Phtm 3,Jun 57
The Empty Platform   Phtm 1,Apr 57
Shadow on the Sand   Phtm 2,May 57

TAYLOR, FRANCES M.
My Adventures With the Sixth
  Sense [a]   GS Jan 30

TAYLOR, HERBERT HALL
The Crime of the Third Chamber
  [a]   GS May 31
Little Brown Dwarf [ts]   GS Aug/Sep 31
When Lincoln Saw His Own
  Phantom [a]   GS Feb 31
Witch Orchard [a]   GS Oct 30

TAYLOR, JAMES
Arthur Machen: Forgotten Master
  of Fantasy [a]   Nyc 8,Apr 73

TAYLOR, JOHN A[LFRED]   [1931-]
US teacher and writer
Arthur   EC 5,1981
Deep Calls to Deep   EC 4,1980
Despair Thy Charm   Wbk 18,1983
Fist in a Box   S&T 58,Jan 81
From Hell   S&T 57,Oct 80
Gloves: 1 pr   S&T 62,Sum 82
Hell is Murky   TZ Nov 82
The Horn of the Hunter   EC 7,1982
The Hounds of Persephone   S&T 49,Oct 78
I Hae Dream'd a Dreary
  Dream   Arg 8,Fal/Win 81
Kedward's Box   S&T 63,Win 82/3
Like a Black Dandelion   TZ Oct 83
The Measure of Your Foot   S&T 55,Apr 80
Passing the Love of Women   EC 6,1982
The Quilt   EC 3,1980
Straight From the Comet's
  Mouth   S&T 47,Apr 78
When the Cat's Away   TZ Sep 81
Winner Take All   S&T 64,Sum 83

TAYLOR, KEITH
Australian sf/fantasy writer
  as Dennis More
The Atheling's Wife   [F]   Ftc Aug 76
Buried Silver [nt]   [F]   Ftc Feb 77
The Forest of Andred [nt] [F] Ftc Nov 76
Fugitives in Winter [nt] [F] Ftc Oct 75
[F - Felimid the Bard]

TAYLOR, L. A.
Double Indemnity   Arg 9,Fal 83
A Shorter History   S&T 65,Win 83/4

TAYLOR, LEON
Life   S&T 9,Jul 70

TAYLOR, MERLIN MOORE   [1886-?]
US journalist and author
The Place of Madness   WT Mar 23

TAYLOR, OLIVER
The Burglar-Proof Vault   MoH 8,Apr 65

TAYLOR, REBECCA
Once [v]   Eld 2,1981

TAYLOR, SAMUEL M.
*Memory Test   MysT Jun 52
  [*Crowell-Collier,1939]

TEALBY, MICHAEL
Here Comes the Bogy Man!   Nek 5,mid-51

TEASDALE, L. F.
Sawdust But no Spangles   Phtm 4,Jul 57

The Haunted Writing Manual   'Ftc Oct 75
One Magic Ring, Used   Ftc May 76
Parker Frightened on a Tightrope
                  Ftc Nov 76
Sound Tract: The Making of a
  Thoroughbred   Ftc May 74

THWAITES, Col. NORMAN G[raham] [1864-?]
The Legend of Newberry Castle   GS Aug 27
My Seance With Margery the
  Medium [a]   GS May 27
Revealed By a Ouija Board   GS Nov 26
"What a Man Sows - "   GS Jan 27

TIBBETTS, GEORGE F[ranklin]
From Out the Vasty Deep   GS May 31
Green Death   GS Dec 31/Jan 32

TIBBETTS, JOHN   [1946-]
US writer, editor and commercial artist
A Dialogue   Eld 6,1979
Dream Along With Me [play] Eld 8,1982
Enough Light [play]   Eld 7,1980
The Game   Eld 8,1982
In Clouded Spring [v]   Eld 8,1982
Jumper [v]   Eld 9,1983
Nightmare [v]   Eld 7,1980
The Traveller   Eld 7,1980
The Well at the Half-Cat   Eld 5,1979

'TIBERIUS'
Witches Song [v]   WWd 2(1956)
*Witches' Song [v]   Phtm 1,Apr 57

TIEDEMANN, M. WILLIAM
The Spacer Walks   S&T 65,Win 83/4

TIERNEY, RICHARD L.
US writer and poet
The Altar [v]   Whsp 1,Jul 73
Apocalypse [v]   FyM 3,Jun 82
Carcosa [v]   ArkC 5,Sum 69
Countdown for Kalara [nt] S&T 56,Jul 80
The Creatures   Eld 3,Mar 78
Cthulhu in Mesoamerica [a]   HPL 1972
Demon-Star [v]   Nyc 6,Feb 72
The Derleth Mythos [a]   HPL 1972
The Doom Prophet [v]   HPL 1972
[*The Doomsday Poems [7v] TZ May 82]
  [*all listed separately below; from
   Collected Poems,1981]
The Dreadful City [v]   Div 5,Oct 74
The Dream   FBDG 2,Dec 72
The Eggs of Pawa   Eld 2,1981
[Evil Dreams: Sonnets of the
  Outer Dark [6v - see below]Nyc 6,Feb 72]
The Evil House [v]   Nyc 8,Apr 73
Found in a Storm-Destroyed
  Lighthouse [v]   HPL 1972
Fulfillment [v]   Nyc 7,Aug 72
The Garret Room [v]   Nyc 5,Oct 71
Gods [v]   F&T 7,1975
Hate [v]   E&O 1,1973
The Hills [v]   Nyc 6,Feb 72
Homesickness [v]   Nyc 9,Jul 74
*Hope [v]   TZ May 82
H.P.L. and the Cosmic Quality
  in Fiction [a]   Div 14,May 76
The Hydrogen Bomb [v]   Div 19,Mar 77
  [see rep. as "To the Hydrogen Bomb"]

The Ice-Woman's Prophecy   FCr 12,Nov 77
  [Chap.4 of rr. "Genseric's Fifth-
  Born Son"]
In Evil Dreams [v]   Nyc 6,Feb 72
In Halls of Fantasy [v] Whsp 2,Dec 73
Jack the Ripper [v]   E&O 1,1973
The Legend [v]   Mac 18,Win 65/6
Madness of the Oracle [v]   Myrd 3,1976
*Madness of the Oracle [v]   TZ May 82
The Man in the Evil Garrett Nyc 18,Apr 83
A Man of Discretion   E&O 1,1973
Minas Morgul [v]   FCr 15,Jan 79
Moubata [v]   E&O 1,1973
Mountains of Madness [v] Mac 14,Win 63/4
*Mountains of Madness [v]   HPL 1972
The Nereid [v]   Div 12,Jan 76
Night Visitant [v]   Whsp 5,Nov 74
Old King Kull [v]   Div 8,Apr 75
*Optimism [v]   TZ May 82
*The Pilgrimage [v]   TZ May 82
The Pinnacles [v]   Nyc 6,Feb 72
Prayer to Zathog [v]   FCr 13,Jun 78
Richard L. Tierney: His Book
  [a]   Nyc 7,Aug 72
Sabbat [v]   ArkS 2,Sep 83
The Scrolls [v]   E&O 1,1973
Sonnet to a Boxelder Bug [v] DMR 1,1975
Tahuantin-Suyu [v]   F&T 7,1975
*This Great City [v]   TZ May 82
To Gorice XII, King in Carce
  [v]   Whsp 4,Jul 74
To Great Cthulhu [v]   ArkC 9,Spr 71
*To Great Cthulhu [v]   TZ May 82
*To Great Cthulhu [v]   ArkS 2,Sep 83
To Mount Sinai [v]   HPL 1972
*To the Hydrogen Bomb [v]   TZ May 82
  [*orig."The Hydrogen Bomb"above]
A Vision on a Midsummer
  Night [v]   Nyc 10,Jan/Feb 75
The Volcano [v]   Nyc 6,Feb 72
The Wendigo [v]   ArkC 6,Win 70
When the Stars are Right [a] E&O 1,1973
Wrath of Tupan   FCr 10/11,Mar 77
Yahweh [v]   Mac 18,Win 65/6
*Yahweh [v]   Div 14,May 76
Zarria [v]   Nyc 6,Feb 72

  completion of fragment by Edgar Allan
  Poe
The Lighthouse   Nyc 14,Mar 78
*The Lighthouse   E&O 2,1983
  [see also comp.of same fragment by
  Robert Bloch]

TIFTON, LEO
  Pseud: see Gerald W. PAGE

'TIGRINA'
  Pseud: see Edythe EIDE

TILBURNE, A. R.
US artist and author [see Artist Index]
  as Lee Tilburne
*Handmade Hero   WT(Can)May 45
  [*Short Stories Feb 10,1944]

TILBURNE, LEE
  Pseud: see A. R. TILBURNE

TILEY, VALERIE   [1955-]
US Veterinarian's Assistant
On a Chill October's Eve [v] SPWAO 2,1982

TORRO, PEL
  Pseud: see R. Lionel FANTHORPE and
  Harry O. MANSFIELD

TOSTIG, ALVIN
  Ant Hell   WST Jul/Aug 72

TOTH, ALBERT
  Beyond Ka-ree [v]   Ggn(9) 1949

TOTHERTON, DAN W.
  Called Back   WT May/Jul 24

TOWNSON, PRIMROSE
  The Permanent Tenant   Phtm 1,Apr 57

TOYE, ERIC
  Deathday [cs]   S&T 30,May 75

TRACY, DON
  The Bald-Headed Man   StS Oct 40

TRAFF, FREDERICK
  *Doctor of Doodling   UTC 13,Jan 42

TRAFTON, THOMAS
  The Castaway Slave [ts]   WT Jul 40

TRAJORE, FRANZ
  In the Second Astral [na4]
                                 MM Jun-Sep/Oct 31
  The Soul Raiders [nt2]   MM Nov-Dec 31

TRANSEAU, T. E.
  The Case of the Man Blind   TB Sep 15,19

TRAVEN, B.   [1882-1969]
  Best known US identity of German-born
  writer & novelist Otto Feige.
  The Third Guest [nt]   Ftc Mar/Apr 53
  *The Third Guest [nt]   Ftc May 66

TREAT, LAWRENCE
  *Coffin House   WT(Can)Sep 44
    [*Short Stories Sep 25,1943]

TREDINNICK, Jr., WILLIAM/BILL [1946-]
  US free-lance author
  Dragons, Snakes and Wiverns [a]   TW 1975
  The Fate That Money Can Buy [WJ] EC 5,1981
  Last Anniversary   Mb 29/30,1977
  Legend of the Vampire [a]   Mb 8,1972
  Pre-Islamic Evil Jinn [a]   Mb 10,1973
  The Shape Changers (Part 1)   Mb 7,1972
  The Shape Changers (Parts 2 & 3) Mb 28,1976

    as Sol Kaneman
  Alone With Fate   [WJ]   Mb 14,1974
  Capo Mafioso's Fate   [WJ] Mb 20,1975
  A Devil in Time Makes   Mb 8,1972
  Faces of Fate   [WJ]   Mb 17,1974
  Fate Levels   [WJ]   Mb 14,1974
  Fate's Send-Off   [WJ]   Mb 24,1976
  Filet [v]   Mb 21,1975
  A Foolish/Ghoulish Mistake
    [v]   Wyrd 6,Win 76/7
  For All the Pre-1950 Igors [v] Mb 25,1976
  I'll Conserve You   Mb 8,1972
  It Will End Here   Mb 20,1975
  One Night With Fate [v]   Mb 29/30,1977
  Searching For Fate [WJ]   Mb 9,1973

The Shape of Fate   [WJ]   Mb 17,1974
There'll Be a Hot Time in the
  Old Mound Tonight [v]   Mb 20,1975
Waiting For Fate   [WJ]   Mb 9,1973
When Fate Summons [v]   Mb 29/30,1977
You Can't Make a Silk Bed Out
  of a Sow's Ear [v]   Mb 28,1976

    as Sol Kaneman & Bill Tredinnick
Eternal Fate   [WJ]   Wbk 13,1978
Fate Dine's Out   [WJ]   Wbk 12,1977
The Fate of Enoch Whately [WJ] Wbk 15,1981
Fate's Private Viewing [WJ]   Wbk 11,1977
The Lamp of Fate   [WJ]   Wbk 11,1977

    as Carmuth Tarokath
Destination [ss]   Wbk 4,1971
[WJ - The Wandering Jew]

TREFON, HENRY
  The Velvet Death [ts]   WT Sep 23

TREMAINE, F[rederick] ORLIN [1899-1956]
  US editor and author
    as Orlin Frederick
  The Throwback   WT Oct 26

TREMAYNE, PETER
  Pseud: see Peter Berresford ELLIS

TRENERY, GLADYS GORDON
  Pseud: see G. G. PENDARVES

TRENT, DICK
  Rue Morgue Revisited   HST 1,1972
  Witches of Amen Ra   HST 1,1972

TRENT, OLAF
  Pseud: see R. Lionel FANTHORPE

TREVOR, ELLESTON [1920-]
  Legal name of UK thriller writer and
  novelist born Trevor Dudley-Smith but
  now better known as Adam Hall.
  The Chicken Switch   SFy 71,Apr 65

    as Trevor Dudley-Smith
  The Immortal Guardian   WS 1(1943)
  Milky Throws a Boomerang   WPL 1(1943)
    [non-fantasy filler]

TREVOR, OTIS
  The Ghost of Death [ts]   WT Jun 23

TRIEM, PAUL ELLSWORTH
  The Evening Wolves [nt2]   WT Jun-Jul 23
  Vials of Insects   WT May 23

TRIMBLE, KAREN G.
  The Awakening [v]   FB Aug 82

TRISLER, T. L.
  Richard Lynn [in]   FCr 3,May 75

TRISSEL, LAWRENCE A.
  My Love [v]   Mac 22,1973

TRITTEN, LARRY
  Three Bananas   TZ Mar 82

TROUT, ROBERT
  *D-Day   MysT Mar 52

TUTTLE, LISA   [1952-]
US writer and critic, now resident in UK
At a Time Very Near the End Shyl 3,Sum 79
The Birds of the Moon   Ftc Jan 79
Colin Wilson [in]   TZ Apr 83
Community Property   Shyl 4,Win 80
A Friend in Need   TZ Aug 81
The Other Room   Whsp 17/18,Aug 82
A Piece of Rope   Shyl 1,Nov 77
Roald Dahl [in]   TZ Feb 83
Sangre   Ftc Jun 77

   + Steven Utley
Uncoiling   Ftc Apr 78

TWAIN, MARK   [1835-1910]
Regular pen name of US humorist and writer
Samuel Langhorne Clemens.
*A Dying Man's Confession   WT Oct 30
*The Undying Head   MoH 1,Aug 63

TYRRELL, M. E.
US clerical worker
The Other Gothic [a] Div 26/7,May/Jul 78
Valley of the Lost Soul Arg 6,Sum/Fal 79

TYSON, ARNOLD
House name used by Harold Hersey and poss-
ibly by one other.
   by Harold Hersey
Aglaia [v]   TB Jun 15,19
The Battle [v]   TB May 1,19
Freedom [v]   TB Apr 15,19

   by poet unknown
Life's Last Song [v]   TB Sep 1,19
Love's Silence [v]   TB Oct 1,19

TYSON, DONALD   [1954-]
Canadian writer
Cruising   TZ Sep 82

TYSON, JEANNE MARIE
Night Landing   Mac 4,Win 58
Two Loves [v]   Mac 5,Sum 59

UCHNO, EDWARD   [1951-]
Blood Money   Ftc Apr 80

ULMER, ROBERT EUGENE
The Headless Horror   WT Apr 25
The Strange Case of Pascal   WT Jun 26
*The Strange Case of Pascal   SMS 2,Fal 66
   [by-line given as Roger Eugene Ulmer]

UNDERWOOD, JOHN
Cosmic Cosmetics [v]   S&T 61,Win 81/2

UNDERWOOD, W. E.
The Death of Time [v]   WT Apr 27

UPPER, JOSEPH
Dregs [v]   WT Oct 28

URBAN, HELEN M.   [1915-]
Pass the Salt   SFy 13,Apr 55

USCHOLD, MAUD E.
Old Ghosts [v]   WT Jan 29

USSACK, INA RAE
The Litter   Mb 18,1974

UTLEY, STEVE[N]   [1949-]
US writer and proofreader
Abaddon   Shyl 3,Sum 79
Dog in the Manger   Shyl 5,Win 82
In Brightest Day, In Brightest
   Night   Ftc Feb 77
The Mouse Ran Up the Clock   Ftc Jan 79
My Lady Sleeping [v]   Shyl 1,Nov 77
Ocean   Ftc Aug 76
Rex and Regina [v]   Shyl 2,Feb 78
To 1966   Chac 2,Spr 77

   as Septimus Dale
Goodbye to All of That   Shyl 1,Nov 77
Report to Montezume   Shyl 4,Win 80

   as Bruce Holt
Mr. Wyatt in Darkest Africa Shyl 1,Nov 77

   + Lisa Tuttle
Uncoiling   Ftc Apr 78

UTTER, VIRGIL
Morgan Le Fay   Ggn 4,Sep 47
Red Star [v]   Ggn(11) 1949
Walpurga's Night [v]   Ggn(8) 1948

VADIS, WALDO Q.   (pseud)
Fornicator 101   WST Jul/Aug 72

VAGOVSKY, DANA
The Statue   EC 4,1980

VALENTINE, DEBORAH
(untitled) [v]   Nyc 18,Apr 83

VAN, HARRY
   Pseud: see Harry V. SCHREINER

VAN DE VERG, LOUISE
The Three   WT Feb 29

VAN DE WATER, VIRGINIA TERHUNE [1865-1945]
US novelist; sister of Albert P. Terhune
Ghosts I Have Loved [a]   GS May 29

VAN DER VEER, KATHERINE
Drums of the Congo [v]   WT Mar 35
Place Names [v]   WT Jan 34
A Ship is Sailing [v]   WT Aug 34

VAN DER VEER, STEWART
The Yellow Specter   WT Apr 26

VAN HELSING, KURT
   Pseud: see T. E. D. KLEIN

VAN HOESEN, ALLAN
But - He Couldn't Kill Her Ghost!
                                GS Sep 26
The Day I Lived Backwards   GS Aug 28

WAGNER, GEOFFRY
Autogeddon   Ftc Oct 62

WAGNER, IRVIN L[eo]
[see Editor Index]
First of the Litter   WD 2,1980
The Imaginary Emperor   Arg 5,Win/Spr 79
The Last King of Landomir Arg 7,Fal/Win 80
Little Mary Module   [v]   Div 7,Feb 75
Nowhere Man   S&T 25,Jul 74
The Seven Steps to Salvation Wyrd 1,Jun 73
Someday We'll Look Back on
  This and Shudder   Div 2,Jul 74

WAGNER, KARL EDWARD   [1945-]
US writer, anthologist and specialty
publisher
Interview   NV 6,Sum 80
Beyond Any Measure [nt] Whsp 15/16,Mar 82
The Coming of Ghor [rr] FCr 10/11,Mar 77
  [Chap.2 of rr."Generic's Fifth-
  Born Son"]
The Dark Muse   [nt] [Kane] MS 2,Sum/Fal 75
*Darkness Weaves   [na2]
  [Kane]   MS 1-2,1974-Sum/Fal 75
  [*orig.version of book, Powell, 1970]
Death Angel's Shadow [v]   MS 1,1974
The Fourth Seal   Whsp 6/7,Dec 76
In Memoriam: Dave McFerran
  [obit]   Agd 1,Aut 80
In the Lair of Yslsl [Kane]   MS 1,1974
The Last Wolf   MS 2,Sum/Fal 75
*The Last Wolf   FyT 2,Win 77
Lee Brown Coye [obit]   FyT 9,Spr 82
Lonely Places   MS 1,1974
Lynortis Reprise [nt] [Kane]   MS 1,1974
Manly Wade Wellman [in]   Chac 2,Spr 77
Midnight Sun [v]   MS 1,1974
Mourning of the Following
  Day [v]   FyT 4,Spr 79
*The Once and Future Kane [a] Shyl 1,Nov 77
  [*REH:Lone Star Fictioneer 1,1975]
The Other One, [Kane]   Esc Fal 77
*The Other One [Kane]   FyT 7,Spr 81
Raven's Eyrie [na] [Kane]   Chac 2,Spr 77
Sing a Last Song of Valdese
  [Kane]   Chac 1,Win 76
Sticks   Whsp 3,Mar 74
13 Best Non-Supernatural
  Horror Novels [list]   TZ Jun 83
13 Best Science Fiction
  Horror Novels [list]   TZ Aug 83
13 Best Supernatural
  Horror Novels [list]   TZ Jun 83
Two Suns Setting   [Kane]   Ftc May 76
Undertow [nt]   [Kane]   Whsp 10,Aug 77
Wasn't Bran Mak Morn a
  Cereal? [a]   DFd 3,Sum 80

  + David Drake
Killer   MS 1,1974
[Kane]

WAIGHT, GEORGE
The Electric Chair   WT Jan 25
*The Electric Chair   MoH 2,Nov 63

WAINWRIGHT, EVELYN
The Voice in the Picture Frame GS Mar 27

WAINWRIGHT, JONAS T.
Fact or Fiction? [col]   Thrl May-Jul 62
  [appears anon. in May issue]

WAIT, ROBERT A.
Waning Moon   UnS May/Jun 35

WAKEFIELD, H[erbert] RUSSELL [1888-1964]
UK writer, criminologist, civil servant
and broadcaster
Obituary   ArkC 1,Sum 67
A Black Solitude   WT Mar 51
*The Central Figure   AFR 1,1947
  [*Ghost Stories,1932]
*An Echo   TMD 1(1934)
  [*They Return at Evening,1928]
From the Vasty Deep   WT Jul 49
Ghost Hunt   WT Mar 48
A Kink in Space-Time   ArkS Sum 48
Messrs Turkes and Talbot   ArkS Win 48
*Old Man's Beard   TU 1(1934)
  [*Old Man's Beard,1929]
Out of the Wrack I Rise   WT Nov 49
The Third Shadow   . WT Nov 50
*The Third Shadow   Phtm 13,Apr 58
The Triumph of Death   ArkS Aut 49
Woe Water   WT Jul 50

WAKEFIELD, JOHN
The 13th Cat   Phtm 3,Jun 57

WALDO, E. HUNTER
  see under Theodore STURGEON

WALDROP, HOWARD
US writer
The Adventure of the Grinder's
  Whistle   Chac 2,Spr 77
All About Strange Monsters of
  the Recent Past   Shyl 4,Win 80
Dr. Hudson's Secret Gorilla Shyl 1,Nov 77
Green Brother   Shyl 5,Win 82
Horror, We Got   Shyl 3,Sum 79
Mono No Aware   HoH Aug 73
Der Untergang des Abenlandes-
  menschen   Chac 1,Win 76
"-The World as We Know't"   Shyl 6,Win 82

WALDRIP, W. F.
A Final Memoir   Eld 6,1979

WALKEN, CHRISTOPHER
US actor
Interview   TZ Oct 83

WALKER, BRUCE   [see below]
I've Got to Believe It   StS Oct 40

WALKER, BRUCE   [see above]
The Witchery of Robert Bloch[a]Nyc 8,Apr 73

WALKER, CEDRIC
The Helping Hand   Nek 5,mid-51

WALKER, DAVID
Death to Him Who Desecrates
  My Tomb [a]   Phtm 11,Feb 58

WALKER, FRANK E.
Phantom Billiards   WT Feb 26

*The Door in the Wall   MoH 9,Jun 65
  [*Daily Chronicle Jul 14,1906]
*A Dream of Armageddon   WT Mar 26
  [*Black & White,1901]
*The Inexperienced Ghost   GS Aug 29
*The Inexperienced Ghost   TU 1(1934)
*The Inexperienced Ghost   MoH 1,Aug 63
  [*The Strand Magazine Mar 1902]
*The Late Mr.Elvesham   PGS 1963
  [*see "The Story of the Late Mr.Elvesham"]
*A Moth - Genus Unknown   GS Oct 27
*The Moth   TMD 1(1934)
*A Moth   MoH 6,Nov 64
  [*Pall Mall Gazette Mar 28,1895]
*The Plattner Story   GS Jun 27
  [*New Review Apr 1896]
*Pollock and the Porroh Man   GS Jul 30
  [*New Budget May 23,1895]
*The Queer Story of Brownlow's
  Newspaper   AFR 3,1947
  [*The Strand Magazine Mar 1932]
*The Red Room   GS Apr 27
*The Red Room   MoH 2,Nov 63
  [*The Idler Mar 1896]
*The Stolen Body   WT Nov 25
  [*The Strand Nov 1898]
*The Story of the Late Mr.
  Elvesham   GS Aug 27
  [*The Idler May 1896; see also rep.
  as "The Late Mr.Elvesham"]
*The Temptation of Harringay   SMS 4,Spr 67
  [*St.James's Gazette Feb 9,1895]
*The Truth About Pyecraft   AFR 1,1947
*The Truth About Pyecraft   MoH 4,May 64
  [*The Strand Apr 1903]
*The Valley of Spiders   WT Dec 25
*The Valley of Spiders   FFy Feb 71
  [*Pearson's Magazine Mar 1903]
*A Vision of Judgement   MoH 3,Feb 64
  [*Butterfly Sep 1899]

WELLS, PAUL ALLEN
  The Silent Man [v]   DH 22,Spr 81

WELLS, RAMA
  Esmeralda   SMS 3,Win 66/7

WELLS, [Frank Charles] ROBERT [1929-]
UK international banker; sf writer
  Song of the Syren [nt]   SFy 70,Mar 65
  Stop Seventeen   Imp 9,Nov 66

WENDELESSEN
  Pseud: see Charles DE LINT

WENDELL, [B.] LEILAH   [1958-]
US writer,artist,publisher and para-
psychologist
  Here at the Edge [v]   DH 25,Sum 82
  Necromantic [v]   FB Dec 81
  Time Upon Time [v]   EC 5,1981

WENTZ, ROBY
  Change   UW Oct 43
*Change   UWB May 44

WENTZ, W[ALTER] J[AMES]
  The Bookseller's Tale   Anu 2,Spr 67
  The Shark King   Wbk 5,1972

WENZEL, SOPHIE LOUISE
  Maiden name: see Sophie Wenzel ELLIS

WENZLER, ELIZABETH ADT
  The Demons of Castle Romnare   WT Jul 26

WERBA, MOLLIE L./MEI-LI
  Corona Mundi [v]   Eld 8,1982
  Night Quest   Eld 2,1981

WERNER, [HANS-] PETER   [1948-]
German-born,US-resident fan artist and
publisher
*The Broken Towers   PtF 1,Sum 78
  [*earlier version in fanzine Pablo
  Lennis]
  Fire on Yellow Mountain   CT 5,Jan 79
  Flight to the Golden Mountain
  [v]   PtF 2,Fal 79
  The Fountain   PtF 1,Sum 78
  A Great King Called Ile Phant
                               CT 6/7,Jul 79
  Is Fantasy & Science Fiction a
  Significant Literature [a] PtF 1,Sum 78

    + Wayne Hooks
  Go Down Moses   PtF 1,Sum 78

WEST, AVERY
  "Giant Spiders Are Attacking
  Our Town"   AH Oct 71
  Revenge of the Witch   AH Aug 71

WEST, DOUGLAS
  Pseud: see E.C. TUBB

WEST, JOHN
  The Psychic Typewriter   G&G(1938)

WEST, JOHN
  Found Money   MysT Nov 51
  The Vanishing Passenger   MysT Jun 52
  The Weeping Woman   MysT 5,1952

WEST, JOHN ANTHONY
  Chanceyville   Shk Sep 60

WEST, JOSEPH A.
  Brandon's Pipe   E&O 1,1973
  The Sadhu   Div 3,Aug 74

    + John Koblas & Eric Carlson
  Carl Jacobi [in]   E&O 1,1973

WEST, L.H.
  Join the Living Dead   Phtm 8,Nov 57

WEST, MICHAEL
  Pseud: see August DERLETH

WEST, WALLACE [G(eorge)] [1900-80]
US pollution control expert
  The Empty Road   WT Jun 30
  Heinrich   SFy 49,Oct 61
  The Incubator Man   WT Oct 28
*The Incubator Man   ASFR 1,1951
  The Last Incarnation   WT Oct 30
*The Last Man   Ftc Apr 79
  The Laughing Duke   WT Feb 32
*The Laughing Duke   MoH 17,Fal 67
  Leasehold   Ftc Oct 78
  Loup-Garou   WT Oct 27

WHITE, WILLIAM A[nthony] P[arker] [1911–
US sf/fantasy/mystery author,   1968]
reviewer, critic and editor
Ye Goode Olde Ghoste Storie   WT Jan 27

   as Anthony Boucher
The Compleat Werewolf [nt]   UW Apr 42
*The Compleat Werewolf [nt]   UWB Aut 45
  [also in *FUW,1948 and *FUWB,1952]
*The Empty Man   Shk May 60
  [*orig."The Anomaly of the Empty
  Man" Mag.F & SF Apr 52]
Footnote to Dunne [a]   ArkS Aut 49
The Ghost of Me   UW Jun 42
*The Ghost of Me   UWB Jun 42
Mr. Lupescu   WT Sep 45
*9-Finger Jack   Shk Jul 60
  [*Mag. F & SF Aug 52]
On a Limb [a]   UW Oct 41
*The Pink Caterpillar   AFR 17,1951
  [*Adventure Feb 45]
The Scrawny One   WT May 49
Snulbug   UW Dec 41
*Snulbug   UWB Win 48
Sriberdegibit   UW Jun 43
*Sriberdegibit   UWB Oct 43
The Star Dummy   Ftc Fal 52
*The Star Dummy   Ftc Aug 69
*Summer's Cloud   TZ Jun 81
  [*The Acolyte Sum 44]
They Bite   UW Aug 43
*They Bite   UWB May 44
*The Way I Heard It   TZ Jun 81
  [*The Acolyte Fal 44]

   as Parker White
Sonnet of the Unsleeping Dead
  [v]   WT Mar 35

WHITE, WILLIE
  Pseud: see Nestor JAREMKO

WHITEFORD, WYNNE
Australian writer
The Non-Existent Man   Ftc Jul 79

WHITEHEAD, CHARLES [1804–62]
UK Popular Victorian writer and man-of-
letters
  [as Editor]
*Lives of Noted Highwaymen[ex]   FC 3,1973
  [*1834 revision of 1711 book]

WHITEHEAD, HENRY S[t. Clair] [1882–1932]
US clergyman and educator
  Bibliography (incomplete)   Lvs 2,Win 38/9
  Obituary   WT Mar 33
Across the Gulf   WT May 26
*The Black Beast [nt][GC] MoH 12,Win 65/6
  [*Adventure during 1931]
Black Tancrede   [GC]   WT Jun 29
Black Terror   [GC]   WT Oct 31
Cassius [nt]   [GC]   ST Nov 31
*Cassius [nt]   [GC]   MoH 5,Sep 64
The Chadbourne Episode [GC]   WT Feb 33
The Cult of the Skull   WT Dec 28
The Door   WT Nov 24
*The Door   WT Aug 33
The Fireplace   WT Jan 25
*The Fireplace   WT Feb 35
The Great Circle [na]   [GC]   ST Jun 32

*The Great Circle [na] [GC] BFT 1,Fal 70
Hill Drums   WT Jun/Jul 31
Jumbee   WT Sep 26
*Jumbee   WT Feb 38
The Left Eye   WT Jun 27
The Lips   WT Sep 29
Mrs. Lorriquer   [GC]   WT Apr 32
The Moon-Dial [nt]   ST Jan 32
*The Moon-Dial [nt]   MoH 32,May 70
The Napier Limousine [GC]   ST Jan 33
No Eye-Witnesses   WT Aug 32
Passing of a God   [GC]   WT Jan 31
*Passing of a God   [GC]   WT Dec 38
*Passing of a God   [GC]   WT Jul 54
The People of Pan   [GC]   WT Mar 29
The Projection of Armand Dubois
  [GC]   WT Oct 26
Sea Change   WT Feb 25
Sea-Tiger   ST Oct 32
The Shadows   WT Nov 27
*The Shadows   AFR 14,1950
The Shut Room   [GC]   WT Apr 30
Sweet Grass   WT Jul 29
The Tabernacle   WT Jan 30
Tea Leaves   WT May/Jul 24
The Thin Match   WT Mar 25
The Trap [nt]   [GC]   ST Mar 32
*The Trap [nt]   [GC]   AFR 6,1948
*The Trap [nt]   [GC]   WTT 3,Fal 70
The Tree-Man   [GC]   WT Feb/Mar 31
*The Tree-Man   [GC]   WT Sep 53
*"Williamson"   [GC]   MoH 17,Fal 67
  [*West India Lights,1946]
The Wonderful Thing   WT Jul 25
[GC - Gerald Canevin]

WHITEHILL, HENRY W.
The Case of the Russian
  Stevedore   WT Dec 24
*The Case of the Russian
  Stevedore   FC 5,1973

WHITELY, T. K.
  Pseud: see Manly Wade WELLMAN

WHITESIDE, STANLEY
The Place Equator   UTC 21,Sep/Oct 43

WHITING, JOHN D.
Old Clothes   WT Aug 32

WHITLEY, GEORGE
  Pseud: see A. Bertram CHANDLER

WHITMAN, WALT[er] [1819–92]
US poet
*Death Carol [v]   WT Mar 26
*Whispers of Heavenly Death [v] WT Nov 25
  [*Leaves of Grass, edition unknown]

WHITMORE, WILL
The Man Who Paid   GS Oct 26

WHITNEY, PHYLLIS A[yame] [1903–]
US suspense/historical/gothic novelist
The Silver Bullet   WT Feb 35
*The Silver Bullet   SMS 16,Sum 70

WHITSON-NORTON, ALICE
The Man Who Died Twice   GS Nov 27

The Last Poet [v]   EC 7,May 82
Lines For Lovecraft [v]   Nyc 14,Mar 78
The Monster   S&T 20,Sep 73
Night Song [v]   BFWK Aut 78
Now We Offer Roses [v]   ToF 1,Spr 82
Overtaken [v]   Nyc 13,May 77
A Phantom of My Youth [a]   Div 20,May 77
Rain Magic [v]   Nyc 9,Jul 74
Realm of the Dead [v]   Mb 8,1972
Refuge [v]   DFd 4,May 83
The Shadow-Shade [v]   Div 21,Jul 77
The Shadow Well [v]   Mb 25,1976
The Slayer in Dreams [v]   Myrd 4,1978
Voices [v]   NF 1,Win 80/1
A Walk [v]   EC 8,1982
The White Faces [v]   Nyc 18,Jan 80
White Lillillaya [v]   Wbk 12,1977

WOLLETT, LEOPOLD J.
    Pseud: see William ELLIOTT

WOLLHEIM, DONALD A[llen]   [1914-]
US writer, editor and publisher
*Aquella   AFR 7,1948
    [*orig."The Planet Called Aquella"
    as by Martin Pearson Super Science
    Stories Nov 42]
Babylon: 70M   MoH 1,Aug 63
*Blind Flight   ASFR 1,1951
    [*see under Millard Verne Gordon below]
*Blue Print   UTC 8,Aug 41
    [*Stirring Science Stories Apr 41]
Bones   SFF Feb 41
*Bones   UTC 7,Jul 41
*Bones   MoH 5,Sep 64
[Castaway - see "The Growing Terror"]
The Coming of the Comet   UTC 20,Dec 42
Doorslammer   MoH 2,Nov 63
The Drums of Reig Rawan   UTC 14,Feb 42
*The Growing Terror   UTC 13,Jan 42
    [*orig."Castaway" Super Science Stories
    May 40]
The Hat   UTC 11,Nov 41
[The Haters - see under collaboration
    with Lowndes below]
*The Horror Out of Lovecraft MoH 27,May 69
    [*a fanzine appearance in 1944]
*The Man From the Future   UTC 17,May 42
    [*Cosmic SF Mar 41]
*Mimic   AFR 3,1947
    [*orig.as by Martin Pearson in
    Astonishing Stories Dec 42]
Miss McWhortle's Weird   ArkC 7,Sum 70
[The Planet Called Aquella - see Aquella]
*Storm Warning   AFR 10,1949
    [*orig.as by Millard Verne Gordon in
    Future Fantasy & SF Oct 42]
[*The Thought Monsters - see collabo-
    ration with Lowndes below]
Umbriel   FT Fal 36
*Up There   AFR 15,1951
    [*orig.as by Martin Pearson in Science
    Fiction Quarterly 7,Sum 42]
Whither Canadian Fantasy? [a]
                                      UTC 20,Dec 42
    as Millard Verne Gordon
*Blind Flight   UTC 20,Dec 42
    [*Stirring Science Stories Mar 42;
    see also as by Wollheim above]
*Cosmophobia   UTC 7,Jul 41
    [*Stirring Science Stories Apr 41]

The Unholy Glass   UTC 21,Sep/Oct 43
    as David Grinnell
The Feminine Fraction   MoH 6,Nov 64
The Garrison   MoH 8,Apr 65

    as Martin Pearson
The Unfinished City   SFF Mar 42

    as Allen Warland
The God of OO   UTC 20,Dec 42

    as Lawrence Woods
[Black Flames - see collaboration with
    Lowndes below]
*The Strange Return   UTC 7,Jul 41
    [*Stirring Science Stories Feb 41]

    as X
*!!!   UTC 8.Aug 41
    [*Stirring Science Stories Apr 41]

    + Forrest J. Ackerman
*Great Gog's Grave   FB Dec 81
    [*pub'd in Avon comic-book in 1940s]

    + Robert W. Lowndes
Black Flames   SFF Apr 41
    [by-lined as by Lawrence Woods]
The Haters   Unk Oct 40
*The Haters   UnkB Oct 40
    [by-lined as by Wollheim alone]
*The Thought Monsters   UTC 6,Jun 41
    [*same as "Black Flames" above, but
    by-lined as by Wollheim alone]

WOOD, Jr., EDWARD D.
US film maker
Hellfire   HST 1972
Scream Your Bloody Head Off   HST 1972

WOOD, EDWIN G.
The Survivor   WT Nov 23

WOOD, JODY SCOTT
The Origin of Species [ss]   Ftc Feb 69

WOOD, KENNETH P.
The Return of Orrin Mannering   WT Sep 35

WOOD, THEODORE SNOW
People vs Bland   WT Jul/Aug 23

WOOD, VALERIE
Roots   EC 1,Jul 76

WOODCOTT, KEITH
    Pseud: see John BRUNNER

WOODFORD, JACK
    Pseud: see Josiah Pitts WOOLFOLK

WOODING, JAMES BENNETT
    + Joseph Faus
The Extraordinary Experiment of
    Dr. Calgroni   WT Mar 23

WOODS, P. F.
    Pseud: see Barrington J. BAYLEY

WOODWARD, ARTHUR
Lord of the Talking Heads   WT Dec 31
*Lord of the Talking Heads   WT May 54

as Harrison Denmark
Monologue For Two   Ftc May 63
A Thing of Terrible Beauty   Ftc Apr 63
[Dil - Dilvish the Damned]

ZELDIS, LEON
  Portrait of Things to Come
                          W&S 5,Jan/Feb 71

ZERR, 'THE MYSTIC MIND'
  Whence The Answer? [a]   MM Oct 31

ZICREE, MARC SCOTT
  America Enters the Twilight
    Zone [a]   TZ Apr 81
  Rod Serling: First Citizen of
    the Twilight Zone [a]   TZ Apr 81
    [also in *GSTZ,1982]
  The Story Behind Richard
    Matheson's "The Doll" [a]   TZ Jun 82
    [also in *GSTZ,1982]
  TV's Twilight Zone [col] TZ Apr 81-Oct 83
  The Twilight Zone: The Final
    Season [a]   TZ Aug 82
  The Twilight Zone: The Third
    Season [a]   TZ Oct 81
  A View Across the Twilight
    Zone [a]   TZ Oct 83

ZIMMER, PAUL E[dwin]   [1943-]
US poet and writer, brother of Marion
Zimmer Bradley
  The Complaint of Agni [v]   Wyrd 8,1980
  Logan [v]   Wyrd 7,Fal 77
  The Shadow of Tugar [v]   FB Aug 83
  A Sudden Storm in Spring [v]
                           Wyrd 6,Win 76/7

ZIMMERMAN, M. G.
  Blurble   Ftc Jun 59

'ZORRO'
  Pseud: see Harold WARD

ZUCKER, ELLIOT
  Hipster From Hell   MP Dec 58

ZYCHOWICZ, JIM
  Dust Under the Bed   Mb 28,1976

                    *****

Artist Index

ADAMS, DUANE
cover
 Wyrd 1980(8)

ADAMS, JEFF
cover
 EvM 1976 Fal.

ADAMS, NEAL [1941-]
US comic-book artist
cover
 DFy 1976 Dec(10).

ADKINS, DAN
cover
 Ftc 1971 Jun

backcovers
 Ftc 1961 Jul,Oct,Nov,Dec
     1962 Feb,Jun; 1963 Mar

ADKINS, SAM S.
backcover
 Arg 1981 Fal/Win(8)

ADRAGNA, ROBERT
covers
 Ftc 1962 Dec; 1964 Jun,Sep;
 StF 1970*Spr(11) [*part Ftc Sep 64]

AINSWORTH, K. P.
covers
 UTC 1942 Mar-May(15-17),Sep-Dec(19-20)
     1943 Sep/Oct(21)

ALLAN, JOHN
Canadian painter, fl.1900
cover
 Kdth 1974(1) [photographic reproduction
     of a painting destroyed by fire in 1903]

AMBROSE, MICHAEL E.
covers
 Arg 1976 Sum; 1977 Spr/Sum

ANDERSON, BRENT
covers
 S&T 1974 Jul(25); 1975 May(30)

interiors
 FCr 1975 May(3) Howard's Women [ap]
     1975 May-Aug(3-4/5) Benji the Bar-
         barian [cs2]
 S&T 1975 May(30) Deathday [cs]

ANDERSON, CRAIG W. [1951-]
US lawyer
covers
 Div 1976 Nov(17)
 Pgn 1980 May(1)

backcover
 Div 1976 Nov(17)

ANDERSON, DENNIS
interiors
 Ariel 1978 Apr(3),Oct(4)

ARFSTROM, JON D[ouglas] [1928-]
Interview E&O 3,1983
covers
 E&O 1983(3)
 WT 1952 Jan,Jul; 1953 Sep

ARMATA, BARB
interior
 NV 1981 Fal(8)

ARNOLD, HERB   [1949-]
cover
 E&O 1973(1)

backcover
 HPL 1972

interiors
 FCr 1975 Aug(4/5) Fantasy Swordsmen[ap]
 HPL 1972   Lovecraft [ap]
 Nyc 1972 Aug(7)   CAS: Portfolio [ap]
 Whsp 1974 Jul(4) The White Ship [ap]

'ARTIFACT'
cover
 TZ 1983 Jun

AUSTIN, ALICIA
backcover
 Chac 1977 Spr(2)

BAHRET, ALVIN
covers
 AD 1975 Win(1),Win(2); 1976 Spr(3)

backcovers
 AD 1975 Win(1); 1976 Fal(4)

BAKER, KEN(?)
cover
 Ftc 1969 Feb

BALL, MIKE
cover
 FCr 1974 Nov(1)

BAMBARA, FRANK
cover
 Wbk 1973(6)

backcover
 EC 1982(6)

BANI, ALESSANDRO
backcover
 Kad 1980 May(2)

interior
 Kad 1981 Jul(4)

BANISTER, MANLY [Miles] [1914-]
covers
 Nek 1950 Spr(1),Aut(3),Win(4)

BARBER, TOM
covers
 WT 1981 Spr(1),Spr(2),Fal(3); 1983 Sum(4)

BARKER, NANCY
backcover
 Div 1977 Jan(18)

BARLOW, ROBERT H.   [1918-51]
covers
 Lvs 1937 Sum(1); 1938/9 Win(2)

BARLOWE, WAYNE DOUGLAS
cover
 Ftc 1980*Jul [*Tomorrow & Beyond,1978]

BARR, GEORGE   [1937-]
covers
 Ftc 1962 Apr,Jun
 FFy 1970 Dec
 StF 1970*Spr(11) [*part Ftc Apr 62]

interiors
 FB 1982 Aug (frontispiece)
 Whsp 1975 Dec(8) color inset 'Red Nails'

BARTH, ERNEST K.
cover
 Ftc 1954 Oct

BARTON
cover
 SN 1960 No.36

BARTON, BERNARD
US pocketbook & commercial artist
cover
 AFR 1951(17)

BECK, C[harles] C[larence] [1910-]
US comic artist
interior
 FCr 1975 Aug(4/5) The Hobbit Portfolio

BEEKMAN, DOUG
cover
 Ftc 1976 Nov

BELARSKI, RUDOLPH [1900-]
US pulp and pocketbook artist
covers
 StS 1939 Feb,Apr (both unconfirmed)
     1940 Apr

BENDER, HOWARD
cover
 Div 1975 Feb(7)

BENNETT, RICHARD
cover
 WT 1942 Nov

BENSEN, ANDREW
cover
 WT 1926 May

BERGEY, EARLE K. [?-1952]
Noted US sf pulp artist
covers
 ASFR 1952(3)
 StS 1939 Aug,Oct,Dec;
     1940 Feb,Jun,Aug,Oct,Dec; 1941 Feb
 TMM 1927 Dec-1928 Apr (possibly did all
     covers, but unconfirmed)

BERKEY, JOHN
Profile/Interview Ariel 4,Apr 78
interior
 Ariel 1978 Oct(4) frontispiece & ap

BERRY, D. BRUCE [1924-]
US commercial artist
covers
 Anu 1968 Aut
 Wbk 1978 No.13

backcover
 Wbk 1979 No.14

interiors
 Wbk 1979 No.14[ap]; 1982 No.16

BERRY, PHIL
covers
 Ftc 1959 Jan

BERTIN, EDDY C[harly] [1944-]
backcovers
 Nyc 1971 Feb(3),*Jun(4) [*Shadow 7,Sep 69]

BETCHER, MARK
cover
 MS 1979(5)

BEVILACQUA, CAROL
covers
Nov 1980 Aut(1); 1981 Win(2),Spr(3)

BICK
cover
UTC 1942 Jan(13)

BIERLEY, JOHN
cover
Ftc 1977 Feb

interior
DFd 1980 Sum(3)

BILLMAN, DAVE
cover
S&T 1976 Jan(34)

backcover
AD 1977 Win(5)

BIRCHALL, JEFF
interior
Mb 1971 No.4 Grotesqueries [ap]

BIRD, CLIFFORD W.
covers
AD 1977 Fal(6)
Div 1978 May/Jul(26/7)
FCr 1977 Nov(12)

backcovers
BL 1977 Mar(3)
FCr 1975 Nov(6); 1976 Feb(7)

interiors
AD 1977 Fal(6) Dream-Quest of Unknown
       Kadath [ill]
Db 1978 Spr(1)
FCr 1975 Aug(4/5) Fantasy Sworsdmen [ap]

BIRKHEAD, SHERYL
covers
Div 1974 Jul(2)

BIRMINGHAM, LLOYD   [1924-]
covers
Ftc 1961 Nov,Dec; 1962 Jan,Mar,Sep,Nov
    1963 Feb; 1964 Dec

BLACKSHEAR, THOMAS
Profile and Portfolio Shyl 5,Win 82
cover
Shyl 1979 Sum(3)

interiors
Shyl 1982 Win(5) Profile & Portfolio
     1982 Win(6) Middle Earth [ap]

BLAIR, JACQUELYN R.
cover
Ftc 1963 Jul

BLAKELY, BRADFORD
cover
Wbk 1981 No.15

interior
Wbk 1978 No.13 [endpaper]

BLISH, JUDITH ANN
   see under Judith Ann LAWRENCE

BOAS, MARCUS
cover
Ftc 1975 Oct

interiors
Chac 1976 Win(1)
PD 1977 No.2 Solomon Kane [ap]
Whsp 1976 Dec(9)

BODE, VAUGHN   [1941-75]
cover
Ftc 1971 Oct [+ Larry Todd]

interior
Anu 1968 Aut(4) Dead Bone [gs]

BOK, HANNES   [1914-64]
Profile Chac 1,Win 76
covers
Biz 1941 Jan
FCr 1978 Sep(14) [+ Stephen Fabian]
FM 1953 Feb/Mar,Jun,Aug,Nov
SFF 1941 Apr,Jun; 1942 Mar
WT 1939 Dec; 1940 Mar,May
    1941 May,Jul,Nov; 1942 Mar
    1973 Fal [+ G.van der Stever]

backcover
Whsp 1982 Mar

interiors
Chac 1976 Win(1)
WT 1944 Jul Weirditties [pic][+ Nichol]
    1951 Mar Weirditties of Science [pic]

BOOTH, FRANKLIN
interior
Ariel 1977 No.2 [endpapers]

BORKOWSKI, JOHN
cover
NV 1981 Spr(7)

BOYER, B. C.
interiors
NV 1979 Sum(4) Creative Images [ap]

BRADFORD, AL
interiors
FCr 1974 Nov(1) [+ Marty Green] [ap]
    1975 Feb(2) [+ Marty Green] [ap]

BRAYMAN, KARI
covers
TZ 1983 Apr

BREIDING, WILLIAM
backcover
Nyc 1980 Jan(15)

BROECKER, RANDY
backcover
FyT 1979 Win(5)

BROSNATCH, ANDREW
covers
WT 1924 Nov,Dec; 1925 Jan-Nov
    1926 Jan,Mar

BROWN, GERALD J. [1950-]
   as Paul M. Cordel
backcover
Arg 1980 Fal/Win(7)

interiors
NV 1977 Fal(1)   Frontispiece
                 Creative Images [ap]
                 Consummation [gs]
    1978 Win(3) Frontispiece

BROWN, HEATHER
interiors
Db 1978 Spr
BFWK 1978 Aut   Frontispiece

BROWN, HOWARD V.   [1878-?]
cover
Kad 1980*May(2) [*Astounding Stories
                  Jun 36]

BROZE, CAM
backcover
F&T 1973 No.2

interior
F&T 1973 No.2 The Continuing Story of
   Joe and Mac [cs]

BRUNDAGE, MARGARET   [1900-76]
Profile & Interview E&O 2,1983
covers
E&O 1983*No.2 [*WT Dec 33]
WT 1932 Sep,Oct; 1933 Mar,Jun-Dec
    1934 Jan-Dec; 1935 Jan-Dec
    1936 Jan-Jul,Aug/Sep,Nov
    1937 Jan,Mar,May,Jun,Aug-Nov
    1938 Jan,Mar,May,Jun,Aug-Oct
    1940 Jul,Nov; 1941 Mar,Sep
    1942 Jul; 1943 May; 1944 May
    1945 Jan; 1953*Nov [*WT Jan 45]

backcover
E&O 1983*No.2 [montage]

BRUNING, RICH
covers
S&T 1976 Jul(37)

BRUNO, FRANK
covers
Ftc 1963 Apr; 1964 Apr
StF 1969*Spr(8) [*Ftc Apr 63]

BULL, REINA M.
covers
SFy 1951/2 Win(3); 1952 Spr(4)

BURCHAM, F. NEWTON
cover
NV   1978 Sum(2)

backcovers
NV   1978 Sum(2); 1983 Win/Spr(9)

interiors
NV   1977 Fal(1) Alienation [gs]
                  Creative Images [ap]
     1978 Sum(2) Sunslayer [gs + C.Pitts]
                  The Dream is Alive [ap]
          Win(3) Creative Images [ap]
                  The Alien & The Elf [cs]
     1979 Sum(4) Chrysalis [cs]
                  The Puppet of Fate [gv]
          Fal(5) Frontispiece [+ C.Pitts]
                  Portfolio [ap]

BURCHETT, RICK
interiors
NV 1979 Fal(5)-1981 Spr(7) Sunslayer
    [gs3] [+ Don Secrease]

BURGE, JERRY   [1931-]
covers
W&S 1971 Jan/Feb(5); 1972 No.8

BURLESON, JOE
cover
TZ 1983 Aug

BURNHAM, LILLIAN
cover
Eld 1979 No.6

backcover
Eld 1979 No.6

BURNS, GENIE
backcover
Div 1974 Dec(6)

BYERS, IAIN
cover
S&T 1983/4 Win(65)

CAESARI, VICTOR
cover
SN 1960 No.31

CALDWELL, CLYDE
covers
Esc 1977 Fal
PD 1977 No.3
S&T 1972 Nov(17)

interiors
Chac 1977 Spr(2)
Shyl 1982 Win(5)   Fantasy [ap]

CALLE, PAUL   [1928-]
cover
WB 1950 Dec

CAMERON, LOU   [1924-]
interiors
MP 1958 Dec Magician of Death [cs]
    1959 Mar She Stalks at Sundown [cs]
M&T 1959 Jan The Vampire Legion [cs]
        Apr Curse of the Living Cross-
bones [cs]

CAMPBELL, CLAYTON
cover
TZ 1981 Nov ['Death Masquerades as a
   Lover']

CANTY, TOM
interior
Ariel 1978 Apr(3)

CAPELLA, RAY   [1933-]
backcover
NV 1975 Sum/Fal(2)

CARSON, DAVE
covers
DH 1978 No.18; 1981 Sum(23)
FyM 1980 Sep(1); 1981 Apr(2); 1982 Jun(3)
FyT 1981 Sum(8)

backcovers
DH   1979 No.20; 1980 No.21; 1983 Spr(26)
FyT 1982 Sum(10)
Kad 1980*Nov(3); 1981*Jul(4)

interiors
Kad 1980 Nov(3) Frontispiece
    1981 Jul(4)
    1982 Jul(5) Frontispiece
Whsp 1982 Aug(17/18)
    1983 Oct(17/18) The Lurking Fear

CARTER, HUBERT
covers
MoH 1966 Sum(13),Win(14)
SMS 1966 Sum(1)

CARTIER, EDD
covers
Unk 1939 Dec; 1940 Feb,Mar,Apr,Jun
UnkB 1939*Dec; 1940*Feb,*Mar,*Apr,*Jun
FUW 1948
FUWB *1952

CASTENIR, RALPH
covers
Ftc 1954 Dec

CAWTHORN, JAMES   [1929-]
covers
SFy 1962 Oct(55); 1964 Feb(63)

backcover
DH   1971(1)

interior
SE   1980(1) Dream of a Doomed Lord [ill]

CHAFFEE, DOUG
cover
Ftc 1971 Dec; 1972 Dec

CHAPLIN, CARL
cover
TZ   1982 Jan

CHARETTE, JOHN
covers
DFy 1978 Jul(17)
Db 1978 Spr(1)
S&T 1978 Oct(49); 1981 Jan(58)

interior
Db 1978 Spr(1)

CHASTAIN, GEORGE
cover
MS   1975 Sum/Fal(2)

interior
MS   1975 Sum/Fal(2)

CHRISTIANA, DAVID
cover
TZ   1982 Dec

CHURCH, WILLIAM
cover
WD   1980 No.2

backcover
NFJ 1976 Sum(1)

CIROCCO, FRANK
cover
S&T 1974 May(24)

backcover
Div 1975 Feb(7)

interiors
FCr 1974 Nov(1)   Fan Art Portfolio [ap]
    1975 Feb(2)   Trader [cs]
         May(3)   Howard's Women [ap]
         Aug(4/5) Day Breaks Over Simla
    [gv - text: Robert E. Howard]

CLARK, TOM R.
cover
Wyrd 1967/7 Win(6)

backcover
FBDG 1977 Oct(4)

CLEWELL, ROBERT
covers
MoH 1970 May(32)
SMS 1970 Spr(15)

CLINE, MICHAEL
interior
E&O 1983 No.3 The Yowlings of Yog-
         Sothoth [ap]

CLINGAN, A. BRUCE
backcover
Div 1975 Jun(9)

CLYNE, RONALD
cover
WT   1946 May

COLE, ADRIAN
cover
DH   1973 No.6

CONKLIN, BRUCE [Stewart] [1954-]
covers
DFy 1978 Dec(18)
NV   1979 Sum(4)
S&T 1980 Oct(57); 1982/3 Win(63)

backcovers
Arg 1979 Win/Spr(5),Sum/Fal(6)
DFy 1980 Nov(23)
EvM 1978 Spr

interior
NV   1978 Sum The Dream is Alive [ap]

CONRAD, RUPERT
covers
BFF 1954 Jan; 1955 No.10
Ftc 1953 Jul/Aug

CONRAD, TIM
interior
Ariel 1978 Apr(3)   The Last Enchantment

CONWAY, BOB
cover
S&T 1977 Jan(40)

backcover
FCw 1977 Feb(3)

DAY, GENE [Howard Eugene] [1950-82]
Canadian artist, fan editor & publisher
covers
  AD   1976 Fal(4)
  BL   1976 Aug(1); 1977 Mar(3); 1978 Jan(4/5)
  DFy 1973 Sum(1),Fal(2); 1974 Mar(3),Jul(4)
         Oct(5); 1975 Jan(6),Sep(7);
         1977 Jan(11); 1979 Oct(21)
         1977 Sep(14)[+ P. Lambo]
  Div 1975 Oct(11)
  FCr 1975 Nov(6); 1976 Feb(7)
  S&T 1975 Sep(32)
  WA   1978 No.2
  Wyrd 1975 No.5

backcovers
  Agd 1980 Aut
  DFy 1973 Sum(1); 1974 Jul(4)[+ P.Lambo]
         1975 Jan(6); 1976 May(8),Sep(9),Dec
         (10); 1977 Jan(11); 1978 Jun(16);
         1979 Jul(20).
  Div 1975 Oct(11)
  FCr 1976 Aug(9)
  Jeet 1977 Apr(1)
  Wbk 1977 No.12

interiors
  AD   1977 Win(5) Pulp Characters [ap]
         Fal(6) The Dunwich Horror [ill]
  Db   1978 Spr(1) Frontispiece
  Eld 1978 Oct(4) Frontispiece
  FCr 1975 Aug(4/5) King Kull [ill]
         1976 May(8) The God in the Bowl [ap]
         Aug(9) Red Nails [ap]
  FCw 1977 Jan(1) [ap]
  TW   1975   Icarus 2000 [cs]
  Wyrd 1975 No.5 Cad Goddeu, the Battle of
         the Trees [gs]

DE LA ROSA, SAM
cover
  FCr 1975 May(3)

interiors
  FCr 1975 Feb(2) [ap]
         Aug(4/5) Conan [ill]

  + Ric Cruz
  FCr 1974 Nov(1) [ap]
         1975 Aug(4/5) The Frost Giant's
         Daughter [ill]; Ancient Sorceries
         [cs: adapted by Jonathan Bacon];
         UFOs [cs: text Pat Boyette]
         1976 May(8) Crimson Cavalier [gv]

DeLAY, HAROLD
covers
  WT   1939 May,Oct; 1941 Jan
         1944 Jan; 1954*Jul [*WT Jan 44]

DE PERSIIS
interior
  Ftc 1953 May/Jun [ap]

DE SOTO, RAPHAEL M. [1904-]
Puerto Rican born pulp/pocketbook artist
Profile CT5 Jan 79
cover
  Ace 1936 Sep

DeWOLFE, RICHARD
backcover
  DFy 1974 Mar(3)

DE ZUNIGA, TONY
  Interview NV5,Fal 79

DESROCHER, JACK
interior
  Ariel 1978 Oct(4)

DiFATE, VINCENT   [1945-]
US sf illustrator
cover
  Whsp 1974 Nov(5)

interior
  Whsp 1974 Jul(4) The White Ship [ap]

DI GIANNURIO, ANTHONY
cover
  WT   1952 Nov

DICKISON, LARRY
  Interview CT 5,Jan 79
covers
  Arg 1980 Fal/Win(7)
  CT   1979 Jan(5)
  DFy 1979 Jul(20)
  NV   1981 Fal(8)

backcovers
  DFy 1978 Jul(17); 1979 Oct(21);1980 Mar(22)
  PtF 1979 Fal(2)

DIETTERLIN, WENDEL   [1550-99]
German artist and engraver
cover
  DH   1974*Apr(8) [*Architectura,1598]

DILLON, LEO & DIANE   [1933-]
  Profile & Portfolio Shyl 4,Win 80

DIXON, VERNA [Lee]
covers
  Div 1974 Jun(1)

DOCKTOR, IRV   [1918-]
covers
  Sus 1951 Sum,Fal

DODS, JOHN
interior
  CT   1978 Jan(3) Grog [ap]

DOLGOV, BORIS
cover
  WT   1946 Nov; 1947 Mar,Sep; 1948 Jan;
         1950 May

DOLLENS, MORRIS SCOTT   [1920-]
covers
  Ftc 1959 Nov
  Gam 1963 No.1,No.2; 1964 No.3

DOOLIN, JOSEPH
covers
  WT   1925 Dec; 1926 Dec

DORE, GUSTAV   [1833-83]
French painter and illustrator
cover
  F&T 1973*No.3

interior
  F&T 1973*No.3 A Sampler [ap]

backcovers
Esc 1977 Fal
FCr 1978 Jun(13); 1979 Jan(15)
FCw 1977 Feb(2)
FyT 1981 Spr(7) ['The Moon Bog']
    1983 Win(12)
Nyc 1978 Mar(14)
TW 1975
Whsp 1977 Aug(10) ['The Book of the Black
    Art']

interiors
Ftc 1979 Jul-1980 Jul Daemon [gs5] [+
    Chip Daemon]
FCr 1975 May(3) Howard's Women [ap]
    Aug(4/5) A Witch Shall Be Born
HPL 1972 Lovecraft [ap]
NV 1980 Sum(6) Frontispiece
Nyc 1982 Jun(17)
Shyl 1977 Nov(1) endpapers
    1978 Feb(2) endpapers
    1979 Sum(3) [ap]
    1980 Win(4) endpapers
    1982 Win(5) Fantasy [ap]
Whsp 1974 Jul(4) The White Ship [ap]
    The Demoniac Footsteps
    [pic]
    Nov(5) Nightmare: A Tribute
    to William Hope Hodgson [ap]
    1977 Aug(10) color inset
    1979 Oct(13/14) Swords & Deviltry
    1982 Mar(15/16) The Red Death [ap]

FACEY, GERALD
covers
SN 1954 Nos.3,4; 1955 Nos.5,7

FALKOWITZ, AMY
interior
FB 1982 May Frontispiece

FALLONE, A. R.
covers
DH 1973 No.5

FARAGASSO, JACK   [1929-]
covers
Ftc 1960 Apr

FARLEY, G. M.
covers
Wbk 1969 No.2; 1970 No.3; 1971 No.4
    1972 No.5

FARRINGTON, K.
covers
Wbk 1976 No.10

FASTNER, STEVE
interiors
Shyl 1978 Feb(2) Frontispiece [+ Randall
    Larson]

FAULKENBERG, JIM
backcovers
F&T 1974 No.6

interiors
Nyc 1976 Apr(11/12)

FERGUSON, Jr., CLAY
covers
FT 1936 Fal
MT 1935 Sum

FINLAY, VIRGIL   [1914-71]
US fantasy artist
    Obituary ArkC 9,Spr 71
covers
[Note: the reprinted covers come from black
and white interiors. Other magazines are
AS, Amazing Stories; FA, Fantastic Adven-
tures; FFM - Famous Fantastic Mysteries;
FN, Fantastic Novels; SS, Startling Stories]

BFT 1970*Fal(1)   [*SS Jan 52]
BC 1970/1*Win   [unconfirmed]
Kad 1979*Oct(1) [*WT Jul 38]
MoH 1967*Spr(15) [*Ftc Nov 64]
    *Sum(16) [*FN May 50]
    *Fal(17) [*FFM Jun 50]
    *Nov(18) [*WT Jun 38]
    1968*Jan(19) [*WT Mar 38]
    *Mar(20) [*WT Jul 37]
    *May(21) [*WT May 38]
    *Jul(22) [*Ftc Nov 63]
    *Sep(23) [*AS Feb 43]
    *Nov(24) [*FN Jan 51]
    1969*Jan(25) [unconfirmed]
    *Mar(26) [*FFM Oct 51]
    *May(27) [*Ftc Sum 52]
    *Sep(29) [*WT Jul 36]
    1970*Feb(31) [*WT Sep 52]
    *Sum(33) [*Ftc May 57]
    *Fal(34) [*WT Jan 39]
SMS 1966/7*Win(3) [unconfirmed]
    1967*Spr(4) [*FFM Sep 42]
    *Sum(5) [*FA Jan 52]
    *Fal(6) [*WT Oct 37]
    1967/8*Win(7) [*WT Dec 36]
    1968*Spr(8) [*WT Jul 36]
    *Sum(9) [*WT Sep 37]
    *Fal(10) [unconfirmed]
    1968/9*Win(11) [*Ftc Fal 52]
    1969*Spr(12) [FN Jul 49]
    *Win(14) [Ftc Feb 57]
    1971*Mar(18) [may not be Finlay]
WT 1937 Feb,Apr,Jul,Dec
    1938 Feb,Apr,Jul
    1939 Jan-Apr,Jun/Jul,Aug,Sep;Nov
    1940 Jan; 1952 May,Sep; 1953 Mar
    1954*Sep [*WT Aug 39]
    1973 Sum [intended for WT Sep 36
    but never used]
WTT 1969/70*Win(1) [*FFM Apr 42]
    1970*Sum(2) [*WT Jul 38]

backcovers
BC 1970/1*Win [unconfirmed]
Ftc 1961 Sep; 1962 Jan,Mar
    1963 Feb,Jul,Nov; 1964 Jan

interiors
BC 1970/1*Win [*FFM Sep 42]
Ftc 1966*Jul [ap:*AS Feb 43,*FA Feb 48,
    *FA Jul 48]
    1973*Feb [ap:*FA Dec 48]
WT 1937 Dec The Vampire [pic]
    1938 Jan "Her Demon Lover" [pic]
    Feb Old Cornish Litany [pic]
    Mar "Like One, That on a Lone-
    some Road"

Apr   La Belle Dame Sans Merci
        [pic]
May   Tam O'Shanter [pic]
Jun   The Skeleton in Armor [pic]
Jul   The Weird Sisters From
        Macbeth [pic]
Sep   Israfel [pic]
Oct   The Horns of Elfland [pic]
Dec   The Blessed Damozel [pic]
1939 Jan   Hence, Loathed Melnahcoly
        [pic]
Feb   Shapes of Men That Were
        [pic]
Mar   Satan, Yawning on his
        Brazen Seat [pic]
Apr   Their Eyes Upturned [pic]
May   Where Crafty Gnomes [pic]
Jun/Jul   We Are No Other Than a
        Moving Row [pic]
Aug   I Can Call Spirits [pic]
Oct   The Hashish Eater [pic]
Nov   Is That the Wind Dying [pic]
Dec   Deep Night, Dark Night [pic]
1940 Jan   Up From the Earth's Center
        [pic]
Mar   Broken is the Golden Bowl
        [pic]
May   The Graves Stood Tenantless
        [pic]
Whsp 1975 Jun Frontispiece

FITZPATRICK, JIM
Irish illustrator, designer & artist
  Interview Agd 1,Aut 80
covers
  FCr 1977 Mar(10/11)
  FyT 1980*Sum(6) [*The Book of Conquests,
        1978]

backcover
  FyT 1977 Win(2) ['Macha/Nemed']

interior
  Agd 1980 Aut 'Nuada Airgedlamh [ill]
  Chac 1977 Spr(2) Celtia [ap]
  Shyl 1977 Nov(1) Tailltu [ap]

FLATOW, HERB
interior
  PGS 1963 "Dear God, Let Me Die!" [pic]

FLETCHER, DAVID L.
  Interview DH 11,Win/Spr 75
cover
  DH 1975 Win/Spr(11)

backcovers
  DH 1975 Aut/Win(12); 1976 Win(15)

FOGLIO, PHIL
backcover
  Div 1976 Sep(16) [+ J. Pearson]

FOSS, RONN
interiors
  FCr 1975 Feb & Aug Volsunga Saga [gs2]
        1975 Aug   Conan [ill]

FOSTER, BRAD W.
backcover
  Nyc 1982 Jun(17)

interiors
  NV 1980 Sum(6) [ap]
  Nyc 1982 Jun(17) Frontispiece

FOSTER, TIM
interior
  FCw 1977 Feb(2)

FOSTER, TOM
interior
  FCr 1975 Aug(4/5) *Fantasy Swordsmen
        [ill:*The Fiction of Robert
        E.Howard McHaney & Lord,
        1975]

FOX, H.
covers
  SN 1957 Nos.11,12; 1958 Nos.15,16
     1960 Nos.34,35; 1961 Nos.38,41,42,44,
        50; 1962 Nos.52-64,66;
     1963 Nos.68-83; 1964 Nos.84-93
     1965 Nos.94-101; 1966 Nos.102-105
     1967 Nos.106,107,109

FOX, MATT
covers
  WT 1944 Nov; 1946 Jul; 1947 May,Nov
     1948 May,Jul; 1949 Mar,Jul,Nov
     1950 Jan,Jul
backcover
  Whsp 1975 Dec(8) [dated 1965]

FRAME, PAUL
cover
  Ftc 1960 Mar

FRANKENBERG, ROBERT [1911-]
covers
  Ftc 1953 Jan/Feb
  StF 1970*Sum(12) [*part Ftc Jan/Feb 53]

FRAZETTA, FRANK [1928-]
  Interview Ariel 1-2,Aut 76-Win 77
cover
  Ariel 1977 Win(2)

backcover
  Ariel 1976*Aut(1) [*Conan of Cimmeria by
        Robert E. Howard, Lancer,1969]
  Eld 1978 Oct(4)
  FCr 1977 Mar(10/11)

interiors
  Ariel 1976 Aut-1977 Win [various]
  Chac 1976 Win(1); 1977 Spr(2)

FREAS, [FRANK] KELLY [1922-]
Noted US sf artist & illustrator
covers
  HoH 1973 Aug
  WT 1950 Nov; 1951 Nov; 1953 Jan

FREEMAN, GARY
backcovers
  Ftc 1980 Apr,Oct

FREEMAN, GEORGE
covers
  DFy 1978 Jun(16)

FRITZ, STEVE
cover
  W&S 1971 May(6)

FROLICH, DANY
cover
  S&T 1972 May(15)

backcover
  Wbk 1972 No.5

interior
  HPL 1972 Lovecraft [ap]

FROMMIG, PETER
cover
  TZ 1981 Dec

FUJITAKE, DENNIS
interior
  FCr 1975 Aug(4/5) Conan [ill]

FULKERSON, JUDE [Judy Jensen]
covers
  Div 1977 Jan(18)
  Spoor 1974 No.1

backcovers
  EC 1976 Jul(1)
  Wbk 1974 No.8

FUQUA, ROBERT
    Pseud: see Joseph W. TILLOTSON

GABRIELSON, ERNEST   [1891-1978]
cover
  Out 1946 Win

GARCIA, MIKE
interiors
  Nyc 1974 Jul(9) [ap]
  Whsp 1976 Dec(9) [ap]
       1978 Oct(11/12)

GARDNER, L. JACKSON
backcovers
  Spoor 1974 No.2

GARNER, MICHAEL J.
covers
  SE 1980 Spr(1)

GARRISON, JIM
covers
  Div 1975 Jun(9)
  F&T 1974 No.5
  S&T 1974 Mar(23)
  Wbk 1973 No.7

backcovers
  Wbk 1973 No.7; 1976 No.10; 1983 No.17
  Whsp 1974 Jul(4)

interiors
  E&O 1983 No.2 Eve Two [ill] Discovery
              [ill]
  F&T 1975 No.7 The Trophy [gs]
  HPL 1972 Lovecraft [ap]
  TW 1975 The Genesis [ap]

GASBARRI, FABIO
cover
  DFy 1978 Jan(15)

backcover
  DFy 1978 Jan(15)

GAUGHAN, JACK [John B.] [1930-]
covers
  Ftc 1963 Mar
  StF 1970*Fal(13) [*Ftc Mar 63]
  WoF 1968 No.1; 1970 No.2,Win(3);
       1971 Spr(4)

backcover
  Ftc 1962 Sep

GEIER, EARL
interiors
  Whsp 1983 Oct(19/20) The Colour Out of
              Space [ill]

GELOTTE, MARK
covers
  BL 1976 Oct(2)
  F&T 1975 No.7
  S&T 1970 Jul(9); 1971 Jun(12),Sep(13)
       1973 May(18),Nov(21); 1974 Nov(27)
       1975 Nov(33); 1976 May(36)

backcovers
  F&T 1975 No.7
  S&T 1971 Jun(12); 1973 Nov(21)
       1974 Mar(23),Jul(25); 1980 Apr(55)
       1983/4 Win(65)

interior
  S&T 1971 Jun(12) [ap]

GERUNG, JON
interiors
  Chac 1976 Win(1) Frontispiece
  Ftc 1979 Jul Sex Queens of Outer Space

GIBSON, BOB
cover
  EC 1981 No.5

GIESEKE, TOM
interior
  Ariel 1978 Oct(4) Frontispiece

GIUNTA, JOHN   [1920?-70]
US comic & magazine illustrator
covers
  WT 1944 Mar; 1948 Nov; 1949 May

GLADNEY, GRAVES
covers
  Unk 1939 Apr,Aug,Nov
  UnkB 1939*Nov

GLASENAPP, LYNN
interior
  FB 1982 May The Lynxidopteron [pic]

GOLLER, LYNN
cover
  BI 1967 Nov/Dec [unconfirmed]

GOODIER, JOHN
interior
  Whsp 1983 Oct(19/20) Pickman's Model[ill]

GORDON, DONNA
covers
  DFd 1980 Sum(3); 1983 Win(4)

HEATH, Jr., DAVID
interiors
  FCr 1974 Nov(1) Fan Art Portfolio
       1975 Feb(2) Fan Art Portfolio
                   Mars Reporter [cs]
            May(3) Our World [cs]
                   Ler's [cs]

HEITMAN
cover
  WT 1923 May

HELSDON, MARTIN
cover
  G&S 1980 No.2

HENDRICKSON, KATHY
backcover
  Ariel 1978 Apr(3)

HERRING, DOUGLAS
interior
  FCr 1975 Aug(4/5) Fantasy Swordsmen [ap]

HERRON, DON
cover
  Div 1974 Oct(5)

backcover
  Div 1974 Sep(4)

HICKMAN, STEVE
cover
  Ftc 1976 May

HICKS, IAN
cover
  DH 1983 Spr(26) [+ G. Crossland]

backcover
  FyT 1982 Win(11) [+ G. Crossland]

HIGGS, MIKE
cover
  DH 1972 No.4

HILBRETH, BOB
cover
  Ftc 1966*Nov [*Amazing Stories Dec 46]

HILDEBRANDT, Bros. [Bob & Tim]
cover
  Ftc 1980*Apr [*Urshurak,1979]

HILKERT, JOHN K.
cover
  ET 1941 Jul

HILL, CATHY
cover
  FB 1981 Oct

interiors
  Whsp 1977 Aug(10) color inset

HILL, LANCE
     as Lance Howlett
covers
  Myrd 1975 Win(1),Aug(2)

HILL, LAWSON W.
backcover
  Myrd 1975 Win(1)

HILL, MARVIN
backcover
  WA 1978 No.2

HINGE, MIKE
covers
  Ftc 1972 Apr,Oct

HJORT, JAMES W.
backcover
  EC 1981 No.5

HODGE, MIKE
interior
  FCr 1975 Feb(2) Fan Art Portfolio
                   Kung Who? [cs]

HOFFMAN, CHRISTOPHER
interior
  TZ 1983 Feb Optoshock! [pic]

HOFFMAN, RAH
interior
  Nyc 1972 Aug(7) CAS: Portfolio

HOGARTH, BURNE   [1911-]
  Interview Ariel 1,Aut 76
interior
  Ariel 1976 Aut(1) Tarzan cs examples

HOLMBERG, RANDY
covers
  NFJ 1977 No.2
  WD 1980 No.3

backcover
  Wyrd 1974 Spr(3)

HORSFALL, SIMON
backcover
  FyT 1979 Spr(4)

HOWLETT, LANCE
  Pseud: see Lance HILL

HUBER, Jr., RICHARD
cover
  FCr 1976 Jan

backcover
  FCr 1976 May(8)

interiors
  FCr 1975 Nov(6) [ap]
  Whsp 1983 Oct(19/20) Nyarlothotep [ill]

HUEY, GUY L[incoln] [1912-]
covers
  MT 1934 Win

HUGHES, BILL
covers
  FFy 1970 Oct; 1971 Feb,Jun

HUNT, JAMES E.
cover
  S&T 1978 Jan(46)

1963 Jan,May,Aug
StF 1970*Spr(11) [*Ftc Aug 62]

KRENKEL, ROY G.   [1918-83]
Noted US fantasy illustrator
cover
  Wbk 1977 No.11

KRUPA, JULIAN S.
cover
  Ftc 1965*Nov [*Amazing Stories Jul 39]

interior
  Ftc 1972*Feb [ap:*Fantastic Adventures
                 May 39]

KRUSZ, ARTHUR
covers
  BFF 1954 May,Sep

KUHLHOFF, PETE
covers
  WT 1945 May,Sep; 1946 Sep

KUNTZE, KURT
cover
  EC 1982 No.7

KUPPERBERG, ALAN
cover
  S&T 1972 Feb(14)

KURAS, THOMAS F.
cover
  EC 1980 No.4

KUROWSKI, CLIFF
cover
  Div 1976 May(14)

backcover
  Div 1975 Aug(10)

LABONSKI, MICHAEL
cover
  WT 1949 Sep

LAKIN, RICHARD
covers
  DH 1979 No.19

LAMBO, PAUL
cover
  DFy 1977 Sep(14) [+ Gene Day]

backcovers
  DFy 1973 Fal(2); 1974 Jul(4) [+ Gene Day]

LANDGRAF, KEN
backcover
  S&T 1977 May(42) [+ 'Simon']

LANOS, HENRI [fl.1886-1911]
French illustrator
interior
  Ftc 1968*May [ap:*When the Sleeper Wakes
                H.G.Wells The Graphic 1898/9;
                taken from book,1899]

LARSON, KEVIN
cover
  TZ 1982 Apr   [*backcover of GSTZ,1982]

LARSON, RANDALL D. [1954-]
interior
  Shyl 1978 Feb(2) Frontispiece [+ Steve
                    Fastner]

LAUGHLIN, CLARENCE JOHN
cover
  Nyc 1983 Apr(18)

LAWRENCE, JUDITH ANN [Mrs Judith Blish]
cover
  Imp 1966 Mar(1)

LAWTON, CLIFF
cover
  BWT 1960

LAYBOURNE, MEL
interiors
  Wyrd 1976/7 Win(6); 1977 Fal(7)

LEACH, STUART
covers
  GS 1931 Oct/Nov; 1931/2 Dec/Jan

LEE, ALAN
interior
  Ariel 1978 Apr(3)

LEE, LARRY
interiors
  S&T 1967 Fal(2) Edgar vs the Tree [cs]
      1968 Spr(3) Nastasi of the Apes
                   Returns [cs]
      1970 Feb(8) The Wizard [cs]

LEE, WALTER
cover
  FB 1983 Aug

backcovers
  FB 1982 Aug,Nov

LENEC, LIDIA
backcover
  AD 1975/6 Win(2)

LESLIE, WALTER
covers
  UTC 1941 Jun(6)-Sep(9)

LEWIS, BRIAN [1929-78]
covers
  SFy 1957 Dec(26)
      1958 Feb(27)-Dec(32)
      1959 Feb(33)-Dec(38)
      1960 Apr(40)-Oct(43)
      1961 Feb(45)-Aug(48)

LINDALL, TERRANCE
cover
  GSTZ 1982

LINTON, JOHN
cover
  Whsp 1975 Dec(8)

backcover
  Whsp 1974 Mar(3); 1975 Jun(6/7)

interiors
  Whsp 1974 Jul(4) the White Ship [ap]

Whsp 1975 Dec(8) A Folio
    1978 Oct(11/12)

LIPPA, LINDA
cover
 TZ 1981 Jul

LITTLE, JOHN A.
covers
 EvM 1974 Dec; 1975 Spr,Sum,Fal,Win
     1976 Spr,Sum,Win

LITTLEJOHN, MICHAEL T.
covers
 EvM 1978 Spr
 WD 1977 No.1

backcover
 EvM 1977/8 Win
 Jeet 1977 Sum(2)

LITTLEJOHN, WILLIAM
backcover
 S&T 1978 Jan(46)

LLOYD, DAVID
covers
 DH 1974 Aut/Win(10); 1977 Sum(17)
     1979 No.20
 DDH 1978 Dec(1)
 FyT 1979 Win(5); 1982 Sum(10);
     1983 Win(12)
 G&S 1982 No.4

backcovers
 DH 1976 Spr(13); 1981 Spr(22)

LOGE, DANIEL
cover
 EC 1976 Jul(1)

LONG, WILF
covers
 UTC 1941 Oct(10),Nov(11),Dec(12)
     1942 Feb(14)

LONGLEY, MARTIN
backcover
 DH 1979 No.19

LUTH, TOM
backcover
 S&T 1976 May(36)

LUTJENS
backcover
 Ftc 1964 Feb

LYNCH, TIM
backcovers
 S&T 1975 May(30); 1979 Jul(52)

LYNN, RICHARD
 Interview FCr 3,May 75
interiors
 FCr 1975 Feb-May(2-3) The Sons of
              Liberty [cs2]

MACABASCO, R.
backcover
 EC 1982 No.9

McCABE, BIL   [?-1982]
[also incidental art under the pseud.
Bukku Be Zaro]
cover [+ Harry O. Morris]
 Nyc 1981 Mar(16)

interior
 Nyc 1977 May(13) [ap]

McCORMICK, PATRICK
interior
 Nyc 1981 Mar(16) endpapers

MacDONNELL, KEVIN G.
backcovers
 S&T 1972 Nov(17); 1973 May(18);
     1974 Jan(22)

McLANE, PAULA
covers
 Ftc 1963 Sep; 1964 Mar; 1971 Aug

MacLEOD, ANGUS
backcover
 Div 1977 Mar(19)

interior
 S&T 1975 Sep(32) Cyanda [cs]

McLEOD, JIM
cover
 Myrd 1978 No.4

McNEILL, MALCOLM
cover
 TZ 1982 Jun

McSHERRY, Jr., F. D.
cover
 Unq 1978 Jan(1)

MAGRITTE, RENE   [1898-1967]
Belgian surrealist painter
cover
 TZ 1981*May   *'The Pleasure Principle'

MAITZ, DON
interior
 Ariel 1978 Oct(4)

MALLY, R. M.
covers
 WT 1923 Jun,Jul/Aug,Sep,Oct
     1924 Jan-May/Jul

MALONEY, TERRY
 (may also be one of the team 'Jarr')
covers
   as Jose Rubios
 SFy 1957 Apr(22)-Oct(25)

   as 'Terry'
 SFy 1956 May(18)

MANLEY, GRAHAM
interior
 FyT 1977 Win(2)

MANSO, LEO   [1914-]
US art director and pocketbook artist
covers
 ASFFR 1953 Jan,Apr

MOSKOWITZ, H. S.
covers
  MM 1931 Jun,Jul,Dec

MOWRY, DAVID
backcover
  DFy 1974 Oct(5)

MOY, GLENN
cover
  Ftc 1974 Mar

MUSGRAVE, REAL
backcover
  FB 1982 May

NAPOLI, VINCENT
interiors
  Whsp 1979 Oct(13/14) Art Folio
(also found extensively in WT in 1940s)

NAPPI, RUDY
cover
  TF 1957 Spr

NAZZ, JAMES
cover
  TZ 1982 Sep

NELSON, T. WYATT
cover
  WT 1932 Aug

NICHOL
interior [+ Hannes Bok]
  WT 1944 Jul   Weirditties

NICHOLSON, RUSS
cover
  G&S 1981 No.3

interior
  G&S 1979 No.1   M.R.James [ap]

NOEL, ARLENE
interior
  Ariel 1978 Oct(4)

NOLDE, EMIL
backcover
  Wbk 1968 No.1

NORDLING, LEE
interiors
  FB 1982 Aug-1983 Aug(not May 83)
            Curtains [cs]
       1983 May Drydock [cs]
            Dec Full Moon [cs]

NUETZELL, ALBERT A[ugustus]
covers
  Ftc 1960 Jan,Aug

OBERDORF, JOHN
cover
  TZ 1982 Feb

ODBERT, JIM
interior
  Whsp 1977 Aug(10) Frontispiece

OERMANN, ROBERT
backcovers
  FCr 1975 Aug(4/5)
  FCw 1977 Jan(1)

OLIFF, STEVE
covers
  Wyrd 1974 Dec(4)

interior
  Wyrd 1976/7 Win(6) Gunfighter [gs]

OLSEN, RICHARD
backcover
  Whsp 1974 Nov(5)

O'NEAL, MICHAEL D.
backcover
  S&T 1981 Apr(59)

OSTERMAN, DAN
cover
  S&T 1970 Feb(8); 1971 Apr(11)

backcovers
  S&T 1970 Feb(8); 1971 Apr(11);
      1972 Feb(14); 1973 Jul(19)

interior
  S&T 1972 May(15) [ap]

OUGHTON, TAYLOR
cover
  Ftc 1959 Sep

PALMER, DELOS
covers
  GS 1927 Dec; 1928 Feb-Jul

PARDEE, CURTIS
interior
  Nyc 1978 Mar(14) endpapers

PARKER, JOHN
cover
  DW 1957 May

PARTRIDGE, NORMAN
cover
  SFy 1954 Sep(10)

PATRICK, TONY
backcover
  Wbk 1983(18)

PAUL, FRANK R[udolph] [1884-1963]
Austrian-born US pioneer sf pulp artist
covers [Note: FA is Fantasic Adventures,
  AS is Amazing Stories, ASQ is Amazing
  Stories Quarterly]
  Ftc 1965*Sep [*FA May 39]
      1966*Mar [*AS Nov 40]
          *May [*AS Sep 44]
          *Jul [*FA Oct 45]
          *Sep [*AS Apr 42]
      1967*Jan [*AS Mar 41]
          *Sep [*AS Jan 41]
      1968*Jan [unconfirmed]
          *Oct [*AS Mar 45]
interiors
  Ftc 1966 Nov *The Land That Time Forgot
            [*AS Feb 27]

```
        1967 Mar *Merritt Portfolio
               [*AS May 27]
        1972 Dec *The Sunken World
               [*ASQ Sum 28]
```

PAVLAC, BRIAN
cover
 NFJ 1976 Sum(1)

PEARSON, JOE
backcover
 Div 1976 Sep(16) [+ Phil Foglio]

PEDERSON, Jr., JOHN
cover
 Ftc 1972 Jun

PELLETIERE, CHRIS
cover
 Wbk 1979 No.14

backcover
 EC 1982 No.8

interior
 Whsp 1979 Oct(13/14) Smoke Ghost

PERL, H. W.
cover
 STB 1946 No.1

PETERKA, JOHANN
interior
 Nyc 1977 May(13) Dagon [ap]

PETILLO, ROBERT
cover
 Ftc 1980*Oct [*Tomorrow & Beyond ed.
          Ian Summers,1978]

PETRIE, Jr., C. BARKER
covers
 WT 1926 Feb,Aug,Oct;
        1927 Jan,Feb; 1931 Feb/Mar

PFEUFER, CARL
cover
 GS 1931 Aug/Sep

PHILLIPS, BARYE [?-1969?]
covers
 Ftc 1952 Sum[+ L.R. Summers],Nov/Dec

PHILLIPS, RALPH RAYBURN
 Profile Nek 2,Sum 50
covers
 Nek 1950 Sum(2); 1951 mid(5)
 Wbk 1968*No.1 [*Shanadu ed. Robert
          Briney,1953]

PIANFETTI, JIM
cover
 Eld 1982 No.8

backcover
 EC 1979 No.2

interior
 Eld 1981 No.2 [ap]

PITTS, CHARLES [1952-]
backcovers
 NV 1977 Fal(1); 1981 Spr(7)

interiors
 NV 1977 Fal(1) Creative Images [ap]
                  Tumblins' [gs]
        1978 Sum(2) Sunslayer [gs] [+ F.
                  Newton Burcham]
                  The Dream is Alive [ap]
        Win(3) Creative Images [ap]
        1979 Sum(4) Creative Images [ap]
        Fal(5) Frontispiece [+ F.
                  Newton Burcham]
        1983 Win/Spr(9) Frontispiece

PITTS, JIM
 Interview DH 9,Sum 74
covers
 Agd 1980 Aut
 Cth 1976 No.1; 1977 No.2; 1978 No.3
 DH 1973 Dec(7); 1974 Sum(9);
        1976 Spr(13),Win(15)
 FyT 1977 Sum(1),Win(2); 1979 Spr(4)
        1981 Spr(7); 1982 Spr(9),Win(11)
 Kad 1981 Jul(4); 1982 Jul(5)
 Nyc 1976 Apr(11/12)

backcovers
 DH 1976 Sum(14)
 FyT 1980 Sum(6)
 Kad 1982 Jul(5)

interiors
 DH 1974 Sum(9) [ap]
 Whsp 1974 Jul(4) The White Ship [ap]
        Nov(8) endpapers
        1975 Dec(8) Ghosts: a Tribute to
                  M.R.James [ap]

POLLACK, J.
cover
 SN 1957 No.10

POLSON, WALTER
interior
 NV 1980 Sum(6) centrefold

POTTER, J. K.
covers
 Nyc 1980 Jan(15); 1982 Jun(17)

backcover
 Wbk 1978 No.13

interior
 Nyc 1980 Jan(15) H.P. Lovecraft: A Legacy
                  of Worms [ap]

POTTS, CARL
backcover
 Div 1975 Apr(8)

POUND, JOHN
covers
 FC 1973 Nos.1,2(?),4,5

POWELL
cover
 SFy 1950 Sum(1)

POWERS, RICHARD M. [1921-]
covers
 BFF 1953 Jul,Sep
 Ftc 1953 Mar/Apr

PRESTON, DANIEL W.
backcover
  Wbk 1969 No.2; 1970 No.3

PRISCILLA, LOUIS
interior
  Ftc 1954 Apr [ap]

PUNCHATZ, DON IVAN
  Profile & Portfolio Shyl 6,Win 82

QUIGLEY, RAY
covers
  WT 1938 Dec; 1940 Sep; 1942 May

QUINBY, EDWARD
backcover
  Wbk 1977 No.11

interior
  Wbk 1978 No.13 Frontispiece

QUINN, GERARD   [1927-]
Irish illustrator
covers
  SFy 1952 Aut(5); 1953 Spr(6)
      1954 Spr(7),May(8),Jul(9),Dec(11)
      1955 Feb(12)-Nov(16)
      1956 Feb(17),Aug(19),Dec(20)
      1957 Feb(21)
      1961 Oct(49),Dec(50);
      1962 Feb(51)-Aug(54)
      1963 Feb(57),Jun(59),Aug(60)

RAE, G. M.
cover
  UTC 1942 Jul(18)

RAINEY, D.
covers
  SN 1960 No.37;
      1961 Nos.39,43,45,47-49,51
      1962 Nos.65,67

RANEY, KEN W.
covers
  AD 1977 Win(5)
  DFy 1980 Mar(22)
  S&T 1975 Jul(31); 1981/2 Win(61)
  SPWAO 1980 No.1; 1982 No.2

backcovers
  BL 1976 Aug(1)
  DFy 1978 Dec(18)
  FCr 1975 Feb(2)
  S&T 1975 Jul(31)
  ToF 1982 Spr(1)

interiors
  BFWK 1978*Aut(1)
  FCr 1975 Feb(2) Fan Art Portfolio
           May(3) Howard's Women [ap]
           Aug(4/5) Beyond the Black River
  NV 1981 Spr(7) Frontispiece
  S&T 1975 Jul(31)-1976 Mar(35) Black Wolf
                              [cs4]
  SPWAO 1980 No.1 The Gallery [ap]

RANKIN, HUGH
covers
  WT 1927 Aug,Dec; 1928 Dec
  WT 1929 Feb,Apr,Jun,Aug,Oct,Dec
  WT 1930 Feb,Apr,Jun,Aug,Oct,Dec

REDONDO, NESTOR
interior
  Chac 1976 Win(1)

REHBERGER, GUSTAV   [1910-]
interior
  Ftc 1953 Sep/Oct [ap]

REISENBERG, S. H.
covers
  TB 1919 Mar 1,15,Apr 1,15,May 1,15,
           Jun 1,15,Jul 1,Aug 15,Oct 1(?)

REISMAN, DAVID
backcover
  FCr 1976 Jan

REYNOLDS, JAMES
covers
  TB 1919 Sep 1, Oct 15

RICE, KEN
cover
  Sus 1951 Spr(?)

RICHARDSON, JOHN ADKINS [1929-]
  Interview NV 2,Sum 78
covers
  NV 1977 Fal(1)

interiors
  HPL 1972   Lovecraft [ap]
  NV 1978 Sum(2) Ted,Red & Willie [gs/ex]

RICHARDSON, SUE
interiors
  FB 1982 Feb Frontispiece
           Nov Frontispiece

RIDGE, GLENN
cover
  Ftc 1974 May

RILEY, DAVID A.
covers
  DH 1972 No.2,No.3
  WW 1970 Jun(1); 1971 Mar(2)

interior
  E&O 1983 No.2 Shub-Niggurath [ill]

RILEY, STEPHEN T.
covers
  Div 1975 Aug(10)
  FCw 1977 Jan(1)
  FBDG 1972 Apr/May(1); 1974 Apr(3)

backcover
  FCr 1978 Sep(14)

interiors
  AD 1977 Fal(6) The Silver Key [ill]
  FCr 1975 May(3) Howard's Women [ap]
      1976 Feb(7) Lovecraft [ap]
  Nyc 1972 Aug(7) Tsathoggua [gv]
      1976 Apr(11/12) Frontispiece
  Whsp 1974 Jul(4) The White Ship [ap]

ROBERTS, KEITH   [1935-]
UK Author and Commercial Artist
covers
  Imp 1966 Apr(2)-Dec(10); 1967 Jan(11)
  SFy 1965 Jan/Feb(69),May(72)-Aug(75)
           Nov(78); 1966 Jan(80),Feb(81)

ROBERTS, LON T.
backcover
  Whsp 1983 Oct(19/20)

ROBERTS, W. J.
covers
  FGS 1938
  TGHH 1939 Dec
(Roberts probably did most of the covers
for the Master Thriller series)

ROBERTSON, RICHARD
interiors
  Whsp 1975 Jun(6/7) color inset (from
            Tower of the Elephant Robert
            E. Howard, D.M.Grant,1975]

RODEN, MICHAEL
backcover
  S&T 1980 Jul(56)

interiors
  Nyc 1983 Apr(18) endpapers
  SPWAO 1980 No.1   The Gallery [ap]

ROGERS, ALVA   [1923-1982]
US pharmaceutical salesman and sf fan
cover
  STB 1946 No.2

ROLAND, HARRY
covers
  Ftc 1973 Jul; 1975 Jun,Aug

ROLAND, MARK
backcover
  Wyrd 1976/7 Win(6)

interior
  Wyrd 1976/7 Win(6) Manabozho and the
            Lacrosse Game [gs]

ROMERO, ED
cover
  S&T 1972 Aug(16)

interior
  S&T 1971 Jun(12) Could You Be Next?[cs]

ROMITA, Jr., JOHN
backcover
  S&T 1972 Aug(16)

RONDEAU, MELODY
interiors
  FB 1982 Aug-1983 Feb Morgoth [cs]

ROWE, DAVID
backcovers
  DH 1972 Nos.2,3

ROY, PIERRE   [1880-1950]
French painter
backcover
  Ftc 1952*Sum [*Danger on the Stairs]

RUTT, J.
interior
  Chac 1977 Spr(2) centrespread

S., R. W.
covers
  Phtm 1957 Apr(1)-1958 Jul(16) all issues

ST. JOHN, J[ohn] ALLEN [1872-1957]
US illustrator noted for his Burroughs
work
covers
  Mystic 1953 Nov
  WT 1932 Jun,Nov,Dec
      1933 Jan,Feb,Apr,May
      1936 Oct,Dec

interiors
  Ftc 1966 Nov *Burroughs Portfolio
            [*AS Mar & Jun 41, FA Jul 41]
      1972 Apr *Slaves of the Fish Men
            [*FA Mar 41]

SALMONSON, JESSICA AMANDA [1950-]
US author [see Author Index]
    as Amos Salmonson
covers
  F&T 1973 Nos.1,2

backcover
  F&T 1973 No.1

    as Joy Long
interior
  F&T 1973 No.4 Demonology of the Pacific
            N.W. American Indian [pic]

SALOMONI, TITO
covers
  TZ 1981 Aug,Oct; 1982 Mar

SANDERCOMBE, W. FRASER [1949-]
backcovers
  EC 1980 No.3
  Wbk 1982 No.16

SANDERS, MICHAEL [see Saunders below]
backcovers
  FCr 1975 May(3)

SASSAMON, GARY
interior
  FCr 1975 Feb(2) Fan Art Portfolio

SATER, S. SCOTT
backcover
  S&T 1974 May(24)

SAUBER, ROB
cover
  TZ 1982 Oct

SAUNDERS, MICHAEL [see Sanders above]
interior
  FCr 1974 Nov(1) Fan Art Portfolio

SAUNDERS, NORMAN B. [1907-]
US pulp/pocketbook illustrator
covers
  AMF 1950 Feb,Apr,Jul,Oct
  EM 1938 Aug,Nov; 1939 Feb,Apr/May
  ES 1937 Aug
  MysT 1951 Nov; 1952 Jan,Mar,Jun,No.5
  US 1941 Apr
  UT 1939 Apr/May-1940 May (probably did
            all covers)

SAVIUK, ALEX
covers
S&T 1967 Fal(2); 1968 Spr(3),Win(4)
    1969 Sum(6),Aug(7); 1971 Mar(10)
    1977 Jul(43)

backcovers
S&T 1969 Spr(5),Sum(6),Aug(7)
    1971 Mar(10)

interiors
S&T 1968 Win(4),1969 Sum(6) & 1971 Mar(10)
        The Hellsman [cs3]
    1969 Spr(5) & 1970 Jul(9)
        The Dawn of Time [cs2]
        Aug(7) A Hasty Passage [cs]
                The Stranger [cs]
    1972 May(15) Why Me? [cs]

SCHELLING, GEORGE [Luther] [1938-]
covers
Ftc 1962 May; 1964 Oct,Nov

backcovers
Ftc 1962 Aug; 1963 May,Jun,Sep

SCHILLING, DAN
cover
Ftc 1973 Nov

SCHMAND, RICHARD & ROBERT
covers
MoH 1969 Jul(28),Dec(30)
SMS 1969 Sum(13); 1970 Sum(16),Fal(17)
WTT 1970 Fal(3)

SCHNOBRICH, GEORGE
covers
NF 1980/1 Win(1)

backcover
NF 1980/1 Win(1)

interior
DFd 1983 Win(4) Frontispiece

SCHOMBURG, ALEX   [1905-]
US painter and sf artist/illustrator
covers
Ftc 1960 Nov; 1961 Jan,Mar,Jun,Sep,Oct
    1963 Nov

SCHROEDER, ERNEST
cover
Ftc 1954 Jun

interior
Ftc 1954 Jan/Feb "The Rime of the
        Ancient Mariner" [ap]

SCHWAB, JAN
backcover
Shyl 1979 Sum(3)

SCHWARTZ, STEPHEN F.
covers
Arg 1981 Fal/Win(8)
Div 1977 Nov(23)
S&T 1979 Jul(52); 1980 Apr(55)

backcovers
NV 1978 Win(3)
S&T 1979 Jan(50); 1982 Sum(62),Win(63)

SCOTT, H. W.
US pulp artist, notably westerns
covers
Unk 1939 Mar,May,Jun,Jul,Sep; 1940 Jan
UnkB 1939*Sep; 1940*Jan

SCOTT, MICHAEL
covers
Nyc 1972 Feb(6); 1974 Jul(9)

interiors
Nyc 1972 Aug(7)   CAS: Portfolio
Whsp 1978 Oct(11/12) endpapers

SCOTT, ROMAN
cover
EC 1982 No.8

interior
Whsp 1983 Oct(19/20) Lovecraft [ap]

SEARS, BROC
cover
FCr 1975 Aug(4/5)

interiors
FCr 1975 Aug(4/5) Conan [ill]
                    Incident [cs]

SECREASE, DON
interiors
NV 1978 Win(3)-1979 Sum(4) Songbringer
        [gs2] [+ Paul Daly]
        Win(3) Creative Images [ap]
    1979 Fal(5)-1981 Spr(7) Sunslayer
        [gs3] [+ Rick Burchett]

SENF, C. C.
covers
WT 1927 Mar-Jul,Sep-Nov
    1928 Jan-Nov
    1929 Jan,Mar,May,Jul,Sep,Nov
    1930 Jan,Mar,May,Jul,Sep,Nov
    1931 Jan,Apr/May-Dec
    1932 Jan-May,Jul

SERVOSS, ALLAN
interiors
Whsp 1975 Jun(6/7) A Folio
        1978 Oct(11/12) Frontispiece

SETTLES, JAMES B.
cover
Ftc 1966*Jan [*Amazing Stories Aug 42]

SEVERIN, JOHN
interiors
Chac 1977 Spr(2) The Eternal Champion
Shyl 1982 Win(5) Fantasy [ap]

SHARP, HENRY
cover
Ftc 1955 Feb

SHERMAN
covers
Ace 1936 May,Jul

SHESKIN, DAVID J.
interior
S&T 1983/4 Win(65) Bezeball - 2082 [pic]

SHONBERG, BURT
cover
  Ftc 1960 Jun

interior
  Gam 1963 No.2 [ap]

SHULTZ, WENDY ADRIAN
US illustrator
    as Wendy Adrian Wees
cover
  G&S 1983 No.5

SILVEY, W. H.
covers
  WT 1953 Jul; 1954 Jan,May

SIM, DAVE
cover
  PD 1977 No.2

interiors
  DFy 1976 Dec(10) Dead Things [ap]
  Db 1978 Spr(1)

SIME, SIDNEY H. [1867-1942]
British artist and cartoonist
  Profile   ArkS Aut 49

SIMON
backcover [+ K.Landgraf]
  S&T 1977 May(42)

SINGER, EVAN
cover
  WT 1954 Mar

SIROIS, AL
covers
  Div 1976 Sep(16); 1979 Feb/Mar(28/9)

SMITH, ANDREW
covers
  MS 1976 Apr(3),Aug(4)

backcover
  FBDG 1972 Apr/May(1) [+ G.Matthews]

SMITH, CHARLES T.
covers
  S&T 1976 Jan(34),Nov(39)

interior
  S&T 1972 Aug(16) Whore of the Worlds
      [cs: text also by Smith under
          pseud 'George Herbert']

SMITH, CLARK ASHTON   [1893-1961]
backcover
  Nyc 1972 Aug(7)

interior
  FCr 1975 May(3) Howard's Women

SMITH, DAWN
backcover
  F&T 1973 No.4

SMITH, KENNETH
  Profile FCr 14,Sep 78
interior
  FCr 1978 Sep(14)

SMITH, MALCOLM
covers
  Ftc 1967*May [*Fantastic Adventures,
              Jun 43]
  Mytic 1954 Mar,May

SMITH, MARGARET
interior
  F&T 1973 No.4

SPANGLEY, RANDAL
cover
  NV 1979 Fal(5)

SPURGIN, RANDALL
covers
  Nyc 1975 Jan/Feb(10)
  S&T 1977 Sep(44)
  Spoor 1974 No.2

backcovers
  Eld 1978 Mar(3)
  Nyc 1973 Apr(8)

interior
  FCr 1975 Aug(4/5) Beyond the Black River
  Nyc 1972 Aug(7) CAS: Portfolio

STANLEY, DORIS
covers
  GS 1928 Aug-Dec

STARSHINE, SYLVIA
backcover
  FyT 1978 Sum(3)

STATON, JOE
covers
  Ftc 1973 Sep; 1974 Nov

STEELE, TED
cover
  UTC 1941 May(5)

STEIN, MODEST
cover
  Unk 1939 Oct
  UnkB 1939*Oct

STERANKO, JIM   [1938-]
interior
  Chac 1977 Spr(2) Mother Was a Lovely
                Beast [ill]

STEVENS, DALTON
covers
  GS 1930 Apr-Dec
      1931 Jan-May

STEVENS, LAWRENCE [Sterne]
cover
  AMF 1949 Dec

STEVENSON, E. M.
covers
  WT 1926 Apr,Jun,Jul,Sep,Nov

STEWART, JOHN
covers
  PD 1976 No.1
  Whsp 1982 Mar(15/16),Aug(17/18)

backcovers
Nyc 1977 May(13); 1981 Mar(16)

interiors
Agd 1980 Aut Witch Tree [ill]
Nyc 1978 Mar(14) Frontispiece
Whsp 1978 Oct(11/12) Averoigne [ap]
     1979 Oct(13/14) Our Lady of Dark-
          ness (frontispiece)
     1982 Mar(15/16) Carib Grotesques
          [ap]
          Aug(17/18) Gunslinger Folio

STINE, ROGER
covers
Shyl 1977 Nov(1); 1980 Win(4)

STONE, BILL
covers
FF 1950 May,Nov

STONEHAM, WILLIAM
cover
TZ 1982*May

STONER, ELMER C.
covers
Wtch 1936 Nov,Dec

STOUT, WILLIAM
covers
Cov 1969 Sep,Nov; 1970 Jan,Mar
 [Sep 69 cover rep.as backcover to
  Cov Mar 70]

STREFF, MICHAEL
cover
Div 1977 Mar(19)

STUCK, FRANZ   [1863-1928]
cover
SE 1980*Win(2)

SUMMERS, LEO RAMON
covers
Ftc 1952 Sum[+B.Phillips],Fal
    1953 Sep/Oct; 1957 Jul
    1958 Mar,Apr,Jul,Aug; 1959 Jul
    1960 Feb,Jul,Oct,Dec
    1961 Feb,Aug; 1962 Feb
WM 1970*Fal(1) [*FA May 52]

backcovers
Ftc 1961 May,Aug;
    1962 Apr,May,Jul,Oct,Nov; 1963 Jan.

SUTBERRY, JERRY
interiors
NV 1978 Win(3) Creative Images [ap]

SWENSTON, STEVE
covers
Wyrd 1974 Spr(3)

backcovers
DFy 1975 Sep(7)
Wyrd 1974 Dec(4)

interior
TW 1975 White Bear & Red Moon [ap]

SYMEON
cover
SN 1960 No.32

TALBOT, BRIAN
cover
DH 1972 No.1

TEMPLAR, SCOTT
cover
BFF 1954 Mar

'TERRY'
    Pseud: see Terry MALONEY

THAYER, JED
cover
Ftc 1959 May

THEOBALD, RAY
covers
OTW 1954 No.1
SN 1954 Nos.1,2; 1957 Nos.9,13
    1958 Nos.14,17-20
    1959 Nos.21-29; 1961 No.40

TIANI, DENIS
covers
ArkC 1971 Win(8)
Div 1976 Mar(13)
Nyc 1972 Feb(6); 1974 Jul(9)

backcover
Nyc 1976 Apr(11/12)

interior
Whsp 1974 Jul(4) The White Ship [ap]

TIBBETTS, JOHN
covers
Eld 1978 Oct(4); 1979 Apr(5); 1980 No.7
    1981 No.2

interiors
Eld 1978 Mar(3) Robert E.Howard [ill]
    1979 No.6   Robert Bloch [ill]
    1981 No.2   August Derleth [ill]

TILBURNE, A. R.
    [see fiction under pseud. Lee Tilburne]
covers
WT 1938 Nov; 1942 Sep; 1943 Jan,Sep,Nov
    1944 Jul,Sep; 1945 Mar;
    1946 Jan; 1947 Jan

TILLOTSON, JOSEPH W.
    as Robert Fuqua
cover
Ftc 1967*Mar [*FA May 39]

TIPTON, DAVE
interior
NV 1979 Fal(5) Artmaster [cs]

TODD, LARRY S.
cover
Ftc 1971 Oct [+ Vaughn Bode]

TOOKER, GEORGE   [1920-]
backcover
Ftc 1952*Fal [*'Dance']

TREVISANI, FRAN[cis John George] [1953-]
US map maker
covers
S&T 1978 Apr(47); 1980 Jul(56)

backcovers
S&T 1979 Apr(51); 1981 Jan(58)

TUCKER, EZRA NOEL
cover
Shyl 1982 Win(5)

interior
Ariel 1978 Oct(4)

TURNER, HARRY
cover
SFy 1950/1 Win(2)

TURNER, ROLAND
covers
OTW 1955 No.2
SN 1955 Nos.6,8

UTPATEL, FRANK
covers
Whsp 1975 Jun(6/7); 1977 Aug(10)

interiors
Whsp 1974 Jul(4) The White Ship [ap]
Whsp 1977 Aug(10) A Folio

VALIGURSKY, ED[ward] [1926-]
covers
DW 1957 Feb,Aug
Ftc 1955 Apr,Jun,Aug,[Oct?],Dec
    1956 Feb,Apr,Jun,Aug,Oct,Dec
    1957 Feb-Jun,Aug-Dec
    1958 Jan,Feb,May,Jun,Sep
    1959 Mar,Apr,Jun,Aug,Oct,Dec
WM 1970*Win(2) [*Ftc Sep 58]
    1971*Spr(3) [*FA Jan 52]

VAN DER STEVER, GARY
cover
WT 1973 Fal [comp. of art by H.Bok]

VAN DONGEN, H[enry] R.
covers
WB 1951 Jan,Feb

VAN VLACK, MERCY
interior
FCr 1975 Feb(2) Fan Art Portfolio

VELEZ, WALTER
covers
TZ 1983 Feb

VESS, CHARLES
covers
FB 1981 Dec
S&T 1978 Jul(48)

interiors
DFd 1980 Sum(3) Frontispiece
    1983 Win(4)
Whsp 1982 Mar(15/16) endpapers

VICTOR, JONATHAN
interiors
FCr 1974 Nov(1) Fan Art Portfolio
    1975 Feb(2) Fan Art Portfolio

1975 May(3) Howard's Women [ap]

VIDMAR, RENE
covers
BFF 1953 Nov; 1954 Jul,No.9

VOLPE, DANTE
cover
UnT 1974 No.1

VOSBURGH, DAVID
covers
Arg 1979 Win/Spr(5)
EvM 1977 Fal

backcovers
BL 1976 Oct(2); 1978 Jan(4/5)
EvM 1977 Fal; 1978 Sum

WALKER, BRUCE
backcover
Whsp 1973 Dec(2)

WALKER, IAN
interior
F&T 1973 No.4

WARD, GERALDINE M.
cover
Hor 1982 No.2

backcovers
Hor 1980 No.1; 1982 No.2

WARREN, JIM
cover
TZ 1981 Apr

WASHBURN
cover
WT 1923 Nov

WAULS, CHERYL
backcovers
Wbk 1971 No.4

WAYNE, BILL
covers
WT 1950 Sep; 1951 Mar

WEES, WENDY ADRIAN
    see under Wendy Adrian SHULTZ

WEILL, IRVIN J.
interiors
WT 1940 Nov-1947 May Superstitions &
              Taboos [pic.series]

WENSKE, HELMUT
backcover
Nyc 1975 Jan/Feb(10)

interiors
Nyc 1973 Apr(8); 1974 Jul(9) [ap]
    1976 Apr(11/12)

WENZEL, PAUL E.
cover
Ftc 1963 Dec

WERNER, HANS-PETER   [1948-]
covers
NV   1980 Sum(6)
PtF 1978 Sum(1); 1979 Fal(2)

backcovers
NV   1981 Fal(8)
PtF 1978 Sum(1)

interiors
NV   1979 Fal(5)
Wbk 1983 No.17   endpaper

WESSO[LOWSKI], HANS W[aldemar] [1894-]
German-born US pulp artist
covers
ST   1931 Sep,Nov
     1932 Jan,Mar,Jun,Oct; 1933 Jan

interior
Ftc 1973 Jul *Invaders From the Infinite
       [*Amazing Stories Quarterly* Spr/
        Sum 32]

WEST, JOSEPH A.
cover
Div 1974 Dec(6)

backcover
E&O 1973 No.1

WHELAN, MICHAEL
Interview Shyl 5,Win 82
cover
Shyl 1982 Win(6)

interior
Shyl 1982 Win(5)

WHIGHAM, ROD
cover
WA   1978 May(1)

WHITE, DAVID
cover
TZ   1982 Jul

WHITEHEAD, DANNY
interior
Ariel 1978 Apr(3) Frontispiece

WILBER, RON[ALD]
covers
Div 1977 Jul(21)
S&T 1976 Nov(39)

backcover
S&T 1974 Nov(27)

WILLIAMSON, AL
interior
Ariel 1978 Apr(3) Alon the Scenic Route
       [gs;from a story by H.Ellison]

WILLIS, PAUL J.
cover
Anu 1966 Aut

WILOCH, THOMAS
interior
Nyc 1983 Apr(18) Frontispiece

WINDSOR-SMITH, BARRY   [1950-]
Interview Ariel 3,Apr 78
cover
Ariel 1978 Apr(3)

interiors
Ariel 1978 Apr(3)
Shyl 1977 Nov(1)   Frontispiece

WING, CHUCK
cover
S&T 1977 May(42)

WINNICK, GARY
covers
Div 1974 Sep(4); 1975 Apr(8); 1977 Sep(22)

backcover
Div 1976 Mar(13)

interiors
S&T 1973 Sep(20) Centrespread
     1974 Sep(26) Darkover: Night of the
                   Sorceress [cs]
     1975 Mar(29) Darkover: The Brigands
                   [cs]

WITTMACK, E. FRANKLIN
covers
WT   1943 Mar,Jul

WOLFE, COREY   [1953-]
covers
FB   1982 May; 1983 Feb,Dec

backcovers
FB   1982 Feb; 1983 May
WOLTERS, FRED
covers
MoH 1964 Nov(6); 1965*Jan(7) [*as No.6]
     1965 Apr(8),Jun(9)

WOOD, DARRELYN
cover
TZ   1981 Jun

WOODS, JOAN HANKE
cover
NV   1978 Win(3)

interior
NV   1979 Sum(4) Frontispiece

WREN, GEORGE
covers
GS   1931 Jun,Jul

WRIGHTE, BRUCE
interior
Db   1978 Spr

WURTS, JANNY
cover
FB   1982 Aug

ZABEL, JOE
cover
S&T 1976 Mar(35)

backcover
S&T 1976 Jul(37)

interior
S&T 1976 Mar(35)   Hero [cs]

ZARO, BUKKU BE
   Pseud: see Bil McCABE

ZILZER, GYULA   [1898-?]
interior
 Ftc 1953 Nov/Dec

ZIRN, RUDOLPH
cover
 DrD 1935 Apr

                    ***

_Editor Index

ABERCROMBIE, ROBERT NYCROFT
Publisher/Editor: Wyrd No.8,1980

ACKERMAN, FORREST J   [1916-]
Associate Editor: BWT 1960

ADAMS, ALLAN M.
Publisher: BI Nov/Dec 67

ADAMS, FRED C.
Editor: Spoor No.1,1974

ALBING, JERRY
Publisher: SFF Feb 41-Mar 42

AMBROSE, MICHAEL E.   [1956-]
Publisher/Editor: Arg May 72(1)-current
   [Fal 83(9)]. [Note: entitled Macabre
   May 72-Sum 76]

ANDERSON, JAMES
Editor: SPWAO No.2, 1982

ANDERSON, WILLIAM T.
Executive Editor: Chl Jul-Nov 81

ARTHUR, ROBERT   [1909-69]
Managing Editor: MysT Nov 51-No.5,1952

ASSAEL, SOL
   + Michael Nahum
Co-Publisher/Editor: OTW No.1,1954-No.2,
   1955; SN No.1,1954-No.109,1967 [Note:
   early issues edited under pseud. John
   Spencer Manning]

AVALLONE,Jr., MICHAEL [Angelo] [1924-]
Editor: TF Spr-Aug 57

BACON, JONATHAN   [1948-]
Publisher/Editor: FCr Nov 74(1)-Mar 77(10/
   11);Jun 78(13)-Jan 79(15); FCw Jan 77
   (1)-Feb 77(3)

BAIRD, EDWIN   [1886-1957]
Editor: WT Mar 23-Apr 24

BAKER, CHARLES L.
Assistant Editor: Eld No.8,1982-current

BANISTER, MANLY [Miles]   [1914-]
Publisher/Editor: Nek Spr 50-mid 51

BARLOW, ROBERT H[ayward] [1918-51]
Publisher/Editor: Lvs Sum 37-Win 38/9

BATES, HARRY   [1900-81]
Editor: ST Sep 31-Jan 33

BAY, G. R.
Editor: MM Jun-Nov/Dec 31

BAYER, JANE
Managing Editor: TZ May 81-Feb 84

BECKER, EDITH L.
Managing Editor: GS Late 1928-early 1929;
   Apr-late 1930

BENJAMIN, JUDY-LYNN
Associate Editor: WoF No.1,1968
Managing Editor: WoF No.2,1970-Spr 71

BENSINK, JOHN
Executive Editor: TZ Dec 83-current

BERGLUND, E[dward] P[AUL] [1942-]
Editor: FBDG Apr/May 72-Oct 77; Spoor
   No.2,1974
Assistant Editor(Fiction): Nyc Jun 71(4)-
   Jan 80(15)
Editorial Assistant (early stages only):
   ToF Spr 82(1)

   + Crispin Burnham
Co-Editor: DMR No.1,1975

BERNHARD, ALAN P.
Associate Publisher: Ftc Apr 79-Oct 80

BERNHARD, ARTHUR
Associate Publisher: Ftc Oct 70-Jan 79
Publisher: Ftc Apr 79-Oct 80

BERRY, JOHN
Assistant Editor: Ftc Nov 73-May 74

BETZ, DANIEL R.
Editor/Publisher: Hor No.1-current

BIRD, CLIFFORD W.
Editor/Publisher: FCr Nov 77(12)

BLOOM, BRITTON
Editorial Assistant: Ftc Jan-Oct 80

BOND, GEORGE
Editor: GS during 1929

BONFIGLIOLI, KYRIL   [1928-]
Editor: SFy Jun/Jul 64(65)-Feb 66(81);
   Imp Mar 66(1)-Sep 66(7)

BRENNAN, JOSEPH PAYNE   [1918-]
Publisher/Editor: Mac Jun 57(1)-1976(23)

BROWN, GERALD J.   [1950-]
Publisher/Editor: NV Fal 77(1)-[Win]84
   (10)

BROWNE, HOWARD   [1908-]
Editor: Ftc Sum 52-Aug 56

BUCHANAN, LAMONT
Associate Editor: WT Nov 42-Sep 49

BURGE, SUSAN
   see under Susan PATRICK

BURNHAM, CRISPIN   [1949-]
Publisher/Editor: Eld Mar 78(3)-current

   + E. Paul Berglund
Co-Editor: DMR No.1,1975

BYRNE, CHARLES RAYMOND   [1916-]
Editor-in-Chief of all Avon Publications,
inc. Avon Fantasy Reader (18 issues), Avon
SF Reader (3 issues) and Avon SF & Fantasy
Reader (2 issues)

CADIGAN, PAT[ricia]   [1953-]
Associate Editor: Chac Spr 77(2)
Editor: Shyl Nov 77(1)
Executive Editor: Shyl Feb 78(2)-No.7,
   1984

CAMPBELL, JOHN W[ood]   [1910-71]
Editor: Unk Mar 39-Oct 43 [ret. UW from
   Oct 41]; FUW, 1948

CARLSON, ERIC A[rne]   [1944-]
Publisher: E&O No.1,1973

   + John J. Koblas
Editor: E&O No.1,1973

   + John J. Koblas & R. Alain Everts
Co-Editor: E&O No.2,1983-current

CARNELL, EDWARD JOHN   [1912-72]
Editor: SFy Win 51/2(3)-Apr 64(64)

CARRINGTON, GRANT
Associate Editor: Ftc Apr 72-Aug 75
[listed as Associate Editor Emeritus
   until Jan 79]

CARTER, LIN[wood]   [1930-]
Publisher/Editor: Kdth No.1,1974
Editor: WT Spr 81-Sum 83

CHADBURN, TOM
Editor: Wtch Nov-Dec 36

CHINN, MIKE   [1954-]
   + John Merritt
Editor: DH No.19,1979-No.22,Spr 81

CIRRITO, JEAN W.
Assistant Editor: Cov Sep-Nov 69
[thereafter Editorial Consultant]

CLAYPOOL, GAVIN
Consulting Editor: FB Oct-Dec 81

CLAYTON, WILLIAM
Publisher: ST Sep 31-Jan 33

CLINGAN, A. BRUCE
Production Advisor: Div Nov 76(17)-Jul
   77(21)

   + C. C. Clingan
Co-Publisher/Editor: Div Jun 74(1)-Sep
   76(16)

CLINGAN, C[hester] C[arl]   [1944-]
Publisher: Div Jun 74(1)-Feb/Mar 79(29)
[Co-Publisher with A.B. Clingan till
   No.16,Sep 76]; Pgn May 80(1)
Editor: Div Jun 74(1)-Nov 77(23) [Co-
   Editor with A.B. Clingan till No.16,
   Sep 76]; Pgn May 80(1)

   + Jon Inouye
Co-Editor: Div Jan 78(24)

   + Jon Inouye, R.S.Harding, Joey Froehlich & R.R. Medcalf
Co-Editor: Div Mar 78(25)

   + R. S. Harding & Joey Froehlich
Co-Editor: Div May/Jul 78(26/7)

COCKRELL, AL D.
   + Irvin L. Wagner
Co-Editor: Wyrd Jun 73(1)-Spr 74(3)

COHEN, SOL
Editor: ASFFR Jan-Apr 53
Publisher/Editor: Ftc Sep 65-Jan 79
[Editor Sep 65-Nov 67,Apr-Dec 69 only];
   StF Spr 69-Fal 70; WM Fal 70-Sum 71;
   SSET Sum 70; S&S Win 74/5

COLBY, MELVIN R.
Editor: ET Jul 41[unconfirmed]; UTC Nov
   40(1)-Sep/Oct 43(21)

COLE, ADRIAN   [1949-]
Editor: DH No.6,1973-Dec 73(7) [No.7 co-
   edited with David A.Sutton]

CONWAY, GERARD F.   [1952-]
Editor: HoH Jun-Aug 73

COVA, FRANCESCO
Publisher/Editor: Kad Oct 79(1)-current

CRAWFORD, GARY WILLIAM
Publisher/Editor: Goth Jun 79-Dec 80

COWIE, GEORGE R.
   + Gordon M.Kull
Co-Publisher/Editor: Vor Nos.1-2,1947

CRAWFORD, WILLIAM L.   [1911-84]
Publisher/Editor: MT May 34-Sum 35;
   UnS Mar 34,May/Jun-Win 35
Publisher: W&S Jan/Feb 71(5)-No.10,1974

CRIST, BRIAN
Editor: Wyrd Dec 74(4)
Assistant Editor: Wyrd No.5,1975

DAVIS, BERNARD G.   [?-1972]
Publisher: Ftc Sum 52-Sep 57; DW Feb-
   Aug 57

DAY, HOWARD E[u(GENE)] [1950-82]
Publisher/Editor: DFy Sum 73(1)-Nov 80
   (23)

DE LINT, CHARLES   [1951-]
Publisher: Db 1,Spr 78; BFWK 1,Aut 78;
   DFd Sum 80(3)-current
Editor: BFWK 1,Aut 78; DFd 4,Win 83

   + Charles R.Saunders
Co-Editor: DFd 3,Sum 80

DEL REY, JUDY-LYNN
   Married name; see Judy-Lynn BENJAMIN

DEL REY, LESTER   [1915-]
Editor: FM Feb/Mar-Nov 53 [last issue
   pseudonymously edited as Cameron Hall]
   WoF No.1,1968-No.2,1970
Associate Editor: WoF Win 70/1(3)-Spr 71

DELACORTE, GEORGE T.   [1894-?]
Publisher: DrD Feb-Apr 35

DELANEY, WILLIAM J.
Publisher: WT Nov 38-Sep 54

DENNIS, WALTER L.
Associate Editor: MT Win 34-Sum 35

DERLETH, AUGUST   [1909-71]
Publisher/Editor: ArkS Win 48-Aut 49;
   ArkC Sum 67(1)-Sum 71(10)

DI PRETE, JOHN
Publisher/Editor: BL Aug 76-Jan 78

DICKSON, LAWRENCE J.
Publisher/Editor: Nov Aut 80-Spr 81

DONALDSON, DALE C.   [1923-77]
Publisher/Editor: Mb No.1,1971-No.29/30,
   1977 [last issue completed by his
   wife, Jane Donaldson]

DRAKE, DAVID   [1945-]
Assistant Editor: Whsp Jul 74(4)-current

DURWOOD, THOMAS
Editor: Ariel No.1,Aut 76-No.4,Oct 78

EFFINGER, GEO[rge] ALEC   [1947-]
Associate Editor: HoH Jun-Aug 73

EISEN, ARMAND
Publisher: Ariel No.1,Aut 76-No.2,1977
Editorial Consultant: Ariel No.3,Apr 78-
   No.4,Oct 78

ELSON, LOUIS C.
Publisher: BFT Fal 70(1)-Mar 71(2);
   MoH Aug 63(1)-Apr 71(36); SMS Sum 66
   (1)-Mar 71(18); WTT Win 69/70(1)-Fal
   70(3)

ELWOOD, ROGER   [1943-]
Editor: Chl Jul-Nov 81

ENG, STEPHEN   [1940-]
Associate Editor: Goth Dec 80

ENGEL, LYLE KENYON   [1915-]
Editorial Director: TF Spr-Aug 57

ERISMAN, ROBERT O.
Editor: UT Apr/May 39-May 40; US Apr 41

ESHBACH, LLOYD ARTHUR   [1910-]
Associate Editor: MT May-Win 34

EVERTS, R[andolph] ALAIN
Publisher: DMR No.1,1975; E&O No.2,1983-
   current; Spoor No.1 & 2,1974
Publisher/Editor: ArkS (2nd series) Jun
   83-current

   + Eric Carlson & John Koblas
Co-Editor: E&O No.2,1983-current

FAIRMAN, PAUL W.   [1916-77]
Associate Editor: Ftc Fal 52-Mar/Apr 53
Managing Editor: Ftc May/Jun 53-Oct 54;
   Aug 56
Editor: Ftc Oct 56-Nov 58; DW Feb-Aug 57

FARRELL, TOM
Publisher: Sus Spr 51-Win 52

FAWCETT, RICHARD
Publisher/US Editor: FyM Apr 81(2)-
   current

FEDER, MOSHE
Assistant Editor: Ftc Oct 72-Jun 75

FENNER, ARNIE   [1955-]
Publisher: Chac Win 76-Spr 77
Assistant Editor: Chac Win 76
Editor: Chac Spr 77
Publisher/Editor: Shyl Nov 77(1)-1984(7)

FESTER, ROBERT F.
Publisher/Editor: WA May(1)-No.2,1978

FRIERSON, PENNY and MEADE
Co-Publishers/Editors: HPL,1972

FRITCH, CHARLES E.
Publisher/Editor: Gam No.1,1963-Sep 65(5)

FROEHLICH, JOEY   [1954-]
  + C. C. Clingan & R. S. Harding
Co-Editor: Div Mar 78(25)-May/Jul 78(27)
  [assisted by Jon Inouye & R. R. Medcalf
  on No.25]

  + R. S. Harding
Co-Editor: Div Feb/Mar 79(28/9)

GAIL, ANNA
Editorial Assistant: Ftc Jan-Oct 80

GANLEY, W. PAUL   [1934-]
Publisher/Editor: Wbk 1968(1)-current;
  EC Jul 76(1)-current
Publisher/Co-ordinating Editor: TW,1975

GARDINER, HELEN
Editor: PGS 1963 (unconfirmed); TTT Fal 63

GARRY, LEON
Publisher: TZ Jul 81-Dec 82

GIBSON, WALTER B.   [1897-]
Editor: TMM Dec 27-Apr 28

GILLINGS, WALTER   [1912-79]
Editor: STB Nos.1-2,1946; SFy Sum 50(1)-
  Win 50/1(2)

GNAEDINGER, MARY   [1898-1976]
Editor: AMF Dec 49-Oct 50

GOHAGEN, OMAR
  Pseud: see Elinor MAVOR

GOLD, HORACE L[eonard]   [1914-]
Editor: BFF Jul 53-No.10,1955

GOLDSMITH, CELE   [1933-]
Assistant Editor: Ftc Oct 56-Mar 57;
  DW Feb 57
Managing Editor: Ftc Apr 57-Nov 58; DW
  May-Aug 57;
Editor: Ftc Dec 58-Jun 65 [as Cele G.
  Lalli from Jul 64]

GOODMAN, MARTIN
Publisher: UT Apr/May 39-May 40; US Apr 41

GORDON, NOAH   [1926-]
Assistant Editor: ASFFR Jan-Apr 53

GRAMMER, ALLEN L[uther]   [1889-1969]
Publisher: Unk/UW Mar 39-Oct 43

GUINN, ROBERT M.   [1911-]
Publisher: BFF Jul 53-No.10,1955; WoF No.
  1,1968

HAHN, KEN
Publisher/Editor: Jeet Apr-Sum 77

HALL, CAMERON
  Pseud: see Lester DEL REY

HALL, DESMOND W.
Assistant Editor: ST Sep 31-Jan 33

HALL, Jr., WILLIAM P.
Publisher: PD No.1,1976-No.3,1977

HAMMELL, DALE
Publisher/Editor: CT Dec 76-Jul 79
  [Co-Editor on last issue with Sharon
  Sinner]
HAMMELL, TIM
Assistant Editor: CT Dec 76-Jan 79

HARDING, RALPH STEPHEN
  + C. C. Clingan & Joey Froehlich
Co-Editor: Div Mar 78(25)-May/Jul 78(27)
  [assisted by Jon Inouye & R.R.Medcalf
  on No.25]

  + Joey Froehlich
Co-Editor: Div Feb/Mar 79(28/9)

HARRISON, HARRY   [1925-]
Editor-in-Chief: Imp Oct 66(8)-Feb 67
  (12)
Editor: Ftc Jan-Oct 68

HARVEY, JON M.
Publisher/Editor: Cth No.1,1976-No.3,1978;
  DDH Dec 78

HECHT, THEODORE S.
Editor: AH Oct 70-Oct 71 [entitled
  Horror Stories from Feb-Oct 71]

HENDERSON, GEORGE
Publisher/Editor: BC Win 70/1

HENNEBERGER, JACOB C[lark]   [1890-1969]
Publisher: WT Mar 23-Oct 38

HERBERT, BENSON   [1912-]
Publisher: STB Nos,1-2,1946

HERON, JOHN
Editor: DH No.18,1978

HERSEY, HAROLD [Brainerd]   [1893-1956]
Editor: TB Mar 1-Jun 15,19
Publisher/Editor: GS Apr 30-Dec 31/Jan 32

HILL, LAWSON   [1956-]
Publisher/Editor: Myrd Win 75(1)-No.4,
  1978; NF Win 80/1

HILLMAN, ALEX   [1900-68]
Publisher: WB Dec 50-Feb 51

HOPPENSTAND, GARY
Publisher/Editor: MS No.1,1974-No.5,1979

HOWLAND, ARTHUR B.
Editor: GS Apr-late 1930

HUGHES, TERRY
Assistant Editor: Ftc Jul 74-Jan 79

HUGHES, TREVOR
Editor: DH No.5,1973

IMBUSH, PAUL
Probable editor of UnkB/UWB Sep 39-Win 49;
  FUWB,1952

INOUYE, JON
+ C. C. Clingan
Editor: Div Jan 78(24)

+ C. C. Clingan, R.S. Harding, Joey
Froehlich & R. R. Medcalf
Co-Editor: Div Mar 78(25)

IRWIN, THEODORE [1907-]
Editor: Sus Spr 51-Win 52

JACOBS, MARK
+ Chris Marler
Co-Publisher/Editor: AD Win 75-Fal 77

JAKOBSSON, EJLER [1911-]
Associate Editor: WoF No.2,1970
Editor: WoF Win 70/1-Spr 71

JOHNSON, LESLIE J. [1914-]
Publisher/Editor: Out Win 46

JONES, STEPHEN [1953-]
Editor: DH Sum 74(9)-Win 76(15);
FyT Sum 77(1)-current

+ David A.Sutton
Co-Publisher: FyT Sum 77(1)-current;
Agd Aut 80(1)

KAGAN, MICHAEL
Assistant Editor: Ftc May/Jun-Nov/Dec 53

KARR, PHYLLIS ANN [1944-]
+ Jessica Amanda Salmonson
Co-Editor: F&T No.7,1975

KATZ, ARNOLD
Associate Editor: Ftc Feb 70-Feb 72

KELLER, HARRY A.
Editor: GS Jul 26-mid 27

KELLY, SEAN
Associate Editor: BMM Oct 65-Jan 66

KLEIN, T.E.D.
Editor: TZ Apr 81-Oct 83
Editor-in-Chief: TZ Dec 83-current

KNIGHT, DAMON [1922-]
Editor: WB Dec 50-Feb 51

KOBLAS, JOHN [1942-]
+ Eric Carlson
Co-Editor: E&O No.1,1973

+ Eric Carlson & R. Alain Everts
Co-Editor: E&O No.2,1983-current

KOGAN, DAVID P.
Publisher: MysT Nov 51-No.5,1952

KRUEGER, KEN [1926-]
Editor: FC Nos.1-5,1973
Publisher/Editor: UnT No.1,1974; Unq Jan
78

KULL, GORDON M.
+ George R.Cowie
Co-Publisher/Editor: Vor Nos.1-2,1947

LALLI, CELE G.
Married name: see Cele GOLDSMITH

LANDIS, ARTHUR H. [1917-]
Publisher/Editor: Cov Sep 69-Mar 70

LARSON, RANDALL D. [1954-]
Publisher/Editor: ToF Spr 82(1)-current

LAWTON, CLIFF
Editor: BWT 1960
[Note: was also Art Editor of Phtm,
and may have been editor of SCMS]

LEE, STAN [1922-]
Publisher: HoH Jun-Aug 73

LEHRMAN, HERBERT A.
Assistant Editor: Ftc May-Jul 66
Associate Editor: Ftc Sep 66-Nov 67
Managing Editor: Ftc Jan-Oct 68

LEVINE, GERALD
Publisher: BMM Oct 65-Jan 66

LINDEN, JUDY
Editorial Assistant: TZ Oct-Dec 82

LINZNER, GORDON
Publisher/Editor: S&T Spr 66(1)-current

LITTLE, JOHN A.
+ David R.Warren
Co-Editor: EvM Dec 74-Spr 75

LOBSENZ, NORMAN [Mitchell] [1919-]
Editorial Director: Ftc Dec 58-Jun 65

LOWNDES, ROBERT A[ugustine] W[ard] [1916-]
Editor: MoH Aug 63(1)-Apr 71(36); SMS
Sum 66(1)-Mar 71(18); WTT Win 69/70(1)-
Fal 70(3); BFT Fal 70-Mar 71(2)

MacADAMS, CAMILLE
Managing Editor: GS early 1929-Mar 30

MacFADDEN, BERNARR [1868-1955]
Publisher: GS Jul 26-Mar 30

McFERRAN, DAVE [1954-80]
Editor: Agd Aut 80(1)

McILWRAITH, DOROTHY
Editor: WT May 40-Sep 54

MAHAFFEY, BEA[trice] [1926-]
Editor: Mystic Nov 53(1)-Aug 55(11)

MALLONEE, DENNIS
Publisher: FB Oct 81-current
Executive Editor: FB Oct-Dec 81;Aug 83-
current

MALZBERG, BARRY N[orman] [1939-]
Associate Editor: Ftc Oct 68
Editor: Ftc Dec 68-Apr 69

MANN, KURT C. S.
Executive Publisher: FC Nos.1-5,1973

MANNING, JOHN SPENCER
Pseud: see Sol ASSAEL & Michael NAHUM

MARCONETTE, WALTER
+ J. Chapman Miske
Co-Publisher/Editor: Biz Jan 41

MARGULIES, LEO [1900-75]
Editor-in-Chief: StS Feb 39-Feb 41
Publisher: WT Sum 73-Sum 74

MARLER, CHRIS
+ Mark Jacobs
Co-Publisher/Editor: AD Win 75-Fal 77(6)

MARX, JOSEPH L.
Editor: Fear May-Jul 60

MASULI, PATRICK
Editor: TTFB Sum 64

MATCHA, JACK [1919-]
Executive Editor: Gam No.1,1963-No.3,1964

+ Charles E. Fritch
Co-Editor/Publisher: Gam Feb-Sep 65

MAVOR, ELINOR [1936-]
as Omar Gohagen
Editor: Ftc Apr 79-Oct 80

MELVIN, CHARLES W.
Publisher/Editor: Esc Fal 77

MENVILLE, DOUGLAS
Editor: FFy Oct 70-Jun 71

MERRITT, JOHN
+ Mike Chinn
Co-Editor: DH No.19,1979-Spr 81(22)

MERWIN, Jr., SAM [1910-]
Associate Editor: BFF Jan-Sep 54

MEYERS, JOSEPH [1898-1957]
Publisher: AFR No.1,1947-No.18,1952;
ASFR No.1,1951-No.3,1952; ASFFR Jan-
Apr 53

MICHAELSON, MICHAEL
Publisher: Ftc Apr 58-Oct 61

MISKE, JACK CHAPMAN
+ Walter Marconette
Co-Publisher/Editor: Biz Jan 41

MITCHELL, CURTIS
Publisher/Editor: FF May-Nov 50;

MORRIS, Jr., HARRY O. [1949-]
Publisher/Editor: Nyc May 70-current
Publisher: FBDG Apr/May 72(1)-Oct 77(4)

MOSKOWITZ, SAM [1920-]
Editor: WT Sum 73-Sum 74

MOWRE, CARSON W.
Editor: DrD Feb-Apr 35

MULLEN, STANLEY [1911-73?]
Publisher/Editor: Ggn Mar 47(1)-No.11,1949

NAHUM, MICHAEL
see Sol Assael for details

NOLAN, WILLIAM F. [1928-]
Managing Editor: Gam No.1,1963-No.3,1964

ODDEY, JAMES D.
Pseud: see David A. SUTTON

OLIPHANT, RONALD
Editor: TB Jul 1-Oct 15,19

ORENSTEIN, S. EDWARD
Executive Publisher: TZ Apr 81-current

PAGE, GERALD W. [1939-]
Editor: W&S Jan/Feb 71(5)-No.10,1974

PAIGE, EVELYN
Assistant Editor: BFF Jul-Nov 53
Managing Editor: BFF Jan 54-No.10,1955

PALMER, RAYMOND A. [1910-77]
Publisher/Editor: Mystic Nov 53(1)-Oct
56(17) [thereafter retitled *Search*]

PARDOE, ROSEMARY A. [1954-]
Editor: DH Nos.1-4,1971/2
Publisher/Editor: G&S No.1,1979-current

PARDOE, W. DARROLL [1943-]
Editor: DH Apr 74(8)

PARKHILL-RATHBONE, JAMES
Associate Editor: SFy Mar 65(70)-Jan 66
(80)

PARTINGTON, CHARLES
Publisher/Editor: SE Spr 80(1)-current

PATRICK [BURGE], SUSAN
Assistant Editor: W&S Jan/Feb 71(5)-
No.10,1974

PERKINS, HENRY AVELINE
Associate Editor: WT May 40-Sep 42

PINES, NED [Lewis] [1905-]
Publisher: StS Feb 39-Feb 41

POE, JOHN
Editor: BMM Oct 65-Jan 66

PROTTER, ERIC
Editorial Director: TZ Apr 81-Dec 82
Publisher: TZ Feb 83-Feb 84

RALSTON, WILLIAM
Publisher: TB Mar 1-Oct 15,19

RAYMOND, JOHN
Publisher: FM Feb/Mar-Nov 53

REEDER, DAVE [1950-]
Editor: FyM Sep 80(1)-current

REGINALD, ROBERT [1948-]
Associate Editor: FFy Oct 70-Jun 71

ROARK, BYRON
Editor: Chac Win 76(1)

ROBERTS, KEITH   [1935-]
Associate Editor: SFy Feb 66(81);
   Imp Mar(1)-Sep 66(7)
Managing Editor: Imp Oct 66(8)-Feb 67(12)

ROBERTS, W. ADOLPHE   [1886-1962]
Editor: GS mid 27-1928

ROSS, JOSEPH   [1929-]
US school teacher, real name Joseph Wrzos
Managing Editor: Ftc Sep 65-Nov 67

ROTH, JOSEPH M.
Managing Editor: GS Jul 26-1928

SABAT, ROBERT
Assistant Editor: TZ Feb-Dec 82
Associate Editor: TZ Feb 83-current

SALMONSON, JESSICA AMANDA   [1950-]
Publisher/Editor: F&T No.1,1973-No.7,1975
   [first 4 issues as Amos Salmonson; last
   issue co-edited with Phyllis A. Karr]

SANTANGELO, JOHN
Publisher: Chl Jul-Nov 81

SAUNDERS, ALFRED and JOSEPH
Publishers: FFy Oct 70-Jun 71

SAUNDERS, CHARLES R.   [1946-]
Editor: Db 1,Spr 78

   + Charles de Lint
Co-Editor: DFd 3,Sum 80

SCHARF, HENRY
Publisher: Fear May-Jul 60

SCHIFF, STUART DAVID
Publisher/Editor: Whsp Jul 73-current

SCHREINER, HARRY
Editor: Thrl Feb-Jul 62

SCHWARTZ, STEVEN
Assistant Editor: TZ Feb-Jun 82

SERLING, CAROL
Associate Publisher/Consulting Editor:
   TZ Apr 81-current

SHAFFER, LILA E.
Managing Editor: Ftc Sum 52-Mar/Apr 53

SHAPIRO, M. J.
Editor: MP Sep 58-Mar 59
Managing Editor: M&T Jan-Apr 59

SHAPIRO, NILS A.
Publisher: TZ Apr-Jun 81

SHAW, ALAN
Assistant Editor: Ftc Aug 70-Aug 72
   [as Associate Editor on last issue]

SHAW, LARRY T.   [1924-]
Managing Editor: MP Sep 58-Mar 59
Editor: M&T Jan-Apr 59

SHEPHERD, WILSON
   + Donald A.Wollheim
Co-Publisher: FT Fal 36

SINNER, SHARON
   + Dale Hammell
Co-Editor: CT Jul 79(6/7)

SMITH, GEOFFREY N.
Editor: DH Spr-Sum 77(Nos.16-17)

SMITH, NICK
Editor: FB Oct 81-current

SPECTOR, MORGAN
Associate Editor: Cov Jan-Mar 70

STAFFORD, GREG
Assistant Editor: Wyrd Dec 74(4)
Publisher/Editor: Wyrd No.5,1975-Fall
   77(7)

STAPLETON, DOUG
Editor: BI Nov/Dec 67

STATHIS, LOU
Assistant Editor: Ftc Aug 75-Aug 76

STECKER, MARC
Editorial Assistant: TZ Jul-Nov 81

STEEGER, HENRY   [1903-]
Publisher: AMF Dec 49-Oct 50

STEIN, IRWIN   [1925-]
Publisher: MP Sep 58-Mar 59; M&T Jan-Apr
   59

STEINHORN, DIANA
Managing Editor: TZ Apr 81 (only)

SUTTON, DAVID A.   [1947-]
Editor: DH Sum 81(23)-current
Associate Editor: FyT Sum 77(1)-current

   as James D. Oddey
Publisher/Editor: WW Jun 70(1)-Mar 71(2)

   + Adrian Cole
Co-Editor: DH Dec 73(7)

   + Stephen Jones
Co-Publisher: Agd Aut 80

SWAN, GERALD G[eorge]   [1902-80]
Publisher: WSM Aug 40; YWS Mar-Jun 42;
   WT(British)1942; WPL 1943; WS 1944;
   OS 1945/6; WSM Nos.1-2,1946; WOM,1949;
   WOL Nos.1-3,1960

SYDDALL, LESLIE
Editor: Phtm Apr 57(1)-Jul 58(16)

TARRANT, CATHERINE   [?-1980]
Assistant Editor: UW Oct 41-Oct 43

TIBBETTS, JOHN
Assistant Editor: Eld No.7,1980 & No.2,
   1981

WAGNER, IRVIN L[EO]
Publisher/Editor: Wyrd Jun 73(1)-Spr 74
    (3); NFJ Sum 76(1)-No.2,1977; WD No.1,
    1977-No.3,1980

WARFIELD, WAYNE
Editor: PD No.1,1976-No.3,1977

WARREN, DAVID R.
Publisher: EvM Dec 74-Sum 78 [assisted
    by Marjorie Warren from Sum 77]
Editor: EvM Dec 74-Sum 78 [assisted by
    John A.Little till Spr 75]; SPWAO No.1,
    1980

WAX, SHELDON [1928-79]
Editorial Director: Fear May-Jul 60

WEISINGER, MORTIMER [1915-78]
Editor (uncredited): StS Feb 39-Feb 41

WERNER, HANS-PETER [1948-]
Publisher/Editor: PtF Sum 78-current

WHEELER, D. E.
Editor: GS Late 29-Mar 30

WHITE, TED [1938-]
Managing Editor: Ftc Apr-Dec 69
Editor: Ftc Feb 70-Jan 79

WIDMER, HARRY
Editor: Ace May-Sep 36; ES Aug 37;
    EM Aug 38-Apr/May 39

WILCOX, ROBERT H.
Editorial Consultant: Ftc Jul 79-Oct 80

WILLIAMS, JOHN W.
Editor: TTT Spr 64

WILLIS, PAUL J.
Editor: Anu Aut 66-Aut 68

WILLIS, RONALD J.
Publisher: Anu Aut 66-Aut 68

WOLLHEIM, DONALD A. [1914-]
Editor: FT Fal 36; SFF Feb 41-Mar 42;
    AFR No.1,1947-No.18,1952; ASFR No.1,
    1951-No.3,1952

    + Wilson Shepherd
Co-Publisher: FT Fal 36

WYN, A[aron] A. [1898-1967]
Publisher: Ace May-Sep 36; ES Aug 37;
    EM Aug 38-Apr/May 39

                        ***

Appendices

I.

INDEX TO SERIES AND CONNECTED STORIES

The following is an index to the common characters or settings that feature in the stories covered in the Issue Index. The first column lists the series name as identified in the Author Index. The second column refers to the writer(s) responsible. Character names are covered by surname only except in the case of nicknames (e.g. Northwest Smith) where entries are given under both names. Similarly for character teams (e.g. Fafhrd and the Grey Mouser) two entries are given. To avoid confusion other less obvious combinations are also given dual entries.

Aihai (Tales of Mars)	Clark Ashton Smith
James Allison	Robert E. Howard
Kid Allison	Robert E. Howard
Amergon	Lew M. Cabos
Anathae (Willis &)	Michael F.X. Milhaus
Anita	Keith Roberts
Arcana	Janet Fox
Simon Ark	Edward D. Hoch
Arquel of Argos	Ray Capella
Artonal	Jessica Amanda Salmonson
Atlanaat	E. Hoffmann Price
Atlantis	Clark Ashton Smith
Averoigne	Clark Ashton Smith
Lefty Baker	Roger P. Graham
Hek Belov	Ed Mackin
Lancelot Biggs	Nelson S. Bond
Blackjack Davy	Galad Elflandsson
James Blood	Gordon Linzner
Brak the Barbarian	John Jakes
Bran Mak Morn	Robert E. Howard
Breck	W. Fraser Sandercombe
Dr. Ivan Brodsky, Surgeon of Souls	Victor Rousseau
Father Brown	G. K. Chesterton
Camber of Culdi	Katherine Kurtz
Gerald Canevin	Henry S. Whitehead
Carcosa	Galad Elflandsson
[see also Cthulhu Mythos]	
Carnacki the Ghost Hunter	
	William Hope Hodgson

Randolph Carter	H. P. Lovecraft
Tommy Caxton	John Brunner
Johnny Choir	Ray Bradbury
Chu-Tang	Gene Phillips
The City States	August Derleth
Clarique	Juanita Coulson
Colum	Charles de Lint
Conan of Cimmeria	Robert E. Howard
[see also continuations by L.Sprague de Camp and Lin Carter]	
Corpse, Adventures of a Professional	H. Bedford-Jones
Steve Costigan	Robert E. Howard
Cranshawe	Gordon M. Hillman
Titus Crow	Brian Lumley
Cthulhu Mythos	

The full Mythos was established by August Derleth from stories originally created by H.P.Lovecraft and his friends. Mythos stories in this Index will be found under the following authors:

F.C.Adams, Michael E. Ambrose,James Anderson, Herb Arnold, A. Aspromatis, Ross F. Bagby, Daniel Bailey, E. Paul Berglund, Zealia B. Bishop, Robert Bloch, Robert J. Borski, Crispin Burnham, Lew Cabos, Ramsey Campbell, Peter Cannon, Lin Carter, William A. Conder, Andrew Darlington, Walter C. DeBill, Jr., L. Sprague de Camp, August Derleth, Gary Drake, Denise Dumars, Robert Eber, Lyle Gaulding, John Glasby, Alan D. Gullette, Charles D. Hammer, Henry

Turlogh O'Brien	Robert E. Howard
Father O'Connor	David Rowlands
Lafayette O'Leary	Keith Laumer
Operation Venus	Landell Bartlett
Ouija Land	Ralph Milne Farley
Pavane	Keith Roberts
The People	Lin Carter
Phillimore (Fillmore)	Marvin Kaye
Placide's Wife (Nita Duboin)	Kirk Mashburn
Plumrose	Ron Goulart
Solar Pons	August Derleth
Prester John	Norvell Page
Hugh Docre Purcell	W. Adolphe Roberts
Judge Pursuivant	Manly Wade Wellman
Pusad	L. Sprague de Camp
Quandar	C. C. Clingan
Rald	Clifford Ball
Prince Raynor	Henry Kuttner
J. G. Reeder	Edgar Wallace
Jame Retief	Keith Laumer
Roderick	John T. Sladek
Santo Domingo	Arthur J. Burks
Dr. Satan	Paul Ernst
Servants of Satan	Seabury Quinn
Mark Shadow	R. W. Sneddon
The Shaver Mystery	Richard S. Shaver
[see also Joel Kos, A.J.Steichart and Raymond A. Palmer]	
Harold Shea	L. Sprague de Camp & Fletcher Pratt
Dr. Shen Fu	Frank Owen
Sherra of Normansk	Paul Collins
John Silence	Algernon Blackwood
Simrana	Lin Carter
Slow Glass	Bob Shaw
John Smith	Lew M. Cabos
Morgan Smith	Robert Weinberg
[see also E. P. Berglund, Gordon Linzner]	
Northwest Smith	C. L. Moore
Sphereworld	Michael J. Bell
The Star Kings (John Gordon)	Edmond Hamilton
Val Stearman & La Noire	R. Lionel Fanthorpe

John Steppling	Frank Owen
Subb-Latha	Don Broyles
Sunslayer	Gerald J. Brown
The Surgeon of Souls (Dr. Ivan Brodsky)	Victor Rousseau
Taine of San Francisco	David H. Keller
Teeheemen	Arthur Thatcher
Theem'hdra	Brian Lumley
Thongor of Lemuria	Lin Carter
Dr. Thorndyke	R. Austin Freeman
Throdrexon & Hamakara	Darrell Schweitzer
John Thunstone	Manly Wade Wellman
Tiana of Reme	Richard K. Lyon & Andrew J. Offutt
Mrs. Tokkin	Wilmar Shiras
The Traveler in Black	John Brunner
Trumpets From Oblivion	H. Bedford-Jones
Venerian Invasion	Nictzin Dyalhis
Operation Venus	Landell Bartlett
Vermilion Sands	J. G. Ballard
Forst of Villefere	Robert E. Howard
The Voidal	Adrian Cole
Otto von Hofstadter	Robert Fester
Prince Vukasan.	Brian W. Aldiss
The Wandering Jew	William Tredinnick
Dr. Warm	Geo. Alec Effinger
Watkin's World	Kenneth Bulmer
Weird Crimes	Seabury Quinn
The Werewolf Clan	H. Warner Munn
The Whole Man	John Brunner
Willie and Rick	Ed Beck
Willis and Anathae	Michael F. X. Milhaus
Dr. Wilson	John Phillifent
Wing Loo	David H. Keller
Witchdame	Kathleen Sky
The Woman in Red	Muriel C. Dyar
Xiccarph	Clark Ashton Smith
Yuggoth, Fungi from	H. P. Lovecraft
Zothique	Clark Ashton Smith

***

II.
HONORABLE
MENTIONS

There have been many magazines this century that have at some time during their life carried a fair percentage of weird fantasy. To list them all would be impossible. The following are a selection which came closest to being included in the main index.

THE AUSTRALIAN HORROR & FANTASY MAGAZINE
First issue: Sum 84
A small press horror/fantasy magazine published in octavo format by Barry Radburn, 234 Jamison Road, Penrith, New South Wales 2750, Australia. Co-Editor: Stephen Studach. The only Australian fantasy magazine (though see also *Void*). Includes fiction by Christine Elphick, Paul Collins, Trevor Donohue and Rick Kennett. Cover by Rama Mithrian.

BALTHUS
4 issues: Mar,Sep 71,1972,1973
A British small press magazine published in large digest format and edited by Jon M. Harvey, 18 Cefn Road, Cardiff, Wales. Contained an interesting blend of articles and fiction dealing with fantasy & horror. Fiction includes, Sep 71: "Ash Shadow" Mark Adlard, "The Smugglers of Penrose" Sarah L. Eneys; No.3,1972: "Curtain Fall" Eddy C. Bertin, "The Champion of the Lake" Robert J. Curran; No.4,1973 "Sang the Stone" Gordon Larkin, "Esau Grist" Bruton Connors. Author Profiles ran Mar 71 "Alan Garner" by Peter Parkin; Sep 71 "A.Merritt" Brian Frost; Nos.3-4 "Arthur Machen" by Jon Harvey. Other articles by David A. Sutton, Mike Ahley, Andrew Darlington and Robert J. Curran.

BORIS KARLOFF STORY DIGEST MAGAZINE
1 issue: Jun 70
A pocketbook collection published in magazine format by Western Publishing, New York. Managing Editor: Wallace I. Green. Consists of eleven horror/mystery stories

comprising the volume *Tales of Mystery* by Dick Wood.
[Info. supplied by Kenneth R. Johnson]

COUNTERTHRUST
1 issue: 1976
A small press fantasy magazine issued by the University of Maryland SF Society under the imprint of Thrust Publications P.O. Box 63, College Park, Md.20740. Editors: Steven L. Goldstein & J. Timothy Tarrants. Intended as an annual exploring all forms of fantasy only the first issue appeared, though its companion sf review *Thrust* continues to this day. Fiction: "Stone God's jest" Damien Broderick, "Wail From the Mist" Michael R. Mikesh, "To Search for Majicks" Steven L. Goldstein, "Figure in Light" Larry Stevens. Also contained transcript of speech given by Roger Zelazny at the Univ. of Maryland in 1973. Cover by Dennis R. Bailey.

DARK SHADOWS STORY DIGEST MAGAZINE
1 issue: Jun 70
Strictly speaking a novel in magazine format, published as a pocketbook by Western Publishing, New York. Managing Editor: Wallace I. Green. Contains "The Interrupted Voyage" by D.J. Arneson, a novel based on the *Dark Shadows* television series.
[Info. supplied by Kenneth R. Johnson]

DIFFERENT
At least 46 issues: Mar/Apr 45-Fal 54
US 'cultural' magazine published by the Avalon Arts Academy, Rogers, Arkansas.

Editor/Publisher: Lilith Lorraine. Stanton
Coblentz served as fantasy story editor.
Early magazine dedicated to publishing
fiction that was 'different' in style and
in which the author 'escapes from regi-
mented plots and imitative styles'. Also
contained much poetry and non-fiction.
Not all fiction was fantasy. Few issues
sighted but stories of interest include:
"The Planet That Committed Suicide"
Stanton Coblentz (Mar/Apr 46), "The Dog"
Francis Flagg (Jul/Aug 46). Originally bi-
monthly large-size magazine, it suspended
publication with issue for Aut 51 (Vol.7,
No.3); was revived as a digest quarterly
from Spr 53.
[Info.supplied by Howard DeVore]

THE DRAGON-FLY
2 issues: Oct 15,1935 & May 15,1936
US small press magazine published and
edited by Robert H. Barlow, DeLand, Florida.
Published mostly verse, short sketches and
mood pieces by members of the Lovecraft
Circle. Issue 1 included "A Dream" Barlow,
"The Epigrams of Alastor" Clark Ashton
Smith, "On Writing in Bed" J. Vernon Shea,
plus verse by Elizabeth Toldridge and
August Derleth. No.2 included "Pursuit of
the Moth" Barlow, "Four Playwrights" by
J. Vernon Shea, further epigrams by Clark
Ashton Smith, and verse by Derleth, Tol-
dridge and E. A. Edkins.
[Info. supplied by Glenn Lord]

EQUINOX
*4 issues; dates of first two not known;
No.3,May 76; No.4,Sum 77.*
Attractive US small press sf/fantasy
magazine published in A4 format by Stellar
Z Productions, 4608 St. Nazaire Road, Pen-
sacola, Florida 32505. Editor: Neal R.
Blaikie. Featured fiction, comic-strips
and verse, plus limited non-fiction.
Fiction includes: May 76 "If Jonathan
Swift" Jon Inouye, "From the Deep" and
"The Unusual Case of Frederick Harrison"
Cthulhu Mythos tales by Gregory E. Nicoll,
"Carmanda" Jessica A. Salmonson and "Star-
walker" by Dan Beck. Sum 77: "The Glorious
Insanity" Andrew Darlington, "Kid on the
Mountain" Jon Inouye, "Edgar Allan Poe and
the Lord of the Winds" Gregory Nicoll, "The
Ranachii Woman" G. R. Muschla, "The Enchant-
ed Pool" Jerry Baker, "Oh For a Vision of
Earth" C. C. Clingan, "The Last Problem"
G. R. Muschla, "The House of the Beast
Within" Gregory Nicoll, "Return of the
Deathmen" Jon Inouye, "A Sound Only the
Deaf Can Hear" Andrew Darlington and
"Wings" Dan Beck. No.4 also contained nine
poems by John Bredon [Steve Eng]. Covers:
May 76 Gene Day; Sum 77 Rick Harrison.

FAMOUS FANTASTIC MYSTERIES
81 issues: Sep/Oct 39–Jun 53
One of the most attractive and collectible of all sf/fantasy pulp magazines, published bi-monthly (quarterly during War
years) by Frank A. Munsey Co., 280 Broadway

New York until Dec 42; thereafter by All
Fiction Field, a subsidiary of Popular
Publications, 205 East 42nd St, New York.
Editor: Mary Gnaedinger. Published mostly
reprints, usually a lead novel and several
short stories. Initially all reprints from
the Munsey archives (*Argosy, All-Story,
Cavalier, Scrapbook* etc) but a later pol-
icy change extended reprints to selections
from other sources. The reprints centred
mostly on early scientific romances or
fantastic adventures, hence the magazine's
exclusion from the Main Index, but it did
publish a fair quota of weird fantasy.
Special items of interest include: "Blind
Man's Buff" J. U. Giesy, "The Whimpus" Tod
Robbins, "The Witch-Makers" Donald Wandrei
(Sep/Oct 39); "Almost Immortal" Austin Hall
"The Man With the Glass Heart" George
Alan England (Nov 39); "Lights" Philip M.
Fisher, Jr., "The Diminishing Draft" Wald-
emar Kaempffert (Dec 39); "Behind the Cur-
tain" Francis Stevens, "The V Force" Fred
C. Smale (Jan 40); "The Ship of Silent Men"
Philip M. Fisher (Feb 40); "The Belated
Tears of Louis Marcel" Perley Poore Shee-
han (Mar 40); "The Devil of the Western
Sea" P.M. Fisher (Apr 40); "Three Lines of
Old French" A. Merritt, "Pegasus" Henry
Kuttner (May/Jun 40); "The Rebel Soul"
Austin Hall, "Half-Past Twelve in Eter-
nity" R.W. Sneddon (Aug 40); "Fungus Isle"
P.M. Fisher (Oct 40); "The Other Man's
Blood" Ray Cummings, "The Sleep of Ages"
Stuart Martin, "The Devil's Bodyguard"
Clyde Irvine (Dec 40); "The Ship of Silent
Men" P.M. Fisher (Feb 41); "Claimed" Frances
Stevens (Apr 41); "John Ovington Returns"
Max Brand (Jun 41); "The Colour Out of
Space" H.P. Lovecraft (Oct 41); "The Lost
Garden" Max Brand (Dec 41); "The Citadel
of Fear" Francis Stevens (Feb 42); An Un-
natural Feud" Norman Douglas (Apr 42);
"Burn, Witch, Burn!" A. Merritt (Jun 42);
"Serapion" Francis Stevens (Jul 42); "Creep,
Shadow!" A. Merritt (Aug 42); "Wild Wullie
the Waster" Tod Robbins, "The Horla" De
Maupassant (Sep 42), "The Elixir of Hate"
George A. England (Oct 42), "The Demois-
elle D'Ys" Robert W. Chambers (Nov 42).

"The Yellow Sign" R.W. Chambers (Sep 43);
"The Derelict" William Hope Hodgson, "The
Mask" R.W. Chambers (Dec 43); "The Ghost
Pirates" W.H. Hodgson (Mar 44); "The Wen-
digo" Algernon Blackwood (Jun 44); "The
Day of the Browne Horde" Richard Tooker,
"The Novel of the White Powder" Arthur
Machen, "The Postman of Otford" Lord Dun-
sany (Sep 44); "The Lost Continent" C.J.
Cutcliffe Hyne, "The Highwayman" Dunsany
(Dec 44); "Before I Wake" Henry Kuttner
(Mar 45); "The Boats of the Glen Carrig"
Hodgson (Jun 45); "Phra the Phoenician"
E.L. Arnold (Sep 45); "The Ancient Allan"
H. Rider Haggard, "The Hashish Man" Lord
Dunsany (Dec 45), "The House of the Secret"
Claude Farrere (Feb 46); "The Willows"
Algernon Blackwood (Apr 46); "The Undying
Monster" Jessie D. Kerruish, "The Novel of
the Black Seal" A. Machen (Jun 46); "The

Secret of the Growing Gold" Bram Stoker
(Aug 46), "The Burial of the Rats" Stoker,
"Daemon" C.L.Moore (Oct 46); "At the
Farmhouse" E.F.Benson (Dec 46); "The
Spectre Spiders" W.James Wintle (Feb 47);
"Allan and the Ice Gods" H.R.Haggard,
"Passeur" R.W.Chambers (Apr 47), "Cater-
pillars" E.F.Benson (Jun 47); "The City of
Wonder" E.C.Vivian (Oct 47); "The Lonesome
Place" A.Derleth (Feb 48); "City of the
Dead" Augusta Groner, "The Messenger" R.W.
Chambers (Apr 48); "The Devil's Spoon"
Theodore du Bois, "The Shadow and the
Flash" Jack London (Jun 48); "The Valley of
Silent Men" E.C.Vivian (Aug 49); "The Star-
kenden Quest" Gilbert Collins (Oct 49);
"Ogden's Strange Story" Edison Marshall,
"No Man's Land" John Buchan (Dec 49); "Morn-
ing Star" H.R.Haggard, "Strange Occurrence
in Clerkenwell" A.Machen (Feb 50); "The
Outsider" H.P.Lovecraft, "Mrs Amworth"
E.F.Benson (Jun 50); "The Weigher of Souls"
Andre Maurois (Oct 50); "Brood of the
Witch-Queen" Sax Rohmer (Jan 51); "The
Threshold of Fear" A.J.Rees (Mar 51); "The
Slayer of Souls" R.W.Chambers, "Lukundoo"
Edward L.White (May 51); "Tcheriapin" Sax
Rohmer (Jul 51); "Monsieur Seeks a Wife"
Margaret Irwin (Oct 51); "The Grey Mahatma"
Talbot Mundy (Dec 51); "The Valley of Eyes
Unseen" Gilbert Collins (Feb 52); "Her
Ways Are Death" Jack Mann (Jun 52); "The
White Wolf" Franklin Gregory (Aug 52); "The
Bat Flies Low" Sax Rohmer (Oct 52); "Skull-
Face" R.E.Howard (Dec 52); "Full Moon" T.
Mundy (Feb 53): "The Wanderer's Necklace"
H.R.Haggard (Apr 53).

The pictorial series "Masters of Fantasy" by Neil Austin ran Aug 47-Apr 50
depicting the following authors: Stephen
Vincent Benet (Aug 48), Algernon Blackwood
(Apr 48), Ray Bradbury (Oct 49), Edgar Rice
Burroughs (Oct 48), Robert W.Chambers (Dec
47), Lord Dunsany (Jun 49), M.R.James (Apr
50), H.P.Lovecraft (Aug 47), Arthur Machen
(Dec 48), A.Merritt (Oct 47); Edgar Allan
Poe (Dec 49), M.P.Shiel (Feb 49), Clark
Ashton Smith (Aug 49), Olaf Stapledon (Feb
50), John Taine (Apr 49), H.G.Wells (Jun
48), S. Fowler Wright (Feb 48).

FFM is perhaps best known for its
interior and cover art by Virgil Finlay
and Lawrence S.Stevens. Some of the work
attributed to Lawrence was the work of his
son Peter and the full extent of his cont-
ribution has yet to be assessed. Covers by
Finlay were 1940 Mar,Aug,Oct; 1941 Feb,
Apr,Jun,Aug,Oct,Dec; 1942 Feb,Apr,Jun-Dec;
1943 Mar,Sep; 1946 Dec; 1947 Feb,Jun,Aug,
Dec; 1948 Feb,Jun. Those by Stevens 1943
Dec; 1944 Mar,Jun,Sep,Dec; 1945 Mar,Jun,
Sep,Dec; 1946 Feb,Apr,Jun,Aug,Oct(son);
1947 Apr,Oct (both son); 1948 Apr,Aug,Oct,
Dec (all son); 1949 Feb,Apr,Jun,Aug,Oct(all
son),Dec; 1950 Feb(son),Apr; 1951 May,Jul,
Oct,Dec; 1952 Feb,Apr,Jun,Oct,Dec; 1953
Apr,Jun. Other covers were by Frank R.
Paul (Apr,May/Jun,Dec 40), Norman Saunders
(Jun,Aug 50; Mar 51; Aug 52; Feb 53),
Raphael de Soto (Oct 50), Steele Savage
(Jan 51).

[See also following entry on *Fantastic
Novels*, and in Main Index for *A.Merritt's
Fantasy Magazine*]

FANTASTIC NOVELS
*25 issues, two series: Jul 40-Apr 41;
Mar 48-Jun 51.*
US sf/fantasy pulp, companion to *Famous
Fantastic Mysteries*. First series pub'd by
Frank A.Munsey Co., New York; Second series
by Popular Publications, New York. Policy
similar to FFM, though with emphasis on
longer works. Items of interest include:
1st series: "Monsier de Guise" Perley
Poor Sheehan (Jul 40), "Through the Dragon
Glass" A.Merritt (Sep 40), "Who Wants a
Green Bottle?" Tod Robbins (Nov 40); "The
People of the Pit" A.Merritt (Jan 41).
2nd series: "The Terrible Three" Tod
Robbins (Nov 48); "Seven Footprints to
Satan" A.Merritt (Jan 49); "The Toys of Fate"
Tod Robbins (Mar 49); "The Living Portrait"
Tod Robbins, "The Elf-Trap" Francis Stevens
(Nov 49), "That Receding Brow" Max Brand
(Mar 50), "Drink We Deep". Arthur L.Zagat
(Jan 51), "The Song of the Sirens" Edward
L.White (Jun 51).

As with FFM interior and cover art by
Virgil Finlay and Lawrence Stevens make
the issues collector's items today. Covers
by Finlay are 1940 Jul,Nov; 1941 Jan,Apr;
1948 Nov; 1949 Mar,Nov. By Lawrence (or
his son Peter) 1948 Mar,May(both son),Jul,
Sep(son); 1949 Jan,May,Jul,Sep (all but Jan
son); 1950 Jan(son),Jul; 1951 Apr,Jun.
Other covers by Frank R.Paul (Sep 40),
Norman Saunders (Mar,May,Sep 50), Raphael
de Soto (Nov 50,Jan 51).

FANTASTIC WORLDS
*5 issues known: Sum,Fal/Win 52;Spr,Sum,
Fal 53.*
US small press sf/fantasy magazine
published quarterly in digest format by,
initially Edward W.Ludwig, 1942 Telegraph
Ave., Stockton, California; and subsequent-
ly Sam Sackett, 1449 Brockton Ave., Los
Angeles 25. Featured fiction, articles,
interviews, verse and reviews. Items of
interest include: "The Arkham House Story"
article by August Derleth, "The Flight of
Azrael" verse by Clark Ashton Smith and
"The Soul Seeker" story by W. Paul Ganley
(all Sum 52); "The Lovers and Others"
article by Philip Jose Farmer (Spr 53);
"Calling Dr. Caligari" article by Robert
Bloch and fiction "Last Day" Bertram
Chandler and "Through Crisis with the
Gonedaidins" David R. Bunch (Sum 53);
"The Question" David H. Keller and "The Mad
Man From Machinery Row" David R. Bunch,
plus an interview with Fredric Brown (all
Fal 53). Later issues not sighted.

FANTASY BOOK
*8 issues. Irregular, No.1[Sum]1947,
No.2[Spr]1948, No.3[Sum]1948, No.4
[Win]1948, No.5[Sum[1949; No.6[Win]
1950; No.7[Fal]1950; No.8[Win]1951.*
A sf/fantasy magazine published irregularly by Fantasy Publishing Co.Inc.,

8318 Avalon Boulevard, Los Angeles 3, CA. Editor: Garret Ford (William & Margaret Crawford). Not to be confused with the current *Fantasy Book* (see Main Index). Despite the title it ran little fantasy, concentrating on sf. Has become collectible because it published the first story by Cordwainer Smith "Scanners Live in Vain" (No.6). Also pub'd "The People of the Crater" Andrew North (pseud.Andre Norton) originally acquired for Crawford's earlier magazine *Marvel Tales* (see Main Index). Other stories of interest, "Black Lotus" Robert Bloch, "Strange Alliance" Bryce Walton (both No.1), "The Ship of Darkness" A.E.van Vogt (No.2),"Gifts of Asti" Andrew North [Norton] "Turnabout" H.S.W. Chibbett (both No.3).

THE GHOST
5 issues: Spr 43, Jul 44, May 45, Jul 46, Jul 47.
Noted small-press magazine published in quarto format by Driftwind Press, North Montpelier, Vermont. Publisher/Editor; W. Paul Cook. Heavily biased toward Lovecraftiana. First issue (48 pages) contained many small essays and poems. Fiction includes "Whom We Call Dead" Edith Miniter. Second issue, which Harry Warner once stated could claim 'to rank as the greatest single issue of any fanzine in history' is most noted for Chapter 1 of E. Hoffmann Price's "The Book of the Dead" being his memories of Farnsworth Wright (see Main Index). Chapter 2 on Robert E. Howard appeared in Issue 3, and Chapter 3 on James F. Morton in Issue 5. Other noted contributions include "The Weird Tale in English since 1890" August Derleth (No.3), "Burrowings of an Old Bookworm" Rheinhart Kleiner (the whole of No.4), and "Ramblings of a Reader and Collector" by H.C. Koenig (No.5).

GHOUL
1 issue: [Sum] 1976
A British horror magazine published by New English Library, Barnard's Inn, London EC 1. Editor: Penelope Grant. A poor attempt at a blend of serious and tongue-in-cheek horror. Most of the contents were spoof items by R. Chetwynd-Hayes under pen names like Hans Clutcher. Two stories: "Ghoul at Large" R.Chetwynd-Hayes and a reprint of "Some New Pleasures Prove" Charles Birkin. An article by Walter Gillings on Edgar Allan Poe was intended as the first of a series on Masters of Horror.

GRIMOIRE
Current, 5 issues: Sum, Fal, Win 82; Spr, Sum 83.
US small press literary magazine published and edited by Thomas Wiloch, 8181 Wayne Road, Westland, Michigan 48185. A surreal fantasy magazine with emphasis on collages and poetry. Most noted fiction by Thomas Ligotti, as follows: "Ghost

Stories For the Dead" (Fal 82), "The Christmas Eves of Aunt Elise" (Win 82), "Dr. Voke and Mr. Veech" (Sum 83). Issues also include fiction by Richard Fawcett, Billy Wolfenbarger, Ruth Berman, Keith Allan Daniels, Bruce Boston, and verse by Denise Dumars, G. Sutton Breiding and Andrew Joron.
[Info. supplied by Billy Wolfenbarger]

GRIPPING TERROR
1 issue, undated (1949/50)
UK pulp magazine published by Hamilton & Co., London. Editor/Publisher not identified but issue assembled by Harry Assael (brother of Sol Assael - see Editor Index). One of the many mock-American publications that appeared after the War. Stories mostly mystery with minor fantasy elements: "When Churchyards Yawn" Thornton Dale, "Murder is Hell" Norman Lazenby, "Death Has No Boundaries" Clarkson Waverly and "Horror From the Swamps" Richard Milne.

THE HORROR SHOW
Current, 4 issues: Win, Sum, Fal 83; Win 84
New small press weird fantasy magazine published in slick format by editor David B. Silva, Star Route 1, Oak Run, CA 96069. Details received too late to include in Main Index, though magazine qualifies. Contents include: Win 83: "Transfusion/ Karen Anderson Lynch, "Mirror Images" Doreen Pecis, "Creatures of Man" Michael Arthur Betts and others by Silva and Randy Grant. Sum 83: 17 stories including "First Contact on Linden Street" Janet Fox, "Review of Latest Arrivals" J.N. Williamson, "Ohio Route 101" Ellen Behrens. Fal 83: 15 stories, including "Beware If They Follow" Rod Little, "Devilment" Janet Fox, "Blood Love" Michael Arthur Betts, "The Ingredient" Donald R. Burleson. Covers: Win 83 Jeff Monje, Sum 83 Calvin Collins, Fal 83 Jim Garison.

LONDON MYSTERY MAGAZINE
132 issues: Dec 49-Mar 82
UK mystery magazine with regular inclusion of weird fiction. Published initially by Hulton Press, 43/4 Shoe Lane, London EC4 and edited by Michael Hall, it suspended publication in Apr/May 52 (No. 15) until revived by Norman Kark, Grand Bldgs., Trafalgar Square, London WC 2 and published as a regular quarterly. Retitled London Mystery Selection from No.36 (Mar 58). Final place of publication: 268-270 Vauxhall Bridge Road, London SW1. The magazine is indexed complete to Dec 80 (No.127) in *Monthly Murders* (Greenwood, 1982). Early issues featured work by Algernon Blackwood, Lewis Spence, H. B. Drake, Russell Kirk, Robert Aickman. Kark's early issues included John Collier, Gerald Kersh, Edmund Cooper, Anthony Shaffer, Shamus Frazer, Denys Val Baker and John Newton Chance. Rosemary Timperley was the

most regular contributor, with L.P.Davies
and (from 1972) Guy N.Smith making regular appearances.

THE MAGIC CARPET MAGAZINE
see ORIENTAL STORIES

MIND, INC.
*Probably 126 issues, though far from
all sighted; May 29-Nov 39 (retitled
Mind in Apr 32 and Mind Magazine in
Oct 32)*
A theological magazine published in
pocketbook format by Mind,Inc., 599 Fifth
Ave., New York. Publisher/Editor: Robert
Collier. Although a Christian philosoph-
ical magazine it carried enough borderline
fiction to attract the interest of coll-
ectors, and has thus remained an enigmatic
fantasy item. It never was a fantasy maga-
zine but completist collectors will be
interested in the following issues which
reprinted stories of note: May 29 "Special
Delivery" Algernon Blackwood; Jul 20 "The
Young King" Oscar Wilde; Oct 29 "The Rush-
ing of Wings" Emma-Lindsay Squier; Dec 29
"A Doer of the Word" Theodore Dreiser,
"Wonder of Women" Jack London; Nov 30 "V.
Lydiat" L.Adams Beck, "The Leather Funnel"
A.Conan Doyle; Jan 31 "Glamour of the
Snow" and "Tongues of Fire" Algernon
Blackwood; Jun 31"Golden Dreams" Washing-
ton Irving; Sep 31 "A Vision of Avdeitch"
Leo Tolstoy; Nov 31 "The Three Questions"
Leo Tolstory and "The Great Stone Face"
Nathaniel Hawthorne.
[Info. supplied by Grant Thiessen]

MYRRH
1 issue: Jan 81
A special fantasy issue of *Art & Story*,
published in slick formar by Art & Story
Publications, Fresno, California 93790.
Publisher/Editor: James D.Denney. Contains
fiction: "Dread Vintage" Nancy Mortensen
and "The Star Sorcerers" John Kelly; a
comic strip adaptation by James Denney of
"The Gift" by Ray Bradbury, and an article
by Woodrow Nichols on "Star Wars and the
SF Film Conspiracy".
[Info.supplied by Nancy Mortensen]

ORACLE
Current: 2 issues, Jun 82, Feb 83
US small-press publication subtitled
'Science-Fiction & Fantasy Anthology Mag-
azine' and produced by SF&F Productions,
Detroit, Michigan 48219. Publisher/Editor:
Dave Lillard. A mixture of stories, most-
ly fantasy, including "The Fabulous Sea
Below" Jessica Amanda Salmonson, "Mandri-
kore" Ken St.Andre, "The God of Thieves"
Michael A.Stackpole and "Vllarn" by Dave
Lillard in the first issue, and "The World,
the Flesh and Maxwell Harrison" Nigel
Sellars, "Rosenberg's Last Case" K.L.
Jones and "In the Land of Oblan-Shar" by
Steve Vance in the second.

ORIENTAL STORIES
*14 issues: Oct/Nov 30-Jan 34 (retitled
The Magic Carpet Magazine from Jan 33)*
US adventure pulp published irregularly
by Popular Fiction Co., Indianapolis, In.,
companion to *Weird Tales*. Editor: Farnsworth Wright. Of interest primarily due to
its inclusion of much fiction by regular
WT writers, mostly historical adventures
with occasional fantasy motifs. *OS* published Otis A.Kline's seven-part series of
the memories of Hamed the Attar starting
with "The Man Who Limped"(Oct/Nov 30).
Other stories of interest include "The
Voice of El-Lil" Robert E.Howard (Oct/Nov
30), "Della Wu, Chinese Courtesan" Frank
Owen and "Red Blades of Cathay" Robert E.
Howard & Tevis Clyde Smith (both Feb/Mar
31), "Hawks of Outremer" R.E.Howard(Apr/
Jun 31), "Four Doomed Men" Geoffrey Vace
[Hugh Cave](Sum 31), "The Blood of Bel-
shazzar" R.E.Howard (Aut 31), "The Sowers
of Thunder" R.E.Howard (Win 32), "Lord of
Samarkand" R.E.Howard, "Scented Gardens"
Dorothy Quick and "The Djinee of El Sheyb"
G.G.Pendarves(all Spr 32), "A Battle Over
the Tea-Cups" August Derleth (Sum 32), "The
Master of Dragons" H.Bedford-Jones and
"Ismeddin and the Holy Carpet" E.Hoffmann
Price (Jan 33), "Kaldar,World of Antares"
Edmond Hamilton (Apr 33), "The Lion of
Tiberias" R.E.Howard and "The Kiss of
Zoraida" Clark Ashton Smith(Jul 33); "Pale
Hands" E.Hoffmann Price and "Death in My
Hands" Paul Ernst (Oct 33), "The Shadow of
the Vulture" R.E.Howard(Jan 34). *OS* also
published the first cover painting by
Margaret Brundage who did 6 covers in all:
Spr,Sum 32, Jan,Apr,Oct 33, Jan 34. The
magazine's first five covers were by Von
Gelb, whilst J.Allen St.John painted the
covers for Win 32 and Jul 33.

POTBOILER
*Current: 7 issues to date, Jul,Nov 80;
Jul 81; Feb,Sep 82; Spr/Sum 83; Win
83/4.*
Canadian small press sf/fantasy magazine published in A4 format (No.2 only
A5 format) by Lari Davidson, Richards Road,
Roberts Creek, British Columbia VON 2WO.
Rather too much emphasis on sf and comic
strip to qualify for inclusion in the main
index, though it does contain several items
of interest and is attractively illustrat-
ed throughout. Of special interest is the
series by Albert J.Manachino "Order of
Business" (Jul 80), "Eugenia and the Necro-
nomicon"(Nov 80), "Eugenia and the Wild
Broom" (Jul 81), "Eugenia and the Pumpkin
Bread" (Feb 82), "The Witch and the Doll"
(Sep 82), "I, Slimerod" (Spr/Sum 83) and
"Moonhog" (Win 83/4). Of further interest
is Issue 4 (Feb 82) which also contains
"The Crystal City Horror" Chet Clingan &
Ron Fortier, "The Neighbor's Shrunken
Heads" Jeffrey Goddin, "The Knight of the
Road" Millea Kenin, "Toad Strangler" Ste-
phen Gresham, "Eejit" William Maddox and
"Jeroboam Henley's Debt" Charles R.Saun-
ders.

PULPSMITH
Current: Spr 81-(quarterly)

US independent literary magazine with an emphasis on bizarre and offtrail fiction, subtitled 'the Curious Magazine'. Published by The Smith, 5 Beekman Street, New York 10038. Publisher/Editor: Harry Smith. Managing Editor: Tom Tolnay. Fiction of interest: Spr 81 "Kicked Straight at Last" David R. Bunch, "The Drone of Wings" Rick Bailey; Sum 81 "Speaking Wolf" Ardath Mayhar; Fal 81 "A Fable for Yesterday" Jeanne F. Drennan; Win 81 "The End of the War" Ardath Mayhar, "Ishbar the Trueborn" George F. Guthridge; Spr 82 "Growing Wings" Alan Davis; Sum 82 "The Task of the Green Bone" Ardath Mayhar, "Lock, Stock and Casket" Loren D. Estleman; Aut 82 "The Great Magic Words Crisis" Thomas Wiloch, "The Eldritch Chronicle" Louis Phillips, "Drawer 14" Talmage Powell; Win 83 "Up Under the Roof" Manly Wade Wellman (from WT Oct 38), "Sunrise" Darrell Schweitzer, "The Witchpricker" Georgette Perry, "Bags" Al Sarrantonio; Spr 83 "In Borges Library" Ken Kalfus, "Escort Service" Dave Pedneau.

SHADOWS OF...
Current, 6 issues to date (No.1 not sighted). No.2 Oct 79, No.3 Aug 80, No.4 Feb 81, No.5 Fal 81,No.6,Spr 82.

US sf/fantasy small press magazine published by Dawn Press, P.O.Box 1696, Norman, Oklahoma 73070. Publisher/Editor: Dawn Atkins. Contains more sf than the title implies. Rise in quality from issue 4 which included interviews with Kelly Freas, Alan Dean Foster and Richard Pini. Issue 5 interviewed Robert Lynn Asprin, and issue 6 Joe & Jack Haldeman. Fiction includes four-part serial "Thrak" by Jeff Morgan (Nos.2-5), "Madmen and Mothers-in-Law" Michael Bracken (No.4), "The Man Who Could Sell Hats to Chinamen" John Maddox Roberts (No.5) and "The Gift of Life, the Gift of Death" Geo.W. Proctor (No.6).

THRILLS
1 issue, undated (1939). Possible second issue.

UK pulp adventure magazine published by Atlas Publishing & Distributing Co., Bride Lane, London. No edited credited, but possibly Paul Imbush. Contained reprints from William Clayton's US pulps of the early thirties, including *Strange Tales*. Contained five stories of which only one, "Duel of the Sorcerers" by Paul Ernst - which took up over half the issue - was fantasy. Other authors were Peter Ellsworth, S.B.H.Hurst, C.M.Rockwell and Roland Phillips. A second issue was announced and may have appeared. It would have featured "Wolves of Darkness" by Jack Williamson and "By the Hands of the Dead" Francis Flagg.

UNDINAL SONGS
Current, 7 issues, Oct 81- (quarterly)

US small press fantasy magazine pub'd

and edited by Leilah Wendell, P.O.Box 70, Oakdale, Long Island, NY 11769. A magazine devoted to necrophilia and vampirism it concentrates mostly on verse and short mood pieces. Two pieces of note include "The Chosen One" by Ann Wilson (No.5,Oct 82) and "The Gravedigger's Long Wait" by Greg Cox (No.6,Jan 83).

UNIQUE TALES
3 issues: Jun 37, Jan,Apr 38 (retitled Unique from Issue 2)

US small press magazine published and edited by Russell Leadabrand, Route 2, Dinuba, California. Neatly printed in small digest format it was one of the last of the great 'thirties' fanzines, although time has dimmed its significance. Items mostly editorially written with many reviews and non-fiction features. Stories include No.1 "A Legend of the Dark Isles" Roy Lundholm, "Diary of Istal Woerton" Russell Leadabrand; No.2 "Perpetuation" Walter Jamieson, "Etunga" Lorin Lovejoy; No.3 "Red Flowers" Russell Leadabrand, "The Only Flower" Jack Curtis and "Words and Music" Roy Lundholm.

VOID
5 issues: [Sum]1975 - 1977

Australian sf/fantasy small press magazine published in digest format by Void Publications, St Kilda, Victoria 3182. Editor: Paul Collins. Emphasis on sf, originally being launched to coincide with the 1975 World SF Convention being held in Melbourne. Later issues contained more fantasy. Items of interest include: "Dreams of Ash, Memories of Fire" Karl Hansen (No.2,1976), "The Jekyll & Hyde Mushrooms" and "The Veiled Pool of Mistorak" Darrell Schweitzer (No.3,1976),"The One Who Spoke With the Owls" Darrell Schweitzer (No.4,1976) and "Lady of the Fountain" Darrell Schweitzer (No.5,1977). Magazine was continued as an original sf anthology series.

WHISPERS FROM BEYOND
1 issue: 1972.

A large format quasi-slick magazine published by Peacock Press, Chicago, Illinois. No editor credited. Calling itself 'a revolutionary idea in the publishing field' it was a reprint of Kurt Singer's anthology *Bloch and Bradbury* [Tower Press, New York:1969] containing six stories by Robert Bloch and four by Ray Bradbury, all reprints.

***

III.
CHRONOLOGICAL
LISTING OF
—MAGAZINES

The magazines are listed in the order of publication of their first issue. Canadian magazines are identified by a [C] after the title. British magazines are listed in italics.

The Thrill Book	Mar 1-Oct 15,19	*Strange Tales*	*Feb 46-Mar 46*
Weird Tales	Mar 23-current	*Outlands*	*Win 46*
Ghost Stories	Jul 26-Jan 32	The Avon Fantasy Reader	Feb 47-1952
Tales of Magic & Mystery	Dec 27-Apr 28	The Gorgon	Mar 47-May 49
Mind Magic/My Self	Jun 31-Dec 31	The Vortex	Spr 47-Fal 47
Strange Tales	Sep 31-Jan 33	The Arkham Sampler	Win 48-Aut 49
Unusual Stories	Mar 34-Win 35	*Weird & Occult Miscellany*	*Apr 49*
Marvel Tales	May 34-Sum 35	The Book of Terror [C]	Dec 49
Tales of Mystery & Detection	*Jun 34*	A. Merritt's Fantasy Magazine	Dec 49-Oct 50
Tales of the Uncanny	*Dec 34*	Brief Fantastic Tales [C]	1949/50
Doctor Death	Feb 35-Apr 35	The Nekromantikon	Spr 50-mid 51
Ace Mystery	May 36-Sep 36	*Science Fantasy*	*Sum 50-Feb 66*
Fanciful Tales	Fal 36	Fantasy Fiction [Stories]	May 50-Nov 50
The Witch's Tales	Nov 36-Dec 36	Worlds Beyond	Dec 50-Feb 51
Tales of Terror	*May 37*	Suspense	Spr 51-Win 52
Leaves	Sum 37-Win 38	Avon Science Fiction Reader	Spr 51-Win 52
Mystery Stories	*1937-1939*	The Mysterious Traveler	Nov 51-Sep 52
Eerie Stories	Aug 37	Fantastic	Sum 52-Oct 80
Tales of Crime & Punishment	*Nov 37*	Avon SF & Fantasy Reader	Jan 53-Apr 53
Fireside Ghost Stories	*1938*	Fantasy [Fiction] Magazine	Mar 53-Nov 53
Ghosts & Goblins	*1938*	Beyond Fantasy Fiction	Jul 53-Jan 55
Eerie Mysteries	Aug 38-May 39	Mystic	Nov 53-Jul 56
Strange Stories	Feb 39-Feb 41	*Supernatural Stories*	*May 54-Sum 67*
Unknown [Unknown Worlds]	Mar 39-Oct 43	*Out of This World*	*Oct 54-Jan 55*
Uncanny Tales	May 39-May 40	*Weird World*	*Win 55-Spr 56*
Unknown [Unknown Worlds]	*Sep 39-Win 49*	Dream World	Feb 57-Aug 57
Tales of Ghosts & Haunted Houses	*Dec 39*	Tales of the Frightened	Spr 57-Aug 57
Weird Story Magazine	*Aug 40*	*Phantom*	*Apr 57-Jul 58*
Uncanny Tales [C]	Nov 40-Oct 43	Macabre	Jun 57-1976
Bizarre	Jan 41	*Screen Chills & Macabre Stories*	*Nov 57*
Stirring Fantasy Fiction	Feb 41-Mar 40	Monster Parade	Sep 58-Mar 59
Uncanny Stories	Apr 41	Monsters & Things	Jan 59-Apr 59
Eerie Tales [C]	Jul 41	*Weird & Occult Library*	*Spr 60-Aut 60*
Weird Tales [C]	May 42-Nov 51	*A Book of Weird Tales*	*Aut 60*
Yankee Weird Shorts	*May 42-Jun 42*	Fear!	May 60-Jul 60
Weird Pocket Library	*1943*	Shock	May 60-Sep 60
Weird Shorts	*1944*	Thriller	Feb 62-Jul 62
Occult [Occult Shorts]	*1945*	Gamma	Sum 63-Sep 65
Weird Story Magazine	*1946*	Magazine of Horror	Aug 63-Apr 71

True Twilight Tales	Fal 63-Spr 64
Prize Ghost Stories	Spr 63
Tales of Terror From the Beyond	Sum 64
Bizarre! Mystery Magazine	Oct 65-Jan 66
Impulse	*Mar 66-Feb 67*
Space and Time	Spr 66-current
Startling Mystery Stories	Sum 66-Mar 71
Anubis	Aut 66-Aut 68
The Arkham Collector	Sum 67-Sum 71
Beyond Infinity	Dec 67
Weirdbook	Apr 68-current
Worlds of Fantasy	Sep 68-Spr 71
Strange Fantasy	Spr 69-Fal 70
Coven 13	Sep 69-Mar 70
Weird Terror Tales	Win 69-Fal 70
Nyctalops	May 70-current
Weird Window	*Jun 70-Mar 71*
Dark Horizons	*1971-current*
The Strangest Stories Ever Told	Sum 71
Bizarre Fantasy Tales	Fal 70-Mar 71
Weird Mystery	Fal 70-Sum 71
Adventures in Horror	
[Horror Stories]	Oct 70-Oct 71
Forgotten Fantasy	Oct 70-Jun 71
Witchcraft & Sorcery	Feb 71-1974
Moonbroth	1971-1977
The Black Cat [C]	Win 71
From Beyond the Dark Gateway	May 72-Oct 77
Macabre/The Argonaut	May 72-current
H.P.L.	Spr 72
Horror Sex Tales	Jul 72
Weird Sex Tales	Aug 72
Monster Sex Tales	Sep 72
Legendary Sex Tales	Oct 72
The Haunt of Horror	Jun 73-Aug 73
Wyrd	Jun 73-current
Whispers	Jul 73-current
Etchings & Odysseys	1973-current
Fantasy & Terror	1973-current
Fantasy Classics	1973
The Diversifier	Jan 74-Mar 79
Fantasy Crossroads	Nov 74-Jan 77
Evermist	Dec 74-Sum 78
Midnight Sun	1974-1979
Spoor Anthology	1974
Unique Tales	1974
Kadath	1974
Sword & Sorcery Annual	1974/5

Astral Dimensions	Win 75-Fal 77
Myrddin	Win 75-Apr 78
The Dark Messenger Reader	
[Eldritch Tales]	Win 75-current
Toadstool Wine	Oct 75
Cthulhu	*1976-1978*
The New Fantasy Journal	Sum 76-1977
Eerie Country	Jul 76-current
Black Lite	Aug 76-Jan 78
Ariel	Aut 76-Oct 78
Chacal	Win 76-Spr 77
Phantasy Digest	1976-1977
The Copper Toadstool [C]	Dec 76-Jul 79
Fantasy Crosswinds	Jan 77-Feb 77
Jeet	Apr 77-Sum 77
Fantasy Tales	*Sum 77-current*
Escape	Fal 77
Night Voyages	Fal 77-Win 84
Shayol	Nov 77-Spr 84
Wax Dragon	1977-1980
Dragonbane [C]	Spr 78
Weird Adventures	May 78-1978
Prelude to Fantasy	Sum 78-current
Beyond the Fields We Know [C]	Aut 78
Dreams of a Dark Hue	*Dec 78*
Ghosts and Scholars	Spr 79-current
Gothic	Jun 79-Dec 80
Kadath (Italian)	*Oct 79-current*
Something Else	*Spr 80-current*
Paragon	May 80
Airgedlamh	*Aut 80*
November	Aut 80-Spr 81
Hor-Tasy	1980-1982
SPWAO Showcase	1980-current
Fantasy Macabre	*Sep 80-current*
Night Flights	Win 80
Rod Serling's 'The Twilight	
Zone' Magazine	Apr 81-current
Chillers	Jul 81-Nov 81
Fantasy Book	Oct 81-current
Threshold of Fantasy	Spr 82-current
The Arkham Sampler	
[2nd series]	Jun 83-current

***

IV.
Geographical Listing of Magazines

The listing is grouped firstly by country. For the United States it is sub-divided by State. All countries are then sub-divided into publishers.

UNITED STATES

ALABAMA
CRYSTAL VISIONS PRESS
809 Cleremont Drive, Huntsville
Escape!

ARIZONA
ULTIMATE PUBLISHING CO.,
Box 642, Scottsdale
Fantastic (Apr 79-Oct 80 only)

CALIFORNIA
CAMELOT PUBLISHING CO.,
2412 West 7th St., Los Angeles
Coven 13

CASTLE PRESS
Leah Court, Oroville
The Diversifier/Paragon

THE CHAOSIUM
Box 6302, Albany
Wyrd (issues 6 and 7 only)

FANDOM UNLIMITED ENTERPRISES
3378 Valley Forge Way, San Jose
Threshold of Fantasy

FANTASY BOOK ENTERPRISES
1441 N. Altadena Drive, Pasadena
Fantasy Book

FANTASY HOUSE
[A division of Flamingo Press]
6045 Vineland Ave., North Hollywood
Fantasy Classics

FANTASY PUBLISHING CO. INC.,.
1855 West Main St., Alhambra
Witchcraft & Sorcery

GALLERY PRESS
5583 W. Pico Blvd., Los Angeles
Horror Sex Tales
Legendary Sex Tales
Monster Sex Tales
Weird Sex Tales

I.D. PUBLICATIONS
8383 Sunset Blvd., Hollywood
Beyond Infinity

NECTAR PRESS, INC.
1521 N. Vine St., Hollywood
Forgotten Fantasy

SHROUD PRESS
5652 Vineland Ave., North Hollywood
Unique Tales

STAR PRESS, INC.
19523 Burbank Blvd., North Hollywood
Gamma

TINTAGEL
Berkeley
Wyrd (No.8 only)

COLORADO
GORGON PRESS
4936 Grove St., Denver
The Gorgon

CONNECTICUT
CHARLTON PUBLICATIONS, INC.
Charlton Bldg., Division St., Derby
Tales of Terror From the Beyond
Chillers

ILLINOIS
PALMER PUBLICATIONS
806 Dempster St., Evanston
Mystic

RURAL PUBLISHING CORPORATION
854 N.Clark St., Chicago
Weird Tales (Mar 23-May/Jul 24 only)

INDIANA
POPULAR FICTION COMPANY
2457 East Washington St., Indianapolis
Weird Tales (Nov 24-Oct 38 only)

IOWA
ANSUDA PUBLICATIONS
P.O. Box 158, Harris
Hor-Tasy

STYGIAN ISLE PRESS
Lamoni
Fantasy Crossroads (to Feb 76 only)

KANSAS
DAEMON GRAPHICS
[formerly Nemedian Chronicles]
P.O.Box 186, Shawnee Mission
Chacal

FLIGHT UNLIMITED
8435 Carter, Overland Park
[see also under Missouri]
Shayol

THE MORNING STAR PRESS
P.O.Box 6011, Leawood
Ariel (first two issues only; see
under Ariel Books, Missouri)

NEMEDIAN CHRONICLES
see Daemon Graphics

YITH PRESS
1051 Wellington Rd., Lawrence
Eldritch Tales
[see also The Strange Press,Wisconsin]

LOUISIANA
GOTHIC PRESS
4998 Perkins Rd., Baton Rouge
Gothic

MARYLAND
HALL PUBLICATIONS
Perryville
Phantasy Digest

MINNESOTA
MINNCONN PUBLICATIONS
P.O.Box 7042, Duluth
Etchings & Odysseys (Issue 1 only)

MISSOURI
ARIEL BOOKS
Suite 2406 Power & Light Bldg., Kansas City
Ariel (Nos. 3 and 4 only)

FLIGHT UNLIMITED
4324 Belleview, Kansas City
[see also under Kansas]
Shayol

NEW MEXICO
SILVER SCARAB PRESS
500 Wellesley S.E., Albuquerque
Nyctalops
From Beyond the Dark Gateway

NEW YORK
ACE MAGAZINES
67 West 44th St., New York
Eerie Mysteries
Eerie Stories

as PERIODICAL HOUSE [sub-imprint]
Ace Mystery

ALBING PUBLICATIONS
Manhattan, New York
[subsequently Manhattan Fiction]
Stirring Fantasy Fiction

AVON BOOK CO.
119 West 57th St., New York
[later AVON NOVELS INC., 575 Madison Ave.,
New York]
Avon Fantasy Reader
Avon Science Fiction Reader
Avon Science Fiction & Fantasy Reader

BETTER PUBLICATIONS
22 West 48th St., New York
Strange Stories

CARWOOD PUBLISHING CO.,
New York
The Witch's Tales

CLAYTON MAGAZINES
80 Lafayette St., New York
Strange Tales

CONSTRUCTIVE PUBLISHING
Macfadden Bldg., 1926 Broadway, New York
Ghost Stories (Jul 26-Mar 30 only)

DELL PUBLICATIONS
New York
Dr. Death

FARRELL PUBLISHING CORPORATION
420 Lexington Ave., New York
Suspense

FUTURE PUBLICATIONS
80 Fifth Ave., New York
Fantasy [Fiction] Magazine

GALAXY PUBLISHING CORPORATION
421 Hudson St., New York
Beyond Fantasy Fiction
Worlds of Fantasy (No.1 only)

GOOD STORY MAGAZINE CO.
New York
Ghost Stories (Apr 30-Jan 32 only)

GRACE PUBLISHING
105 East 15th St., New York
The Mysterious Traveler Magazine

GREAT AMERICAN PUBLICATIONS
270 Madison Ave., New York
Fear!

HEALTH KNOWLEDGE INC.,
140 Fifth Ave., New York
Magazine of Horror
Startling Mystery Stories
Weird Terror Tales
Bizarre Fantasy Tales

HILLMAN PERIODICALS INC.
535 Fifth Ave., New York
Worlds Beyond

KENSINGTON PUBLISHING CORPORATION
21 East 40th St., New York
  Weird Tales (Spr 81–Sum 83 only)

LEAGUE PUBLICATIONS
205 East 42nd St., New York
  Prize Ghost Stories
  True Twilight Tales

MAGABOOK, INC.
136 East 67th St., New York
  Fantasy Fiction/Stories

MAGNUM PUBLICATIONS
11 West 42nd St., New York
  Monster Parade
  Monsters & Things

MANHATTAN FICTION PUBLICATIONS
  see Albing Publications

MANVIS PUBLICATIONS
[a subsidiary of WESTERN FICTION]
RKO Bldg., Radio City, New York
  Uncanny Tales
  Uncanny Stories

MARVEL COMICS GROUP
575 Madison Ave., New York
  The Haunt of Horror

PAMAR ENTERPRISES INC.
122 East 42nd St., New York
  Bizarre! Mystery Magazine

PERIODICAL HOUSE
  see Ace Magazines

POPULAR PUBLICATIONS
205 East 42nd St., New York
  as Recreational Reading Inc.
  A.Merritt's Fantasy Magazine

RECREATIONAL READING INC.
  see Popular Publications

REPUBLIC FEATURES SYNDICATE
39 West 55th St., New York
  Tales of the Frightened

SHORT STORIES, INC.
9 Rockefeller Plaza, New York
  Weird Tales (Nov 38–Sep 54 only)

STANLEY PUBLICATIONS
261 Fifth Ave., New York
  Adventures in Horror/Horror Stories

STREET & SMITH PUBLICATIONS
79–89 Seventh St., New York
  The Thrill Book
  Unknown/Unknown Worlds

TEMPEST PUBLICATIONS
2 West 45th St., New York
  Thriller

TZ PUBLICATIONS
800 Second Ave., New York
  *Rod Serling's 'The Twilight Zone'
  Magazine*

ULTIMATE PUBLISHING CO.
Oakland Gardens, Flushing
[see also under Arizona]
  Fantastic (Sep 65–Jan 79 only)
  Strange Fantasy
  The Strangest Stories Ever Told
  Sword & Sorcery Annual

Weird Mystery

UNIVERSAL PUBLISHING & DISTRIBUTING CO.
235 East 45th St., New York
  Worlds of Fantasy (Nos.2 – 4 only)

WEIRDBOOK PRESS
Amherst Branch, Buffalo
  Weirdbook
  Eerie Country
  Toadstool Wine

WHISPERS PRESS
70 Highland Ave., Binghampton
  Whispers

WINSTON PUBLICATIONS
157 West 57th St., New York
  Shock

ZIFF-DAVIS PUBLISHING CO.
366 Madison Ave., New York
[1 Park Ave., New York after 1958]
  Dream World
  Fantastic (Sum 52–Jun 65 only)

OREGON
MALVERN ENTERPRISES
616 NE 118th St., Portland
[formerly in Bellevue, Washington]
  Moonbroth

PENNSYLVANIA
FANTASY PUBLICATIONS
Everett
  Marvel Tales
  Unusual Stories

PERSONAL ARTS COMPANY
931 Drexel Bldgs., Philadelphia
  Tales of Magic and Mystery

THE SHADE PUBLISHING COMPANY
1008 West York St., Philadelphia
  Mind Magic/My Self

TEXAS
SIMBA PUBLICATIONS
Huston
  Fantasy Crossroads (No.12 only)

VIRGINIA
GOLDEN GOBLIN PRESS
P.O.Box 323, Arlington
  Anubis

WISCONSIN
ARKHAM HOUSE
Sauk City
  The Arkham Sampler (First Series)
  The Arkham Collector

THE STRANGE COMPANY
P.O.Box 864, Madison
  Spoor Anthology
  The Dark Messenger Reader
  Etchings & Odysseys (No.2 onwards)
  The Arkham Sampler (Second Series)

CANADA

ADAM PUBLISHING COMPANY
28 Wellington St. West., Toronto, Ontario
[later renamed Norman Book Co., at 95
  King St. East, Toronto before returning
  to the above address]
  Uncanny Tales

AMERICAN NEWS COMPANY
474 Wellington St. West, Toronto
  Weird Tales

CK PUBLISHING
84 Adelaide St. West, Toronto
  Eerie Tales

MEMORY LANE PUBLICATIONS
594 Markham St., Toronto
  The Black Cat

METROPOLITAN PUBLISHING CO.
Toronto
  The Book of Terror

NORMAN BOOK CO.
  see Adam Publishing Co.

SHADOW PRESS
Box 207, Gananoque, Ontario
  Dark Fantasy

SODA PUBLICATIONS LTD.
750 Bridge St., Richmond, British Columbia
[subsequently 1235 Nelson St., Vancouver,
  British Columbia]
  The Copper Toadstool/The Storyteller

STUDIO PUBLICATIONS
2842 Bloor St. West, Toronto
  Brief Fantastic Tales

TRISKELL PRESS
P.O. Box 9480, Ottawa, Ontario
  Dragonbane
  Beyond the Fields We Know
  Dragonfields

UNITED KINGDOM

ATLAS PUBLISHING & DISTRIBUTING CO.
18 Bride Lane, London
  Unknown/Unknown Worlds

BADGER BOOKS
  see John Spencer & Co.

BRITISH FANTASY SOCIETY
  [address varies]
  Dark Horizons

COMPACT BOOKS
  see Roberts & Vinter Ltd.

DALROW PUBLICATIONS
Dalrow House, Church Bank, Bolton, Lancs.
  Phantom

GANNET PRESS
77 Claughton Rd., Birkenhead, Cheshire
  Weird World

THE HAUNTED LIBRARY
11b Cote Lea Square, Southgate, Runcorn,
  Cheshire
  Ghosts and Scholars

WILLIAM C. MERRITT
335 City Road, London
  Weird Tales (1946 reprint issue only)

NOVA PUBLICATIONS LTD.
25 Stoke Newington Rd., London (and
  various address changes)
  Science Fantasy (to Apr 64 only)

PAN VISUALS
Legh St., Patricroft, Manchester
  Something Else

PEP PUBLISHERS
Croydon, Surrey
  Screen Chills and Macabre Stories

ROBERTS & VINTER, LTD.
42/44 Dock St., London
  Science Fantasy (Jul 64-Feb 66 only)
  Impulse

SPECTRE PRESS
18 Cefn Road, Mynachdy, Cardiff, Wales
  Cthulhu
  Dreams of a Dark Hue

JOHN SPENCER & CO.
24 Shepherd's Bush Rd., London
[subsequently 131 Brackenbury Road, London]
  Supernatural Stories
  Out of This World

STRATO PUBLICATIONS/THORPE & PORTER
East Street, Oadby, Leicester
  Beyond Fantasy Fiction
  Fantastic
  Weird Tales (1949-1954 only)
  (all British editions of US magazines)

SWAN PUBLICATIONS
Edgware House, Burne St., Marylebone,
  London [subsequently 17 Chapel St.,
  London, then 40 Crundale Ave., London]
  Weird Story Magazine
  Yankee Weird Shorts
  Weird Tales (1942 reprint only)
  Weird Pocket Library
  Weird Shorts
  Occult/Occult Shorts
  Weird and Occult Miscellany
  Weird and Occult Library

UTOPIAN PUBLICATIONS
London
  Strange Tales

VEEVERS & HENSMAN LTD.
Burnley, Lancashire
  A Book of Weird Tales

WORLD'S WORK LTD.
Kingswood, Surrey
  The Master Thriller series
  Mystery Stories

ITALY

KADATH PRESS
Corso Aurelio Saffi 5/9, Genova
  Kadath

***

BIBLIOGRAPHY

Details for all magazines were taken directly from the magazine issues. In some instances, by way of precaution, items were double checked against existing indices as listed below. Much of the biographical information came from direct contact with the authors. Standard reference works such as *Who's Who, Who Was Who* and *The Dictionary of National Biography* were used as well as books cited below. Most bibliographical data came from the collection and records of Mike Ashley, and further books consulted are listed below.

Berglund, Edward P. with Loay Hall and Randall Larson. "A Listing of Cthulhu Mythos Stories Appearing in Non-Professional Magazines" *Fandom Unlimited* No.3: 19-21 (Spring 1977)

Bleiler, Everett F. *The Guide to Supernatural Fiction.* Kent, Ohio: The Kent State University Press, 1983.

Carter, Lin. "A Complete Bibliography of the Mythos" in *Lovecraft: A Look Behind the Cthulhu Mythos.* New York: Ballantine, 1972. Pp. 183-189.

Cockcroft, T. G. L. *Index to the Weird Fiction Magazines.* 2 vols. Lower Hutt, New Zealand: privately published, 1962/64.

Cockcroft, T. G. L. *Index to the Verse in Weird Tales.* Lower Hutt, New Zealand: privately published, 1960.

Contento, William. *Index to Science Fiction Anthologies and Collections.* Boston, Mass: G. K. Hall & Co., 1978.

Cook, Michael L. *Monthly Murders.* Westport, CT: Greenwood Press, 1982.

Day, Bradford M. *The Complete Checklist of Science-Fiction Magazines.* New York: privately published, 1961.

Day, Bradford M. *An Index on the Weird and Fantastica in Magazines.* South Ozone Park, NY: privately published, 1953.

Day, Donald B. *Index to the Science-Fiction Magazines, 1926-1950.* Portland, OR: Perri Press, 1952. Revised by L.W. Currey and David G. Hartwell, Boston: Mass: G. K. Hall, 1982.

Evans, William H. "Fantasy in The Blue Book Magazine". *Fantasy Commentator* I: 59-68 (No.4, December 1944)

Franson, Donald. "Fantasy Pseudonyms" in *Lore*, I: 92-103 (No.7, September 1966)

Hasse, Henry. *Index to Fantasy and Science Fiction in Munsey Publications.* Los Angeles, CA: FPCI, undated (1979?)

Hoffman, Stuart. *An Index to Unknown and Unknown Worlds.* Black Earth, Wisc: Sirius Press, 1955.

Jones, Robert K. "Index to Weird Menace Pulps" in *Popular's Weird Menace Pulps* by Robert Jones, Evergreen, Col: Opar Press, 1972.

Jones, Robert K. "The Thrill Book" originally in *WSFA Journal* March-November 1970. Version consulted as updated and expanded in *Xenophile* March 1977, pp. 4-10.

McGhan, Barry. *Science Fiction and Fantasy Pseudonyms.* Dearborn, Mich: Misfit Press, 1976. Revised and expanded, 1979.

McHaney, Dennis & Glenn Lord. *The Fiction of Robert E. Howard.* Privately published, 1975.

Metcalf, Norm. *The Index of Science Fiction Magazines, 1951-1965.* El Cerrito,

CA: J.Ben Stark, 1968.

Murray, Will. "The Unknown Unknown" in *Xenophile* No.42: 11-15 (Sep/Oct 1979)

Owings, Mark with Jack Chalker. *The Revised H.P. Lovecraft Bibliography*. Baltimore, MD: The Mirage Press, 1973.

Pavlat, Bob and Bill Evans. *Fanzine Index*. Originally printed in 1952. Published and re-set, Flushing, NY: Harold Palmer Piser, 1965.

Reginald, R. *Science Fiction and Fantasy Literature, A Checklist, 1700-1974*. Detroit, Mich: Gale Research, 1979.

Roberts, Peter. *British Fanzine Bibliography*. Dawlish, Devon, England: 3 vols., privately published, 1977/79.

Sieger, James R. *Stories of Ghosts*. Evergreen, Col: Opar Press, 1973.

Strauss, Erwin S. *Index to the S-F Magazines, 1951-1965*. Cambridge, Mass: MIT SF Society, 1966.

Tuck, Donald H. *The Encyclopedia of Science Fiction and Fantasy*. Chicago, Ill: Advent, 3 vols., 1974, 1978, 1982.

Use has also been made of articles published in the magazines covered by this index, and I would make special reference to the non-fiction items listed under the entries for L. Sprague de Camp, R. Alain Everts and Sam Moskowitz.

ERRATA AND CORRIGENDA

The receipt of the details on the Canadian *Weird Tales* as noted on page 286 was too late to allow correction of the early stages of the Author Index. The following additional printings should therefore be included.

AMES, LEONA MAY
*Return [v]   WT(Can)Jul 43

ARTHUR, JAMES
*Ears of the Dead [v]   WT(Can)Sep 42

ARTHUR, ROBERT
The Book and the Beast   WT(Can)Sep 42
    [This precedes its US publication in
    WT Mar 43. It also appeared in the
    corresponding WT(Can)Jul 43]
*Ghost For a Night   WT(Can)Jan 43

AVRETT, ROBERT
*Devil's Swamp [v]   WT(Can)Jan 43

BALL, CLIFFORD
*The Little Man   WT(Can)Nov 43

BARKER, S. OMAR
*Judge Bean's Bear [v]   WT(Can)Mar 43
    [*Short Stories Mar 25,1942]
*Ol' Sancho [v]   WT(Can)Mar 43
    [*Short Stories Jul 10,1941]
[Note: neither of these poems appeared
    in the US edition of WT]

BARNARD, JOHN M.
*Flight of Time [v]   WT(Can)Jan 43

BLOCH, ROBERT
    as R.J. Comber
*The Bat is My Brother   WT(Can)Mar 46

BRYAN, BRUCE
*Return From Death   WT(Can)Nov 43

CALHOUN, HOWELL
*The Plumed Serpent [v]   WT(Can)Sep 42

COBLENTZ, STANTON A.
*To the Moon [v]   WT(Can)Nov 44

COLE, ALONZO DEEN
*The Gipsy's Hand   WT(Can)Jan 43

COMBER, R. J.
    Pseud: see Robert BLOCH

COUNSELMAN, MARY ELIZABETH
*Twister   WT(Can)Sep 43

DRAKE, LEAH BODINE
*Bad Company [v]   WT(Can)Sep 42

GARFIELD, FRANCES
*Forbidden Cupboard   WT(Can)Sep 43

GARY, KEN
*A Weird Prophecy [ts]   WT(Can)Mar 43

GREEN, JULIA BOYNTON
*Painted Cave [v]   WT(Can)Jan 43

HAGER, SUDIE STUART
*Inheritance [v]   WT(Can)Sep 42

HOWARD, ROBERT E.
*The Ghost Kings [v]   WT(Can)Sep 44
*Recompense [v]   WT(Can)Nov 44

***

About the Compiler

FRANK H. PARNELL was born in London and has published numerous short stories in the field of science fiction and fantasy. He possesses an extensive collection of weird fantasy magazines and has contributed to *The Encyclopedia of Science Fiction* by Peter Nicholls. He currently resides in Suffolk, England.